International Political Economy in Context: Individual Choices, Global Effects

To Pam, Donna, and Amy

International Political Economy in Context: Individual Choices, Global Effects

Andrew C. Sobel

 |

Los Angeles | London | New Delhi
Singapore | Washington DC

Los Angeles | London | New Delhi
Singapore | Washington DC

FOR INFORMATION:

CQ Press
An Imprint of SAGE Publications, Inc.
2455 Teller Road
Thousand Oaks, California 91320
E-mail: order@sagepub.com

SAGE Publications Ltd.
1 Oliver's Yard
55 City Road
London EC1Y 1SP
United Kingdom

SAGE Publications India Pvt. Ltd.
B 1/I 1 Mohan Cooperative Industrial Area
Mathura Road, New Delhi 110 044
India

SAGE Publications Asia-Pacific Pte. Ltd.
3 Church Street
#10-04 Samsung Hub
Singapore 049483

Acquisitions Editor: Elise Frasier
Development Editor: Nancy Matuszak
Production Editor: Astrid Virding
Copy Editor: Judy Selhorst
Typesetter: C&M Digitals (P) Ltd.
Proofreader: Scott Oney
Indexer: Kathy Paparchontis
Cover Designer: Auburn Associates, Inc.,
                 Baltimore, Maryland
Marketing Manager: Jonathan Mason
Permissions Editor: Adele Hutchinson

Printed in the United States of America

Library of Congress Cataloging-in-Publication Data

Sobel, Andrew Carl, 1953-

International political economy in context: individual choices, global effects / Andrew Sobel. — 1st Ed.

p. cm.
Includes bibliographical references and index.

ISBN 978-1-60871-711-8 (pbk.)

1. Economics—Political aspects. 2. Globalization. 3. International economic relations. 4. Nation-state. 5. World politics. I. Title.

HB74.P65S63 2013
337—dc23   2012012484

This book is printed on acid-free paper.

SUSTAINABLE FORESTRY INITIATIVE

Certified Chain of Custody
Promoting Sustainable Forestry
www.sfiprogram.org
SFI-01268

SFI label applies to text stock

12 13 14 15 16 10 9 8 7 6 5 4 3 2 1

Brief
Contents

Detailed Contents

Figures, Tables, and Maps

FIGURES

TABLES

MAPS

Preface

Positioned at the nexus of politics and economics, international relations and international political economy involve broad and diverse subjects that touch all our lives in significant ways. By definition, any gateway text to a subject is incomplete. It can, at best, provide a solid foundation for more advanced study and stir student interest in further exploration of its subject matter. Constructing this book presented many challenges: what to include and what to exclude; what approaches to adopt and which ones to omit; how much history and contextual detail to include versus how much theoretical abstraction is needed; how much economics versus how much political science; whether to approach the topic with macro or micro tools; whether to afford primacy to the structure of relations between nation-states or to open up nation-states to consider the mechanisms of domestic politics. Another challenge involved how to develop students' empathy for the difficulties that policy makers face in selecting policies in a complex social system where seemingly sound choices can turn bad and produce unexpected outcomes. *International Political Economy in Context: Individual Choices, Global Effects* tackles these challenges in a systematic way, from building blocks and micro tools to the many forces at work in the global economy of the past and present.

Many in political science separate international relations from international political economy, applying distinctions such as the "high politics" of security versus the "low politics" of economic relations. I find this separation to be a false, misleading, and intellectually damaging dichotomy. Because their field of study is a science, political scientists must look for explanations and processes that generalize from one setting to others. If man is "a political animal," we should establish what we mean by *political* and how the mechanisms of politics work. The theories and explanations that help us make sense of political behavior are likely to be similar across domestic and international arenas and across issue areas, whether security, economic, or social. Separating the study of security and conflict from the study of economic relations in the international arena suggests that politics works completely differently in one sphere than in another. Others have made this dichotomy and suffered serious consequences. Napoleon, a warrior, dismissed England as a "nation of shopkeepers," and Mao Zedong ("All power comes from the barrel of a gun") called the United States a "paper tiger." The shopkeepers and the paper tiger eventually prevailed in the political-military sphere because of their activities and capabilities in the political-economic arena. Societies that have prevailed and dominated the rules of the game in international affairs have been first and foremost great political economies with economies and polities that can then support political-military capabilities, and not the other way around. The Soviet Union amassed an impressive military but lost the Cold War to the economic prowess of the U.S.-led global capitalist political economy. The United Kingdom and the United States dominated international affairs during the 1800s and 1900s, respectively, becoming hegemons through the strength of their economies and their policy choices in the political-economic arena. Success in political-economic affairs spills over to the security sphere. Creating a false dichotomy between substantive spheres of political activity and neglecting connections across them is therefore dangerous not only in terms of policy but also in terms of our understanding of political behavior.

Questions of pedagogy and ontology are often ignored by students being introduced to the study of a social science. The genesis of this project, however, offers important insights into this volume's approach, which is different enough from the approaches of other texts in international political economy and international relations to merit some attention. I have adopted a political economy approach in this text, but students should note that, in general, competing approaches exist in the study and analysis of international political and economic relations, even if one analytic approach dominates a text. Students should question and challenge ideas and frameworks, continually assessing the power and validity of all approaches. In laying out the pedagogy of the approach that dominates this text, I hope to help them do so intelligently, productively, and with healthy skepticism.

WHY THIS TEXT?

For many years I was frustrated with the introductory texts in international political economy and international relations. Many do an excellent job at describing an array of important topics—whether giving details about international conflict, the International Monetary Fund and the World Bank, international monetary and trade arrangements, the activities of multinational corporations, or the problems of development. They tend, however, toward atheoretical, nonanalytical, and nonpolitical descriptions of events, and static descriptions of the mechanisms of trade, finance, migration, and international political economy. Although in some cases they offer excellent descriptions of *what* has occurred, they make little attempt to develop explicit theoretical frameworks explaining *why* things happen in global political and economic relations, refraining from grounding policy choices in the deliberations and competitive environs of domestic politics and decision-making processes, complete with their strengths and constraints. What analysis does appear in most of these texts takes the form of macro theory, which relies on system structure and monolithic nation-states to account for behavior in the global arena. Individual decision makers, the institutions and organizations of government and society, and subnational actors are missing from such accounts, or, at best, they are presented as automatons reacting in a deterministic fashion to the vicissitudes of the international system. Many of my friends in microeconomics find the very notion of macro theory implausible because of the relative absence of individuals as decision makers, but it is an appropriate description of a causal argument built on a perception of monolithic nation-states acting within a particular global context. I include aspects of those macro approaches—liberalism and realism—in this text as a means of demonstrating their weaknesses and arguing the need for examination of microfoundations in the domestic political economy to explain international political and economic relations.

These macro approaches failed to resonate with me during my intellectual development, as I had difficulty placing myself in a decision maker's shoes as required in making the calculations and choices demanded by these approaches. Indeed, when I placed myself in that context, I often made choices that conflicted with what was prescribed by the macro approaches. This contradiction seems to characterize real policy makers' choices as well, for all too often their decisions conflict with those anticipated by macro approaches to political and economic behavior.

This point was brought home to me after al-Qaeda attacked on September 11, 2001. At the time, I was teaching a large introductory class on international relations, and, as expected, the attack sparked frequent questions and debates as students tried to make sense of world affairs. The events of 9/11 highlighted the roles of individuals and nonstate actors in global affairs, and the difficulties of understanding the actions of terrorists within the boundaries of the macro frameworks underscored the weaknesses and limitations of those approaches. In fact, I had plenty of theory and tools that helped students better understand the events of 9/11 and those after, but those tools came from micro political economy, which was on the syllabus for later in the course. These micro tools focused on individual preferences, constraints on individual choice, incentives and disincentives to individuals, and strategic interactions of individual choice and calculations. I saw clearly that a text such as *International Political Economy in Context: Individual Choices, Global Effects* was needed, and my frustration that semester intersected with the persistence and persuasiveness of Charisse Kiino, now publisher for political science at CQ Press. At a conference several years earlier, she had approached me about writing a text for international political economy. I initially resisted, because I thought the project would interfere with my research program on globalization, risk, and the changing role of the state. Circumstances and Charisse's persistence eventually converged to convince me that I should accept her offer.

EXPLANATORY FRAMEWORK

Of necessity, I made several working assumptions that define the boundaries of what this text does and does not do. First, it is meant for a course in analytical political science, not politics or current events. It is designed to help students probe, dissect, and analyze political behavior, not to promote memorization and regurgitation of facts and events. Some beginning students know a lot about politics, which is of great use for those interested in political science, but such knowledge is not to be confused with political science. They may be history buffs, political "junkies," or well-informed on current events, but they probably comprehend little political science despite knowing a lot of "stuff" about day-to-day politics.

Students may have tremendous native abilities, but they are diamonds in the rough until they have developed and honed their skills. The process of education is a technological and capital-intensive transformation of human labor and abilities. This text focuses on developing a particular set of systematic tools for explanation or exploration of the phenomena we study in political science. It emphasizes explanatory frameworks for social behavior that are based on a rational choice approach to political economy.

Second, I assume that a text that students read is better than one they do not read, even if the text they neglect covers more material more thoroughly. My experience on a university campus continually reminds me that time is a scarce resource. Students must allocate their time and resources among multiple courses and community life. I adjusted my expectations for this text by limiting the material to be presented, but without sacrificing the comprehensiveness of core topics that instructors will want to cover. I constrained the boundaries of the text in the belief that accomplishing a few key objectives well is better than a diffuse effort covering a broader area. In the spirit of lowering the barriers to students' success at grasping and playing with the frameworks in this text, I limited the use of footnotes and references to other sources. Such cites are useful in more advanced undergraduate and graduate courses, where students are expected to develop depth and expertise, but at this level they can only distract from the big ideas. For those students who want to move beyond this text, I include suggestions for further reading at the end of each chapter. These supplementary reading lists can also guide instructors as they tailor the text to their needs and objectives.

Third, I assume that students can absorb, digest, and process news and events available through the media and histories. As a consequence, I focus on theories, frameworks, information, and tools that are harder to grasp on one's own. I do not attempt to provide extensive factual background or details about the world beyond what is necessary to empirically test and demonstrate the theoretical foundations of the text and to accomplish the core objective of the text, which is to develop a set of systematic tools that help make sense of the facts, construct stories about relationships, and test interpretations. How much contextual background and history to include is a difficult balance to strike: too much can distract from the text's primary focus on theoretical tools and perversely encourage students to spend time memorizing details, but developing such tools in the absence of sufficient background and history is pointless and potentially pathological. Context matters! Details and facts are potentially useful, but not independent of explanatory frameworks. Students will find it necessary and worthwhile to read and analyze other texts, periodicals, magazines, and newspapers in conjunction with reading this volume. I firmly believe the best social science, like the best physical science, is a constant back-and-forth between theory and empirical testing of theory. Theory without empirical testing can quickly become ideology. And empiricism without theory limits our ability to see the big picture, make generalizations, recognize similar phenomena, and draw connections that inform us about the world we live in.

In addition to serving as a core text for a range of courses in international political economy, this book can be used as a core or complementary text in an introductory international politics course to teach the microfoundations of political behavior and underscore the role of global exchange (not conflict) in that curriculum. The political processes highlighted should be the same across substantive areas—domestic or international, security or economics. Textbooks reflect the teaching strategies of their authors, but teachers inevitably take different approaches to their courses and materials. Ten political scientists asked to design a particular course will create ten different syllabi with some important similarities and some important differences; often similar topics will be covered, but in different orders and from different perspectives. This volume reflects my general approach to teaching international political economy and international affairs, but I tried to design a text that could be used in a number of courses, in a variety of approaches, and at various levels of instruction. This flexibility requires that instructors thoughtfully integrate the text into their courses in the manner most complementary to their own approaches. I am aware of this need for flexibility even as the author of this text.

Indeed, you may be familiar with my first volume with CQ Press, *Political Economy and Global Affairs*. This new text, *International Political Economy in Context: Individual Choices, Global Effects*, derives from that original book and has benefited greatly from the thoughtful and compelling feedback from faculty who used the first volume as well as those who strongly considered using it. The improvements made based on that feedback turned out to be substantial, and ultimately prompted a new structure, organization, and content, all in an effort to make the book better fit the courses for which it's used. At the same time, I recognize that many instructors still will modify it based on their preferences. Those who used *Political Economy and Global Affairs* will easily find their way through this new book.

ORGANIZATION OF THE BOOK

International Political Economy in Context explains the micro political economy approach to political behavior, underscoring the ways in which the micro approach clarifies our understanding of global affairs. Part I on "Building Blocks to Examines Global Political Economy and Conflict" focuses on primary assumptions and structural/macro conditions of economic and political geography in the global arena. This section provides students with an introduction to the concepts and theories that form the foundation for understanding international political economy, as well as an assessment of macro approaches and a rationale for why this book takes a micro approach. Part II, "Micro Tools," builds on the preceding chapters as it delves into the micro-level conditions and mechanisms, and their shortfalls, that influence political and economic outcomes. Though the discussion in these chapters is immersed in the micro approach—looking at how domestic concerns and interest groups may influence actors' decision-making and set priorities that are not objectively logical—the narrative regularly takes note of how this micro examination fits within the big picture of international political economy. Finally, Part III, "Context," uses those primary assumptions and micro-level arrangements to make sense of the changes in the global political economy over the past two hundred years. This covers the periods from the end of the Napoleonic Wars through industrialization and the development of globalization and the Atlantic economy, to the breakdown in globalization and cooperation during the interwar years. It also covers the revival of globalization during the Bretton Woods period and the transition post–Bretton Woods, and concludes with the current era of global financial liberalization, its crises, and responses to those crises. Those of you familiar with my first book will have noticed that in this book, the section "Micro Tools" now comes before the "Context" section precisely in order to better equip students to understand the context through the lens of the micro approach. That is, they can now see micro tools in application.

Several chapters from *Political Economy and Global Affairs* have also been restructured and combined in this book to streamline similar discussions, eliminate redundancies, and create stronger connections between concepts and context. In chapters 1 and 4, I have moved to chapter appendices several sections that use social choice and game theory examples to illustrate intransitive or suboptimal social outcomes as a consequence of voting or social traps. These changes are intended to provide instructors with greater flexibility in how they include some of the more formal approaches to the concepts being covered.

This new book also features critical new content: chapter 6, "The Role of Hegemonic Leadership and Its Micro Foundations," and chapter 14, "Into the Future: Political and Economic Market Failures and Threats to Globalization." Hegemony is a critical component of producing cooperative outcomes in the international arena and stabilizing that arena at times of potential economic and political dislocation, and chapter 6 explores this in depth. Chapter 6 summarizes the emergence of hegemonic leadership, its foundations in a political economy's mechanisms of public and private finance, and how such a political-economy promotes productive political-economic relations, encourages the expansion of globalization during good times, and manages dislocations during hard times that could undermine globalization and lead to increased conflict in the system.

Chapter 14 brings the section on context up to date. It presents an empirical examination of global affairs after the financial and regulatory liberalization of the 1980s onward. Reforms and liberalization in national financial arenas revived a relatively moribund global financial arena and led to innovations that made capital more accessible across national borders, which increased the density and frequency of global financial relations but also increased the frequency and severity of financial crises that began to appear in the 1980s with the savings and loan crisis, the 1987 October market break, currency crises, and most recently the 2008 freeze in the credit markets and the European sovereign debt crisis. These increasingly severe financial crises pose systemic risks to international cooperation, globalization, and the global political economy and provide excellent opportunities for examining the core concepts and problems tackled in this text, and for examining political and economic market and regulatory failures on the part of governments and private enterprises, threats to the processes of global capitalism and globalization, the role of U.S. hegemonic leadership in containing those threats, and the prospects for continued U.S. leadership or succession to that leadership.

International Political Economy in Context also improves upon the pedagogical features in my prior book, with an eye toward enhancing students' ability to grasp key information and concepts. Readers will find a running "call-out glossary," boxes placed throughout the text that contain definitions of key concepts, set near where those concepts are discussed in the chapters to encourage comprehension and to serve as quick study aids. In addition, more international political economy examples appear throughout the chapters, and more connections are drawn between the micro approach and how it all relates to the big picture of international political economy.

Instructors can make use of the resources available online for this book, including a test bank and comprehensive set of PowerPoint lecture slides, downloadable jpeg files of all tables and figures, and solutions to end-of-chapter exercises. Access them at http://college.cqpress. com/sites/sobel-instructor. Adopters of my previous book can also make use of a transition guide that supports a smooth and easy transition to this new text. The online resources for students include practice quizzes, vocabulary flash cards, and chapter summaries, and can be found at http://college.cqpress.com/sites/sobel.

ACKNOWLEDGMENTS

I have been lucky to teach at Washington University in St. Louis, where I have taught students with strong analytical capabilities. Their feedback has improved the content and design of this text. My graduate teaching and research assistants have made valuable contributions to this project: Zdravka Brunkova, Gyung-ho Jeong, Michael Popovic, Scott Schmidt, and Jianmin Zhang read and commented on several chapters. Paul Scharre, Jeremy Caddel, and Chia-yi Lee provided tremendous assistance in developing the exercises, outlines, and Power Point presentations for instructors and for the Web materials for students. My graduate teaching assistants over the past six years have provided input and questions that have found their way into my exams. Some of these contributions are now questions at the ends of the chapters or part of the resources available to faculty. I also roped several undergraduate research assistants into the project: Amelia Boone, Zahra Egal, Seema Kanwar, Sagar Ravi, and David Rogier read drafts, researched facts, and helped to construct tables and the exercises at the ends of chapters. Several other undergraduates provided significant assistance: Jonathan Caplis, Maggie Hughes, Stephen Quinn, and Shelby Wolff. The College of Arts and Sciences at Washington University provided resources and means by which I could include these talented undergraduates in this project.

My involvement traces to Charisse Kiino in her role as a persistent, convincing, and supportive editor at CQ Press. The project is a result of her initial vision. She has moved upstairs and I now work with acquisitions editor Elise Frasier, who has been a strong and persistent supporter and guide for this revision. Also at CQ Press, Michael Kerns as the development editor for my first book offered thoughtful, useful feedback and strict deadlines. For this project, Nancy Matuszak worked as the development editor. Her suggestions were invaluable and are incorporated throughout the text. It is much better consequently. I thank Judy Selhorst, who did a fantastic job as the copy editor for this new version and production editor Astrid Virding ably handled the project to completion. I really enjoyed writing this book, then reworking it and writing new content, and just when I thought I had it right after repeatedly writing and rewriting chapters, the editorial staff at CQ Press made additional suggestions that improved the organization of the text and its prose. My colleagues at institutions around the country who served as reviewers for CQ Press—among them, J. Lawrence Broz, University of California, San Diego; Kerry Chase, Brandeis University; John Conybeare, University of Iowa; David Fisk, University of California, San Diego; Scott Gates, International Peace Research Institute, Oslo; Tobias Hofmann, College of William and Mary; Mike Jasinski, University of Wisconsin–Osh Kosh; David Leblang, University of Virginia; Quan Li, Texas A&M; Eloise Malone, United States Naval Academy; Waltraud Q. Morales, University of Central Florida; James Morrison, Middlebury College; Nathan Jensen, Washington University in St. Louis; Maria Sampanis, California State University, Sacramento; Susan Sell, George Washington University; Beth Simmons, Harvard University; Jeffrey Sosland, American University–Tenley Campus; and Gregory White, Smith College— dedicated substantial time to provide excellent feedback and suggestions. Their comments have greatly improved the text.

I thank Pam Lokken for reading and rereading draft upon draft of this book and all my other projects. She has provided tremendous support and encouragement over the years, and I look forward to more of the same. Finally, I want to thank the folks at Einstein's Bagels, Sharky's Grill, and Gary's Dewey Beach Grill for providing much-needed sustenance during my intensive writing periods. To all those named here and those who wish to remain anonymous, I extend my thanks and appreciation. As always, any remaining problems are solely the responsibility of this author.

Part I

Building Blocks to Examine Global Political Economy and Conflict

Introduction: Political Economy, Rationality, and Social Science

I consider that a man's brain originally is like a little empty attic, and you have to stock it with such furniture as you choose. A fool takes in all the lumber of every sort that he comes across, so that the knowledge which might be useful to him gets crowded out, or at best jumbled up with a lot of other things, so that he has difficulty in laying his hands upon it. Now the skillful workman is very careful indeed as to what he takes into his brain-attic. He will have nothing but the tools which may help him in doing his work, but of those he has an assortment, and all in the most perfect order. It is a mistake to think that little room has elastic walls and can distend to any extent. Depend upon it there comes a time when for every addition of knowledge you forget something that you knew before. It is of the highest importance, therefore, not to have useless facts elbowing out the useful ones.

—*Sherlock Holmes, in Arthur Conan Doyle, A Study in Scarlet, 1887*

This book adopts a political economy approach to examining world affairs in an era of expanding globalization. In this chapter we begin to build a foundation for this approach. First, we define what we mean by *globalization*, then we introduce the basic framework of political economy, and finally we consider what it means to poke and prod social behavior as social scientists. Before we go into greater depth, what is political economy? Moreover, what is international political economy and how does it differ from just plain political economy?

Political economy refers to a specific theoretical approach that focuses on the rational calculations and choices of individuals, and how those choices interact to produce social outcomes in world affairs. What makes this book's approach different from a political economy approach to domestic politics is the added consideration that such choices and aggregation processes occur in settings, and with consequences, that span national boundaries. From a political economy perspective, the logic of decision making in both domestic and world affairs is the same. The context,

Political economy encompasses a variety of approaches to social behavior. Macro political economy investigates associations between political activities and substantive performance of an economy. A micro political economy approach focuses on the processes that influence, motivate, and constrain the choices of individual political actors. In this micro approach to political economy we seek to examine the processes of choice that lead to government policies and to social, economic, and political outcomes. This approach seeks to investigate and construct the microfoundations of macro outcomes. A micro political economy approach can be used to examine individual decisions and social outcomes across a wide variety of settings. In this book, it is applied to questions in the arena of international affairs, international cooperation, and globalization.

however, differs in important ways that have profound implications for arriving at productive or damaging social outcomes. The implications of the important differences in structure and context that separate domestic from international affairs are what set this book's approach apart from a straight political economy focus and will become more explicit and apparent later in this chapter and the next.

SIMILARITIES ACROSS DOMESTIC AND INTERNATIONAL POLITICS

Many in political science separate the study of international relations from international political economy, applying distinctions such as the "high politics" of security versus the "low politics" of economic relations. They also separate the study of domestic politics from international politics. These distinctions are misleading and intellectually damaging. Political scientists look for explanations and processes that generalize from one setting to others. This is one characteristic that makes political science a science. If man is "a political animal," we should establish what we mean by *political* and how the mechanisms of politics work. The theories and explanations that help us make sense of political behavior are likely to be similar across domestic and international arenas and across issue areas, whether security, economic, or social. The key difference will be in the dependent variable, or what we seek to explain, and not in the independent variables—the mechanisms and explanations of why political actors do what they do. Separating the study of security and conflict from the study of economic relations in the global arena, or from the study of domestic politics, suggests that politics works completely differently in one sphere than in another. Others have made this dichotomy and suffered serious consequences. In the 1500s, Philip II of the Spanish Habsburg Empire, a military superpower of its time, sought to quell a rebellion against Spanish rule by the provinces of the Dutch Netherlands, a far smaller political and demographic entity. Napoleon, a warrior, dismissed England as a "nation of shopkeepers," and Mao Zedong ("All power comes from the barrel of a gun") called the United States a "paper tiger." The Dutch, the shopkeepers, and the paper tiger prevailed in the political-military sphere because of their activities and capabilities in the political economic arena. The Dutch Netherlands, the United Kingdom, and the United States dominated international affairs during the 1500–1600s, 1700–1800s, and 1900s onward, respectively, becoming hegemons through the strength of their economies and the policy choices they made in their domestic political economic arenas. The Soviet

Union amassed an impressive military but lost the Cold War and disintegrated because of its inability to compete with the economic prowess of the U.S. political economy. Success in political economic affairs spills over to the security sphere. Creating a false dichotomy between substantive spheres of political activity and neglecting connections across them is therefore dangerous not only in terms of our understanding of political behavior but also in terms of policy.

Let's start by examining the broad and shifting structure of world affairs, which is characterized by capitalism and an increasing globalization of social, political, economic, and cultural relations across national boundaries. This increasing globalization of human interactions across national boundaries presents national policy makers, public and private, with tremendous opportunities to enhance the well-being of their societies and communities, but it also creates pitfalls and challenges that, if poorly addressed, could damage and undermine that well-being. A political economy approach to world affairs will help us recognize those opportunities and challenges, enabling us to understand why societies sometimes act productively and sometimes perversely in terms of aggregate social welfare, and, for those of us interested in improving social outcomes, may provide a road map that will allow us to avoid potholes in our journey through life.

GLOBALIZATION AND GLOBAL CAPITALISM: CONNECTING MARKETS AND COMMUNITIES

Global relations of various kinds play a growing and important role in our day-to-day lives. Economic, social, cultural, and political relations within and across nations have shifted dramatically over the past two centuries, and they continue to change at a rapid rate. These transformations contribute to the process called **globalization,** which affects social relations between and within

> **Globalization** consists of the processes by which people in one society become culturally, economically, politically, strategically, and ecologically closer to peoples in geographically distant societies.

nation-states. Globalization consists of the multiple processes by which people in one society become culturally, economically, politically, strategically, and ecologically closer to peoples in geographically distant societies. These processes include the expansion of cross-border trade, the production of goods and services through multinational corporations, the movement of peoples, the exchange of ideas and popular culture, the flow of environmental degradation and disease from one nation to another, and the routine transfer of billions of dollars across borders in nanoseconds. They connect communities, cultures, national markets for goods and services, and national markets for labor and capital. The food we consume, the clothes we wear, the jobs we perform, the air we breathe and the water we drink, the cars we drive, the transport that delivers our goods, the information we access, the capital that powers our economies, the services and computers we use, the places we travel to, the education we seek, the diseases we contract, and just about every aspect of our day-to-day lives have some international component. This book seeks to help students develop the tools they need to understand why policy makers, public and private, make the choices they do in an era of increasing globalization.

One characteristic of globalization is the prospect for some incidence of convergence across nations as markets and societies become increasingly exposed to each other and increasingly integrated. The more integrated economies become, the more closely we should observe prices for commodities and labor across those economies converging. Still, there is little reason to expect complete—or even near—convergence in many arenas of social life. A continued divergence in commodity and labor prices across markets demonstrates the persistence and stickiness of distinct national political economies in the face of globalizing pressures. Moreover, the services that states provide to their citizens can vary quite dramatically from state to state. Such differences represent differences in social contracts—the bargains between governments and their peoples. The modern nation-state is far from dead or from being brushed aside by the trend toward globalization.

One factor that has contributed to economic convergence is the advance of **global capitalism,** which is a particular form of social and economic relations connecting national economies. After the collapse of the communist regimes of the Eastern bloc in the late twentieth century, capitalism emerged as the preeminent form of social and economic organization in the global political economy. In global capitalism, exchange across nations occurs primarily in markets, where consumption choices are voluntary, determined by supply and demand, and coordinated by price mechanisms. Markets can be located in physical structures such as buildings, on docks, in town squares, or in cyberspace, where exchanges are conducted via computer keystroke. Markets are wherever merchants and consumers gather to exchange commodities and services.

Global capitalism is a particular form of social and economic relations connecting national economies, by which exchange across nations occurs primarily in markets, where consumption choices are voluntary, determined by supply and demand, and coordinated by price mechanisms. **Decentralized** economic systems are those in which consumption, production, and allocation choices are voluntary, determined by supply and demand, and coordinated by price mechanisms. **Centralized means of allocation** are distribution mechanisms that are more hierarchical and authoritative than the voluntary, consensual nature of a market.

Markets aggregate individual activities and produce collective outcomes. They are relatively **decentralized** mechanisms for allocating goods, capital, and services within and across societies. This mode of exchange differs from more **centralized means of allocation** such as government-administered distribution mechanisms that are more hierarchical and authoritative than the voluntary, consensual nature of a market. In this book, we extend the framework of market exchange beyond the boundaries of economic exchange to encompass political exchange as well. When economic and political markets work well, they are a wonderful means of aggregating individual preferences, conveying tremendous amounts of information, and producing collective outcomes. They tell us about the preferences of consumers and voters in society, about the productive capabilities of producers and policy makers given the distribution of resources in society, and about the most efficient ways to coordinate the choices of consumers and voters with those of producers and policy makers.

The expansion of globalization means that economic production and consumption choices in one nation are increasingly influenced by similar choices in other nations. For many years, economists used **closed-economy models** to examine economic conditions in a society. They ignored economic factors and conditions external to a nation, thinking about the nation's economy as if it were a secluded island. But with the transformation of national capitalist relations into increasingly global capitalist relations, closed-economy frameworks have given way to **open-economy models,** in which connections across national economies are considered to be important factors in a nation's economic and social welfare and the politics that surround it. Imports and exports now constitute at least a third of the economies of advanced industrialized nations, and for many, such as Germany, the size of the tradable sector is even larger.

> **Closed-economy models** approach the examination of economic conditions in a society by ignoring economic factors and conditions external to the nation and considering the nation as an isolated entity. **Open-economy models** are political economy models in which connections across national economies are considered to be important factors in a nation's economic and social welfare and the politics that surround it.

The extent of global influence on our lives may vary depending upon where we live, our nationality, our income, our profession, and the openness and strength of our national political economy. However, the world is figuratively shrinking, as activities in one nation spill over to influence activities in other nations with greater and greater frequency. Almost certainly, the connection of economic markets across borders will influence choices and actions in national political markets. The shifts in global economic activity spawn debates about the changing roles of markets and states, about the risks individuals face in this changing state of affairs, and about whether those risks can or should be managed and, if so, by whom. At the heart of these debates rests an extraordinary tension between economic and political forms of social organization. Global capitalism is based on market exchange and an economic geography that spans national borders. With globalization, economic relations are increasingly formed and shaped by global market forces. In theory, these forces do not recognize the political boundaries of nation-states, yet national borders define political arenas and are the dominant form of political geography in theory and in practice. Political relations are defined by the modern nation-state system. Thus national boundaries organize political life, but economic life spans those boundaries. Political organization, authority, and geography do not overlap with the economic geography of globalization. This tension between sovereignty and interdependence will return again and again in our study of modern international affairs. As billionaire currency trader George Soros noted, "We can have a market economy, but we cannot have a market society."

Creating such connections across national boundaries brings good and bad consequences. Globalization can improve the well-being of many, but it also creates new risks and problems for societies. Globalization and global capitalism can blur the economic boundaries of the nation-state, spill over into noneconomic areas of social activity, and challenge the policy autonomy of national governments. In this shifting arena, significant challenges, perils, and opportunities confront governments, societies, firms, policy makers, and individuals. Many praise globalization, while others rail against it. Yet others see both its good and bad consequences and argue for managing the negatives while promoting the positives. This divisive effect goes beyond academic debate to visceral public arguments that evoke conflicting passions and fears. Demonstrators at the meetings of the World Trade Organization and the International Monetary Fund, at the Word Economic Forum in Davos, Switzerland, and at other international economic conferences have regularly protested globalization and the transformations in global capitalism.

Many worry about the potential for increasing income inequality and wealth concentration that accompanies market exchange if it is not mitigated by government policies that redistribute opportunities, resources, and wealth—even if individuals are better-off than they were the year before, and the year before that. But concern about globalization extends beyond economic consequences. Many fear its homogenizing effect on the distinct identities and cultures of different societies, as Nike, McDonalds, Starbucks, Coca-Cola, and other symbols of global capitalism insinuate themselves into national economies and consciousnesses. Immigration, another process of globalization, can bring new labor and vitality to some societies, but it can also challenge notions of national identity. Organizations and groups can advocate for fellow citizens to support national producers or resist inflows of foreign goods, people, and ideas, but such choices rest largely in the hands of individuals in market and democratic societies. Perhaps worried about the fate of the classic French bistro in the face of competitive pressures from McDonalds and other fast-food chains, Jack Lang, a former French minister of culture, warned:

> The disappearance of languages and cultural forms is the great risk today. Diversity threatens to be replaced by an international mass culture without roots, soul, color, or taste.[1]

These debates, protestations, and concerns will continue, both because globalization and international political economic relations are complex and incompletely understood phenomena and because the dominant form of political organization does not mesh with the dominant form of economic organization in the global political economy.

Autarky is a policy that seeks self-sufficiency and isolation from the global economy.

Despite such worries about globalization and its consequences, societies and governments rarely seek complete isolation from the global economy—a status called **autarky,** or self-sufficiency. Autarky

---

[1]Quoted in Walter LaFeber, *Michael Jordan and the New Global Capitalism* (New York: W. W. Norton, 1999).

and isolationism are sure paths to retarding the future growth and welfare of a society. Political economies that have tried to insulate themselves, or have been isolated by external sanction, from global exchange have lagged behind. This is the story of Cold War containment, Iran, Iraq, Venezuela, and North Korea. To be sure, risks to some individuals, families, and communities do accompany the significant societal payoffs to be expected from interacting with the global political economy, and we should not be naively optimistic about the resulting dislocations. Many of these effects will be relatively short-term, but they will nevertheless be costly to those who suffer them. This is true of any major social transformation, regardless of how beneficial the change may be for society in the long term. Change is inherently costly to anyone who prefers the status quo, who fears the uncertainty of the future, or who is underequipped in terms of the skills needed to adapt to change. Here we see the roots of the conflicted politics of globalization: many stand to benefit from the transformations it will bring, but some legitimately fear the potential costs to them, their families, and their communities.

At the societal level, the potential gains from the global exchange of goods, services, capital, and ideas far outweigh the benefits of self-sufficiency and isolationism, even if such strategies were plausible. Hiding our national heads in the global sand or retreating behind xenophobic national barriers based on fear of foreigners cannot be advanced as a plausible policy for dealing with the world unless we want to consign our economies, polities, and societies to second-class status. Policy makers are confronted with the challenge of reaping the rewards of globalization for the majority in their societies while managing the dislocation of the few. On the international front, they may resort to either unilateral or multilateral strategies to manage the effects of globalization on their societies— either adopting policies without the cooperation and coordination of other governments or attempting to coordinate policies with those of other governments. On the domestic front, policy makers must decide how to manage the inevitable dislocations (hopefully short-term) to the minority who will be negatively affected, for this minority could deny or dampen the benefits of globalization to the majority if they are effective at political action.

THE PAST AS PROLOGUE

Despite recent fascination with globalization and the belief by many that it is a new phenomenon, the transformations in global political economic relations of the later decades of the twentieth century are not unique in the history of human affairs. Significant cross-border market exchange has existed for many centuries. The Dutch became the first commercial and financial global hegemon in the 1600s. They propelled the expansion of global trade and market exchange. Amsterdam became an international financial center. The English and London would replace the Dutch and Amsterdam as the center of global commerce and finance by the 1700–1800s. Global capitalism emerged as the dominant form of international

Pedestrians walk past the skyline of Shanghai's financial district. Since Chinese authorities began liberalizing their economy more than thirty years ago, China has been the fastest-growing economy in the world, averaging more than 10 percent growth per year over the period. This economic transformation stems from China's engagement with the global capitalist economy and has resulted in hundreds of millions of Chinese being lifted out of poverty. China has become the world's largest exporter and second-largest importer, attracts capital investment, and sends millions of students abroad to study and gain skills to benefit the Chinese economy further.

exchange by the late 1700s–early 1800s. Nevertheless, this transition has been halting, plagued with breakdowns, interludes, and reversals along the way. Part III of this book explores the advance and retreat of globalization over the past several hundred years, providing a historical backdrop of important shifts and processes in world affairs.

WHAT IS POLITICAL ECONOMY?

The primary task of this book is to help students of world affairs develop a political economy approach to examining international relations and international political economy. First, what is political economy? The term encompasses a variety of approaches. For some, description of macro political economic activities constitutes political economy. Macro political economy investigates associations between political activities and substantive performance of an economy. Macroeconomic numbers such as gross national product (GNP), gross domestic product (GDP), national debt and deficit, inflation, unemployment, exchange rates, size of the public sector, balance of trade, central bank interest rates, investment, money supply, and productivity describe the state of the national political economy, all supplying information about a nation's aggregate welfare. We use such descriptive characteristics to infer how well or poorly governments are performing in managing their economies, and what areas governments and societies need to target for improvement. From a macro political economic perspective, these descriptions can serve as dependent variables that are influenced by government policy choices, or they can be considered as independent variables that motivate and influence a government's choice of policies. In either case, the substantive questions revolve around the nexus of government and economic behavior: How do government actions affect the state of the economy, or how does the state of the economy affect government actions? Many approaches to international political economy focus on such macro depictions. These depictions are important at both the domestic and international levels, and they can be a component of our discussion of political economy, but they differ from the micro approach emphasized throughout this book.

The micro political economy approach focuses on the processes that influence, motivate, and constrain the choices of individual political actors. We will emphasize the rationality, preferences, capabilities, calculations, strategies, and choices of individual political economic actors in social settings where their choices interact with the choices of others to produce the social outcomes we observe. In this approach, political economy describes the processes of choice that lead to government policies and to social, economic, and political outcomes. This approach seeks to investigate and construct the *micro* foundations of *macro* outcomes. Individual choices aggregate to produce macro outcomes, but we need to understand why individuals make the choices they make if we are to understand and thus be able to influence broader social outcomes in the world. We can then use these microfoundations to explain why decision makers make the choices they do, how context affects their individual calculations, and how individual choices aggregate to produce the social outcomes that we observe.

These processes are just as relevant to understanding decisions about war and conflict as they are to understanding why governments implement some economic policies and not others. Conceptualizing political economy in this way, we attempt to discover the inner workings, or causal foundations, of actions in political arenas. We focus on the calculations and choices of individuals in social settings, the incentives that influence these calculations and choices, and the processes by which individuals interact, compete, bargain, compromise, and even fight over policies, elections, regulations, and rules. The choices of numerous actors in the political sphere interact and aggregate to produce the social, economic, and political outcomes that are reflected in the macro political economy. They affect the allocation of gains and losses in society, creating winners and losers. From our micro perspective, political economy is a story about the processes and means by which members of society decide on policies and rules of the game that allocate gains, losses, and risks.

So why is this micro approach to politics considered political economy, and not political anthropology, political sociology, political psychology, or some other strategy of analysis? Simply, we assume that political actors use a specific form of logic—an economic logic—when evaluating alternatives as they engage in the processes of political bargaining and behavior. This approach to decision making compares the costs and benefits of alternative strategies and the likelihood of different outcomes given the possible actions of others. In this text, we apply this political economy approach to understanding world affairs, but it can be used to gain insight to social phenomena that are not exclusively international, such as migration, voting decisions and rules, judicial activity, political and civil liberties, ethnic conflict, discrimination, gender rights, fiscal policies, health care, and other political activities.

THREE CORE ASSUMPTIONS WITHIN THE MICRO POLITICAL ECONOMY APPROACH

Three powerful assumptions underpin the tools of explanation developed in this book. First, *we live in a world of scarce resources.* Second, *political actors seek to survive.* Third,

Scarcity is the concept that all items and resources that we consume—those produced by human beings and those produced by nature—exist in some finite amount, regardless of the demand for those items; this is a key assumption because it generates the conditions for competition, cooperation, and conflict over the distribution of resources and opportunities. **Costs** are the goods that we forgo when we choose to consume particular items.

decision makers act as if they are rational. Let's consider each of these more carefully, for the logic of our micro political economy approach builds on these assumptions. Making these assumptions, and others, explicit also creates better opportunities to challenge them. Unstated assumptions prove more difficult to challenge because they offer greater wiggle room, whereas more explicit approaches encourage rigorous testing and build a healthy skepticism into the process of investigation.

Scarcity

Scarcity is a key assumption, as it generates the conditions for competition, cooperation, and conflict over the distribution of resources and opportunities. It creates the possibility for relative winners and losers to emerge. In a world of plenty—a world absent scarcity—men and women could consume whatever they want, whenever they want, without impinging on the choices of others. No competition or conflict over the distribution of resources would exist, nor would there be a need for compromise or cooperation to overcome barriers to the distribution or allocation of resources. Selfish actors—gluttons—could consume as much as they wanted without diminishing the supply of resources for others. Hunger, impoverishment, jealousy, and want would not exist or make sense. In such a world, envy and *egoistic* (selfish) actions would be meaningless, as they would create no costs for others and would not affect an individual's own opportunities or those available to others. Neither money nor any other medium of exchange would have value, for all could consume what they wanted without concern for the rules of supply and demand. **Costs,** those things that we forgo when we choose to consume particular items, would become meaningless, as no costs would exist. We would not have to forgo consumption of some items because we elected to consume other items. A world without scarcity would translate into an absence of constraints on consumption, as well as an absence of the conditions that spawn distributional conflict, competition, and cooperation. A world without scarcity would be literally a Garden of Eden.

Unfortunately, we do not live in such a garden of unlimited resources. All items we consume—those produced by humans and those produced by nature—exist in some finite amount, regardless of the demand for those items. In a world of scarce resources, items in high demand and low supply become expensive and valuable relative to items in high supply and low demand. Scarcity may appear as a budgetary constraint, such as how much money is in one's wallet; as a resource constraint, such as height and strength; or as an information constraint, such as incomplete information or limited ability to process information. In a world of scarcity, mechanisms of exchange become important. Scarcity creates the conditions for politics, which is a use of coercive means to determine the rules of social, political, and economic exchange, to allocate resources, to divide the proverbial pie, and to decide who gets what, why, and how. Politics imposes a nonvoluntary component upon exchange and allocation. For example, if you vote for the Democrat but the Republican wins, you still must consume the political policies enacted by the Republican.

Politics helps create rules for social, economic, and political exchange and allocation within and across communities. Such rules, if violated, can trigger penalties and punishment. We call such rules **institutions,** a concept that we examine more carefully in chapter 8. These institutions or rules may be formal or informal.

> **Institutions** are the formal and informal "rules of the game," laws, and practices that structure the incentives of individuals.

Examples of formal institutions include constitutions, electoral rules, statutory laws, and regulations. Examples of informal institutions are habits, norms, and loosely defined social practices. Formal institutions enjoy formal sanctioning mechanisms such as governments to enforce rules and apply penalties for lack of compliance, whereas informal institutions lack such explicit enforcement mechanisms. Informal institutions can arise from a variety of sources, such as common beliefs and practices, differences in power, the emergence of societal norms, religious prescriptions, folklore, and voluntary cooperation. Informal rules are nonstatutory, but they may prove just as forceful as formal rules in motivating and constraining human activity. The use of threats, penalties, and punishment is by definition coercive, as these measures constrain human choice (that is, without such constraints a person would choose differently), but they may be necessary to encourage social, economic, and political exchange that can be socially beneficial within and across national boundaries. The rules of exchange and allocation produced in political arenas create relative winners and losers in political economies. Constructing a law, rule, or regulation, or invoking a social practice one way versus another, affects the distribution of resources and influ-

Antiglobalization protesters regularly voice their opinions at Group of 8 and Group of 20 (G-8 and G-20) summits of world leaders. Here, in reaction to the G-8 meeting in Paris during May 2011, activists from the humanitarian nongovernmental organization Oxfam pose as (from left) Russian president Dmitry Medvedev, British prime minister David Cameron, U.S. president Barack Obama, French president Nicolas Sarkozy, Italian prime minister Silvio Berlusconi, German chancellor Angela Merkel, Japanese prime minister Naoto Kan, and Canadian prime minister Stephen Harper playing poker, with the stakes being the health of the world economy. Such demonstrations reflect the intensity of opposition among critics of globalization and the pressures that policy makers must confront and manage in formulating policies and laws related to the processes of globalization.

ence in societies. Altering such institutions moves the boundaries of distribution and allocation; therefore, laws and regulations themselves can become targets of fierce competition, sometimes leading to cooperation and compromise, sometimes to conflict.

Political Survival

The second assumption on which the tools in this book build is that political actors and governments want to survive—to stay in office and in power—and will act to survive. In democratic electoral systems, these actors work to enhance their prospects for reelection. In less democratic systems, political actors may instead work to build constituencies among those groups that can protect them, such as the military or select segments of society. We call the group essential to a political actor's survival the *selectorate*. The assumption that survival is an important goal helps us to analyze the choices made by policy makers, by asking how political actors view such choices as affecting their prospects for political survival.

This assumption does not imply that politicians have no preferences about the state of the world or about the public policies that affect the state of the world, but it does suggest that they evaluate policies for achieving those preferences within a context that involves assessing how their choices will affect their ability to survive politically and whom they must satisfy to survive. A politician who finds her policy preferences in conflict with her ability to survive faces difficult choices and trade-offs. Such conflict is very common, and it underpins much of the cynicism about politics that is generated when politicians seem to compromise their policy preferences in order to stay in office. However, if selecting policies independent of considerations about reelection and political survival should lead to her political demise, the politician would not be able to promote her policy preferences in the future, whereas her opponent, who has different policy preferences, would. Compromising on policy preferences to improve the odds of political survival is thus akin to retreating in order to fight another day.

Rationality

Our third assumption is that people behave as if they are rational. This is not to claim that people really are rational beings, but rather that they behave and make choices *as if* they are. Explicitly assuming that people behave as if they are rational, regardless of whether they really are, embeds decision making within a particular logic that can be applied to politicians, policy makers, and interested parties. This logic is key to systematic and consistent investigation of the actions of such actors within political economies, for it provides a powerful and explicit lever for analyzing behavior and understanding decision making.

What do we mean by *rationality*, and why is it such a useful tool? Rationality describes a particular process of choice. This focus on the choices of individuals is called

methodological individualism. It amounts to a claim that individuals—not larger units of aggregation such as nations or societies—make choices. A variety of approaches exist to investigate the choices of individuals: cultural anthropologists

> **Methodological individualism** is a focus on the actions and choices of individuals—not larger units of aggregation such as nations or societies.

place their primary focus on the effects of culture on individual choice; sociologists emphasize the influence of group dynamics on individual choice; and psychologists look at psychological, emotional, biological, and subliminal constraints on individual choice. The assumption of rationality in this book on political economy focuses our attention on a particular means by which individuals choose among alternatives under constraints of scarcity.

RATIONALITY, PREFERENCES, AND SELF-INTEREST EXPLORED

Because the assumption of rationality is central to the micro political economy approach of this text, we need to take a closer look at some mechanics of this assumption and how it interacts with the first two assumptions about scarcity and political survival. Assuming that political economic actors behave as if they are rational means that we assume they can systematically order their preferences over the state of the world, along with the expected outcomes of their choices, and that the ordering will be consistent over time and in their self-interest. There are many ways that preferences could conceivably be ordered: randomly, as in drawing them blindly from a hat; alphabetically; or by some other arbitrary scheme. The rationality assumption holds that preferences are ordered in terms of self-interest.

Ordering Preferences

To understand the ordering principle that underpins rationality and our approach to individual choice, we first must ask, what are preferences and self-interest? At the level of the individual, **preferences** are simply statements about individual wants such as food, wealth, entertainment, security, community, justice, status, respect, influence, fairness, and liberty. These preferences include material wants as well as social and spiritual wants; a want can be a preference over the state of the world, as the state of the world is instrumental in affecting the distribution of other wants. **Self-**

> **Preferences** are statements about individual wants, including material wants as well as social and spiritual wants. **Self-interest** is the notion that people make choices based on their hierarchies of preferences and their budgetary constraints.

interest is simply a statement about how an individual's preferences affect her interpretation of her position in the world. Economists call this *utility,* which is shorthand for everything that affects an individual's expected satisfaction. Will a particular choice increase or decrease an individual's utility? Self-interest assumes that individuals will select choices by seeking to improve their utility, or expected satisfaction. Utility sometimes refers to goodies such as economic wealth or income, which are relatively easy to measure. But utility can also include noneconomic goodies such as health, social status, happiness, family, or some other aspect of life that an individual values, which can be relatively difficult to measure. Remember, we have assumed that decision makers, or political actors, will seek to survive and to advance their interests. So one criterion for evaluating and comparing preferences is determining how they affect the survival and status of the decision maker.

This approach to investigating decision making involves the following assumptions:

- People act as if they can discriminate among their preferences.
- People act as if they can order their preferences in terms of most to least desirable.
- People can evaluate and rank possible outcomes of their choices in terms of their preferences because they recognize that there may be some discontinuity between a choice based on a preference and the actual outcome.
- People will choose to obtain an expected outcome that is higher in their ranking rather than a lower one given their budgetary, resource, or information constraints.
- People will be fairly consistent in their choices and preferences over time and, if presented with the same list of preferences and outcomes at different times, will rank them similarly.

Assuming that people behave *as if* rational and that they can place their preferences along a single dimension based on their self-interest—thus creating a hierarchy of preferences from most to least preferred—is a vast simplification and potentially a tenuous one, but it is nonetheless useful as the first step in adopting rationality as an analytic tool. It supplies a systematic way of discriminating across preferences and alternative outcomes and of evaluating different courses of action. We can employ this assumption of rationality to understand why a decision maker might choose one action over another. It enables investigators to examine alternative courses of action or strategies for achieving the actor's objectives and to evaluate those strategies in terms of their potential to produce the preferred objectives and of their likely costs. This tool allows investigators and individuals to evaluate the trade-offs between costs and benefits, to weigh disadvantages and advantages.

Rationality under Scarcity and Political Survival

Our three core assumptions work together to shape our inquiry. Understanding the assumption of rationality returns us to the scarcity and political survival assumptions. In a world of plenty, we would not have to consider the criteria that guide individual choices, because decisions would not matter in terms of consumption opportunities. Irrelevant to the distribution of resources, political survival would also be meaningless. But scarcity places costs on decision making because making choices involves forgoing other possibilities, affects distributional outcomes in society, and makes political survival relevant. The assumption of scarcity creates both a need for decision criteria to make trade-offs and a demand upon politicians to act in their self-interest in terms of political survival. Rationality is one such decision criterion, and it is constrained by scarcity. Decision makers' time, energy, and capabilities are scarce resources. They may need to make choices with incomplete information, limited by the demands of time and handicapped by the dilemmas of trying to forecast an uncertain future. Such constraints can affect a decision maker's process of choice and force her to allocate more time and effort to some decisions than to others. Together, these assumptions help us to investigate why a political actor may focus on one objective over another, by making it clear that a decision maker does not value all objectives equally but discriminates across a wide range of objectives as she allocates her limited time and energy.

Rationality prescribes the more efficient choice, determining which strategy can be expected to deliver the largest payoff, given a preference ordering and given the cost constraints. When the expected costs of obtaining the most preferred objective are too high, the assumption of rationality allows us to evaluate the trade-offs between secondary objectives, strategies to obtain those objectives, and the cost of each strategy. The assumption of rationality means that we expect decision makers to choose the course of action that is most likely to produce the best outcome for them given costs and benefits across the alternatives. For example, despite a general trend toward trade liberalization—which is consistent with their own dominant preference for free trade over government intervention in trade—policy makers in the United States occasionally create and maintain barriers to trade. Such barriers have been imposed on products such as textiles, shoes, steel, and automobiles. At first glance, this practice appears nonrational, because it seems to conflict with the preference ordering of policy makers. But policy makers also want to survive, and we can assume that this preference generally dominates other preferences. If supporting free trade in a particular sector, such as textiles or shoes, would severely threaten a politician's ability to survive because it would produce dislocated and unhappy voters, we should expect that politician to support a less costly policy. If enough politicians were threatened in this way, we would find an explanation based on rationality for the adoption of trade barriers in particular sectors.

Putting our three core assumptions together suggests that as policy makers operate in a world of scarcity, they will act to further their policy preferences within the limits of their ability to survive, and they will follow a logic based on rationality to do so. This means that they will act in their self-interest—broadly defined as a calculation of how their choices will affect their ability to survive and prosper, given the alternatives. Ideally, their self-interest will be compatible with societal welfare, but there are no guarantees that the interests of policy makers and those of the broader society will overlap significantly.

Two Properties of Preference Ordering: Completeness and Transitivity

Next we consider two important properties that are involved in using preferences and rationality to examine behavior: completeness and transitivity. **Completeness** establishes that two alternatives are comparable and can be placed in a hierarchy. If we can say that an individual prefers one alternative to another (or vice versa) or is indifferent between the two, we are establishing qualities about the alternatives that constitute completeness. **Indifference** means, quite literally, that an individual is indifferent between alternatives, that they are equal but still comparable. Completeness is a useful concept because it allows us to study an individual and say that she prefers one alternative to another or is indifferent, and then to expect her to behave according to that preference ordering.

Completeness is the quality that defines two alternatives as both comparable and capable of being placed in a hierarchy. **Indifference** is the state of impartiality, or lack of preference, between alternatives that are equal but still comparable. **Transitivity** is the quality that defines three or more alternatives as comparable and capable of being placed in a hierarchy of preferences. A **hierarchy of preferences** is the ranking of preferences along a single dimension based on self-interest—creating a hierarchy from most to least preferred.

Transitivity extends the logic of comparability that is reflected in completeness to more than two alternatives. Transitivity means that three or more alternatives are comparable and can be placed in a hierarchy of preferences. For example, imagine that an individual has to choose among three alternatives for dinner: steak, chicken, and fish. She begins by first looking for completeness, or comparability between two alternatives, by comparing each pair of alternatives: steak and chicken, chicken and fish, and steak and fish. Her preferences are transitive if she prefers steak to chicken, chicken to fish, and steak to fish, because this pattern permits a strict ordering or **hierarchy of preferences.** If we were trying to understand her preferences so that we could take her to dinner for her birthday, determining that she has a strict hierarchy of preferences would make our task easier. Even if she were indifferent between several alternatives, her preferences would still be transitive if they could be arranged in order and we could therefore anticipate what restaurants would give her the greatest satisfaction for her birthday celebration.

Unfortunately, not all choice situations are this simple. In relatively rare cases, individuals display complete but intransitive preferences. For example, our birthday celebrant may prefer steak to chicken, chicken to fish, but fish to steak. Every alternative is comparable, which satisfies completeness, but we cannot build a strict hierarchy across the three alternatives. This leaves us with the dilemma of where to take her for her birthday dinner if we want to provide her with the greatest expected satisfaction. We might say that individuals who can fulfill a condition of completeness but not transitivity are nonrational or confused, or perhaps that life is complicated and rational people can have preferences that fall along more than a single dimension. Both life and the investigation of choices are much simpler when we can establish a preference ordering that falls along a single dimension, as in figure 1.1; then we can simply anticipate choices being made for more preferred over less preferred alternatives, given the constraints of resource scarcity. But if we add another dimension to the choice of food—such as the ambience of the restaurant, whether it is quiet or loud, as in figure 1.2—both the investigation of individual choice and the choices themselves become far more complicated. This added complexity creates uncertainty about individual choice and interjects considerations of costs or trade-offs into the selection of one alternative over another. Figures 1.1 and 1.2 offer useful visual tools for examining the distribution of preferences over outcomes. Each is a spatial depiction, or what is called a **spatial model** of an individual's preferences.

A **spatial model** is a useful visual tool for examining the distribution of preferences or policy in geographic or geometric space. An **intransitive collective outcome** is a social preference ordering constructed through the aggregation of the preferences of individual group members and in which the group outcome does not represent a strict hierarchy of social preferences.

In reality, this problem is relatively rare for individuals. When forced to select between alternatives, individuals can usually produce a complete and transitive preference ordering—they are able to force their individual preferences into a strict hierarchy. But the dilemma of intransitive preferences is quite likely to arise in the construction of the preference orderings of collectivities such as groups, societies, or electorates by means of some democratic voting rule or market exchange mechanism. The aggregation of individual preferences by such means can often produce an **intransitive collective outcome,** even if all the individuals voting have expressed complete and transitive preferences. This possibility opens the door to troubling questions about whether democratic and market processes of choice in economic and political exchange can actually maximize the social welfare function of society—whether individuals voting in accordance with their complete and transitive preference orderings can indeed produce a complete and transitive collective preference ordering that optimizes the social welfare of society. If individuals and groups confronted with three or more alternatives satisfy the condition of completeness but not that of transitivity, this element of uncertainty presents potential hindrances to our use of rationality as an analytical tool. (The appendix to this chapter offers examples of individual and collective preferences in the political arena that are complete but intransitive.)

This conceptualization of preference ordering describes a particular logic that assumes rationality and a specific process by which individuals select among alternatives. Even if individuals have intransitive preferences, we can use this logic as a tool to investigate choices in politics, economics, and other avenues of life. This logic allows us to evaluate

| FIGURE 1.1 | **Complete and Transitive Preference Ordering along One Dimension** |

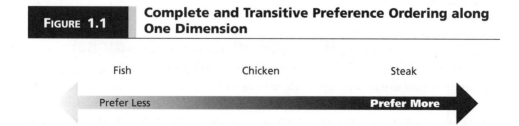

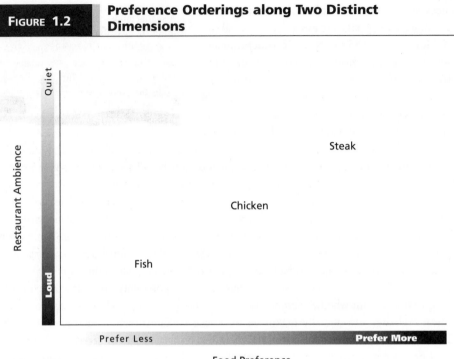

FIGURE 1.2   Preference Orderings along Two Distinct Dimensions

the preference orderings of individuals over the range of alternatives they consider and to consider the trade-offs and costs across such alternatives. This process amounts to a cost-benefit analysis of possible alternative choices, in which we consider the preference ordering of outcomes, whether these outcomes satisfy conditions of completeness and transitivity, the likelihood of obtaining each alternative outcome given our available strategies and resources, and the cost of obtaining each alternative outcome. This type of analysis offers a strategy for understanding past choices and anticipating future choices. We can anticipate that decision makers will select courses of action that are most likely to produce the best outcomes on their hierarchies of preferences, given cost constraints. This logic provides the foundation for a systematic strategy to examine why decision makers make the choices they do.

CONTEXT AND THE INTERDEPENDENCE OF CHOICES: OPPORTUNITY FOR STRATEGIC BEHAVIOR

We must be careful in building upon the assumption of rationality. Even after ordering preferences and determining whether they have properties of completeness and transitivity that fall along a single dimension to produce a consistent ordering, choice may not be straightforward. We should consider two important reasons why: *choice is not independent of context*; and *choice is not independent of the actions of others.*

Choices occur within contexts. Taken independent of context, rationality becomes a trivial—or worse, pathological—assumption. Context influences costs and the likelihood of obtaining particular outcomes. The same rational decision maker may select one strategy in one context and another strategy in another context. This does not mean that the decision maker behaves nonrationally, but that a change in context can affect her evaluation of the trade-offs, costs, and gains involved with different strategies. The policy maker who decides to lower trade barriers during a period of economic expansion may resist such a policy change during a period of economic contraction. The policy maker who advocates military intervention in Somalia, Iraq, or Serbia for humanitarian reasons may resist such intervention in Rwanda or North Korea. Politicians who advocate placing limits on whaling in order to protect a species from risk of extinction may not be inclined to impose limits to protect fishing stocks facing similar consequences. A shift in context produces this change, not a shift in rationality. Rational action is embedded in context. Therefore it is important to study decisions within their contexts, which inform us about the options and constraints that decision makers encounter.

The second reason for apparent inconsistency is that choice is not independent of the actions of others. This complication is a function of the structure of context, of who the other parties are within a context, the preferences of those different parties concerning outcomes, their individual choices, and the mechanisms that aggregate those individual choices to produce a social or collective outcome. Interesting outcomes in social settings are generally consequences of the interactions of multiple individuals' choices and actions. Most interesting social outcomes, those depending on the actions of more than a single person, are produced by the interactions of multiple individuals and their strategies. This interdependence raises the opportunity for strategic behavior, in which individuals are aware that an outcome depends on the interaction of their choices with others' choices, so they try to select strategies that anticipate what others may do or manipulate the context to affect others' choices. If my most preferred outcome depends on my choice of strategy and a specific choice of strategy by another person, but that person would never make that specific choice, then my selecting a strategy to obtain that preferred outcome is fruitless. It might even prove perverse, if the interaction of such choices should produce a far worse outcome than if I had compensated for the other person's likely choice by making another choice accordingly.

GAME THEORY: MODELING CONTEXT AND INTERDEPENDENT CHOICES

"You mean, the theory of games like chess." "No, no," he said. "Chess is not a game. Chess is a well-defined form of computation. You may not be able to work out all the answers, but in theory there must be a solution, a right procedure in any position. Now real games are not like that at all. Real life is not like that. Real life consists of bluffing, of little tactics of deception, of asking yourself what is the other man going to think I mean to do."

—John von Neumann, in William Poundstone, *Prisoner's Dilemma* (1992)

Game theory is the systematic study of rational choice in strategic settings.

Game theory, the systematic study of rational choice in strategic settings, is a useful tool for modeling and investigating social behavior that involves rational calculation and interdependent choices. Strategic settings are those situations in which outcomes depend on the interactions of the choices of two or more individuals. Decision makers must consider the strategies of others in this decision context, their likely choices, and how those choices interact to produce individual and collective outcomes. Figure 1.3 uses several simple games to illustrate how individual choices interact to produce an outcome, and how the same rational individuals may behave differently if the context varies. The games in figure 1.3 are models of decision settings or contexts in which two decision makers must decide among alternative strategies. By definition these models are simplifications, but they capture some important underlying dynamics of a choice situation.

In these games, each decision maker, or player, has a choice of two strategies, *A* or *B*. The payoffs the decision makers will obtain if their choices intersect are located in the cells of figure 1.3. In each cell, the payoff for Player 1 is shown before the comma and that for Player 2

FIGURE 1.3   Strategy and Choice in Different Contexts

GAME A

	Player 2's Choice	
Player 1's Choice	Strategy *A*	Strategy *B*
Strategy *A*	20, 10	5, −1
Strategy *B*	−1, 5	0, 0

GAME B

	Player 2's Choice	
Player 1's Choice	Strategy *A*	Strategy *B*
Strategy *A*	20, 10	5, 15
Strategy *B*	10, 20	−5, −5

appears after the comma. For example, in Game A, if Player 1 and Player 2 both select Strategy A, Player 1 will receive 20 and Player 2 will receive 10. If we assume that the decision makers will act as if they are rational, we can rank all the outcomes or payoffs in terms of the players' preferences (more is better in this example): given the possible outcomes in Game A, Player 1 prefers 20 to 5 to 0 to −1 (20 > 5 > 0 > −1) and Player 2 prefers 10 to 5 to 0 to −1 (10 > 5 > 0 > −1). These preference orderings are complete and transitive. Now, each player must consider the other player's expected behavior given her preferences and choice of strategies, and then select the strategy that can be expected to produce the greatest benefit contingent upon the other player's choice of strategy.

> **Dominant strategy** is a strategy that a player would select regardless of the actions of other players. The **invisible hand** is an idea proposed by Adam Smith, who theorized that an unseen force guides self-interested individual behavior in competitive markets to promote the welfare of society without deliberate intent.

This is a nice game, as both players can obtain their best outcomes by selecting Strategy A. Player 1 knows that Player 2 prefers the outcome produced by Strategy A, and Player 2 knows that Player 1 prefers the outcome produced by Strategy A. There is no tension or conflict in this game because both players can select their preferred strategies and obtain their preferred outcomes. Each has a **dominant strategy,** which is the one she would select regardless of what the other player does. In this case, the dominant strategy produces the best collective outcome, 20 10, and everyone is happy! This is the situation that eighteenth-century economist and philosopher Adam Smith envisioned in *The Wealth of Nations* with his argument about the functioning of the **invisible hand** in efficient markets. In such settings, individuals only need to act sincerely, choosing their most preferred outcomes to obtain the best possible collective outcome.

> A **stable equilibrium** is a situation in which no actor can improve her situation by unilaterally making another choice. This demonstrates the importance of the interaction of choices in social settings. This is also called a Nash equilibrium.

In Game A, a dominant strategy exists for both players, whereby the intersection of their choices—their payoffs—is stable, and neither player can improve her payoff by unilaterally selecting another strategy. This is called a **stable equilibrium,** or, in game theory terms, a **Nash equilibrium,** named after its inventor, John Nash (who was the subject of the book and award-winning film *A Beautiful Mind*). This idea transformed microeconomics, and Nash won the Nobel Prize in Economics for its invention. Equilibrium is nothing more than a situation in which activity has stopped; there is no switching of strategies. Aside from this quality of stability and its value for predicting and explaining behavior, there is nothing inherently special or attractive about equilibrium, which may be normatively good or normatively bad.

An international agreement about fishing rights that allocates catch shares and ensures survival of a fishing stock would be a normatively good equilibrium from the perspective of those who think species preservation is a good outcome. Being locked in ethnic conflict or a civil war might also be equilibrium, if neither side could improve its prospects for survival by unilaterally selecting another strategy. But we would likely consider this situation as normatively perverse, for the equilibrium promotes continued killing and destruction.

Game B changes the context or structure of the interaction between the same decision makers. In terms of payoffs, Player 1 prefers 20 to 10 to 5 to –5 (20 > 10 > 5 > –5), while Player 2 prefers 20 to 15 to 10 to –5 (20 > 15 > 10 > –5). Again, these preference orderings are complete and transitive. In this situation, Player 1 has a dominant strategy, Strategy A, which she will select regardless of Player 2's choices. Player 1 prefers 20 to 10 and 5 to –5, which are the different outcomes she can expect between Strategies A and B, dependent upon Player 2's choice of strategy. So Player 1 will always select Strategy A in this game. If Player 2 recognizes that Player 1 has a dominant strategy of A, she can make her decision contingent on that knowledge. If she wanted to maximize her payoff without any knowledge of Player 1's strategy, she would choose Strategy A, with the expectation of obtaining 20 should Player 1 choose Strategy B. But, as Player 2's payoff results from the intersection of her choice with Player 1's choice, she would receive only 10 instead of the expected 20, because Player 1 will have selected Strategy A. What a disappointment! There is no way Player 2 can obtain 20 because Player 1 has no incentive to shift strategy. But if she recognizes that Player 1 will always choose Strategy A, Player 2 can do better for herself by choosing Strategy B and obtaining a payoff of 15, which is much better than 10. By acting strategically—selecting a strategy that does not reflect her most preferred outcome in an absolute sense but represents her best choice given the structure of her interaction with Player 1—she will do better.

> A **social trap** is a situation in which what appears to be an individual's maximizing, self-interested choice for obtaining a preferred outcome results in a subpar outcome both for the individual and for the larger group or society; this unexpected outcome occurs because of the structure of interactions of the choices made by multiple individuals.

In both games, we had rational decision makers, but their choices changed with the shift in context. Context is not trivial; in fact, it is critical to understanding choices, as social settings can influence payoffs by determining how choices interact. We return to game theory models later to illustrate how contexts can produce social traps in economic and political markets. A **social trap** is a situation in which what appears to be an individual's maximizing, self-interested choice to obtain a preferred outcome actually results in a subpar outcome both for the individual and for the larger group or society. This unexpected outcome occurs because of the structure of interactions of the choices made by multiple individuals.

OUTCOMES VERSUS CHOICE: USING THE RATIONALITY ASSUMPTION

The preceding section and the appendix at the end of this chapter highlight an important distinction between choices and outcomes. One might reasonably ask why, if policy makers behave as if they are rational, their choices sometimes produce costly and seemingly perverse outcomes. Should we not expect rational decision makers to be reasonably successful in attaining their preferences, and only occasionally to fail in their efforts? And if their choices fail to attain their preferred outcomes, shouldn't they be able to avoid extremely costly and perverse outcomes? When we observe bad outcomes—such as the destructiveness of total war, the failure of a trade policy, an international financial crisis, or the extinction of a fish species due to overfishing in international waters—does this mean that policy makers intended to produce such outcomes through the careful and rational comparison of alternatives and strategies?

Did the leaders of European nations in 1914 rationally intend to reduce the population of Europe by approximately ten million people when they entered into World War I? Did Hitler rationally seek the outcome of fifty-five million dead, thirty-five million wounded, some three million more lost and unaccounted for, his own death, and the complete destruction of his Germany when he took the steps that would embroil much of the globe in World War II? When Congress enacted the Smoot-Hawley Act in 1930, dramatically raising tariffs on U.S. imports and provoking other nations to raise their tariff rates, did Smoot, Hawley, and the other legislators who voted in favor really want to torpedo the global economy? Did President Herbert Hoover, as a rational decision maker, known for his humanitarian efforts in Europe after World War I, consciously elect to promote economic disarray and human suffering when he decided to sign the Smoot-Hawley Act against the advice of more than one thousand economists? The answer to all these questions is, unequivocally, No! But, then, how can rationality help us to understand choices that produce such perverse outcomes?

Backward Induction

These examples illustrate a very important lesson for how we use the rationality assumption to investigate human behavior: *the consequences of choice differ from the motivations of choice*. It may seem obvious, but it is important to understand that a decision differs from an outcome. As the simple games in figure 1.3 illustrate, in social settings (those that involve more than one person), outcomes result from the interaction of choices but are not the choices themselves. Otherwise, a person's choice to play a lottery game would be equivalent to winning. The rationality assumption helps us to investigate the individual motivations leading to decisions, but it does not necessarily explain the consequences of those decisions. If we assume that people operate as if they are rational, we can look at a decision situation and work backward to try to understand the rational calculations that could lead to the decision under examination. This process, which is called **backward induction,** is a very powerful tool for probing history and understanding politics.

> **Backward induction** is an analytical tool for trying to understand why people make the choices they make. One starts by examining a decision and asking what would lead a rational decision maker to make such a choice. By working backward, one attempts to understand the rational calculations that could lead to the decision.

Backward induction places the primary focus of analysis on the decision rather than on the outcome of that decision. It involves starting with a decision—not its outcome—and asking what did the decision maker hope to accomplish with her choice, what were her objectives, how did she rank those objectives, and how did she understand the preferences and likely choices of others that could impinge on her actions? How does her choice of a particular strategy allow us to evaluate her understanding of the trade-offs between objectives and the cost of the strategies to obtain those objectives? The assumption of rationality means that we expect a decision maker to choose a course of action most likely to produce the best outcome given costs and benefits. This expectation gives us a tool to help us re-create the scenario of a decision we hope to understand, even if the outcome of that choice appears nonrational. We try to put ourselves in the decision maker's shoes. We look for supporting evidence in the historical record, in archives, in interviews with participants to an event, and in any data that provide a glimpse of the context in which the decision was made. The assumption of rationality provides a logical framework in which to evaluate that information. Under the rationality assumption, we do not expect decision makers to make random choices or to select their second or third preferences if their first choices have equal or lesser costs. Consequently, we seek to understand how a decision maker came to view her choice as the best option given her understanding of the costs and benefits of alternative strategies.

Focusing on an outcome is very different from focusing on motivation when we investigate the choices that have produced an outcome. Outcomes attract our attention because we hope to understand what causes crises and disasters, as well as what promotes good and fruitful outcomes in the global political economy. But to focus on an outcome as we try to understand the choices leading to that outcome represents a potential trap that ensnares many investigators. Outcomes result from the interaction of choices made in a world where decision makers are limited in the time and energy they can devote to any single choice, where they are not fully aware of other decision makers' understandings of the world, and where they are not equipped with functioning crystal balls. An outcome may occur as expected and predicted, it may be unanticipated, it may produce unintentional consequences, or it may be just one of many possible outcomes that could have occurred—but decision makers have weighted all those possible outcomes with a probabilistic evaluation that has proven to be accurate or faulty.

An Example of Backward Induction

Let's return to the Smoot-Hawley Act of 1930 as an example. Smoot-Hawley raised U.S. tariff barriers to heights not seen before or since. In retrospect and with 20/20 hindsight, Smoot-Hawley looks like one of the worst, most destructive policies ever implemented in American politics. Were Smoot and Hawley seeking such infamy when they introduced their legislation and nurtured its passage through Congress? Did they consciously seek to create a disaster in the global economy and fuel a global depression that helped lead to World War II? Were they hoping that their names would be forever associated with an unmitigated policy disaster? If we were to begin with the outcome of worldwide economic depression and contraction that followed Smoot-Hawley and employ the rationality assumption and backward induction, we would be assuming that policy makers wanted to encourage a worldwide economic catastrophe.

A more appropriate research strategy to understand the passage of Smoot-Hawley, however, would ask under what conditions legislators would view the Smoot-Hawley Act as a rational strategy or a best choice given their understanding of the costs and benefits of different strategies. What did Smoot and Hawley and the supporting members of Congress expect to accomplish when they passed the legislation? Clearly they did not expect what happened, or we would have to call them crazy or sick. More likely, they were civil servants seeking to promote the welfare of their constituents and to enhance their own prospects for reelection. These goals required cushioning their constituents during a time of economic downturn and uncertainty. Jobs, livelihoods, and communities were being threatened, creating a situation that could easily translate into disgruntled voters. In response to this situation, the Smoot-Hawley legislation sought to transfer the costs of the economic downturn—job losses and other dislocations—to workers and producers in other countries by erecting barriers to their access to U.S. markets. Protecting U.S. markets for U.S.-produced products by raising the costs of imported products, Smoot-Hawley was an attempt to shift the costs of economic hardship overseas.

Senator Smoot and Congressman Hawley had good reason to believe in the soundness of their strategy, for it had worked numerous times in the past. Indeed, the U.S. economy grew up as a highly protected economy with high barriers to entry in particular sectors, and the U.S. Congress had raised tariff protections in the agricultural sector as recently as 1922 without destroying the global economy. But the position of the U.S. economy in the global context had changed by 1930, so that their actions instead contributed to a process of impoverishment, which ensured their electoral demise.

An outcome may attract us to a particular problem, but the focus on choice permits us to seek out the motivations and expectations underpinning the choice, to conduct an autopsy in order to learn what went wrong or what went right. Asking what decision makers expected to achieve is the first step toward understanding the microfoundations of the macro outcomes that we observe in the world. This approach offers a useful strategy for analysis of the decision-making process. Often we do not have access to decision makers at the time of their choices—we cannot be flies on the wall, or parties to their mental musings and policy deliberations. Sometimes these political actors are dead, sometimes they are retired, sometimes they have selective and retrospective memories that rearrange history to make them look better, and sometimes they are leaders in other countries about whose motivations we have limited information. Ultimately, we want to have some means of inferring why policy makers did what they did, or what they will do. Retracing the process of rationality, along with our other core assumptions, provides us with tools to help us in our attempts to explicate and anticipate choices.

THE PURPOSE AND PROCESS OF SOCIAL SCIENCE

In this volume we approach the study of world affairs as a scientific activity—a social science—that describes the processes by which we generate, assess, and accumulate knowledge. As we examine and attempt to understand world affairs of the past, present, and future, we need systematic tools and frameworks to assist our efforts. We want to avoid relying on one-shot, ad hoc explanations, which treat each event or situation as unique. All events are unique if we dig deep enough and describe them in their most finite details, yet as social scientists seeking to generalize from one situation to another, we are more concerned with the commonalities across phenomena than their uniqueness. Without systematic frameworks that help us categorize social phenomena, recognize commonalities across events, and enable us to generalize lessons from one situation to another, we will be at a great disadvantage in anticipating and understanding world affairs—we will always be surprised by events.

In the study of global affairs, social scientists focus on a spectrum of behavior that ranges from violent conflict to productive cooperation across national boundaries. For the most part because of my own specialty, this book tends to focus on international political economic relations, not on war. But cooperation and conflict are related as two sides of the same coin. The explanatory frameworks or mechanisms of political behavior should be similar regardless of the phenomenon we want to understand—whether conflict or more cooperative outcomes of economic exchange. If politics are politics, then the same explanatory frameworks should operate in a variety of situations, domestic or international, in war or peace. The settings may shift, but the theories and tools we use to account for political behavior should remain relatively constant. This approach explicitly assumes that similar processes and mechanisms are at work across the different fields of political science and that the boundaries separating the different fields—such as comparative politics and international relations—are artifacts of organization and specialization, not differences in explanatory mechanisms.

Social scientists engage in a variety of activities: description, explanation, prediction, and prescription. In this text I emphasize the task of explanation, use description, and largely neglect prediction or prescription. Social scientists engage in all these activities as part of their discipline, but they tend to specialize and focus more heavily on one activity over the others. In the pursuit of explanation, social scientists employ a variety of theoretical frameworks as they explore the range of human activity. In political science, multiple, or competing, approaches robustly coexist, as no single unified explanatory or theoretical framework has prevailed. In any science, explanatory approaches become more prominent or fade depending upon how they perform relative to alternative approaches. First, let's consider what I mean by *science* in this book, and then proceed to define the activities that constitute its practice.

Social Analysis as Social Science

Science is about the process of research. Unlike physical and life scientists who practice bench science in laboratories, and often under controlled conditions, day-to-day activities in the world and history serve as the dominant laboratories for social scientists. They rarely have the luxury enjoyed by many physical and life scientists to conduct experiments in controlled laboratory settings where all inputs are carefully measured and one input (called an intervention or independent variable) can be varied at a time so the scientist can then look for a change in outcomes (the dependent variable) that can be attributed to the change in the input, or independent variable. A controlled laboratory setting allows the scientist to insulate the experiment from other inputs that could affect the outcome. This control of the experimental environment and of the intervention allows for more comfortable assessments about **causality,** or whether the change in the input *A* actually caused a change in the outcome *B,* and, if so, how much change and why. If the physical scientist worries about control of the intervention and about potential threats to causal claims, she can often design experiments to address such potential threats. For example, she can design an experiment that involves multiple groups whose members are randomly assigned; one group (the treatment group) receives the intervention, and the other group (the control group) does not. Random assignment helps to disperse preexisting characteristics in the experimental population that could influence the outcome separate from the intervention, or independent variable, of interest. Randomizing ensures that such characteristics are relatively equally distributed across the different groups, thus equalizing the groups and negating the ability of such characteristics to threaten the causal test of the experiment.

> **Causality** is the direct connection between a cause and an effect; a relationship in which a change in input *A* brings about a change in outcome *B.*

Controlled experiments and random assignment are powerful tools in the design of research, but they are tools that are often unavailable to social scientists. Unfortunately, relatively small portions of the phenomena that most of the social sciences seek to understand are conducive to experimental research settings, and, even then, questions remain about the applicability of the research findings to the nonexperimental world. Instead of sterile and controlled experimental settings, the current world and history serve as the settings where political scientists explore and test their theories. Political scientists obtain some of their data from controlled laboratory settings, but most of their data come from uncontrolled research settings such as the forensic probing of past and current events, the conduct of elite and mass interviews and opinion surveys, exploration of historical archives, examination of government reports of economic and social statistics, analyses of media reporting, consideration of legislative voting behavior, and other activities that occur outside the laboratory.

The absence of control by the researcher means that she cannot assign an intervention to a particular group and not to another, nor does she get to distribute the subjects being studied (governments, decision makers, voters, businesses, and so on) among the different groups. For example, political scientists do not designate some people to live under authoritarian regimes and others to live under democratic regimes in order to evaluate the effects of regime type on citizen behavior; they do not assign war to some nations and not to others in an effort to determine the effects of war on society; they do not impose economic recession on some societies and not on others so as to examine the influence of economic downturns on political and social behavior; and they cannot lower barriers to international trade in some societies and not in others in order to evaluate the impacts of free trade on domestic politics.

The lack of control and assignment by political science researchers creates tremendous obstacles for analyzing and testing causal relationships, which can affect the strength and confidence of their causal claims. Unlike the laboratory researcher, who can control or manage many outside forces that might affect an experiment, the political scientist generally has no such control—which makes it far more difficult for her to assert confidently that *A* causes *B*. Self-assignment by the subject or the phenomenon being studied creates a possibility for selection bias, which can contaminate a causal claim. The reason a state, society, organization, or individual is in one category or another may be found in some underlying characteristic that causes the outcome of interest and not the independent variable of interest. Consequently, social scientists must often take greater leaps of faith in making their causal claims than physical and life scientists do. Recognizing this absence of control is not to belittle the endeavor of social scientists or the results of their research; rather, it highlights the greater obstacles that social scientists encounter as they undertake their tasks.

Already a tough challenge owing to the lack of control over the research setting, the process of social science is further complicated by an additional factor: the subjects of social science research, human beings, exercise choice. At least on the surface, they change their minds. One day a person eats fish, another day, chicken, and another day, meat. In one election a person votes Republican; in another, Democratic. A policy maker who claims to be a proponent of free trade may promote freer trade in one industry but advocate trade protections in another. Physical laws governing the bonding of chemical elements, chemical reactions, movement of objects through space, behavior of neutrons and electrons, or genetic patterns appear immutable—or at least the physical scientist can specify under what conditions the relationships dictated by the laws of nature do not hold. Social scientists are far from being as successful as physical scientists at creating general laws of behavior in their fields, or in specifying under what conditions those laws do or do not hold. Ironically, perhaps the only successful overarching law of behavior in the social sciences is the one that states how difficult it would be to generate such laws.

Despite the differences separating the physical and life sciences from the social sciences, there are tremendous similarities across the two spheres that make them sciences and separate them from the humanities. I emphasize four key similarities here: *the is versus the ought, systematic and rigorous exploration, cumulative progress,* and *generalizability versus uniqueness.* The difference between the *is* and the *ought* is simply the difference between how the world does work and visions of how we want it to work. How we desire the world to work is a **normative** statement. Our individual visions of an ideal world are loaded with our individual values. How the world actually operates is a **positivist** statement, regardless of whether we like the outcomes or not. The *ought,* the ideal, can and will vary from person to person, but how the world does work, the *is,* does not—although as individuals we may have different interpretations of that reality. One of the objectives of positivist social science is to limit those different interpretations. This contrast underpins the difference between **positive theory** and **normative theory.** Normative philosophers empha-size the *ought.* Physical and social scientists both care about the normative state of the world—they have preferences about how the world should be, but their basic research gener-ally attempts to explain what does happen, not what ought to happen. Positivist scientists engaged in basic research strive to uncover the *is.* Sometimes this distinction can be uncom-fortable for investigators, as they discover that the world operates in a manner contrary to their normative preferences or values. But changing such undesired outcomes in the world requires understanding the mechanisms that produce those outcomes.

> **Normative** refers to how we desire the world to work in the ideal. Individuals are likely to have different normative outlooks on the world. **Positivist** refers to how the world actually oper-ates regardless of whether we like that world or not. **Normative theory** is a statement about how we want the world to work, what "ought to be." **Positive theory** is a model for how the world actually works, "what is," rather than how we might want the world to function.

Both physical and social scientists seek to explore the world systematically and rigorously in an attempt to develop causal understanding of physical and social phenomena, respec-tively. They seek to build and test causal explanations about how the world works in their particular areas of interest. Systematic, rigorous exploration involves clear and explicit state-ments about how one set of factors, known as **independent variables,** relates to another factor, the **dependent variable,** or how and why change in the independent variables may cause shifts in the dependent variable. This systematic positing of relationships differs significantly from simply asserting or demonstrating a relationship. It involves construction of a logical formulation of how one set of factors relates to another—a causal path. There are crucial differences between estab-lishing causality and discovering an association or correlation between one set of factors and another. *Correlation* suggests only a connection between different factors: it tells us that fac-tors covary in relation to each other, but not why they covary. *Causality* requires more than demonstration of a covariance: it is an attempt to tell *why* factors covary in relation to each.

> The **dependent variable** is the phenomenon or outcome that a social researcher is attempting to explain, a factor that is influenced or caused by an independent variable. **Independent vari-ables** are factors that, when changed, cause a shift in another factor (the dependent variable).

Claims of causality require a story, a theory, that links the independent and dependent variables. For example, since the end of World War II, the expansion of international trade is positively associated with economic growth. This is a descriptive statement that tells us that trade covaries with economic growth, but it does not tell us why. Within this simple statement of association, we lack a story that explains whether trade causes economic growth, whether growth causes trade, or whether, perhaps, the relationship is simply **spurious**—the two factors really are not related, and just by happenstance they covary. Now, if we say that trade exposes

> **Spurious** refers to a false association, such as when two or more phenomena seem to covary yet there is no direct causation or any real underlying association. This can be the result of coincidence or perhaps an unseen factor that is associated with the phenomena that appear to be associated.

producers to greater competition that disciplines production and encourages economic specialization and economies of scale, then we have a plausible causal story that tells us why trade contributes to economic growth.

A scientist, physical or social, has the responsibility of developing and considering competing explanations, alternative theories, and causal paths. Positing a causal relationship is only part of the process; another part is the systematic and rigorous empirical testing of that posited relationship. This testing is critical for evaluating the validity of the posited causal explanation—for evaluating the *is* versus the *ought*—and for selecting among a variety of plausible but competing explanations of the same behavior. The scientific process—the rigorous design of empirical tests of competing theoretical arguments—does not actually prove theories as much as it disproves them. The rigorous design of empirical tests helps to rule out some explanations and increases confidence in others. Such rigor is clearly more difficult for social scientists than for physical scientists, for the reasons discussed earlier.

Both physical and social scientists seek to develop cumulative bodies of knowledge and understanding that build and improve upon previous work. This focus reflects the fact that science is an ongoing, progressive enterprise. New generations of scientists build upon the foundations established by the work of past researchers, developing a body of knowledge that contributes to future research and understanding. This cumulative effort differs from the endeavors of the arts and humanities. For example, our drama is not better than Shakespeare's or our art better than that of Rembrandt or Michelangelo, just because we have had centuries to build upon their work. But if we are successful as scientists, our physical science is better than that of Galileo Galilei, a seventeenth-century astronomer, and our social science is better than that of Max Weber, a German sociologist of the late nineteenth and early twentieth centuries—even if they might prove to be better investigators than we are if we could transport them through time to the present.

Finally, physical and social scientists concern themselves with their ability to generalize from one relationship or phenomenon to others. They search for commonalities across phenomena as opposed to the uniqueness of such phenomena. A social scientist may study a particular case, but she does so in the hope that by understanding the specific case she can generalize the findings and so extend her understanding to other cases and settings. Social scientists seek to be able to generalize from one setting to another. Theory and empirical testing provide the backbone of this process. Social scientists engage in empirical testing of theories in multiple settings, seeking to reproduce their findings in support or rejection of given theories, but always with the goal of finding robust explanations of human behavior that work in a variety of settings. Students of the arts and humanities may revel in the uniqueness of a phenomenon, but social scientists relish the discovery of characteristics that undermine claims of uniqueness and distinctiveness.

Tasks of Inquiry: Describing and Explaining What Happened and Why

Now let's turn to the four tasks of social science: description, explanation, prediction, and prescription. *Description* is the process of telling *what* happened; it is a recounting of events. Those engaged in description act as storytellers and perform a great service. Without description we do not have a history of our past or a good understanding of the contexts in which we operate. Without such understanding, our choices are more likely to prove dysfunctional, even pathological. Those engaged in the endeavor of description may implicitly convey a story about *why* something happened or the causality of the event in question, but the process of description does not explicitly require an explanation of why something occurred. Descriptions in world politics tend toward highly detailed accounts of how the participants behave. By their focus on particular events, descriptions often emphasize the uniqueness of events and behavior. Journalistic accounts of world affairs generally fall into the category of description. This text engages in some description of global political economic relations (in Part III) to provide context for evaluating and using tools of explanation.

Introducing tools of *explanation* is the primary goal of this text. As political scientists interested in global affairs, we want to know *why* certain phenomena occur—such as war, peace, growth, development, democracy, financial distress, trade barriers, alliances, international investment, migration, and environmental decay—not simply *what* occurs. Explanation is the process of trying to understand the causal relationship between independent and dependent variables. We hope to understand why and how changes in the independent variables will produce changes in the dependent variable. Simply asserting a relationship between independent and dependent variables does not constitute an explanation, only an association. Explanation is the goal of theories that link the dependent variable to the independent variables. Such theories are attempts to make sense of why people behave the way they do in specified settings, or why they make the choices they make under specified conditions. A good theory is logically constructed, which means that each step of the theory, a step along a causal path, attempts to follow rigorously, logically, and consistently from the previous step. This deliberate progress contrasts with ad hoc or off-the-cuff argumentation, which amounts to assertion, even if intelligent assertion.

Another term for theory is **model.** By definition, models or theories are simplified intellectual constructions that propose relationships. By simplifying or extracting core, primitive relationships among variables, models provide tools for recognizing similarities across social behavior. This process may enable us to generalize our discoveries about social behavior in one setting to understand similar behavior in another setting. In an incredibly complex world, loaded with information and noise, models help us determine where to look,

> A **model** is an intellectual construction that postulates a causal relationship across a set of variables, thus providing a tool for examining similarities across social behavior. By definition a model is a simplification of the world being examined.

what to ignore, and what to expect. They establish frameworks for collecting, connecting, and evaluating information about the world and then interpreting events. They help us distinguish important from trivial information. Sometimes our models are wrong, and we overlook or misinterpret important information. If our models prove consistently inaccurate and unhelpful, then we seek to construct new models. But if our models prove useful and stand the test of continual reexamination and application, then we gain confidence in them.

Multiple explanations are plausible and likely for almost any interesting social behavior. How do we choose among competing explanations, particularly if several seem plausible? Political scientists evaluate models of political behavior by examining their theoretical construction, but also through empirical testing. At a theoretical level, we assess the plausibility and usefulness of a model's assumptions and its internal consistency and logic. Empirically, we test a model's validity, or how accurately the model reflects the actual relationship in the laboratory of the real world. As mentioned earlier, this is generally a more

> **Validity** is the accuracy of a model or claim. **Testable hypotheses** are assumptions about behavior that can be evaluated with information from the empirical world. **Data** are information, quantitative or qualitative, that can be applied to a question of interest.

difficult laboratory than the typical controlled laboratory setting enjoyed by physical scientists. Political scientists rarely have direct control over the settings or the range of factors that can influence human behavior. Consequently, in most cases the political scientist's conclusions about causality are necessarily weaker than those of physical scientists. Within the constraints of such lower expectations, does a model do well at explaining what it claims to explain? How does a model fare in comparison with other models? Good theories produce **testable hypotheses** or conjectures about behavior that can be evaluated with information, which we call **data**, from the empirical world. Data can be quantitative or qualitative. Investigators can compare expectations produced by the different models and then use empirical tests to select among competing explanations. If they are successful, other researchers can build upon their findings, creating a cumulative body of research and knowledge. Good scientific investigation requires constant reexamination and the creation of opportunities to be proven wrong. Testing and retesting the same logic across multiple settings helps to reject some explanations for social behavior and can build robust explanations that are cumulative and serve to advance our understanding of social behavior.

Whereas description is a process of telling what happened and explanation is the task of telling why it happened, *prediction* is the process of telling what will happen. Prediction is a primary concern for those engaged in policy making. Policy makers want to know what is going to happen, with the goal of being able to affect what happens or at least gain some warning so they can prepare to manage the consequences. Soothsaying, fortune-telling, and divine prognostication are forms of prediction, but not the type meant here. Prediction for a social scientist is more than a random, unsystematic, mystical gaze into the future. For a social scientist, prediction is based upon systematic frameworks or models of human behavior. Like the logically and systematically derived hypotheses used to test models of explanation, predictions derive from such models—implicitly or explicitly. The testing of models of explanation can engender confidence that translates into predictive capabilities of the successful models. Sometimes we use the past to test the predictive capacities of our models. Yet, the fact that we have identified good predictive models does not mean that we necessarily know why things happen. Nor does understanding why things happen necessarily produce good predictions. As E. B. White wrote in 1948:

> The so-called science of polling [*a favorite activity of many political scientists*] is not a science at all but mere necromancy. People are unpredictable by nature [*the effect of choice*], and although you can take a nation's pulse, you can't be sure that the nation hasn't just run up a flight of stairs, and although you can take a nation's blood pressure, you can't be sure that if you came back in twenty minutes you'd get the same reading. This is a damn fine thing.[2]

Finally, some social scientists engage in *prescription*, or the advocacy of specific policies for implementation. This activity separates those social scientists engaged in basic research from those in applied work, distinguishing those who try primarily to understand why things happen from those who work to change what will happen. These tasks are not independent, but collegial. The most effective prescription builds on understandings of causal processes that are illuminated by those engaged in the task of explanation. Knowing why things happen, the causal path, can give applied social scientists and policy makers valuable insights about where and how best to intervene to alter social outcomes, about where and how to use scarce resources to change behavior in societies. Prescribing policy without some systematic notion of the underlying processes is little more than random prescription, or throwing money at problems. Yet this may be the best that policy makers can do in some situations, given the difficulty of uncovering the root causes and mechanisms of complex social behaviors.

TWO EXAMPLES OF THEORETICAL FAILURES: LIBERALISM AND REALISM

Our journey to develop the political scientist's theoretical toolbox requires that we quickly outline, evaluate, and discount two popular and prominent approaches, realism and liberalism, that have dominated the teaching of international relations and international political economy for decades. (*Liberalism* as used here refers to the processes of market exchange and not to a position on the left-right spectrum of politics.) While realism and liberalism are useful theories up to a point, it should quickly become evident by the yardstick of what we

---

[2]E. B. White, "Polling," *New Yorker,* November 13, 1948; bracketed italics added.

have defined as science that excessive reliance on these is bad social science if part of our endeavor, as scientists, is to test our theories continually against the empirical world in order to reject theories that fail to provide useful analytical leverage over important social behavior. This is important not simply for academic musing and as part of the normal progression of science, but because these frameworks are used to inform policy deliberations that affect the lives and welfare of individuals and their communities. Two examples will illustrate the significant shortcomings of realism and liberalism to explain international political behavior, enabling us to move on to develop a framework that is more useful.

Liberalism: The Mutually Beneficial Exchange of Trade and Globalization

In 1930 Congress passed the Smoot-Hawley Act, the last general tariff adopted and implemented in the United States. Almost since the founding days of the Republic, tariffs (trade barriers that increase the cost of imports by imposing taxes on them) had been a focus of much congressional activity. Until the passage of the constitutional amendment enabling the income tax, tariffs had been a major source of federal government revenues. Debates and divisions over trade policy colored early U.S. history. Shortly after the country's founding, Alexander Hamilton endorsed trade protections as a tool to stimulate economic activity in nascent American industries. In the latter 1800s, the issue of tariffs became a significant source of conflict between Republicans and Democrats, with the Republicans generally favoring tariffs and the Democrats pushing to lower trade barriers. E. E. Schattschneider, a political scientist whose research on U.S. politics in the mid-twentieth century was seminal to the development of political science as a science, wrote that "the history of the American tariff is the story of a dubious economic policy turned into a great political success. The very tendencies that have made the legislation bad have made it politically invincible."[3]

The Depression-era bill, named for its creators, Senator Reed Smoot (R-Utah) and Representative Willis Hawley (R-Oregon), imposed tariffs on more than twenty thousand imported goods and raised tariff rates to their highest level in U.S. history. Many political scientists and economists view the Smoot-Hawley Act as among the most damaging interventions by government into the economy—and one of the worst pieces of legislation—in U.S. political economic history. They argue that the Smoot-Hawley tariffs added to the depth and duration of the Great Depression. Because of the position of the United States as the largest and richest political economy in the global arena, U.S. policy choices such as Smoot-Hawley spilled across national boundaries and influenced economic, social, and political activity in other countries, in this case causing unemployment and economic distress among other nations' laborers and producers.

Other governments, seeking to address the contagion of economic ills wrought by Smoot-Hawley on their constituents, retaliated by raising their tariffs and trade barriers.

---

[3]E. E. Schattschneider, *Politics, Pressures and the Tariff* (New York: Prentice Hall, 1935), 283.

Over the next several years, impediments to international exchange continued to increase, and the volume of world trade declined drastically. As imports and exports fell, the economic activity associated with those imports and exports also declined. The decline in trade slowed economic activity, added to economic uncertainty, cut off avenues for expansion and recovery, and fed the social and political dislocations of the Depression years. Political parties on both the extreme right and the extreme left took advantage of the economic distress to build support among the disaffected and so advance their political agendas. Hitler, Mussolini, Franco, and others mobilized widespread popular discontent to take command of their respective governments. World War II followed. Certainly other factors contributed as well, but the breakdown in the processes of globalization abetted by the Smoot-Hawley tariffs played a major role in the progression of events leading to the war.

Liberalism, one significant approach to international relations, argues that trade and the processes of globalization constitute a win-win situation for all parties engaged in exchange. Since David Ricardo's seminal essay on the political economy of foreign trade in 1817, economists and policy makers had come to understand and recognize the consequences of comparative advantage in international trade and its ability to improve the aggregate welfare of societies that participated in international exchange. Economists had come to accept as law the pure utilitarian gains that trade provided: overall, societies benefited from more—not less—trade, regardless of the circumstances. The precepts of liberalism demonstrated that trade in all situations would lead to an enlargement of market exchange. This would expose producers and labor to greater competition, which would condition the productive forces of societies, enable greater gains from specialization, lead to more efficient use of productive resources, and enlarge the consumption possibilities of those in society—essentially increasing their real incomes. Paul Samuelson, the first American to win the Nobel Prize in Economics and one of the preeminent economists of the twentieth century, called comparative advantage the only big idea that economics produced that was both nontrivial and surprising.

Why would two Republican members of Congress propose legislation that rejected common knowledge and produced such damaging outcomes? Why would other Republicans support this legislation? Why would a Republican president, Hoover, sign it into law? And why would U.S. society tolerate such antitrade practices, which would predictably damage the nation's social welfare—raising prices for consumers, limiting their consumption possibilities, and effectively lowering their real incomes? Why would the United States—a country that professed a belief in market exchange and the mechanisms of capitalism—adopt such high levels of tariff protection when such policies intervened in market exchange, reduced the efficiency and gains from market exchange, and threatened the welfare of its own people?

We cannot claim that the Republican supporters of Smoot-Hawley were ignorant of economic arguments against government intervention in market exchange and against their legislation in particular. After all, they were members of a political party that had for decades been unabashed supporters of laissez-faire capitalism and limited government intervention in the economy. The Republican Party represented the business and economic elites who strenuously resisted government intervention in domestic economic activities. With some exceptions, such as Teddy Roosevelt, the Republican Party reliably championed corporate capitalism against the interests of labor and small enterprise, as Republican business elites fondly embraced the tenets of social Darwinism and the survival of the fittest in economic affairs. Moreover, in case these Republican legislators had a temporary brain freeze and had forgotten the connection of trade to market exchange, more than one thousand economists, including all the top experts, signed a letter imploring Congress to reject Smoot-Hawley and asking President Hoover to veto the legislation. Why, then, would policy makers favor policies that they knew would limit the gains to their society, and even potentially harm it?

Moreover, this intervention by the government in market exchange was not an unusual event. Earlier in the decade a Republican-dominated Congress had passed the Fordney-McCumber Act, which increased tariffs on agricultural imports. As Schattschneider noted, tariffs had been an enduring part of U.S. economic policy for much of U.S. history, despite the awareness of the aggregate social welfare gains from trade. Republican support for tariffs had a long history. Following the Civil War, a partisan divide had emerged over tariffs, with Republicans generally supportive of and Democrats usually more opposed to such measures. We cannot argue that Democrats actually understood market economics and the purported benefits of capitalist market exchange better than Republicans did during this period. As mentioned earlier, many influential Republicans had long been forceful proponents of laissez-faire capitalism and social Darwinism—whereby the discipline of free market exchange created economic winners and losers, rewarding the winners and forcing the losers to adjust their economic activity. In contrast, many leading Democrats had advanced a populist and more progressive agenda, which advocated using the tools of government to constrain laissez-faire and corporate capitalism. Given this history, Democrats would seem more likely than Republicans to advocate government intervention to rein in the harshness of social Darwinism and to cushion workers and small businesses from the potential violence of the rapid adjustments generated by market exchange.

The framework of liberalism provides no explanatory mechanisms to account for such seemingly socially perverse choices. Did Senator Smoot and Representative Hawley set out intentionally to damage the national economy and destroy the global economy, prolong the Great Depression, and generate conditions conducive to another world war? Unlikely! Should we conclude that Smoot, Hawley, other members of Congress, and the president all elected to act irrationally at the very same time to endanger the global economy at a time of great fragility? No! But this explanatory dilemma highlights weaknesses in liberalism as a theoretical framework for understanding important processes and events in international affairs. The moving parts of the theory of liberalism cannot account for such devastating choices by informed and intelligent policy makers. Smoot-Hawley and other similar policy choices are not trivial problems for the explanatory framework of liberalism. Problems in this framework might be overlooked if they produced only minor problems, but the resulting problems are often not minor. In the case of Smoot-Hawley, the resulting decline in trade fed the depth and duration of the Great Depression, which led to the political extremism that underpinned the downhill slide into World War II, during which approximately fifty-five million people perished.

Schattschneider wrote that the conditions surrounding bad economic policy such as the tariff actually made such policy "politically invincible," or undefeatable. He argued that the institutional makeup of the U.S. political system promoted the tariff despite its poor economic policy prospects. U.S. political institutions—"the rules of the game"—structured political bargaining and the partisan divide in a way that made elected representatives amenable to flawed public policy such as Smoot-Hawley. This explanatory framework provides a mechanism where the independent variables—the institutional setting of U.S. politics—produce a decision-making context where public policy makers might rationally and intelligently select a policy that is inconsistent with the precepts of liberalism. Liberalism has no mechanisms to explain such a seemingly contradictory choice. It lacks those independent variables or moving parts. Schattschneider's explanation suggests that we would still be burdened by these poor policy choices if the rules of the game, the political institutions, had not changed. And in 1934, Congress did indeed pass legislation that changed the rules of the game. The Reciprocal Trade and Tariff Act (RTTA) was an institutional reform that shifted some responsibility for U.S. tariff levels to the executive branch. Congress gave the president the ability to unilaterally negotiate and adopt reductions of up to 50 percent in existing tariffs without consulting lawmakers. The president could not impose new tariffs, for that prerogative rests constitutionally in the power of the House of Representatives to create taxes, but the president could now reduce existing tariffs within the guidelines established by Congress. This new rule started a long decline in U.S. tariff levels and a liberalization of access to U.S. markets. Given the size of the U.S. economy and its position in the global economy, this trend helped promote an expansion in international exchange and contributed to an increase in global social welfare. Within the space of four years, the United States had adopted policies diametrically opposed to Smoot-Hawley.

In this historical example, we encounter many of the broader topics that are the focus of this book. First, a government enacts a policy—Smoot-Hawley—that is inconsistent with its society's long-term welfare, although another policy would produce a better outcome for society as a whole. This policy making produces a suboptimal collective outcome, which we call a *social trap* or *political market failure*. Second, there is breakdown in economic market exchange as international trade declines precipitously, which we call an *economic market failure*. Third, as we noted, the U.S. government is divided along partisan lines, which reflect *cleavages* that can produce different coalitions and alignments of interests in domestic society. Fourth, we see the importance of the rules of the political game, which we call *institutions*. A dramatic change in the rules of the game from the 1930 Smoot-Hawley Act to the 1934 RTTA provided an opportunity to observe the consequences of institutional change, as Schattschneider's politically invincible tariff became vulnerable. Finally, all of these observations concern activities and actions that originate within a specific political economy, and yet their consequences spill across borders to influence other political economies and the global arena itself. We cannot account for any of these activities using only the framework of liberalism, as the key explanatory components are missing. We will revisit liberalism, especially in chapters 3 and 4, as it will provide a baseline for recognizing and evaluating political and economic market failures.

Realism: The Nation-State System and the Distribution of Power

Now let's turn to another influential theory in international affairs, **realism,** or **realpolitik**. Realism uses only a few moving causal parts, or independent variables, to explain behavior in the international arena. Realism focuses primarily on the structure of international relations—the nation-state system—and the distribution of power or capacity to exercise influence in the international arena. Since the Treaty of Westphalia in 1648, relatively autonomous political units called nation-states have dominated the political organizational and structural landscape of modern international affairs. This does not mean that international affairs involve only nation-states, just that nation-states have been the primary and dominant form of political organization in world affairs since the advent of the modern nation-state system in 1648. The governments of these nation-states purportedly exercise exclusive authority, which is known as **sovereignty**, over their domestic affairs. Theoretically, this authority is free of intrusions by other governments or societies. This is a creative fiction that is sometimes observed when useful but is frequently violated, especially with the advance of globalization that links societies together. Moreover, this system lacks any centralized authority that overarches the decentralized nodes of political authority resting in the hands of the governments of these nation-states. Despite the presence of an organization such as the United Nations, there is no government to govern the governments of the nation-states. The nation-state system lacks any overarching authority or binding international law with credible enforcement mechanisms to mediate and resolve disputes between countries, to punish those violating the rules of the game, or to manage uncertainty and constrain governments. Political scientists have labeled this structure a state of *anarchy*.

This anarchical structure of international political relations creates a dilemma for governments in terms of advancing their societies' needs. They must rely on their own capacities, or what we call **power**, rather than on international treaties and law. So realism is defined by the structure of political organization that creates a *self-help* system. This

Realism, or **realpolitik**, is an approach to international relations that emphasizes the reliance of governments on their own means, rather than on international treaties and law. It focuses on power, self-help, and material outcomes, rather than moral constraints to address a world of what is, not a world of what ought to be. **Sovereignty** is the principle that the government of the state is the supreme legitimate authority within its territorial borders; in terms of international relations, it means that, theoretically, no state can exercise legitimate authority within another state's boundaries. **Power** consists of the tools, the means, to influence outcomes and achieve one's own ends; it is the ability to prevail and overcome.

structure is one key explanatory variable in the theory of realism. The ability of governments to engage in self-help, which we lump together under the category of power, constitutes a second key variable in the theory. Not all governments have the same capacity to exercise power. This leads to another variable, or explanatory moving part, called *hierarchy.* Hierarchy is defined by where a government's capacity to exercise influence stands in relation to the capacities of other governments in the nation-state system. Realists attempt to use these three moving parts—structure, power, and hierarchy—to explain behavior in the international arena such as conflict, competition, cooperation, the forming of alliances, and the forming of trade relationships.

Realists make no assumptions about the beneficence of others or about the reliability of international legal obligations in the context of anarchy. Realists assume that governments will use their self-help tools, or power, to survive and, they hope, prosper, perhaps at the expense of others and regardless of any normative notions of morality and humanity. Their ability to do so is conditioned by their position in the international hierarchy of such self-help abilities, or power. This may seem like a pessimistic view of human behavior, but realism does not preclude cooperation, prosperous coexistence, and normatively desirable outcomes. Instead, it argues that obtaining such outcomes requires governments to recognize the proclivities of others and to act to constrain activities that can undermine such outcomes. For realists, the ends justify the means. Realism is a strategy for dealing with the state of anarchy in international affairs. The state of anarchy may describe a world of disorder within a brutal state of nature, a dog-eat-dog world where conflict and disorder are ever present, or it may describe a world of order and stability, an arena characterized by cooperation and agreement. The framework of realism suggests that the differential abilities of states can actually produce a hierarchy among states, generating a structure within the state of anarchy. The mechanisms of power and hierarchy in the theory of realism may provide a means by which order can exist in such a self-help structure, allowing states to engage in cooperative and peaceful exchange, resolution of disputes without violence, and compromise.

Realism assumes that goal-oriented policy makers will not knowingly opt for policies that damage their states' survival, their states' positions in the international hierarchy, or their states' abilities to prevail in international affairs. This suggests that decision makers should opt for policies that address threats to their survival or could affect their positions in the international hierarchy. Any other policy choices would be outside their national interests as defined by the moving parts of the theory. This approach has many merits. It is elegant and simple. In addition, realism highlights the structural dilemmas of the global arena, but it falls short of being able to account for many important outcomes in world affairs for many of the same reasons that liberalism is flawed. Its moving parts cannot account for important behavior in global affairs.

For example, realism cannot account for U.S. involvement in the Vietnam War, or its outcome. In the context of realism, why would a superpower at the very top of the international hierarchy (in terms of capacity) engage in a conflict with a peasant economy far down that international hierarchy? North Vietnam was not a threat to U.S. survival, or to the U.S. position in the international hierarchy. Nor could the United States improve its position in the international hierarchy by engaging in a conflict with Vietnam. Moreover, given the critical moving parts of the theory—the capacity for self-help and position in the international hierarchy—how can realism account for the United States losing the conflict? This loss was apparent to U.S. policy makers as early as the mid-1960s, as revealed by the tape-recorded conversations between then Secretary of Defense McNamara and President Johnson, and by the memo sent by Assistant to the President Patrick Moynihan to President Nixon in April 1969, in which he wrote, "Unless I am mistaken, America has 'lost' its first war. Four years, $65 billion, and 212,022 casualties have not enabled the most powerful nation on earth to overcome the resistance of a vastly out-gunned, out-numbered enemy." Were U.S. policy makers simply misinformed about the stakes, or could some other theoretical approach perform better in accounting for U.S. policy choices? A similar theoretical failure applies to the Soviet invasion of Afghanistan in 1979, which ended with failure and the withdrawal of the final Soviet troops in 1988. Again, the Soviet Union was one of the two modern superpowers, sitting near the top of the international hierarchy, and Afghanistan was far down the international hierarchy. In terms of the moving parts of realism, what could a successful or unsuccessful war do for the Soviets in terms of their position in the international hierarchy, and how could they possibly lose? Realism cannot account for either the choice to go to war or the outcome. Can another approach to political behavior do better? Let's turn to a more recent case that illustrates the shortcomings of realism.

On September 11, 2001, terrorists hijacked several U.S. commercial airplanes and flew those planes into targets in the United States—the World Trade Center towers in New York and the Pentagon in the Washington, D.C., area. U.S. intelligence agencies quickly determined that a nonstate or nongovernmental organization (NGO), al-Qaeda, was behind the attacks on U.S. soil. There are many different types of NGOs in the world that play roles in international affairs—they include the International Red Cross, Doctors without Borders, the Soros Foundation, the World Economic Forum, and yes, terrorist organizations that operate across national borders. U.S. authorities knew that al-Qaeda was operating out of training camps located primarily in Afghanistan, a nation-state. An attack by one state on another state would be considered an act of war under international law, but the 9/11 attack was carried out by a nonstate actor upon a state—a murkier area in international law that led to debates over whether this was an act of war or an act of criminal violence. As the state of Afghanistan harbored the training camps and base of operations for al-Qaeda, U.S. policy makers held Afghanistan responsible for the heinous acts precipitated by this particular NGO. This is consistent with a principle in international law called *sovereignty*. The principle of sovereignty asserts that a government has the primary responsibility for its territory and that others cannot impinge on that sovereignty, which also means that a government has primary responsibility for any act that originates on its soil—whether by the government or by a nonstate actor.

Using the principle of sovereignty, U.S. policy makers asked the government of Afghanistan to arrest the terrorists for the crimes committed on U.S. soil and surrender (extradite) them to U.S. authorities. If they refused, then under the same principle, responsibility for the acts of terrorism would then also fall on the government of Afghanistan. As we know, the Taliban government of Afghanistan refused, which essentially transformed the terrorist act by a non-state organization into an act of war by one state on another. Under international law, this more than satisfied any preconditions for U.S. forces to invade Afghanistan in search of al-Qaeda and to confront the Afghan government. This was the beginning of the formal war on terror, where the full weight of the U.S. security establishment was engaged.

The war on terror that began with the attacks by al-Qaeda and the invasion of Afghanistan quickly morphed into a war in Iraq. U.S. policy makers asserted a connection between Saddam Hussein's government in Iraq, terrorism, and the threat of weapons of mass destruction. U.S. policy makers demanded that international weapons inspectors, specifically inspectors from the International Atomic Energy Agency (IAEA), have full access to Iraqi weapons facilities. This led to a tug-of-war between the governments of Iraq and the United States. Under the umbrella of a United Nations resolution and U.S. congressional authorization, U.S. forces invaded Iraq and quickly vanquished the Iraqi military and overthrew Saddam Hussein's government. Within a short time, several hundred thousand U.S. troops had boots on the ground in two land wars in the Middle East. These conflicts became the longest ongoing wars in U.S. history—longer than the Civil War, longer than World War II, and longer than the Vietnam War. They were also very costly wars in human, monetary, material, and psychological terms.

Can realism help account for the events of 9/11 and following, for the actions of al-Qaeda, for the actions of the Afghan government, and for the choices made by U.S. policy makers? In a very limited manner the answer is a conditioned yes, but realism fails to account for much of the important behavior observed. We have already noted that as an elegant and simple theory, realism makes no assumption about the beneficence of others or about the reliability of international legal obligations in the context of anarchy. Instead, realism assumes that governments operate in an international state of anarchy and will use their self-help tools, conditioned by their position in the international hierarchy, to survive and prosper, perhaps at the expense of others and regardless of any notions of morality. So realism focuses our attention on state actors, power, and hierarchy in the international arena.

The first dilemma is that there are no moving parts for nonstate actors such as al-Qaeda in the theory. In what category do we place an organization such as al-Qaeda and its actions? Of course we can accommodate realism and call the terrorists criminals. Realism does recognize that NGOs and criminal activity can exist, but it does not really have an explicit mechanism for dealing with an NGO that declares international war on states and their societies. Is it merely another NGO, an organized interest group? If so, then does it make sense for a military superpower to mobilize its entire national security establishment to combat a special interest? Right away, we see a dilemma with realism.

Second, how can we explain the actions of the government of Afghanistan? Using the mechanisms of power and hierarchy in the theory of realism, the United States clearly sits atop the international hierarchy. Afghanistan is far down the hierarchy, a thirteenth-century political economy in a twenty-first-century world. We have noted that realism assumes that goal-oriented policy makers will not knowingly opt for policies that damage their states' survival, their states' positions in the international hierarchy, or their states' abilities to prevail in international affairs. This suggests that decision makers should opt for policies that address threats to their survival or could affect their positions in the international hierarchy. Any other policy choices would be outside their national interests as defined by the moving parts of the theory. A militarily insignificant state was confronted by the demands of a global superpower. Resistance would essentially be suicidal, but resistance is what Afghan policy makers chose. They knowingly opted for policies that damaged their state's survival. We might be able to explain their decision calculus, but not within the boundaries of realism. Perhaps something at the domestic level of politics can account for their decisions, but we cannot gain much, if any, analytic insight using the moving parts of realism—system structure, power, and hierarchy. Using these moving parts, the choices of the Afghan policy makers appear nonsensical.

Third, can realism account for the actions of the Iraqi government? Ironically, the choices of the Iraqi government might be the only actions that can be explained adequately with the moving parts of realism. The government of Saddam Hussein resisted U.S. pressures and calls for international weapons inspectors, but at almost every escalation of the crisis before the U.S. invasion the Iraqi government moderated its resistance and seemed to be partially acceding to U.S. demands. The government of Iraq seemed to be playing a game of chicken with the United States, a military superpower with far greater capabilities. But the government of Saddam Hussein also seemed to recognize the differences in power and position in the international hierarchy, informed by its experience from the first Gulf War in 1991. Rather than reject U.S. demands outright and commit suicide, like the government of Afghanistan, the government of Iraq partially responded to U.S. demands at every step of the process leading up to war. The Iraqi government continually ran up to the line in the sand, but, in retrospect, it seemed careful not to cross that line. It appeared willing to make concessions to avoid damaging the state's survival. Perhaps Saddam Hussein and his advisers miscalculated, but they clearly seemed to recognize that war with the United States would be suicidal. Other theoretical approaches to political science might provide a different account of Iraqi actions—such as playing to the domestic Iraqi audience and political survival—but those actions do make sense within the context of realism. Saddam Hussein's government resisted but then made concessions at every step of the process leading to war.

Finally, can realism account for U.S. actions? Beyond having to respond to an attack on U.S. soil and defending the national space against physical attack, realism falls far short as a useful theory here. First, the attack by an NGO terrorist organization was not going to endanger U.S. power or position in the international hierarchy. Nor were the governments of Afghanistan or Iraq capable of fundamentally damaging U.S. power or position in the international hierarchy. Perhaps we can use realism to account for why the United States initially responded to al-Qaeda and to Afghanistan for sheltering al-Qaeda, but we cannot explain the waging of decade-long wars by the United States against states far down the international hierarchy. The costs of the wars in Afghanistan and Iraq have likely done more to damage U.S. power, prestige, and position in the international arena than anything Afghanistan or Iraq could have done through rational calculation and actions consistent with realism. In many ways, U.S. actions in these cases were incredible overreactions within the framework of realism. The bargaining actions over weapons inspections and transparency by the United States vis-à-vis Iraq are consistent with realism, but the Iraqis consistently made concessions that, if continued, could have avoided outright war. Why, within the framework of realism, would the United States have elected to enter a war that would be excessively costly given its stated objectives and given the viability of other, cheaper, strategies to achieve those objectives? Furthermore, there was no indication that such a conflict would improve the U.S. position in the global hierarchy or enhance the power or prestige of the United States. Perhaps the conflict would achieve other objectives, but those do not lie within the boundaries of realism and how realism defines national interests. Perhaps other theories in political science can do better?

The structure of international relations, the capacity to influence others, and the distribution of that capacity to create a hierarchy of more to less capable governments are clearly important characteristics in international affairs (and we will examine them more carefully in chapter 2), but they are insufficient to account for many important situations in global affairs, as illustrated by the examples above. Realism neglects the political activities and strategic manipulation that can take place between individuals and groups within domestic political arenas. To circumvent such apparent discrepancies with realist theory as those illustrated above, proponents of realism often resort to ad hoc explanations that rely on independent—causal—variables that do not exist in realism. They may assign causal weight to interest group activity; variations in internal political dynamics or partisanship; domestic institutional variations across states, such as authoritarian versus democratic, presidential versus parliamentarian, or winner-take-all versus proportional electoral rules; or some other factors that political scientists in the fields of American or comparative politics find influential, but these factors are not part of the explanatory framework of realism. This reliance on causal mechanisms or independent variables that are exogenous to—not included in—the theory of realism but are prevalent in other fields in political science highlights the shortcomings of the theory and suggests that we might be better served by a theory or theories that include such variables.

A theory whose moving parts frequently fail to account for significant and nontrivial outcomes that affect social welfare is of questionable usefulness and should encourage a search for alternative theoretical frameworks that perform better when tested against the empirical world. This is the forward progress and practice of good science. The practice of good science is central to producing a better, evolving, academic understanding of social behavior, and also essential to well-informed policy making that seeks to learn from past experience and mistakes. This sets the stage for a discussion of what it is that scientists, specifically social scientists, do.

CONCLUSION AND SOME OTHER PITFALLS

In this chapter we have discussed the purposes and processes of social science. We have defined also what we mean by a micro political economy approach in this text and the three assumptions that lie at the heart of that approach, offering powerful and elegant tools to leverage our investigation and understanding of political behavior. We must remember that these are simplifications. We do not know whether political actors actually are rational and actually want to survive, but these assumptions are useful. Even with such powerful assumptions and tools, the analysis of political behavior is difficult. Strategic settings complicate the dilemma of connecting preferences, choices, and outcomes in the social world.

Several other problems also hamper this process, both for investigators trying to understand choices and for policy makers trying to make choices in strategic settings. Two of these problems warrant mention. First, decision makers generally operate under some degree of uncertainty: they have incomplete information about the world, about their possible choices, about the preferences and possible choices of others, and about how multiple decision makers' choices will interact. The games represented in figure 1.3 model interactions of complete information, in which all players know the payoffs and possible strategies; this omniscience greatly simplifies the search for preferences and dominant strategies. Dilemmas exist for decision makers even in such simple interactions, but the game becomes infinitely more complicated when a decision maker encounters a real-world strategic challenge armed with incomplete information about her choices, the preferences of others, and the structure of her interaction with others.

A fallacy of composition is a situation in which an outcome is different from what was expected based on simple extrapolation from its component parts. It may be greater or less than the sum of its parts.

Second, we cannot assume that choices in strategic settings interact in linear fashion. This means that we cannot just add individual choices together to arrive at an outcome, for they may not interact additively. An outcome may be different from simply the sum of individual choices. In this situation, which we call a **fallacy of composition,** the outcome is different from the sum of the parts: perhaps greater, perhaps less, but different. These two problems—incomplete information and the fallacy of composition—raise the possibility of unanticipated outcomes, which are unintentional consequences of choice. No policy maker is capable of looking down a decision path and fully anticipating the consequences of her choices and those of others. Some uncertainty about the future, some risk, always remains.

Now, as Holmes said to Watson, "the game is afoot. . . ."

APPENDIX: EXAMPLES OF COMPLETE AND INTRANSITIVE PREFERENCES

Let's examine completeness and transitivity in two scenarios, looking at preference ordering over outcomes, first by an individual and then by a collectivity or group. The latter is the more interesting and important case for societies relying on elections and markets to determine public preferences and produce social outcomes, and, as we will see, it is a problematic case for the normative qualities that many of us value in democratic societies. Since the properties of completeness and transitivity are logically consistent, relatively straightforward, and fairly easy to grasp in terms of rationality, we will intentionally construct cases wherein the preference orderings in the individual and collective scenarios are complete but intransitive. This is actually quite difficult in the individual case, but it happens fairly easily and often in the case of collectivities.

Why is this pattern of completeness plus intransitivity so difficult to illustrate in the individual case? When forced by constraints such as scarcity, individuals can usually construct a preference ordering between two alternatives that fulfills the condition of completeness, or among three or more alternatives that satisfies the condition of transitivity. This ordering process requires several simplifying presumptions that might be considered heroic. The first presumption is that individuals are well informed about the differences between alternatives and can distinguish those differences. This is a demanding criterion, but it is important for our use of rationality to examine social behavior and for the recognition of potential pitfalls of the rationality assumption. When we relax this presumption, individuals can still be rational yet make choices that appear inconsistent with rationality because of their being poorly informed or confused; they are still rational, but they are working with incomplete information. This recognition will focus our attention on the constraints of information in decision-making contexts.

For example, a wine expert should be able to rank-order two wines easily based on taste, and if a third wine were added to the tasting, the expert should be able to rank it vis-à-vis each of the other wines, so that the ordering would be transitive. If another wine were to be added, again the expert could make a paired comparison to establish completeness of preferences. The wines would all be comparable pair by pair, and when all the choices were put together, the property of completeness would also be consistent with the property of transitivity. We assume that a fully informed wine expert could produce such complete and transitive preferences. In reality, however, few individuals are master sommeliers. Most people would probably be able to do a paired comparison, comparing any two wines against each other and thereby establishing completeness, but they would likely falter in attempting to create a transitive ranking of preferences over a large number of wines. Are these nonexperts nonrational, or do they just have insufficient knowledge and experience with wine? The latter is more likely the case. If so, they are still rational, but confused by their informational shortcomings—no doubt an accurate assessment for most of us.

Our second presumption—also quite rigid—is that preferences do not change. We know empirically that tastes do change and evolve, but presuming fixed preferences is a simplifying condition that provides us with analytical leverage to examine choices. By holding this one component of the decision process constant, we can look at variations in other parts of the process and attribute variations in behavior, in choice, to those inconstant components. Presuming that preferences are constant means that the moving parts in this approach to choice are information and context. As a consequence, we look for variations in those parts to explain choices that look inconsistent with a rational decision maker's assumed preference ordering.

We can construct a situation in which an individual political actor—for instance, a judge in the European Court of Justice (ECJ), the high court of the European Union (EU)—has complete but intransitive preferences. In her deliberations, the judge weighs how her decisions affect three different outcomes: the legal process, justice for individuals, and EU integration. We can examine her preferences over outcomes for completeness by conducting a paired comparison of the weighting she gives each outcome in her deliberations. When comparing the importance of the legal process to justice for individuals, she values the process of law more than justice for individuals; we can say that legal process defeats justice. When comparing justice for individuals to EU integration, her preference for justice defeats EU integration. Finally, when comparing her weighting of the legal process and EU integration, we discover that EU integration defeats the legal process. We've established completeness, as each pair is comparable. To summarize her paired comparisons:

legal process > justice

justice > EU integration

EU integration > legal process

Yet, if we look closely at her paired comparisons, we discover that her preferences are intransitive. Rationality and the property of transitivity dictate that if she prefers process to justice, and justice to EU integration, she should prefer process to EU integration. But she actually weights EU integration over legal process in her deliberations, which means that her judicial decisions may cycle across alternatives if her deliberations involve considering the effects on all three outcomes. To her colleagues on the bench and to observers of the court who make strict assumptions about rationality, her decisions appear nonrational, poorly informed, or confused—not a good way to build a consistent and coherent body of law that will help guide social behavior. An informed observer may consider this problem manageable, however, as long as the judge's deliberations involve making a decision that will affect only two of the alternatives. This situation of intransitive preferences can be problematic for those trying to observe and understand social behavior, but it is actually quite rare at the individual level.

Unfortunately, the problem of complete and intransitive preferences can occur regularly when we are examining collective decision making such as elections and markets, which aggregate the preferences of many individuals to produce a collective preference ordering. Therefore the second scenario, involving a collectivity's preference orderings, is much more relevant for our study of political behavior. Every democratic society adopts voting rules to aggregate individual preferences among alternatives. There are a variety of voting rules—such as unanimity, majority, plurality, and proportionality—that can transform individual preferences over outcomes into a social preference. For simplicity's sake, we use a simple majority—or winner-take-all—rule in the following, but another choice of voting rule would not make a difference in our example.

Also for the sake of simplicity, the society in our example is made up of three individuals. These three members of society, or voters, evaluate their choices among particular policies according to how the policies influence three big social outcomes: social justice, democratic rule, and economic growth. Each voter makes a complete and transitive preference ordering over these outcomes.

Voter 1 values social justice (A) over democratic rule (B),

democratic rule (B) over growth (C), and

social justice (A) over growth (C).

Voter 2 values growth (C) over social justice (A),

social justice (A) over democratic rule (B), and

growth (C) over democratic rule (B).

Voter 3 values democratic rule (B) over growth (C),

growth (C) over social justice (A), and

democratic rule (B) over social justice (A).

These paired comparisons produce an individual transitive ordering as follows:

Voter 1:   social justice > democratic rule > growth

Voter 2:   growth > social justice > democratic rule

Voter 3:   democratic rule > growth > social justice

An election decided by a majority rule transforms these individual preferences into a social or collective preference. We find that social justice is preferred to democratic rule (A defeats B) by 2 to 1. Democratic rule is preferred to growth (B defeats C) by 2 to 1. So far, so good, but growth is preferred to social justice (C defeats A), also by 2 to 1. If our collective preference ordering were to be transitive, social justice would have defeated growth (A defeats C). However, the collective's preference ordering is intransitive; the outcomes of elections can cycle across the three alternatives.

The **Condorcet paradox** is a situation in which a voting rule aggregates individual preferences that are complete and transitive but produces a collective outcome that is intransitive and cycles because the preferences of the aggregated majority are in conflict with each other.

The lack of a fixed hierarchy of preferences makes society look confused or nonrational, but it is produced by individually rational behavior. This problem, known as the **Condorcet paradox,** can occur under any voting rule in a democratic society. Kenneth Arrow, a Nobel Prize winner, proved that except in a dictatorship, where only one individual decides, any voting rule to create a social ordering among alternatives can produce an intransitive ordering even though the individuals making up the social group have complete and transitive preferences. This dilemma means that it is impossible for democratic societies to construct a social welfare function from individual preference functions. This realization opens a chink in the normative appeal of democracy, if we value democratic voting rules solely for their ability to map individual preferences accurately into a social welfare function that maximizes collective welfare. Democracy has many other appeals, however.

KEY CONCEPTS

autarky (p. 8)

backward induction (p. 25)

causality (p. 29)

centralized means of allocation (p. 6)

closed-economy models (p. 7)

completeness (p. 18)

Condorcet paradox (p. 50)

costs (p. 12)

data (p. 34)

decentralized (p. 6)

dependent variable (p. 31)

dominant strategy (p. 23)

fallacy of composition (p. 46)

game theory (p. 22)

global capitalism (p. 6)

globalization (p. 5)

hierarchy of preferences (p. 18)

independent variable (p. 31)

indifference (p. 18)

institutions (p. 13)

intransitive collective outcome (p. 19)

invisible hand (p. 23)

methodological individualism (p. 15)

models (p. 33)

Nash equilibrium (p. 23)

normative (p. 30)

normative theory (p. 30)

open-economy models (p. 7)

political economy (p. 4)

positive theory (p. 31)

positivist (p. 31)

power (p. 40)

preferences (p. 15)

realism (p. 40)

realpolitik (p. 40)

scarcity (p. 12)

self-interest (p. 15)

social trap (p. 24)

sovereignty (p. 40)

spatial model (p. 19)

spurious (p. 32)

stable equilibrium (p. 23)

testable hypothesis (p. 34)

transitivity (p. 18)

validity (p. 34)

EXERCISES

1. What is the difference between an independent variable and a dependent variable? Give one example each of an independent and a dependent variable pair.

2. Which of the following are variables?

   Foreign aid levels   Barack Obama

   3 percent growth   Birthrates

3. Assess whether each of the following statements is a claim of causality or of correlation:

   a. Economic growth almost always accompanies population increase. *correlation*

   b. Trade promotes peace because it increases the costs from war. *causality*

   c. Tourism rises all over the world during the years that the Olympics are held. *correlation*

4. Identify the independent and dependent variables in each of the following statements:

   a. Knowledge is advanced by systematic research.

   b. The more foreign aid a country receives from the United States, the more likely that country is to vote consistently with the U.S. position at the United Nations.

   c. Low labor costs encourage the construction of U.S.-owned factories in Southeast Asia.

   d. Authoritarian regimes discourage international investment.

   e. The more educated a nation, the larger the voter turnout in national elections.

5. What is globalization? Give an example of global integration.

6. Why are some societies and peoples resistant to globalization?

7. What are the four similarities across the physical and social sciences that distinguish them from the humanities?

8. Why do social scientists emphasize cumulative knowledge, and how does this differ from the humanities?

9. What are the four primary activities of social scientists?

10. What do we call the analytical strategy that focuses on individual choice?

11. What do we call the state of a decision maker's preference if she must choose between two alternatives that are comparable, but she does not prefer one alternative or the other? What kind of behavior might this account for?

12. In game theory, what do we call the situation in which no player in a social interaction can improve her outcome by unilaterally choosing another strategy?

13. Consider the game illustrated below. Does a dominant strategy exist for either or both players? If so, what is it for Player 1? For Player 2?

	Player 2's Choice	
Player 1's Choice	Strategy A	Strategy B
Strategy A	2, 1	0, 0
Strategy B	0, 0	1, 2

14. Explain Nash equilibrium. Give examples of good and bad equilibria.

15. Why do political scientists use backward induction? Why is it more beneficial to look at the desired outcome than at the actual outcome?

16. Equilibria are appealing for understanding social behavior, but are they inherently good normatively? Why or why not?

17. Assume Iran and Kuwait are (the only) members of an oil cartel. Each may choose to expand or restrict its output of oil. The table below shows each side's profits (in billions of dollars) for these possible outcomes. (Iran's profits are in bold.)

	Kuwait	
Iran	Expand	Restrict
Expand	**$50**, $25	**$65**, $15
Restrict	**$30**, $40	**$60**, $35

a. What is Kuwait's dominant strategy: expand, restrict, or depends on what Iran chooses?

b. Which of the following outcomes is the Nash equilibrium? Both expand oil production, both restrict oil production, Iran expands oil production and Kuwait restricts, or Iran restricts oil production and Kuwait expands.

c. Is any one of the following outcomes better for both than the Nash equilibrium? Both expand oil production, both restrict oil production, Iran expands oil production and Kuwait restricts, or Iran restricts oil production and Kuwait expands.

FURTHER READING

Axelrod, Robert. 1984. *The Evolution of Cooperation.* New York: Basic Books.

Dixit, Avinash, and Barry Nalebuff. 1991. *Thinking Strategically: The Competitive Edge in Business, Politics, and Everyday Life.* New York: W. W. Norton.

Lave, Charles, and James March. 1975. *An Introduction to Models in the Social Sciences.* New York: Harper & Row.

Poundstone, William. 1992. *Prisoner's Dilemma: John Von Neumann, Game Theory, and the Puzzle of the Bomb.* New York: Doubleday.

Riker, William. 1986. *The Art of Political Manipulation.* New Haven, CT: Yale University Press.

Schelling, Thomas C. 1978. *Micromotives and Macrobehavior.* New York: W. W. Norton.

———. 1980. *The Strategy of Conflict.* Cambridge, MA: Harvard University Press.

Structure, Nation-States, Power, and Order in an International Context

L'état c'est moi.

—*Louis XIV, 1651*

The previous chapter began to raise the issue of how context can affect the choices of rational policy makers. Context can transform social interactions, alter beliefs about what strategies are appropriate, influence evaluations of what others' choices might be in given situations, and affect perceptions of possible benefits and possible costs. In this chapter we begin by examining some structural characteristics of the international system that help to define the context within which policy makers operate, specifically the nation-state system. As noted in chapter 1, rational policy makers may make particular choices in one context, but change the context and the very same rational decision makers will make other choices. For more than four hundred years the nation-state system has been the dominant context in which policy makers and individuals have made choices in international affairs. This context imposes significant constraints and pressures on policy makers, constraints and pressures that differ dramatically from the contextual setting of domestic politics. We next move to the tools and capabilities that governments and other actors use to influence outcomes and the activities of others in the global arena. Although our focus in this book is on global political economy, the tools and the approach we develop here are applicable in a wide variety of political settings. We can apply the logic of rational self-interested decision makers operating in an environment of scarcity to both domestic and international political arenas. There is, however, an important structural distinction between the study of politics in international arenas and the study of politics in domestic arenas. This difference, which reflects the current international context, colors our analyses of global affairs, international politics, and international political economy by adding another independent variable to our explanations.

THE CONTEXT OF INTERNATIONAL VERSUS DOMESTIC POLITICAL ARENAS

International politics and international political economy take place in an arena that lacks a central overarching authority. No central government exists as in domestic political arenas. Although some domestic political arenas have more effective, fair, capable, just, and legitimate governments than others, domestic political arenas are nonetheless generally characterized by the presence of a central, overarching authority. But there is no central or world government with legitimate governing authority over the actions of all those living on the planet, no world government with binding authority to implement and enforce international laws over national governments. Because the absence of a supranational government is important to our understanding of global political economic relations, this distinction between political arenas with central authority and those with no central authority must be included as an independent variable in our analyses.

For centuries, the nation-state has been the dominant unit of political aggregation in world affairs. This helps explain the term *international relations,* or relations between nations. As the key defining unit of political geography in world politics, nation-states must be considered from several angles: What are their origins, what makes them similar, what differentiates them, what makes some more capable than others, why do we care about nation-states, and how does a global system structured around nation-states affect world politics? As we begin to explore the concept and history of nation-states and the nation-state system, we will encounter key terms such as *legitimate authority, identity, nationalism, sovereignty, anarchy, self-help, power,* and *influence.* All represent concepts that are central to our understanding of the influence of context on world politics.

NATION-STATES: INFLUENTIAL POLITICAL ORGANIZATIONS IN THE GLOBAL ARENA

A **nation-state** is a form of political organization. In the past, other forms of political organization have been influential in the global arena: city-states, empires, feudal kingdoms, commonwealths, leagues, and others. In the future, new forms may emerge to supplant the state as the primary unit of

> A **nation-state** is the primary unit of political aggregation in world affairs, combining the collective identity of a *nation* with the legal entity of a *state.*

political aggregation in world affairs. Some new forms of political aggregation may be emerging already, such as the supranational governmental structure of the European Union. Currently, the EU appears subordinate to its member states, but its structure and reach are changing. The EU experiment in supranational governance may fail because of internal contradictions; it may continue to meander along, managing internal turmoil and tensions that threaten to unravel the interstate cooperation that underpins the EU; or it may someday challenge and perhaps supplant the governmental structures, reach, and authority of its member states. In Honduras we can observe a new experiment in political organization with the creation of free market cities, which will be self-governing and semi-independent from the Honduran state. It is important to recognize that the nation-state, even though it is currently the dominant form of political geography in the global arena, is not the only means of organizing political space in world affairs. For the time being and the foreseeable future, however, the vast majority of cross-border political and economic relations in the global arena will be between nation-states. We can gain greater understanding of the term *nation-state* by dividing it into its two components: *nation* and *state*.

States and Their Defining Characteristics

A state is a legal entity that can undertake and accept legal commitments, such as treaties and other obligations, through its representative authority or government. Much as an individual can enter into contracts and other commitments, a state can make such contractual commitments. From this perspective, a state is a legal abstraction that can assume the same responsibility under law that individuals can. A state can enter into contracts within its national boundaries or across national boundaries. This premise sits at the heart of constitutions and bodies of domestic law and regulation, which are contracts between states and their citizens. It also underpins international law, international organizations, and international treaties. In the agreements that create international treaties or international governmental organizations (those organizations whose members are nation-states), the basic assumption is that states, like individuals and firms, can enter into binding legal commitments. Of course, states may renege on their agreements, just as individuals and firms sometimes fail to live up to their commitments. Nevertheless, such agreements are viewed as contracts similar to those that individuals, firms, and other organizations undertake within national political arenas. However, as we will shortly see, because of the structure of modern international relations, such contracts or treaties between states are not backed with the same weight of law, adjudication, and enforcement as are contracts and agreements made within national boundaries.

Aside from their function as legal entities, states have several other very important characteristics. First, a state has a defined geographic territory. In the modern nation-state system, states are the only international actors that technically control territory. Of course, private property ownership does exist in most states around the world. Even though individuals may own their homes and companies may own buildings and land, their ability to exercise property rights over a defined geographic area is determined by the state. Through law, states define property rights and delegate them to others. States may follow different practices in defining private property and assigning property rights. Some states retain greater control of property than do others, which explains why notions of private property vary from one country to another.

Second, a state has a population that inhabits its geographic territory. The characteristics of populations may vary from state to state. A state's population may be rich or poor, old or young, highly educated or not, healthy or unhealthy, diverse or homogeneous, or identified by some other feature or quality. But each state has a population that is connected to its territory. These are the people who provide revenues to the state, staff its militaries, propel its economy, and constitute its society.

Third, every state has a government to represent some component of the people who inhabit its territory. Governments vary in this notion of representation. Differences in representation help explain some of the differences in government activities from nation to nation. A government may represent a broad swath of society, as democratic governments do, or it may represent some more parochial and narrow segments in society, as patronage or authoritarian regimes do. In chapter 1, we defined the portion of society upon which political leaders depend for their political survival as the selectorate. The concept and makeup of selectorates vary from state to state. The state apparatus of a government is considered the source of legitimate coercion within a society. Governments use police forces to enforce their laws, regardless of whether or not those laws are fairly constructed and enforced. The government may not be the only possible source of coercion and violence in a society, but it is the only legitimate source. Of course, that very legitimacy is often a matter of conflict and dispute.

Functional Equality and Specialization: What Every State Does, but Some Better than Others

Within the current nation-state system, all states are functionally equal. Does this mean that all states are equal? Are the United States and Ecuador equal? Clearly they are not equal on most dimensions. The United States has a much bigger economy, more extensive territory and a larger population, a more capable military, a higher per capita income, longer life expectancies, and so on. So what does **functional equality** mean and why is it relevant? Functional equality is a comparative statement about what states do—the functions states undertake—rather than a statement about how well they perform those functions. Regardless of their abilities, all states attempt to perform similar essential functions, such as defining notions of property, extracting taxes, providing for the common defense, developing legal systems to impose order on social relations within state boundaries, devising means such as courts and regulators to adjudicate disputes in society, creating police agencies to enforce both the legal structure and judicial resolutions, and representing some interests (however defined and implemented) in the society.

> **Functional equality** is the principle that, regardless of their abilities, all states attempt to perform similar essential functions; they are equal not in how they perform such functions, but only in that they all attempt to perform them.

Again, all states are equal not in how they perform such functions, but only in that they all attempt to perform them. This functional equality means that governments and their societies do not take advantage of specialization in the international arena in terms of the activities of government. For example, the French government may excel at tax collection, the Swedish government at provision of social services, the Russian and Chinese governments at domestic spying and surveillance, the Japanese government at managing industrial policy, and the U.S. government at the provision of national security. Yet governments and societies do not purchase such public commodities from whichever governments are the best producers. The Russian and Chinese governments do not hire the U.S. government to provide for their common defense, nor do the Mexican and Nigerian governments contract with the French government for tax collection. Governments do not engage in exchange relations with other governments to implement the functions of government. They all attempt to perform the same basic functions, regardless of their capabilities and effectiveness.

> **Specialization** is an economic practice whereby each producer does not attempt to produce the entire range of commodities, but rather produces a commodity or supplies a service in which the producer has a comparative advantage.

The functional equality of states and their lack of specialization in the provision of government commodities differ dramatically from the global economic arena, where international trade and market exchange enable consumers and producers to take advantage of specialization in the production of nongovernment commodities. With **specialization,** a producer does not attempt to produce the entire range of commodities desired by her society, but instead relies on her community to supplement her production of some commodities with other commodities she may want. Producers concentrate on the production of particular commodities and trade for others they do not produce. When humankind was in its hunter-gatherer stage of economic activity, or even during the early stages of the transformation from hunter-gather communities to pastoral-agricultural communities, a high degree of functional equality from producer to producer existed. With economic advance, however, individual producers began to specialize in production, trading the output of their labors for commodities they did not produce. Such specialization of nongovernmental commodities occurs within states and increasingly across states with the globalization of exchange.

Efficiencies of the Market and Fragmentation of Government Services

> **Economies of scale** are the efficiency gained in producing a commodity from the concentration of activities and resources that are required to produce it. **Economies of knowledge** are the efficiency gained from learning about how to produce a product.

Economies of scale and economies of knowledge can increase the efficiency of production of a commodity. **Economies of scale** occur with the concentration of resources in that production—producing more of a commodity may be more efficient owing to the aggregation of activities and resources that are required to produce it. **Economies**

of knowledge occur with gains from learning about how to produce a product—the more we do something, the better and more efficient we may become at doing it. **Efficiency** is simply a statement about how much is produced for a fixed amount of labor and other inputs to production. More efficient producers produce more with the same amount of labor and other resources than do less efficient producers. All other things being equal, specialization in production generally produces efficiency gains. In economic life, we can develop specialization in our productive activities, which focuses our individual efforts on producing a narrower range of products, and then exchange our products for the wider variety of other products we desire. Such specialization allows us to produce and consume more commodities than if we individually had to produce all the products we want.

We live in domestic and global political economies in which economic actors take advantage of specialization. As we will see in future chapters, market mechanisms in the global political economy condition production, promote specialization, and generate gains in efficiency in economic arenas. But states do not take advantage of possible gains in efficiency from specialization in the production of governmental goods. The characteristic of functional equality in terms of government activities, which occurs across national governments, can present formidable dilemmas for the well-being of communities. The resulting fragmentation in the provision of governmental services can lead to inefficient governance, producing redundancies in management of such services and a lack of economies from scale and knowledge, as well as unwillingness to share governmental resources with those who live in communities under different governmental arrangements. Despite the inefficiencies and problems for overall social welfare created by governmental fragmentation and functional equality, people often prefer such governing arrangements over more efficient forms of organizing political space. They often prefer less optimal to more optimal governing arrangements because they are their governing arrangements and not those of another society, even if that other society is more efficient in the delivery of specific policy goods.

National Policy Autonomy and Interdependence

This difference between the functional equality of government activities in the nation-state system and the specialization that characterizes the production of economic commodities across nation-states highlights an interesting and important component of modern international relations. We live in a global political economy wherein the dominant production of political commodities—defense goods, social welfare goods, and other government services—is structured and conditioned *within* national polities, but the production of economic commodities is increasingly structured *across* national economies. This difference in settings raises the possibility of tensions between the production of political

> **Interdependence** refers to the connections and relations across nations, the degree to which activities in one nation spill over to influence activities in other nations. **National policy autonomy** is the ability of a government to maintain independence in producing political commodities and in forming and enforcing its own policies.

and economic goods, since the mechanisms that condition and discipline the production of government and nongovernment goods diverge dramatically. In one arena, the domestic polity acts as the disciplinary mechanism, while in the other arena, economic processes that do not recognize national boundaries discipline behavior. This difference is at the crux of the tension between **interdependence** (the connections across nations) and **national policy autonomy** (the production of political commodities for local consumption), and it helps to account for the production of political commodities that may impinge on the production of economic commodities.

For example, take the international production and trade in steel. With trade, the global market rewards efficient and competitive producers of steel and penalizes less efficient producers. Consumers will prefer to purchase steel from more efficient and competitive producers because their products will be less expensive for comparable quality. Less efficient producers of steel must transform their production capabilities to meet the challenge of global competition, or they will lose business, falter, and possibly fail. This is the discipline of the global market: those penalized by trade must find a way to use their productive resources more efficiently. Of course, the less competitive steel producers (and their labor force) may appeal to their politicians for some form of government intervention in the economic arena to protect their enterprise—a tariff, a quota, or a subsidy—that alters the supply or the price of foreign steel in the domestic market or the cost of producing domestic steel. The government may intervene in international trade to affect the price and, consequently, the production of steel. In this case, a national government becomes the disciplinarian of steel production and circumvents global market forces. Workers and companies in the domestic steel industry evade the discipline of the global market, but foreign producers of steel face the discipline imposed by the government that has made the intervention. Here economic producers respond to government incentives, and not to the efficiency demands of the market.

Equality and Effectiveness

Despite the characteristic of functional equality, in reality some states are more effective than others and more capable at performing the functions they undertake. Some governments are better than others at tax collection, provision of social services, national security tasks, and building infrastructure that is conducive to economic activity. Governments that are effective in one arena are often effective in multiple arenas. Theoretically, we could rank-order states from most to least capable in terms of their effectiveness and capabilities for the tasks they undertake, thus sketching a **hierarchy** in the international arena based on capabilities. Many of us already do this informally, on a case-by-case basis, when an international dispute arises between states. Whether we observe a trade dispute, a dispute over fishing rights, an international negotiation about pollution, an extradition

A **hierarchy** is the structure of the international arena in which nation-states are ranked in terms of their effectiveness and capabilities.

dispute, a disagreement over information sharing in the process of a criminal investigation, or a war, we often project the outcome based simply on our estimation of the differences in the capabilities of the involved states, their governments, and their societies. We call this difference in capabilities a difference in power.

Nation: Development of Collective Identity and Social Cooperation

Let's turn to the *nation* part of the term *nation-state*. A **nation** is a form of collective identity or community identification that is based on some common or shared knowledge. Unlike the physical, geographic entity of the state, it is an abstraction, for neither this common knowledge nor the collective identity can be seen or touched. It is thus more difficult to measure or observe than the physical entity of the state. Yet the conception of nation is critically important, as it reflects a highly potent form of collective affinity that can motivate individuals to engage in extraordinary activities. Policy makers can enlist this collective identification to influence their societies to participate in collective action. The common knowledge that underlies the identity of nation builds upon a grouping of individuals who share one or more characteristics that help to define who is a member of the specific community and who is not. By definition, the idea of community is based upon the recognition of boundaries between members and nonmembers of the community. Common characteristics that make individuals feel part of the same grouping can thus serve as a basis for the construction of identity and community.

> A **nation** is an abstract form of collective identity or community identification that builds upon a grouping of individuals who share one or more characteristics that help to define who is a member of the specific community and who is not.

A nation is a grouping, but not all groupings are nations. All of us belong to a variety of groups that contribute to our identities. The difficulty in observing and measuring the concept of nation arises from the fact that we live in social settings that are filled with clubs, associations, religious groups, community groups, and other organizations that contribute to identities. You might be a member of a fraternity or sorority, a labor union, a political party, a business or professional association, and/or a specific profession; a follower of a particular faith; or an emigrant from a particular country. Your gender, race, and class are other groupings with which you identify. Such collective associations help form the basis of our identities, but they are not all part of the collective identity called nation, which is a social institution that political elites can mobilize and manipulate in pursuit of collective action.

How do we distinguish between a nation and some other grouping that contributes to collective identity? This is not a simple or straightforward task, but some general characteristics do help. First, most people self-identify their attachment to a grouping called nation. When asked about nationality, one might reply Russian, American, British, Indian, Cuban, or Palestinian, but one would not say American Medical Association, al-Qaeda, or Pi Sigma Alpha. Second, national identity is more all-encompassing than most other collective groupings. Third, individuals may have hierarchies of group identification, making possible a rank-ordering of group associations in terms of their importance to individuals' identities. We may be members of multiple groups, but some motivate us more than others. When the identity of nation is activated and elevated in importance during times of strife and state crisis, an individual's other collective identities tend to take a subordinate role. Fourth, nation is one of the few identities that large numbers of people seem willing to kill and die for. This characteristic is what makes nation as an identity so powerful a force—if this concept of identity can inspire large numbers of people to make the ultimate sacrifice, it can surely be a strong motivation for other endeavors. Religion, as another such source of identity, can motivate in the same way. In contrast, it would be rather hard to believe that many members of a college fraternity, the American Bar Association, or the United Auto Workers would be willing to kill and die for these associations.

Unlike a state, a nation is not necessarily tied to physical geography. People can share the collective identity of a nation although they do not have a territory or a government that is recognized under the tenets of international law. Before 1947, the Jewish nation existed, but not the state of Israel. The Palestinian nation is currently fighting for the right to be a state. The Kurdish people in northern Iraq, southeastern Turkey, and northern Iran constitute a nation and want to become a state. In Spain, Basque nationalists fight for statehood and independence. The Navajo, Mohicans, Sioux, and Comanche may have lost their territory in wars with the United States, but they still remain nations. Vietnamese nationalists resisted Chinese domination, later French colonialism, and then American political-military intervention to fight for the creation and preservation of the Vietnamese state. Biafran nationalists tried to secede from Nigeria in the early 1970s, but two other nations, the Hausa and Fulani, fought the dissolution of Nigeria, resulting in a bloody civil war. Bangladeshi nationalists in East Pakistan sought, and finally obtained, independence from Pakistan; they created the state of Bangladesh. With the demise of the Soviet bloc in 1989–1991, independence movements based on national identity arose all over Eastern Europe and Central Asia, transforming the political map as new states emerged. The countries of Bosnia and Herzegovina, Croatia, Macedonia, Serbia and Montenegro, and Slovenia were part of the former state of Yugoslavia. Czechoslovakia split into the Czech and Slovak Republics. Estonia, Lithuania, Latvia, Georgia, Ukraine, Armenia, and other nations broke away from the Soviet Union and obtained statehood.

Some of these transformations from nation to nation-state occurred relatively peacefully, but others followed brutal conflicts of national unification and independence, terrorism, and abuse of individual political and civil liberties. Not all attempts to create state boundaries that coincide with the boundaries of national identification succeed. The persistence of nationalist civil conflict in many states shows the potential incongruence between states and nations. Since the breakup of the Soviet Union and the end of the Cold War, most combat deaths have occurred in civil wars, which represent battles over the concept of nation, rather than in interstate conflicts.

Moreover, states can exist without nations. State boundaries in Europe emerged from centuries of conflict and state building, which drew upon the construction of national identities that were based on the state and the allegiance of individuals to the state. But the drawing of state boundaries in Africa took place in European capitals. These boundaries are legacies of colonialism, and they do not necessarily coincide with the emergence of particular national identities within those boundaries. The people living within particular sets of boundaries may not share a collective identity that coincides with the state, or the state may place several national identities in conflict, which can result in civil war, so-called ethnic cleansing, and discrimination—as in Rwanda, Zimbabwe, and Sudan. Even the Western European states, the United States, and other modern nation-states were not spared this dilemma of incongruence between nation and state, for the evolutionary nation building they experienced was also marked by a history of violence and civil conflict. Indeed, violence is often a part of nation building—just ask any Native American, the descendants of men who served in the U.S. Civil War, residents of Kosovo, or the men and women of Iraq today.

A Palestinian celebrates in the Gaza Strip in August 2005 in anticipation of the withdrawal by Israel from Palestinian territories it had occupied since 1967. Behind him is Neve Dekalim, a Jewish settlement established like many others to strengthen Israeli claims to the land by creating facts on the ground. The Palestinians remain a nation without a fully formed state, as Jews were before the creation of the state of Israel in Palestine. The Palestinian-Israeli conflict is, at its core, a dispute between two nationalities staking claim to the same piece of land.

Building National Identity

Successful construction of a sense of nation, or *nationalism,* amounts to the evolution of individuals into a group with an extraordinarily potent form of common identity. How do large masses of individuals come to identify themselves with a nation? How do individuals develop a collective identity that is aligned with a nation and may be stronger than their personal ambitions? What integrative forces contribute to the development of a nation? Let's first consider the influence of the key characteristics of a state—common territory and common government—on the evolution of national identity. A common territory can be integrative if individuals transfer their emotional ties to a territory to a collective identity attached to that territory. A common government, whereby people live under common political institutions, can also be integrative if the individuals living under the authority of that government come to accept its laws, institutions, and practices. Physical territory and common government can be integrative, but they can also be divisive if the groups within that territory have competing collective identities. As illustrated by the examples above of nations that exist without congruent states, territories, or governments, common territory and government are not necessary conditions for the development of nation. If nation is the dependent variable, common territory and government can be important contributors to nation, but they are not the critical independent variables for its development.

If nation is the dependent variable, a common economy is also not the critical independent variable for development of nation, for it is not a necessary condition for development of a national identity. The Kurds have rarely, if ever, lived within a common economic framework, but they share a strong bond of national identity. Between the time when they were driven from Jerusalem centuries ago and the formation of the modern state of Israel, Jews were scattered across many state territories and did not share a common economy, yet they retained a common identity as a nation. Other nations are spread across a variety of states and hence come under a variety of economic arrangements. Moreover, merely living under a set of common economic arrangements may fail to be a compelling integrative force. The inhabitants of the Basque regions of Spain operate within the Spanish economy, employ the euro, and accept that their economic futures are greatly influenced by Spanish economic institutions, yet the Basques strongly resist identifying themselves as Spanish. In the European Union, many countries have converted their currency to the euro, but they do not consider themselves part of a single nation called Europe. So far, they have maintained their distinct national identities even as they adopt some common economic tools.

A common culture, common religion, or common language may contribute significantly to the evolution of a group into a nation. Individuals who eat the same foods, wear similar clothing, listen to similar music, appreciate and revere similar art, speak the same language, employ similar expressions and slang, practice the same religion, and engage in similar social practices share a common culture, and this sharing can be integrative and help to develop a common identity. After all, people who share cultural characteristics tend to be more alike than not. However, although Australians, British, Americans, Canadians, and New Zealanders share a common language, they do not consider themselves part of a single nation. Argentineans, Chileans, Spaniards, Mexicans, and Costa Ricans speak a common language and practice a common religion, but they do not identify themselves as belonging to a single nation. In Miami and Los Angeles, significant portions of the population use Spanish as their primary language, but they identify with the nation of people making up the United States, despite this preference for a language that is not dominant outside their local communities. English serves as the secondary language in many Chinese American, Japanese American, Serbian American, Croatian American, and other ethnic American households and neighborhoods, yet those households and neighborhoods are vital parts of the U.S. nation.

Japanese Americans and German Americans served valiantly in the U.S. armed forces during World War II even though Japan and Germany were the enemies. Again, if nation is the dependent variable, common culture, common religion, and common language are not the critical independent variables for the development of nation. They can help, but they are not necessary or sufficient conditions.

Perhaps sharing a common political ideology can serve as the integrative force that promotes the development of nation? A common political ideology is a shared set of beliefs about the relationship between governments and their peoples, about the role of government in society, about what people can expect from government and what government can demand from people. Common political ideology differs from common government, which is a key component of a state, for people can live under a common government and yet hold distinctive political ideologies—including those that contradict their government. Moreover, people who live in many different states can share a common political ideology. Does this mean that they are part of the same nation, yet part of different states? Possibly, but in most of these cases, these people who live in different states and share an ideological perspective are not part of the same nation. During the Great Depression and for many years thereafter, some Americans held socialist and communist political ideologies even though they lived under governing structures that rejected such ideologies. Many of them shared an American national identity with those who supported another political ideology—same nation, different political ideology. In authoritarian states as well, there may be groups that support political ideologies that differ from those held by the governing regimes. The political challenges to Eastern bloc governments from 1989 to 1991 and the Arab Spring that began in 2011 are examples of citizens of states challenging the governing frameworks of their states, but sharing a common national identity with their political opponents. These examples suggest that common political ideology, while potentially a force for integration into a common national identity, is not a necessary condition. People can belong to a nation and yet hold different political ideologies.

What about a common history? Does sharing a common past ensure the development of nation? Consider states that have experienced large immigrations. During the 1800s and early 1900s, large waves of immigrants arrived in the United States and other parts of the New World from a variety of Old World countries. People emigrated from Norway, Sweden, Ireland, the United Kingdom, Germany, Russia, the Baltic republics, Italy, China, and other places to become residents of the United States, Canada, Argentina, Chile, and Australia. Many of these immigrants sought to become members of those states' nations, to share in the common knowledge and common national identity of the people of their destination states. They did not share a common history, but they sought to share the common identity of belonging to the same nation. These New World destinations developed strong nations and integrated new members into those nations despite the lack of shared histories. Governments can use the teaching of a common history to foster an integrative common knowledge and identity, but it is not a necessary condition for the development of nation.

Common territory, government, political ideology, culture, religion, language, and history can be integrative forces, but a nation may emerge even in the absence of these integrative forces, or these forces may be present where a nation does not exist. If none of these shared characteristics is a necessary and sufficient condition for the development of nation, what is? A shared sense of common destiny or common future is the critical component. The past, where people have been, is less important than where people are going. Linking individual destinies together to develop a group destiny sits at the heart of the concept of nation. Israelis, Palestinians, Kurds, French, Americans, Mexicans, Iranians, and Hutus become members of their respective nations when they share an identity based on future, not past, hopes and associations. As in the Horatio Alger stories, which emphasize the opportunities for success that await those coming to American shores with little or nothing and regardless of their pasts, the successful nation-states of the New World built impressive collective national identities in a relatively short period of time. Those nation-building success stories were based on the emergence of a sense of a common destiny shared among people looking to the future, without extensive common pasts, without much accumulated culture, often with several different languages and religions, and sometimes under changing governmental arrangements and state-society bargains.

The Importance of Nation in World Affairs

This abstract concept of national identity can work to governments' advantage in terms of extracting and mobilizing resources for state activities, promoting responsible community behavior and participation, and constraining threats to community and government authority. The combination of an abstract nation with a concrete state—the development of a nation-state—is an extremely powerful phenomenon. The governments of states whose people enjoy common knowledge about their national identity can manipulate that knowledge to increase their own authority over their peoples and their territories. Such governments can exploit the sense of national identity to ask more of their citizens than can governments whose populations have not developed this quality of nationalism, and they can extract greater individual sacrifice for the welfare of the larger group or nation. The governments of nation-states can draw more resources from their populations per capita than can the governments of mere states; they are more successful at collecting taxes, as those being governed are willing to contribute larger portions of their personal wealth if they believe in a shared national destiny. Governments can thus take advantage of the social institution of identity to motivate the actions of individuals in their societies, for people with a collective sense of the future are more willing to forgo current consumption to invest in the future. They are less likely to hide their revenues from their governments, more likely to ante up to the state coffers voluntarily, and more likely to contribute their energies and those of their children to societal endeavors. This same pattern of voluntary activity is repeated across strong nation-states, where national identity overlays the people's physical residence.

Nation-states are also better at getting their youth to contribute several years of their lives to national service. Consider the effect of national identity on eighteen-year-olds in nation-states, who are generally more willing to risk their lives in the service of their nations than are those in states that have not developed a sense of nation. This same feeling of nationalism can also increase a government's effectiveness at managing affairs in the domestic political arena. The governments of nation-states can ask more of their people for domestic programs, even for redistributive programs that are designed to benefit other members of the society.

Entrepreneurial governments may seek to promote the development of national identity in order to create a responsive citizenry and to reduce divisive localism. Many, if not all, governments face the dilemma of governing populations made up of diverse groups. Diversity may be more apparent in states with heterogeneous racial, religious, or ethnic composition, but even apparently homogeneous societies are composed of assorted groups that impose competing demands on individual identity. Such separate demands place cross-cutting pressures—pressures that overlap and compete—on individuals, which can lead to community divisiveness and undermine the collective purpose of the larger group.

The Rise of Modern Nationalism

States and nations have existed for centuries, but as more distinct than connected phenomena. The linkage of nationalism to the state is a relatively new trend. The Glorious Revolution in England, the American and French Revolutions, and Napoleon and the Napoleonic Wars ushered in modern nationalism, which represents a transformation from an elite to a mass form of collective identity and the development of mass attachments to the state. Prior to these transformations in state-society relations, only small elite groups identified with the power and policies of their states; mass loyalty, if it existed, was directed toward the monarch. Most of a state's inhabitants had no significant attachment to the state or the government of the state. One lord of the manor looked similar to any other feudal king to peasants, serfs, and those with no political rights or identity. Armies were predominantly professional armies, heavily composed of mercenaries. In some cases, the workers of the land could be mobilized for temporary military service, but this was part of the contractual obligation imposed on those workers by the feudal lord and not a product of collective identity.

The rise of nationalism and national identification with the state coincided with the huge growth in the size of militaries, broad conscription to fill the ranks, and the expansion of rights of citizens in exchange for their contributions to national service. Napoleon invented the modern civilian army with the *levée en masse,* which led to a dramatic increase in the size of militaries as governments drew upon their inhabitants for military service. The boundaries of citizenship were expanded as the quid pro quo—an exchange between the state and the people for the participation of the masses in the military. This form of conscription differed from the press-gangs and coerced service of those seeking to avoid prison that had been the traditional means of forcing an unfortunate minority, those apprehended in the wrong place at the wrong time, into the military service of the government. In contrast, the mass conscriptions, begun under Napoleon and soon adopted throughout Western Europe and later the United States, applied to large segments of males in societies, rich and poor, regardless of religion.

To expand the base of conscription beyond the limited numbers who volunteered required an upgrading of public records and better accounting within societies. Many of the states becoming modern nation-states began to take national census counts in the early to mid-1800s, some even earlier. These national accountings gathered information for the state about the number of citizens, where they lived, and their approximate well-being. These data provided the records governments needed both to implement universal conscription for military service and to know whom to tax.

Serving together, training together, and living together helped to develop bonds among the conscripts, whose lives (and futures) depended on one another. Successful political leaders then sought to transfer this bond of loyalty from the small group to the larger nation-state. The military became a school for embedding a modern national identity in the mass population. Broad-based conscription contributed to a dramatic increase in the number of people who identified with the state's power and policies, and in their willingness to sacrifice for the state. The recasting of identity and of the bargains made between the state and its residents transformed the state's capabilities, which changed the nature of warfare. Wars became more deadly as governments mobilized larger and larger armies made up of everyday citizens.

Governments of states can seek to develop common knowledge about collective national identity in order to expand the capabilities of the states, but national movements within states can also press for the creation of new states. This sometimes can lead to civil conflict or civil war between groups living within a common political geography but having different collective identities. Such civil conflicts are artifacts of nation and state building, some successful and others not. The nineteenth century saw the rise of national movements that advocated statehood and independence. Territorial consolidations and unification in Germany, Italy, and the United States merged fragments into large states and also built national identities congruent with physical states. Nationalists overcame significant barriers to building nation-states. The activities of Italian nationalists such as Giuseppe Mazzini, Count Camillo Benso of Cavour, and Giuseppe Garibaldi led to the making of Italy by 1870. Count Otto von Bismarck, the Prussian leader, succeeded in unifying distinct German entities into a single German state by the Franco-Prussian War in 1870. In the United States, President Abraham Lincoln led a war to preserve and cement national union; one result of the U.S. Civil War was the elevation of central government and national identity over state government and more localized identity. Such nationalist movements have also been active in state building in the twentieth and twenty-first centuries. In the mid-1900s, nationalist movements in Africa and South Asia led to the creation of many new states as colonial governments were pushed aside. In 1945, 51 states signed the Charter of the United Nations as the original members. With the addition of Montenegro and South Sudan in 2006 and 2011, respectively, U.N. membership had grown to 193 states. While many of these states are still developing coherent national identities, their membership in the United Nations speaks to some degree of national identity that overlaps with their geography.

By the late 1800s, the more successful states were those whose governments had somehow managed to expand their support from a small cadre of elites to the masses, which shared in the collective identity. Then and today, *failed states* are partly defined by the failure of their governments to create common knowledge about collective identity, which enshrines a bargain between the state and mass society that encourages allegiance and sacrifice by the masses for the state.

If history provides any insight, conflicts over nation building can prove extremely deadly. This is an important lesson to remember as we watch contemporary conflicts over nation building in places such as Sri Lanka, Central Asia, Rwanda, and the fragments of the former Yugoslavia. Today, those in the advanced industrialized states may deplore the violence that characterizes many of these modern nation-building efforts, but they need only look to their own histories to see examples of the violence and destruction that can occur during the process of territorial consolidation and construction of national identity.

Often, however, a national identity that is tied to the state and that can overcome competing identities fails to emerge. The former Yugoslavia is an example of the difficulties a government faces in managing the tensions between local and national identities. For almost fifty years after World War II, the government of Yugoslavia appeared to have managed successfully the crosscutting pressures of a handful of strong and diverse local ethnic identities—Serbian, Croatian, Bosnian, and others. But the death in 1980 of Marshal Tito, the Yugoslav leader, the dissolution of Soviet control over the Eastern bloc nations at the end of that decade, and the ensuing manipulation of ethnic identities by local political leadership eventually revealed that those regional ethnic identities were stronger than Yugoslav nationalism. Yugoslavia fragmented under these pressures and produced militarized conflict between Bosnians, Serbs, Croatians, and inhabitants of the region surrounding Kosovo.

What do governments do to promote common knowledge about national identity? Educational systems provide exceptional vehicles for socializing citizens with a sense of broader community and national identity. The expansion of public education and the mandating of required schooling for youth have been seen as devices to improve the quality of the workforce, but these are also tools for embedding a sense of community, national civics, and respect for the processes of government. In the 1870s, the Germans started singing *Deutschland über Alles*. Students in American classrooms began reciting the Pledge of Allegiance in the 1890s. Most U.S. students take classes in American civics and government during their K–12 years, and sometimes at higher educational levels. This practice of civic education is repeated around the world. What better way to develop an attachment to the state than to inculcate beliefs and knowledge through the educational mechanisms of society?

In addition to the formal institutional settings of schools, governments have other tools for building common knowledge about identity. Required military and public service can help build broad national identity and attachment to the state. Public holidays, parades, and folklore help build civil mythologies that contribute to a sense of group identification. Some of these efforts advance attachment and identity to groups smaller than a nation, but many contribute to the development of national identity. Manifest destiny, Horatio Alger and the American Dream, the Thousand-Year Reich, George Washington and the cherry tree, Lord Nelson and the Battle of Trafalgar, the French Revolution and the rise of republican government, Napoleon's military success, and other civil myths and military exploits are examples of the mythologies that governments can promote to overcome crosscutting allegiances and contribute to a sense of belonging to a community that extends beyond the boundaries of individual, family, or other smaller group associations.

Origins of the State System: Empire and Fragmentation

What are the roots of the state system that, together with markets, dominates relations in today's global political economy? The modern state is a relatively new form of political organization, dating from the Treaty of Westphalia in 1648, which ended the Thirty Years' War in Europe. Before that extended continental conflict, the political map of Europe displayed a variety of political forms—empires, states, feudal kingdoms, or other entities—where networks of transactions and authority relationships cut across the boundaries of physical geography (see map 2.1).

States are significant political entities, but they are not the only possible form of significant political and geographic consolidation. An **empire** encompasses far more territory under a single political entity than does a state. As the fifth century dawned, the Roman Empire dominated the political geography of Europe and the Mediterranean, consolidating much of the territory from North Africa to Ireland under centralized and organized governance. In a more modern attempt at empire, Adolph Hitler wrote in *Mein Kampf* about his vision of a Thousand-Year Reich, in which Germany would create a territorial and political empire through military conquest and then govern much of the world. He came uncomfortably close to achieving his vision.

> An **empire** is a political entity that incorporates far greater territory under a single political authority than does a modern nation-state.

After six centuries of rule, the Roman Empire fell apart. Germanic tribes threatened, captured, and assimilated Roman settlements in Western Europe, and the centralized political and territorial control fragmented into localized fiefdoms. Charlemagne and his Franks tried to re-create political and territorial empire in Europe around 800, but their efforts were short-lived, as barbarians from the East overran the Frankish Empire. By 1000, the political map of Europe reflected a large number of small, localized political entities. Feudal relations between lord and peasant defined social order and authority in these agricultural economies, which remained isolated from other parts of the world in both economic and political terms.

Crosscutting Authority: Lords, Popes, and the Holy Roman Emperor

Around this time, the Roman Catholic Church was actively extending its spiritual influence and authority by assimilating Franks, Germanic tribes, barbarians, and others into Christianity. Soon, the reach of the Church began to exceed that of small and highly localized political entities, and its religious authority began to compete with the secular, nonreligious authority of the local feudal lords. The inhabitants of these feudal entities faced three major, crosscutting authority relationships, each placing separate demands on their resources.

| Map 2.1 | **Europe in the Sixteenth Century** |

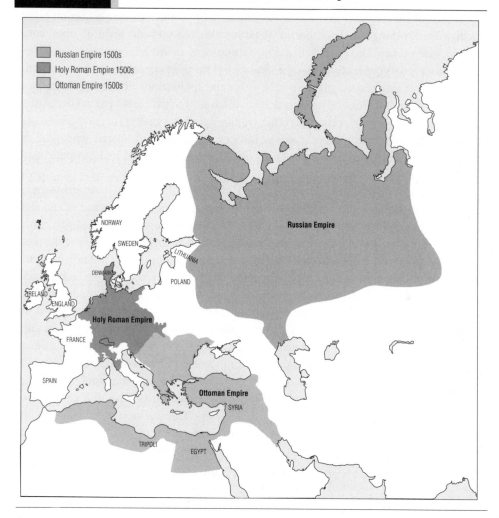

Russian Empire 1500s
Holy Roman Empire 1500s
Ottoman Empire 1500s

Source: Bruce Buena de Mesquita, *Principles of International Politics* (Washington, DC: CQ Press, 2003). Used by permission.

First, a line of political authority existed between the local lord of a feudal domain and his subjects. In many cases, these small feudal fiefdoms were little more than isolated handfuls of villages and farms, whose inhabitants—peasants and an emerging class of traders and merchants—owed their obedience to the local feudal lord. Under this hierarchical relationship, the local lord, their king, made demands on their labors and extracted his due in terms of their agricultural production, physical labor, and economic enterprise.

The religious and spiritual power of the pope created a second channel of authority, which also needed support from the lower orders. Priests extracted resources from their local populations by making demands on local lords and their subjects, passing collection plates, soliciting alms, tithing, and other forms of taxation, which took the form of labor, commodities, and money. The Church had a novel means of creating incentives for donating such resources to its coffers. Whereas the local lords sent their tax collectors into the farms and villages to exact payment, often with the threat and application of force, the Church was able to appeal for donations by promising eternal salvation, threatening eternal damnation or excommunication, or offering some other religious perk or penalty. The local representatives of the Church (friars, abbots, priests, bishops, cardinals, and others) employed the influence of the local lord in their activities, but they also challenged and competed with such secular authority.

A third track of political authority placed the Holy Roman Emperor in a hierarchical relationship with the inhabitants of the lands where the Roman Catholic Church had extended its spiritual reach. The emperor was a secular political authority, already a king who governed a physical territory, but also the figure whom the Church had anointed as defender of the faith. This arrangement, which provided the Church with a means of projecting military force at a time of religious proselytizing and rapid expansion of Christianity, invested the Holy Roman Emperor with a mix of secular and nonsecular power and authority. Like the local feudal authorities, the emperor needed resources to govern his local lands, but he also required the means to engage in a wider range of activities at the behest of the Church. To pay for such activities, the Holy Roman Emperor needed to cast his revenue nets beyond his immediate lands, placing him in competition with the local kings and the Church for resources.

Amid these three channels of authority, no single one had a clear monopoly of political authority over any given territory. Political and religious authority were thus confounded and in competition for the same pool of scarce resources. This situation might not be problematic when all three channels agreed on objectives and the means to obtain those objectives, but any disagreement could create a source of tension and a foundation for cleavage and conflict. Disagreements among the Church, the emperor, and local lords over objectives or demands on the resources of the local populations would inevitably put such overlapping authorities at odds in a world of scarcity, and there was no established hierarchy or other mechanism to resolve such conflicts peacefully.

Transformation of Social and Economic Organization

Economic and social activity in Europe was undergoing significant transformation at the same time these three channels of political and religious authority were evolving. The destruction of the Roman Empire by tribes from the East had left a vacuum of large-scale political authority in Europe. Social and economic activity fragmented without the centralized adjudication mechanisms of the Roman governors and the enforcement power of the Roman legions. Brigands and thieves plagued the countryside, inhibiting wide-scale economic and social activity and forcing people to band together in search of protection and shelter from the violence. Eventually, local lords emerged as a means of protection against such threats, but the military forces of these lords were little more than gangs of thugs in the employ of individuals whose power was based on their having been more successful in the exercise of violence than the leaders of competing gangs. The inhabitants of these communities, ruled by their thuggish leaders, exchanged the fruits of their labors for security, sometimes willingly but often under the threat of force.

As local lords consolidated their authority and provided protection for the societies within their domains, towns started to grow into centers of economic activity, trade, and new forms of social and economic organization. The new forms of economic activity led to the creation of wealth, the development of commercial classes, and eventually the introduction of money systems to replace barter. The economic tentacles of these emerging urban centers reached farther and farther into the countryside as farmers brought their goods to market, but such tentacles were vulnerable and required protection. The expansion of commercial areas and the growth of trade between such areas required security and order to protect merchants, provide contracting mechanisms, adjudicate complaints, and enforce the rulings of the adjudicators. These activities, in turn, required resources such as men, weapons, and money.

Who had such resources? The towns and their commercial areas were becoming locations of surplus resource accumulation, or wealth. In search of security, the emerging commercial classes there were willing to form coalitions with political entrepreneurs, the local feudal lords, who obtained resources from them in exchange for providing protection for their commercial activity. The commercial classes gained security and order, which nurtured continued commercial expansion; the lords gained greater and greater tools of coercion. Such protection arrangements enabled communities to reach farther and farther into the countryside, and exchange increased between communities.

Consolidation of Territory and Authority

The expansion of exchange between communities brought local lords into contact with other local lords. Sometimes these contacts led to competition and conflict over the authority to adjudicate exchange and enforce laws, the distribution of wealth, and the access to resources to pay for the military protections of territory and exchange. The more entrepreneurial lords used the economic surplus from their emerging commercial classes to challenge their competitors. They acquired more advanced weaponry and larger militaries, which enabled them to overcome the resistance of other nobles and to consolidate and expand their territorial influence. As they became rulers of larger and larger territorial spaces, they needed more and more resources to administer that territory, which meant more bureaucracy and larger armies to administer and collect taxes. This expanding spiral—territorial expansion by local nobles, elimination of political rivals within that territory, centralization of the mechanisms of coercion (military), and development of bureaucracy to administer those areas (cumulating taxes and resources)—characterized the formative years of state building in Europe. Successful thugs became lords, successful lords became kings, successful kings challenged the authority of other kings, and eventually some would challenge the authority of the Holy Roman Emperor and even the pope.

The Instability of Crosscutting Lines of Authority

The crosscutting lines of political and religious authority between the local lords, the pope, and the Holy Roman Emperor eventually proved unstable. Tensions emerged as these authorities competed for resources and allegiances. In 1517 Martin Luther challenged the spiritual authority of the pope by nailing his list of demands for reform to the door of his church. Luther was seeking peaceful reform and change, but his hammer blows instead mobilized the tensions between the crosscutting lines of authority and unleashed destructive religious wars.

In competition with the Roman Catholic Church over resources and authority over their subjects, many German princes supported Luther's proposed reforms and tried to impose them within their territories—a movement known as the Reformation. Whether these renegade princes sincerely supported Luther's ideas or merely saw in them a strategic opportunity to consolidate their authority, their actions nevertheless challenged the religious authority of the Church and caused a split in its ranks. Support for Lutheranism spread throughout central Europe, but not all principalities and kingdoms adopted the reforms; many remained loyal to the Church. The Church, the Holy Roman Emperor, and the lords loyal to the Church sought to reassert the authority of the Church in a movement known as the Counter-Reformation. This schism produced conflicts between principalities over the issue of religion, between the agents of the pope and those principalities turning away from the dictates of Roman Catholicism, and between the Holy Roman Emperor (as defender of the faith) and those rebellious principalities.

The sixteenth and early seventeenth centuries, the period of the Reformation and Counter-Reformation, were dominated by violent wars motivated by this challenge to the power of the Church in Rome to impose its religious authority on territories governed by local political rulers. These conflicts culminated in the Thirty Years' War, in relative terms among the deadliest wars in European history: one in four males of Germanic heritage died in this conflict over religious and secular dominion. The peace agreement that ended this war established the state as the dominant form of political authority and organization, and it continues to be so to this day.

THE TREATY OF WESTPHALIA AND SOVEREIGNTY: REDRAWING THE LINES OF POLITICAL AUTHORITY

The Thirty Years' War ended in 1648 with the signing of the Treaty of Westphalia, which redrew the lines of political and religious authority in Europe (see map 2.2). The treaty resolved the debate over who had the authority to determine the religion of a territory—the most important political question of the time—and formally ended the problem of the crosscutting authorities and multiple loyalties that had characterized Europe before the onset of the religious wars. The Treaty of Westphalia established the principle that the king, or sovereign, of a territory had the sole legitimate authority to determine the religion of the inhabitants of that territory. This principle severely curtailed the authority of the pope and the Holy Roman Emperor, who thus became secondary to kings in terms of political authority and political geography.

| Map 2.2 | Europe in 1648 |

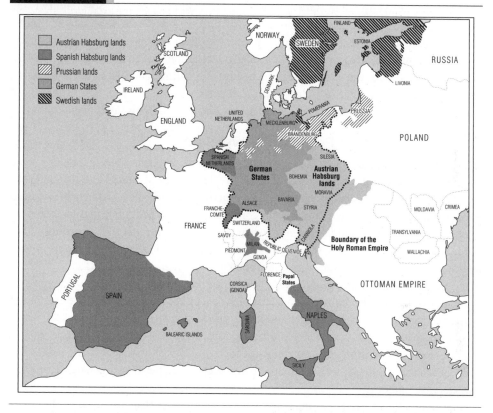

Source: Bruce Buena de Mesquita, *Principles of International Politics* (Washington, DC: CQ Press, 2003). Used by permission.

The Treaty of Westphalia established territoriality as the dominant basis for Europe's political map. Geographical area became the most important criterion for organizing political space under a single dominant authority. A territory and the people living within that territory belonged to the king or sovereign. The Church and the pope could still wield some influence over these inhabitants, particularly in spiritual affairs, but under the treaty, the authority of the religious establishment was subordinated to that of the crown.

> The **Westphalian state system** is the modern state system, whereby the government of a state, and by definition a territory, is considered the sole legitimate authority within its territorial boundaries. **Sovereignty** is the principle that the government of the state is the supreme legitimate authority within its territorial borders; in terms of international relations, this means that, theoretically, no state can exercise legitimate authority within another state's boundaries.

This change in the organization of political authority—the creation of a dominant secular authority attached to a specific geography—gave birth to the modern state system and introduced the principle of each state's sovereignty within its territorial borders. We call this arrangement the **Westphalian state system** in recognition of its origins. **Sovereignty** is the principle that the government of a state, and by definition a territory, is the supreme legitimate authority within the state's territorial boundaries. This concept has become one of the most important organizing principles in modern international relations and law. In theory, it means that no state can exercise legitimate authority within another state's boundaries, which implies that each state is independent in the management of its domestic affairs and that the state's political authority within its geographic boundaries is sacrosanct.

The Principle and the Practice of Sovereignty

In theory, sovereignty supplies a nice, clean organizing principle for international affairs—you stay out of my domestic affairs and I will stay out of yours—but the empirical world is rarely so clean and well behaved. In practice, sovereignty is frequently infringed upon. At best, sovereignty is a creative and convenient fiction that policy makers embellish when they find it useful and try to ignore when they find it a hindrance. It is a concept that is much more pliant and more often contested than conceded in the abstract discussions of international law. The processes of globalization create particular challenges to the principle of sovereignty, for they bring one state's population into contact with the inhabitants of other states. The gains from international exchange occur because the productive energies of different states are pooled into larger and larger production structures and markets, which encourage specialization across national boundaries. But these globalizing processes also produce costs for societies and can challenge the authority of states, most often inadvertently, when the actions of a government are limited by activities that originate beyond the borders of the state.

To make matters more confusing, governments sign treaties that commit them to follow defined practices and particular behaviors. Such restrictions can constrain the latitude of governments to enact the policies they prefer, thus limiting their policy autonomy. For example, a government may commit by international agreement to control the fishing catch of its nationals, to constrain the production of specific pollutants by industries within its territorial boundaries, or to institute specific civil and human liberties to protect its citizens. Do such external agreements, which limit the autonomy of governments within their territorial borders, constitute infringements on sovereignty?

We resort to two possible explanations to counter this apparent breach of the principle of sovereignty. First, we can declare that some basic principles of human rights trump the principle of sovereignty—that some rights are inalienable and cannot be infringed, even by sovereign governments. By making this statement, we are accepting the premise that when principles conflict, some principles are more important than others. Yet if this reasoning applies, it can apply only to a limited number of principles. Moreover, this is not a very satisfying rationale, given the origins of the principle of sovereignty, which emerged originally as a means of subordinating individual religious choice to the state. It is difficult to argue that basic human rights and individual dignities outrank sovereignty on the hierarchy of principles when the concept of sovereignty itself originally empowered the state to manage individual religious choice, which many would claim as a basic human right.

Second, we can argue that governments' decisions to negotiate international agreements or to open their borders to exchange are voluntary choices. In such cases, governments have not lost their sovereignty but have voluntarily ceded their policy autonomy as a sovereign choice. They have assigned or delegated their sovereign responsibilities to others, in an act of self-restraint. In practice, national governments in the global arena, absent a central authority, are regularly engaged in negotiating their sovereign authority. As the political scientist Stephen Krasner has noted, in such a system, sovereignty has always been up for grabs. The ongoing tensions between policy autonomy and international interaction, between sovereignty and interdependence, are an inevitable part of the modern nation-state system.

Common Violations of the Principle of Sovereignty

Given the difference between sovereignty in principle and sovereignty in practice, what does it mean when a government violates the concept of sovereignty by exercising influence in another state's domestic affairs? An infringement on sovereignty is technically a hostile act, but in practice the meaning of the intrusion depends on the seriousness of the violation and its consequences. War is the most extreme form of infringement, but much less violent challenges to sovereignty occur regularly. Americans would respond unfavorably to a foreign government's purchasing advertisements supporting one candidate or another in an American election, yet the trade or labor policies of another government may help one U.S. political party build support within a specific constituency. Many governments of Arab nations argue that American politicians support Israel because of the influence of the American Jewish lobby, which they claim is manipulated by the Israeli government. Whether this charge is true or not, the Arab governments make it to create anger against Israel among Americans by suggesting that U.S. foreign policy (a sovereign choice) is being manipulated by the Israeli government. Ironically, the Arab governments use this strategy in an attempt to influence political debate within the United States—which is technically an infringement on sovereignty that is very similar to the behavior they attribute to the Israeli government.

The Federal Open Market Committee (FOMC) of the Federal Reserve, a key policy-making committee of the U.S. central bank, meets regularly to discuss and adopt policies that will affect the supply and cost of money in the United States, with the goal of managing the country's macroeconomic conditions. However, because of the central position of the U.S. economy in the global economy, the choices of the FOMC, a part of a U.S. government agency, also affect economic conditions in many other nations. FOMC choices influence the cost and supply of capital in the United States, but also in other states. Shifting the cost and supply of capital in the United States influences the investment and consumption of industries and inhabitants within the United States, which has the added effect of slowing or accelerating global economic activity. The fact that policy choices by a U.S. government agency can have a large impact on economic activity in other nations could be considered, technically, an infringement on the principle of sovereignty. But to avoid such infringement on the sovereignty of others, the Federal Reserve would have to refrain from taking actions that are in the interest of the U.S. economy, which would be an infringement on the sovereignty of the United States.

These examples highlight the tension between a key organizing principle of modern international relations—policy autonomy or sovereignty—and the connections across national borders that produce the increasing interdependence that is a characteristic of modern global affairs. The concept of sovereignty underpins the modern state system, but it is a concept that competes and conflicts with other core characteristics of globalization in a state system. Focusing on the concept of sovereignty helps us to understand sources of tension and conflict in the system, as this concept highlights the different bases for political and economic organization in global relations.

ANARCHY: CONFLICT, COMPETITION, AND COOPERATION IN THE GLOBAL ARENA

Anarchy is a characterization of the relations between states in the global arena, where the lack of an overarching central authority to resolve disagreements creates a social context that is open to competition and cooperation, dispute and disagreement, negotiation and compromise, and, sometimes, violent conflict.

The combination of scarcity, the position of the state as the dominant form of political organization in an international system that lacks a central authority, and the principle of sovereignty creates a global social context that resembles Thomas Hobbes's description of the state of nature, wherein life is "solitary, poor, nasty, brutish, and short." We call this condition a state of **anarchy**. What is anarchy, and what is its relevance to how political activity that occurs *between* nation-states differs from the political activity that occurs *within* nation-states, in their domestic arenas? Since the Treaty of Westphalia, the government of a state has been the dominant authority within that state's domestic arena. There is a hierarchy of legitimate authority within a state: all other authorities are subordinate to the authority of the state. The existence of this hierarchy means that a dominant central authority exists within the state to govern, to help structure social relations, to mediate and adjudicate disputes, to extract and allocate scarce resources, and to enforce laws.

International relations, those interactions in the global arena between states, are characterized by the absence of such a central authority. With the Treaty of Westphalia and the establishment of the dominance of sovereign authority, all states are, in principle, equal in their authority over their domestic arenas. There is no central authority or formal hierarchy in the global arena to perform the functions that the government of a state performs in the domestic arena. No dominant central authority in international relations looms over national authorities to resolve disagreements and disputes between such authorities. By definition, any such external authority would impinge on each state's sovereignty.

We do have bodies of international law and principle, but they are formed by cooperative agreements—international treaties—that are negotiated by sovereign state governments. Technically, these laws are not binding on states that are not signatories to the international agreements creating them. Moreover, they do not appear to be binding even on signatories if the governments decide to ignore or reject their obligations. In the absence of a central authority to enforce such obligations, reneging on them does not often bear the same costs as violating domestic laws in domestic political arenas. A government that reneges on its international agreements rarely faces the threat of incarceration; it may be ostracized in the court of public opinion, treated as a pariah by other governments, and sanctioned through a variety of other measures, but these are penalties applied by competing authorities in the international arena. International law does not carry the same weight as domestic law, for its application relies on the self-constraint of sovereign governments and the willingness of sovereign governments to impose penalties on other sovereign governments.

Absent a recognized central authority with the legitimacy to coerce and cajole, the activities of functionally equal states often do conflict. Sovereign governments may have conflicting agendas, especially given the assumption of scarce resources. If a sovereign government implements policies that affect others—especially if it does so in a negative way—then it likely violates the sovereignty of those other states. But within the state system of social relations, the lack of an overarching central authority to resolve such disagreements creates a social context that is open to competition and cooperation, dispute and disagreement, negotiation and compromise, and, sometimes, violent conflict.

Self-Help Dispute Resolution under Anarchy

How do such disputes between sovereign governments get resolved? Governments must rely on their own capabilities and tools to obtain their preferred ends—a **self-help system** that returns us to Hobbes's notion of the state of nature. Creatures in a state of nature, without an external restraint mechanism to resolve disputes, depend on their own means of survival, not on the goodwill of others or on a collection of principles that others might willingly violate. Instead, they develop tools and strategies to increase their chances to survive and prosper. Not all succeed.

> A **self-help system** is one in which creatures in a state of nature, without a legitimate central authority to resolve disputes, must rely on their own means to survive. The term is used to refer to the global arrangement whereby governments, lacking an overarching central authority, must resort to their own capabilities and tools in order to obtain their preferred ends.

Do the demands of self-help in a state of anarchy preclude cooperation and compromise, mandating violence since only the strong will survive? On the contrary, turning to cooperation and compromise, while reserving conflict as a last resort, provides a strategy that has proven successful in such an environment—a victory of brains over brawn, of coalition building over individual self-reliance. Centuries ago, individuals and families were eventually successful in defeating the raids of marauding hunter-gatherers by banding together into small pastoral communities. How do we know this? A look at the more successful societies in the world today reveals the heirs of the cooperative pastoral society strategy and no exemplars of the marauding strategy. We can find some descendants of the barbarian marauders among less successful political economies, but not among the advanced industrialized political economies. Strategies of cooperative social behavior appear to have been more conducive to surviving and prospering than were strategies of noncooperation and conflict.

The state of anarchy helps to account for the fact that states are functionally similar and do not take advantage of specialization of function. Governments are not willing to contract their survival, or their people's well-being, to other governments in a world that lacks a dominant central authority to enforce such obligations. Policy makers are willing to sign treaties limiting or outlawing human rights abuses, categories of weapons, slavery, and economic and environmental policies that may impose undue hardships across national borders, but they refrain from placing blind faith in the self-restraint and good intentions of the other signatories when there is no central authority to ensure their compliance. As a measure of insurance against the anarchic state of social relations in the state system, governments insist on developing their own tools and devices in their attempts to get others in the international arena to behave in accordance with their interests. This reliance of governments on their own means, rather than on international treaties and law, underpins the theory of realism discussed in chapter 1.

HIERARCHY: LOOKING FOR ORDER AND PREDICTABILITY

Describing the international arena as a state of anarchy or a state of nature does not mean that it necessarily lacks order and predictability. Relations between governments can be quite predictable. Implicitly, we know in advance that Ecuador will not resort to military force to resolve a fishing dispute with the United States. Implicitly, we recognize that the preferences of the U.S. government are likely to condition international environmental negotiations more than the policy preferences of the government of Ghana. Implicitly, we assume that European Union preferences on agricultural policies will have greater influence over the patterns of global agricultural production and trade than the preferences of Kenya. Such predictability suggests that some systematic mechanisms exist to provide a degree of order and stability in international relations. Can we make the mechanisms that generate such order more explicit?

Hierarchies can help create order in social relations and allow some predictability about such relations. Order and predictability are important, for they allow people to plan ahead and to select appropriate strategies given some reliable assumptions about how others will behave. The simplest, and perhaps the most useful, device for examining international relations is a hierarchy based on differences in the abilities of state and nonstate actors to influence outcomes—what political scientists call differences in *power*. Such a hierarchy differs from the power structure within a domestic political arena, where the dominant authority of the central government is embedded in a legal system and overshadows other forms of authority that may exist in society. Power underpins domestic governance, but it is cloaked within legal frameworks.

POWER DEFINED AS A RELATIVE CONCEPT

Power is an abstract concept that is difficult to define, observe, measure, and quantify precisely, yet it is the currency of politics. As many economists focus on differences and changes in wealth to examine the economic sphere, many political scientists look to differences and changes in power as a key to understanding political behavior and outcomes. In their quest to examine this critical concept, however, political scientists give it a variety of meanings. Power has been defined as a set of attributes or capabilities, as the processes of influence, as the ability to control resources, as the capacity to influence the behavior of others and events, and as the ability to manipulate the structure of social interactions. For our purposes, **power** refers to the tools, the means, to achieve one's own ends. Power is the ability to prevail and overcome obstacles, to achieve a desired outcome by influencing the environments and choices of other decision makers.

> **Power** consists of the tools, the means, to influence outcomes and achieve one's own ends, or the ability to prevail and overcome obstacles.

Power is a relative phenomenon in social affairs. Having more or less power takes on meaning and relevance only within the context of social interactions. Evaluation of a political actor's power becomes useful as a method of political analysis in comparison with the power of others and in assessment of its effect on the behavior of others. Power is an aspect of every relationship, adversarial or friendly, although it is generally more apparent in adversarial than in friendly relations. If both sides to a political interaction agree on an outcome, the application of power may not be obvious; its role becomes more apparent if the parties disagree. Yet power is at play in both cases.

As power involves a relationship between parties, we should recognize that each party in a relationship has some power over the other. Influence is not unidirectional, flowing only from one party to another. Instead, the application of power involves a flow of influence in both directions. My exercise of influence over you, in order to affect how you behave, also means that you exercise influence over me, for you have affected how I behave. This relative power exchange assumes that without the exercise of influence, you and I would both have behaved differently than we have done. So, even when the very strong attempt to exercise influence over the very weak to change their behavior, the very weak have exerted some influence over the very strong. Simply assuming that the U.S. military has greater capabilities than the Taliban opposition in Afghanistan underplays the fact that the exercise of power by the U.S. military in Afghanistan also means that the Taliban influences U.S. actions. This reciprocal effect is often neglected when analysts try to understand politics by using differences in power capabilities to think about political behavior, but it becomes more apparent when the idea of costs is considered.

The exercise of power can produce great benefits for those who prevail, but such benefits are rarely, if ever, cost-free. The use of power imposes costs, even on the winner. For example, attempting to alter another state's behavior through military means imposes human and economic costs on a state even if it wins the conflict: people die or are injured and their talents are lost to the future; the direction of economic resources and human energy into military preparations means that those resources are not being applied to other endeavors; and families and communities are diminished by the loss and injuries of their members. These are costs. Attempting to influence another government's behavior by means of economic sanction and political pressure diverts resources from other activities, and it may deny the benefits of economic interaction to the state applying the sanctions. These are costs. Attempting to influence another state's policies through foreign aid and other forms of assistance requires a government to tax its own people to garner the necessary resources, which might have been used otherwise. Again, these are costs. Such costs are important to consider when we analyze political behavior. Politicians consider the expected benefits of exercising power, but they must also weigh the expected costs in light of the likely outcome. Sometimes what appears to be the best outcome in terms of benefits turns out to be a poor choice, given the costs of obtaining that outcome.

USING THE TOOLS OF STATECRAFT AND DIPLOMACY TO INFLUENCE BEHAVIOR

Our discussion of power becomes more concrete if we consider the various kinds of pressure that governments, politicians, and policy makers employ as they seek to influence the behavior of others. In both domestic and international arenas, public or private policy makers can resort to a range of strategies to affect the incentives and calculations of the target actors by shaping their perceptions of the costs and benefits of different courses of action. In international affairs, we think of these options as the tools of statecraft and diplomacy, which can be sorted into a set of categories that range along a spectrum of influence (see figure 2.1) from the most passive (persuasion) to the most violent (force).

FIGURE 2.1	The Spectrum of Policy Makers' Tools for the Exercise of Power

Persuasion

Persuasion, the most passive of the tools of statecraft, encompasses the art of discussion, the skillful use of language and logic, argument and debate, entreaty and cajoling, education, and diplomatic negotiation. It is the art of convincing others to see things your way by demonstrating the soundness of your logic and leading them to see your preferred policy as consistent with their best interests. A vast amount of activity in the global arena falls into this category of power relations. Governments routinely exchange diplomatic missions and send messages with the primary intent of persuading other governments and their policy makers to think in a particular manner or to adopt a particular policy or approach. They manipulate the public release of information through the media and other channels in an attempt to change the thinking and alter the behavior of others. Governments also use these tools of persuasion to influence the activities of nonstate actors such as businesses, charities, foundations, aid groups, and other nongovernmental organizations.

Offer of Rewards

The next category on the spectrum of power and influence involves the offer of rewards. As governments and other actors in global affairs seek to manipulate the behavior of others, they may dangle the temptation of positive benefits if the targets of influence will change their behavior accordingly. These promises may include such rewards as the potential for future lucrative contracts and investment, favorable preferences in future trade negotiations, an increased potential for foreign aid and assistance, a promise of assistance in future interactions with other parties, or even the promise, stated or implied, not to obstruct a choice of action in the future. Some such promises may be viewed as extortion or bribery. For example, during the run-up to the 2003 Iraq war, the U.S. government offered substantial resources to the Turkish government in an attempt to convince it to allow U.S. military forces to use bases in Turkey as staging areas for the planned invasion. This attempt at manipulation proved unsuccessful, but it demonstrates the practical efficacy of the offer of rewards. In another example, developing states often seek election to the rotating openings on the U.N. Security Council, as governments holding such seats can offer to vote with the United States in exchange for foreign assistance.

Granting of Rewards

The promise or offer of rewards in the future is not the same as the actual delivery of rewards today, which is generally more costly than making a promise. Granting a reward in exchange for a change in behavior, or a particular choice of action, is a common tool of influence. For example, the more advanced economies in the European Union made substantial capital transfers to less advanced EU economies in order to obtain their cooperation in concluding the Maastricht Treaty, a core agreement in the formation of the EU. Portugal and Ireland used such financial transfers to fund infrastructure development and growth policies. The U.S. government supplied significant foreign aid to Israel and Egypt as part of the deal to get those governments to join in signing the peace agreement known as the Camp David Accords. The Marshall Plan committed vast resources to the reconstruction of Western European states after World War II in exchange for those Western European governments' cooperation in containing the Soviet Union. Persuasion, the promise of rewards, and the delivery of rewards are the sweet and tempting carrots of the carrot-and-stick metaphor.

Threat of Punishment

Cheap talk is an insincere, empty threat, promise of reward, or commitment.

The alternative to the carrot as a tool of influence is the harsh and threatening stick, which constitutes not a single strategy but a variety of strategies that continue along the spectrum of influence. Much as the promise or offer of reward is not actually the provision of a reward, the threat of punishment is not actually the application of punishment. Threats to impose economic sanctions, to increase tariffs or other barriers to entry to a state's markets, to abrogate treaties of cooperation, to scale back foreign assistance, to withdraw from agreements, or to isolate a state diplomatically constitute potential consequences in the future if the targets of such threats should fail to adjust their behavior. The threat of punishment may be direct and explicit or subtle and implied, but in either case, the target of such a threat is faced with the problem of trying to estimate its credibility, as the possible implementation of the threat lies in the future. If the target of a threat or promised reward estimates that there is no prospect of the threatened punishment's or promised reward's implementation, then the threat or promise is not credible. Empty threats or promises of reward constitute **cheap talk,** which can be quite damaging to the parties making the empty promises if it undermines the credibility of future threats or promises that may be sincere. In that case, a target may choose to ignore very real threats or promises, resulting in high costs both to the party trying to exercise influence and to the target of that intended influence.

For example, in 2001 the United States imposed steel tariffs on foreign producers to protect its domestic steel industry. Foreign producers and their governments brought a case to the World Trade Organization (WTO) claiming the U.S. actions violated U.S. international obligations under the WTO treaty, of which the United States was a signatory; in fact, the United States was the leading force in establishing the international trade organization. After going through the adjudication process and obtaining a positive ruling from the WTO, other governments were authorized to impose retaliatory tariffs against a variety of U.S. products if the U.S. tariffs were not reversed before a set deadline. U.S. policy makers viewed the threat of retaliatory tariffs as credible, and so, faced with the threat of costly punishment that outweighed the benefits of the steel tariffs, they reversed course on the protective steel tariffs before the deadline. A contrary situation developed when U.S. policy makers announced a policy of deterrence and containment against the Soviet Union and its allies in the late 1940s. Although they asserted that the umbrella of deterrence included South Korea, the Soviets and their allies calculated that the United States would not defend South Korea—that the

U.S. threat was empty. History tells us that the Soviet interpretation of the U.S. threat as cheap talk was a miscalculation that proved extremely costly to both sides.

Nonviolent Punishment

Proceeding along the spectrum of influence, the next category that involves the use of the stick is the implementation of nonviolent punishment. This strategy moves beyond the threat of punishment to the actual application of penalties, such as those mentioned earlier as threats. The application of forms of punishment short of the use of military force can still be harmful and disruptive if it imposes hardships on members of the target government or its society. Recall of an ambassador, closing of a diplomatic consulate or embassy, withdrawal of diplomatic recognition, a negative vote in an international body such as the U.N. Security Council or the WTO, imposition of economic sanctions, economic boycott, withdrawal from a cooperative economic or political-military agreement, termination of foreign assistance, cancellation of preferential trade arrangements, and public castigation are examples of strategies of nonviolent punishment that are meant to convince another party to alter its behavior or to punish a party for its activities in hopes of ending or discouraging those activities in the future.

For example, the policy of containment of the Soviet Union, begun under President Truman in the late 1940s, formed the backbone of U.S. foreign policy until the collapse of the Eastern bloc governments in 1989–1991. One component of containment imposed controls on what could and could not be exported from the United States and its allies to the Soviet Union and its allies. The objective of such controls was to deny the Soviets specific gains from trade with the United States and its allies, but the controls also denied the gains of such trade to the United States and its allies. Containment was intended to degrade Soviet capabilities over time and to impose hardships on Soviet policy makers and their constituents. The designers of the policy hoped that imposing hardships on the average Soviet consumer would eventually create dissension in the Soviet economy. In retrospect, the policy seems to have worked, as frustration within the political economies of the Eastern bloc boiled over in the late 1980s.

How did containment impose nonviolent punishment? Withholding trade access and limiting the export of particular commodities to the Soviet Union forced the Soviets and their allies to alter their production structures. The Soviets' inability to take advantage of participation in the larger global economy and the resulting specialization it would create in the Soviet production structure generated inefficiencies in the economies of the Soviet Union and its allies, which led to shortages of consumer goods. In another example of nonviolent punishment, President Jimmy Carter instituted a boycott of the 1980 Summer Olympic Games, which were held in Moscow, and imposed new trade sanctions on the Soviets after they invaded Afghanistan in 1979. These sanctions were not meant to reverse Soviet policies in Afghanistan, but to impose penalties on the Soviets for such policies and to affect their future calculations about military adventurism and expansionism.

In the 1990s, the European Union and its member governments imposed barriers on the importation of hormone-treated beef from the United States, claiming that such beef posed public health hazards. As public health responsibilities for constituents are among the tasks of modern governments, this was not a straightforward barrier-to-trade dispute. WTO rules enable governments to intervene in international trade to protect the health and safety of their constituents. The U.S. government and U.S. cattle producers objected and challenged the claims that hormone-treated beef posed health hazards for humans, insisting, Show us the data! They claimed that the EU and its members were, under the guise of an international agreement, erecting a barrier to entry merely to protect the interests of European agricultural producers. As all the governments involved in this dispute were signatories of the WTO, the WTO had jurisdiction over the dispute. Consequently the U.S. government, representing the interests of U.S. cattle producers, brought the case to the WTO for adjudication. After adjudication hearings and the presentation of reams of scientific evidence and argumentation by both sides to the dispute—Show us the data!—the WTO found the Europeans at fault. The WTO found no scientific basis in the data for the public health claims. The Europeans objected and reformulated their barriers to entry, which brought new arbitration. The WTO ruled again in favor of the United States and its cattle producers. The WTO then authorized the United States to impose tariffs to redress the damage to U.S. producers.

Force

The final category on the spectrum of influence involves the use of military force, which holds the potential for the most violent application of power. Not all uses of military force actually turn violent, however. Sometimes the use of force is only threatened or implied; the actual application of force depends on the response of the target of influence. Military blockades (such as the naval quarantine of Cuba during the Missile Crisis of October 1962), port calls by warships in trouble spots (showing the flag), flyovers by warplanes, moving troops into situations that would be in harm's way if hostilities were to break out (such as the basing of American troops in Germany during the Cold War and along the demilitarized zone in Korea), and the extension of military assistance to another country in the form of military advisers to help train local troops (such as those the United States sent to Vietnam before 1965 and to the Philippines following September 11, 2001)—all are examples of the use of military force in hopes of influencing outcomes without resorting to actual violence.

Sometimes the implied use of force fails to convince another actor's policy makers to alter their activities. Then the original policy makers must confront the choice of whether or not to actually initiate violence. The use of force in a situation where it has been previously threatened or implied is not straightforward. In economic terms, projecting military force abroad is expensive enough, but putting a state's youth in danger is also politically and socially costly, as it disrupts families and communities. These potential costs mean that policy makers will hesitate to turn to such measures unless they believe the situation warrants them. Policy makers must weigh the differences in costs between threatened and actual use of force (following through on the threat), the costs of not using force once it has been threatened (the costs of crying wolf), the importance of the preferred outcome, and the likelihood that the preferred outcome will be attained through the use of force. We like to think that policy makers are sufficiently farsighted and they try to calculate all the possible costs and benefits to the use of force in advance, but the world is a complex place. Policy makers usually have their agendas full of problems demanding their attention, which means a problem might not get the full examination it deserves (a decision maker's time is a scarce resource). Moreover, as noted in chapter 1, outcomes are the results of interdependent choices. In 2002, U.S. policy makers miscalculated the duration and costs of conflict in Afghanistan and Iraq. This was partly a consequence of a murky information environment, but it was also a consequence of how their choices interacted with those of decision makers in those countries.

In another example, consider the meeting of Germany's Adolf Hitler and British prime minister Neville Chamberlain at Munich in 1939. English and French policy makers calculated that by appeasing Hitler at Munich they could forestall a major European conflict, even after they had threatened the use of their military forces to challenge Hitler's territorial grab. Critics of the Munich settlement assert that the British and French accommodation emboldened Hitler by undermining the credibility of their threats to use violence and, hence, increased the likelihood of the very conflict they were trying to avoid. Now labeled the Munich Appeasement, this abortive settlement has become one of the most potent analogies in diplomatic history, cited repeatedly to discredit accommodation as a policy choice. Raising the specter of Chamberlain at Munich can end, or at least seriously influence, policy debates over the use of military force, as it strongly suggests the possibility of very costly consequences for failing to act.

Obviously, physical force has been used throughout history as an important tool of influence and statecraft. Battlefields testify to its use; families of wars' casualties serve as visible reminders of its costs; academics engage in grand research projects designed to improve our understanding of war; historians, political scientists, anthropologists, sociologists, and psychologists publish reams upon reams of research into the use of armed conflict as a tool of influence; and protesters routinely demonstrate against the use of military power as a tool of statecraft. Despite the horror of militarized conflict and most policy makers' desire to avoid it, states and statesmen keep returning to the use of force as a viable instrument for exercising power. This situation is probably inevitable given the social context of a self-help state system that lacks a legitimate central authority to resolve and adjudicate disputes. Nevertheless, we should recognize that military force is only one tool of influence, and one that is used infrequently relative to the others. A focus on military conflict alone provides an incomplete examination of the uses of influence and power, neglecting other forms that are more characteristic of day-to-day interactions in the global arena.

ANALYZING POLITICAL BEHAVIOR: WEIGHING THE COSTS AND BENEFITS OF THE TOOLS OF STATECRAFT

Policy makers use the tools of statecraft and diplomacy to create incentives for other policy makers to act one way instead of another by affecting calculations of expected costs and benefits. If persuasion, the promise or imposition of rewards, or the threat or imposition of punishment are to alter the cost-benefit assessments of a target of influence in the global political economy, these strategies of influence must motivate that target's policy makers to compare their proposed course of action against alternative choices. As policy makers seek to affect the behavior of others, they must evaluate what tools might influence the calculations of others, as well as the probability of successfully exercising influence with each tool, and at what cost. Remember, the use of power imposes costs on the loser and also on the winner. Trying to alter another policy maker's choice requires the use of resources that might have been used for another activity. It is critical to consider such costs, as doing so gives us a powerful tool for analyzing political behavior. When we assume that policy makers consider the benefits and the costs of different applications of power (the likely outcomes and their rewards or penalties), we can weigh the expected benefits of each strategy against its expected costs and try to understand why a policy maker selects a particular strategy. We can use backward induction to infer how policy makers may have perceived the costs and benefits as they weighed their choices.

Generally, the tools of influence impose increasing costs and conflict as we move along the spectrum of influence from persuasion through force (see figure 2.2). These costs can affect prospects for the political survival of policy makers as well as for the well-being of their larger societies. We can reasonably assume that policy makers will try to limit their individual costs and their societies' costs given their policy objectives. They will attempt to select the best forms of influence in terms of the cost, efficiency, and efficacy in obtaining desired outcomes. They seek to avoid overkill, for using a more costly tool of statecraft when a less costly strategy would succeed proves inefficient, detracts from the expected gains from a change in behavior by the target of influence, affects the credibility of their own efforts, and

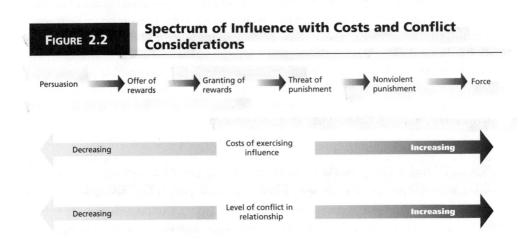

FIGURE 2.2 **Spectrum of Influence with Costs and Conflict Considerations**

Persuasion → Offer of rewards → Granting of rewards → Threat of punishment → Nonviolent punishment → Force

Decreasing ← Costs of exercising influence → **Increasing**

Decreasing ← Level of conflict in relationship → **Increasing** can damage how a polity views the leaders attempting to exercise influence. For instance, the United States in the twenty-first century is capable of exercising overwhelming power in terms of military capabilities, but these resources are excessive tools for exercising influence in many situations. The 1991 Gulf War demonstrated the effectiveness of U.S. military power in defeating conventional military forces, but in many situations the use of such military force would be too inefficient and too costly. Despite U.S. military success during the Vietnam War, in Afghanistan, and in Iraq, the long-term objectives of U.S. policy makers have proven elusive in those arenas and at very high costs—both to the societies engaged and to the political survival of the policy makers. Actions have consequences, some good and some bad. Governments rarely resort to force as a first option. Even Hitler resorted to diplomatic strategies to build his Third Reich before turning to war.

FINDING ORDER IN ANARCHY: POWER CAPABILITIES AND ATTRIBUTES

Although the modern international system has been described as a state of anarchy, order can arise in this system based on differences in power capabilities and the attributes that contribute to those capabilities. Such a **power hierarchy** reflects the varying capabilities of different states and

> A **power hierarchy** is a structure that reflects differences in the capabilities of different states and their policy makers to employ the tools and strategies of influence as they think about trying to affect the behavior of others.

their policy makers to employ the tools and strategies of influence. Policy makers from different states may not have the same range of options when placed in similar circumstances, even though their states are functionally equal. The U.S. president has a wider range of options than does the president of Mexico when his state is confronted by a national security threat that arises halfway around the world. A German government's offer of preferential trade arrangements is likely to carry more influence than the same offer by the government of Ghana. A threat of economic boycott by the Japanese government will have greater weight than a threat of economic boycott by the Peruvian government. Policy makers in Mexico, Ghana, and Peru may want to exercise the same influence over outcomes as the policy makers of the United States, Germany, and Japan, but their ability to do so differs.

Motivation versus Capability in the Hierarchy of Influence

This difference in power, in the hierarchy of influence, highlights the difference between motivations and capabilities. It calls attention to the difference between the range of tools that policy makers can theoretically employ and their actual ability to use such tools. Policy makers from different states may have identical motivations in terms of advancing the welfare of their states and similar preferences over public policy and outcomes, but they have different capabilities for achieving their goals. Surely the leaders of Senegal, Azerbaijan, Poland, and other states would like to occupy the place held by the United States as the dominant state in terms of influencing the framework and practices of the global political economy. In this regard, they are similarly motivated and comparable to U.S. policy makers, but this is a comparison only of motivation and preferences, not of capability. Motivations and the spectrum of influence generalize across governments and policy makers, but the ability to select and implement strategies on this spectrum of influence is state and case specific.

Differences in capabilities across states and the willingness by their policy makers to use those capabilities constitute the key to a hierarchy of influence, for such differences can create order in a state of anarchy. So what underpins differences in capabilities of policy makers and governments? Where do we look if we are trying to understand why one state has prevailed over another, or who will prevail in a future test of power and will in the global arena? Policy makers do not simply select a tool of influence without considering the likelihood of its success and the costs of exercising influence. This twofold assessment requires that they consider the ability and will of the target to resist—which means that they must try to evaluate the power capabilities and will of those they wish to influence and compare their own capabilities and will. So we need to move beyond the tools and strategies of influence to consider the capabilities that underpin the ability, or inability, of policy makers to use those tools and strategies.

Because power is a relative phenomenon in social affairs, the analysis of social behavior involving power requires an evaluation of differences in the power capabilities of those involved in a social and political interaction and the willingness to use such capabilities. Power, however, is much more difficult to quantify and to observe than is wealth or money, the currency of economics. As a shortcut to attain a rough indication of a state's relative power, therefore, political scientists often substitute observable measures of the state's attributes and capabilities—such as gross domestic product, degree of industrialization, exposure to international trade, age distribution of the population, and numbers of active-duty military personnel—for unobservable power. This substitution is reasonable, since policy makers draw upon a state's attributes and capabilities when they seek to exercise influence, and power should be positively associated with these same attributes. This logic simply means that if all else remains unchanged, an increase in a key attribute will correspond to an increase in power, and a decrease in a key attribute will correspond to a decrease in power. Even if we can produce some empirical assessment of capabilities, we must still consider the will of policy makers to use those capabilities. This is a much more difficult task.

Tangible Attributes That Contribute to Power

Given that many of a state's attributes are more observable and measurable than the phenomenon of power, let's consider some features that can contribute to power. Both tangible assets and intangible resources contribute to a state's capabilities. What is the difference between these two components of a state's power potential? **Tangible attributes** are generally naturally occurring

Tangible attributes are naturally occurring resources or physical assets that people can employ and manipulate to advance their agendas.

phenomena—resources that can be touched, observed, and sometimes counted, as well as employed and manipulated by people to advance their agendas. Minerals, petroleum, arable land,

> **Intangible attributes** are resources that are created and transformed by people and contribute to a state's capabilities.

population, climate, forests, rivers, mountains, and other natural physical assets fall into this category. **Intangible attributes,** as the name suggests, are less concrete. They are created and transformed by people. Economic, political, and social organization make up this category. Tangible and intangible attributes can contribute to power independently, but their *interaction* can create tremendous shifts in the power capabilities of a state. Many states have comparable levels of tangible resources but differ markedly in their ability to use them to influence the behavior of others. Tangible assets are important, but intangible resources are key to unleashing their potential to produce a significant transformation in a state's power potential.

What tangible assets affect a state's power potential? Many physical features can contribute to the power potential of a state, but let's focus on four broad categories: geography, climate, population, and natural resources. In general, large is better than small in terms of how these categories affect the power potential. A state's geography—size, topography, and location—can affect its ability to exercise power and prevail. The Russians, and later the Soviets, used the vast reaches of their territory as part of their defensive strategy to absorb and eventually repel attacks by the armies of Napoleon and Hitler. But great physical expanse can also be a hindrance if it inhibits economic exchange, increases the difficulty of defending points of potential attack, presents obstacles to supply of forces, and creates problems for communication and control.

Some states must deal with difficult topography that creates barriers to mobility and economic exchange, whereas other states have natural highways such as rivers that aid in transit and trade. Some states are isolated, while others are surrounded by many neighbors. Some are islands; others have contiguous land borders with their neighbors. Some states' borders and territory present physical barriers to entry and exit that can inhibit the flow of people and commodities, while the physical geography of others is easily passable. Oceans, mountains, rivers, and sheer distance may create potential obstacles to invasion forces, but such barriers can be overcome. European feudal lords and kings believed that the Alps protected their region from invasion, but Hannibal brought his troops and their elephants over that mountainous barrier when he invaded the Roman Empire. During World War II, both the Japanese and, later, the Americans crossed oceans to invade the territory of their enemies. Many attribute the emergence of England and the United States as world powers to their physical isolation from continental Europe, as well as from other potential predators and competitors. A state may have weak neighbors that it can influence, or it may be influenced by stronger neighbors. As former Canadian prime minister Pierre Trudeau noted, when the United States sneezes, Canada catches a cold. All the members of the European Union have equal voting power within the EU structure, but Germany, as the largest and most central political economy in Europe, seems to carry more weight in EU decisions and policies than do other member states.

Climate is another tangible feature that can affect the power capabilities of a state, but its influence is not straightforward. Inhospitable climates can slow economic enterprise, but they may also deter invasion and help defeat attackers. The Russian winter and spring were almost as responsible as the czarist and Soviet armies in slowing and then reversing the attacks of Napoleon's and Hitler's armies. Desert sands can clog modern economic machinery and modern tools of warfare. Dense rain forests hold valuable resources that can be used to influence others, but they are also great resources for guerrilla campaigns against invading armies, as has been demonstrated in the Philippines, Burma, and Vietnam. Climate can also affect the progress of industrialization and economic activity. Before the advent of air conditioning, the heat and humidity of tropical and equatorial climates slowed the pace of work and exacted a toll on machinery and human productivity—only "mad dogs and Englishmen" tended to work at midday during the summer in India—while states with more temperate climates faced no such barriers to economic activity. Some climates are more conducive to agricultural production, so that some states have more productive arable land than others solely because of their geographic location. This physical feature affects the ability of a state's population to feed itself and others, and food resources are potential tools of influence in international affairs. Yet, in some cases, modern systems of climate control negate these climatic effects.

Large states usually support larger populations than small states, but not always. All else being equal, human assets are a resource for both military and economic enterprise. States with large populations can generally maintain larger militaries than small states, and larger populations can often support larger economies and create greater economic surpluses than smaller populations. Societies can redistribute such surpluses to other activities, such as the exercise of influence. But population size is not the sole consideration in the importance of a state's people as a resource. The age distribution of a population also plays a role, for even if large, an aging population may be a less productive resource than a younger population in a less populated state.

In the twenty-first century, most of the world's advanced industrialized political economies face the dilemma of aging populations; in some cases, their populations are also decreasing. Declining birthrates, improved health care, increased longevity, and constrained immigration mean that the average age in many of these societies is increasing, even as many populations shrink. This limits the replacement of retiring workers with new, young productive workers, which means that, over time, fewer and fewer workers are supporting more and more pensioners. This is problematic and places increasing fiscal pressures on societies and governments in terms of tax revenues and social expenditures. For the largest four EU states—France, Germany, Italy, and the United Kingdom—just to maintain their 1995 population size at current fertility rates, the United Nations has estimated that they would need to triple the number of immigrants allowed to enter those countries each year. To stabilize and maintain the ratio of workers to pensioners at current fertility rates, these four EU states would need to increase immigration by thirty-seven times over current levels. This amounts to almost nine million new immigrants of working age each year. These are extraordinary and unprecedented levels, and politically infeasible in these societies given popular opposition to broad-scale immigration. Over the next decade China, even though its population will likely continue to expand, will encounter the problem of an aging population and a changing ratio of workers to retirees. It is interesting to note that the United States is the only major advanced industrialized society with a growing population—that population is aging, but slowly. Between relatively high fertility and significant migration, the United States enjoys a fairly robust population replacement rate.

States with a disproportionate number of retirees or workers nearing retirement may encounter difficulties in staffing their militaries, maintaining momentum in their economies, and providing social welfare. An effective military depends on a large pool of youth from which to draw troops. An expanding economy relies on a supply of labor to perform its work. Constraints on the labor supply can slow economic growth. States with aging populations face dilemmas in choosing between financing military programs and infrastructure improvements and funding social welfare provisions, pensions, and retirement systems; between investing in productive enterprise and expending resources on a segment of the population that has retired from economic production. With an increasing share of a state's population in retirement, an increasing tax burden falls on the younger population even to maintain the status quo in government expenditures. This budgetary constraint can limit a state's ability to use its resources to exercise influence in the global arena.

Other characteristics of a population—growth rates, job skills, educational levels, and general health—can affect a state's power capabilities. An expanding population places demands on a society's support systems, but a fruitful and capable populace that is growing in size increases the possibilities that citizens will make discoveries and develop strategies that can increase the state's power potential. High levels of education are heavily responsible for the economic success of the advanced industrialized societies in the past and the present, and for their likely success in the future. Education acts as a multiplier of human talent; it represents an investment of capital in human labor potential, which transforms that potential and increases its productivity. This leads to increased productivity and higher wages. This generates greater surplus per capita, which can be reallocated to other activities—such as national security and diplomacy, construction of infrastructure, and provision of social welfare goods—that make a society stronger and more effective in world affairs.

Health and nutrition can affect a state's capacity to exercise influence, its position in the global power hierarchy, and its future prospects. Healthy populations are more economically productive, provide better pools of manpower to staff militaries, and place smaller burdens on government and societal systems, which leaves more resources to be used elsewhere. Something as simple as prenatal health care makes a significant difference in the long-term health and productivity of a state's population. Healthy children with good diets perform better in school than do sick and malnourished children, and this translates into differences in productivity and capability later in life. We can look at measures of health care provision, disease, and caloric intake to assess a state's current and future capabilities in the global political economy.

For example, many African states currently face health crises of immense magnitude: a huge proportion of their people are infected with HIV/AIDS, malaria, and other diseases, and many suffer from severe malnutrition. Treating such conditions demands a significant commitment of resources just to maintain life. The costs of antibiotics, antiretroviral drugs to treat HIV, antimalaria campaigns, and emergency food programs; the demands on health care workers and medical facilities; the burdens shouldered by families and their community resources—all these stresses are overwhelming, even in developed countries with far smaller afflicted populations. For a developing state, such stresses are catastrophic in terms of prospects for economic development. Even if adequate treatments and programs are affordable and available, the demands on health care workers and family members for home health care and support limit the numbers of people available for productive economic enterprise or military service. Compared with unhealthy populations, healthy populations can be expected to be more productive in any activity.

Large states often harbor greater natural resources, but not always. States with more arable land are usually better able to feed themselves and others than are states with less arable land, but not always. A state endowed with rich farmland may fail to take advantage of its ability to produce food and other crops if its society is engaged in civil conflict. The economic advances of the nineteenth and twentieth centuries, which led to tremendous shifts in the global power hierarchy, depended on access to natural resources. Such resources, once they are extracted and mobilized, sustain modern economic enterprise: coal and iron fueled the Industrial Revolution of the 1800s, and oil, metallurgy, chemicals, and electronics were essential to the economic growth of the twentieth century. Being self-sufficient in the resources that supply such economic activities is not a necessary condition for development, however. Nor is it even efficient on an economic dimension, for international trade provides a means of importing resources as inputs to economic activity.

In the global political economy, trade, specialization of production, and the import of raw materials make immutable sense economically. Trade and the resulting specialization of productive activities improve the economic welfare of a society, but they reduce self-sufficiency and increase reliance on the productive activities of those beyond the state's borders. The networks of global exchange also offer policy makers levers by which they can attempt to influence the activities of others. This is not an argument for self-sufficiency. First, the economic gains and improvement in welfare from global exchange generally far exceed the costs and risks posed by increased exposure to political manipulation. Second, interdependence goes both ways along such networks. Such networks and interdependence increase the viability of the entire range of the tools of influence, as well as the potential costs of using such tools.

Having natural resources within a state's boundaries may offer some advantage that affects the state's power potential, but not always. Controlling such resources may insulate a state from the influence of others and may provide tools for use in influencing others, or it may expose the resource-rich state to greater external influence. Since the 1973 Arab-Israeli war, the oil-producing states of the Middle East, through the mechanism of the Organization of Petroleum Exporting Countries (OPEC), have used the world's dependence on oil as a political tool to exercise influence over policy debates in other states. OPEC's actions and the Iranian Revolution produced the oil crises of the 1970s, huge increases in energy costs, and long lines at gas pumps in the United States and other parts of the world. The higher costs of energy slowed economic activity and contributed to inflation in the advanced industrialized societies, but it also stalled economic progress in the developing world. Such intentional and inadvertent manipulation of energy supplies has prompted ongoing policy debates in many states about how to reduce their dependence on Middle Eastern oil and how to insulate domestic political arenas from the influence of these oil-producing states.

Controlling such resources, however, can also expose the oil-rich states to external pressures. These same political economies that have used oil as a tool to exercise political influence in recent years were themselves dominated and manipulated in some form or another over the century preceding the oil crises they precipitated in the 1970s. Would these states have attracted such attention if they did not possess such a valuable resource? Whether it is true or not, many in the Arab world interpret U.S. military activity and interest in the Middle East as part of a policy to ensure stable access to the energy resources of their region. These states' prominence and influence on the world stage flows from their oil production, but this resource also provides incentives to governments of oil-importing states to try to influence the activities of the oil exporters. Their petroleum reserves give them a tool of potential influence over the actions of others, while the same reserves make them the targets of influence by others.

Sensitivity and Dependence

The ability to use a natural resource as a tool of influence depends on a variety factors. First, natural resources are not all alike. Economies and societies need some resources more than others, which raises issues of **sensitivity** and **dependence**. A political economy that is not sensitive to or dependent on a particular resource enjoys a condition of autarky, or independence from that resource, which is therefore unlikely to be useful as a tool to influence its activities. In contrast, a state that is sensitive to or dependent on a particular resource is vulnerable to influence because of it. Differences between sensitivity and dependence are matters of degree: states that are only sensitive to

Sensitivity is a component of a state's power potential reflecting the fact that economies and societies need some resources more than others; a state that is sensitive to the availability of a particular resource is vulnerable to potential manipulation and influence because of it, but less so than a state that is dependent on that resource. **Dependence** is a political economy's reliance on a particular resource, which thus makes the state vulnerable to influence.

> **Substitutability** is the prospect that economic enterprises and societies will find new sources of a commodity or substitutes for that commodity at affordable prices.

the availability of a particular resource are less exposed to potential manipulation and influence than are states that are dependent on it.

What affects a state's level of sensitivity or dependence? One important factor is the prospect of **substitutability.** Can economic enterprises and societies find new sources of the commodity or substitutes for the commodity at affordable prices? In the 1970s, when the OPEC cartel managed to manipulate both the supply and the price of petroleum, OPEC members transformed their economic leverage into political leverage. The cohesion of the OPEC cartel and the ability of its key members to collude prevented defections that would have undermined their production agreements, and so they were able to restrict the worldwide supply of oil. For the consumers of oil products, discovering and developing new sources of petroleum or other forms of energy takes substantial time and money. Even under the best possible conditions, such alternatives would not be available for decades, and then only after considerable investment. Users of petroleum had no real alternatives, at least not in the short or intermediate term. Banana- and copper-producing states attempted to mimic the success of the OPEC cartel by creating banana and copper cartels that would set production targets for the purpose of manipulating supply and increasing revenues from exports of these resources. Unlike oil, however, bananas and copper were commodities for which consumers soon found affordable substitutes and alternative supplies. Consumers switched from bananas to other fruits or bought bananas from other suppliers. Consumers of copper wire substituted aluminum wire or found copper producers who would operate outside the cartel.

> The **elasticity of demand and supply** is the relative changeability in consumer demand or producer supply associated with a change in price; inelastic demand or supply is relatively inflexible regardless of price, while elastic demand or supply will change with a change in price.

These cartel examples demonstrate differences in the **elasticity of demand and supply** for particular commodities. Changes in world oil production are relatively slow, while demand for oil production is relatively high and inflexible, regardless of price. Demand for oil will not change markedly even with significant increases in the price, and this condition of *inelastic* demand and *inelastic* supply endows oil producers with potential tools of influence in the political arena. In the case of banana consumption, a significant increase in the price of bananas was met by a shift in consumption to other fruits. Consumer demand for bananas was flexible and affected by price—a condition of *elastic* demand. Even if the supply of bananas were inelastic, the willingness of consumers to substitute other fruits for bananas, and the ease with which they could do so, undermined the ability of the banana cartel to manipulate the banana market and use its resource to gain political influence. A similar set of conditions limited the ability of the copper cartel nations to manipulate price in the market so as to use copper as a tool of political influence. Clearly, oil is a special commodity with unusual properties of supply and demand.

The Limits of Tangible Resources as Tools of Influence

The phrases *not always* and *all else being equal* recur in discussions of tangible, physical attributes. Such resources contribute to potential power capabilities, but a focus solely on tangible assets can obscure key differences that separate states' ability to prevail and to influence others. Although large states that enjoy significant endowments of tangible resources often prevail and are effective at exercising power over smaller states that are less endowed, sometimes smaller states with fewer tangible resources prevail instead. The Dutch Netherlands dominated the global political economy for much of the seventeenth century even though it had a smaller population, less arable land, and fewer resources than many other states. It did so in the face of the far greater size and military potential of the Spanish Habsburgs and French kings. The United Kingdom dominated the global political economy for much of the eighteenth and nineteenth centuries, even though it had a smaller population, fewer mineral and coal reserves, and less arable land than many other states. For half a century, Israel has prevailed in military conflicts with adversaries that enjoy much larger populations, territories, and resources. The peasant economy of Vietnam persisted and prevailed first in a conflict with the larger and wealthier advanced industrialized state of France and then over the even more impressive political and military power of the United States. In the 1980s, the feudal warlords of Afghanistan battled and prevailed over the forces of the Soviet Union, one of the world's superpowers at the time. By the measure of population, China and India should have surpassed the United States as dominant states in the global political economy, but the beginning of the twenty-first century finds the United States as the world's sole superpower. Discrepancies in power potential based on tangible resources do not always predict success in world affairs.

Intangible Attributes That Contribute to Power

The intangible resources that contribute to a state's power are less concrete and physical than its tangible assets. Of the many such intangible resources, we can focus on three broad categories: economic organization, political organization, and social organization. Why do we consider organization as an intangible resource? Can't we observe organizational structures in states? Granted, many states have defined formal organizational structures that can be depicted in flowcharts and formal diagrams, but these structures tell us little about the effectiveness of organization or how organization actually works to affect the states' capabilities.

More than in the case of tangible assets, understanding the contributions of intangible resources to a state's power potential is key to understanding what separates more influential from less influential political economies. How do organizational resources affect a state's ability to prevail and exercise influence in international affairs? Many states enjoy an abundance of tangible resources, but some exploit their naturally occurring resources more effectively than others. Differences in the organizational capabilities of governments, economic actors, and societal actors help account for differences in the ability to exploit, transform, and more efficiently employ the tangible attributes of power. Economic, political, and social organization contribute to power by affecting the mobilization and transformation of tangible resources such as population, physical resources, and geography. People, petroleum, iron ore, arable lands, rivers, and other physical assets are not as useful in their raw forms as they are once they have been transformed by education and socialization, metallurgy and smelting, application of modern fertilizers and irrigation systems, and the construction of cargo vessels and dams. Organization acts as a multiplier of tangible resources by transforming them into something greater than they are in their naturally occurring state.

Political, economic, and social organization are not independent resources; rather, they are overlapping and potentially synergistic. Greater economic organization contributes to more sophisticated, productive, and diverse economies, which provide governments with greater economic resources for influencing the behavior of others. More sophisticated political organizations are better able to contain societal conflicts, manage individual risk and uncertainty, extract and reallocate resources from their societies, and create environments conducive to economic activity. Social organizations help to develop communities and community identities, build social coalitions, manage individual risk and uncertainty, defuse social conflict, and reduce risks to contracting and exchange. Social organizations become vehicles to articulate preferences and needs in political arenas, and they help to support group interests in economic arenas.

Economic Organization and Development

Even though political organization, economic organization, and social organization are overlapping and synergistic arenas, let's consider each separately. Economic organization focuses on the ability to incorporate, manage, and transform resources in economic activity. How efficiently does a country's economy employ the tangible resources at its disposal? For economists, one of the great puzzles to decipher is what accounts for growth. All economies are not equal: some are larger than others and some have expanded at more rapid rates than others. Over time, some have grown very rapidly (today's developed economies) and some have grown much more slowly if at all (today's developing economies). Some of this inequality might be explained by differences in population, in the rate of population change, in physical resource base, in discoveries of tangible resources, or in investment patterns. The classic growth model in economic theory contains two independent variables: capital and labor. In this model, increasing the outcome of the dependent variable of growth requires an increase in either capital or labor.

Empirical evidence suggests that the classic growth model in economic theory is insufficient to account for modern economic growth. Very little separated rich from poor political economies before the late 1700s. Per capita incomes and output were remarkably similar across rich and poor states. From the early 1800s onward, this pattern changed, and dramatically so. National political economies were increasingly differentiated by their varying outputs from comparable amounts of tangible resources. Some appeared to use their resources more efficiently and productively, as they enjoyed much greater output per worker.

The economies of what became the modern industrialized states expanded much more rapidly than could be explained by changes in the supply of capital or labor, and much more rapidly than did the economies we now call developing economies. Economists revised the classic growth model by adding technology as an independent factor to help explain changes in growth. Technology is more than the phenomenon responsible for semiconductors or the chips in computers and cell phones, or the chemical and biological creations of pharmaceuticals. Technology involves much more than scientific breakthroughs, insights, or outcomes. Technological change includes the processes of scientific investigation, the processes of transforming scientific insights into applied products, the processes of transforming labor, and the processes of organizing workplaces and production.

Henry Ford's doubling of the daily wage and introduction of the assembly line transformed the means of producing automobiles. The higher wage attracted better workers and a more stable workforce; the assembly line encouraged efficiencies from economies of scale and learning. Ford's innovations, which became known as Fordism, were technological changes in production structures and the organization of economic activity. Similarly, differences in the organization of national educational systems help to account for differences in economic activity across nations. Changes in educational systems through state-mandated education requirements and through the development of postsecondary and graduate educational institutions have transformed labor and the processes of invention and innovation. German universities transformed the field of chemistry, which revolutionized the production of dyes and helped turn Germany into an economic and political powerhouse. The advent of the land-grant system in the United States led to tremendous investment in agricultural, mining, and forestry research, with significant spin-offs in our understanding of chemical, biological, and economic processes. After World War II, the G.I. Bill opened university doors to new populations of students, which led to a significant transformation in the U.S. labor force. The National Defense Education Act of 1958 encouraged the development of math, science, and engineering skills, which helped lead to technological invention and innovation. Such technological changes in the processes and organization of education affect the organization of economic activity. Such changes, and others in the organization of economic activity, have revolutionized production in many industries, transformed the skills of labor and increased worker productivity, led to more efficient use of resources, and increased social welfare. These examples demonstrate the importance of organization for transforming inputs to economic activity.

Economic organization increases the overall wealth and welfare of a society. States that stagnate in the organization and transformation of economic activity have less surplus to be invested, taxed, and reallocated to other endeavors. Your parents, society, and government have invested part of their surplus in your education, an investment in future productivity. Governments tax surplus to fund infrastructure investment, social welfare programs, education, research and development, foreign policy, and national security—all activities that contribute to the potential to influence the behavior of others in the global arena. Surplus is not simply a function of overall economic size, for a state with a large population can have a larger

TABLE 2.1	**Gross Domestic Product and Gross National Income per Capita by Income Classification, 2010**	
	GDP (in $ millions)	GNI per capita
World	**76,287,673**	**11,058**
Low-income states	993,078	1,246
Low-middle-income states	8,969,795	3,701
Upper-middle-income states	24,511,227	9,904
High-income states	41,868,508	37,183

Source: Data are purchasing power parity (ppp) and are from the World Development Indicators database, World Bank.

gross national income (GNI) than a state with a smaller population but still have a smaller surplus. Surplus is a function of both overall economic size and the productivity of each worker (GNI per capita). Table 2.1 shows differences in GNI and GNI per capita incomes across a range of political economies. States with higher GNI per capita can extract more resources from each worker than can states with lower GNI per capita. In this table, the high-income states are the advanced industrialized economies of the Organization for Economic Cooperation and Development (OECD) that dominate activities and the rules of the game in the capitalist global political economy. Even a cursory glance at the table reveals that economic success correlates highly with the capacity of governments to exercise influence in world affairs. The effect of economic organization on the accumulation of wealth and surplus is an important contributor to a state's power potential and ability to prevail in global affairs.

Unlike acres of arable land, population size, petroleum or mineral reserves, and other tangible assets, intangible resources such as economic organization are difficult to measure. The effects of organization may be observable, but organization itself is much more difficult to observe and measure directly. Economists have devised some useful measures of the consequences of economic organization that can be used as proxy (substitute) measures of economic organization. These substitutions assume that economic organization will affect economic outcomes. Measures such as GNI, gross national product (GNP) or gross domestic product (GDP), productivity or GNP per capita (GNP/n), level of industrialization, and percentage of the labor force engaged in agricultural production tell us a lot about the organization of economic activity, quality of workforce, societal wealth, and accumulation of surplus.

Political Organization and Development

The success of economic organization relies heavily on the organization and capacity of the political arena. Economic actors operate within political arenas and under rules constructed by politicians and policy makers. Political arenas define property rights and the rights of economic actors to the fruits of their labor, provide tools such as currencies that can facilitate exchange, establish contracting procedures and adjudication mechanisms such as courts and regulatory agencies to resolve disagreements in the economic arena, back those property rights and dispute adjudication mechanisms with the enforcement mechanisms of the state, and affect the macroeconomic environment through taxes, programs, regulation, and manipulation of money supply. As states are functionally equal, they all attempt to perform such functions. But political arenas vary in how and how well they perform these functions. Some governments are better than others at stabilizing and managing risk and uncertainty for economic actors from the political arena, which allows economic actors to have more confidence in their forecasts, better manage risks to their activities, and take greater chances on future outcomes. Such governments work with their societies, and their actions encourage private economic activity and help advance the broader well-being. Other political arenas are more predatory, with economic and political elites effectively preying upon their broader societies; this creates disincentives for private economic activity and damages overall social welfare even as those elites prosper. Political arenas that nurture productive economic activity are those that encourage economic actors to lengthen their time horizons and place greater bets on the future by expanding investments that will be repaid, if successful, in the future.

Political development and organization sit at the heart of government capacity to provide an arena conducive to economic activity, investment, and risk taking on the future. Political organization is the capacity of a political system to carry out tasks imposed on it domestically and internationally. A government's ability to perform well depends on its ability to extract, mobilize, and allocate resources; to convince members of society to act in the collective interest; to manage conflicts in society that could create divisions, turn violently divisive, or undermine confidence in the future; and to engender confidence in a broad swath of society to take risks on the future with personal resources. These are difficult tasks. No clear blueprint exists for well-intentioned politicians and policy makers who want to create a political and societal arena with such characteristics. If political development were simple and formulaic, then we would observe far more politically and economically developed states in the world today.

To complicate matters, not all politicians and policy makers seek the best possible long-term outcomes for their societies. Some politicians are not well-intentioned; rather, they seek to benefit personally from policies that they know will cause social ills. Even well-intentioned political leaders face short-term narrow pressures that create hurdles to their political survival and may run counter to long-term societal welfare. We began with an assumption that politicians seek to survive. Political survival may depend more on policies that appeal to short-term special interests and narrow constituencies than on policies meant to address broader and more long-term societal interests. All societies have divisions, groups, and individuals with divergent preference orderings that pressure politicians to act in the short term and often at the expense of the long-term welfare of their societies. Societies that effectively manage such forces through their political organization and the development of constructive political institutions prove far more successful than other societies in managing the domestic arena, expanding domestic economic and social opportunities, and increasing the capacity of the state to act in world affairs. Such societies are in the minority on the world stage, however.

Let's quickly consider the mechanisms of political development, institutions, and organization and how they operate. If success is defined broadly in terms of overall societal welfare and not in terms of narrow segments of society, then successful instances of political development, political institutions, and political organization are those that encourage investment in the future (risk taking in society), manage societal conflict and disputes constructively, and succeed in advancing the long-term welfare of society. Successful political organization engenders respect for the authority of the state that does not rely solely on state tools of violent coercion, constructs a rule of law that encourages respect and tolerance for the rights of others, encourages notions of fairness that extend beyond dominant societal subgroups, provides protections for minorities, and restrains the inclinations among members of society to resort to violence rather than to peaceful methods of dispute resolution.

All this is easier said than done! Just think how many governments of failed states cannot convince enough members of society to cooperate instead of fight, to adjudicate disputes peacefully through established legal mechanisms instead of through violence, to contribute resources to the state for reallocation to others (taxation as a contribution to the future), or to send their children off to distant schools (another contribution to the future welfare of society). Skilled and dedicated workers at the World Bank, the U.S. Agency for International Development (USAID), the United Nations Development Program (UNDP), and numerous other development organizations have been trying to promote such conditions in developing political economies since the end of World War II. Despite their skill and commitment, they have met with far less success than desired. The news media are filled with stories about civil wars, failure to establish civil societies and national identities, breakdowns in civil societies, political leaders' abusive use of the tools of coercion against segments of their own populations, economic failures, and policies that discriminate against some portions of states' populations to enrich those who have special connections to the political leadership of the states.

Societies are made up of individuals. Individuals usually have group associations that affect their decision calculus, but they still must make choices about their actions in society. These choices and how they aggregate provide the microfoundations of societal outcomes. So we want to ask how political development, institutions, and organization might influence individual preferences and decision processes, and how they affect the aggregation of individual preferences and choices to produce societal outcomes. For successful political development to occur, political organizations and institutions must affect the individual-level calculations of a broad swath of society and create incentives for individuals to make choices that improve their well-being and at the same time contribute to the general well-being of their broader society. Less successful political development also affects the incentives of individuals in societies, but it promotes individual actions that may be individually rational but are at odds with the greater social welfare.

Political development, institutions, and organization consist of far more than the physical edifices of the state. Buildings, monuments, and governmental infrastructure are physical manifestations of the state, but they are only limited indicators of the development of the political arena. States with high degrees of societal conflict and violence could easily have large government mechanisms, such as militaries and police, to combat that conflict, but the high level of violence tells us that political development, institutions, and organization have failed to constrain individual calculations and actions that work against overall societal welfare, or to provide mechanisms that enable the peaceful adjudication of conflict and promote compromise. How do political development, institutions, and organization convince individuals to become stakeholders or shareholders in the future of national society, to compromise and peacefully adjudicate disagreements, so they will forgo short-term individual rewards to gain long-term benefits for themselves and society? The temptation to garner short-term gains at long-term expense is a social trap, a suboptimal equilibrium like those described in chapter 1. Earlier in this chapter we examined the importance of national identity and nationalism, based on a sense of common destiny, for transforming a state into a nation-state. Common destiny means having a similar stake in the future, or shareholding. Nationalism and political development evolve hand in hand, not as independent processes. Nationalism is a tool that can be used artfully by political entrepreneurs to advance the process of political development, but it can also be mobilized to discriminate against segments of society.

At the heart of political development and the development of shareholding in society are the linkages that connect members of society to the state, the masses of the population to the political elites. Remember that power and influence involve relationships, which work in both directions. So we need to ask, What are the channels by which elites are connected to the masses and groups in society, and what are the mechanisms by which elites motivate those masses and groups? This is a question about elites' ability to act as **agenda setters** and entrepreneurs, creating demands and preferences in society from the top down. But we also need to ask, What are the channels by which masses communicate their preferences and demands to elites? This is a question about **representation** and the ability to convey demands and preferences in society from the bottom up. How sophisticated and encompassing are such channels? This is a question about how much of society they incorporate, and about the reach, depth, and effectiveness of the channels of communication and influence.

> **Agenda setters** are actors whose actions constrain the choices of others and direct them toward a limited menu of choices. **Representation** consists of the processes and mechanisms in society by which demands and preferences are conveyed from the bottom up.

What mechanisms can link society to the state's political elites? In the political sphere, elections, public opinion, legislatures, political parties, class-based organizations, narrowly defined special-interest groups, bureaucracies, courts, and media are conduits of communication and influence. These can be employed to develop identity and stakeholding, create political institutions and incentives to affect individual choice, aggregate and mobilize interests, extract and reallocate resources, extend representation, provide leadership, manage societal conflict, foster the development of civil society, and develop bargains between the state and society such as the modern welfare state. Signals, information, and pressures move in both directions along these channels: from the political elites to the broader society, and from the broader society to the political elites. The breadth and depth of these channels—how much of society they encompass and organize—help political scientists investigate the nature of participation and representation in the political arena, bottom-up demands and responsiveness of political elites to those demands, and top-down political manipulation in societies.

As with economic organization, effective political organization acts as a multiplier, interacting with other tangible and intangible resources of a state. Governments and societies that have broadened the base of political participation and enhanced the channels of representation connecting political elites and masses have proven more successful at extracting and allocating resources for societal ends. Such societies are far more capable of manipulating the tangible and intangible assets at their disposal, which increases the power potential of the state. Later in this text, we will examine more extensively the influence of such forms of political development and organization on the calculations and activities of members of society, and their consequent impacts on public policy and the global political economy.

As analysts of political behavior trying to understand why things happen in world affairs, we want to try to evaluate the contribution of intangible resources such as economic, political, and social organization. But intangibles are difficult to observe and measure. For economic organization, we use measures of economic outcomes as substitutes for direct measures of the processes of economic development and organization. Proxy measures and assessments of political development and organization are more difficult to construct than their economic counterparts. The connection between political outcomes and the processes of political development and organization are more tenuous. Nevertheless, some measures have been advanced to try to capture differences across states in political development and organization.

Political scientists have developed tools for assessing the institutional climate of a state. Measures of tax avoidance and tax compliance tell us about the capability of the state to extract resources and the willingness of its society's members to pay their taxes—both proxy assessments of the level and depth of political organization and development. Nobody really likes paying taxes, and tax evasion is a common phenomenon in many political economies, so the effectiveness of a government in obtaining tax revenues tells us about the ability of the state and also the willingness of the taxpayers to contribute to society. Examinations of government budgets provide information about the ability of states to allocate resources to various types of programs, which can tell us about the breadth and reach of the channels of political organization. Does government fund a wide range of programs to address the interests of a broad set of constituencies in society, or do its programs target a much narrower segment of society, a patronage clientele? Government turnover, electoral participation, competitiveness of elections, stability of the electoral process, regime change, public opinion assessments, connections between local and national political organizations, adjudicatory fairness of the legal system, and candidate recruitment are other indicators used in the assessment of political development and organization.

Some economic variables can prove useful in the assessment of the organizational capacity of a state. Government policies seek to influence specific macroeconomic conditions such as inflation, unemployment, stability of the exchange rate, investment and savings, and liquidity and money supply. As policy makers try to influence such conditions, they encounter pressures from within their domestic political economies that encourage short-term, politically expedient choices that can amount to long-term macroeconomic mismanagement. Measurements of such variables can tell us how well governments succeed or fail in managing target conditions and how well they succeed or fail in constraining short-term political pressures that could be detrimental to long-term social welfare. These performance evaluations, in turn, provide information about government capacity and the level of development and organization of the channels connecting policy makers to society. Governments cannot unilaterally attain their preferred outcomes on such macroeconomic conditions, for the actions of private economic actors are critical to such outcomes. How well governments do in attaining their preferred outcomes depends on their ability to convince private economic actors that those are the appropriate targets. Well-developed channels and connections between policy makers and private economic actors are essential to successful manipulation of such macroeconomic conditions.

Interest rates on government financial instruments can also offer information about the political capacity and development of governments. Interest rates on bonds are the cost of capital for the borrower. If you purchase a government bond as an investment, you are lending money to that government. The interest rate on the bond is the fee the government pays you for your loan. As a lender you will demand higher fees, or payments for your money, as the risk or uncertainty of your investment increases. If we assume that more politically developed and organized societies and governments are better able to manage such risk and uncertainty, this superior capability should be reflected in the cost of capital. Governments that are more capable—have greater political development and organization—should pay less to borrow capital than governments that have less political development and organization. Again, this proxy measurement assumes a strong association between the intangible resources of political development and organization and the ability of the state to overcome problems and prevail.

Social Organization and Development

Among the other intangible resources that can affect the capacities of societies and governments are cultural and social organization, which can help to build identities, create civil societies, and generate networks within communities and states. Social and cultural identities and networks can be as useful as economic connections in motivating people—more useful in many cases. Religious, cultural, and social organizations can create dense, active networks that can be transformed into tools to organize and mobilize interests, place demands on governments, and affect activities within political and economic arenas. Strategic policy makers can mobilize social and cultural networks to advance political agendas. The political movements surrounding humanitarian assistance, abortion rights, stem-cell research, gay rights, terrorism, and ethnic conflict become more powerful as they tap into social and cultural networks and organization.

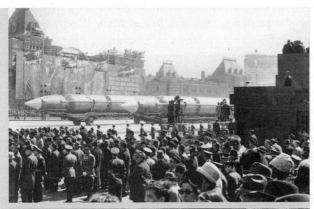

This May Day parade in Moscow and Boeing assembly plant in Washington State illustrate differences in the use of resources and paths to international influence: guns versus butter and military versus economic. In assessing means to power, many people focus almost instinctively on military tools, such as the missiles being displayed in Red Square. They tend to overlook other sources of influence, as in this case the transformation of productive assets into commercial airliners. Boeing's planes will be sold in global markets, influence global activity, and connect the world through modern transport. Production activity such as Boeing's functions as a multiplier in a political economy, promoting economic advances and generating wealth that can be used to influence others. In retrospect, the economic organization of the United States proved more influential than the military organization of the Soviet Union.

CONCLUSION

The context of international relations differs from that of domestic politics. This fact is an independent variable that we must consider when trying to account for behavior in global affairs, but it is not the only variable, as we shall quickly see. In the modern nation-state system, each government is the supreme legitimate source of authority and coercion within the state's boundaries, but the international arena lacks such a legitimate central authority to prescribe formal rules and laws and to adjudicate and enforce them. Consequently, international affairs have been described as a state of nature or anarchy, wherein behavior is guided by the law of the jungle and the survival of the fittest. Each government must rely on its own capabilities to advance its objectives, and the development of a collective identity, or nation, can assist it in that quest. This context of anarchy does not mean that conflict is inevitable and constant, or that cooperation and peaceful resolution of disputes are unlikely. Instead, from purely a contextual perspective, order can emerge in such an anarchical system from the distribution of capabilities across states and the existence of a hierarchy based on that distribution.

Why do we care about tangible and intangible resources, about power and hierarchy in global affairs? Differences in the distribution of tangible and intangible resources translate into differences in the power capabilities of states in the international arena. They establish a basis for hierarchies among autonomous, sovereign units. Such hierarchies are important in global affairs, given the absence of a central authority and the resulting anarchical state of affairs. They provide order to anarchy. Anarchy is often equated with disorder, sometimes accurately. Differences in power can produce violence, as wars and disputes attest, but differences in power can also provide tools for obtaining cooperative and productive outcomes in international affairs. Differences in capabilities and the hierarchies built on them can restrain governments from acting as if they were in a violent state of nature, convincing them instead to act as part of a community. The violence of conflict in the global system can distract our attention from the extraordinary amount of cooperative behavior in an arena that lacks a rule of law provided by a central authority, its adjudication mechanisms, and its enforcement mechanisms. A tremendous amount of cooperation and agreement is necessary to maintain the current daily flow of vast quantities of goods, services, capital, people, and information across national boundaries, yet no central authority exists to support those flows, protect contracts, resolve disputes, and punish those who cheat. Hierarchies can replace the formal mechanisms of central authority with an informal mechanism based on differences in power distribution, but not always. The informal mechanisms of hierarchy can break down and lead to violence and chaos, just as the formal authority mechanisms of domestic political arenas can break down and lead to civil conflict.

Intangible assets make the greatest difference in states' power capabilities, as they organize human activities and act as multipliers of tangible resources. Differences in the organization of political, economic, and social life separate subsistence states that have few surplus resources to expend on influencing the activities of others in the global arena from states with abundant surpluses that can be allocated to support more advanced and expensive strategies of statecraft. Political and economic revolutions produced changes in power capabilities that enabled the Dutch Netherlands to gain influence far disproportionate to its physical and demographic size in the 1500s and 1600s, the United Kingdom to exert disproportionate influence over European and international relations in the nineteenth century, the United States to exercise inordinate influence over world affairs since World War II, and the West to dominate the organization of world affairs from the 1500s until today. Hierarchies affect the "rules of the game," or how international affairs are organized, the nature of conflict, and the form of exchange. As we advance in the twenty-first century, pundits and policy makers are already discussing possible changes in the global hierarchy with the economic successes in China, India, and Brazil.

Advances in political, economic, and social organization and development tend to make a state a more effective international actor. If advances in political, economic, and social organization and development interact and produce synergisms, states and societies can undergo amazing increases in their power potential and their ability to affect the behavior of others and to resist pressures from others. Such differences in power and position in hierarchy can provide good indicators for explaining and understanding why some prevail and some falter, and for predicting what preferences will dominate in global affairs. Hierarchies based on differences in power provide tools for managing the potential disorder of anarchy, which may be necessary to overcome the barriers to cooperation that exist in a system lacking central authority. From a political economy perspective, power capabilities and hierarchies provide all sorts of valuable qualities. They can create equilibria, reduce uncertainty, narrow the ranges of choices available to decision makers, stabilize expectations, and enable cooperation.

KEY CONCEPTS

agenda setters (p. 103)

anarchy (p. 78)

cheap talk (p. 84)

dependence (p. 95)

economies of knowledge (p. 58)

economies of scale (p. 58)

elasticity of demand and supply (p. 96)

empire (p. 70)

functional equity (p. 57)

hierarchy (p. 60)

intangible attributes (p. 91)

interdependence (p. 59)

nation (p. 61)

nation-state (p. 55)

national policy autonomy (p. 59)

power (p. 81)

power hierarchy (p. 89)

representation (p. 103)

self-help system (p. 79)

sensitivity (p. 95)

sovereignty (p. 75)

specialization (p. 58)

substitutability (p. 96)

tangible attributes (p. 90)

Westphalian state system (p. 75)

EXERCISES

1. Describe the main characteristics of a state.

2. The United States and South Africa are two very different countries, but they are functionally equal. Explain how these two countries can be functionally equal and yet so different at the same time.

3. What is common knowledge, and how does it contribute to the concept of nation?

4. What is a nation, and how does it differ from a state?

5. Can a nation exist without a state, or vice versa? Give an example of a state that does not function as a nation as well.

6. What are some of the forces that build common knowledge and help to integrate people into a nation?

7. As students of international relations in general and international political economy specifically, why do we care whether states become nation-states?

8. Before the Thirty Years' War, most Europeans lived in settings where they faced three cross-cutting lines of authority. What were the different authorities, what problems resulted from this crosscutting of authority, and why?

9. The United States enacts domestic tax and labor policies, but these policies can affect economic activities in Japan. How does this create a problem for the concept of sovereignty?

10. How does the structure of political activity in international politics differ from that in domestic politics? What are the implications of this difference?

11. Hobbes wrote that in a state of nature, life is "solitary, poor, nasty, brutish, and short." Does this apply to international relations? If so, how and why?

12. Many factors can contribute to the formation of a nation, but many of them are not necessary or sufficient contributions. Name some of the factors that can be helpful but are not necessary or sufficient. What is the one quality that does seem to be necessary and sufficient for the development of a nation? Now, thinking about these different factors, what does "necessary and sufficient" mean?

13. Explain the tension between sovereignty and interdependence.

14. Generally, what is the most costly tool of influence for a state or policy maker in international politics?

15. Why do policy makers worry about the costs of exercising power in world affairs?

16. Cite an example to explain how the United States has used its power to influence affairs in the international political economy. Which tools of statecraft were used?

17. Explain how education and health affect a state's power capabilities.

18. On October 22, 1962, after reviewing newly acquired surveillance photographs, President John F. Kennedy informed the world that the Soviet Union was building secret missile bases in Cuba, a mere ninety miles off the shores of Florida. After weighing such options as an armed invasion of Cuba and air strikes against the missiles, Kennedy decided on a less dangerous response. In addition to demanding that Soviet premier Nikita S. Khrushchev remove all the missile bases and their deadly contents, Kennedy ordered a naval quarantine (blockade) of Cuba in order to prevent Russian ships from bringing additional missiles and construction materials to the island. Name two tools of statecraft relevant to this example and cite which action illustrates each.

19. Governments have a variety of options when it comes to influencing the behavior of others in world affairs. We call these options the tools of statecraft, or tools of influence. Name three broad strategies of influence and give an example of each.

20. Explain how elasticity of demand affects an economy that is sensitive to a particular resource as compared with that economy's condition of autarky (independence) in relation to another resource.

21. The success of China in the twenty-first century is beginning to raise questions about the global hierarchy and what state will set the rules of the game for the global arena in the future. Is the United States still the predominant political economy as it has been since the mid-twentieth century, or is it being supplanted by China? Conduct an analysis of the power capabilities of China and the United States using concepts discussed in this chapter.

22. When we think about power in international affairs, we often focus on military size. Table 2.2, which shows numbers of military personnel, tells one story about the distribution of power in international affairs. Table 2.3 tells another story. Using the data from 1880, construct two different hierarchies of power based on these two tables. What might account for the differences in the distribution of capabilities from table 2.2 to table 2.3?

TABLE 2.2	Military and Naval Personnel, 1880–1914 (in Thousands)				
	1880	*1890*	*1900*	*1910*	*1914*
Germany	426	504	524	694	891
France	543	542	715	769	910
Russia	791	677	1,162	1,285	1,352
United States	34	39	96	127	164
Austria-Hungary	246	346	385	425	444
United Kingdom	367	420	624	571	532
Japan	71	84	234	271	306

Source: Adapted from Paul Kennedy, *The Rise and Fall of Great Powers* (New York: Random House, 1987), 203.

TABLE 2.3	Total Industrial Potential in Relative Perspective, 1880–1938 (U.K. in 1890 = 100)				
	1880	*1890*	*1913*	*1928*	*1938*
Germany	27.4	71.2	137.7	158	214
France	25.1	36.8	57.3	82	74
Russia	24.4	47.5	76.6	72	152
United States	46.9	127.8	298.1	533	528
Austria-Hungary	14.0	25.6	40.7	—	—
United Kingdom	73.3	[100]	127.2	135	181
Japan	7.6	13.0	25.1	45	88

Source: Adapted from Paul Kennedy, *The Rise and Fall of Great Powers* (New York: Random House, 1987), 201.

FURTHER READING

Alter, Peter. 1985. *Nationalism*. London: Edward Arnold.

Art, Robert J. 1980. "To What Ends Military Power?" *International Security* 4 (Spring): 4–35.

Brubaker, Rogers. 1996. *Nationalism Reframed: Nationhood and the National Question in the New Europe.* Cambridge: Cambridge University Press.

Carr, E. H. 1946. *The Twenty Years' Crisis, 1919–1939.* 2nd ed. London: Macmillan.

Clausewitz, Carl von. 1982. *War, Politics, and Power.* New York: Penguin Books.

Machiavelli, Niccolò. 2003. *The Prince and the Discourses.* New York: Penguin Books.

Morgenthau, Hans J. 2006. *Politics among Nations: The Struggle for Power and Peace,* revised by Kenneth W. Thompson. 7th ed. New York: McGraw-Hill Higher Education.

Nye, Joseph S., Jr. 1990. *Bound to Lead: The Changing Nature of American Power.* New York: Basic Books.

Organski, A. F. K., and Jacek Kugler. 1981. *The War Ledger.* Chicago: University of Chicago Press.

Oye, Kenneth, ed. 1986. *Cooperation under Anarchy.* Princeton, NJ: Princeton University Press.

Rothgeb, John M., Jr. 1993. *Defining Power: Influence and Force in the Contemporary International System.* New York: St. Martin's Press.

Schelling, Thomas C. 1967. *Arms and Influence.* New Haven, CT: Yale University Press.

Snyder, Jack. 2000. *From Voting to Violence: Democratization and Nationalist Conflict.* New York: W. W. Norton.

Strange, Susan. 1988. *States and Markets.* London: Pinter.

Sun Tzu. 1971. *The Art of War.* New York: Oxford University Press.

Waltz, Kenneth. 1959. *Man, the State, and War.* New York: Columbia University Press.

———. 1979. *Theory of International Politics.* New York: Random House.

3

Economic Liberalism and Market Exchange in the Global Arena

> [Every individual] generally, indeed, neither intends to promote the public interest, nor knows how much he is promoting it . . . he intends only his own gain, and he is in this, as in many other cases, led by an invisible hand to promote an end which was not part of his intention. Nor is it always the worse for the society that it was no part of it. By pursuing his own interest he frequently promotes that of the society more effectively than when he really intends to promote it.
>
> —*Adam Smith, 1776*

Over the past four hundred years the global political economy has been increasingly characterized by processes, exchange, and production and consumption of goods, services, and resources that take place within markets and are disciplined by supply, demand, and price. The last major group of political economies embraced market exchange as the dominant form of production and transfer of goods, services, and ideas across national boundaries with the end of the Cold War between the U.S. bloc and the Soviet bloc. Already the dominant approach to international economic activity, market exchange became the unambiguous winner of the ideological battle between very different forms of organizing domestic and international political economic relations, between decentralized market exchange and hierarchical central planning. It was a conflict over the rules of the game in political and economic affairs. Since the Russian Revolution and the creation of the Soviet Union under Lenin, the Soviet Union and its allies had rejected market exchange and championed central planning and allocation. Mikhail Gorbachev, who ascended to the leadership of the Soviet Union in the 1980s, introduced significant policy changes. He initiated economic reforms, labeled perestroika, that introduced market mechanisms and pressures to the Soviet economy. These reforms encouraged consumer demands, decentralized decision making and industrial management, and supported private economic initiatives. Gorbachev also adopted political reforms, called **glasnost,** that helped to unleash individual choice and broader citizen participation in political life. The Soviet economic and political reforms spilled over into Eastern Europe. In 1989 the populations in several

> **Glasnost** refers to the political reforms initiated by Mikhail Gorbachev that helped to unleash individual choice and broader citizen participation in the political life of the Soviet Union in the 1980s.

Eastern European states rejected communist rule, and the rest of Eastern Europe soon followed. Growing nationalist and ethnic forces within the Soviet republics pressed for greater political decentralization and fragmentation. By fall 1991, republic after republic within the Soviet Union announced secession and declared independence. The Soviet Union disintegrated. The events of 1989–1991 ended the Cold War competition between the different forms of organizing domestic and global political economic relations. Market exchange in the economic arena and democratization in the political arena seem to have prevailed, at least for the foreseeable future.

In chapters 1 and 2 we noted the possibility of tension between the geography of international economic activity and the political geography of the nation-state system. Now let's more carefully consider the underpinnings of global capitalism, or the exchange of goods, services, skills, and information within and across national borders through market mechanisms. We focus on global capitalism because it is the dominant form of economic exchange in the global political economy and it colors all aspects of economic, political, and social relations within and across societies. We can create various categories for the processes that underpin global capitalism, but for simplicity let's say that they fall into three broad categories: the production of goods and services, financial market integration, and the movement of human capital. These categories are not independent of one another. Indeed, they overlap a great deal—this is clear particularly once we recognize that labor and capital are commodities just like other goods that are priced and traded in markets.

ECONOMIC LIBERALISM: COMPETITIVE MARKETS AND SOCIAL OUTCOMES

Economic liberalism is rooted in the writings of Adam Smith, David Ricardo, John Stuart Mill, Thomas Malthus, and scores of philosophers and economists who followed. At the heart of economic liberalism is exchange within **competitive markets.** Remember the modifier *competitive,* for it has a very precise meaning to which we will return in the next chapter, but a meaning that is often overlooked or obscured in discussions about the efficacy and value of market exchange. Competitive economic markets are decentralized mechanisms that coordinate the allocation, distribution, and use of the raw materials,

> **Competitive markets** are decentralized mechanisms that coordinate the allocation, distribution, and use of the raw materials, labor, and capital that go into economic activity. They are mechanisms of symmetric and voluntary exchange among nonhierarchical parties.

labor, and capital that go into economic activity. Markets perform these functions by affecting the calculations and incentives of consumers and producers, aggregating and coordinating their behavior, and encouraging production and consumption of some commodities while discouraging the production and consumption of other commodities. The choices of consumers and producers are decentralized and nonhierarchical. Market exchange is relatively symmetric, involving voluntary contractual relationships. Nonmarket mechanisms

Self-interest is the notion that people make choices based on their hierarchies of preferences and their budgetary constraints.

also exist that coordinate the allocation and use of resources—production and consumption choices—in a society. Many of these mechanisms differ from the market mechanism in that they are hierarchical and often involve less than voluntary relationships. Governments, religious orders, organizations, families, and business firms are just a few examples of such nonmarket mechanisms.

How do markets work? In competitive markets, producers of goods and services meet potential consumers of those commodities. Consumers have preferences regarding what they want to consume, and, in a world of scarce resources, they face budget constraints on their consumption choices. Because they cannot consume everything they desire, they must discriminate in their consumption, as discussed in chapter 1. In decentralized markets, we assume that consumers base their choices on hierarchies of preferences and budgetary constraints—the size of their wallets. They make trade-offs based on their **self-interest** and on their budgets. Producers also face budgetary constraints as they purchase the inputs to their productive activities. This economic framework requires us to make no noble assumptions about human motivations—only that humans are self-interested (or egoistic) and that they behave as if they are rational. Working with these less than idealistic assumptions allows us to examine the actions and preferences of human actors to see if they conform to the conditions of completeness and transitivity, which we also considered in chapter 1.

The Price Mechanism Coordinating Supply and Demand

Markets aggregate individual choices by means of a **price mechanism,** which coordinates consumption preferences, or **demand,** with producers' activities, or the **supply** of specific goods and services. The price mechanism influences the use of societal resources by changing the behavior of producers and consumers, given the supply of commodities and services

A **price mechanism** is the cost factor that coordinates individual consumption preferences (demand) with producers' activities (the supply of specific goods and services). **Demand** is the market force that represents the aggregation of individual consumption preferences. **Supply** is the amount of specific goods and services produced in response to consumer demand.

and the demand for those commodities and services as conditioned by their costs. The market and its price mechanism discipline producers and their production choices: if they offer commodities or services that consumers do not want, do not want at the price offered, or do not want in the quantity produced, producers face incentives to change what they produce, the price of what they produce, or the quantity of what they produce. If producers do not adjust to such demands, they will find the well-being and even the survival of their enterprises threatened. Consumers will reward producers who respond to their demands and penalize producers who do not. Similarly, the activities of producers affect the incentives and demands of consumers, for consumer choices may change as producers change what they offer and the prices at which they offer it.

Adam Smith called this dynamic process the **invisible hand** of the market—an unseen force that guides self-interested individual behavior in competitive markets and promotes the welfare of society without individuals' deliberate intent. Noble human motivations are not needed to attain good collective outcomes, for if the market mechanism works as hypothesized, then individual self-interested choices aggregated through competitive market mechanisms will produce good collective outcomes automatically, and regardless of the motivations of those parties involved in market exchange. This is the stable equilibrium described in chapter 1, where no party to an exchange can improve her payoff by unilaterally selecting another strategy.

> The **invisible hand** is an idea proposed by Adam Smith, who theorized that an unseen force guides self-interested individual behavior in competitive markets to promote the welfare of society without individuals' deliberate intent.

Gordon Gekko, in Oliver Stone's 1987 movie *Wall Street,* reveled in this sentiment with his pronouncement, "Greed is good." In 2009, in the wake of the economic global calamity that began in 2007, Lloyd Blankfein, the head of Goldman Sachs, an investment bank, echoed this sentiment when he said that banks are "doing God's work. We're very important. We help companies to grow by helping them to raise capital. Companies that grow create wealth. This, in turn, allows people to have jobs that create more growth and more wealth. It's a virtuous cycle." We will revisit and examine this sentiment in the next chapter when we consider potential shortcomings in the market mechanism, but it is important to recognize that producing a good collective outcome does not mean that all parties find that outcome optimal. A good collective outcome simply means that the collective outcome is enhanced; it is not necessarily an optimal outcome for all parties affected by market exchange.

In effect, the invisible hand is a giant information mechanism that polls members of a society about all their wants and desires, their cost constraints, and the ability of producers to adjust their activities to meet those wants and constraints—an amazing task. Neither today's most sophisticated computers nor those expected in the foreseeable future can offer the computing and storage capacity necessary to replicate the outcomes that are coordinated by price mechanisms in competitive modern markets.

Factors of Production: The Allocation of Land, Labor, and Capital

Markets coordinate the use of different resources in society through the invisible hand of the price mechanism. The production of commodities requires a mix of resources, which generally fall into three broad categories: land, labor, and capital. Knowledge and technology might also be considered critical resources involved in economic production, but for

Factors of production are the inputs to economic production—land, labor, and capital. Factor endowment is the distribution of factors of production in a specific economy; each economy has a different factor endowment based on relative abundance of resources.

simplicity we focus here on land, labor, and capital. Economists call these inputs **factors of production.** Each nation has some mix of land, labor, and capital—a combination referred to as its **factor endowment.** Different allocations and mixes of factors of production across nations are the differences in the factor endowments of those nations.

These differences are not static; they can change over time with population change, discoveries, consumption, technological shifts, and economic growth or decline.

Land

The physical resources available in nature—such as arable land, water, and raw materials, whether animal, vegetable, or mineral—are categorized as **land.** Sometimes such resources are easy to find and use, but more often some combination of labor, intelligence, and capital must be expended to transform them from their natural state into useful form. Humans develop tools to hunt and trap animals or to fell trees, tame beasts of burden to help in farming, create strategies to harvest fish, dig mines to extract coal and iron, drill holes to find oil, and invent biochemical processes to transform that oil into fuel and other petrochemical products.

Land refers to the raw materials and physical resources available in nature, such as arable land, water, and raw materials, whether animal, vegetable, or mineral. Labor is the effort that men and women put into producing a commodity.

Labor

The second factor of production, **labor,** consists of the efforts that men and women put into producing a commodity, whether extracting a resource from the ground, planting and harvesting a crop, milling or refining a raw material, inventing, or teaching. This resource category encompasses blue-collar, white-collar, physical, menial, and mental labor. Population size, age distribution, and gender breakdown—as well as societal attitudes and rules about who should work and for how long—affect the amount of labor that is available in an economy. Prohibiting child labor, creating retirement insurance or some other form of social security, requiring schooling up to a specified age, or limiting the length of the workweek and workday shrinks the physical size of a labor pool even if such activities improve the quality and productivity of labor. Qualitative aspects such as health and education affect the ability of labor to generate outputs. Qualitative improvement of this productive ability requires the interaction of labor with another factor of production.

Capital

Capital is a factor of production that people construct, or invent, and then use to transform the other factors of production—land and labor—to make them more productive.

Capital differs from the other factors of production in one important characteristic: it does not occur naturally. People construct, or invent, capital and then use it to transform the other factors of production to make them more productive. Capital can be invested in the training and education of labor; in the development of tools, technologies, and skills to transform raw materials, such as to make crude oil into plastics and other synthetics; in the invention of fertilizers and crop technologies that increase agricultural output per acre farmed or per worker; in the building of plants and factories to improve the efficiency of the manufacture of commodities; in processes of production innovation; and in scientific laboratories and research facilities to further discoveries that may improve the productivity and welfare of society. The college or university you attend is an example of the massive application of capital to transform a factor of production (you) into a more productive member of society. The investment of capital in your training through higher education increases your value and capability as an input to production. Would you trust someone without benefit of such an investment to perform surgery on you? This application amounts to an increase in human capital, a synergistic interaction of labor and capital.

Capital is the critical ingredient in the mix of the factors of production; the abundance or scarcity of capital separates more advanced and wealthier political economies from those that are less developed and less affluent. A society that enjoys an abundance of capital can usually make more productive use of its labor and land than can societies that are comparably endowed in those factors but have less capital.

THE NORMATIVE APPEAL OF ECONOMIC LIBERALISM: INDIVIDUAL CHOICE, LIBERTY, AND EFFICIENCY

Liberal market exchange appeals to many on moral grounds. It embraces individual choice, free will, and a notion of efficiency with which it can generate broader social gains. Such moral appeal depends on the condition that markets work as envisioned by theory. We will return to this condition in the next chapter. Much of the normative appeal of economic market exchange stems from its foundation in individual choice and free will. In theory, market exchange liberates individual choice and free will. The parties to market exchange voluntarily participate in that exchange based on their individual choice. They choose one commodity over another, make trade-offs across commodities based on need and price, and decide what to exchange and when. Nobody tells you that you must purchase or sell a commodity in a market. These concepts, individual choice and free will, are powerful and seductive because people generally dislike having their actions dictated by others, even if those at the top of a hierarchy harbor the best intentions for members of their group. Even in hierarchies with relatively benign leaders who seek to advance the broader interests of their communities, such as those in many businesses, organizations, and governments, people find working in a hierarchy unpleasant at times. Some of this unhappiness arises from hierarchical intrusions on individual liberty and autonomy. Consequently, market exchange can be viewed as the expression of the preferences and wants of the participants, and the hierarchy of those preferences. This allows interpersonal comparisons of utility, or how individuals value some commodities over others, and comparison of those preference orderings across individuals.

Efficiency is a comparative gauge of the inputs of land, labor, and capital that go into the production of individual goods or services; an efficient market optimizes the use of the resources that go into economic activity to satisfy the aggregated wants and preferences of the members of society. **Productivity gains** are improvements in efficiency that occur when producers discover a means to reduce inputs per unit of production.

If markets work well, they enhance social welfare and are socially efficient. What do we mean by efficiency? The term **efficiency** has multiple usages in relation to economic activity. In terms of production, it is a comparative gauge of the inputs of land, labor, and capital that go into the production of individual goods or services. How much land, or raw material resources, goes into the production of the commodity? How much labor—often defined by the number of hours of labor required—is needed to produce a unit of the commodity? How much capital is required to produce a unit of the commodity? More efficient production involves fewer inputs, or costs, per unit of output than does less efficient production. **Productivity gains,** or improvements in efficiency, occur when a producer discovers a means to reduce the inputs per unit of production or increase output without increasing inputs. Such gains are made when labor becomes more effective in less time or when a producer discovers a way to reduce the input of raw materials. More often than not, producers achieve such productivity gains by transforming labor or resources through the application of capital.

Efficiency has a broader significance in terms of market exchange. An efficient market optimizes the use of the resources that go into economic activity to satisfy the aggregated wants and preferences of the members of society. No absolute standard of efficiency can apply to every society and market, for what is efficient differs across societies, depending on the desires of their members. Markets maximize social welfare when the market mechanism accurately aggregates those preferences and leads to the production of goods and services that best meet those desires—in other words, when no other level of production of goods and services could produce greater overall societal happiness. This does not mean that every individual obtains her or his most preferred outcome. In fact, efficiency means something quite different. Optimal, efficient markets that facilitate the production and consumption of goods and services given the mix of individual preferences in society rarely optimize those preferences in society. What efficient exchange does is minimize the collective dissatisfaction and optimize the collective satisfaction of those individuals in society engaged in exchange. The production of any other level of goods and services might make some specific members of society better-off, but, given the preferences of all members of society, it would make society as a whole worse-off. At any given moment, an efficient market reflects an allocation of resources and efforts that is in equilibrium, wherein movement to another allocation could not advantage one member of society without hurting another and lowering the overall satisfaction of the mix of preferences in society.

Proponents of competitive markets find them morally attractive because they depend on individual choice, involve relatively symmetric and voluntary contractual relationships among nonhierarchical parties, and, *if they work properly,* should result in good societal

outcomes given the aggregated preferences of members of society. Effective market mechanisms lead to
the optimal allocation of a society's scarce resources
given the preferences and resource constraints of
society and its members. They increase productiv-

> The **production possibilities curve** is the outer
> boundary of what an economy could conceiv-
> ably produce given the resources and prefer-
> ences of society.

ity, maximize use of the factors of production, and expand the range of consumption possibilities for a society in response to the efforts of its members. Real wages increase, which
means that, in the aggregate, members of society can purchase more with their labor. In
economic lingo, an efficient and competitive market places a society on the frontier of the
production possibilities curve, or the outer boundary of what a society could conceivably
produce and consume given its resources and the preferences of its members. This is an
aggregate statement about the collective condition of the society—the social outcome—and
not about the lot of particular individuals in the society.

MARKET EXCHANGE AS THE BASIS OF INTERNATIONAL TRADE: MECHANISMS AT THE CORE OF MODERN GLOBALIZATION

Market exchange within national boundaries can lead to more efficient use of societal
resources, but what about market exchange across national borders? International trade can
link national markets to create a larger, more efficient global market. As philosopher and
economist John Stuart Mill explained in his classic text *The Principles of Political Economy,*
published in 1848:

> The benefit of international exchange, or in other words, foreign commerce (Setting
> aside its enabling countries to obtain commodities which they could not themselves
> produce at all) . . . consists in a more efficient employment of the productive forces of
> the world.

International trade based on market exchange is a cornerstone of the expansion of globalization, global capitalism, and the development of a modern global political economy. Yet trade
is not the sole mechanism of global liberal exchange, nor may it be the most important. The
flow of capital through overseas investment, immigration, and the outsourcing of employment from one nation to another are also significant processes by which people in one society become culturally, economically, politically, strategically, and ecologically closer to
peoples in geographically distant societies. These processes rival trade in terms of their influence on political economies and their capacity to transform political economies. Economists
suggest that these different processes can serve as economic substitutes for one another.
Outsourcing, migration, and international investment may look different from trade in
goods and services, but at their foundations they are similar. Trade in goods and services

simply embeds labor and capital in the goods and services being exchanged across borders. Again, this highlights the tension between economic geography and political geography in the modern global arena. Even though these processes might serve as economic substitutes and produce similar macroeconomic outcomes in terms of global output, they are not substitutes in terms of political geography. They influence what types of jobs will be created and where, and who will pay taxes, how much and where; they affect the fiscal rewards that government and specific societies reap, as well as those societies' abilities to translate surplus into public policies.

Extending market exchange across national borders is not simple, straightforward, or noncontroversial in some circles. Even today, after several centuries of the expansion of global capitalism and despite academic study and evidence, debates continue within polities about the value and wisdom of international trade. In such debates, the mechanisms underpinning international market exchange and the effects of trade are often misconstrued. Some believe that the mechanisms of international exchange create greater interdependence across national political economies, enhancing welfare and promoting universal harmony. Others view international exchange as a threat to sovereignty, a hindrance to national political economies, and potentially damaging to the welfare of their societies.

Many have depicted globalization and international exchange as a zero-sum relationship between states (that is, a situation in which one party's gain results in another party's loss). Critics have rallied to the antiglobalization ranks for fear of losses in jobs, investment, and economic opportunities. Those seeking to restrict such exchange and globalization frame them as a competition among nations rather than a positive-sum relationship whereby both parties to an exchange benefit from the exchange. The virulence and persistence of such negative attitudes appear with increasing regularity during electoral campaigns, during economic slowdowns that threaten economic opportunities, and as the pace of globalization accelerates and exposes societies to transformation from the status quo. Such negative attitudes and concerns persist despite the overwhelming recognition among economists that the mechanisms of international exchange generally produce welfare gains for society as a whole regardless of how those gains are distributed among the individuals who constitute a society.

In his bid for the American presidency as an independent in 1992, Ross Perot warned of a "giant sucking sound" that would be heard because the U.S. economy would lose jobs to the Mexican economy if the North American Free Trade Agreement (NAFTA) were ratified. Eight years later, another independent candidate, Ralph Nader, warned of similar job losses and the exit of investment capital from the United States as a result of globalization. Unions, manufacturing workers, and owners of semiskilled manufacturing enterprises have raised similar fears about the flight of jobs and capital from the more advanced political economies to the developing political economies. These claims raise the specter of a one-way highway on which all capital, job creation, and trade flow in one direction, eventually impoverishing the Northern political economies and enriching the Southern political economies. These claims amount to zero-sum thinking. Such claims may be useful in mobilizing political support and obstructing international exchange, but they misrepresent the facts and contradict the logic and empirical evidence of trade. Without doubt, current and future election cycles will witness similar attacks on the processes of globalization: questioning the merits of trade, disparaging the outsourcing of employment, challenging immigration, and criticizing overseas investment.

Such debates and disparagements highlight the importance of understanding globalization and international exchange, how it works, and how the expansion of market exchange across national borders affects the welfare of societies and the structure of production and consumption in societies. In the following subsections, we examine the mechanisms that make up the process of international exchange: absolute advantage, comparative advantage, factor endowments, factor intensities, the balance-of-payments mechanism, and the exchange-rate mechanism.

Absolute Advantage: An Early Principle of International Trade

Centuries ago, a principle called **absolute advantage** guided the practice of trade between nations. This principle holds that if one trading partner is more capable and efficient at producing particular commodities than its other trading partners, then it should specialize in the production of such commodities and trade for goods on which others enjoy absolute advantage. Absolute advantage reflects a comparison of production costs for the same commodity across borders—comparing the cost of producing apples to apples, and oranges to oranges. A useful means of comparing production costs is to focus on the labor cost, or the amount of labor time needed to produce a commodity. This process of comparison forms the basis of the **labor theory of value.** More efficient producers have lower labor costs, or lesser amounts of labor per unit of production, which constitutes one measure of productivity per unit of production.

> **Absolute advantage** is a nation's ability to produce a particular commodity more efficiently than other nations. The **labor theory of value** is a means of comparing production costs that focuses on the labor cost, or the amount of labor time needed to produce a commodity.

Under the concept of absolute advantage, the justification for trade across national boundaries was to obtain commodities that a nation's workers could not produce more efficiently than workers abroad. One nation might be more proficient than others at producing semiconductors, automobiles, corn, aspirin, or some other product. Conceivably, a nation could produce all goods more efficiently than any of its potential trading partners in a commodity-by-commodity comparison; this nation would enjoy an absolute advantage in every form of production. For example, workers in the United States might be more proficient than workers in France at producing cars, semiconductors, software, corn, cheese, wine, and most other products. With absolute advantage as a guide, there would be no justification for Americans to import any of these commodities from France, since a commodity-by-commodity comparison demonstrates that French labor is less efficient and hence the French products are more costly than comparable products produced in the

United States—that is, American labor produces the same products in less time than French labor. Trade guided by the principle of absolute advantage limits the gains from trade available to societies.

Comparative Advantage: A Revolution in Thought

In 1817 David Ricardo, an intellectual, economist, stockbroker, and member of the British House of Commons, published a series of essays under the title *On the Principles of Political Economy and Taxation.* One of these essays, "The Political Economy of International Trade," revolutionized economics. In this essay Ricardo developed the principle of **comparative advantage,** which has since become the foundation of modern international trade and is one of the most elegant and influential ideas in economics. In so doing, he supplied the intellectual underpinnings for trade among nations regardless of their productive capabilities and advantages. How does this principle differ from absolute advantage, and what does the difference mean for international trade? Whereas absolute advantage looks at the relative efficiency of production by comparing product against like product across borders, comparative advantage looks at relative efficiency not just product by product, but also across products. So where absolute advantage compares apples to apples and oranges to oranges across states in terms of their costs of production, comparative advantage compares apples to apples, oranges to oranges, and also apples to oranges both within and across political economies in terms of their costs of production. When the gaps in efficiency between two trading partners are greater for some products than for others, one trading partner has a comparative advantage in the product with the greatest gap in efficiency.

> **Comparative advantage** is a nation's ability to produce a particular commodity with a greater margin of efficiency over its trading partners than it enjoys in the production of other commodities. This principle is the foundation of modern international trade and the basis for the principle of specialization.

Examples Illustrating Specialization

In the example above using the United States and France to consider the concept of absolute advantage, American labor enjoys an absolute advantage over French labor for those products it produces at a lower per unit labor cost. However, this comparison neglects the possibility that American labor might be more efficient at producing software than it is at producing cars or wine. In this example, even though the United States has an absolute advantage over France in the production of software, cars, and wine, American labor might be much more efficient (enjoying a large absolute advantage) than French labor at producing software but only a little more efficient (enjoying a small absolute advantage) in the production of automobiles or wine. Thus the United States would have a comparative advantage in the production of software.

For an example closer to home, assume that your class valedictorian will be better at most careers than the rest of her cohort. She has an absolute advantage over her colleagues whether she chooses law, business, physics, engineering, medicine, psychology, writing, or political science. But despite having an absolute advantage over her colleagues, she may find her abilities more suited to one career over another. This is her comparative advantage, as she fits all career choices better than her peers (her absolute advantage), but some more than others (her comparative advantage). Given the assumption of scarcity that underpins the approach to political economy in this book, and recognizing that her labor is a scarce resource, the valedictorian must make a choice among careers. She will do well in any career but better in some than in others.

The same scenario is true in the example comparing American and French labor. The American labor force is more productive than the French labor force, but there are a limited number of work hours in a week and therefore limits to the total number of work hours for a nation's workforce given the size of the working population. These factors are not easily manipulated—the size of the American or French labor force cannot be increased overnight. So, given these constraints on labor, what should American labor produce if it has an absolute advantage and can produce everything more efficiently than the French? Recall that in this example, American labor is far more efficient at producing software than at producing cars or wine. Such relative differences in efficiency within a nation's production capabilities and across nations for particular goods constitute the underpinnings of comparative advantage. They create the opportunity for trade to enhance economic welfare even for a nation that enjoys absolute advantage in producing every good. How can this be so?

By taking advantage of relative disparities in production costs (differences in the amount of labor needed to produce a unit of each commodity), a nation can enhance its aggregate welfare through **specialization** in the production of those products for which it has a greater comparative advantage and trading for those goods for which it has a lesser comparative advantage, even if there is an absolute advantage in all products. By specializing in those commodities with the greater comparative advantage (or smaller absolute disadvantage) and exporting those products, a nation's population can use the earnings from the exports to purchase products with a smaller comparative advantage and still have more of all commodities to consume. In the language of economics, a society

> **Specialization** is an economic practice whereby each producer does not attempt to produce the entire range of commodities, but rather produces a commodity or supplies a service in which she has a comparative advantage. **Consumption possibilities** are the consumption frontier for a nation; the maximum amount of economic goods that can be utilized in a society.

that engages in trade and takes advantage of specialization has expanded its **consumption possibilities.** The following brief hypothetical example illustrates the difference between absolute advantage and comparative advantage.

A Hypothetical Example of Absolute and Comparative Advantage

By the mid- to late 1800s, the cost of transport had declined dramatically, increasing the potential appeal of international exchange by significantly reducing the transaction costs.

For the purpose of simplicity in our example, we assume that such transaction costs are now negligible. Focusing on the production and exchange of two commodities, grain and textiles, between the United States and the United Kingdom, we use the labor theory of value—meaning that the value of a commodity is determined by its labor content—to price these commodities. This method of valuation simplifies our example and eliminates the need to adjust for different national currencies and their exchange rates, although the same relationships would hold using multiple currencies.

Before we begin to think about trade, let's examine what a single day of a worker's labor produces in each political economy, as shown in table 3.1. Our first conclusion is that the United States enjoys an absolute advantage in the production of both grain and textiles (cloth), because its labor force has higher productivity than British workers in both products—60 bushels of grain versus 20, and 20 yards of textiles versus 10. According to absolute advantage (the economic logic preceding David Ricardo's insight), the welfare of the United States cannot be improved by the nation's importing either of these commodities from the United Kingdom. Conversely, the United Kingdom can improve its social welfare by importing both of these products from the United States, but it must have earnings from exports to pay for these commodities, and our stylized model precludes production and trade in other commodities.

Now let's consider this same example through the lens of comparative advantage. First, we look for relative differences in the extent of the U.S. advantage in production across the two products. The United States enjoys a three-to-one advantage in grain production (60 versus 20 bushels) and a two-to-one advantage in textile production (20 versus 10 yards). Even though the United States enjoys an absolute advantage in producing both commodities, it has a greater relative advantage in the production of grain. U.S. labor is more efficient at producing grain than it is at producing textiles. The reverse is true for the United Kingdom: even though it has an absolute disadvantage in both products, its relative disadvantage is greater in the production of grain than in the production of textiles. Thus the United States has a comparative advantage in the production of grain, and the United Kingdom has a comparative advantage in the production of textiles.

We can illustrate these differences in relative advantage by pricing these commodities in relation to each other without considering trade. In the United States, 60 bushels of grain can

TABLE 3.1	A Hypothetical Exchange	
	Grain production per day	Textile production per day
United States	60 bushels	20 yards
United Kingdom	20 bushels	10 yards

purchase 20 yards of cloth—or 3 bushels of grain purchases 1 yard of cloth. In the United Kingdom, 20 bushels of grain can purchase 10 yards of cloth, or 2 bushels of grain purchases 1 yard of cloth. This means that textiles are cheaper in the United Kingdom than in the United States. Flipping the example to consider the price of grain in each political economy before trade, 1 yard of textile can purchase 3 bushels of grain in the United States but only 2 bushels in the United Kingdom. Grain is cheaper in the United States.

Here we begin to observe the potential gains from trade for both the United States and the United Kingdom, even though the United States enjoys an absolute advantage in the production of both commodities. Without international trade, a U.S. grain worker can use her 3 bushels to purchase 1 yard from a U.S. textile producer, but with international trade she can take her 3 bushels of grain and purchase 1.5 yards from a U.K. textile producer. U.S. consumers can still consume the same amount of grain they always consumed, but now they can also consume 50 percent more textiles—a clear improvement in their consumption possibilities and welfare despite the absolute advantage of the United States in the production of both commodities. Without international trade, a British textile worker can use her 1 yard to purchase 2 bushels from a U.K. grain producer, but with international trade she can use that same 1 yard to purchase 3 bushels from a U.S. grain producer. U.K. consumers can still consume the same amount of textiles they always consumed, but now they can also consume 50 percent more grain—a clear improvement in their consumption possibilities, caloric intake, and welfare.

A U.S. grain worker should be willing to engage and excited about the prospect of engaging in international trade with a British textile producer because it expands the amount of commodities she can consume for the same amount of labor, and the same is true of a U.K. textile worker. This is also true of consumers in both societies. This means that even with an absolute advantage, the United States can expand its consumption possibilities and welfare if it exports the product for which it enjoys a relatively greater production advantage and imports the product for which it enjoys a relatively smaller production advantage. Of course, this equation does not work to the advantage of grain producers in the United Kingdom or textile producers in the United States, both of whom will discover that their products are at a disadvantage against those of their foreign competitors, even though the U.S. textile producer enjoys an absolute advantage over the U.K. textile producer. Producers and workers in the grain sector in the United Kingdom and the textile sector in the United States will face uncomfortable choices about how to adjust to their lack of comparative advantage. The mechanism of international exchange thus creates incentives for U.S. textile producers to improve their efficiency and lower their prices vis-à-vis grain production, to shift away from textile production and toward grain production or some other form of production that enjoys a comparative advantage, or to appeal to the state and its control over political geography to intervene in the economic geography of trade even if such intervention creates costs for the broader society. The same is true for British grain producers.

Revisiting Factors of Production: Labor Theory of Value to Factor Endowment

Let's add an interesting twist, or economic innovation, to comparative advantage that will contribute to our understanding of the political economy of globalization. Ricardo's principle of comparative advantage, like the principle of absolute advantage it replaced, relied on a labor theory of value. Comparative advantage was defined as a favorable difference in the relative costs of production, which derived from a comparison of labor costs per unit of production across commodities. This approach does not explicitly consider other potential inputs to production, such as the availability of raw materials, climate, investment in training that might make labor more productive, or investment in research that might lead to discoveries that could transform production. In short, it ignores the other two factors of production, resources (land) and capital. These inputs are implicitly embedded in the labor theory of value, as they can make labor more productive, but they are not considered explicitly. Agricultural labor becomes more productive with good soil and adequate rainfall. Coal miners became more productive with the introduction of the steam engine and power drill. Bankers became more productive with the invention of savings, credit, and investment mechanisms. Textile manufacturers became more productive with the introduction of the water-powered mill and the power loom. They are able to produce more in less time.

David Ricardo was a financial broker, country gentleman, member of Parliament, journalist, and one of the foremost economic thinkers in history. His 1817 treatise *On the Principles of Political Economy and Taxation* articulated his famous theory of comparative advantage, which transformed thinking about international trade. In this treatise, Ricardo made other extraordinary contributions to economic theory: a labor theory of value and a theory of growth. Together these pieces formed a consistent approach to economics now known as the classical or Ricardian School of economics.

Factor Endowments and Heckscher-Ohlin

In the 1920s, two Swedish economists, Eli Heckscher and Bertil Ohlin, made more explicit the role of inputs other than labor. They transformed the principle of comparative advantage based on a labor theory of value into an economic principle based on differences across nations in their allocations of productive inputs—or factor endowments. Their approach, which became known as the **Heckscher-Ohlin model,** was later refined by other economists, most notably by Wolfgang Stolper and Paul Samuelson, in the Stolper-Samuelson theorem introduced in 1941.

> The **Heckscher-Ohlin model** is an economic framework that states that differences in factor endowments across nations produce comparative advantages. **Factor intensities** are the different quantities of the factors of production necessary to produce a commodity.

The Heckscher-Ohlin model emphasizes differences in the distribution of factors of production across national boundaries and builds on several propositions. First, commodities differ in the relative quantities of the factors that are necessary to produce them. We refer to these different quantity requirements as **factor intensities**—some use more capital, some more labor, and some more land. Producing airplanes, which requires more capital than producing corn, is a *capital-intensive* industry. Producing cotton, which requires more land than producing an accounting service, is *land-intensive.* Second, countries differ in their factor endowments. Some have more capital per laborer and some less; some have more capital per usable natural resource (land) and some less. Nations that have more labor relative to land are called *labor abundant.* Nations that are resource rich relative to their labor resources are called *land* or *resource abundant.* Nations with a lot of capital per laborer or relative to land are called *capital abundant.*

For example, the United States is capital and land abundant but labor poor. Despite its huge physical geography, China is labor abundant but land poor. China is currently undergoing a transition in its factor endowment, however, as it appears to be moving from being a capital-poor economy to a more capital-abundant economy. Mexico looks similar to China because it is labor abundant but land poor, and its capital intensity seems to be improving over time. Japan is capital and labor abundant but land poor. The imports and exports of a political economy provide important clues to its factor endowment and the relative scarcity or abundance of its inputs to economic production.

Given the conditions of supply and demand, abundant factors tend to be relatively less expensive inputs to production than are scarce factors. This difference in cost creates relative advantages and disadvantages across types of production, given differences in the factor intensities of products and the factor endowments of states. Differences in factor endowments interact with the differences in factor intensities across commodities and services to create comparative advantages between countries in producing different products and services. A country can benefit from international trade by specializing in the production of those commodities and services whose factor intensities match its factor endowments while trading for those products and services whose factor intensities fit less well with its factor endowments. This outcome, conditioned by the market, is the fundamental insight of the Heckscher-Ohlin model. With international trade, labor-abundant economies should specialize in production of labor-intensive commodities and export those in exchange for land-intensive commodities. Land-abundant economies should specialize in producing land-intensive products and export those in exchange for labor-intensive products. The same is true for capital—states with abundant capital will have a comparative advantage in producing commodities that are capital-intensive, whereas those states where capital is scarce will be at a comparative disadvantage trying to produce capital-intensive commodities.

The Stolper-Samuelson Extension

The **Stolper-Samuelson theorem** is an extension of the Heckscher-Ohlin model that recognizes that the liberalization of trade will benefit abundant factors of production in an economy.

The **Stolper-Samuelson theorem,** an extension of the Heckscher-Ohlin model, recognizes that the liberalization, or greater opening, of trade benefits the abundant factors of production in an economy. Such factors are in greater supply than are scarce factors of production, and, consequently, their prices as inputs to production will be relatively lower. Producers will be encouraged to employ lower-cost inputs to production, and those producers who require relatively higher-cost inputs will be penalized by market forces. Over time, the shift toward production that employs relatively abundant factors of production due to their lower costs will raise the relative prices of the abundant factors in an economy as demand for those factors increases, but not as fast as the costs of scarce factors of production. With more liberal trade, the price of capital will eventually increase in the capital-abundant economy, the price of labor will increase in the labor-abundant economy, and the cost of resources will increase in the land-abundant economy.

Over time, if there are no trade barriers, this dynamic will cause the prices of factors of production to converge across national boundaries. Conversely, increased barriers to trade will protect scarce factors of production from the competition of their abundant counter-parts located in other states, increase the costs of those factors, and reward relatively expensive and inefficient factors of production. The consequences of more or less liberal trade can spill over into political arenas by generating winners and losers from economic activity, influencing the preferences of those winners and losers, creating cleavages in society, and affecting those groups' capabilities to form coalitions along cleavage lines and influence political outcomes (see chapter 7).

Regardless of whether the mechanism of comparative advantage derives from a labor theory of value or from factor endowments, the gains from trade are based on the efficiency gains produced by specialization. The production possibilities in any state are bounded: a nation cannot produce petroleum by-products without oil, or a nuclear power plant without highly trained (capital-intensive) labor. But with trade and the resulting specialization in production, a nation's factor endowment is applied toward those forms of production in which it is most efficient. The resulting efficient use of resources leads to larger gains in what society can consume for the same amount of labor.

The logic that underpins Heckscher-Ohlin and modern trade theory also helps account for why corporations might invest in overseas operations and outsource employment, and why individuals might choose to migrate. Understanding that differences in factor endowments across states mean that the costs of production for any particular commodity or service can vary across states, and that the return to one's labor can vary across states, can provide significant insight as to why people, jobs, investment, and production cross borders. Employers that move production facilities and jobs offshore are often seeking more cost-effective means of production. Workers who migrate are generally seeking better wages, working conditions, and opportunities. People rarely relocate for less income and less opportunity. The individual incentives created by differences in factor endowments help account for overseas investment, location of production facilities abroad, outsourcing of jobs, and migratory patterns. In macroeconomic terms, this leads to a more efficient use of the inputs of production given the wants and preferences of those who constitute the global marketplace. This helps demonstrate why trade, outsourcing, overseas investment, and migration might be considered policy substitutes at the macro level. But at the micro or individual level—within political economies, communities, and families—these processes can distribute their effects quite differently. Some individuals, families, communities, and societies may reap rewards, whereas others suffer hardships.

The Balance of Payments: Regulating Trade and Capital Flows in the Global Political Economy

How can the zero-sum claims discussed at the beginning of this section on trade mechanisms persist and thrive in the face of economic theory and facts? Such claims survive because they are politically useful: they help protect people from change and take advantage of people's fears and distrust of foreigners. Antitrade and antiglobalization arguments build and depend on poor understandings of how international exchange works and the central role of the **balance of payments** in international exchange. The balance-of-payments mechanism sits at the heart of international exchange, where it serves as a giant thermostat, regulating and equilibrating trade and capital flows in the international political economy.

> A **balance of payments** is an accounting of all the goods, services, and capital exported and imported across national borders, reflecting a nation's economic interactions with those in other nations.

The balance of payments reflects a nation's economic interactions with other nations. It is an accounting of all the goods, services, and capital exported and imported across national borders. In economic theory, the balance of payments tends toward a long-run equilibrium whereby, over time, a nation's imports will balance out exports, and vice versa. Such an outcome may not be reached in any particular year or over a limited number of years, but over many years the balance of payments will tend toward equilibrium. This balance-of-payments equilibrium is not a description of the relationship between any two political economies but of the relationship of any political economy with the rest of the system. The balance-of-payments mechanism is divided into two primary categories: the current account and the capital account.

The Current Account

The **current account** is a part of the balance-of-payments account that comprises the imports and exports of goods, services, and several ancillary items.

The **current account** describes the import and export of goods, services, and several ancillary items. It tells us about the effect of a state's domestic demand on production and employment beyond the state's borders and about the influence of foreign consumption on a state's employment and production within its borders. A surplus in the current account means that the state is exporting more goods and services than it imports, which results in an inflow of capital based on the net difference between imports and exports. A deficit in the current account means that the state imports more goods and services than it exports, which produces an outflow of capital.

When someone in the United States purchases a BMW manufactured in Germany, the U.S. current account is debited and Germany's current account is credited; when a U.S. firm purchases the services and banking advice of Deutsche Bank, the U.S. current account is debited and Germany's current account is credited; when a German travel agency purchases the services of a U.S. tour agency, the U.S. current account is credited and the German current account is debited; and when a student from Germany studies at a U.S. university, the U.S. current account is credited and the German current account is debited. Credits constitute foreign obligations and payments to domestic factors of production; debits represent domestic obligations and payments to foreign factors of production. Credits fuel employment in the domestic arena, while debits create jobs abroad.

Credits and debits create demand for currencies. Foreigners who owe U.S. producers obligations—credits in the U.S. current account—need to obtain U.S. dollars to pay off those claims, which creates a foreign demand for U.S. dollars. Conversely, U.S. firms or citizens with foreign obligations—debits in the U.S. current account—must obtain foreign currencies to pay those claims, which creates a domestic demand for those foreign currencies. Much of this currency exchange goes unobserved, even by those purchasing the foreign goods or services. The American who purchases the German-made BMW does not actually obtain euros to pay for that purchase, for most transactions take place in the domestic currency of the location where the transaction occurs. However, a behind-the-scenes settlement process for such international transactions places demands for currencies to settle international obligations. We will quickly see the importance of this process as the supply and demand for currencies affect the prices of different nations' goods and services, influencing demand and providing a tremendous equilibrating force in the balance-of-payments mechanism.

The Capital Account

The **capital account** comprises capital inflows and outflows related primarily to investment at home and abroad, not consumption. Such investments fall into several different categories. **Foreign direct investment (FDI)** is investment in the control of productive facilities overseas—whether full control or only partial control. FDI is defined as a significant ownership position—a 10 percent stake or greater—in a company abroad. FDI occurs when Ford builds a production facility in Mexico, BMW constructs a factory in the United States, IBM opens a semiconductor plant in Thailand, or the Swiss firm Nestlé purchases the Ralston Purina Company in St. Louis, Missouri.

The other major component in the capital account is **portfolio investment,** which does not create control of an overseas facility, as does FDI. This is defined as a stake of less than 10 percent in an entity abroad. Credits or debits in the portfolio category include the sale or purchase of foreign stocks and bonds (financial instruments and obligations), borrowing from a foreign bank, and lending capital to foreign borrowers. Again, credits and debits reflect obligations of foreign parties to domestic parties or of domestic parties to foreign parties. These obligations translate into foreign demands for the domestic currency, or domestic demands for foreign currencies, when it is time to square accounts.

> The **capital account** is a part of the balance-of-payments account that comprises capital inflows and outflows related primarily to investment at home and abroad. **Foreign direct investment (FDI)** is investment in control of productive facilities overseas—usually defined by an investment that amounts to control of 10 percent or more of a company's equity. **Portfolio investment** is investment that amounts to less than 10 percent of equity in a firm, which ensures that investors cannot exercise any control over the firm; a major component in the capital account that does not create control of an overseas facility.

Long-Term Equilibrium and the Exchange-Rate Mechanism

The **exchange-rate mechanism (ERM),** determining the value of one currency versus another, provides a means of adjustment in the balance-of-payments mechanism and its equilibrating tendency. A state's currency is its face to the global economy and contains important information about the stability and efficacy of the state's government, its macroeconomic condition, and the demands on its producers and the wants of its consumers. Unfortunately, reading such information is not always easy. How does the changing demand for currencies, necessary to settle the obligations reflected in the balance of payments, generate equilibrating pressures on the balance of payments and affect the flow of goods, services, and capital over time? In the mid-1700s, David Hume provided the intellectual underpinnings for explaining why the flow of goods, services, and capital across national boundaries would tend toward a balance in the long run, with some years in deficit and some years in surplus but always returning toward a balance. Hume's writings on "specie flow," the flow of money, provided elegant and powerful insights grounded in a quantity theory of money. Hume viewed money as a commodity that is exposed to the forces of supply and demand—demands such as the need to meet foreign obligations. Simply, if a nation's

> The **exchange-rate mechanism (ERM)** is the mechanism that determines the value of one currency versus another and provides a means of adjustment in the balance-of-payments mechanism.

domestic money supply decreases because of the need to purchase foreign monies to fulfill foreign obligations, as accounted in the balance of payments, there is less domestic money to purchase goods and services or to pay labor in the domestic market. This reduced money supply puts downward pressure on the prices of domestic goods, services, and labor, as there is less money to go around. This decreased supply of money in circulation is the primary cause of price deflation in a political economy. Hume's 1753 essay "Of the Balance of Trade" provides a nice mental example:

> Suppose four-fifths of all the money in Great Britain to be annihilated in one night, . . . what would be the consequence? Must not the price of all labour and commodities sink in proportion and everything be sold *cheap*[*er*]? (emphasis added)

Conversely, if a state's balance of payments is in surplus—exports exceeding imports—foreigners must obtain that country's currency to meet their obligations. This situation results in a repatriation of the national money, which increases the supply of the state's currency in the home market and leaves less abroad. With an increase in the supply of domestic money, prices of domestic commodities, services, and labor can increase. This increased supply of money in circulation is the primary cause of price inflation in a political economy. Or, as Hume went on to hypothesize:

> Suppose that all the money in Great Britain were multiplied fivefold in a night, must not . . . all labour and commodities rise to such an exorbitant height . . . ?

Contractions in domestic money supplies in states experiencing balance-of-payments deficits are accompanied by increases in money supplies of those states experiencing balance-of-payments surpluses. As expansion of the money supply in those surplus countries produces an increase in the prices of their domestic goods, services, and labor, those products and services increase in price in overseas markets also. This increase in prices, at home and abroad, then leads to a decrease in the attractiveness of the products and services relative to those produced overseas in nations experiencing balance-of-payments deficits. Put together, prices related to domestic production fall in states experiencing balance-of-payments deficits because of the shrinking quantity of money, whereas prices related to domestic production rise in nations experiencing balance-of-payments surpluses because of the expanding quantity of money. Prices of domestic goods and services become comparatively cheaper than foreign goods and services in the deficit states but comparatively more expensive in the surplus states. This relative shift in the prices of goods and services produced overseas versus those produced at home enters into the calculations of consumers possessing limited resources. It shifts their consumption choices and puts self-correcting pressure on the balance of payments.

This money flow lies at the heart of the international trading system. States experiencing balance-of-payment deficits or surpluses will incur changes in domestic money supplies that, over time, produce changes in domestic prices in relation to foreign prices, which lead to changes in consumption of domestic versus foreign goods and services. This ongoing process generates a pendulum effect in the balance of payments—deficit to surplus, surplus to deficit, and on and on. Many refinements and discoveries have been appended to Hume's specie flow model since the 1700s, but the basic mechanism still applies. Changes in the quantity of money, and the resulting changes in prices of domestic goods and labor, result in a self-correcting balance-of-payments mechanism. If the shrinkage in domestic money supply produces a decline in a country's prices for domestic goods, services, and labor, the country's products and services decline in price in overseas markets also. A decrease in these prices, at home and abroad, then leads to an increase in the attractiveness of the products and services relative to those produced by overseas producers, all else being equal.

But, of course, everything else is not equal. Governments—again, the nation-state political geography—can distort this process by growing or shrinking money supply independent of the balance-of-payments mechanism. A variety of motivations apart from trade can drive policy makers to use monetary policy to increase or decease their national money supplies, and in so doing they may go against the discipline of market forces that are produced by the global economic geography, in effect *sterilizing* the consequences of those market forces. In practice such monetary manipulations will have similar influences on price inflation or deflation with the increase or decrease of money supply related to trade, but for very different motivations. Policies that manipulate money supply in the domestic arena, independent of the equilibrating mechanism of the balance of trade, have international consequences in a globalized economic geography as they are transmitted abroad through the exchange-rate mechanism and other processes of financial integration, outsourcing, and multinational operations. Some of these consequences can be quite market distorting and are capable of imposing significant benefits or costs on other societies.

THE ROLE OF FINANCIAL INVENTION AND INTEGRATION IN EXPANDING GLOBAL CAPITALISM

One important process of global capitalism has been the ongoing invention and integration of financial mechanisms and markets. This includes the creation of money, the acceptance of money as a tool of exchange, the evolution of stable currencies, the development of exchange-rate mechanisms that translate the value of one currency into another currency, the invention of mechanisms of credit that expand the pool of capital available for investment and growth, the development of financial markets involving increasing investment across national boundaries, and the deepening and increasing diversity of those financial markets within and across national borders. Without the invention of such processes and instruments, states' abilities to trade across borders and to manage the risks associated with such trade would be severely limited, and so consequently would be the globalization of relations in which activities within one state become increasingly tied to activities in another state. Moreover, without the invention and advance of such financial processes and instruments, development and economic advancement in societies would be limited by the capital that could be raised within individual states' borders. With global financial integration, societies can enjoy expanded access to a critical input to economic development beyond national borders. Let's quickly consider some of the mechanisms that underpin the process of financial integration: money, investment, financial innovation and market development, and the increasing diversity and depth of the global financial network based on those markets.

Money: A Functional Approach

Money is any medium of exchange that can store value and serve as a unit of accounting and exchange. A national money helps to create a bond between users of this currency and their state. **Credit** is the delayed payment for the exchange of resources, goods, or services. It involves the promise of payment at a future date for a transaction that takes place at an earlier time and includes any type of deferred payment. This makes exchanges possible even if the consumer of the goods being exchanged does not have the resources to pay for the goods at the time of the exchange. This expands the range of exchange over time and creates the opportunity for more economic activity and growth, as individuals and societies are able to consume beyond their immediate constraints.

An examination of modern economic activity within and across national boundaries reveals the importance of **money** and **credit**.[1] Before the use of money and credit, exchange was defined by barter—that is, the exchange of goods or services for other goods or services. The bartering process imposed significant transaction costs and created barriers to exchange. The invention of money and credit revolutionized exchange. Exchange by means of money and credit was far more efficient than barter and helped stimulate the growth of exchange over time and space. To understand why requires asking, What is money? The answer to that question may appear obvious to anyone who carries bills and coins in a wallet, purse, or pocket, but the idea of what constitutes money is actually much more sophisticated and nuanced. Money can be anything—physical, legal, or conceptual—that performs several key functions: it serves as a tool of exchange, as a storehouse of value, and as a unit of accounting.

A Tool of Exchange

As a tool of exchange, money serves as a means of payment, a device to meet the contractual obligations of an exchange. This method differs from a traditional barter economy, in which people exchange one commodity for another commodity—a bushel of corn for two chickens, a basket of beans for a pail of paint, a gallon of fuel for a pair of jeans. With barter, each party to an exchange must actually want or need the other's commodity if the trade is

---

[1]This section draws on the discussion in Benjamin J. Cohen, *The Geography of Money* (Ithaca, NY: Cornell University Press, 1998).

to occur. The owner of the corn must want the chickens, and the owner of the chickens must desire the corn. Exchange would not occur without the coincidence of these mutual wants. Further, both parties must be in the right place at the right time. Consequently, barter is a relatively inefficient form of exchange, as it can occur only if the farmer with chickens happens to want corn and finds a farmer with corn who happens to want chickens.

Money eliminates the inefficiencies of barter by removing the need for each party to coincidentally want the other party's commodity. Instead, one party can sell its commodity and, with no immediate consumption need for another commodity, wait for another time to make a consumption decision. Money breaks the single barter transaction into multiple transactions and expands the number of parties potentially engaged in such transactions over time and space.

A Storehouse of Value

In order to serve as a means of payment to replace barter, money must come to be a storehouse of value. Successful money holds its value over time, maintains its purchasing power over time, and is recognized as having those properties over time by contracting parties. Money takes on value and holds value over time when a social grouping bestows that quality upon it by means of common agreement and understanding among the members of the group. This stockpiling of value in money may involve voluntary agreement among the group members (a market solution), or it may result from nonvoluntary imposition and enforcement of a common understanding (a government solution). For example, in the 1700s and early 1800s societies were awash in many different monies—private and public. Banks issued their own monies, governments issued monies, and sometimes other organizations created monies (again, the term includes anything that serves as a tool of exchange, a storehouse of value, and a unit of accounting). As governments defined particular monies as legal tender—meaning that they could be used to settle claims and had special standing in courts of law—the numbers of different monies in societies decreased. Some monies lost value and others gained or remained stable in value. Many of those that lost value disappeared. Government monies were usually empowered by a definition of legal tender that led to their increasing use and a squeezing out of private monies. Yet private monies still exist and continue to be used. Some examples include airline points (or frequent-flier miles), credit card rewards points, and private-party coupons such as Groupon and the shopping cents-off coupons that are often found in Sunday newspapers.

Not all governments' currencies are equal in terms of their ability to store value, and consequently such currencies are not all equal as tools of exchange. Even though we recognize that governments are functionally equal (they all tend to issue some form of money, just as they all endeavor to provide national security, adjudication and enforcement of law, and other government services), we can observe a wide range of capability in the performance of their functions. The same is true for money. Some governments are more successful than others at creating and maintaining money that holds value over time, and consequently is preferred as a tool of exchange. A national currency conveys all sorts of information to actors in the global political economy about the government's capacity to manage macroeconomic conditions, to affect economic and political volatility, and to support a sound and stable currency. A state's currency—how it behaves and how others in the international arena employ that currency—provides information about the government's capacity, or its power. A state's currency can be viewed as the face of the state's political economy to the global arena. Governments often limit the use of other states' currencies within their national borders, as a matter of sovereignty, but the ability of a state to dictate what currency is used in international exchange is far more limited. During different eras of global capitalism, parties to cross-border exchange have come to prefer specific currencies. During the late 1500s and the 1600s, traders involved in international exchange preferred using the Dutch guilder or financial instruments denominated in guilders for international transactions. During the 1700s and 1800s, financial instruments denominated in British pounds replaced the guilder as the preferred currency of international transactions. Since the end of World War II, the U.S. dollar has assumed the mantle of the currency preferred for international transactions. Today, the dollar is still the heavily preferred currency for international transactions. The European Union's euro and the Japanese yen are a distant second and third in terms of international usage.

Money that maintains purchasing power over time and is commonly recognized by different parties permits immediate barter transactions to be broken into multiple transactions over time. It also expands the size of the market, allowing individuals to go from trading mostly with those they know and trust to being able to trade with those of no acquaintance. With the use of money, the owner of the chickens does not have to trade for bushels of corn to rid herself of her chickens; she can sell her chickens and then wait to purchase something she prefers to corn. She can exchange her chickens for money and know that the money will be good at some later time because it stores value. This practice limits her risk and uncertainty about the person to whom she sells her chickens. Money as a storehouse of value expands the range of economic activity, improves consumption possibilities by expanding the time horizon of economic transactions, and creates greater efficiencies as people purchase only what they want.

A Unit of Accounting

Finally, if money serves as a tool of exchange and a storehouse of value, it must come to hold some commonly agreed-upon value. This definition imbues it with the ability to serve as a unit of accounting for the valuation of goods, services, and wealth. We can record output, property values, and labor costs by means of a common accounting standard even when we are not trading. Such a means of accounting provides a way to compare the economic activity of yesterday with that of today, and then again with that of tomorrow. It allows us to assess differences across economic activities. Measurement and accounting are integral to modern economic activity.

Exchange-Rate Mechanisms

Exchange across national boundaries involves a variety of monies. This can complicate international trade, and if enough uncertainty exists about the value of one money for another, a breakdown in trade can result. One may exchange one currency for another, one state's money for another, to manage the barriers to transactions across national boundaries and in different currencies. Effectively this means treating currencies as commodities and trying to estimate the value of one for another. This involves what is called an exchange-rate mechanism (ERM)—a strategy or device for estimating the value of one currency for another or a currency's exchange rate in terms of another currency or commodity such as gold or silver. ERMs can emerge in a variety of ways. They might be produced by international agreement among governments, be created by the law of supply and demand in currency markets, or simply emerge as a consequence of convergence on common usage between private actors engaged in exchange.

Expanding Access to a Larger Pool of Capital

The globalization of financial relations involves the processes that lead to increasing capital mobility across national borders and the global integration of national capital market mechanisms. These produce a global financial network, which is the nervous system of the global economy. Increasing capital mobility, the opening of national borders to capital flows, is the result of national governments making choices not to limit the inflow or outflow of capital. Just as governments can intervene in international trade by adopting protectionist policies to impose the political geography of the state on the economic geography of markets, they can also intervene in the processes of accumulation, allocation, and flow of capital among savers, investors, and borrowers across state borders. Governments have the ability to impose capital controls that limit the inflow and outflow of capital. They can limit access to who can purchase foreign currencies, impose taxes on international capital flows to discourage such movements, require citizens to surrender foreign monies, and use law and regulation to constrain financial institutions from moving capital across borders. Policy makers who impose such controls may do so for a variety of reasons: to limit volatility in their local economies, to manage money supply, and to limit the outflow of capital and encourage investment in economic enterprise at home, among others. Today we live in a period when most governments have decided not to impose significant controls on the global movement of capital, but this has not always been the case. In the years immediately following World War II, the majority of governments imposed some form of capital controls as they sought to rebuild economic infrastructure and productive capacities that had been ravaged by war. In many states, such controls lasted until the 1980s. Conversely, the pre–World War I period saw only limited attempts to restrict the international flow of capital. So the changes in international financial integration and changes in capital controls are not unidirectional.

A decline in barriers to international capital flows increases opportunities for savers and borrowers. Borrowers that can operate across national borders find a larger pool of capital that they can access, and potentially at lower costs. Ideally, this adds to their economic efficiency by lowering their costs and enabling them to do more with their resources. Borrowing in capital markets abroad is principally an activity of governments, large firms and other organizations, and financial institutions. Yet individuals such as you and me may be unknowingly accessing the larger pool of global capital if our local financial institutions use global capital markets to obtain the capital to make our student loans, car loans, mortgages, and other loans. An increase in capital mobility and market integration across borders also provides savers and investors with expanded opportunities to diversify their financial investments and their risks. State boundaries, public policies, and state-specific activities separate national economies. These contribute to differences in economic outcomes across states. Some have higher growth rates than others, some have better rule of law and respect for economic contracts than others, some have better-educated and -socialized workforces than others, some are more corrupt than others, some have better infrastructure than others, and some produce more highly valued commodities than do others. Such differences create the potential for different rates of return on investment and different levels of risk to investment. By lowering barriers to international capital mobility and increasing global financial integration, investors and savers are able to enlarge their search for places to put their capital to work, to find opportunities that meet different levels of risk tolerance, and to diversify their risks and investments. If done well, diversifying investments across national boundaries can reduce volatility and increase rewards.

Such activities increase global financial integration, creating networks that link national economies. Often this is productive and leads to a more efficient use of capital resources and greater economic gains. Yet these networks can also transmit shocks and dislocations from one political economy to another. A financial failure in one country might act as a contagion and transmit financial distress to other countries. In 1983 an inability by several developing governments to continue paying for financial obligations they incurred in New York, London, Paris, and other financial markets quickly spread to other countries. This situation, which became known as the Third World Debt Crisis, threatened the stability of banks in the major international financial centers and consequently increased the costs of capital worldwide. In 1997 a currency crisis that began in one Southeast Asian political economy quickly spread to other political economies in that region as traders in private global currency markets challenged governments' abilities to maintain the value of their currencies. Numerous governments were forced to devalue their currencies significantly. Because of the change in the price of their national currencies vis-à-vis the dollar, students from Taiwan, Korea, and other countries who were attending universities in the United States found that their tuition bills almost doubled overnight. In 2007 and 2008 a financial crisis in the United States, the center of global financial integration, quickly spread through the networks of global financial integration to other political economies. Major financial institutions in Europe faced insolvency because of their investments in U.S. financial instruments that went bad. The global economy slowed and went into recession as a consequence of this financial crisis.

These examples demonstrate the contagion possibilities of financial distress in a world of increased financial integration. This does not mean that global financial integration is bad, just that it is not always good. Global financial integration and diversification have benefits and costs just as do any other social processes, and those costs and benefits should be considered and weighed. Global financial integration and diversification can increase access to capital and lower its cost for economic activities that generate employment, improve quality of life, raise living standards, and potentially transform communities for the better. The very same processes, however, connect markets and societies in unpredictable ways that can spread distress across communities. This suggests that we should recognize the gains that can derive from financial globalization, as with the other processes driving globalization, but also remain cautious about the potential costs of such integration. It also accounts for much of the political debate that swirls around the topic of financial globalization.

LABOR MOBILITY: CREATING LINKAGES ACROSS STATE BORDERS

Most people in the world live near where they were born and raised, or move within a fairly limited geography. With industrialization and the increasing sophistication of economic enterprise, the largest movement of populations has been from rural to urban areas. Despite romantic depictions of noble, rugged individuals working the land, huge numbers of people have left their agricultural communities to move to urban areas in search of economic opportunities. This pattern is most pronounced in advanced industrialized societies, but we can observe such population transitions to some extent in almost all states. This is a function of the changing patterns of the geography of economic activity. Yet, with a few noteworthy exceptions, this physical relocation of people has taken place overwhelmingly within political economies and not across state borders.

During the 1800s and early 1900s people did migrate in great numbers from state to state, first from Eastern Europe to Western Europe, and then most often from the Old World to the New World. Changes in transportation and economic conditions spurred large movements of people. Irish, Polish, Italian, Norwegian, Jewish, Chinese, and other peoples left their communities and moved in great numbers to the New World. They moved primarily to seek better economic opportunities, and they helped drive the rapid economic expansion of the New World. Migration motivated by economic gain is self-limiting. People seeking improved economic outcomes will move to those environs where they believe such opportunities exist and will stop when such opportunities cease. But some people who migrated to the New World during this period had noneconomic motives. Some moved to be with family, others to avoid religious discrimination, and others to gain political and civil liberties; some were forcibly relocated as slaves. Few state prohibitions inhibited the movement of people during this period. Such movements were relatively limited before the 1800s because of the high costs of travel and the limited wealth of those seeking to migrate, not because of any state limitations on migration. In the early 1900s, states began erecting legal obstacles to the flow of people across their borders—passports, visas, quotas, tax penalties, and others. This shows the tension between the economic geography of global capitalism, which increased the mobility of labor across borders, and the political geography of the state, which now sought to control such flows.

Migration continues today and has a significant influence on the economic future of communities, because immigrants can bring new skills and energy that can spark development or they can impose costs as they place costly demands on their new communities and their presence creates tension. Contentious political debates concerning immigration tend to focus attention on the latter, but the former generally has been a more significant force. It depends on who the immigrants are, their skills and education, their age and health, and a variety of other factors that can affect what they bring to or take from a society.

Migration has been the typical means of relocating labor inputs to production, but it is just one form of labor mobility across national borders. Employers can move labor abroad by shifting production abroad and moving their workers overseas. For example, U.S. oil companies that bored wells in the Middle East often did so with workers from places such as Texas and Oklahoma. Another form of relocating work abroad but not actually moving workers across state borders is outsourcing, in which the location of the job moves but the worker does not. This often reduces labor inputs in the country from which the job is moved (a nice way of saying workers are let go) and increases labor inputs in the country to which the job is moved (new workers are hired). Examples of outsourcing include establishing customer-service call centers for U.S. companies in India and opening laboratories across borders to hire scientists and researchers from other states. The process of moving jobs abroad has been made simpler in the past few decades by technological advances in travel, communication, and information processing. Just as with investment abroad, organizations move labor abroad or outsource labor for a variety of reasons: to access labor with particular skills, to lower the costs of production, to access markets abroad, to take advantage of different time zones and workdays, to access raw materials and resources, and to avoid tax and regulatory requirements, among other reasons.

The changes in labor mobility over the past several centuries, from migration to multinational relocation of production facilities and offices to outsourcing, reflect the increasing sophistication, diversification, and linkage of labor markets across state borders. As with the other major processes of globalization, the mobility of labor and the integration and diversification of labor markets across state boundaries has benefits and costs. Such integration and diversification can increase access to labor and lower its costs for economic activities that generate employment, improve quality of life, raise living standards, and potentially transform communities for the better. Yet the very same processes connect markets and societies in ways that can also generate unemployment and distress within communities. This suggests that we should recognize the gains that can derive from such processes of globalization but also remain cautious about the potential costs and how societies might address those costs. These conflicting potentials help account for the ongoing political debates around the issues of migration, relocation of production facilities abroad, and outsourcing.

CONCLUSION

David Ricardo's principle of comparative advantage overcame major obstacles to international exchange. Ricardo's insight transformed thinking about international exchange and led policy makers to reconsider the gains and losses from international exchange. The concept of comparative advantage showed that all sides could gain from the expansion of trade and the specialization of production—that trade is a positive-sum, not a zero-sum, relationship regardless of absolute advantage. Ricardo's discovery, combined with Hume's insights about the relationship of prices to monetary flows based on exchange, underpins our understanding about the benefits of international economic exchange and the balancing mechanism that regulates such exchange. The recognition of the benefits of international exchange advanced by Ricardo and by scores of later economists—a recognition that is well supported by empirical research and has become accepted orthodoxy in economics—leads to predictions and prescriptions about the policies that liberal political economies should pursue.

Our analytic frameworks should allow us to describe the characteristics of a liberal system and to predict what we should observe, given the expectations that arise from our understanding of liberal economic exchange. First, if market exchange leads to maximum economic growth, efficiency, and the greatest advances in aggregate economic welfare, we should expect that policy makers in a liberal political economy who value such outcomes will pursue policies that encourage greater market exchange in the domestic arena. Such policies should produce the greatest level of satisfaction in their polities. Therefore, we should expect to see policies in the domestic arena that promote, rather than obstruct, market exchange. We should expect politics and economics to remain separate arenas except in those areas in which public policy could help to promote market exchange—as in defining property rights, adjudicating and enforcing contracts, promoting disclosure so that buyers and sellers are equally well-informed about the products being exchanged, ensuring competitive markets, and managing other forces that could undermine market exchange.

Next, if promoting market exchange in the domestic arena is good, then expanding such exchange to take advantage of specialization and discipline in larger and larger markets would be better. If aggregate social welfare is enhanced by market exchange because the invisible hand coordinates the use of factors of production given society's wants and desires, then coordinating larger and larger pools of factors of production should only increase the efficiency of the invisible hand and the overall satisfaction of society. Policy makers in liberal political economies should seek to promote greater trade and exchange across borders, regardless of the actions of other states' policy makers. They should seek to lower barriers to entry at home and abroad because increased market exchange enhances the social welfare of their populations, and they should enact such policies unilaterally if others do not. From a liberal perspective, if other states' policy makers choose to maintain discriminatory barriers to trade, they are only hurting their own populations—which is no reason for liberal policy makers to adopt similar policy stances and detract from the social welfare of their own polities.

What about conflict in an international political economy based on liberal market exchange? Chapter 2 notes that conflict may be an inherent component of a global political economy built around nation-states as the dominant form of political organization. Does economic liberalism produce the same expectations? Since benefits are distributed in a liberal international political economy in a way that is mutually beneficial—a positive-sum scenario wherein the absolute gains are positive for those adopting liberal economic policies—should we expect any degree of inherent conflict or persistent cleavage in the international political economy? On a theoretical level, should rational policy makers adopt nonliberal policies that are detrimental to the social welfare of their society? The answer appears to be no; there is no basis in liberal economic theory for such policies. Greater interdependence leads to increased welfare for societies engaged in more open exchange. This social welfare argument for interconnectedness provides the foundation for expectations that interdependence increases harmony and reduces tensions between countries, regardless of the nation-state system.

In *On the Principles of Political Economy and Taxation,* David Ricardo posed just such a benevolent and harmonious view of trade and globalization:

> Under a system of perfectly free commerce, each country naturally devotes its capital and labour to such employments as are most beneficial to each. The pursuit of individual advantage is admirably connected with the universal good of the whole. By stimulating industry, by rewarding ingenuity, and by using most efficaciously the peculiar powers bestowed by nature, it distributes labour most effectively and most economically: while, by increasing the general mass of productions, it diffuses general benefit, and binds together, by one common tie of interest and intercourse, the universal society of nations throughout the civilized world.

Expectations of enhanced social welfare from increased interdependence lead to expectations about the policies of governments toward trade with other states and about the nature of international politics. In an international arena dominated by market exchange and liberal rules of the game in economic interactions, we should expect politics and economics to remain separate arenas except in those areas in which public policy can help to promote international exchange and interdependence. As a large component of any political arena, economic welfare should encourage cooperative international political relations and public policies to reflect a benign rather than a malevolent interdependence. As in domestic political arenas, we should expect policy makers to enact policies between states that promote greater trade and exchange across borders. Conflict can interrupt such relations, so we should expect policies that reduce rather than exacerbate international tensions.

What is the purpose of international organizations such as the International Monetary Fund, the World Bank, the World Trade Organization, the United Nations, the World Health Organization, and numerous other multilateral development organizations? What types of policies and frameworks should we expect to see such organizations promote? What is their role? From a liberal economic perspective, we should expect to see such organizations encouraging discussions, debates, and policies that would promote interdependence and international exchange. They should be constructive mechanisms for providing infrastructure advantageous to exchange across borders and for helping to reduce barriers to the coordination that would aid such exchange. Certainly, some barriers to exchange across borders are more difficult to circumvent than those within borders, for different states have different rules about private property and the exchange of property, different notions of contracts, different rules of adjudication and enforcement, and different monetary systems. These differences can produce barriers to exchange, even unintentionally. From a liberal economic perspective, international organizations can help by addressing such problems and influencing governments to adopt policies that will enhance their societies' social welfare.

The expectations just described are consistent with a liberal economic framework. To summarize, if markets work as anticipated in economic theory, we should expect to see particular forms of political behavior in domestic and international arenas. From a liberal economic perspective, we should expect the following behaviors:

- Policy makers pursue policies that encourage greater market exchange in their domestic arenas.
- Politics and economics remain separate domestic arenas except in those areas in which public policy could help to promote market exchange.
- Policy makers enact policies that promote greater trade and exchange across borders, regardless of the actions of other states' policy makers.
- Greater interdependence produces increased harmony and reduced tension between nations.
- Politics and economics remain separate arenas in international relations except in those areas in which public policy could help to promote international exchange and interdependence.
- International organizations are constructive mechanisms for provision of infrastructure advantageous to economic exchange across national borders and reduction of barriers to coordination that would aid such exchange.

These expectations provide a baseline, or yardstick, for evaluating market exchange and government policies in the global political economy, for considering the strengths and limitations of such theories, and for determining when such theories approximate empirical behavior and when (and why) they do not. So why do we observe protectionist policies, obstructions to the international mobility of capital, limits to migration, and virulent criticisms of outsourcing, international trade, multinational corporations, international investment, and migration in avowedly liberal political economies? This question is the focus of the next chapter.

KEY CONCEPTS

absolute advantage (p. 121)

balance of payments (p. 129)

capital (p. 116)

capital account (p. 131)

comparative advantage (p. 122)

competitive markets (p. 113)

consumption possibilities (p. 123)

credit (p. 134)

current account (p. 130)

demand (p. 114)

efficiency (p. 118)

exchange-rate mechanism (ERM) (p. 131)

factor endowment (p. 116)

factor intensities (p. 127)

factors of production (p. 116)

foreign direct investment (FDI) (p. 131)

glasnost (p. 113)

Heckscher-Ohlin model (p. 127)

invisible hand (p. 115)

labor (p. 116)

labor theory of value (p. 121)

land (p. 116)

money (p. 134)

portfolio investment (p. 131)

price mechanism (p. 114)

production possibilities curve (p. 119)

productivity gains (p. 118)

self-interest (p. 114)

specialization (p. 123)

Stolper-Samuelson theorem (p. 128)

supply (p. 114)

EXERCISES

1. What is the role of preferences in a competitive market? What do preferences have to do with self-interest?

2. Explain how the three functions of money are at work when you save your earnings from a part-time job and use them to buy your favorite music.

3. Why are international monetary arrangements important to international trade?

4. Explain how a deficit in your nation's current account affects workers and producers in another country.

5. Nations differ in their factor endowments, or distribution of the factors of production, which means that they are comparatively rich in some factor or factors but lacking in other factor(s). From what you know, or using resources in your school's library or on the Internet, describe

the factor endowments for Russia and for Denmark. In each case, which factors are relatively abundant and which are relatively scarce?

6. Explain the difference between absolute advantage and comparative advantage.

7. What is the long-term tendency of the balance-of-payment mechanism? Why?

FURTHER READING

Caves, Richard E., Jeffrey A. Frankel, and Ronald W. Jones. 2002. *World Trade and Payments.* 9th ed. Boston: Little, Brown.

Cohen, Benjamin J. 1998. *The Geography of Money.* Ithaca, NY: Cornell University Press.

Hume, David. (1741) 1987. "Of the Balance of Trade," in *Essays, Moral, Political, and Literary.* Reprint, Indianapolis: Liberty Fund.

———. (1752) 1906. *Political Discourses.* Reprint, New York: Walter Scott.

Kenen, Peter. 2000. *The International Economy.* 4th ed. Cambridge: Cambridge University Press.

Krugman, Paul. 1999. *Pop Internationalism.* Cambridge: MIT Press.

Ricardo, David. (1817) 1996. *The Principles of Political Economy and Taxation.* Reprint, Amherst, NY: Prometheus Books.

Roberts, Russell. 2001. *The Choice: A Fable of Free Trade and Protectionism.* Upper Saddle River, NJ: Prentice Hall.

Part II
Micro Tools

The Micro Approach to Political and Economic Markets in Theory and Practice

This chapter and the rest of Part II construct a microfoundation for the concepts and frameworks raised in the preceding three chapters. The discussion in this section will help us understand how individuals, groups, and societies arrive at their choices and actions that lead to the good and bad social outcomes that we observe in the international political economy.

Most of the time we do the right thing if we have enough information and enough time to think about it.

—*President Bill Clinton, Riverside Church, New York City, August 29, 2004*

There are known knowns. These are the things we know. There are known unknowns. That is to say, there are things that we know we don't know. But there are also unknown unknowns. These are things we don't know we don't know.

—*U.S. Secretary of Defense Donald Rumsfeld, on the war on terrorism, 2003*

At the heart of this approach is the self-interested individual, a minimalist assumption about human behavior. We use this methodological individualism to examine how economic and political market exchange works, how it fails, how it produces good social outcomes, and how it creates social traps that can damage individuals and their communities.

INDIVIDUAL PREFERENCES, SOCIAL OUTCOMES

In this chapter we explore how individual preferences aggregate to produce social outcomes in economic and political arenas. Sometimes such aggregation leads to productive social outcomes, sometimes it leads to social traps that are perverse and destructive to society, but almost always it produces an outcome that falls short of the ideal outcome given the distribution of individual preferences in society. We focus on economic market exchange and democracy because the world has been trending for centuries toward these ends, because market exchange dominates international exchange, and because market exchange and democracy provide an elegant theoretical baseline against which we can compare economic and political exchange that does not conform to market exchange or falls short of such exchange. We treat political exchange in democracies as a form of market exchange—political market exchange—and political exchange in nondemocracies as political market failure. Evaluating, examining, and critiquing the current global political economy demands a clear understanding of the theoretical frameworks that sit at its core. These frameworks provide baselines, or points of comparison, for evaluating the choices of market and political actors. They help investigators and policy makers to develop expectations about how the global political economy should function—to which they can compare actual outcomes. They illuminate inconsistencies between the theoretical frameworks and empirical behavior. These ideal types offer baselines for evaluating how well economic and political markets function, where and why they might fail, and some potential ways to adjust our theoretical frameworks.

By constructing theoretical baselines for how capitalist markets and democracies are supposed to aggregate individual preferences in an ideal world to produce social outcomes, we can then assess how well they perform such functions empirically and how this should affect our understanding of economic and political market activity. This is very important, for without a clear understanding and expectation of how markets and democratic political arenas are supposed to work, what they are supposed to do, and how, how can we assess how well they function or fail in promoting economic exchange and political cooperation across national borders—the key to modern globalization? In chapter 3, we examined the broader consequences of market exchange in the context of capitalism, globalization, and growth. Now we take a closer look at the foundations of economic and political market exchange in market economies and participatory polities. In so doing, we treat the processes of exchange in markets and democratic polities as alike in their theoretical foundations, objectives, and empirical problems.

ECONOMIC AND POLITICAL MARKET EXCHANGE

In chapter 3, we discussed how liberal market exchange appeals to many people on moral grounds. People like the opportunity to make choices in markets because such actions embrace the idea of individual choice and free will. Choices in economic markets are voluntary consumption decisions, or votes, on economic commodities guided by individual preference. The same appeal applies to democratic processes in political arenas. Political arenas, especially democratic political arenas, can likewise be viewed as markets, wherein individual political choice is liberated by representation and electoral mechanisms. Choices in such political markets are consumption decisions, or votes, on political commodities, be they politicians or policies. The parties to such exchanges in economic and political arenas value the concept of voluntary participation and the explicit rejection of hierarchical intrusion upon freedom of choice and individual autonomy. People rarely claim that their lives would be better if government were less democratic and more authoritarian, or if they had to consume economic commodities that they did not want. When members of nondemocratic societies venture to voice their concerns and suggest alternatives, they generally call for expanding the base of representation and limiting the ability of the few to constrain the actions of the many. Sometimes this produces rebellion and change, as in the French, Mexican, and Russian Revolutions, the battles to extend suffrage to women in the United States and other nations, the civil rights movement in the United States, the breakdown of the Soviet bloc beginning in 1989, and the Arab Spring beginning in 2011.

Members of democratic societies also complain about their governments and demand reforms when politicians and policy fail to produce desired outcomes. In many democratic states, carping over politics seems to be a favorite national pastime, surpassing soccer or baseball. Interestingly, demands for reform in democratic societies often contain the same prescription as reform demands in nondemocratic societies: that representation be improved and not diminished. When democratic governance and representation fail to produce good policy outcomes in societies, members of such societies tend to blame a breakdown in the channels of communication—a breakdown in representation itself—between those elected as representatives and those being represented. In such cases, the demands from society are to fix representation, to improve the channels of communication, and to make government more representative of the people.

In ideal settings, market exchange and democracy express the preferences and wants of the participants to those processes and the hierarchy of such preferences. Under the best conditions this enables interpersonal comparisons of utility—how individuals value some economic and political commodities over others. This interpersonal comparison is easier in the case of economic exchange than in the case of political exchange, for reasons we will discuss shortly. Moreover, in the ideal, such economic and political exchange has the added benefit of producing socially efficient outcomes that can lead to gains in social welfare. As noted in chapter 3, efficient economic and political markets maximize social welfare when they accurately aggregate the preferences of members of society and generate the economic and political goods and services that best meet those desires—in other words, when no other level of production of economic and political goods and services could produce greater overall societal happiness. Efficient exchange minimizes the collective dissatisfaction and optimizes the collective satisfaction of those individuals in society engaged in exchange, but it usually does not maximize any individual's preference in society. Such moral appeal depends on the mechanisms of economic market exchange and democratic political exchange operating as envisioned by theory. So let's first ask whether we can apply the logic of the economic market to political exchange. Then we will consider the ideal theoretical conditions under which economic and political markets produce efficient social outcomes that maximize social welfare and minimize collective dissatisfaction. In so doing, we will recognize important similarities between economic and political markets—both in how they operate and in how they fail—but also some important differences.

MARKET EXCHANGE IN THE POLITICAL ARENA: RATIONAL CONSUMERS AND PRODUCERS

Applying the economic arena's logic of the market mechanism to political arenas provides a powerful analytical tool for examining politics. But let's first ask whether this is a reasonable analytical strategy—can we extend the market analogy to politics? In economics, markets are aggregation and allocation mechanisms, coordinating rational, goal-oriented individual behavior of consumers and producers, which choreographs the use of society's scarce resources. Politics is also a social aggregation and allocation process—it aggregates preferences and choices, coordinates and allocates the use of resources in society, and produces social outcomes. As a famous political scientist wrote, "Politics is about who gets what and how." If the market analogy is to apply, we must have the following reasonable expectations: (1) that citizens act as rational consumers of political goods; (2) that politicians, policy makers, and bureaucrats act as rational producers of political goods; and (3) that the exchange between citizens as consumers and politicians as producers of political goods conforms to our expectations of what constitutes market exchange.

Can we assume that citizens, politicians, policy makers, and bureaucrats act as if they are rational consumers and producers in an exchange relationship? Do they act as if they are making trade-offs across political goods based on their ranking of the alternatives, the costs of the different alternatives, and the expected utility of one choice over another? Is it reasonable to assume that when citizens vote, they are attempting to exercise their preferences about the agendas and actions of political parties, public policies and programs, politicians, government bureaucrats, and their bureaucracies? Is voting an attempt to purchase a political outcome? When people vote, do they exchange their votes for the possibility that a preferred politician and her agenda will ascend to office, a preferred outcome on a referendum will attain, or a preferred party and its policy agenda will prevail? If so, they are participating in an exchange relationship as rational consumers, with policy makers, politicians, bureaucrats, and political parties as the producers of political goods.

On the production side of political exchange, do politicians, policy makers, public bureaucrats, and political parties seek support from voters and the populace by marketing political goods? Do they seek to peddle public policies, sell their agendas, and market candidates? What happens to politicians, political parties, policy makers, and bureaucrats if they succeed in marketing their products and agendas, and what happens if they fail? If they succeed, are they rewarded as successful economic producers are in a market—do they gain market share and influence? If they fail to sell their products and agendas, are they penalized in the way that unsuccessful producers are in economic markets—do they lose market share and influence, or even go out of business? If successful and unsuccessful producers in political arenas experience fates similar to successful and unsuccessful producers in economic markets, the market analogy gains traction and applicability to political behavior. From this perspective, citizens and politicians do seem to fit the analogy of rational consumers and producers of political commodities.

THE MECHANISM OF POLITICAL EXCHANGE

Even if political consumers and producers act as if they are rational, do the means of their exchange approximate those of market exchange? Is the market mechanism an appropriate and useful characterization of political exchange? A variety of market and nonmarket types of exchange occur in societies. In all but the most repressive authoritarian regimes, consumers and producers of political commodities do not unilaterally determine the supply, demand, and price of those political commodities. In most political arenas, the interaction of numerous producers (politicians, parties, and policy makers) and numerous consumers (voters and citizens)—and the aggregation of their choices and actions—create the social outcomes we observe in political arenas. This interaction of political producers and consumers draws our attention to the aggregation processes in political arenas, the mechanisms by which individual choices interact and are compiled to generate social outcomes. Are the aggregation mechanisms in political arenas akin to those in economic markets?

Elections are an appropriate place to begin evaluating whether we can view political exchange as a market relationship between producers and consumers of political commodities. Elections constitute a decentralized mechanism for aggregating societal preferences. They are built around individual choice. If we look around the world, we quickly recognize that elections are only one way to organize political life. Many people live in political arenas where the exercise of political choice at the ballot box is an anomaly. Autocracies, monarchies, and anarchies do not offer meaningful, stable electoral processes. This does not mean there is an absence of political exchange, but that the transfer of political commodities between political producers and consumers takes place through some aggregation mechanism other than individual choice in a decentralized political market—generally a more centralized hierarchical mechanism. Here, the rules of exchange are, generally, more arbitrary, ad hoc, and circumscribed than in arenas with stable electoral processes. Individuals in such systems can still exercise choice by voting with their feet in protest or rebellion, but their ability to obtain political commodities by exchanging their votes at the ballot box is limited or nonexistent.

Democratic and decentralized political arenas seek to provide individuals with voice (influence) over their political circumstances by granting them property rights over their votes, which they can exchange for political commodities such as policies and politicians. An election is an aggregation device that creates the opportunity for individuals to exercise their property rights over their votes. Ideally, this aggregation device accurately assembles individual choices and preferences into an outcome that generates the greatest amount of social welfare in the political arena. Just as a variety of market mechanisms exist in economic exchange, a range of electoral forms dot the political landscape. For example, members of the U.S. Congress are elected by a plurality rule, whereby the "winner takes all." This rule means that the candidate with the most votes wins the election, and the people who voted for losing candidates do not obtain a share of the representation proportional to the votes their candidates received. In systems such as the European parliamentarian democracies, even those who vote for candidates who do not receive a plurality of the vote (the largest vote share) receive some proportional representation in the legislature, if their candidate's share of the vote exceeds a predefined threshold (for example, 10 percent of the vote).

Voluntary versus Nonvoluntary Exchange

The differences across the examples described here suggest a potentially important difference between economic market exchange and political exchange—the potential for nonvoluntary consumption in political exchange. In economic markets, the parties to an exchange participate voluntarily as they exchange property rights over one commodity for property rights over another. They do not knowingly consume a commodity that they do not wish to consume. We can assess consumers' interpersonal utility for one commodity versus another by what they consume and how much they are willing to spend. This voluntary quality of consumption choices underpins the normative appeal of economic market exchange: it enshrines the rights and liberty of the individual.

Yet nonvoluntary consumption of political commodities appears to occur with great frequency in political arenas. Nonvoluntary consumption is most evident in states governed by authoritarian regimes, which often redistribute societal resources by hierarchical fiat, denying political consumers any property rights over their votes and political consumption decisions. An exchange takes place in this arena, but we cannot make any assumptions about the voluntary nature of that exchange, and we hesitate to claim improved social welfare where most citizens have had no say in the exchange. These regimes are clearly not efficiently functioning political markets, but the market analogy can still provide a useful framework for considering such authoritarian political arrangements as examples of market failure and diagnosing the damage such regimes do to social welfare.

Nonvoluntary consumption also appears to take place in political arenas that enshrine the notion of individual electoral choice, such as the European and U.S. examples cited earlier. In these political arenas, voters cast their votes for particular candidates or policies, but, for example, those who voted for Al Gore in the 2000 U.S. presidential election or for John Kerry in 2004 still had to consume George W. Bush and his administration's policies. Those who voted for John McCain in 2008 are consuming policy goods produced by Barack Obama's administration even if they prefer other policies. The McCain and Obama campaign platforms differed on both domestic and international policies, such as how to respond to issues of global economic recovery, immigration, and the wars in Iraq and Afghanistan.

In the United States, when a voter's preferred candidate or policy loses in an election or referendum, the voter still has to consume the specific political commodity she voted against unless she then moves to another political geographic region that is more to her liking in terms of the production of political commodities. Certainly, throughout history, many people have migrated from one society to another for political reasons. Almost without exception, migrating people have searched for more liberty and choice in their consumption of political commodities, not less. But exit is often difficult: economic means, language, family and social ties, culture, space as a scarce resource, legal barriers to exit and entrance, and geographical affinity may all affect the ability of an individual to migrate in order to avoid consumption of a particular political commodity. We could sidestep our dilemma of voluntary versus nonvoluntary political exchange by asserting that individuals consume an assortment of social, political, and economic commodities and must make trade-offs across such commodities because we live in a world of scarce resources. Because we make trade-offs across goods, we cannot always have our cake and eat it too, as the saying goes. This is true, but it does not negate the distinction between a voluntary, symmetric exchange in a decentralized market (where parties are viewed as equal in terms of their choice to participate in the exchange) and an exchange that involves asymmetric authority of one party to direct the actions of others (where one party enjoys more influence over the exchange than do the other parties).

If our losing voter remains in place, does this decision indicate whether she is subject to voluntary or nonvoluntary consumption of a political commodity? Our answer lies in why our voter votes. If she votes because she values the process more than any specific outcome, then it is voluntary exchange even if she dislikes the specific outcome. Her participation purchases and legitimates the broader democratic process, not any specific political good. Many people vote because they value the process of democratic politics, peaceful resolution of political differences through electoral processes, and societal compromise even if they disagree with specific outcomes. But if our voter's candidate or policy loses in the election and the voter does not find inherent merit in the process that produced that outcome, her subsequent consumption of the political commodity produced by the election is nonvoluntary. Nonvoluntary political exchange may not improve social welfare if people value particular outcomes over processes. In fact, it can detract from individual liberties, depending on what commodity political consumers must consume.

Inevitably, in political settings with asymmetric authority, even good democratic settings, some political exchange will involve some nonvoluntary consumption. Both authoritarian and democratic regimes employ asymmetric authority and hierarchical imposition, but they do so to significantly different degrees. Unlike voluntary exchange, nonvoluntary transactions pose a dilemma for the evaluation of the individual benefit, social efficiency, and social welfare that may result. We have no standard for making comparisons concerning interpersonal welfare. With nonvoluntary transactions we cannot assess how much voters actually value a candidate or policy they did not support. We can observe trade-offs, costs, and prices in voluntary exchange, as well as consumption choices that allow us to assess the value of commodities purchased and not purchased by individuals. But with nonvoluntary exchange, such as voting for the losing candidate or policy and then having to consume the winning candidate or policy, we cannot determine how much our losing voter values the winning candidate or policy. She must consume the winning candidate or policy regardless of the costs to her. This nonvoluntary quality undermines our ability to assess the relative gains or costs to society. Here we have to make a leap of faith!

Social Choice and Voting Rules

A **voting rule** defines the process by which societies decide on the political commodities they will consume. As discussed earlier, a wide variety of voting systems are employed around the world. Voting rules such as dictatorial rule, majority rule, plurality rules, supermajority rules, unanimity, and other rules are all mechanisms that aggregate the political preferences of a society's members—or some of its members—and coordinate those preferences with the production of political commodities by politicians, governments, and political parties. Each system has its strengths, weaknesses, and trade-offs. Drafters of national constitutions and designers of electoral systems must weigh the strengths and weaknesses of different voting rules and definitions of political property rights as they seek to build the structure for political exchange in their societies. The choice of voting rules affects policy choices, which in turn affect both domestic and international affairs. The political processes that guide a government's actions in domestic affairs are the same processes that guide its choices in international affairs.

A **voting rule** is a mechanism that defines the process by which societies decide on the political commodities they will consume; a wide variety of voting rules are employed around the world. **Social choice theory** is a body of inquiry concerned with the aggregation mechanisms or voting rules that compile the preferences of society's members.

The fact that a voter must consume the winning candidate or policy regardless of whether that outcome reflects her preferences raises an important question: Are some types of aggregation mechanisms or voting rules more effective than others at accurately and efficiently compiling and protecting individual choices in a political arena and producing outcomes that also improve social welfare? A school of inquiry called **social choice theory** studies voting rules and other aggregation mechanisms, seeking to understand which processes most accurately compile the preferences of society's members, optimizing individual liberty and social outcomes. Voting rules such as majority rule, plurality rules, supermajority rules, and unanimity are designed with the intention of aggregating individual preferences to produce a social outcome. Each voting rule has its strengths, weaknesses, and trade-offs in terms of efficiently aggregating individual preferences, enhancing social welfare, protecting minority rights, and limiting the problem of nonvoluntary exchange. To date, however, no voting rule in political exchange overcomes all the problems of nonvoluntary consumption, nor is such a voting rule likely to be developed, given the theoretical requirements of such a rule. This dilemma also is true of economic exchange, but there it is far less visible to the average observer.

Despite the potential of nonvoluntary exchange, the market analogy offers a powerful and useful tool for examining political behavior—if we guard against naïveté and remain aware of the prospects for nonvoluntary exchange. Just as it does in the economic arena, using the market framework to examine choices and exchange in political arenas offers a baseline from which to evaluate how well political exchange works in terms of efficiently and accurately connecting individual preferences with social outcomes. Moreover, the framework provides tools for determining when and why exchange in political markets falls short of the idealized case.

THEORETICAL PREREQUISITES OF EFFICIENT AND COMPETITIVE MARKETS

The normative attractiveness of economic and political market exchange comes from their theoretical potential, in comparison with other types of economic and political allocation mechanisms in society, to improve social and individual outcomes while still protecting individual liberty and voluntary choice. No other level of production of political and economic goods could produce greater overall societal happiness. In the ideal case, the production of such goods lies on what is called the *production-possibility frontier,* as seen in figure 4.1. As we move along this particular production-possibility frontier, we get different mixes of two commodities—guns and butter—but each mix uses societal resources efficiently and produces the maximum amount of societal happiness and minimizes collective dissatisfaction. We call this frontier **Pareto optimal,** meaning that we cannot move off this frontier to improve the welfare of some specific members of society without damaging the welfare of others and of society as a whole, given the preferences of all members of society. This is an equilibrium wherein another distribution of resources and efforts cannot benefit one member of society without hurting another and lowering the overall efficiency of the production and consumption of economic and political goods given the mix of preferences in society.

> The **Pareto optimal** is a situation or equilibrium wherein another distribution of resources and efforts cannot benefit one member of society without hurting another and lowering the overall efficiency of the production and consumption of goods, given the mix of preferences in society.

A Pareto optimal frontier, however, while approachable, is rarely obtained. Some economic and political markets do better than others, and some do dramatically better. As noted earlier, the empirical world always falls short of the idealized theoretical world. Despite theory, no economic and political markets are perfectly competitive, and no such markets perfectly and efficiently aggregate individual preferences to produce ideal social outcomes. If they did, we would not observe government interventions in international exchange that damage more of their societies than they help. Subsidies, quotas, limits on

FIGURE 4.1	The Production-Possibility Frontier of Political and Economic Goods

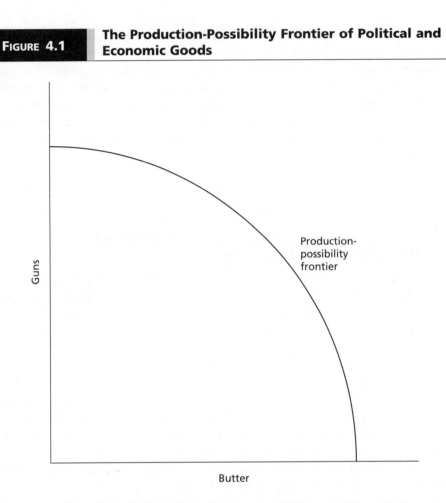

immigration, and other protectionist measures may help specific segments of societies, but they tend to damage more people in a polity than they help by increasing costs of consumption and reducing consumption possibilities. Such policy choices move societies away from their Pareto optimal frontiers. Nor would we view an absence of intervention in areas where more people would be helped than hurt, such as in areas of environmental degradation. Here a lack of policy choice shifts societies away from their Pareto optimal frontiers. Obtaining desirable outcomes depends on economic and political markets working as closely as possible to how they were theoretically envisioned—or at least not failing too badly. What conditions are important for markets to work as envisioned and to produce socially desirable outcomes based on the aggregation of decentralized nonhierarchical and voluntary individual choices? Our answer lies in what constitutes competitive markets and what conditions must be present for such markets to exist.

In the ideal, for economic and political markets to take individual preferences and transform them accurately and efficiently into collective outcomes, they must meet the following demanding prerequisites: (1) all parties to an exchange have clearly defined property rights and can negotiate, monitor, and enforce contracts at relatively negligible costs; (2) no individual buyer or seller, or cartel of buyers or sellers, can manipulate the price mechanism; (3) transactions in the markets have no effect on third parties; and (4) all parties to an exchange enjoy complete or full information. Let's examine each of these conditions in the context of political exchange.

Clear Property Rights and Low Transaction Costs

Competitive economic and political markets require clear definition of **property rights** and the ability for market participants to negotiate, monitor, and enforce contracts at relatively negligible

> **Property rights** are rules defining the ownership of property.

costs. Participants in a competitive market must enjoy a clear understanding of who owns what, as the exchange of goods and services in a market involves the exchange of property rights over those goods and services. What does this mean in the context of political exchange? In political markets, citizens trade their votes for goods produced by politicians, policy makers, bureaucrats, and political parties. They can also trade their labor and financial resources by working on campaigns, making contributions to campaigns, advocating public causes, or funding efforts on behalf of such causes. Clear definition of property rights means that there is no ambiguity over who can vote or what they can contribute in exchange for political commodities. With clear definition of property rights, citizens own the property rights over their votes, the labor they can donate to political causes, and their financial contributions to political activities. They can freely exchange these forms of support for the promise of political goods, and politicians know whether their supporters can deliver at the ballot box.

Clear definition of property rights in political exchange also means that there is no ambiguity about whether policy makers can or cannot deliver the political commodities that they offer in exchange for voter support. For example, in student elections, such as those for seats on a student council and class officers, candidates often run on platforms that promise greater student oversight and input to school policy and performance, better food in the school cafeteria, or improvements in the functioning of the school library or computing systems, despite the fact that members of the student council and class officers do not have the ability or authority to make such changes. They do not own or control the property rights over such policies—that is, they do not have the ability to exchange improvements in such areas for their colleagues' votes. The property rights for such changes lie in the hands of school administrators, local government, and, ultimately, taxpayers and voters. If fellow students vote for candidates based on such promises, they misunderstand who owns the rights to make such changes.

Transaction costs are the costs of negotiating, monitoring, and enforcing the terms of an exchange or a contract. **Uncertainty** describes a situation in which decision makers have incomplete information about their world, their and others' property rights, their possible choices, the preferences and possible choices of others, and how multiple decision makers' choices will interact.

The costs of determining such property rights and negotiating, monitoring, and enforcing the terms of an exchange or contract are called **transaction costs**—the costs of doing business or engaging in exchange relationships. **Uncertainty** or confusion over property rights can increase transaction costs. The more uncertain property rights are, the more parties to an exchange must expend effort and resources to protect themselves—for example, who wants to buy a house or a car from someone who might not own that house or car? Such uncertainty means that the costs of negotiating, monitoring, and enforcing the terms of an exchange are no longer negligible. It adds costs to an exchange and generates inefficiencies that detract from the overall value of the exchange. If transaction costs become sufficiently large, they undermine the social efficiency of economic or political market exchange. They may even undermine or limit exchange.

In political arenas, an election, a referendum, a legislative act, or a political promise constitutes an exchange between voters and policy makers. The costs of negotiating, monitoring, and enforcing the terms of such exchange must be small or negligible if the exchange is to be efficient. For example, in the American South after Reconstruction, African Americans were systematically discriminated against in political arenas. Barriers such as Jim Crow laws were constructed to prevent African Americans from registering to vote and exercising their political franchise. Even if such citizens could have clearly asserted their property rights over their votes, the transaction costs of doing so were prohibitive and often included violence. Southern whites used legal obstructions, psychological and physical harassment, beatings, and lynchings to deprive African Americans of their rights in political markets. In another example, the transaction costs of voting against Saddam Hussein and his party in Iraqi elections were prohibitively high for Iraqi citizens, even though there was little ambiguity about who had the right to vote. Election observers from the United Nations, the Carter Center in Atlanta, and other organizations routinely monitor elections and plebiscites in emerging democracies, looking for evidence of voter fraud or tampering (ambiguity over the property rights of a vote) and systematic intimidation or discrimination against a particular segment of society (significant transaction costs). Both can undermine efficient and competitive political exchange.

Voters must also be able to assess easily whether policy makers are fulfilling their commitments, and policy makers must be able to evaluate easily whether voters are voting as promised. Are politicians delivering the policy goods that they promised in exchange for votes and support, and are voters actually casting their votes and throwing their support as promised? The more difficulty or uncertainty voters and policy makers encounter in determining whether the other party to a political exchange is actually fulfilling its part in the terms of the exchange, the more likely that one party or another can cheat. If voters know that policy makers cannot easily monitor their support, voters can more easily assert their support in exchange for a political good but then not deliver their support at the ballot box. If policy makers know that voters will have a difficult time evaluating whether the policy makers have lived up to their commitments, they can more easily claim to have delivered policies that they did not.

Even if it were possible to overcome such uncertainty, citizens and policy makers would have to invest substantial resources in monitoring each other's actions. Thomas Jefferson viewed an active free press as necessary for democracy, as the press would seek out and provide information that could help overcome voters' uncertainty about their policy makers. If successful, a free press can monitor the activities of voters and policy makers and so help to overcome the uncertainty of both about the political exchange, but this investment of social resources is, nevertheless, inefficient. If the actions of politicians and voters were transparent and easily monitored, a press—free or not—would be unnecessary. With greater and greater uncertainty, political exchange becomes less and less efficient and may even break down. Ambiguities over who can vote, how citizens can participate in political life, and what political commodities are to be exchanged can detract from the value of political exchange and create inefficiencies in political markets: voters feel disenfranchised and stay home, while politicians ignore constituent needs, become corrupt, and use their positions to redistribute societal resources to special interests, cronies, or family.

The ambiguities and uncertainties about property rights and the transaction costs for monitoring exchange relations that are seen within domestic arenas are magnified in exchange and political relationships across national boundaries. Differences in language, culture, systems of laws and contracting, business organization, and informal practices have significant effects on relations across borders, adding uncertainty and nonnegligible transactions. These are surmountable, or else we would not observe the extraordinary amount of cross-border exchange and cooperation that characterizes globalization, but they do add inefficiency to the process.

Competition and Manipulation of Market Exchange

A variety of factors affect transaction costs, the prospects of competitive exchange, and the efficiency advantage of market exchange as compared with other forms of allocation. Efficient economic and political markets require competition, so that no individual buyer or seller, or cartel of buyers or sellers, can manipulate the price and supply of an economic or political commodity. When a single producer is able to manipulate the price of a commodity by affecting the supply of that commodity in a market, that producer is said to have a **monopoly.** We call the market condition in which sellers of a commodity are so few that the actions of any one of them or of some in collusion will materially affect price and have a measurable impact on competitors

A **monopoly** is a market condition in which a single producer is able to manipulate the price of a commodity by affecting the supply of that commodity in a market. An **oligopoly** is a market condition in which the actions of a few sellers materially affect price and have a measurable impact on competitors and consumers. **Price takers** are all participants in economic exchange whose actions cannot individually control or manipulate prices; in efficient and competitive markets, all parties to an exchange are price takers—that is, they must accept the prices determined by the invisible hand of the price mechanism.

and consumers an **oligopoly.** In a competitive market, enough producers supply the commodity that any attempt to manipulate supply would fail. This competition factor also exists on the demand side: there is no single consumer, or collusive cartel of consumers, whose actions can affect the demand for a commodity and hence gain the ability to manipulate the price of that commodity. Participants in efficient and competitive markets are all **price takers,** meaning that no one individually controls the price.

In competitive economic markets, price is dictated by supply and demand as coordinated by the price mechanism. Producers or consumers who try to manipulate the price of a commodity will fail as long as a sufficient number of other producers or consumers are in the market. If a single seller or buyer (or cartel of sellers or buyers) can manipulate supply or demand, that seller or buyer gains the ability to manipulate price and has incentives to manipulate the market to increase her individual welfare. Under these circumstances, resources will not be employed efficiently to meet the wants and desires of the members of society. A monopoly or oligopoly of producers will lead to decreased consumption of goods in general. Consumers are harmed by increased costs and decreased consumption, which outweigh possible gains to the monopolist in the form of increased profits. The same is true if a single consumer (or cartel of consumers) can manipulate demand and, consequently, price. Producers will be harmed by decreased profits and lower production, and the costs to society will outweigh the gains to the consumer who has manipulated price. Competitive markets rely on Adam Smith's invisible hand functioning without manipulation.

Monopsonists are single buyers who are able to manipulate the price of a commodity by affecting the demand for that commodity in a market. A monopsony contains a market condition in which a single buyer is able to manipulate the price of a commodity by affecting the demand for that commodity in a market. **Oligopsonists** are members of a cartel of buyers that manipulates price and has a measurable impact on competitors and consumers. An oligopsony contains a market condition in which the actions of a few buyers will materially affect price and have a measurable impact on competitors and consumers.

As in economic markets, a key condition for competitive and efficient political markets is that no single provider or consumer—or collusive cartel of providers or consumers—of political commodities such as policies or politicians can unilaterally manipulate and determine the terms of political exchange (supply and price in economic markets). Consumers of political commodities must be able to choose among viable alternatives. There must be sufficient competition in political arenas so that producers of political commodities cannot act as monopolists or oligopolists, or consumers as **monopsonists** (single buyers) or **oligopsonists** (one of very few buyers). A monopolist in a political market acts as an authoritarian provider, not providing her citizens with alternatives or allowing citizens to select an alternative. Cleopatra, Julius Caesar, Hitler, Stalin, Saddam Hussein, and other dictators stifled political competition and prevented their citizens from selecting alternatives to their leadership. By intimidating or eliminating their opponents, they prevented political competition. The citizens of their states had no effective choices among the political commodities they consumed, nor could they easily or comfortably exit those arenas or refuse to contribute to the provision of those commodities. Authoritarian leaders essentially manipulate the supply and price of political commodities in their political arenas.

Effective political competition underpins healthy democracies. Competitive elections and other representative devices provide mechanisms for consumers of political commodities to articulate *meaningful* preferences among alternatives. Under such conditions, the producers of political commodities must care about consumer preferences, which conditions the producers' activities. Otherwise they put their political survival at risk. Voters in competitive democracies can decide whether to continue consuming the political products of an incumbent regime or to throw the bums out and opt for another set of political commodities offered by an alternative regime. Effective political competition enables societies to constrain their policy makers, to accept or reject their policies, and to choose among alternatives. In competitive political markets, elections and other forms of representation—such as public opinion, interest group activities, litigation in courts, and debate in the media—are aggregation mechanisms comparable to the price mechanism in economic markets. They provide signals to producers of political commodities that can influence their decisions about what political commodities to supply and how much, or what not to provide.

In competitive political markets, producers of political commodities who ignore consumers risk their own political survival, for elections are the ultimate form of term limits in such markets. Producers of political commodities cannot use the political arena to pursue their narrow individual interests irrespective of the broader societal interests. Political competition pushes politicians to take the public's needs into consideration. The mechanisms of competition in political markets coordinate the individual needs of politicians and the individual needs of political consumers to produce social outcomes that are inherently more socially efficient than those produced by a monopolist. You may not appreciate this outcome if you are the potential monopolist, but you should if you are not the monopolist. Effective political competition coordinates supply and demand in the production of political commodities.

The requirement for producers of political commodities to ensure competitive and efficient political markets also applies to the demand or consumption side of the political exchange. In a competitive and efficient political market, no single consumer, or cartel of consumers, can unilaterally affect the demand for a political commodity, determine an election, or extract special privilege against the will of the broader society. Concerns about special-interest politics, insider access, and the influence of money on politics are all essentially concerns about the ability of narrow swaths of society to manipulate the provision of political commodities and distort the political marketplace. The ability of narrow segments of society, cartels of producers or consumers, to use the political arena to distort exchange is readily apparent in international trade. Agricultural producers in a number of societies (France, Japan, the United States, Denmark, and many others) have been able to obtain public policies such as tariffs, quotas, and government subsidies for their economic sectors even though these protectionist policies damage the majority in each of their societies.

Special-interest politics raises the possibility that the votes of specific individuals or groups may count more than others in the political market and that the provision of political commodities would look different if such special interests did not exist or were constrained from exercising disproportionate influence.

Many societies have attempted to constrain special interests in order to limit the emergence of cartels of consumers of political commodities. Many nations' constitutions seek to protect their societies against influential cartels of political consumers by creating institutions that define and protect specific rights, such as the voting franchise, political speech, religious practice, and access to due process. They prohibit the trading of such rights as political commodities. Many constitutions prohibit voters from selling their votes to other voters, even if it is a voluntary surrendering of the right to vote, in order to limit the ability of any individual or narrow group to garner disproportionate influence over the production of political commodities—an influence that would distort political exchange and generate social inefficiencies. Imagine that Bill Gates, one of the richest men in the world, could use his wealth to purchase your voting franchise. Would you sell your vote for ten dollars, one hundred dollars, one thousand dollars, or more? If you could sell your vote, Bill Gates could use his wealth to purchase enough votes to determine the outcome of an election or referendum.

How much competition is enough to create the possibility for socially efficient political exchange? Clearly, a single producer of political commodities is insufficient. Political consumers with no alternatives cannot refuse to consume the monopolist's goods or drive the monopolist out of political business. Of course, people may be able to emigrate or revolt, but this will not help to break the monopolist's stranglehold by creating political competition and alternative producers of political commodities. If one is not enough, are a large number of producers of political commodities required to ensure a competitive and socially efficient political market? Not necessarily. A competitive political market requires only enough producers of political commodities to offer consumers of those commodities a choice of another policy or politician if one producer ignores their preferences. When political consumers—citizens and voters—can switch their choices and substitute another political commodity, they can discipline producers who fail to respond to their demands.

In the United Kingdom, can citizens who voted for winning Labour Party candidates in one election switch their votes to Liberal Democrat or Conservative Party candidates in the next election if they become dissatisfied with the performance and policies of the Labour Party? Does such a switch, or threat of a switch, by voters constrain politicians from acting as monopolists in the production of political commodities? Can German voters withdraw their support from a Christian Democratic government to support a Social Democratic government instead? Can U.S. voters shift their support from a Republican politician to a Democrat? A competitive political market requires only enough alternatives among producers of political commodities so that voters can shift their support in order to discipline politicians. Just as the price mechanism coordinates supply and demand in a competitive and efficient economic market, elections coordinate supply and demand in a competitive and efficient political market. As for the question about how much competition is enough to create the possibility for socially efficient political exchange—it does not take a lot. The necessary number will be a function of the voting rules and electoral institutions of the society. Under some institutional arrangements, two producers of political commodities can be enough to create a competitive political market and enhance social efficiency, and more than two could be inefficient. We explore such an example at the end of this chapter.

Externalities

Another important condition for competitive and efficient economic and political markets is that transactions in such markets have no effects—costs or benefits—on third parties. Such influence is called an **externality.** *Third parties* are those people who are not directly or willingly involved in an exchange but are affected by that exchange. Externalities can be positive or negative, and both can affect the efficiency of a market, impose undesirable transaction costs, and influence the production and consumption of economic and political commodities. Let's consider several examples.

> An **externality** is the effect of a transaction on a third party that is not directly involved in the exchange. **Free riding** is a collective action problem in which individuals have no incentive to contribute to the provision of a public good because they cannot be excluded from consuming that good even if they fail to contribute.

Think of national security as a commodity that is purchased by members of society. Everyone wants some level of national security or defense, but such goods are expensive. Some optimal level of defense could be provided if the voluntary mechanism of economic markets were efficient at allocating resources to national security. In such a market, we could pass a hat and ask members of society to contribute to the purchase of defense goods, individuals would purchase shares of the level of national security they desired, and the resulting outcome would be socially optimal. Yet such commodities have an interesting quality that could lead to their underprovision in a voluntary market. If you and most other members of society pay for defense goods to defend our territory, I will get the benefit of national security regardless of whether or not I pay my share. I cannot be excluded from the provision of this commodity. This quality is called a *positive externality,* for without being partner to the exchange of resources for national security, I get to consume that commodity nonetheless. This is known as **free riding,** or consumption of a commodity without contribution.

The presence of positive externalities in market exchange encourages rational individuals to shirk their responsibilities to contribute. After all, if I can get national security, or some other good, without paying my fair share, then I can use the resources that I was expected to contribute to national security instead for other goods—more clothes for my family, better schools for my children, a new car, or other private goods. If I can make this calculation, so can other rational individuals in society. If enough people believe that they will get the benefit of national security without contributing, or if enough people believe that the commodity will be underprovided because of the presence of too much free riding by others in society, society may face a dilemma of insufficient contributions to provide adequate national security. Under such conditions, if I did contribute to national security, my contributions and those of others would not purchase enough security because of all the free riders. I would then be a sucker to contribute. This logic and the problem of positive externalities can thus lead to a suboptimal amount of national security or, worse, an unraveling of the provision of the national security that we all want—a social trap.

The problem of positive externalities can easily lead to an underprovision of collective goods in the global political economy. At international summits, governments can agree in principle that we should reform our activities that contribute to environmental distress such as climate change, threaten the long-term viability of fisheries in international waters, or lead to dumping of toxic materials beyond national limits in open waters. Yet, despite the lofty statements that are often issued jointly by governments at such conferences, governments and their societies attempt to shirk their responsibilities and free ride on the positive actions of others.

There are, however, devices to limit such shirking. Forced contributions through mandatory taxes, the threat of government penalties, or an ability to create, monitor, and enforce contractual agreements with defined obligations for the parties can limit shirking. We could organize a community of potential contributors and negotiate a multiparty contract among the members of the group, but people can violate contracts. So ensuring that enough people act in accordance with the multiparty contract requires monitoring the contributions and sanctioning those who do not meet their obligations. These strategies involve nonnegligible transaction costs in the political marketplace, as it is expensive to monitor and enforce compliance with contracts. Resources that could go into defense are channeled into monitoring and enforcing agreements, or ensuring tax compliance. Such transaction costs are inefficient compared with the ideal case of provision of political commodities by purely voluntary exchange. They mean that the amount of national security and other goods purchased by a society is less than what an efficient market would produce, but voluntary market exchange for this type of good generates positive externalities that threaten the very provision of the good. Societies with good national security apparatuses overcome this free-rider, positive-externality dilemma by resorting to nonvoluntary, nonmarket mechanisms.

Environmental pollution offers an example of a *negative externality* and nonvoluntary consumption by third parties not directly or willingly involved in an exchange. Take the case of coal-fired power plants in the midwestern region of the United States. For years those plants spewed a form of pollution into the atmosphere that drifted east and became acid rain, which damaged the ecosystems of lakes in the northeastern United States and across the border in Canada. Fish stocks in those lakes declined precipitously. Many lakes became sterile as a consequence of acid rain. Environmental regulations that required the power plants to use cleaner coal and add cleaners and scrubbers to their exhaust stacks eventually led to a dramatic decrease in the level of harmful pollutions that contributed to acid rain.

How was acid rain a negative externality? The production and consumption of energy generated by the midwestern power plants took place almost exclusively between producers and consumers in the Midwest. Because of weather patterns, however, lakes in the Midwest were relatively unaffected by the acid rain caused by the power plants' emissions. Those living in the affected northeastern United States and in southeastern Canada did not participate in the production and consumption of energy from the plants in the Midwest. They did not receive energy or payments for energy. They were third parties to the exchange of that energy—people not directly or voluntarily involved in the exchange—but they were affected by the exchange. Activities that took place in the Midwest forced significant costs on people in the northeastern United States and southeastern Canada. The acid rain associated with the power plants' emissions resulted in health problems for residents and changes in recreational activities in the affected area, prompted legal suits to constrain midwestern producers from using dirty coal and to force plant upgrades, necessitated large-scale programs to rectify changes in the pH levels of lakes by adding base chemicals, created diplomatic recriminations and tensions between the United States and Canada, and required studies to assess the environmental effects of energy generation by midwestern plants. These third-party costs were not reflected in the production and consumption decisions of energy producers and consumers in the Midwest. This example and the next demonstrate the close interconnection between economic and political markets, and how individual choices within an economic exchange can spill over to the political arena and across national borders, affecting relations between states.

Policy makers often face requests from domestic economic producers in their societies for protections from competition from foreign economic producers. Agricultural producers in advanced industrialized societies often seek government protections and assistance against competition from agricultural commodities from developing political economies. These producers organize and offer to exchange votes, campaign contributions, and other forms of political support for government intervention in international trade. In response to such pressures, governments may do nothing or they may initiate tariffs, subsidies, quotas, or other barriers to trade—thereby exchanging a public policy for political support. Policy makers in Europe, the United States, and Japan have extended substantial protections to farmers in their respective countries. Indeed, agricultural subsidies are the largest component of the European Union budget.

If these societies were populated only by policy makers able to provide such policies and economic producers seeking such policies, this would be an efficient exchange in a political market, and the government would be highly responsive to constituent needs. But these societies also include workers in industries other than those seeking protections from foreign producers. These people consume goods from the protected sectors of the economy. Few of those who live in an advanced industrialized state are part of the agricultural sector, yet all who live in that state consume agricultural products. Not part of the exchange between the protected sector and the government, these nonagricultural workers and families must now pay higher prices for the products from this protected sector of the economy, which reduces their ability to consume other things. The political exchange between the government and the sector seeking protections has imposed costs on other people in society who did not take part in the political exchange. Some survey research suggests that many people appear willing to accept such third-party externalities to protect the jobs and industries of fellow citizens of their states, but would they be willing if they knew that the cost of the third-party externality deprived them of one thousand dollars, two thousand dollars, or more of consumption possibilities?

Some degree of third-party externalities may be almost inevitable, given the persistent likelihood of nonvoluntary consumption in political exchange, but we must ask: At what point does a negative or positive third-party externality severely distort political exchange and heavily damage social outcomes? Many third-party externalities are relatively insignificant, and in some situations, the parties being damaged are aware of the externalities and are willing to bear the costs. In other cases, the parties to a political exchange that generates a third-party externality are willing to provide some compensation to mitigate the costs of the externality. Nevertheless, if severe enough, externalities, positive or negative, can undercut the benefits of market exchange and detract from the efficient allocation of resources that advances overall societal welfare, as the costs to third parties exceed the benefits to the parties directly involved in the exchange.

Workers clean a beach in the Gulf of Mexico affected by the *Deepwater Horizon* oil spill. The oil spill imposed tremendous negative externalities on the Gulf's fishing and travel industries and (for the readers of this book) on college students who had planned to travel to the Gulf Coast for spring break.

Complete Information

In a perfect world, competitive and socially efficient economic and political exchange would require that all parties to an exchange enjoy relatively complete or full information. They would have relatively equal access to any information that is important to the exchange, and such access would be relatively easy and affordable, so that no party to the exchange would be ill informed about the terms of the exchange. None would be deprived of information that is important to the exchange. **Asymmetric information,** whereby one party to an exchange knows more about the commodity being exchanged than do the other parties, can introduce an unfair advantage that detracts from the efficiency of the exchange. Asymmetric information is one form of **incomplete information.**

Let's first think about how information can affect the efficiency of economic market exchange and then extend our analysis to political markets. Imagine that you want to purchase bananas at the supermarket. You have a choice of bananas imported from Africa or bananas from Latin

> **Asymmetric information** occurs in a situation in which one party involved in an exchange knows more about the commodity being exchanged than the other parties do. **Incomplete information** occurs in a situation in which parties to an exchange or interaction are not fully informed about the resources and preferences of the other parties engaged in the interaction.

America. Significant differences exist between Latin American and African bananas in terms of variety, quality, and cost of production. Such differences contributed to a trade war involving the European Union, the United States, and Latin American and African states that produce bananas or are the markets for those bananas. In a competitive market, where all sellers and buyers are equally well-informed, such differences should map into consumer choice. Let's say that African bananas cost less but Latin American bananas taste better. In a market where consumers and sellers are all fully informed, some people will purchase Latin American bananas and others will purchase African bananas. Both groups will be guided by their different preferences in taste and cost. Some people will purchase African bananas even if Latin American bananas are considered better tasting, as they will willingly trade off better taste for lower cost. They are conscious of this trade-off and make their decisions with full information.

In this market, buyers can easily distinguish between the types of bananas, and they know if a banana is incorrectly priced. The supermarket's produce manager cannot charge too much for the cheaper banana by substituting it for the other without changing the price. Nor will she charge too little and cheat herself by underselling the market rate for the more expensive banana. Full information means that voluntary exchange will take place at the real market price, given the wants and desires of society. There will be no inefficiencies created by paying too much or too little, which would lower the ability of buyers to consume other products.

What if you cannot differentiate between African and Latin American bananas? Like most people, you are probably not an agronomist with a specialty in banana cultivars, and becoming one would require a significant investment in resources, which would not likely be an efficient use of your time and resources just so you could tell the difference between banana types when you are at the supermarket. So, you are at the market and having a problem distinguishing Latin American from African bananas. But the produce manager at the market has no such problem, because she is a banana professional, has been dealing with bananas for years, and can easily differentiate between varieties of bananas. Moreover, she knows that consumers will pay more for Latin American bananas because they believe that Latin American bananas are superior. Yet she pays less for African bananas and knows that most of her customers can barely

In July 2005 this Costa Rican banana worker prepares newly harvested bananas for shipping. In August, the World Trade Organization (WTO) ruled that a new European Union (EU) tariff on imported bananas was illegal and discriminated against nine Latin American banana-producing nations. These countries had been involved in a long-running trade dispute with the EU—known as the "banana wars" of the 1990s—in which they accused the EU of erecting preferential trade arrangements that favored former colonies in the African, Caribbean, and Pacific (ACP) group. The WTO ruled that EU practices during the banana wars discriminated against U.S. and Latin American companies, and it gave the EU until January 2006 to introduce a new set of tariffs for the fruit. In 2007, the EU entered into trade negotiations with Colombia, Peru, Costa Rica, El Salvador, Honduras, Guatemala, Nicaragua, and Panama to address this dispute. In 2010 the negotiations produced a settlement in which the EU agreed to a progressive reduction of its import tariff on bananas originating in these countries.

tell the difference between a banana and a plantain, let alone differences across varieties of bananas. She has asymmetric information—which she decides to use to her advantage. She goes to her distributor and purchases African bananas, but she displays them under the label of Latin American bananas. She charges her customers for Latin American bananas even though they are getting African bananas. In this way, she increases her profit margin, but at the expense of her customers, even if they are unaware.

This misuse of asymmetric information creates inefficiencies in the market. Banana consumers are paying too much for African bananas, believing they are Latin American bananas; they are being cheated. They might well be happy with African bananas, but they should be paying less for them. Then they would have more resources left over to buy other commodities, such as kiwis, blueberries, cars, cameras, or college educations. The produce manager is both gouging her customers and limiting their other consumption choices. Moreover, Latin American banana producers are harmed, as consumers unknowingly shift their consumption away from that commodity. This means less revenue for Latin American producers, which could affect economic conditions in their countries, perhaps lowering wages, creating unemployment, and feeding political instability. Reputable produce managers—those who do not take advantage of consumer ignorance by selling African bananas as Latin American bananas—are also damaged, because their profit margins are narrower than those of the disreputable produce manager, and this unfair advantage may either drive the reputable stores out of business or force them to adopt dishonest strategies in order to compete.

In this situation, buyers with asymmetric information face difficulties distinguishing good sellers or good products from bad sellers or bad products. This problem, called a

pooling equilibrium, leads to inefficiencies in the production and consumption of goods and services, as consumers are making their choices based on false or inadequate information. As the likelihood increases that consumers cannot distinguish good from bad products, or good from bad sellers, they may pay too much for products from less reputable sellers and too little for products from good sellers. This outcome damages the consumer and the good seller but advantages the less reputa-

> **Pooling equilibrium** is a dilemma caused by incomplete or asymmetric information whereby consumers face difficulties distinguishing types such as good sellers or good products from bad sellers or bad products. **Separating equilibrium** is the ability to distinguish types such as good sellers and good products from bad sellers or bad products, a solution to the dilemma created by a pooling equilibrium.

ble seller and her products—because people rarely admit that they are selling inferior products. This problem affects production and consumption in society, creating inefficiencies that are simply the difference between what is produced and consumed under asymmetric information and what is produced and consumed under conditions of full information. Facing a dilemma of sorting out good from bad claims, consumers need to create a **separating equilibrium** from a pooling equilibrium. In a separating equilibrium, buyers can distinguish among types of products and sellers.

Now let's consider how information affects exchange in political markets. Ideally in political markets the parties to an exchange would be equally informed about the terms of the exchange and would be able to observe all the nuances of such exchange. There would be no private or privileged information that would give one side or another an unfair advantage in the exchange or that could be used strategically to manipulate the exchange. Voters would be able to distinguish accurately between candidates, parties, and their policies. Producers of political commodities would be able to recognize accurately the preferences and demands of those to whom they want to sell their commodities (e.g., members of the selectorate such as voters).

Yet some individuals and groups in political arenas know more than others about policy issues or political candidates. These people may use their information advantage to educate the citizenry, legitimately and sincerely, with the aim of reducing informational deficiencies and promoting better-informed public debate about policy issues—often such people are members of the news media or academic experts often interviewed in the media. Here, people who enjoy an information advantage may use that advantage simply to reduce the information asymmetries in an electorate. However, other players in political arenas may strategically use an information advantage to gain added leverage for their own preferences in political exchange. To manipulate the production of policy in exchange for support (a political exchange), politicians and their staffs may selectively pick and choose whom to educate and mobilize, what information to publicize and what information to keep private, what information to ignore or bury, and how they interpret or cast information. Shockingly, politicians may be inclined to be less than honest in their portrayal of issues as they pursue political survival and the success of their policy agendas (who would have guessed?), but such behavior is completely consistent with our initial assumptions about the goals and incentives of politicians. In search of political survival and support for the political commodities they peddle, politicians and political parties have developed increasingly sophisticated strategies for advertising their issues, building selective lists of which citizens they should call to educate about controversial issues, and determining which potential voters to remind about an upcoming election and which ones not to remind.

The ability of political actors to manipulate an information environment strategically and distort the social efficiency of political exchange depends on the presence of asymmetric information. Let's examine the Iraq conflict as an example of asymmetric information in political exchange. In 2002–2003, President George W. Bush and members of his administration argued that the presence of weapons of mass destruction (WMDs) in Iraq violated United Nations resolutions and presented a clear and present danger to the security of the United States. In the midst of the brewing international crisis, U.N. weapons inspectors reentered Iraq after a hiatus of approximately five years to try to ascertain the state of the country's weapons programs. Unable to obtain full U.N. support or widespread international cooperation, President Bush rejected the mission of the U.N. weapons inspectors and opted for a military solution, war. The arguments put forth to justify the U.S. military operation to the U.S. population and Congress highlighted the threat posed by Iraq's WMDs and the dangers of waiting for confirmation of their existence. Critics of the Bush administration decried the rush to war and argued for giving the weapons inspectors more time to complete their mission in Iraq. The public debate between supporters and critics of the administration's policy focused on whether Iraq did or did not have WMDs—specifically, had the Iraqi weapons programs been dismantled as promised after the first Gulf War? This debate continued after the triumphant U.S. invasion of Iraq, as U.S. weapons inspectors failed to uncover stockpiles of such weapons.

Was this question about the existence of WMDs the right focus for the political exchange between policy makers and the U.S. public that led to the invasion of Iraq by U.S. forces? Probably not, given the history of U.S. national security policy and nuclear defense strategy since World War II. Within that context, the debate should have focused on the security threat to the United States—what threat such weapons would pose to the United States and its allies, what strategies could best manage such a threat if it existed—rather than exclusively on the alleged existence of weapons of mass destruction. After all, the Soviets had possessed WMDs since Stalin. At the height of the Cold War, the United States and the Soviet Union each had more than ten thousand deliverable nuclear warheads, enough firepower to destroy life as we know it on earth. With successive arms control agreements that have limited delivery vehicles, the numbers of deliverable weapons have decreased in U.S. and Russian arsenals, even though the numbers of warheads remain high. This catalog doesn't even take into consideration the biological and chemical weapons in the U.S. and Soviet arsenals. The People's Republic of China, the United Kingdom, France, Israel, India, Pakistan, and North Korea—and now perhaps Iran—are members of the "nuclear club," while many other nations have some biological or chemical tools in their arsenals that may qualify as weapons of mass destruction. In terms of brutality and threat, Stalin and the Soviets dwarfed Saddam Hussein and Iraq. In a conventional war in Korea, China and North Korea had fought the United States and its allies to a standstill. Israel sits in violation of numerous U.N. resolutions. All these facts are problematic, given the terms of the Bush administration's argument leading up to the Iraq war. Why did earlier U.S. policy makers not select preemptive war in response to other states' development of nuclear weapons capacity?

In their framing of the policy question and subsequent debate, President Bush and members of his administration made the existence of Iraqi WMDs the crucial determinant of U.S. policy—not the threat of such weapons to the United States or whether such a threat could be managed by some action other than war. They succeeded in framing the debate along these lines, as voters, the media, and political opponents alike focused on the existence of WMDs in the hands of Saddam Hussein: Do they exist or don't they? Critics of the administration argued for giving the U.N. inspectors more time, but what if the inspectors had been given more time and then had found weapons of mass destruction? By the terms of the debate, those same critics would then have been obliged to support U.S. military action. The manipulation of the information environment thus prevented consideration of alternatives if WMDs were actually proven to exist during the run-up to war. The Bush administration used the debate to restructure U.S. national security policy dramatically by incorporating, for the first time, a stated policy of preemption. U.S. presidents had always had the option of military preemption at their disposal, but it had never been an official linchpin of U.S. military strategy. Under this restatement of U.S. national security policy, the very existence of weapons of mass destruction was sufficient to justify—even require—military preemption.

Let's consider this policy choice in the context of a different and more complete information environment. For more than forty years following World War II, U.S. national security strategy had been built around the theory of deterrence and containment: if you smack me, I will smack you back, hard, and perhaps even destroy you. Policy makers and strategists believed that a stable threat of assured retaliation and destruction was the best strategy to prevent an attack in the first place. Why would an enemy attack the United States if such action guaranteed swift and sure destruction? Would rational leaders of adversarial governments willingly commit suicide by inviting the destruction of their societies? In order to maintain the necessary stability, this policy required a clear ability to retaliate, the ability to survive an attack and deliver a devastating counterblow, and a target to retaliate against. Another state would offer such a target because its specific geographic location could be attacked. U.S. military procurements during the Cold War sought to ensure the requisite intelligence capacity, early-warning systems, and armaments for a stable and survivable military response to make threats of deterrence credible.

Where was the discussion of the Iraqi threat in terms of this tradition in U.S. national security policy? Had U.S. capabilities eroded so much as to preclude consideration of deterrence and containment as a viable alternative, or had Iraqi capabilities increased so greatly since the Gulf War that any logic of continuing such a policy was undermined? Quite the contrary: the collapse of the Soviet Union and its sphere of influence had left the United States as the sole military superpower in the world, the relative military capabilities of the United States had only grown more formidable since the 1991 Gulf War, and the advance of smart weaponry had extended the U.S. advantage over potential rivals and provided policy makers with options that were more accurate and flexible than those available during the Cold War. By contrast, the capabilities of the Iraqi military had substantially decayed since the Gulf War, when U.S.-led coalition forces easily threw Iraqi troops out of Kuwait. More than a decade of trade embargoes and sanctions had limited the ability of the Iraqi army to upgrade its weapons, or even to service and maintain the weapons it retained at the end of the Gulf War. U.S. military jets continued to enforce a no-fly zone in the north and south of Iraq. The Iraqi armed forces could not even conduct military operations by air against rebellious factions within their own territory under the no-fly zones. With or without weapons of mass destruction, any military conflict between the United States and Iraq would clearly have been one-sided. The U.S. advantages meant that even if Iraq had WMDs, any use of those weapons would be suicidal. Was the Iraqi leadership suicidal?

If containment and deterrence remained credible and effective policies, why was the potential for continuing these policies absent from the debate during the run-up to war? We could simply blame the Bush administration for manipulating the information environment and narrowing the terms of the debate over policy options, but this excuse would be too easy. In our political economic framework, we expect political actors to attempt to manipulate the terms of political exchange for self-interested ends, but such tampering should prove difficult in a relatively complete information environment, where all parties to the political exchange (consumers and producers) have relatively equal access to information with low transaction costs. Under these conditions, an information environment cannot be manipulated to emphasize some aspects of a policy problem and neglect others. Relatively complete information, or transparency, would surely have prompted voters, political opponents, and the media to challenge the Bush administration to engage in a debate over deterrence and containment, rather than to quickly shift focus to preemption. The absence of such discussion signals, in hindsight, a failure by the media, the political opposition, and the voters to act as informed political consumers, as is necessary for socially efficient political exchange.

As in economic exchange, the underlying dilemma facing consumers of political commodities is to break a pooling equilibrium—distinguishing good sellers or products from bad sellers or products—into a separating equilibrium, which allows them to distinguish accurately and efficiently among political actors and their policy agendas. Consumers of political commodities can counter the advantage of asymmetric information by becoming informed about issues, policies, and politicians or by developing strategies that enable them to participate in political exchange as if they are well-informed. Political consumers can look for shortcuts that allow them to act as if they are well-informed even though they are not. For example, political consumers can mimic the behavior of other voters who are better informed and whose preferences and values they share or admire; they can take the advice of special-interest groups that generally represent their preferences. In these cases, less informed political consumers piggyback on the efforts of more informed political consumers.

Effective competition in economic and political markets also helps to constrain the dilemma of asymmetric information if such competition provokes debate and increases the availability of relevant information—both access to that information and the skills needed to evaluate and process it. Competition in the economic and political marketplace, provided by multiple producers of economic and political commodities, can also constrain the problem of asymmetric information if the strategic use of asymmetric information is relatively evenly distributed across the competing producers—in other words, if they all mislead equally and effectively, counterbalancing each other. Information asymmetries may well be the single largest threat to political and economic market exchange.

The effectiveness of economic and political market exchange in allocating resources efficiently depends on the extent to which those markets work as theoretically envisioned. Ideally, the aggregation mechanisms of efficient economic and political markets should ensure that no conflict exists between individual choice and collective welfare in the structure of individual interactions. In theory, at least, the aggregation mechanisms of economic and political markets take self-interested individual behavior and produce nice social outcomes. These frameworks provide theoretical baselines from which to measure how well economic and political markets actually function in the empirical world.

AN EXAMPLE OF POLITICAL MARKET EXCHANGE: ELECTIONS, THE MEDIAN VOTER, AND SELECTION OF POLICY

Let's consider a highly stylized example of exchange in a political market. In order to provide a baseline for comparison, we will assume that the conditions for a socially efficient political market exchange do exist. This means that consumers and producers of political commodities—voters, politicians, policy makers, and political parties—are well-informed about political issues, public policies, and the preferences of others in the political arena. There is no threat of asymmetric information. Moreover, effective competition exists in the political marketplace to discipline consumers and producers of political commodities. Voters have sufficient choice among competing parties and politicians to restrict the potential of monopolistic manipulation of the political arena. We will also assume that the threat of third-party externalities is limited, property rights are clear, and transaction costs are negligible—in other words, producers and consumers of political goods have no incentives to be ill informed, to avoid participating in political exchange, or to cheat or *strategically* manipulate others in political exchange. The only exchange we anticipate under these conditions is *sincere* exchange between the producers and consumers of political commodities, and we expect the political arena to provide an aggregation mechanism, such as elections, to coordinate production and consumption of political goods. Political consumers choose among competitive political producers by casting their votes in an election.

This brings us to the social aggregation mechanism, or voting rule, that acts similarly to the price mechanism in economic markets. We need not worry about nonvoluntary consumption here, as we assume that a voter's participation in an election is a voluntary vote to ratify the process of exchange, even if the voter's own preference loses in the election. As noted in chapter 1, there are a wide variety of voting rules to aggregate individual preferences to generate a social outcome. For our example here, we posit a political system that uses a winner-take-all or first-past-the-post voting rule, one of the simplest voting rules: a **plurality rule.** This means that the candidate, referendum, or policy that wins the most votes in an election takes the whole prize—whatever position or facet of government control was at stake in the election. We expect every voter or political consumer in the system to participate in each election. Why? Because with clearly defined property rights, a relative absence of transaction costs, no potential for manipulation of the election by a monopolist (or monopsonists, oligopolist, or oligopsonists), and relatively full information, a political consumer has no incentive to avoid participating in a political exchange and every incentive to participate in order to try to obtain an outcome close to her preferred outcome.

> A **plurality rule** voting model is one in which the candidate, policy, or referendum with the most votes wins the election—a winner-take-all system.

Returning to one of our original assumptions—politicians seek to survive—let's further postulate that governments, parties, and politicians seek to win elections, continue in office, and control the distribution of political commodities in society. In democratic systems with our choice of voting rule, a political party, or coalition of parties, is selected by a plurality of voters in a competitive election to form a government and control the levers of governance. Such elections occur at regular intervals, for systematic, regular elections are the formal institutional paths stipulated in a constitution or some other legal framework. Losing parties accept electoral outcomes and do not attempt to seize control of the government by extra-electoral means. And, most critical for political market exchange, the governing party or parties must preserve political freedom, political speech, and open access to political information, for these conditions are essential if consumers of political commodities are to be well-informed and avoid the trap of asymmetric information. Restrictions on political and civil liberties such as freedom of speech and association amount to imposing transaction costs and erecting barriers that damage socially efficient political exchange.

In our stylized model, a political party is a group of people who seek by election to accede to control of government. The members of the group generally share similar but not necessarily identical preference orderings of individual and societal outcomes, and they view control of the government as an integral component to achieving those outcomes. By controlling the government, they will be better able to promote their objectives, even if those goals are purely selfish—such as greed, power, and prestige. In fact, we make no assumptions about the nobility of individual motivations, although we do trust in the ability of competitive political markets to mobilize and constrain such egoistic private interests for public good. Hence, political parties and the policies advanced by political parties are constructed simply to win elections and government control.

A voter in this democratic system looks at the political parties and their policy agendas as statements about the political commodities these parties and their candidates are offering. With two or more parties, the voter as political consumer evaluates the alternatives across the producers, compares her expected utility from different electoral outcomes, and votes for the party (candidate) that generates the greatest expected utility. In a two-party system, the voter attempts to build a ranking between the alternatives that exhibits the property of completeness; for three or more parties, she attempts to build a ranking that has the property of transitivity, as described in chapter 1. A voter may rationally choose not to vote for a party whose platform and positions promise the greatest expected utility but whose chance of winning the election seems small. This is a significant problem in a multiparty system, but not in a competitive two-party system, as we will see.

We have assumed that the primary objective of political parties is to win elections and gain control of government. A party that proves continually unsuccessful at winning elections should rationally shift strategies and adopt policy positions that appeal to more voters; otherwise, it risks becoming irrelevant, marginalized, and ultimately defunct as a producer and purveyor of political commodities. Running such a risk is a difficult choice for party members who are motivated by power, status, and greed. So, if rational, they will push their party to change its policy proposals to make them more appealing to political consumers, the voters. The interaction of voters and parties in elections can thus propel changes in party positions and in the political commodities offered by parties.

How does a losing party make such changes? What is a winning strategy for a political party in developing the political commodities it offers to political consumers? Are choices in policy offerings and changes in those offerings random, or can we make systematic statements—predictions—about a party's choices of policy positions? As political parties and their members compete for electoral victory and control of government, they attempt to offer voters a basket of political commodities that will separate them from their competitors while, at the same time, considering the makeup of the electorate. Differentiating your party from another would be relatively easy if you did not need to consider electoral prospects; a political party that is unconcerned about electoral victory could select policy positions anywhere in the political spectrum and far away from other political parties. But we have assumed that the purpose of political parties is to win elections and control government. This desire to win constrains both policy choice and a party's ability to differentiate itself from other parties, and thus it provides us, as political analysts, with leverage to make systematic statements about what policy positions a party is more or less likely to adopt.

This process of analysis brings us to consider the makeup of the electorate, the body of political consumers. First, we must ask, are voters' preferences on one policy issue related to their positions on other issues? Do individual voters have some underlying theory, or

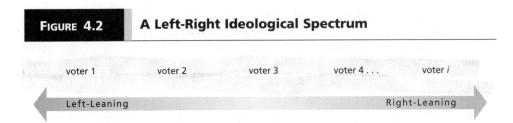

FIGURE 4.2   **A Left-Right Ideological Spectrum**

voter 1   voter 2   voter 3   voter 4 . . .   voter *i*

Left-Leaning   Right-Leaning

framework of beliefs, about state-society relations that makes their preferences on different issues more than random? For the sake of simplicity, political scientists often portray this underlying framework, or ideology, as a position on a left-right political spectrum (see figure 4.2). Voters may be distributed along this dimension in a unimodal, single-peaked pattern like the familiar normal distribution, or bell curve (see figure 4.3), or they may be arrayed in a bimodal or polymodal pattern with multiple peaks, or in some other distribution (see figure 4.4).

FIGURE 4.3   **A Unimodal Distribution of Voters along an Ideological Spectrum (in This Case a Normal Distribution or Bell Curve)**

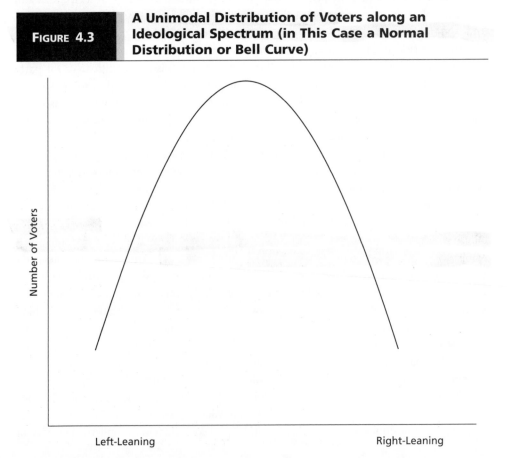

Number of Voters

Left-Leaning   Right-Leaning

FIGURE 4.4	**A Polymodal Distribution of Voters along an Ideological Spectrum (in This Case, a Twin-Peaked Distribution)**

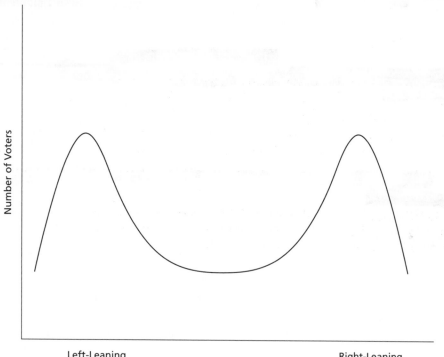

Left-Leaning   Right-Leaning

For analytical ease, let's assume that voters are normally distributed along this left-right spectrum. (We can relax this assumption later.) Remember that political parties seeking electoral success must find policy or ideological positions that appeal to a plural-

> The **median voter** is the voter who is located exactly in the middle of all the voters arrayed on a political spectrum.

ity of the voters. Therefore, in a two-party, winner-take-all system, if $N =$ total number of voters, the winning party must appeal to $N/2 + 1$ of the voters, or 50 percent plus 1, to win an election and control government. Who is the critical voter in this election, the voter who determines who wins and who loses, and where is she located on the left-right political spectrum? The voter who determines the outcome of the election is located exactly in the middle of all the voters arrayed on this spectrum. We call her the **median voter.** In this system, by voting in an election, you move the position of the median voter toward your policy preferences as you affect the size of N; by not participating, you move the median voter position away from your policy preferences. Hence the importance of participation in elections, for abstaining only contributes to an electoral outcome that is more distant from your own preferences on the left-right spectrum.

Knowing that they need the support of the median voter if they are to win in this electoral system, the two competing parties will move toward the median voter and, consequently, toward each other. (We make no prediction that individual voters will move toward the median voter's position, just parties.) Each party's extremists—by definition those located farthest from the median voter—will prefer their party to the other party even as the parties converge on the median voter, as long as their party remains closer to their end of the ideological and policy spectrum. The two parties cannot completely converge, for if they become exactly alike, or are perceived as being exactly alike, their extremists may opt out of the election—as was the case with the disenchanted voters who claimed that there was no difference between the Republican and Democratic Parties in the 2000 U.S. elections.

Convergence on electoral strategies, platforms, and policy promises in order to attract the median voter does not, however, guarantee either the delivery of such policies or their stability if delivered. In a society with a normally distributed electorate and a winner-take-all rule, the pressures of election will drive policy toward the median voter and produce relatively stable outcomes. In a society with large extremist components—a bimodal distribution with weighting toward the extremes, as in figure 4.4—parties will similarly converge on electoral positions, issues, and promises, but, having gained office, the winner will be pulled toward her party's extremists and pressured to adopt policies that are more radical than those preferred by the median voter and very radical compared to those preferred by supporters of the opposing party. In such a system, both democracy and policy performance are far more volatile.

In a two-party, winner-take-all system, convergence of party strategies and policy promises is almost inevitable, given our assumption that individuals coalesce into parties and then develop policies expressly to win elections. If we push harder on this model of political competition and political exchange, we can deduce that a durable, stable third party will prove unsuccessful and dysfunctional for voters. Two parties constitute an equilibrium in this system. Let's explore why. Based on our initial assumption that individuals coalesce into parties to seek control of government by election, we have determined that the optimal electoral strategy is to appeal to the median voter. But in a winner-take-all, three-party system, at least one party is likely to fail, fail, and fail again in its attempts at electoral success, because there will always be at least one party between this third party and the median voter. The third party is therefore not viable in the long term, and this situation confronts its members and leadership with a dilemma. In the search for electoral success, this party's repeated failures may drive its voters to the competing party with the most similar views—effectively killing the third party. Or this perpetually losing party may be inclined to merge with another party, joining forces to improve the chances for electoral success—again effectively killing the third party. This process of consolidation is likely to continue in a three-or-more-party, winner-take-all system until each of the two parties left standing has a good chance of electoral victory.

A third party in this system, however ephemeral, will push the electoral outcomes and the political commodities produced by the winning party away from that party's preferred position on the left-right spectrum. Assuming that voters cast their ballots for the party closest to their individual positions, a third party is going to take votes away from the next-closest party located between the third party and the median voter, and closest to the third party's position. Thus Ross Perot took more votes away from George H. W. Bush than from Bill Clinton in 1992, and Ralph Nader took more from Al Gore than from George W. Bush in 2000. Perversely, this process drives the electoral outcome toward the option most distant from the preferences of the third party's voters. This ironic outcome would be less likely to occur in a system with a proportional voting rule, wherein a party can achieve some electoral success and representation in a legislature by winning a vote total that is above a prescribed threshold but less than a plurality. But under this type of multiparty electoral rule, the desire to control the levers of government will encourage the formation of coalitions among parties located near each other on the left-right political spectrum.

Thus an understanding of both the relevant voting rule and the distribution of preferences in a society offers insight into the nature of that society's politics. A voting rule, which provides the electoral institutional structure of a polity, will systematically help determine both the number of viable political parties its system can support and the nature of political competition and exchange therein. The distribution of voters will offer systematic leverage to explore the stability and durability of political exchange and policy implementation. Are voters (political consumers) unimodally and normally distributed, or polymodally distributed? A unimodal distribution acts as a magnet, pulling party positions and policies toward the central tendency of the distribution, the peak. In a society with large extremist components, a polymodal distribution with weighting toward the extremes, parties may still converge on electoral positions, issues, and promises to attract more moderate voters—particularly with a winner-take-all electoral rule. Proportional electoral rules, in contrast, may empower and stabilize more extreme polymodal distributions. Regardless of the electoral rule, however, once the winning party is in office, the attraction of large numbers of extremist voters in a polymodal electorate will push the party or coalition of parties to adopt policies that are more radical and more in line with the preferences of the party's extremists than the policies preferred by the voters near the center of the political distribution.

INTERNATIONAL AFFAIRS IF THE CONDITIONS FOR EFFICIENT ECONOMIC AND POLITICAL EXCHANGE HOLD

Let's apply the logic of economic and political exchange to international affairs. If economic and political markets work as predicted, and the mechanisms of social aggregation accurately compile individual preferences in societies to produce social outcomes that maximize overall happiness in societies and minimize overall dissatisfaction, and we operate in a context as described by the structure of the invisible hand, then we should expect to observe the following behavior in international affairs:

- Policy makers pursue policies that encourage greater market exchange.
- Politics and economics remain separate except in those areas in which public policy could help to promote market exchange or improve inputs to production, and where economic resources could promote more informed political participation.

- Policy makers in liberal political economies enact policies promoting greater trade and exchange across borders.
- International organizations act as constructive mechanisms that provide infrastructure advantageous to economic exchange across national borders and help to reduce barriers to coordination that would aid such exchange.
- Greater interdependence produces increased harmony and reduces tensions between nations.
- Global economic relations expand and flourish.
- Interdependence, the growth in linkages across borders, becomes self-sustaining.

In theory, the predictions of economic liberalism and political democracy are normatively appealing, but their appeal must be more than theoretical. How well do such theories account for behavior in the social world? Does the empirical world live up to theoretical expectations, or does it fall short? If it falls short, by how much and why? This comparison of theory to the empirical world is critical for trying to understand individual choices, the interactions of such choices to produce social behavior, and the effects of structure and context on outcomes. Rarely does any form of social behavior comport perfectly with social science theory, so investigators must consider the extent to which empirical behavior deviates from a theory's expectations. Part III of this book demonstrates that for much of the nineteenth century and the twentieth century before and after the two world wars, observed behavior in the global arena does reflect the above predictions on average, but not uniformly and without exception, and some of the deviations are incredibly significant. So the logic of economic and political market exchange works fairly well in a world characterized by increasing economic and political liberalization, but not as well as anticipated. Let's consider why.

Market Failure and Suboptimal Social Outcomes

A **market failure** is a situation in which market exchange fails to allocate societal resources as efficiently as theoretically anticipated, so that a society produces and consumes less than the optimal levels of goods and services.

The pragmatic appeal of economic and political relations based on individual choice depends on the aggregation of such choices producing good social outcomes as well as good individual outcomes. Such outcomes require that the stringent assumptions underpinning economic and political market exchange hold relatively well. But what if those assumptions are seriously compromised, and the aggregation of individual actions produces only so-so, or even poor, collective outcomes?

Two major categories of problems potentially threaten the appeal of economic liberalism and political democracy based on individual choice: market failure and social traps. First, what happens when the restrictive prerequisites of efficient exchange in such markets do not hold? The theoretical conditions necessary for a perfect market do not exist in the empirical world. When the core conditions for efficient competitive economic and political markets are violated, there is a **market failure**—the failure of the market to employ the resources of society most effectively given the distribution of preferences in society. Exchange still occurs in most instances of market failure, however; only in the most extreme cases does exchange break down completely. Second, even if the assumptions do hold relatively well, what if the structure of social interactions turns out not to be an invisible hand situation, wherein individual choices interact and aggregate to produce optimal social and individual outcomes, but instead a social context wherein individual choices interact and aggregate to produce suboptimal social and individual outcomes despite the rationality of the decision makers? This situation is the social trap that we discussed in earlier chapters.

UNDERSTANDING MARKET FAILURE

Clear definition of property rights, negligible transaction costs, no possibility for producers or consumers to manipulate supply or demand unilaterally, no third-party externalities, and full information are demanding requirements that are never completely met in exchange situations, economic or political, outside the theoretical world. What happens when we fall short of meeting such requirements in our exchange relationships? Failure to meet any of these conditions undermines the gains of efficient market exchange and, by definition, leads to market failure. Such imperfection does not necessarily mean we should abandon economic and political markets as a form of social, economic, and political organization. Exchange in imperfect markets may still produce better individual and social outcomes than can be gained from alternative forms of social organization that address the distribution of economic and political goods. But we should seriously consider the flaws of market exchange in the real world and ask to what extent such requirements are violated, what damage is done to social welfare by imperfections in political and economic market exchange, how that damage is produced and exacerbated, and how such shortfalls can be mitigated by corrective measures. In effect, we need to act as social forensic pathologists, conducting autopsies of imperfect exchange in political and economic markets to determine how and why things can go wrong when the requirements for efficient market exchange are loosened.

Incomplete Property Rights and Nonnegligible Transaction Costs

Confusion over property rights can limit exchange and increase transaction costs. The more uncertainty there is on this issue, the more parties to an exchange must expend efforts and resources to protect themselves against ambiguous property rights. In economic and political markets such efforts may include hiring lawyers and drafting extensive contracts in attempts to anticipate ambiguities and loopholes in property rights and the expectations of exchange, as well as arranging for auditors to monitor exchanges closely or to mediate disputes arising from discrepancies and disagreements in exchange.

In political markets, ambiguity about property rights over votes distorts the one-person, one-vote principle in elections. In many southern American states, Jim Crow laws embedded this failure in law by limiting African Americans' access to the voting booth following

Reconstruction. Reports of voter fraud, lost ballots, and dead people voting (and voting, and voting) are more examples of political market failure related to uncertainty over the property rights of voting and the transaction costs of clarifying those rights. Treaties between nations are exchange agreements. For example, we will limit our production of greenhouse gases in exchange for *w,* we will limit our number of long-range nuclear weapons in exchange for *x,* we will lower our tariff rates in exchange for *y,* or we will come to your defense as an ally in exchange for *z.* Many treaties, however, are drafted in intentionally ambiguous language that confuses the signatory nations' obligations. For example, many military alliances require members to come to the aid of any allies that have been attacked, but not one that has initiated hostilities. The U.S. Senate failed to ratify the League of Nations Charter following World War I because its terms did not permit the U.S. government to exercise discretion about committing American troops to collective security operations. The United Nations Charter provided greater discretion to governments on the choice of providing troops for U.N.-sanctioned collective security operations (thus the Soviet Union's military did not join in the United Nations effort in the Korean War).

The international trade agreements of the post–World War II era allow nations to impose import barriers if their producers and workers are damaged by unfair competition, but the term *unfair* is intentionally left ambiguous, open to interpretation and adjudication. Without such loopholes, many, if not all, nations would have refrained from signing the General Agreement on Tariffs and Trade (GATT) and the WTO agreement. Ambiguity may be necessary to obtain sufficient consensus to arrive at a treaty, but the gray areas that are open to interpretation produce uncertainty over property rights and obligations in the exchange that forms the basis of the treaty. Such uncertainty over property rights means that the costs of negotiating, monitoring, and enforcing the terms of the exchange agreement are no longer negligible—this uncertainty adds costs and generates inefficiencies that detract from the overall value of the treaty. If these transaction costs become sufficiently large, they can significantly damage the efficiency of the exchange, and consequently harm the social welfare of the parties to the treaty.

Manipulation of Supply and Demand

What happens to efficient exchange if individual producers or consumers (monopolists or monopsonists), or cartels of producers or consumers (oligopolists or oligopsonists), can manipulate the supply or demand for a particular commodity in an economic or political market? For example, the Organization of Petroleum Exporting Countries has garnered such influence in the production and supply of oil because its small membership controls a disproportionately large share of the world's oil production. By colluding to set production targets (numbers of barrels of oil produced), OPEC can manipulate the price per barrel and increase the individual gains of its members, even if the price per barrel does not reflect what an efficient market would charge. The success of OPEC depends on several key characteristics of oil. First, there is a relatively inelastic demand for oil, and substitution of new supplies or alternative fuels is not easy or cost-efficient in the short term. Inelastic demand means that regardless of price, the demand for oil will remain relatively constant (see figure 4.5). Consumption choices concerning oil products will be relatively uninfluenced by the price of oil, for energy and oil are at the heart of any modern or modernizing political economy. We live in a world powered and heated primarily by petroleum products and by-products, where agriculture relies on fertilizers that are petroleum dependent, and where petroleum-derived plastics and other materials are used extensively in consumer goods. The lack of substitutability means that alternative sources of oil or energy, other than those controlled by OPEC, are either not readily available at a reasonable price in the short term or, if cost-effective, not capable of being developed in the short term. Inelasticity of demand and lack of substitutability for oil provide OPEC members with the ability to manipulate supply and therefore price, if they can successfully collude. If OPEC members successfully collude, then they can reap greater profits from their production of oil—far greater than what they would garner in an efficient market. Consumers of petroleum-based products thus pay more for those products than they would in an efficient market and consequently have fewer resources with which to consume other commodities. This higher price is the inefficiency, or cost, of imperfect market exchange in oil.

FIGURE 4.5   A Relatively Inelastic Demand Curve

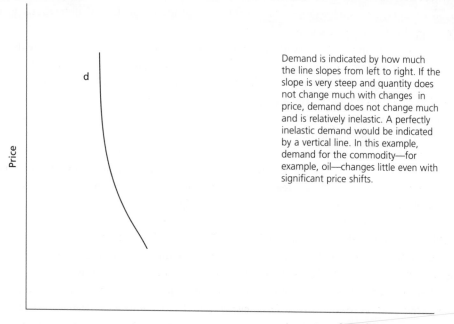

d

Demand is indicated by how much the line slopes from left to right. If the slope is very steep and quantity does not change much with changes in price, demand does not change much and is relatively inelastic. A perfectly inelastic demand would be indicated by a vertical line. In this example, demand for the commodity—for example, oil—changes little even with significant price shifts.

Price

Quantity

Such collusion to manipulate supply or demand also occurs in imperfect political markets. Political parties work to limit the number of viable candidates in elections, to constrain voters' consumption choices. Interest groups that form to advance concerns and place policy demands on politicians may be advantaged in obtaining their policy preferences versus individuals with similar interests who never succeed in forming groups. Political parties and interest groups pool individual resources and voices to create forces in political markets that are potentially more powerful and manipulative than the force of the lone voter. Citizens have little choice in the purchase of government services, since governments are by definition monopolists in the use of the legitimate forces of coercion in society and in the provision of other governmental services. As citizens, we do not get to purchase our national security from a market of national security providers, our social services from a market of social service providers, or our tax collection from a market of tax collectors. Political markets are constrained in their range of choices, and many of the exchanges they offer are nonvoluntary. A citizen must pay for and receive government services regardless of her desire for those services because the purchase of them is a collective decision. She cannot decide to purchase the national security offerings of the United States, the health care of Sweden, the tax collection of France, the road infrastructure of Germany, the legislative representation of Italy, and the courts of the Netherlands. Demand is indicated by how much the line of the demand curve slopes from left to right. If the slope is very steep and quantity does not change much with changes in price, demand does not change much and is relatively inelastic. A vertical line would indicate a perfectly inelastic demand. In this example, demand for the commodity—for example, oil—changes little even with significant price shifts.

In general, collusion by producers or consumers generates inefficiencies that are damaging to collective welfare, but important exceptions exist: natural monopolies such as utilities with high and expensive barriers to entry or too little political collusion that contributes to political fragmentation and conflict. Monopolies or oligopolies do usually lead to an overall decrease in consumption and provision of goods; consumers are harmed by increased costs and decreased consumption. These negative consequences outweigh possible gains to the monopolist in increased profits. The same is usually true if a single consumer, a monopsonist, or cartel of consumers, oligopsonists, can manipulate demand and, consequently, price. Producers will be harmed by decreased profits and lower production, and the costs to society outweigh the gains to the consumers who have manipulated price.

Third-Party Negative and Positive Externalities

Third-party externalities constitute another significant contributor to market failure. As discussed above, these are the costs (negative externalities) or benefits (positive externalities) imposed on individuals who are not directly involved in an exchange that thereby diminish or enhance the individual's welfare. If severe enough, third-party externalities can significantly undercut market exchange and detract from the efficient allocation of resources, given the aggregate wants of members of society. Negative externalities impose costs on individuals not party to an exchange and damage overall societal welfare when the costs to the third parties exceed the benefits to the parties directly involved in the exchange. The earlier example of environmental pollution is a classic example of a negative externality; other examples are abuses of common-pool resources, such as public parks and ocean fisheries, that are misused to benefit a few at the expense of many.

Positive externalities impose societal costs by a different path. They encourage free riding, or consumption of an exchange without contribution. If enough people believe that they will receive a positive externality from an exchange without contributing to the provision of the good or commodity involved, they have an incentive to free ride on those who are willing to pay for the exchange. Free riders, if successful, will enjoy the commodity being exchanged without having to pay for it—they get to have their cake and eat it too. But if enough members of a community calculate that they can free ride on such exchanges, society may face the dilemma of insufficient contributions to provide a particular good that the members of society actually desire. Perversely, the incentive to free ride to enjoy a positive externality can winnow away the provision of the commodity that offers positive externalities to others, leading to an underprovision of a commodity or good that many desire. This problem is exacerbated if those who are willing to pay for such goods resent the free riding by others in society, feel like suckers, and decide not to pay for the goods after all. This reversal generates a vicious cycle leading to market failure.

The dynamics of positive externalities create a social trap. We earlier explored this dilemma in the context of providing national security, but it is prevalent in the provision of any goods that contribute to the infrastructure of a polity or economy. We all want to live in a society of educated people, we all want to drive on nice roads, we all want good power-transmission facilities, we all want clean public parks and forests, and we all want to make well-informed decisions in the voting booth. Trouble arises, however, when many hope that others in society will bear the burden and subsidize the provision of such societal goods while hoping to receive the benefits of such provision without incurring the costs. In chapter 5, we return to the free-rider problem in the context of collective action, to unpack the structure of this problem and better understand why individuals free ride even when it damages their self-interest.

The presence of positive externalities leads to a suboptimal amount of such goods. There are mechanisms through which societies can limit free riding and shirking of contribution. We could, for instance, organize a community of potential contributors and negotiate a multiparty contract among the members of the group. Contracting is a part of everyday life in societies. Private individuals and entities enter into formal and informal contracts committing them to specific actions and obligations, and governments and their societies enter into public contracts—reflected in laws and regulations—specifying the obligations of the governments to their societies and of members of society to their governments and to other members of society. But people can violate contracts. Ensuring that they act in accordance with their contractual commitments requires monitoring the terms of the contract and the actions of the parties to the contract, and sanctioning those who do not meet their obligations. This process involves nonnegligible transaction costs, which generally increase with the number of parties to a contract and its complexity. Monitoring and enforcing compliance with contracts is costly and detracts from the production and consumption of the goods that the parties to the contract desire. In terms of the defense example, resources that could go into production of defense goods are instead channeled into the monitoring and enforcement of agreements regarding contributions to defense. Such transaction costs mean that the amount of national security purchased by a society is less than what an efficient market would produce, but probably more than voluntary market exchange would generate under the influence of positive externalities.

Threats of Incomplete and Asymmetric Information

Incomplete or asymmetric information can also undermine efficient economic and political market exchange. The earlier discussion of complete information provided important insight into the critical role of information in exchange relationships. In selecting commodities, in economic markets or in political markets, consumers or voters must differentiate across a range of options when they make their consumption decisions. Often significant differences separate commodities, but to distinguish among such differences, consumers must be informed. In a competitive market where all sellers and buyers are equally well-informed, such differences should map into consumer choices that accurately reflect the consumers' preferences given their resource constraints. Some people will purchase one commodity over others, vote for one candidate over others, or choose one public policy over others. Such choices will be efficient, as consumers will be opting for the commodity, candidate, or policy that best meets their tastes, given the constraints of cost. A seller of a political or an economic commodity cannot substitute one commodity for another without the consumer's awareness. An informed consumer cannot be misled about her choice, and she will know if it is priced accurately.

What if consumers are insufficiently informed to differentiate accurately between products, politicians, or policies that they might choose to consume? In a complicated world wherein individuals consume a vast array of commodities in political and economic markets, consumers cannot possibly be experts in all their consumption decisions. Even if they wanted to be fully informed about all their choices, trying to obtain such expertise would be inefficient, even paralyzing, as their resources and time for such research are limited. Because their time, energy, and capacity to acquire and process information are limited, consumers inevitably will make some choices with incomplete and asymmetric information, whereby the seller of a commodity knows more about the commodity than the consumer does.

People may have problems distinguishing one politician from another ("they're all alike"), one political party from another, one policy from another, or one product from another. But experts or the sellers of a commodity do not face the same dilemma. They have asymmetric information, which they can use to their advantage. Sellers of less desired products can advertise in an attempt to mislead consumers about the true nature of their products and so inflate the desirability of their products. This practice pressures other sellers of more desirable products to advertise in order to try to inform consumers about the true quality of their products. Both cases impose costs on exchange, reduce its efficiency, and detract from overall social welfare. Consumers may purchase the wrong goods or pay too much for a commodity, and sellers of good commodities may gain less than they would if everyone were equally well-informed.

The very presence of political campaigns and commercial advertisements and the extraordinary expense involved in these endeavors serve as stark evidence of the extent to which asymmetric information affects our consumption choices. If we were really well-informed, political or economic advertising would be useless. Rational companies and politicians would not pay for advertising if it did not affect consumer or voter behavior, and it can only do so if consumers and voters operate with incomplete or asymmetric information. Ironically, advertising may serve to exacerbate the dilemma produced by asymmetric information, because advertisements meant to inform accurately look the same as advertisements meant to mislead.

With incomplete and asymmetric information, consumers or voters face difficulties distinguishing good sellers, good products, good politicians, or good policies from bad sellers, bad products, bad politicians, or bad policies. Earlier we labeled this dilemma a pooling equilibrium, which leads to inefficiencies in the production and consumption of goods and services, or in the production and consumption of political commodities, as consumers or voters are purchasing goods and services or casting their votes and supporting public policies based on false or inadequate information. Consumers and voters can be misled, cheated, and manipulated so that they may not be purchasing the goods they think they are purchasing or voting for the political outcomes they want. This result is partly the responsibility of the consumers or voters who expose themselves to the possibility of being misled and manipulated by not expending the time and energy necessary to become informed consumers or voters.

One might simply say, "Let the buyer beware," and assume that voters or consumers should become sufficiently informed to make intelligent decisions that reflect their true preferences or be willing to bear the costs of their ill-informed choices without complaint. Becoming sufficiently informed is easier said than done, however, because to be well-informed about every consumption choice demands an amazing amount of information and ability to process that information. Protecting oneself against being misled and manipulated by all sellers of products in economic markets, or by all politicians in political markets, would require an impossible investment of resources and a mind with processing power far exceeding a supercomputer of a capacity yet to be invented.

Imagine how much time and effort would be required to make our every consumption decision in political and economic markets a well-informed decision. First, we would have to be able to differentiate clearly across products, politicians, and policies. Second, we would have to be able to evaluate the prospects of the different products, politicians, and policies to produce our desired outcomes. Third, we would have to be able to distinguish sincere policy makers or sellers who mean what they say from the strategic policy makers or sellers who say what is necessary to achieve their desired outcomes, regardless of whether their statements are accurate or not. Furthermore, many transactions in modern economies and polities involve exchange over time and space. For example, we select politicians and policy makers for a period of time, and they deliver political goods over that period. Essentially, we buy a basket of political goods at one point with the expectation that they will be delivered at some time in the future. This is a contract, but an incomplete contract with plenty of opportunities for the creation and exploitation of loopholes. Fourth, all of this evaluation happens in a social setting, so even if one consumer or voter develops such a capacity, the social outcome depends on the choices of many voters and consumers. None of these are trivial impositions—the transaction costs, information costs, and contracting problems are not trivial.

Essentially, consumers and voters face the challenge of sorting out good from bad claims. They need to transform the pooling equilibrium into a separating equilibrium. Recall that in a separating equilibrium, buyers and voters can accurately distinguish among products, sellers, policies, and politicians. Information dilemmas and nonnegligible transaction costs increase the likelihood that consumers cannot distinguish good products from bad products, good sellers from bad sellers, good politicians from bad politicians, or good public policies from bad public policies. They may pay too much for bad products from less reputable sellers and too little for good products from good sellers. They may cast their votes for politicians who do not reflect their true preferences and vote against politicians who better represent their preferences. They may support policies that do not reflect their true preferences at the expense of policies that better represent their preferences. Such confusion damages the consumer, the voter, the good seller, the good politician, the good policy, and society. It advantages the less reputable seller and her products, and the less representative politician and her policies. This problem affects production and consumption of economic and political goods in society by distorting the ideal of efficient economic exchange and political representation, which is simply the difference between what is produced and consumed under asymmetric information and what is produced and consumed under conditions of full information.

CONTEXT AND SOCIAL TRAPS: CYCLING, COORDINATION, AND COOPERATION PROBLEMS

Let's quickly consider a second category of problems that can lead to the suboptimal provision of individual and social welfare—social traps. The dilemma posed by social traps is in the aggregation mechanism—how individual choices interact and aggregate to produce social and individual outcomes. We have considered how individual choices in liberal

economic markets and democracies will aggregate to produce individual and societal benefits *if* they work according to their theoretical constructions, *if* some critical assumptions are
met, and *if* the context of social interaction wherein an individual's choices interact with
those of others is as expected. It is this last condition that concerns us now. Social traps
are often a function of the failure of the requisite demands for efficient exchange, but the
context of social interaction can also lead to an aggregation of those choices that produces
suboptimal individual and social outcomes. Collective and individual outcomes are sensitive
to context and to the interaction of one actor's choices with the choices of others. A rational
individual's choices can remain the same but produce different outcomes if the context or
aggregation mechanism of the choices is changed. Context—the structure of interaction of
individuals' choices—can produce social traps that cause what appear to be maximizing,
self-interested choices by individuals seeking to obtain their preferred outcomes to result in
subpar outcomes for the individuals and for the larger group or society.

When markets work as hypothesized, their contexts are assumed to engender no conflict
between the self-interested actions of individuals and a good collective outcome that optimizes social welfare. These contexts reflect the invisible hand phenomenon discussed in
chapter 1 and illustrated in figure 1.3, whereby we expect that individuals will act in their
self-interest and that the aggregation mechanism of the invisible hand will combine their
choices to produce optimal social and individual outcomes. The aggregation mechanism of
the invisible hand in economic markets, or a similar voting rule in political markets, ensures
that no conflict exists between individual choice and collective welfare in the structure of
individual interactions.

But what if we operate in a context that differs markedly from the invisible hand context?
In chapter 1 we considered how decisions by policy makers could lead to perverse social and
individual outcomes because of the structure of their interaction. In one example, decisions
by national policy makers in the 1920s and 1930s to adopt protectionist measures appear to
be individually rational decisions, given the context of choice and the alternatives available
to any individual government. Opting for protectionist measures was a rational, maximizing
choice for governments, considering their options. Like a snowball rolling down a hill, however, the context produced a vicious cycle of individually rational policy choices that
extended and deepened the Great Depression. But the possibility of a single government's
resisting the downhill momentum would have looked even more foolhardy. If a government
had resisted implementing such barriers to international exchange, even as most other
nations did so, that noble government would have likely imposed even higher costs on its
population. Seemingly good choices, given the context, produced bad outcomes.

Several categories of problems can characterize the structure of social interactions—
interdependent choices—and produce suboptimal outcomes for both individuals and their
societies. Let's consider two categories of such problems: cycling and coordination dilemmas, and cooperation problems. (In the appendix to this chapter, we use game theory to
explore the dynamics of such problems.) Cycling and coordination dilemmas are typical of

social contexts and interactions where multiple equilibria exist. Those engaged in such interactions may or may not have a strong preference for one over another equilibrium, but the dilemma is in coordinating strategies to arrive at one equilibrium where nobody has an incentive to shift policies. Without coordination, decision makers can opt for policies that lead to suboptimal outcomes. This will lead to changes in decisions at the next opportunity, and perhaps the next and the next, until equilibrium is attained. Any equilibrium produces a better payoff than cycling, and once the players are at one of the equilibria, none has an incentive to change strategies. This problem can be resolved through the coordination of interdependent choices through communication—signaling and committing to a decision strategy that is observable by others—or by luck. Once the problem is resolved, an equilibrium obtained, no party has an incentive to change strategies unilaterally, so the equilibrium is stable and lasting.

In international affairs, sea and air transit involve coordination problems that could hinder trade, travel, and transport. What color running lights should we use on our ships and planes? Do we put the red running lights on the port or starboard side of ships, on the left or right side of planes? Do we bear to the left or the right in shipping channels? Do planes flying east adopt a different altitude or flight path than planes flying west? Do small or large ships enjoy the right-of-way? Do the answers to these questions vary from country to country? All involve safety and commerce issues characterized by multiple equilibria and a potential to cycle. Not settling on a particular equilibrium can produce hazards at sea and dangers in flight. Resolving such problems generally requires only coordinating choices so that all parties play by the same rules. An international conference, or a unilateral choice by a nation with a large maritime or air transit sector, would likely be sufficient to resolve such a cycling or coordination dilemma, as no parties would strongly prefer one equilibrium to another.

Coordination problems such as territorial disputes after long and expensive conflicts might prove stickier to resolve, but they remain a cycling problem. Imagine that two nations have disagreed for years over a boundary dispute. Because the dispute is expensive, sometimes breaking into armed conflict, both governments and societies are tired of the dispute and wish for resolution, but coming to a resolution involves making choices among a variety of new boundaries that could be drawn—these possible boundaries represent multiple equilibria. Both parties will prefer any equilibrium that resolves the dispute rather than continuing the dispute, but each party prefers a different equilibrium. Once a resolution is negotiated, it will be a stable equilibrium, for the only alternative will be a return to tensions, as neither party will be able to move the resolution unilaterally to another equilibrium. This cycling problem is stickier to resolve than the simple adoption of transit rules, as both governments to the boundary dispute will be hesitant to commit to a strategy that ensures the other government's preferred equilibrium outcome. The continuation of cycling, however, will only translate into a continuation of tensions until the boundary dispute is resolved.

Cooperation dilemmas are more difficult to resolve than coordination problems. With a cooperation problem, decision makers do have dominant strategies, but the interaction of those dominant choices produces a suboptimal outcome. If the different actors could cooperate and resist playing their dominant strategies, they could achieve better individual and collective outcomes. But the structure of the interaction pushes each actor toward her dominant strategy of noncooperation in order to minimize risk for fear that other parties to the interaction might not cooperate. The prisoner's dilemma game is the classic depiction of this social trap.

Cooperation dilemmas appear frequently in international affairs. Let's return to an earlier example that we touched on early in this book. The beggar-thy-neighbor strategies of the years between World Wars I and II fall into this category of a social trap generally, and they fit the prisoner's dilemma specifically. Tariff policies such as 1930's Smoot-Hawley Act sought to obtain improved economic outcomes for domestic producers and labor at the expense of foreign producers and labor. In the case of Smoot-Hawley, if foreign governments had not retaliated against the increase in U.S. tariff barriers, U.S. producers and workers would have gained significantly while foreign producers and workers would have lost significantly—a good outcome for U.S. producers and workers, the worst of all worlds for foreign producers and workers, and a suboptimal outcome for the global economy.

But the dynamics of the context, a social trap, led foreign governments to retaliate. The intersection of mutual beggar-thy-neighbor policies was a stable equilibrium, but it produced suboptimal outcomes for U.S. producers and workers, for foreign producers and workers, and for the global economy. Severe unemployment, decline of international trade, and national and global depressions were not good for anyone. If enough governments had restrained their actions and committed to cooperation, the problems of the Depression era would not have been as severe and durable. Individuals, companies, nations, and the global economy would have been better off. But the dilemma lay in the individual incentives to opt for uncooperative strategies, and these incentives were not altered or constrained. If governments could have chosen to cooperate by not raising tariffs, not engaging in currency devaluations, and maintaining more open access to trade, the Great Depression would have been shortened and the collective outcome improved. But all the critical parties defected, adopted beggar-thy-neighbor policies in order to shift the costs of adjustment abroad, and, consequently, deepened and extended the economic downturn.

The same dynamic is at work in the formation of collusive, noncompetitive cartels that wish to manipulate the supply of particular commodities and their prices in markets. As noted in the earlier example of OPEC, the oil cartel members meet regularly to determine production targets (number of barrels of oil produced) for each member. Yet the incentive for individual members is to overproduce and sell more barrels than their production targets, in the hope that they can reap extra revenues if other members adhere to their stated targets. If one OPEC nation has an incentive to overproduce, others do as well—which can result in more oil at lower prices in the market. If OPEC fails to overcome the cooperation dilemma that is intrinsic to the members' interactions, the outcome will be suboptimal for OPEC and for OPEC members, but it will be good for the larger global economy of consumers and producers. Resolving such cooperation dilemmas proves difficult—otherwise, we would see more cartels such as OPEC manipulating supplies and prices of commodities. Resolving some cooperation problems, such as beggar-thy-neighbor policies in the international arena, can be good for individuals and for societies, but resolving the cooperative problems of market collusion can produce poor social outcomes on a broader scale. Ironically, both situations have similar underlying dynamics and constitute the same social trap.

> The **shadow of the future** is a concept indicating how much we value the future as compared with the present and how the future affects our present choices. A **discount rate** is the degree to which we allow the future to influence our current choices; a higher discount rate means that we place less value on the future than we do on the present.

Aspects of social interaction that alter individual incentives and expand the importance of the future for players—such as reputation or the prospect of frequent and repeated interactions—may help to overcome barriers to cooperation in such circumstances. This effect depends on how much social actors care about future interactions and about whether their choices today will affect their interactions tomorrow. The more we value future interactions, the more we expand the **shadow of the future** over our current choices. In economics, this influence inversely corresponds to a **discount rate** for the future. A higher discount rate means that we place less value on the future than we do with a lower discount rate—we discount the future at a higher rate. Rarely do we value any future as much as we value the present, but the more we value the future, the more the future influences our current choices. This consideration puts the phrase "Carpe diem" ("Seize the day," or "Live for today") in another light.

Even when a relatively high value is placed on the future, cooperation in such social situations is difficult to obtain and hard to maintain, but the world is filled with examples of cooperation in overcoming this form of social trap. Tools and mechanisms external to the structure of the social trap can influence individual incentives, promote cooperation, and limit the temptation to defect. Trust, reputation, social norms of cooperation such as the Golden Rule, moral suasion, community pressure and ostracism, social networks, binding contracts, side payments and bribes, hierarchy and enforceable rules, and other tools of compulsion can help to constrain this form of social trap and thus promote better individual and collective outcomes.

CONCLUSION

The social efficiency of economic and political exchange depends on the extent to which market mechanisms, voting rules, and other aggregation mechanisms produce collective outcomes that sincerely and accurately aggregate the preferences of individuals over economic and political commodities such as goods, services, policies, and politicians. If the key conditions for socially efficient economic and political market exchange—clear property rights, low transaction costs, competitive exchange, fully informed participants in the economic and political market, and limited third-party externalities—hold or are approximated, the possibility for strategic manipulation of the economic and political arena by one or more parties declines dramatically, and the likelihood of socially efficient economic and political market exchange increases regardless of all the selfish predilections of the individual members of society. Just as in economic markets, socially efficient exchange in a political market requires not that members of society be noble and altruistic, but that the key conditions hold so that the voting or political aggregation mechanisms accurately compile individual preferences. Fully informed consumers in such competitive economic and political markets will condition the producers of economic and political commodities through the aggregation mechanisms of economic exchange, voting, or other forms of political participation.

In a nice, elegant system wherein everything works according to theory, simply observing market exchange or political mechanisms that aggregate preferences in a society offers a useful framework for understanding the nature of the society's economics and politics. Unfortunately, the empirical social world is more complex and often deviates from the ideal. The core conditions for efficient, competitive political and economic market exchange are often violated and so produce market failure and social traps. The presence of social traps and the factors contributing to market failure create opportunities and incentives for strategic behavior, which means taking advantage of social situations in which one's actions interact with the actions of others. This behavior can involve manipulating an information environment for personal gain, negotiating loopholes in contacts, avoiding compensating third parties damaged by negative externalities, acting collusively with other producers or consumers in economic and political markets to manipulate supply and price of economic and political commodities, manipulating agendas toward specific ends, and structuring situations to increase the likelihood of one outcome over another.

Market failures and social traps are common in day-to-day life, in domestic affairs, and in international affairs. Sometimes these problems are relatively trivial, detracting from overall social and individual welfare but not undermining generally constructive social, political, and economic interactions. At other times, however, such problems severely damage the well-being of individuals, businesses, and societies. Economic and political market exchange still occurs in most instances of market failure; only in the most extreme cases does exchange unravel completely. Failure to meet the stringent requirements for economic and political market exchange does not necessarily undermine arguments for such exchange or suggest that another form of exchange could perform better in terms of social welfare, but it does open the door to such considerations. The fact that markets fail does not mean that we should abandon market exchange for some other form of exchange relations, such as authoritarianism in political affairs or centralized allocation and planning in economic affairs. Debates concerning the social welfare effectiveness of market exchange versus some other form of exchange center on the degree of market failure and whether mechanisms can be devised to limit the extent of market failure. At times of excessive economic and political market failures such as the Great Depression, the recession and global credit crisis that began in 2007, or the

EU sovereign debt crisis that began in Greece in 2010, those dislocated begin to question globalization, capitalist exchange, and who is being represented in democratic polities. Such challenges can lead to improvements in the scaffolding supporting economic and political market exchange to address previous inefficiencies, or they could perversely lead to outcomes that are even more damaging to socially efficient economic and political exchange.

The dilemmas produced by social traps and market failures are not easily resolved. No easy or ironclad fix exists for such social dilemmas. Yet some societies manage such dilemmas and failures better than others, and these societies generally enjoy better economic welfare, greater political liberties and civil rights, and more civil societies. In successful market economies and democratic polities, much government regulation concerning market exchange, appropriate behavior in the political arena, and the responsibilities of economic and political actors exists in an attempt to constrain economic and political market failure and protect such exchange. For example, effective rule of law with fair adjudication and enforcement mechanisms can provide strategies for managing ambiguities over property rights and obligations in exchange. Even though such tools impose transaction costs on market exchange, they can help reduce other costs and reduce the overall inefficiency of imperfect market exchange. Courts and treaties can ask parties to an exchange to internalize the costs of producing an externality, adding those costs to the exchange and limiting the externality. Parties to the exchange might be required to compensate third parties for the burden of the externality or to correct the production of the externality. The rule of law and regulation can be used to limit threats to economic and political market exchange from incomplete and asymmetric information. Disclosure, transparency, contracting provisions, lemon laws, and campaign finance laws are attempts to reduce information problems and level the playing field between producers and consumers, between politicians and voters. The existence of relatively well-functioning democratic market economies demonstrates the potential for formal and informal mechanisms to limit, though not eliminate, market failure in economic and political arenas. This sentiment is captured in the well-known remark attributed to President Abraham Lincoln: "You may fool all the people some of the time; you can even fool some of the people all the time; but you can't fool all of the people all the time."

APPENDIX: USING GAME THEORY TO EXPLORE CYCLING AND COORDINATION PROBLEMS

The tools of game theory enable us to explore the internal dynamics of cycling and coordination problems in world affairs. In cycling and coordination dilemmas, similar to many real-world interactions in domestic and international affairs, multiple equilibria exist as in the example depicted in figure 4.6—the upper-left and lower-right quadrants. Given the payoffs in this scenario, neither individual has a preference for one equilibrium or the other; no dominant strategy exists for either player. The dilemma is in coordinating strategies. If Player 1 selects Strategy A and Player 2 chooses Strategy B, or Player 1 picks Strategy B and Player 2 opts for Strategy *A*, the interaction of their choices produces suboptimal individual and social outcomes (0, 0). This context creates a cycling problem when the game is played again, as both players will likely shift strategies to try to obtain the better outcome. If the initial choice of strategies has produced a suboptimal outcome and both players then shift strategies, a suboptimal outcome will result again. They will cycle, or chase each other around the quadrants, in search of improving individual and collective welfare. Only when one player does not change strategy, or discovers a means to signal her choice beforehand, will the intersection of choices arrive at one of the two equilibria. Having arrived at one of the equilibria, neither player has an incentive to shift strategy—this is a stable equilibrium.

FIGURE 4.6	**A Cycling Game with No Distributional Advantage**

Player 1's Choice	Player 2's Choice	
	Strategy *A*	Strategy *B*
Strategy *A*	1, 1	0, 0
Strategy *B*	0, 0	1, 1

We call this game a coordination problem because neither actor has a preference for one or the other equilibrium—just a preference for arriving at one of the equilibria. Either equilibrium produces a better payoff than cycling, and once the players are at one of the equilibria, neither has an incentive to change strategies. In this case, no distributional differences separate the equilibria, so both players are indifferent over the choice of equilibrium. But different distributional outcomes across multiple equilibria can still create a cycling problem, as depicted in figure 4.7. Here, two equilibria exist as in figure 4.6, but now the two players prefer different equilibria. A cycling problem exists until they arrive at one of the two equilibria, which will become stable even though one player preferred a different equilibrium. Once the cycling stops at one of the equilibria, neither player can unilaterally shift strategies in order to move the outcome to another equilibrium. Each player will prefer any equilibrium to cycling, even if the players prefer different equilibria. This cycling problem will prove stickier to resolve in situations with distributional differences across multiple equilibria and different preferences for those equilibria among the players, but it remains a cycling problem nevertheless.

Figure 4.8 depicts a type of social trap called a **prisoner's dilemma.** This game also reflects

A **prisoner's dilemma** is a particular form of social trap that requires the actors to cooperate and to resist playing their dominant strategies in order to achieve a better collective outcome, although the structure of the interaction pushes each player toward her dominant strategy of noncooperation.

FIGURE 4.7	A Cycling Game with Distributional Consequences

	Player 2's Choice	
Player 1's Choice	Strategy A	Strategy B
Strategy A	2, 1	0, 0
Strategy B	0, 0	1, 2

aggregation dilemmas and mechanisms that are inherent to many interactions in domestic and international affairs, but it represents a more difficult social trap than the coordination problem of the cycling game. The prisoner's dilemma is a cooperation problem because it requires the actors to cooperate and to resist playing their dominant strategies in order to achieve a better collective outcome, but the structure of the interaction pushes each player toward her dominant strategy of defecting (noncooperation). Let's consider why.

FIGURE 4.8	A Prisoner's Dilemma Game

	Player 2's Choice	
Player 1's Choice	Cooperate	Defect
Cooperate	–2, –2	–11, 0
Defect	0, –11	–5, –5

The strategy of defecting is dominant for both players, because the payoffs for defecting trump the payoffs for cooperating. But if each player selects her dominant strategy, both will receive suboptimal individual payoffs (–5, –5) and the collective outcome will be suboptimal (–10). If both players choose to cooperate and commit to playing that strategy, they can improve their individual outcomes (–2, –2) and the collective outcome (–4). Unfortunately, the structure of the situation contains a social trap: if one player chooses to cooperate, the other player can improve her individual outcome dramatically by not cooperating and choosing to defect. This strategy will deliver the best possible outcome for the noncooperative player (0), the worst possible outcome for the cooperative player (–11), and a worse collective outcome than if both players had selected their dominant strategies (–11). The tension in this structure therefore promotes noncooperation in order to minimize risk.

KEY CONCEPTS

asymmetric information (p. 168)

discount rate (p. 194)

externality (p. 165)

free riding (p. 165)

incomplete information (p. 169)

market failure (p. 182)

median voter (p. 179)

monopoly (p. 161)

monopsonists (p. 162)

oligopoly (p. 162)

oligopsonists (p. 162)

Pareto optimal (p. 157)

plurality rule (p. 176)

pooling equilibrium (p. 171)

price takers (p. 162)

prisoner's dilemma (p. 197)

property rights (p. 159)

separating equilibrium (p. 171)

shadow of the future (p. 194)

social choice theory (p. 156)

transaction costs (p. 160)

uncertainty (p. 160)

voting rules (p. 156)

EXERCISES

1. What are two key differences between political and economic markets?

2. If a monopoly or oligopoly is a manipulation of the price mechanism in economic markets, what are the comparable manipulations in political markets?

3. What role do the mass media play in a political market?

4. What constitutes competition in the political sphere?

5. Why must all participants in efficient and competitive markets be price takers?

6. What is the difference between a positive externality and a negative externality? Why is free riding associated with positive externalities? Give examples of a positive and a negative externality in international relations not cited in this book. Explain how they work.

7. Why is information important to efficient market exchange?

8. What are the conditions for social efficiency in political exchange?

9. Explain the importance of information for a competitive and efficient political market.

10. Construct a hypothetical distribution of a society's voters and then deduce the nature of the politics in that society based on the distribution.

11. Who and what is the median voter?

12. Describe and explain two voting rules. How do these rules influence political exchange?

13. Identify three factors that contribute to inefficiency in political markets.

14. We have noted the importance of social traps in accounting for what appear to be nonrational social outcomes produced by rational choices. Provide an example in international affairs and explain why it is a social trap.

15. Political and economic markets are susceptible to market failure. What does this statement mean?

16. What do we call the situation in which no actor in a social interaction can improve her outcome by unilaterally choosing another strategy?

17. What is the difference between coordination problems and cooperation problems? Which kind is easier to resolve?

18. How does the structure of the Westphalian state system create the potential for a social trap?

19. Below is a game of a social interaction. Does either player have a dominant strategy in this game? Is there a social trap in this interaction? Provide a real or hypothetical example of this interaction in international affairs.

	Player 2's Choice	
Player 1's Choice	Strategy A	Strategy B
Strategy A	5, 5	−10, 20
Strategy B	20, −10	−50, −50

FURTHER READING

Akerloff, George. 1970. "The Market for 'Lemons': Quality Uncertainty and the Market Mechanism." *Quarterly Journal of Economics* 84, no. 3: 488–500.

Axelrod, Robert. 1984. *The Evolution of Cooperation.* New York: Basic Books.

Coase, Ronald H. 1937. "The Nature of the Firm." *Economica* 4: 386–405.

Dixit, Avinash, and Barry Nalebuff. 1991. *Thinking Strategically: The Competitive Edge in Business, Politics, and Everyday Life.* New York: W. W. Norton.

Downs, Anthony. 1957. *An Economic Theory of Democracy.* New York: Harper & Row.

Hirschman, Albert O. 1970. *Exit, Voice, and Loyalty.* Cambridge, MA: Harvard University Press.

Miller, Gary J. 1992. *Managerial Dilemmas: The Political Economy of Hierarchy.* Cambridge: Cambridge University Press.

North, Douglass. 1990. *Institutions, Institutional Change, and Economic Performance.* Cambridge: Cambridge University Press.

Ordeshook, Peter C. 1992. *A Political Theory Primer.* New York: Routledge.

Peed, Mike. 2011. "We Have No Bananas: Can Scientists Defeat a Devastating Blight?" *The New Yorker* (digital edition), January 10, 28–34.

Polanyi, Karl. 2001. *The Great Transformation: The Political and Economic Origins of Our Time.* 2nd ed. Boston: Beacon.

Riker, William. 1986. *The Art of Political Manipulation.* New Haven, CT: Yale University Press.

Schotter, Andrew. 1981. *The Economic Theory of Social Institutions.* Cambridge: Cambridge University Press.

———. 1984. *Free Market Economics: A Critical Appraisal.* New York: Palgrave Macmillan.

Shepsle, Kenneth A., and Mark S. Bonchek. 1997. *Analyzing Politics: Rationality, Behavior, and Institutions.* New York: W. W. Norton.

Spence, Michael. 1974. *Market Signaling.* Cambridge, MA: Harvard University Press.

The Dilemma of Collective Action: Who Organizes, Who Does Not, and Why

The High Contracting Parties, in order to promote international cooperation and to achieve international peace and security by the acceptance of obligations not to resort to war, by the prescription of open, just and honorable relations between nations, by the firm establishment of the understandings of international law as the actual rule of conduct among governments, and by the maintenance of justice and a scrupulous respect for all treaty obligations in the dealings of organized peoples with one another, agree to this Covenant of the League of Nations.

—*Preamble to the Covenant of the League of Nations, 1919*

Politics is the interaction of diverse interests to produce social outcomes with distributional consequences in a world of scarcity. Such interactions range from cooperative to conflictual, from peaceful to violent; some produce good social outcomes, and others damage social welfare. In order to understand past outcomes and anticipate future social interactions, we need to consider how interests aggregate to produce a collective outcome. We need to think about why some interests successfully mobilize to advance their collective interests and others do not, why some interests in society become actively engaged in the political arena even as other interests remain dormant. Why do some groups emerge to promote their interests? Moreover, why do other groups fail to mobilize successfully even as survey data suggest strong societal support for the social goods they would support if they did become organized? This is not a straightforward empirical question, because it is difficult for researchers to examine groups that fail to materialize in order to understand why. After all, how does a researcher examine something that does not exist? Luckily, theory provides some leverage along with the struggles that groups encounter as they seek to form or as they decay.

Trying to answer these questions requires analyzing how individuals interact in groups. We need a theory of group behavior that helps us to understand when individuals will join groups and contribute to group objectives and, conversely, when individuals will not contribute to group goals even if they are members of the group and would benefit from obtaining the group's preferred outcome. What happens at the individual level either to promote or to undermine productive social outcomes? Why do individuals with mutually compatible interests fail to contribute to group outcomes that would be good for those individuals and their groups? Arriving at such an understanding will provide some insight into collective action and the provision of collective goods (or bads). This chapter examines these questions, explores some of the strategies used to overcome barriers to collective action, and leads to a discussion in the next chapter of a strategy that is particularly relevant to international political economy. The aim of the chapter is to help us understand why only some interests successfully organize to communicate their preferences and agendas to national policy makers concerning issues related to international affairs, such as migration, trade policies, agricultural subsidies, foreign aid, tax policy, and climate change.

A PARADOX OF COLLECTIVE ACTION

Initially, many social scientists believed that individuals with similar preferences in society would coalesce into interest groups to press their jointly held preferences. This approach assumed that individuals would willingly contribute resources, time, and effort to group activities that could further their individual long-term interests. Pushed to its logical conclusion, this assumption suggested that all individuals with similar preferences would voluntarily form groups and contribute to collective action, and that the many interest groups we observe in relatively open societies should constitute all the potential group interests in those societies. Yet we are immediately confronted by an empirical paradox: many individuals with similar preferences fail to form groups to promote their collective interests, and, therefore, many collective interests remain latent in society. We observe potent trade associations, strong labor unions, and intimidating associations of manufacturers, but consumer associations are weak at best. As individuals we all prefer some level of national security, nice public parks, clean air and water, good schools for our children, and sound infrastructure such as roads, bridges, ports, and robust electrical grids, among other collective goods, but as individuals we fail to contribute voluntarily our share of the resources necessary to purchase such goods. We do not spontaneously form or join interest groups to contribute to the provision of such social commodities. Moreover, not only do individuals often fail to form groups and contribute voluntarily to their long-term interests, but also sometimes individuals actually act contrary to those interests. This is another example of situations that produce social traps, those settings where rational individual calculation might actually lead to choices that produce less preferred collective outcomes.

This problem occurs again and again. We favor conservation and clean air, but we purchase inefficient cars, waste energy, and avoid clean-energy technologies. We like clean and plentiful water, but we grow lawns instead of other plants; use chemical fertilizers that damage groundwater, rivers, and lakes; and opt for energy production that produces acid rain. We water our lawns despite severe drought conditions. Walmart parking lots are filled with vehicles sporting bumper stickers denoting labor union membership and admonitions to "Buy American," yet much of the merchandise the owners of those vehicles purchase from Walmart is produced abroad by labor that competes with American workers. We worry about the viability of ocean fisheries, but we happily consume Chilean sea bass and other overfished species at our favorite restaurants. We fret over emissions of greenhouse gases that contribute to global warming, but we fail to cooperate to limit those emissions in order to improve environmental conditions for ourselves, our children, and our grandchildren. Again and again, public opinion surveys show that we prefer nice social outcomes and policies such as peace, growth, education, foreign aid for disasters, health care, clean environments, and collective security. Yet individuals fail to contribute sufficient resources voluntarily to try to achieve such outcomes. Moreover, individuals resist nonvoluntary contributions (e.g., taxes) to fund initiatives to obtain those outcomes.

Ironically, many interest groups coalesce and overcome barriers to collective action in order to resist policies that would improve social welfare. Producers form cartels to manipulate supplies and prices of goods, industrial polluters form coalitions to resist green legislation and environmental reforms, and industry trade associations lobby for special tax provisions and subsidies that redistribute public resources to what has become known as corporate welfare—public resources that benefit private corporations that have robust and healthy balance sheets. OPEC is one of the most obvious examples of collusion to manipulate the supply and price of a commodity—this cartel regularly engages in actions to manage the supply of oil entering the world's markets in order to maintain a floor under energy prices and ensure revenues. Some groups appear schizophrenic: pharmaceutical companies construct coalitions to lobby for increased government contributions to medical research (a help to social welfare) but resist attempts to impose competitive pressures on the prices of their drugs (a hindrance to social welfare).

DISMANTLING THE SOCIAL TRAP: SELF-INTEREST AND COLLECTIVE OUTCOMES

At the heart of collective action, explaining why some interests succeed and others fail to overcome the barriers to cooperation, is a tension between individual rationality and the context of choice. A social trap exists. Returning to our initial assumption that individuals act as if they are self-interested, we must consider how self-interested actors interact to attain—or not attain—collective outcomes and how social context affects such interactions. If rational individuals fail to contribute to group activities that promote gains in individual and social welfare, we must surmise either that they do not recognize their self-interest (an information dilemma) or that they are well-informed but believe refraining from contributing to the collective action offers them a greater cost-benefit outcome regardless of the desirability of the collective outcome. The first problem reflects the asymmetric information dilemma discussed in earlier chapters, but let's focus on the second problem here. This situation is a social trap whereby individual rationality conflicts with collective rationality, as self-interested individuals select actions that undermine collective interests, even though those individuals would prefer the collective outcome. Let's unbundle this social trap to understand the dilemma of collective action.

What Is a Collective Good?

When speaking of collective interests, many use the term *public good,* but this concept carries a more restrictive definition that is unnecessary for our purposes, so here we use *collective good* instead. A **collective good** has two defining qualities: nonexcludability and jointness of supply. The first, **nonexcludability,** means that if you are a member of a group for which a collective good exists, you can consume that good regardless of your contribution to the collective effort—you cannot be excluded. The impossibility of exclusion allows noncontributors, or free riders, in the collective to consume the collective good despite their noncontribution. For example, if you shirk on paying your taxes—your public obligations—but enough other people contribute sufficient resources to the government to produce the collective good of national security, you can still enjoy national security. The group cannot say that everyone in Connecticut receives national security except you (and other shirkers). Clean air, national security, clean water, the Internet, and highways are such collective goods. Not all nonexcludable goods are "good," however; pollution is also a collective good by this definition—or, if you prefer, a collective bad.

The second defining characteristic, **jointness of supply,** means simply that one person's consumption of a good does not restrict its consumption by other members of the collective (or group). That is, your consumption of a good does not constrain my ability to consume that good if we are members of the same group. If the United States is the collective, and national security is the collective good, people in Utah can consume security even as people in Connecticut consume the same good. The consumption of national security by the citizens of Connecticut does not prevent Utah residents from consuming the same security.

These two defining conditions of a collective good are also the keys to the social trap that

> **Collective goods** are public commodities that, if available to one member of a group, must be available to all members of that group. **Nonexcludability** is a characteristic of collective goods: all members of the group must have access to the good regardless of whether or not they contribute to the collective effort; examples can be positive, such as military protection, or negative, such as pollution. **Jointness of supply** is a characteristic of collective goods whereby one person's consumption of a collective good does not restrict its consumption by other members of the group.

> **Free riding** is a collective action problem in which individuals have no incentive to contribute to the provision of a public good because they cannot be excluded from consuming that good even if they fail to contribute.

creates barriers to collective action and the provision of collective goods. Jointness of supply and nonexcludability of a good constitute externalities that create barriers to the provision of public goods, even if all people prefer to live in a world with such public goods. They create opportunities for individuals to consume a collective good without contributing to its provision, to **free ride** on the actions of other members of the group.

Initial Expectations about Provision of Collective Goods

Let's examine the dynamic of collective good provision. When should a self-interested individual contribute to the provision of a collective good? Rational individuals weigh costs against expected benefits, the expected rate of return against the costs of contribution. So, if

C_i = costs for individual i,

GB_i = gross benefits for individual i, and

NB_i = net benefits for individual i,

then the cost-benefit calculation for individual i is

$$NB_i = GB_i - C_i.$$

Following the cost-benefit logic, we would expect individual i to contribute to the collective activity if

$$NB_i > 0,$$

and to refrain from contributing to the collective activity if

$$NB_i < 0.$$

The basic equation merely states that we expect individuals to contribute to the provision of collective goods if their gains from the provision of such collective goods outweigh their costs. Given the logic in this equation, we should anticipate groups forming and contributing to collective action whenever individual expected net gains are positive. This logic seems irrefutable, yet we are constantly confronted by the underprovision of collective goods and the failure of latent groups to coalesce and become active. Let's return to the equation to try to make sense of this paradox.

Positive Externalities and Incentives to Free Ride

If individual i believes that other members of her group will contribute to the provision of the collective good, and individual i believes that their contributions will be sufficient to ensure the provision of the collective good, then individual i will have an incentive to free ride and not contribute. She may decide to act as a third party, treating the collective good as a positive externality of an exchange between others. If the collective good will be provided when

$$NB_i = GB_i - C_i \text{ and } NB_i > 0,$$

and individual i anticipates that the collective good will be provided even without her contribution and that, because of jointness of supply and nonexcludability, she will still be able to consume the collective good because of her membership in the group, she can calculate that if she shirks her contribution, her payoff will be

$$NB_i + C_i = GB_i.$$

As $NB_i + C_i > NB_i$, she recognizes that she does better by free riding than by contributing. She can enjoy the collective good and save her cost of contributing to its provision for some other consumption choice. She can have her cake and eat it too!

The Unraveling of Collective Good Provision

There is, however, a significant and deeper problem with this logic than simply the decision by one member of the group to free ride. We assume that all decision makers are rational and capable of making the same calculations as individual i, who decided to free ride. This means that other members of the group should also rationally consider free riding and attempt to have their cake and eat it too. It is this calculation made individually by many members of the group that can unravel the provision of the collective good. If enough members of the group decide to free ride by failing to contribute to the provision of the collective good, that good will be underprovided or not provided at all—rational individual calculations threaten a collective outcome that is desired by those very individuals. Returning to the example of the provision of national security, if we pass a hat for voluntary contributions to national security, we are unlikely to obtain enough to fund even a fraction of our defense establishment, yet we all want national security.

To make matters worse, the presence of numerous free riders can upset members of a group who do contribute to the collective good, even if the condition $NB_i = GB_i - C_i$ and $NB_i > 0$ is still met for those contributors. Rational or not, individuals who underwrite the provision of collective goods may believe that they are being played for suckers if too many members of their group free ride. Disgruntlement over bearing a disproportional share of a burden may not be rational if the collective good is desirable and the cost-benefit calculation remains positive, but it is, nonetheless, a human emotion that can erect barriers to collective action.

Even if some group members will still contribute to the provision of a collective good in the presence of free riders, another problem looms that could affect the provision of the collective good. With fewer members contributing, there is no reason to assume that the cost of providing the good will decline. Assuming a fixed cost for the collective good, the prospect of more free riders and fewer contributors produces an obvious problem: the cost to each contributor will increase. Returning to the basic equation, this means that the calculation may change for contributors who made an initial decision to contribute when they believed that

$$NB_i = GB_i - C_i \text{ and } NB_i > 0.$$

With fewer contributors, the size of C_i increases. At some point, as fewer members contribute and C_i increases for each contributor, the cost-benefit calculation for those willing to contribute will shift, so that

$$NB_i < 0.$$

When this happens, no one will voluntarily contribute to the collective good, even if all members of society would prefer that outcome. The provision of a socially beneficial collective good, desired by many individuals, unravels.

ANOTHER PARADOX: COLLECTIVE ACTION DESPITE THE SOCIAL TRAP

This social trap of free riding, which threatens the provision of collective goods, turns the original question on its head. We began by assuming that a collective good would be provided if the benefit to society and to individuals outweighed the cost of provision. This assumption led to a conclusion that all affordable collective goods desired by society (or the group) would be provided. But this conclusion is empirically false. Now we have a theoretical mechanism for understanding why rational individuals free ride by failing to contribute to a collective outcome they prefer and consequently undermine the collective good. Pushing this mechanism to its logical but socially perverse conclusion, we should observe the provision of collective goods infrequently. Here we meet with another paradox: empirically, we do see an underprovision of collective goods given the original traditional logic, but we also observe the provision of too many collective goods given the logic of the social trap of free riding.

Many collective goods are provided despite this social trap. People cooperate far more in providing collective goods than we should expect, given the dynamic of the social trap, the tension between individual rationality and desired social outcomes. Explaining the provision of collective goods despite the social trap requires uncovering the existence of mechanisms that help latent groups overcome barriers to collective action, including the incentives for individuals to free ride on other members of their group.

MECHANISMS FOR OVERCOMING BARRIERS TO COLLECTIVE ACTION

What explains the difference between situations in which collective action succeeds and those in which it fails? Specifically, we need to examine what mechanisms can limit individuals' incentives to free ride and convince them to contribute to a collective good. In this section, we consider five categories of devices that can influence the incentives of individuals: compulsion, selective incentives, entrepreneurship, piggybacking, and group size. These mechanisms affect individual calculations by changing their evaluations of the costs (C_i) and, consequently, the net benefits (NB_i).

Compulsion

Compulsion is the exercise of one form of influence to shift the incentives of individuals to contribute to the group effort. It involves the use of power and hierarchy in social relations. Compulsion threatens punishment (perhaps by force), exclusion, or some other penalty for defection from contributing to the collective good. Compulsion transforms a

> **Compulsion** is the exercise of power and hierarchy to shift the incentives of individuals to contribute to the group effort, thus essentially transforming a voluntary exchange into a non-voluntary exchange of resources in order to obtain a collective good.

voluntary exchange of resources to obtain a collective outcome into a nonvoluntary exchange of resources to obtain a collective good. It uses hierarchy to impose individual costs or penalties for noncontribution and transforms the relatively symmetrical exchange characteristic of economic market exchange to an asymmetrical exchange, which is more often typical of political exchange. For compulsion to be successful, it must be credible.

For example, the forced extraction of contributions through national tax structures tempers an individual's inclinations to free ride on the provision of public parks, education, highways, clean air, clean water, and stable adjudication of property rights and disputes. The presence of tax structures is not sufficient to ensure contribution, however; tax avoidance troubles many societies. A credible threat of compulsion behind a tax structure can help to overcome this barrier to contribution. If members of a group would otherwise elect to free ride absent the threats of adjudication and sanction, tax structures compel contributions by means of underlying threats that change the cost calculation of noncontribution and shift the incentives of individuals. Hierarchies, through the threat and use of sanctions, can transform the incentives of individuals to contribute to a collective good.

The mechanism of compulsion works to overcome barriers to collective action in domestic and international arenas. For example, if more powerful nations press for compliance, other governments may lower trade barriers, refrain from practices that damage international exchange, or contribute to collective security arrangements. Members of the Warsaw Pact, the Eastern bloc collective security alliance during the Cold War, contributed to the provision of the collective good of security partly because of the hierarchical influence of the

Soviet Union and its ability to extort contributions through implicit threat of compulsion and, ultimately, explicit punishment.

The governments participating in the Bretton Woods negotiations, which created the rules of the game and the institutional foundations of the post–World War II global economy, agreed to a set of international economic practices that required substantial and expensive resources to promote liberal economic exchange and stability. These cooperative agreements amounted to commitments to the provision of collective goods that would help to restore the health of the global economy. The United States shouldered much of the burden. Policy makers in many states faced frequent temptations to free ride and defect from the Bretton Woods system. Sometimes policy makers succumbed to such temptations, yet they rarely did so in any significant manner that threatened the system. Why? One plausible reason lies in the penalties that the international hierarchy could potentially have imposed on problematic governments or pariah states. In particular, the unambiguous position of the United States at the top of this hierarchy and the network of relations built around U.S. leadership could have created significant problems and penalties for a state defecting from the collective action provisions. Defectors could have incurred penalties from the international governmental organizations (IGOs; also known as intergovernmental organizations) overseeing the system, from the United States as the linchpin of the system, or from others in the system more generally.

U.S. policy makers used the U.S. position as an occupying power in Germany and as the dominant political economy in the immediate aftermath of World War II to dominate discussions over the design of the North Atlantic Treaty Organization (NATO), its command and control structure, the nature of the weapon systems adopted by NATO nations, its force structure, battlefield tactics, and overall strategy. Again, because of its position and capabilities in the international hierarchy, the United States dominated the design of other IGOs such as the Association of Southeast Asian Nations (ASEAN), the International Monetary Fund (IMF), the World Bank, and the GATT. One nation did not equal one vote in the creation of the postwar international organizations that were designed to limit collective action problems.

Certainly, many nations received great benefit and assistance from the U.S. contributions to intergovernmental organizations, yet they did not free ride as one might anticipate. A pure strategy of free riding would suggest that they would not contribute anything if U.S. policy makers were willing to bear the full burden of collective goods provision. Yet they contributed bases, troops, and other resources to the collective good. One potential explanation for this willingness to contribute is the ability of the United States to compel cooperation by threatening to exclude nations that failed to do so. Not that governments had to contribute at a level proportional to the U.S. effort, but the contributions had to be significantly larger than free riding. U.S. policy makers used a variety of strategies to extract contributions from the members of the collective. In the cases of Germany, Japan, and South Korea, the presence of large numbers of U.S. forces providing security for those countries enabled U.S. compulsion. In other cases, a fear or implicit threat of a U.S. retreat to isolationism or protectionism helped to induce cooperation. U.S. policy makers could argue that U.S. taxpayers would not foot the bill if others chose to free ride. The special position of the United States, like that of the United Kingdom in the late 1800s, empowered this implicit threat. Given the size and position of the U.S. economy throughout the post–World War II period, if U.S. policy makers had chosen to free ride on the rest of the collective, any provision of collective goods would have been seriously damaged even if all other governments contributed far more than their fair shares. This situation highlights the special case of the U.S. as a hegemon, or dominant power, in the post–World War II period. (We examine hegemony as a special category of collective goods provision in the next chapter.)

The Soviet Union also employed compulsion in its sphere of influence in the post–World War II period. Soviet policy makers compelled participation in and contribution to the collective security arrangement called the Warsaw Pact and to the economic arrangement called Comecon. These organizations did for the Eastern bloc what NATO, the GATT, the IMF, the World Bank, and others did for the Western bloc and many nonaligned nations. Poland, Hungary, Czechoslovakia, Bulgaria, and others could not simply free ride, even if they so desired. Soviet compulsion was most visible during the 1956 Hungarian revolution and the 1965 Czech Spring, when Soviet tanks and troops put down uprisings antithetical to Soviet purposes.

Selective Incentives

Another strategy to help secure contributions to collective actions, a **selective incentive,** involves the private transfer of additional benefits above and beyond the collective good to specific members of the group in order to induce their cooperation in the provision of the collective good. A selective

> A **selective incentive** is an additional benefit beyond the collective good provided to latent group members in order to change their cost-benefit calculation and induce cooperation in the provision of the collective good.

incentive provides an exclusive benefit that may help to change the cost-benefit assessment of latent group members. Targeting specific group members, it shifts the calculation of net benefits (NB_i) by providing an additional payoff, albeit targeted and private. If the incentive were to be provided to all group members, it would no longer be a selective incentive; rather, it would be a good more similar to a collective good.

Selected incentives can be tangible physical rewards or less tangible rewards such as reputation, pride, or community identification. Tangible rewards, or side payments, take many forms in global affairs. The developed political economies offered a program called Generalized System of Preference (GSP) to obtain support from governments of developing states for the agenda of the GATT, and later the WTO. To exporters from qualifying developing nations, the GSP offered reduced tariff barriers to developed states' markets—a benefit that could potentially level the playing field, provide a comparative market advantage, and provide a boost in their competition with producers from more established political econo-mies. Only developing states qualified for GSP status; developed states were excluded, which made GSP a targeted selective incentive that was designed to obtain support from developing nations for the collective good of liberal economic exchange in the global economy.

Selective incentives hold many military alliances together. The collective good of military alliances is security, but many states obtain more than national security for their contribu-tions to such alliances. In the NATO alliance, some governments and communities receive selective incentives in the form of rent payments for military bases for U.S. troops stationed in Europe. Governments have obtained special deals on weapons and training, and many local economies have enjoyed positive externalities as the location of military facilities has led to the expansion of housing and local economic enterprise.

Governments of major states fill their foreign aid budgets with side payments and selective incentives. For example, three of the largest recipients of U.S. foreign development assistance are Israel, Egypt, and Pakistan. Foreign aid is a very small part of the U.S. government's budget—about nine-tenths of 1 percent and shrinking—but the lion's share of that assistance targets these three nations. Why? The transfers to Israel and Egypt are part of the side pay-ments that President Jimmy Carter used to convince the Israelis and Egyptians to compromise and agree to the historic Camp David Accords. Each nation received selective goods that were exclusionary and specifically targeted to support the collective good of Israeli-Egyptian peace and a decrease in regional instability. U.S. foreign assistance to Pakistan grew dramatically after the terrorist attacks on the World Trade Center and the Pentagon on September 11, 2001. The subsequent war on terror is a collective good, but obtaining Pakistan's contribution to this collective good has required extensive side payments. U.S. assistance to Pakistan is a tar-geted selective incentive that excludes other nations from consuming these side payments. Such private incentives can be revisited if the target does not adequately contribute to the collective good—that is, if it does not essentially live up to the implicit or explicit terms of the agreement. This has become an issue with Pakistan, given the possibility that members of the Pakistani government have aided factions hostile to NATO activities in Afghanistan.

Selective incentives are strategies of reward and sanction targeted at specific members of a group to elicit their cooperation for a broader collective objective. Such incentives are read-ily apparent in everyday life. Membership appeals from the Sierra Club, National Public Radio (NPR), the Public Broadcasting Service (PBS), and local museums and zoos routinely offer canvas tote bags or umbrellas emblazoned with the organizations' logos to individuals who agree to contribute to their activities. Such a contribution involves both a collective good and a selective incentive. The success the Sierra Club achieves in working for the pro-tection of the environment, the special programming provided by NPR and PBS, and the exhibits at museums and zoos are the collective goods. Tote bags or umbrellas are the selec-tive incentives, or side payments, given in return for contributions, but they are more than merely material rewards—they are symbols that advertise the contributors' commitment to the provision of collective goods and, consequently, help to establish the contributors' good reputation, status, and identity in the community. Such intangibles can be extremely powerful selective incentives; anyone can purchase a tote bag or umbrella of similar quality without any advertising more easily and far more cheaply than by making a sizable contribution to a collective good. Yet a simple stroll down any busy city street provides evidence of the appeal of such selective incentives.

As a member of a university community, you will eventually be approached to contribute to the collective good of higher education: soon after you graduate, you will begin receiving calls and letters asking that you contribute to your alma mater. If you decide to do so, your donation will involve both a contribution to the collective good of higher education and a selective incentive to you, as the university publicly acknowledges your gift. Aside from the warm, fuzzy feeling of personal satisfaction you enjoy when making your contribution to such a noble endeavor, your side payment is the reward of public recognition for your contribution.

Entrepreneurship

Entrepreneurship offers another strategy for overcoming barriers to collective action. **Entrepreneurs** are people who help to generate collective goods when they act in their private interest. Although their actions may produce collective goods, they are less

> **Entrepreneurs** are people who help to generate collective goods when they act in their private interest.

motivated by their concerns about the group outcome for the sake of the group than they are by the fact that the group outcome is instrumental to some private objective they wish to obtain. They help mobilize collective action as an instrumental step to achieving their private objectives. Seeking to advance their narrowly defined career interests, such as gaining election, politicians try to transform latent interests in society that fail to provide collective goods into active, privileged groups that do produce collective goods for their members. In such cases, the politicians function as entrepreneurs because their private agendas coincide with the promotion of the collective agenda. This process has been called "the public use of private interests."

Entrepreneurs reduce costs to the individual (C_i) by providing energy, organizational skill, and inertia to the provision of collective goods. Relatively latent, unorganized constituencies, such as women and environmentalists, became more active and engaged in politics when political entrepreneurs created active organizations and movements that focused on issues relevant to those constituencies, such as children's issues, women's rights, gender equity in the workplace, clean air, clean water, and protection of endangered species. By creating the organizations and movements, entrepreneurs mobilized members of these latent groups and transformed them into active groups that contributed to the provision of collective goods. At the same time, the political entrepreneurs increased the likelihood that those who cared about such issues would turn out to vote, consequently advancing their own electoral interests.

Neighborhood Watch programs, which provide the collective benefits of greater security and community, are often started by active entrepreneurs in the neighborhoods where they are established. These programs do not appear spontaneously. Most people care about their neighbors, but their watchful energies and concern often remain unorganized and latent. Overcoming the barriers to the active cooperation that is needed for such a program usually requires the organizational energy and impetus provided by a dedicated individual, or individuals, whose efforts produce collective benefits in terms of neighbors watching out for their neighbors and greater communal interaction. The entrepreneur gains the same collective benefits as the rest of her neighborhood, but she also receives private benefits in terms of reputation, self-esteem, and community leadership.

Similar to Neighborhood Watch programs are many military alliances, such as NATO and the Warsaw Pact, that rely on the entrepreneurship of a leader—the United States and the Soviet Union, respectively, in these cases. Another example is the leadership of the AARP (formerly known as the American Association of Retired Persons), the members of which gain influence and stature if they can expand the organization's membership base by educating older Americans about issues relevant to their later years of life. The efforts of the AARP have helped to transform older U.S. voters into a powerful political constituency that is concerned with health care for the elderly, retirement, and social insurance issues—all collective goods for the membership of the AARP. The AARP has been so successful in its political capacity that U.S. policy makers are more motivated to promote programs to benefit the elderly and retired than they are to promote programs related to children and the active workforce—a potentially perverse policy outcome if we are interested in economic expansion and growth as a collective good. Meanwhile, the leaders of the AARP, the entrepreneurs, gain personal stature, income, and power in the political arena, becoming power brokers whom politicians ignore only at their electoral peril.

Piggybacking

> **Piggybacking** is a mechanism for the provision of collective goods by which established organizations add new concerns and interests to their agendas.

Another mechanism that helps to account for the provision of collective goods despite individual incentives to free ride is **piggybacking,** which occurs when already established organizations add new concerns and interests to their agendas. The civil rights movement in the United States, for instance, used religious organizations to gain footing, organize support, and promote activities to challenge racial segregation and discrimination. Social justice is not inconsistent with the objectives of churches, mosques, and synagogues, but these institutions were founded to take care of religious needs and feed the soul, not to advance social issues publicly and politically. Congressman John Lewis, the Reverend Martin Luther King, Jr., the Reverend Jesse Jackson, the Reverend Ralph Abernathy, and many other African American religious leaders piggybacked civil rights onto the missions of their religious organizations. Churches played a similar role in organizing support for women's suffrage early in the twentieth century.

Another example is provided by labor unions, which were originally established to overcome barriers to collective action by workers in order to promote their interests in negotiating with management and to protect workers against arbitrary and capricious actions by management. Over the years, union leaders have transformed their organizations into significant political forces on a wide range of issues. Today, union leaders use their organizations, which were established to advance collective bargaining and arbitration, for the articulation and advancement of a much wider range of policy issues, such as pensions, trade protections, health care, and environmental issues. It seems unlikely that unions would have initially emerged to advance any of these issues, but once they existed, union leaders could piggyback new issues onto the unions' organizational infrastructure. Large, well-established unions have offices and staffs located in Washington, D.C., and other capitals, where they supply organizational capabilities that can be directed to new issues and the pursuit of new collective goods. Their established organization thus provides unions with disproportionate leverage and staying power in U.S. politics, despite the shrinking proportion of the U.S. labor force they now represent.

In international affairs, many U.S. labor unions have piggybacked international trade issues onto the organizational structures they developed to advance other issues. In the 1940s, 1950s, and 1960s, these unions either looked benignly on free trade or even favored lower barriers to trade. Since the 1970s, however, many unions have taken a more active interest in trade policy and have grown increasingly protectionist. The unions have been so successful in piggybacking trade onto their membership representation structures that they have helped place debates over fair trade, outsourcing of jobs, environmental regulation, and child labor standards on the agenda of U.S. electoral politics. In Poland in the mid-1980s, the trade union Solidarity took the lead in pushing for political reforms that led to the downfall of the nation's Communist government. Again, political reform and rebellion were piggybacked onto an established union organization.

Created early in the twentieth century to represent workers and advocate on their behalf against management, unions are now mobilized to promote policies on a much wider range of issues in a phenomenon known as piggybacking. Here, in a 2005 effort to stop the Central American Free Trade Agreement (CAFTA), a regional trade arrangement between Costa Rica, the Dominican Republic, El Salvador, Guatemala, Honduras, Nicaragua, and the United States, representatives for Citizens Trade Campaign help volunteers organize at the Capitol Hill Presbyterian Church before meeting with members of Congress at the Capitol. The Stop CAFTA lobbying effort was organized by various Pennsylvania unions.

Group Size

Group size is another important consideration among the reasons individuals with common interests in a collective good may or may not overcome barriers to collective action and the temptation to free ride. Small groups generally have an advantage over large groups in overcoming barriers to collective action. First, in small groups, individuals are much more likely to know many, if not all, of the other group members personally, and this familiarity increases the usefulness of ostracism, friendship, companionship, isolation, moral persuasion, respect, admiration, blackballing, censure, and other tools of social pressure in motivating behavior. These tools can be used to impose social rewards and penalties on individuals for contributing or failing to contribute to the group outcome. Such social pressure, which acts as an incentive for individuals by affecting NB_i and C_i, is more likely to work successfully in small-group settings, where the bonds of friendship and familiarity serve to increase the personal costs of noncontribution. In large groups, conversely, anonymity works against these social incentives to collective action. Individuals in large groups are less likely to be known to or familiar with other group members. The bonds of friendship cannot be used to promote behavior where no friendship exists, and it would be equally difficult to ostracize an anonymous target or to employ respect as an incentive when little likelihood exists for repeated social interactions.

Divisibility is the interaction of group size with the total amount of a collective good; an individual's willingness to contribute may lessen if the benefit of the collective good decreases with its consumption by an increasing number of group members.

Second, in a small group, each individual's contribution may be more critical to the provision of a collective good. A small number of free riders can easily undermine the collective effort in a small group, whereas in a large group a significant number of free riders may be less critical. Awareness of this group size sensitivity is more likely to alter the calculations of individuals in the small group, in comparison with those in the larger group, and to increase their likelihood of contributing to group action.

Relaxing the assumption of jointness of supply enables us to consider how the **divisibility** of a collective good interacts with group size to affect the willingness of individuals to contribute to the collective good's provision. If a collective good is in fixed supply, the size of the group can influence the size of each group member's share of that good. In such cases, each group member's share will diminish in larger groups, which affects NB_i for each individual. If you are someone who enjoys consuming the collective good of a tranquil and unspoiled public park, are you more likely to contribute to its provision if only a small number of other people consume the same good or if a huge number of people use the park daily? Finite divisible collective goods can make contributions to the good more attractive in smaller rather than larger groups because the individual's consumption of the collective good will be greater in the small group than in the large group. The divisibility factor is thus a problem of crowding, whereby the benefit of a collective good decreases with its consumption by an increasing number of group members.

For example, international fishing treaties limit tonnage of catch to ensure the health and survivability of a fishery, which is a collective good. Such treaties usually limit catch by nationality, so if the number of Canadian fishing vessels increases but the catch limits remain fixed, the individual Canadian fisherman's benefit from the collective good declines. This problem may encourage some fishermen to cheat by catching more than the limit allowed by the fishing treaty, or, worse, it may lead to revocation of the treaty.

Contrary to the problem of finite and divisible collective goods, some collective goods have an increasing returns quality: the benefits from these collective goods increase with more contributors; net benefits to the individual and net benefits to society increase with more participation. International trade is one such good, as more and more participation rewards specialization, produces greater consumption possibilities for individuals, and increases social welfare. Agreements to limit emissions of greenhouse gases are another collective good that provides increasing benefits to individuals and their societies as participation in the provision of the good increases. Some collective goods may require larger groups simply because of their costs of provision.

Cartels and oligopolies that manipulate supplies and prices of a commodity are also examples of the effect of size. Such cartel activity can undermine the greater public good, as it distorts efficient market prices and reduces overall consumption possibilities, but price-fixing is a collective good to a cartel's members. An economic sector with a small number of producers may more easily surmount barriers to collusion on supply and price than can a sector with a large number of producers. For example, the Organization of Petroleum Exporting Countries benefits from its relatively small number of members, who are relatively homogeneous, as most are closely tied by geography and political-religious interests. Because of its small membership and relatively high homogeneity, OPEC can more easily coordinate production targets, determine if a member state produces more than its negotiated quota, and exert pressure on a member that cheats. Compare OPEC to a potential cartel of rice producers. The larger number of rice producers, their geographic dispersion, and their heterogeneity create more difficult barriers to successful coordination. Whereas the key OPEC producers are geographically proximate and fairly homogeneous on many dimensions, the major rice producers are more widely dispersed and of much greater diversity in backgrounds. This distance factor presents obstacles to having meetings to fix the supply and price of their rice, affecting who will attend and where, as well as obstacles to monitoring whether members are adhering to their negotiated quotas and to pressuring members to comply. Greater heterogeneity means that the members likely have fewer shared characteristics to support trust and cooperative arrangements.

Free trade agreements provide good examples of small-group dynamics. Economists generally view liberal, freer, trade arrangements as collective goods. Yet subnational politics often intervene to obstruct sweeping international agreements that would further liberalize the trading regime for all 190+ signatories of the World Trade Organization. Negotiations among smaller groups of states, subsets of WTO members, might enable the lowering of remaining trade barriers for members of that subgroup, where negotiations among the full group of WTO signatories might fail. Often the pathway to such free trade agreements by a subset of WTO members is conditioned by geographic proximity or special bilateral relations on nontrade issues.

Brazilian president Dilma Rousseff, left, and her counterpart from Paraguay, Fernando Lugo, met in June 2011 at the opening of the XLI Mercosur presidential summit in Asunción, Paraguay. They signed cooperation agreements on aquaculture, road integration, and digital television. Mercosur—a regional trading bloc created in 1991 and comprising Argentina, Brazil, Paraguay, and Uruguay—aims to develop a common market in the Southern cone by gradually reducing tariffs on trade between member states. The small-group dynamics of the organization helped overcome barriers to developing the common market. Bolivia, Chile, Colombia, Ecuador, Panama, and Venezuela are associate members of Mercosur.

Some Other Collective Action Considerations

Compulsion, selective incentives, entrepreneurship, piggybacking, and group size are important to understanding when and why collective action will be successful, but other characteristics of groups and societies can also play a role. The discussion of nationalism in chapter 2 raised the potential of shared values and characteristics in motivating a particular form of group called a nation. All groups by definition have some shared characteristics that separate those in the group from those outside, and the nature of those shared characteristics can affect the willingness of group members to contribute to collective outcomes. Conceivably, more homogeneous groups may have lower barriers to collective action than more heterogeneous groups, for people tend to interact more closely with people like themselves than with people different from themselves. People who share neighborhoods, religious institutions, schools, political parties, and social clubs tend to have more in common with others in their setting than across such settings. This homogeneity can increase the social pressures and incentives that help to induce contributions to a collective endeavor in the presence of temptations to free ride.

We need to be careful here, however, as earlier we noted that some states are incredibly diverse and yet successful at developing a common identity and acting in the collective interest. As we consider the role of homogeneity versus diversity in group dynamics, we need to ask about the nature and intensity of the shared characteristics that define a group's boundaries. Do the foundations of group organization rest on social, economic, or political footings? Social foundations can provide extrarational motivations for individual choices that may not exist in groups based on economic foundations. Social networks, religious teachings, cultural identification and influences, social group norms and conventions, and other intangible social pressures can promote collective action in groups based on such qualities, whereas groups based on economic foundations may have more difficulty relying on extrarational motivations for collective action, as their members have joined these groups because of initial economic calculations that focused primarily on tangible costs and benefits. Groups with political foundations are more difficult to pigeonhole, because their members may be heavily influenced either by extrarational considerations about their community or by narrower individual considerations of benefits.

CONCLUSION

Reducing collective action to its core components reveals the social trap that hinders cooperation, but it also highlights some strategies to overcome this trap. The problem of the provision of collective goods rests at the heart of many cooperation dilemmas in domestic and international affairs. In large groups, the temptations to free ride are individually rational, even if free riding detracts from social and individual welfare. Changing or constraining the nature of interactions within groups offers opportunities to overcome this threat to cooperation and collective action. Reducing the size of the efficacious group, providing selective incentives, compelling cooperation and contribution to collective activities, using political entrepreneurs whose public actions advance their private interests, employing homogeneity and social pressures, and piggybacking on top of established organizational activities offer general strategies to promote collective action. In the next chapter we consider the special case of provision of collective goods in international affairs by a single member of the group. We call this group member the *hegemonic state*. This state has capacities that far outdistance those of other members of the group, abilities that may enable it to provide collective goods to the group unilaterally if it has the will, regardless of others' contributions to the collective goods. Hegemonic stability theory offers a special situation wherein a single state, or group member, can unilaterally provide a collective good and finds such provision rational.

KEY CONCEPTS

collective good (p. 205)	entrepreneurs (p. 213)	nonexcludability (p. 205)
compulsion (p. 209)	free riding (p. 205)	piggybacking (p. 214)
divisibility (p. 216)	jointness of supply (p. 205)	selective incentive (p. 211)

EXERCISES

1. For years, political scientists believed that collective goods would be provided if $NB_i = GB_i - C_i$ and $NB_i > 0$. What are NB_i, GB_i, and C_i? The logic embedded in this formula suggests that any actor for which $NB_i > 0$ would contribute to the provision of the collective good that leads to NB_i, and that, consequently, the collective good would be provided. Yet history is replete with examples of situations where $NB_i = GB_i - C_i$ and $NB_i > 0$, but collective goods

were underprovided. Explain why and use the equation to demonstrate your logic. Provide and explain an example of this problem in world affairs.

2. Several strategies can circumvent the underprovision of collective goods. Name two possible solutions to collective goods provision and give a description of how each works. Provide and explain examples from world affairs of these strategies at work overcoming collective action problems.

3. What factors limit individuals' incentives to free ride and motivate them to contribute to a collective good?

4. Labor unions have employed piggybacking to advance issues beyond labor issues. What are some examples of labor union piggybacking?

5. How does cartel behavior simultaneously undermine and create a collective good? Earlier in the book, we discussed the ability of the members of OPEC to overcome collective action problems in order to manipulate the supply of oil. Take another commodity, such as bananas or copper, and use the formula $NB_i = GB_i - C_i$ and $NB_i > 0$ to construct an explanation for the failure of producers of that commodity to overcome barriers to collective action.

6. Many governments in the world have signed and ratified the Kyoto Protocol's limitations on emissions of greenhouse gases in order to retard the depletion of ozone in the atmosphere—a collective good. The United States and China have refused to accept and ratify this international agreement. What does this refusal by two of the leading producers of greenhouse gas emissions mean for the provision of the collective good of reduced ozone depletion? Use the formula $NB_i = GB_i - C_i$ and $NB_i > 0$ to explain your reasoning. Given the dynamic in the formula, how should other governments react? How would you advise the members of an international environmental organization to obtain U.S. cooperation?

FURTHER READING

Greenberg, Paul. 2011. *Four Fish: The Future of the Last Wild Food*. New York: Penguin Books.

Hardin, Russell. 1982. *Collective Action*. Baltimore: Johns Hopkins University Press.

Kurlansky, Mark. 1998. *Cod: A Biography of the Fish That Changed the World*. New York: Penguin Books.

Olson, Mancur. 1965. *The Logic of Collective Action*. Cambridge, MA: Harvard University Press.

———. 1982. *The Rise and Decline of Nations*. New Haven, CT: Yale University Press.

Schultze, Charles L. 1977. *The Public Use of Private Interest*. Washington, DC: Brookings Institution Press.

The Role of Hegemonic Leadership and Its Micro Foundations

The international economic and monetary system needs leadership, a country that is prepared, consciously or unconsciously, under some system of rules that it has internalized, to set the standards of conduct for other countries and to seek to get others to follow them, to take on an undue share of the burdens of the system, and in particular to take on its support in adversity by accepting its redundant commodities, maintaining a flow of investment capital, and discounting its paper.

—*Charles P. Kindleberger, The World in Depression, 1929–1939, 1986*

In chapter 5, we noted the potential for the special case of hegemonic leadership in the international system to overcome barriers to collective action, avoid social traps, and produce mutually beneficial outcomes. In this chapter we expand our examination of hegemonic leadership. We focus specifically on a particular form of such leadership, one that embraces and promotes liberal economic exchange—market exchange—across national borders. We will examine what such leadership does in providing collective goods to the international system, assess how those collective goods influence choices and actions that aggregate to produce global outcomes, review the foundations of hegemonic capacity, and consider such leadership in historical perspective.

GROWING GLOBAL EXCHANGE UNDER A LIBERAL HEGEMON

For the past four hundred years, the rules of the global game have tended, with some interruptions, to reflect a growing preference for liberal exchange and increasing openness to the flow of goods, services, capital, and sometimes labor across national boundaries. This has unleashed the power of comparative advantage, spurred specialization across political economies, prompted economic expansion, led to improvements in overall social welfare for many communities, and advanced the globalization of economic and social relations.

A major contributor to this dynamic has been the presence of a political economy with the capacity to unilaterally promote, manage, and stabilize a system conducive to such relations regardless of the actions of others in the international system. We call this political economy a **liberal hegemon.** Liberal hegemonic leadership has been viewed as essential for cooperative international relations that enhance social welfare and limit economic, political, and social dislocations. The Dutch from 1500 to 1700, the British from 1700 to 1900, and the Americans in the twentieth and twenty-first centuries acted as commercial and financial hegemons during eras of expanding globalization, dominating international trade and financial affairs in the global arena and supporting the scaffolding for global capitalist exchange.

The dilemmas that hegemonic leadership helps resolve are those lurking behind many of the social traps that we encounter in world affairs and that are addressed in this book. In the nation-state system, national boundaries define the dominant political geography, yet the geography of economic activity increasingly has crossed and challenged political geography to produce a global political economy dominated by liberal market exchange or global capitalism. States and markets are two fundamentally different strategies for distribution of gains and losses—one centralized, the other decentralized. The two geographies, political and economic, can create frictions and traps that often require international cooperation in order to achieve productive economic and political relations. Such cooperation is difficult to build and hard to sustain with a political geography dominated by relatively autonomous nation-states. National policy makers encounter substantial obstacles to cooperation—temptations to free ride, uncertainty and distrust, short-term electoral pressures, incentives to engage in predatory or beggar-thy-neighbor activities, and problems of monitoring and accountability, to mention just a few.

How does such a political economy exercise its influence and support rules that promote capitalist exchange and cooperative behavior across borders? Does a liberal hegemon impose and dictate such rules of the game? Is cooperation extorted and compelled? Or does a liberal hegemon induce support for such rules of the game through more subtle, nuanced, less coercive, and, even, unintended encouragement? A liberal hegemon fosters an environment in which cooperation and liberal economic exchange are incentive-compatible for national policy makers and their selectorates. By *incentive-compatible,* I mean that such an environment and the choice to cooperate in liberal economic exchange are consistent with the preferences of the hegemon's policy makers and the preferences of policy makers and societies in other political economies.

In creating such an environment, a liberal hegemon provides a handful of collective goods that influence the cost-benefit estimations of those policy makers and their selectorates. These goods increase the gains of cooperating around liberal market exchange across borders, raise the costs of defection from such policies, reduce temptations for national policy makers to adopt policies that shift costs of adjustment to economic dislocations abroad, and help manage crises that could threaten stability and growth in the global economy. A liberal hegemonic state essentially establishes rules of the game for global political economic affairs. Such rules guide choices and help overcome barriers to the cooperation essential for productive market exchange across borders. The rules act as constraints on choices, with the aim being to limit damaging actions and increase incentives for more socially productive choices. A liberal economic hegemon creates such rules by providing scaffolding that reduces uncertainty and risk in cross-border market exchange and interaction. This scaffolding includes collective goods that help lubricate and sustain international cooperation and socially productive economic interactions during good times while managing and limiting dislocations during bad times; such dislocations can lead to instabilities that undermine cooperation in the global political economy. A hegemonic state is that political economy with the capacity and will to bear a disproportionate share of the responsibility for providing such key collective goods.

HEGEMONIC LEADERSHIP AND GLOBAL STABILITY

For some the term **hegemony** carries pejorative connotations. Some argue that a hegemonic state leads by coercion, whereas others make a case for benevolent hegemony. This distinction is more semantic and confusing than helpful. Whether one views a state that dominates the rules of the international game of political economic exchange as coercive or benevolent likely depends on where one sits in the system, one's preference for some rules of the game and not others, and how one does or does not benefit from those rules. Rather than dwell on normative distinctions between coercive and benevolent hegemony, let's adopt a positivist and behavioral perspective to focus primarily on what a hegemon does and how. Remember from chapter 1 that positivist approaches focus on the *is,* in contrast to the focus on the *ought* in normative theory. Nevertheless, one cannot ignore the tremendous normative implications of hegemonic leadership, be they stability, cooperation, productive mutual economic relationships, growth of interdependence, expansion of asymmetric mercantilist relations, excessive rent extraction, or manipulation. These drive much of the debate over hegemonic leadership—who has it, whether it is good or bad, and, if it is good, whether such leadership is essential for the overall social welfare of the international system.

> **Hegemony** is the predominance of one state over other states and the rules of the game in the system. A **liberal hegemon** is that state with the capacity to unilaterally promote, manage, and stabilize a system conducive to liberal economic relations. **Hegemonic stability theory (HST)** concerns the situation in which a capable and willing hegemonic state unilaterally provides collective goods to overcome obstacles that hinder cooperation and cross-border market exchange.

Independent of the benevolent-coercive debate, many social scientists equate a dominant state overseeing a clear and stable hierarchy among states with peace and economic expansion and, conversely, periods of uncertain hierarchy with periods of conflict and unrest. This argument about the importance of hegemonic leadership for cooperation, peace, and stability has become known as **hegemonic stability theory (HST).** Charles Kindleberger, an economic historian and one of the strongest proponents of HST, views a successful leader as one that can unilaterally establish and support rules of the game that stabilize expectations, manage risk, and promote cooperation and mutually beneficial exchange across national borders in good and in bad times. Preferring the term *responsibility* to *hegemony,* he argues that during uncertain times, when the system hits significant shocks, "for the world economy to be stabilized, there has to be a stabilizer—one stabilizer."[1] In Part III of this book, we test conjectures about the role of hegemonic leadership and its contributions to productive globalization, economic growth, and relative peace by examining the variations in hegemonic capacity from Pax Britannica during the 1800s to the years between the two world wars of the twentieth century to the Pax Americana of the post–World War II period.

During Pax Britannica the British used their wealth, markets, and capabilities to provide key collective goods that endowed the United Kingdom with leverage to exercise global leadership, set the rules of the game, and promote a stable liberal international economic order. Kindleberger blames the collapse in hegemonic leadership following World War I for a breakdown in cooperation, reversals in globalization, and the traumatic interwar years. Under Pax Americana, the ability of the United States to establish the rules of the game and provide collective goods (militarily and economically) to its bloc during the Cold War reduced uncertainty, encouraged exchange and cooperation, and advanced a liberal international economic order that enhanced stability and growth in the postwar era.

Using such evidence, proponents of HST note that periods of sustained liberal hegemonic leadership are marked by increased international cooperation, beneficial cross-border exchange, economic expansion, accelerating globalization, and improved social welfare. They question whether, absent hegemonic leadership, states can cooperate sufficiently to ensure stable rules of the game that promote mutually beneficial exchange and cooperation in the global arena. Without such leadership, policy makers across states face heightened instability in expectations, increased concerns that their counterparts in other states might defect and adopt beggar-thy-neighbor policies that shift the costs of adjustment to economic dislocations away from their polities and to their neighbors, and calculate that by unilaterally adopting cooperative policies they cannot change the dynamic leading to destructive economic outcomes and may only increase the magnitude of the potential costs to their societies. National policy makers encounter expanding pressures to defect for short-term gains or temptations to free ride on the cooperative activities of other states. They face increasing incentives, and decreasing disincentives, to adopt policies that might enable their societies to gain at the expense of others by shifting the costs of economic, political, and social hardships abroad. After all, political leaders almost always prefer that someone else's constituency bear the costs of adjustment during economic downturns. Such policies can spiral into a vicious

---

[1]Charles P. Kindleberger, *The World in Depression, 1929–1939,* rev. ed. (Berkeley: University of California Press, 1986), 304.

cycle of tit-for-tat policy retaliation across national borders. This can unravel cooperation and undermine rules of the game critical to socially productive economic exchange across borders, producing greater economic volatility, heightened international social and political unrest, and perhaps even war.

This describes a classic social trap where the rational calculations of decision makers aggregate to produce socially suboptimal outcomes. These suboptimal outcomes can be avoided if decision makers can be induced to make other choices. From the perspective of HST, only a hegemon can induce such cooperation by being able and willing to overcome the free-rider problem, bearing the costs unilaterally of providing key collective goods that promote cooperation and exchange across borders—collective goods that constrain the proclivities of policy makers toward destructive economic nationalism.

LIBERAL HEGEMONS AND IMPORTANT COLLECTIVE GOODS

Kindleberger suggests that a political economy, acting as the system leader, provides five key collective goods: "maintaining a relatively open market for distress goods; providing countercyclical, or at least stable, long-term lending; policing a relatively stable system of exchange rates; ensuring the coordination of macroeconomic policies; and acting as a lender of last resort by discounting or otherwise providing liquidity in financial crisis."[2] Consistent with the definition of collective goods presented in chapter 5, these collective services are relatively nonexcludable to any society that wants to participate in the global economy and follow the rules of the game. Let's start by examining each of these five functions, and in so doing recognize that each is intricately connected to finance—provision of capital to support consumption and growth, means to settle payments, and tools to manage currency risks, trade risks, and other shocks such as inflation or deflation.

Open Market for Distress Goods

The first function, maintaining a relatively open market for distress goods, seems more like a trade good than a financial good. What is a market for distress goods and what does it do in the context of global economic growth and cooperation? It is a sufficiently large political economy that is able and willing to maintain its openness to goods from abroad even during harsh economic times. This is critical to providing an opportunity for other countries to obtain capital through the sales of such goods that might spark a virtuous cycle of economic activity and expansion. Maintaining such openness is difficult for policy makers whose constituencies face hardships themselves. Times of economic stress can raise the prospects of deflationary pressures in economies—less money chasing more goods. Imports add

---

[2]Kindleberger, *The World in Depression*, 289.

to such downward pressures on prices. To reduce such pressures and protect the prices of goods made by their domestic producers, national policy makers face temptations to raise barriers to imports—to improve the ratio of money to goods. When economic stress and deflationary price pressures affect a single state, or only a few states, the system might be able to accommodate the raising of barriers to imports in those states.

But if economic stress is systemic and the temptation to erect obstacles to imports is widespread, a situation arises where everyone may raise barriers to imports. This reduces export earnings. Drastically reducing capital inflows from export earnings can limit the capital needed to spark consumption and fuel growth—less trade, smaller export earnings, and less capital at home to stimulate domestic prices and investment. In their efforts to constrain deflationary pressures, national policy makers may participate in interactions that have the cumulative effect of exacerbating the very problems they seek to limit and trapping political economies in a vicious downward cycle—a social trap and a political market failure. By providing a market for distress goods at times of systemic stress—essentially demonstrating a costly commitment to incur at least possible short-term losses for domestic producers—a nation creates an opportunity for other nations' exporters to sell their goods into that market. This generates export earnings and expands money supply in the exporting nations. Increasing the supply of capital in the exporting nations, which stimulates demand, creates upward pressures on prices, promotes growth, and lessens pressures to erect and sustain barriers to imports. Maintaining a market for distress goods becomes a safety outlet and financing mechanism that can transform a vicious cycle into a virtuous cycle that generates growth, improves economic outcomes, reduces perverse pressures on policy makers to enact policies that can damage international cooperation, and enhances the gains from globalization. It is remarkable how insightful and robust Hume's specie flow theory from the mid-1700s remains (see chapter 3 to refresh your memory regarding Hume's theory).

Countercyclical Lending

The second function, providing countercyclical lending, is more obviously a financial tool. Countercyclical lending works with trade to help stabilize the supply of capital and the economic system. During times of economic vitality in a hegemonic economy, lenders in that economy tend to invest more at home than abroad. Through trade, capital flows into other economies in the system as consumers in the hegemonic economy increase their consumption, including purchases of imported goods. Economic slowdown in the hegemonic economy leads to a decline in consumption, which decreases the outflow of capital from the hegemonic economy via the trade mechanism. Yet such slowdowns in the domestic economy of the hegemonic state can lead to increased investment abroad as lenders from the hegemonic economy look elsewhere for growth opportunities. This is the essence of countercyclical lending. When the economy of the hegemon prospers, overseas lending tends to slow relative to domestic lending, and when the hegemon encounters a domestic economic slowdown, overseas lending expands relative to domestic lending.

Stable Exchange-Rate System

The third function, managing a relatively stable system of exchange rates, is also clearly financial. Policy makers worry about exchange-rate stability because it affects their domestic prices, the competitiveness of their goods and services in the tradable sector, and expectations of risk and uncertainty in cross-border exchange. An exchange-rate mechanism that is out of equilibrium—where some currency or currencies are undervalued and others are overvalued—will produce disproportionate claims of the undervalued political economies on the overvalued political economies and pressures to redress the imbalance. This rebalancing can occur through borrowing, currency revaluation, employment, wages, or intervention in the trade arena. These pressures become more severe during hard times, when political economies face slowdowns in trade and constraints on borrowing and liquidity. At such times policy makers may seek to restore the competitiveness of their exports. Currency depreciation can become an attractive policy instrument. Policy makers rarely object if their currencies depreciate relative to other currencies, but they do worry if their currencies appreciate relative to other currencies. Consequently, competitive currency depreciation by one political economy might well incur similar responses by other political economies—a tit-for-tat beggar-thy-neighbor response. Competitive devaluations could lead to chaos in the exchange-rate system, which is the worst of all worlds for trade, since uncertainty in the price mechanism affects the willingness of importers and exporters to enter into forward-looking contracts—those that are settled long after the actual transfers of goods and services occur. The ability of policy makers to manage pressures that push them to engage in competitive currency manipulation is key to the avoidance of economic conflict via the exchange-rate mechanism. Policy makers in a hegemonic economy must be able to contain and manage market pressures that challenge an exchange-rate system. Their tools include the ability to promote international coordination that reduces currency instability and the capacity to finance shortfalls in others' current accounts.

The Federal Reserve serves both as the lender of last resort for the U.S. economy and as the lender of last resort for the global economy, given the position of the United States as the hegemonic leader, or system stabilizer, for the global economy. As lender of last resort, the Federal Reserve creates liquidity in the system when no other institution or market will. In its role as the primary mechanism of U.S. monetary policy, the Federal Reserve also tries to protect the stability of the exchange-rate system.

Macroeconomic Policy Coordination

The fourth function, coordinating macroeconomic policies, involves managing monetary and fiscal policies within a hegemon's political economy and eliciting coordination of those policies across national economies. National policy makers use monetary and fiscal policies for a variety of purposes—for example, to stimulate or restrict growth, redistribute income, sterilize capital inflows, influence resource allocation, and address shocks. If used effectively, these policy levers can help produce and maintain macroeconomic stability within a political economy. Across political economies such macroeconomic coordination faces more daunting challenges. Here, policy makers can use the tools of economic statecraft, such as dialogue, diplomacy, negotiations, conferences, and treaties, as means of promoting macroeconomic coordination across borders. But through their monetary and fiscal choices, policy makers within the hegemonic state can also unilaterally help manage and coordinate macroeconomic contexts via the central position of their monetary and capital markets in the global economy and the networks created by investors and borrowers in those markets. For example, following the 2008 credit crisis that began in the United States and led to a global recession, the U.S. Federal Reserve used monetary policy to pump several trillion dollars into the U.S. economy and, consequently, the global economy. The Federal Reserve did so by purchasing financial assets from financial institutions, governments, and other entities and placing those assets in the Fed's balance sheet. At the same time, the U.S. government used fiscal policies such as stimulus programs and tax cuts to pump additional capital into the economy. Altogether, the actions of the Federal Reserve and the U.S. government added more than four trillion dollars to the global economy at a time when private holders of capital had become risk averse.

Why is macroeconomic coordination important? Macroeconomic policy choices have benefits and consequences, or trade-offs. These trade-offs can be between growth and price stability—inflation, or unemployment—or between domestic and international consequences. Such policies have the capacity to affect global stability when policy makers weigh the trade-off between the domestic and international consequences of their potential macroeconomic choices. At times, policy makers, intent on addressing conditions in their own domestic political economies, may implement policies that impose costs on other political economies. If this leads their counterparts in other states to use macroeconomic policy tools to address their domestic ills and protect their economies from such externally imposed costs, then everyone could be worse-off. If enough states focus entirely on the domestic consequences of their policy choices, independent of the interaction of those choices across national borders, this can produce a classic social trap. In this trap, rational decision makers select policies that in isolation appear likely to improve the conditions of their societies but in conjunction with choices made by policy makers elsewhere in the system have outcomes that prove mutually dysfunctional.

What makes a hegemon so important to the coordination of macroeconomic policies and constraints on national policy makers in their use of macroeconomic policies to redistribute costs abroad? Only a dominant political economy is credible enough to help coordinate actions to avoid poor macroeconomic choices. Absent the participation of the hegemon, or possibly a small number of significant economies, the prospect for productive coordination of policies across states declines dramatically. Even if policy makers in other states want to make socially productive choices, domestically and internationally, their actions would be for naught or at least more costly absent the participation of the dominant political economy.

Lender of Last Resort: Managing Liquidity in the Global System

The fifth function, acting as lender of last resort, involves injecting liquidity during an economic downturn or crisis. During downturns, especially financial or economic crises, private sources of capital such as banks and investors in capital markets become risk averse and less willing to put their capital to work. Out of fear of the future, they seek to preserve the capital they have rather than expose that capital to risks. This shrinks the supply of capital, reduces liquidity, and raises capital costs. These are procyclical forces that can exacerbate a crisis, especially when politicians face pressures from their selectorates to provide relief when their societies encounter such downturns, even if this means implementing policies that could damage other societies and provoke retaliation that leads to greater damage to all involved. Ironically, such pressures may be particularly acute in democratic societies. Addressing the liquidity crunch is critical to breaking the downward trend, increasing the supply of affordable capital to stimulate investment and growth, and reducing pressures on national policy makers to adopt policies damaging to long-term growth and international cooperation. A lender of last resort attempts to address such shortfalls when other lenders flee. For private financial players to act as effective lenders of last resort, short-term private interests must be consistent with longer-term public interests. At times of excessive fluctuation, economic distress, and uncertainty, short-term private interests and long-term public interests can easily become time inconsistent because private lenders of last resort worry about their responsibilities to a narrower range of risk-averse owners or shareholders than a national population and over a more proximate period of time.

Given the procyclical nature of private capital, a government agency such as a finance ministry or central bank often proves the most effective in fulfilling the lender-of-last-resort function for a political economy. Compared with private holders of capital, a government serving as such a lender can draw on a broader base of capital and policy instruments to manage money supply and economic fluctuations. A public lender of last resort, whether a bank or agency, is often explicitly and formally charged with maintaining stability, managing money supply, and providing for the public interest. Its short-term preferences are to limit crises when they occur, unlike the short-term objectives of private holders of capital, who want to preserve their capital at times of dislocation. In practice, some public lenders of last resort perform better than others at representing broad public interests versus narrow particularistic interests.

A successful lender of last resort diffuses risk and increases the likelihood of countercyclical infusions of capital at a time of contraction or monetary constriction. Lenders of last resort attempt to lean against the wind and persuade private banks and investors in capital markets to increase access to their capital during times of slowdown or decrease access at times of inflationary expansion. If such a lender succeeds in managing an economic downturn, then it works to limit wild fluctuations that concern private holders of capital, so that the private holders become increasingly willing to put their capital back to work. A lender of last resort can use a variety of policy tools to interrupt such cycles, increase liquidity, encourage holders of capital to begin lending their capital, and, ideally, constrain pressures on national policy makers to implement policies that try to improve the lot of domestic constituents at the expense of foreigners. A lender of last resort can manipulate the interest rates at which private banks borrow capital, change reserve requirements, sell or buy bonds to affect money supply, and use other means of discounting to affect money supply and credit.

A hegemonic state provides this function not only for its domestic economy but also internationally for the broader system. The lender of last resort for the international arena leans against the wind in attempting to convince private holders of capital to put their capital stocks to work and at risk during slowdowns and crises, but does so on a much broader scale and across national boundaries. Performing this function requires having private capital markets and banks integrated into global networks so that when a hegemon leans against the wind and pumps liquidity into the domestic and international arena, private capital markets and banks in the hegemonic state and in other states follow suit. The earlier example of the Federal Reserve and the U.S. government using monetary and fiscal policies to increase capital in the system dramatically following the 2008 financial crisis illustrates how a political economy can act as lender of last resort for the entire system.

SOURCES OF HEGEMONIC CAPACITY: ARISING FROM CHALLENGES TO POLITICAL SURVIVAL

What are the sources of the capacity for a society to provide such key collective goods to the system? What enables a government and society to provide the functions discussed in the preceding section, to establish and maintain the rules of the game in the global arena, and to act as the system stabilizer during periods of economic stress? Many, if not all, governments and societies would like to sit at the top of the international hierarchy, establish the rules of global interactions, and be the state that other political economies rely on during crises that threaten global social welfare. Some have tried and failed. Many countries are not even in the running. Over the past five centuries, only three political economies have gained such a position in the international system, and their success was not a matter of intentional design with hegemonic leadership as the objective. Instead, the Dutch Netherlands, the United Kingdom, and the United States acceded to hegemonic leadership as a consequence of successful domestic political and economic reforms that were responses to crises and threats to political survival in their domestic arenas. For example, the New York stock market crash of 1929 and the ensuing banking crisis that fueled the Great Depression revealed that American financial markets were corrupt and full of insider trading, and that they were arenas in which strategic actors could manipulate price and supply. A lack of transparency and regulation favored a privileged few at the expense of the general public. Absent the crises of the 1920s and 1930s, would the rules of the game have been reformed to protect the integrity of the markets? It is worth repeating that hegemonic capacity was not an intentional construction by the governments and societies that became hegemonic leaders. It was an outcome, a consequence, of actions taken by policy makers to address dilemmas in the status quo and crises that threatened their societies' welfare and their own political survival. Societies changed because they were confronted by significant shortcomings in the status quo. Their responses were less a consequence of coherent planning than they were piece-by-piece institutional reforms scattered across a wide range of governance, fiscal, monetary, and financial areas.

Moreover, hegemonic capacity is not created in a short time and does not occur in a vacuum. It is a consequence of international investors and borrowers choosing among different states' governance and financial arrangements, rewarding successful strategies and penalizing less successful strategies. The rise of a political economy to a position of leadership rests significantly on the failings of other political economies. Reforms adopted in the Dutch Netherlands, the United Kingdom, and the United States proved successful as they were tested against the strategies and institutional arrangements of other nations. Liberal hegemony emerged as a consequence of an evolutionary process in which investors and borrowers chose among different nations' financial arrangements, rewarding successful strategies and penalizing less successful strategies. They literally voted with their contracts and capital. Success and failure were motivated by problems and objectives other than global leadership.

By now it should be increasingly apparent that the key collective functions underpinning liberal hegemonic leadership are to a great extent financial, fiscal, and monetary mechanisms. A hegemonic state provides capital to support consumption and growth, establishes a means to settle payments, and creates tools to manage currency risks, trade risks, and other shocks such as inflation or deflation. To perform these collective functions, a political economy must be sufficiently large, have access to tremendous sources of capital, and be able to influence the use of that capital to provide private and public goods to the system during economic good times and hard times. The following are four critical foundations underpinning the ability to provide such collective services: a political economy's governance arrangements, its public and private financial arrangements, the credibility of those arrangements, and the development of a global financial network around those arrangements. These four foundations affect the capacity for liberal hegemonic leadership.

PUBLIC FINANCE AND HEGEMONIC PROVISION OF COLLECTIVE GOODS

A positive relationship between sound financial arrangements and good governance is essential to productive social and economic outcomes in market economies. In *The Wealth of*

Nations, Adam Smith wrote that the Bank of England served "as a great engine of the state."[3] Nurturing and advancing this relationship was at the very heart of Alexander Hamilton's Report on Public Credit, submitted to the U.S. Congress in January 1790. Hamilton's report provided a rationale for the first central bank in the United States and for the development of a public debt market. His arguments prevailed despite populist opposition.

In terms of capacity, a potential liberal hegemon is a special case among those political economies where productive financial arrangements and stable governance have coevolved. Any political economy that can perform the collective functions discussed in the preceding section must have access to tremendous sources of capital and be able to influence the use of that capital to provide collective goods to the system during good economic times and bad. Here we focus on five aspects of public arrangements that underpin the provision of such functions: rule of law, taxation, public debt, lender of last resort, and willingness to expose the national currency to international use as a reserve currency and a means to settle cross-border transactions.

Rule of Law

Rule of law is a broad, overarching term. For good reason it has become a popular recommendation in the arena of development. Effective rule of law is foundational to successful development, and any political economy with the potential to become a liberal hegemon has overcome barriers to development. It clarifies and protects private property rights and consequently affects the incentives of individuals and enterprises. Viewing capital as a commodity that trades in a marketplace, rule of law delineates the ownership properties of capital and how it can be traded. It defines the responsibilities of borrowers and lenders, which are key to the incentives to accumulate, lend, and invest capital. Without fair rule of law that clearly lays out such responsibilities, along with complaint and adjudication procedures to resolve contracting ambiguities, risk and uncertainty threaten exchange. An important aspect of the rule of law is its ability to limit and address failures in the marketplace that negatively affect the incentives of individuals to accumulate capital and the willingness of those who hold capital to lend and invest their capital. Much of the ability, or inability, to limit market failures falls in the realm of regulation that targets specific problems such as asymmetric information and transparency, cronyism and corruption, fraud, and adjudication of disputes. Good regulatory arenas help constrain such threats to effective market exchange but are not so onerous as to impose excessive costs that discourage exchange, creativity, and risk taking.

Asymmetric information and poor transparency can negatively affect the incentives of holders of capital to engage in financial dealings and expose their capital if they think one party to an interaction knows something valuable that other parties do not, and if the rules of the game empower and enable that asymmetry. Severe enough problems of asymmetric

---

[3] Adam Smith, *An Inquiry into the Nature and Causes of the Wealth of Nations* (1776), bk. 2, chap. 2.

information and transparency can lead to complete breakdown in the exchange of capital, a liquidity crunch. In a potential hegemon, this would undermine the ability of public and private actors to access the capital necessary to perform the collective functions described above.

Cronyism, corruption, and fraud can have similar consequences for the accumulation and exchange of capital. These affect perceptions of fairness, expectations about the rate of return on capital, and, consequently, the incentives to accumulate, lend, and invest capital. A political economy or capital market that is viewed as rigged or that benefits a particular group independent of economic capability will find huge obstacles to acquiring the critical mass of capital necessary to perform the collective functions discussed above or to develop the network of relationships required to manage economic and financial problems in the system. Those able to accumulate capital in such an arena will often hide their capital from those in positions of power through clever accounting or flight abroad. In effect, such arenas become self-limiting as they undermine the increasing returns characteristic of an effective capital market.

No system works perfectly, even those with the best intentions. Property rights can never be fully specified. Contracts specifying property rights and obligations in any exchange relationship are incomplete because of nontrivial transaction costs, problems of monitoring, and dilemmas of adjudication and policing. Successful capital market mechanisms mediate between savers and borrowers. Capital markets become large when they overcome barriers to anonymous exchange between lenders and borrowers. But this anonymity, the growth of transactional distance between lenders and borrowers, compounds potential dilemmas of monitoring, transparency, incomplete contracts, and disputed property rights. Successful political economies overcome such dilemmas when they develop adjudication mechanisms that settle disputes with perceived consistency and fairness. For capital market arrangements to move successfully beyond national boundaries in terms of transactional geography, such adjudication mechanisms must be viewed as attempting to treat all parties fairly, evenly, and without national bias. Foreign lenders and borrowers of capital must perceive that the adjudication process, the rule of law, applies equitably for nationals and foreigners. Outcomes in the adjudication process must be viewed as relatively independent of nationality; otherwise, national bias is simply a version of cronyism, with similar consequences for the accumulation and redistribution of capital.

Taxation

Taxation is another key public arrangement affecting the capacity of a society to provide the collective functions that underpin liberal hegemonic leadership. Taxation draws on the resources of society through public extraction and redistribution of society's wealth. Few relish paying taxes, but taxation is essential to modern society. Oliver Wendell Holmes reportedly called taxes "the price we pay for a civilized society." There are good and poor tax systems. Good systems enable governments to develop reliable sources of capital and allow them to anticipate revenues from year to year and to budget those revenues. Reliability protects against volatility in government revenues that limits long-term planning, which is important for investment in the scaffolding that supports productive social and economic activity over time.

Good tax systems are perceived as relatively fair. This means that all classes and groups in society are taxed to contribute to societal outcomes. In fair systems no group systematically evades the burden or responsibility of taxation. For example, in the Spanish Habsburg Empire, members of royalty were exempted from taxes. At the time that the Dutch revolted from the Habsburg Empire in the mid-1500s, the Spanish monarchy, a military superpower of the time, could not draw upon the wealthiest segment of the society to help pay for the conflict. Meanwhile, the rebel Dutch did tax across a broad swath of society to help pay for their rebellion. The Spanish system was relatively unfair, placing disproportionate burdens on particular segments of society, whereas the Dutch used a fairer system that spread the burden. Perceptions of fairness affect incentives to evade and to pay taxes. Fair systems, those distributed across all classes and groups (with notable exceptions, such as religious institutions and orders), tend to encounter less opposition and tax avoidance. The transaction costs of collecting taxes are also lower in fair systems. This leads to greater efficiency and more revenues, as more members of society contribute and with less extraction and monitoring costs. Fairness is positively related to legitimacy and stakeholding in a society, but it is also instrumental in helping with reliability and predictability of revenues and, consequently, planning and investment for the future.

Taxation also contributes to a government's ability to borrow from private holders of capital. Reliable and fair tax mechanisms produce dependable revenue streams, which signal prospective purchasers of government debt about the government's ability to service that debt and meet its obligations over time. Effective taxation contributes to the ability to incur public debt by providing credible mechanisms to finance that debt over time. Connecting a stream of revenue such as taxes to a financial obligation enables a government to borrow more and at lower costs. A reliable and fair tax system effectively serves as a form of collateral to secure debt. Linking a fair and reliable tax system with the ability to borrow capital is a central ingredient of a hegemon's capacity to provide liquidity and act as lender of last resort for the system.

Public Debt

An effective public debt market is a necessary condition for any modern state, especially one that attempts to act as the system stabilizer and provide the collective functions discussed earlier. How is the ability to issue government bonds and run a public debt an important contributor to stable governance and, in the special case of the system leader, hegemonic capacity? Many assert that debt is a problem, not a "blessing" as asserted by Hamilton in his *Report on Public Credit*. All societies encounter emergencies with financial demands that fall outside the boundaries of normal taxation and planned budgets based on anticipated revenues. Even the most successful and stable political economies face unexpected emergencies that defy foresight and overwhelm funds set aside for such crises. Wars, earthquakes, epidemics, climatic disasters, economic crises, and other emergencies can easily produce demands on governments that exceed their revenues. Delaying responses to such emergencies until taxation raises sufficient capital could create social unrest and political instability that might threaten government survival.

Governments could wait until such emergencies take place to create **public debt** by introducing and selling instruments of government debt, but waiting for an emergency to create a market for public debt has pitfalls that lead to increased costs and uncertainty for success. Without a history in public debt, a government does not have an opportunity to develop a reputation as a borrower. Is the government reliable, will it meet its debt obligations, or will it renege? Without a history of borrowing, or with a poor reputation, governments are compelled to pay higher risk premiums on loans needed to address emergencies or budget shortfalls that exceed government revenues from taxation. This can be very expensive capital, which may create future dilemmas for a government as it attempts to service its debt and may even increase the incentives for policy makers in the future to renege on those obligations. Prospective lenders recognize such probabilities and may be reluctant to lend to a government without a history in public debt at a time of crisis, even with the additional risk premiums. Having an active public debt market provides prospective lenders with experience about the government as a borrower. A good reputation will reduce borrowing costs and increase the likelihood that a government trying to address unexpected crises will find the financing to do so.

> **Public debt** is the debt owed by government. It is created when a government borrows to fund the difference between government receipts and government expenditures during a year. Governments borrow in public debt markets by issuing securities, bonds, and bills.

Public debt also acts as a constraint on a government's incentives to inflate money supply instead of raising taxes. Inflation is a hidden tax and a means to finance expenditures in the short run, but it detracts from the face value of notes in the public debt market. This reduces the incentives for investors to purchase or hold such notes, as they anticipate erosion in the value of their investment. This raises borrowing costs by increasing the risk premium—interest rates—to compensate for the risk of inflation. If inflation is severe enough, such incentives will fail to convince many investors to take such risks with their capital. An active public debt market can help constrain the incentives of politicians to inflate money supply instead of asking constituents to contribute more through taxation. A public debt market with low risk premiums reflects a political economy with developed financial mechanisms that can handle unanticipated emergencies and expenditures and can also balance the short-term temptations of policy makers to inflate money supply with their long-term interests of reasonable borrowing costs in the public debt market. Development of an efficient and reliable government debt market also helps in the development of private capital markets as individuals become acclimated to lending and investing through such instruments.

Lender of Last Resort

All modern political economies have some organization or organizations that perform the functions of a **lender of last resort** for their

> A **lender of last resort** is a financial institution or government agency that acts countercyclically to ensure an adequate supply of capital during economic crisis, providing a collective good.

domestic political economies. These functions include, foremost, the management of money supply, but they can also involve regulation, bank supervision, provision of insurance or other backstopping for the banking system to protect against systemic risk, operation as a clearinghouse, and promotion of transparency in the banking system. Today, lenders of last resort typically take the form of public or quasi-public central banks, but in the past some private banks, or systems of private banks, performed such functions. The creation of a public central bank as lender of last resort rests primarily on the argument that private banking systems cannot be trusted to operate effectively in this role without strong external constraints or regulation. Competitive pressures among private banks can lead to destabilizing volatility and procyclical fluctuations, which can end in banking panics that spill over to produce severe economic dislocations in society. Proponents of a public central bank argue that a noncompetitive central bank, not devised to maximize profit and politically insulated, is often more capable of overcoming such volatility and acting countercyclically. Clearinghouse activities, monetary management, and bank supervision are more efficient if carried out by a single entity and are likely to be more transparent in the hands of a public entity than a private one.

Central banks are the primary tool by which modern states manage their money supply. Every public central bank is statutorily charged with at least one primary mission: price stability. Some public central banks are also tasked with another mission of equal weight: growth. With an objective of price stability, policy makers manage money supply to contain pressures that can inflate prices and undermine the value of capital assets held over time. Policy makers seeking to promote growth can increase money supply to lower the costs of capital as an input to production (supply-side stimulus) and increase the availability of capital to encourage greater consumption (demand-side stimulus).

Price stability and growth are often in tension with each other. From the objective of promoting growth, too much price stability limits the supply of capital available to purchase goods, expand production, and hire workers. This can produce damaging deflationary pressures that inhibit growth in a political economy. From the objective of price stability, monetary policy that is too liberal risks inflation that damages capital formation and currency stability. This creates the incentive to consume rather than to save or invest or to find a means of saving that bypasses capital instruments denominated in a currency experiencing inflation. To avoid an inflationary currency, holders of capital may seek to move their capital abroad to purchase assets denominated in a more stable currency. They may seek to invest their capital in assets that hold their value over time even as the national currency depreciates, perhaps by storing value in durable goods whose prices will appreciate with inflation. If inflation damages the incentives for members of a society to save or invest in financial

> **Price stability** exists when prices remain relatively the same over time. In an economy, this means that it experiences neither inflation or deflation. Price stability is a function of money supply in an economy: too much produces price inflation; too little leads to price deflation. It is often in tension with the use of monetary policy to promote growth.

instruments, then it comes full circle and undermines growth. Ironically, too great an increase in money supply to stimulate growth and employment can spill over to create an inflationary spiral that undermines asset values, causes stagnation, and leads to less growth and increased unemployment.

Managing the trade-offs between price stability and growth is a difficult balancing task for monetary policy makers. Many political economies try to circumvent the tension between price stability and growth by creating a statutory hierarchy in preferences over macroeconomic outcomes, generally with price stability dominating other objectives. Some political economies task their central banks with the responsibility only for maintaining price stability and limiting inflation. The defunct German Bundesbank and the current European Central Bank are examples of central banks focused on price stability above all else. The U.S. Federal Reserve and the Bank of England are examples of central banks that try to balance the dual objectives of growth and price stability.

A state that emerges as a liberal hegemon performs the lender-of-last-resort functions for the global arena. The hegemon's central bank and financial mechanisms effectively become the central bank for the broader system. A singular focus on price stability to protect against the ravages of inflation may be a sufficient objective for a lender of last resort in a national arena, but not at the global level. The lender for the global system must address the tasks of both price stability and growth. It must be willing to promote growth and risk inflation by manipulating money supply to inject liquidity and stimulate economic activity countercyclically and without hesitation at times of economic crises, systemic threats, and possible global contractions. A lender of last resort with a dominant preference for price stability over growth will be slow, if willing at all, to risk price inflation at home by creating sufficient liquidity to address a global economic crisis. Price stability to the exclusion of growth limits a society's ability to emerge at the hub of a network of global financial relations.

National Currency as an International Reserve Currency

Discussion of the lender of last resort for the global system leads to the final necessary, but still insufficient, aspect of public financial arrangements. A potential hegemon must be willing to expose its national currency to international use as a reserve currency, a means to settle cross-border transactions, and a storehouse of value. A potential system leader must be willing to have its currency become a transactional currency with a functional geography that extends beyond national boundaries. This requires a commitment to the open flow of capital and a rejection of capital controls as a policy alternative. Exposing a nation's currency to international use adds complications to the calculus for that nation's monetary policy makers, as it involves risks of losing some control over money supply and capital resources. The construction of hegemonic capacity derives partly from others' willingness to use the hegemon's currency to settle cross-border obligations and to hold as a reserve asset. This is central to the creation of networks that place a political economy at the hub of the relationships that are essential to managing international economic and financial shocks. A national lender of last resort with a primary focus on domestic price stability may be less willing to expose its currency to such a role—to create sufficient liquidity in its currency to enable its use as a reserve asset, a means of settling accounts, and a tool to promote growth in the system. A national lender of last resort with a primary focus on domestic price stability would worry that creation of such liquidity for international uses—to lubricate the international economic system—could threaten domestic price stability if brought home. Yet this willingness to expose one's currency internationally, to risk price inflation to promote growth and manage international distortions, sits at the heart of the reach of a potential hegemon's monetary policies by leading to the construction of a network of relations that are key to managing systemic economic and financial crises.

PRIVATE FINANCE AND THE HEGEMONIC PROVISION OF COLLECTIVE GOODS

Private as well as public financial arrangements contribute to the emergence of large and effective capital markets that encourage capital accumulation, formation, application, and perhaps even hegemonic capacity if such markets emerge at the hub of a network of global financial relationships that provide a society with an ability to promote growth during good times and manage systemic crises during downturns. Below, we focus on a handful of important nongovernmental characteristics: capital market size, market diversification, market depth and liquidity, market transparency and clearinghouse mechanisms, and the absence of informal barriers to cross-border participation.

Capital Market Size

Capital markets are those financial markets where enterprises and governments issue and trade financial obligations with maturities longer than a year.

Surpassing some threshold of **capital market** size is almost self-evident as a necessary qualification for attaining hegemonic capacity. The collective functions discussed earlier are primarily financing mechanisms to inject liquidity that encourages investment and growth and finances consumption and exchange, both pro- and countercyclically. Doing so productively for a single national political economy requires some relatively efficient means of transferring resources from those with capital surpluses to those short of capital in order to finance their activities. The demands on private and public mechanisms to perform such functions adequately for a single political economy are substantial. Many societies fall short of meeting such needs. Demands grow exponentially for a political economy that can perform these collective functions for the global system. A political economy with the ability to exercise leadership must have access to extraordinary sources of capital and be able to influence the use of that capital to inject liquidity into the system during economic good times and hard times. Large capital markets, by their size, are testaments to their ability to attract both savers and borrowers.

Capital Market Diversification

Capital markets in successful political economies take a variety of forms—banking systems, securitization of debt in bond markets, equity markets, money markets, futures and derivatives markets, currency markets, venture capital markets, and others. Many political economies rely heavily on one form or another. A potential hegemon must have a diversified portfolio of capital market mechanisms. Diversity enables holders of capital to find different levels of risk, to match their risk tolerance with instruments across different markets, and to alter their exposure during times of crisis. Multiple forms encourage competition in the private marketplace for capital. Competition leads to innovation, which can produce greater efficiency in the accumulation and redistribution of capital resources. These characteristics of diversity contribute to the attractiveness of a political economy's private capital markets and can induce an increasing return dynamic that expands the pool of accessible capital and enhances a political economy's capacity to provide liquidity during good and bad times.

Capital Market Depth and Liquidity

Such capital markets must also be deep and liquid, characteristics that are endogenous to their size and success. Depth and liquidity help investors manage the risk to their capital over time and make such markets attractive. In deep markets—that is, markets with vast amounts of assets—even large transactions usually leave asset prices relatively stable. Deep markets help limit investor risk from volatility and large unexpected shifts in asset prices, and so are relatively more orderly than less deep markets. In liquid markets, investors can easily move their assets in or out of investments—an immediate market exists for transactions, with little to no lag in the conclusion of purchases or sales of assets. Liquid markets reduce risks by protecting investors from the dilemma of holding assets they do not want but cannot trade quickly.

Depth and liquidity make for more orderly markets. They limit risks from volatility and from the dilemma of holding assets investors may not want. These qualities help attract domestic and international capital. International capital is integral to the accumulation of sufficient capital resources and the creation of the cross-border networks that are essential to hegemonic capacity and to managing systemic economic dislocations. As more international capital flows into such markets, they move beyond being just national capital markets that bring together domestic savers and borrowers. The flow of international capital into these markets increases global financial integration, linking investors and borrowers of different nationalities and financing economic activities far beyond the national boundaries of such markets. This creates a global financial nervous system that links economic activity, private economic actors, public policy makers, and regulators across borders.

Market Transparency and Clearinghouse Mechanisms

Transparency and clearinghouse mechanisms are integral to these large markets. Transparency means that trades, positions, associations, and other activities that can influence prices are readily apparent and available to most, if not all, informed participants engaged in exchange. The admonition "Let the buyer beware" rests on an assumption about the ready availability of relatively complete information and transparency. Public regulatory activities such as legally mandated and monitored disclosure and reporting requirements affect transparency, but so do many activities in the private sphere. All good-size financial markets involve private organizations that serve as clearinghouses that transfer property rights quickly and unambiguously. With a good clearing mechanism, records of market activity are readily accessible to those completing exchanges and those contemplating exchanges. Good private market organizations publicly report trading activity relatively quickly after the completion of trades. Transparency, clarity, and efficient completion of exchange limit threats to market activity from asymmetric information, incomplete property rights, time, insider trading, cronyism and corruption, and unfair manipulation. They help enhance confidence that a market is fair and trading is legitimate.

Openness and Absence of National Bias

For a political economy and its capital markets to emerge at the hub of a network of global financial relations, the state's borders must be relatively porous to the international flow of capital. This requires willingness on the part of the political economy to allow its currency to become an international transactional currency, to allow its currency to move beyond the limits of national geography, and to reject capital controls. These are public policy choices made in the public arena, but private activities can also influence international access to a political economy's capital markets. Social arrangements and business practices can work, intentionally or not, to discriminate against nonnational investors and borrowers. Informal practices can discriminate by creating pathways that advantage national participants over international participants. Such practices create barriers to entry and an insider-trading advantage for those in the club versus those outside. Strong national bias generally works by undermining transparency and obscuring the informal rules of the game to outsiders while providing informational and bargaining advantages to insiders. In effect, this places outsiders at a competitive disadvantage. This is a form of market failure created by national geography.

Such national bias limits the attractiveness of markets to international investors and borrowers. This constrains the construction of cross-border financial networks, which are essential to creating the capacity to exercise leadership and to address systemic problems. A relative absence of national bias in business and social practices and a willingness to ignore nationality as a basis for business dealings are essential for a political economy to develop global capital markets that are welcoming to both national and international participants. Some national bias is inevitable, but a global market is marked by a relative absence of such bias compared with national markets, which are more inward looking.

CHANGE AND DEVELOPMENT OF HEGEMONIC CAPACITY IN A GLOBAL FINANCIAL NETWORK

How does a political economy develop such capacities? Developing the sound governance and financial capacities that sit at the heart of a sophisticated global financial network and underpin hegemonic capacity is far easier said than done. Political economies are not naturally imbued with such abilities. Developing them demands a significant change in the status quo that has characterized all societies at one time in their pasts. Historically, political authority has generally emerged to advance and protect the narrow interests of a relatively small, privileged group, who often prey on the rest of the groups in their societies. Such elites seek to consolidate and advance their position in society, even to the neglect or detriment of the broader society. They protect their position of economic and political power, advancing policies that improve the welfare of their broader societies and enhance their place on the global stage only if those policies also reinforce or improve the elites' narrowly privileged position. Consequently, at the origins of every form of political authority—nation-states, fiefdoms, city-states, feudal kingdoms, tribes, and other forms of political economic organizations—the financial status quo is dominated by arrangements that favor privileged elites, encourage cronyism, lack transparency, support arbitrariness and corruption, obscure financial obligations, and distort legal recourse to those claims. The economic and financial practices that evolve in nascent and emerging systems reflect asymmetries in power and interests. The foundations of modern, productive, and socially efficient governance and finance are nonexistent in such systems.

Moreover, the status quo is highly resistant to socially productive change because it threatens the privileged and powerful. These socially perverse forms of political economic organization are generally self-reinforcing absent some dramatic change. Practices in such systems are resistant to change, much to the frustration of those engaged in fostering development. Those in privileged positions in society employ the tools of government, force, corruption, family connections, and cronyism to hold on to their positions. They resist shifts that could threaten their privileged position and often seek to limit the competition that contributes to political, economic, and social mobility in a society.

If such systems are robust, how can a socially vicious status quo or equilibrium be disrupted to generate reforms that transform public and private financial arrangements into those that are more socially productive? Significant crises or shocks such as war, severe economic downturn, or revolution play a critical role in transformation. They create opportunities to discredit and disrupt a socially dysfunctional status quo that rewards insiders, cronies, and elites at the expense of the broader society and economic efficiency. A shock that challenges the foundations of political authority, social structure, and economic organization provides an opportunity to alter the status quo. This can produce changes in governance and the financial rules of the game. Some changes can be productive, opening up avenues for new economic actors to achieve success and producing more efficient outcomes, economically, socially, and politically. These alter economic and social relations for the better in the long term, even transforming a political economy's position in the global arena.

However, productive change is not always a consequence when severe shock and crisis challenge the status quo. Many policy makers, political economies, and societies respond poorly when confronted by serious challenges. Governments often learn the wrong lessons and respond poorly to shocks. Many policy makers, when confronted by crises, stick with the status quo and create barriers to change in the social, political, and economic order; some adopt changes that are more illusory than real; and others adopt changes that, while well-intentioned, fail to lead to real reform. Governments can limp along, sometimes as weak or partially failed states, without enacting reforms that help address the ills of their societies.

Even in the best cases of well-intentioned reformers, a great deal of what some call luck operates in the evolution of hegemonic capacity. Rationally designed reforms following a shock can be well-intentioned yet still fail or produce unintended outcomes, given the difficulty of fully anticipating how reforms will actually operate in a world of interdependent choices. For societies that reform their governance and financial arrangements in response to dramatic shocks, the potential for such reforms to create the capacity for leadership in the global arena is determined by whether the new rules of the game develop credibility, how people respond to those reforms over time, whether a critical mass of economic actors respond positively, and whether the actions of those economic actors create a global network of financial relationships.

Credibility of Public and Private Financial Arrangements in the Global Political Economy

If a sufficiently large political economy adopts and implements effective governance and financial reforms following a shock, there is no assurance of its emergence as a global financial center or its ascendance to liberal economic leadership. The reforms must first come to be viewed as credible commitments to fair, transparent, and legally protected capital formation, accumulation, and exchange. To develop the necessary credibility, new regulatory arrangements and rules of the game must be tested. Following a crisis that challenges the status quo and promotes changes in the rules of the game, economic actors and private holders of surplus capital approach new arrangements with some trepidation. They are unsure of how the new arrangements will operate and whether they will work. They are suspicious of commitments to reforms by public and private authorities that were more often than not involved in the failed practices of the past. Perhaps the reforms are merely cheap talk—illusory shifts lacking real substance. Should economic actors trust the reforms and put their capital stocks at risk? Are the reforms credible? And, even if they have been sincere in their intentions in adopting the reforms, do public and private authorities have the capacity to implement the new rules of the game?

One significant obstacle to such reforms quickly obtaining credibility is that those adopting reforms control the levers of power. The very source of their capacity to change the rules of the game and adopt reforms is also a source of their capacity to renege on those changes should they decide to. No third party or overarching authority exists in the nation-state system to sanction governments that arbitrarily ignore the rules of the game they have constructed to guide relations within their national boundaries. For their commitments to be credible, governments, by their position in the domestic hierarchy, must exercise self-restraint. History is rife with examples of governments reneging on their commitments—defaulting on their debts, suspending constitutions, being selective in the enforcement of laws, and other rejections of the statutory rules of the game. There is no magic strategy in institutional design that immediately graces reforms in such contexts with credibility.

Holders of capital who have recently experienced severe trauma to their societies and portfolios are likely to be risk averse and to protect their assets even if reforms purportedly embrace transparency, mechanisms that promote fairness (such as oversight and adjudication of complaints), and other countervailing mechanisms that appear to limit arbitrary actions by those in positions of authority. During and following an economic or financial crisis, such risk-averse, conservative responses limit the exchange of capital between those with surplus capital and those in need of capital for their economic endeavors. Usually, economic actors adopt a wait-and-see strategy to evaluate the sincerity and efficacy of reforms, rather than take reforms at face value. They wait and see how the system performs at times of normalcy and stress. Time and testing provide holders of capital with information about the credibility and efficacy of reforms following severe shocks. If good reforms become credible, then the financial capabilities and complexity of the political economy will expand.

Increasing Returns and Network Externalities Necessary to Become a Global Capital Financial Center

Good and sincere reforms and rules of the game do not ensure that a large political economy and its financial arrangements will become a significant, even hegemonic, player in the global arena. Many well-regulated and effective financial arenas in large political economies remain local or regional markets with limited capacity and reach. Many well-run, stable, and fiscally reliable governments with good mechanisms of public finance exercise only limited reach and influence outside their national boundaries. Successful global capital markets enjoy a disproportionately increasing return dynamic that attracts more and more capital, which produces an increasingly dense network of relationships that become self-reinforcing and increasingly influential over the choices of others.

Successful capital markets enhance transparency, reduce transaction costs, offer strategies to hedge and manage risks, stabilize expectations, reduce volatility, and generate long-term stability that affects rates of return and predictability. Such markets tend to attract capital, more capital, and then more capital. This creates deep and liquid markets. The bulk of internationally mobile capital likes such qualities and searches out such markets, particularly at times of increased risk and uncertainty. In the case of a market that emerges as a global market, this market has outdistanced most others in terms of size, liquidity, depth, and attractiveness to new capital. The more capital it attracts, the more other capital finds it attractive.

As a market grows larger, moving from local to regional and perhaps to global, it becomes more densely connected through networks of complex relationships that span national boundaries. During times of global economic expansion, savers and borrowers become connected across national borders through such markets. Capital access improves and capital costs decline within such networks. A deep, liquid market that is connected across national boundaries generates network externalities that are mutually reinforcing. It also creates a web of relationships that often generate mutual, coherent, and consistent incentives across public and private spheres. These can be mobilized to help manage economic or financial shocks that threaten the system. At the hub of this global financial network are the hegemon's capital markets, its regulators, and its policy makers. As the source of financial collective goods to the system, public and private decision makers in other countries are attentive to suggestions and actions originating in the hegemon's public and private financial institutions. Having private capital markets at the center of global financial and economic relations is a necessary condition for liberal hegemony, but it is not sufficient, given the reluctance of private actors to engage in countercyclical efforts during a severe downturn. During bad times a public actor—a government acting as lender of last resort and assembling consortia of capital to rescue a system in crisis—must be both willing to manage and manipulate the network created during good times and capable of doing so.

Hegemonic influence is a form of soft power embedded in the structure of relationships that emerge as a consequence of governance and public and private financial arrangements—a global nervous system centered on the dominant political economy. It is easier to cooperate and play within the rules of the game supported by a liberal hegemon during good times. Most everyone likes the financier and tolerates its regulators during expansionary times, when capital is plentiful and affordable. The global financial nervous system that connects political economies is often underappreciated during good times. Yet this same system transmits economic dislocations across borders, which can raise doubts about the rules of the game. The network that transmits economic dislocations across national boundaries also provides channels along which a liberal hegemon can exert influence by providing collective goods and liquidity that encourage international cooperation, limit the emergence of dislocations, and, ideally, contain dislocations when they do occur—to stabilize rather than destabilize.

ALTERNATIVE EXPLANATIONS OF THE SOURCE OF HEGEMONIC LEADERSHIP

Let's quickly consider and discount two important competing explanations for the source of hegemonic leadership: size and the establishment of stable and productive property rights. The latter is often subsumed under the category of rule of law. One commonly advanced argument is that the largest state acts as the hegemon. Many use economic, military, or demographic size as a proxy for the processes that spawn the capacity for global leadership, but without explicitly examining the domestic foundations of this leadership. From this perspective, some measures of dominance might include GNP or GDP, output per capita, indices of industrialization, shipping tonnage, and military size.

Another explanation is that stable, well-established rule of law and property rights underpin successful political and economic development and, consequently, also hegemonic capacity. Good rule of law and property rights are relatively important, as no political economy will grow efficiently beyond small-scale economic exchange without such institutions. Without doubt, successful political economies require well-established rule of law and property rights that reduce uncertainty, stabilize expectations, lower transaction costs, increase transparency, improve contracting, and provide incentives for self-interested individuals to engage in individually and socially productive exchange. A commercial and financial hegemon will have such rule of law and property rights, for they are essential to its economic growth and success. Predictable, well-established property rights are necessary components of a hegemon's makeup but are not sufficient conditions to create the capacity for hegemonic leadership. Many societies develop productive property rights. The modern industrialized world is full of examples of political economies with property rights that contribute to good economic and social outcomes for those societies.

History enables us to recognize quickly that these two popular explanations for hegemonic capacity—size and rule of law—are incomplete and insufficient. History shows that size is relatively important, but a hegemonic state might not necessarily be the largest state—economically, demographically, or physically. Size alone is not sufficient to give a state the capacity to perform these functions. History also demonstrates that all the hegemonic states of the modern state system—the Dutch Netherlands from 1500 to 1700, the United Kingdom from 1700 to 1900, and the United States since the mid-1900s—enjoyed good property rights, but they were not alone in doing so in their eras.

In the case of the United States in the twentieth century, both size and rule of law look like plausible explanations for U.S. hegemonic capacity. Yet size alone cannot account for the absence of U.S. leadership during the interwar years, the emergence of Dutch commercial and financial hegemony in the 1600s, or British leadership from 1700 until 1900 in the face of a French economy that was far larger and more populous. As a predictor, size would be wrong in two of the three cases of liberal hegemonic leadership since 1600.

In 1566, seventeen provinces rebelled against the control of the Spanish Habsburg Empire—the most powerful military empire in Europe. The Dutch provinces had adopted rules to protect the foundations of commerce and economic exchange. Contracts were respected and enforced, debt obligations met, taxes raised, and the practices of commerce honored. This enhanced the ability of the Dutch to raise capital during times of crisis. With only about 1.5 to 2 million inhabitants, the seven northern provinces (the Dutch United Provinces) resisted Habsburg Spain's attempts to reassert control, successfully staving off the world's most powerful military and an empire far more populous. During the conflict, the Dutch established a governance and financial framework that contributed to their emergence as a commercial and financial hegemon.

Within a short time, Dutch ships carried more freight in the Baltic than did the Hanseatic League, the Germans, or the Danes; more tonnage in the North Sea and along the north European coast than did British, French, or Spanish vessels; and more goods in the Mediterranean than did Portuguese, Spanish, or Italian ships. Dutch shipping came to dominate trade in herring, salt, lumber, spices, and textiles. Amsterdam surpassed Antwerp of the Spanish Netherlands to become the dominant market hub of overland trading routes as well as sea trade. The Dutch guilder became the preferred currency for pricing and settling international transactions. The Bank of Amsterdam and Dutch financial markets became the central clearinghouse for international finance. Remarkably, by the early to mid-1600s, the Dutch became the first global liberal entrepôt after enduring political and economic conflicts with the Spanish, British, and French and despite their relatively small demographic and geographic size. The commercial hegemony of the Dutch Netherlands lasted for about a century, its financial hegemony almost two centuries, before being eclipsed by the British. Dutch power and influence over the rules of the international game far exceeded what might have been expected given the nation's size; the Dutch Netherlands was dwarfed demographically, militarily, and economically by several major European powers. The Spanish Habsburg Empire, France, and the United Kingdom were far larger political economies with much larger populations.

The British case is another example in which size alone is an insufficient explanation for hegemonic leadership. Following the invasion of England by Dutch forces led by William of Orange in 1688 and the changes wrought in British political and economic life by the Glorious Revolution, the United Kingdom would eventually surpass the Dutch Netherlands as the commercial and financial hegemon in the global arena. The Dutch invasion of England and the Glorious Revolution in 1688 brought important changes in the relationships among the Crown, Parliament, and society. William and Mary's conquest infected English governance and state-society relations with many of the same characteristics and institutions that helped the Dutch rise to commercial and financial hegemony. Changes in the relationship between the Crown and Parliament constrained the Crown from reneging on its financial obligations, changed the rules of borrowing for the government, altered the nature of property rights in society, and spurred financial market development. These changes improved the efficiency and attractiveness of London's capital markets. These markets stimulated English growth, funded English overseas expansion, financed more than a century of sporadic warfare with France, led to London's rise as the center of global finance, and made the British pound the dominant currency for pricing international transactions and settling international accounts.

London, with its capital markets and merchant bankers, would soon pass Amsterdam as the center of global finance. Sovereign bond issuances in London financed state consolidation, government development, infrastructure projects, and public and private activities in many countries. H.M. Treasury, the Bank of England, London's capital markets, and English merchant bankers would soon sit at the hub of commercial and financial relations in the global economy. The position of London's capital markets and the appeal of exporting goods to British markets provided British policy makers and private financiers with tools to promote a liberal global economy and manage economic crises—to establish and maintain the rules of the global economy.

In regard to the variable of size, this might not seem unusual, for England had always been a larger political economy than the Dutch Netherlands. But how does size explain England and not France becoming the hegemonic state? British hegemony emerged in the face of the far larger, more populous economy of France. During the 1700s and early 1800s, France competed politically, militarily, and economically with England for global influence. Centrally placed on the Continent, France dwarfed England in terms of physical and demographic size. Before the Industrial Revolution,

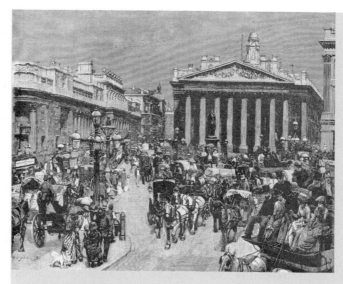

As London became the center of global finance, British policy makers gained tremendous tools to help manage the global economy, promote cooperation, and address dislocations that could threaten globalization. At the heart of this capacity sat the Bank of England, H.M. Treasury, London banks, and British capital markets. Pictured here are the Bank of England and the Royal Exchange.

France enjoyed a larger economy in absolute terms. Nevertheless, England—with a population far smaller, with fewer gold reserves, and with less territory—emerged as the commercial and financial hegemon, setting and maintaining the rules of the game in the global economy. Only after the British economy embarked on the Industrial Revolution did British output and economic prowess actually exceed those of other nations, but only for a short time, because the United States and Germany, which industrialized later than the United Kingdom, both passed the British by the late 1800s. By 1900 the United States had become the largest economy, yet the United Kingdom remained the commercial and financial hegemon of the system until World War I. Size above some threshold may be a necessary but not sufficient condition for setting the rules of the game for the global political economy.

U.S. leadership following World War II is the sole case where sheer economic size and the hypothesized essential financial institutional arrangements overlap. It is the confounding of these factors that makes the Dutch and British cases so important for gaining understanding of the relationship between domestic financial arrangements and hegemonic leadership. U.S. leadership was overdetermined, as the United States had by far the largest economy in the world at the end of World War II and the financial capacity and institutions essential to stimulating and stabilizing the global economy. U.S. economic size and capacity as a share of the global economy were unparalleled.

Even before the end of World War II the United States demonstrated its ascension to the role of commercial and financial hegemon by hosting and guiding the Bretton Woods negotiations. These led to international agreements and a postwar framework of international governmental organizations that supported U.S. efforts to promote the globalization of market relations. During the latter half of the twentieth century, U.S. policy makers worked with these IGOs, as well as U.S. capital markets and private financiers, to manage economic and financial dilemmas that threatened global economic stability and market exchange.

CONCLUSION

History provides important evidence that the rule of law and property rights should be discounted as necessary and sufficient conditions to account for liberal hegemonic capacity. Without doubt, successful political economies require well-established rule of law and property rights that reduce uncertainty, stabilize expectations, lower transaction costs, increase transparency, improve contracting, constrain socially destructive predatory behavior by elites, and provide incentives for self-interested individuals to engage in individually and socially productive exchange. A commercial and financial hegemon has such rule of law and property rights. Yet, even though they are necessary conditions for commercial and financial leadership in the global arena, they are not sufficient conditions. Many societies develop productive property rights and good rule of law. The modern industrialized world is full of examples of political economies with property rights and good rule of law that contribute to productive economic and social outcomes for those societies. The Dutch, the British, and the Americans all enjoyed such conditions, but they were not alone in their eras—although examples of good property rights and good rule of law were far scarcer in the 1500s than in the 1900s. Many states with good rule of law and property rights did not develop the capacity to establish the rules of the global game and sit at the center of global economic activity.

Some level of size and good rule of law and property rights are necessary conditions, but, by themselves or even together, they are insufficient to account for a state emerging as a liberal commercial and financial hegemon. Many nations are sufficiently large but do not acquire the capacity for liberal hegemony. Many nations develop sound rule of law and property rights and yet fail to develop an ability to provide important collective goods to support international cooperation during good times and bad. Some nations may be large enough and enjoy the necessary institutions, yet fall short of being able to act as a liberal hegemon despite a desire to assume such a role.

At the core of hegemonic capacity and leadership sit important mechanisms of public governance, public finance, and private finance. These mechanisms are essential to the emergence of a financial center in a political economy that is really a global financial center. This places that political economy at the heart of a global network and provides it with the tools to promote economic expansion not just at home but globally as well. It also creates the capacity and tools to help manage and limit economic downturns that could damage international relations, undermine the cooperation essential to productive globalization, and produce destructive policies that fuel rather than limit such downturns.

Important Caveat

This chapter focuses on the role of public and private financial arrangements in underpinning the capacity to exercise critical leadership in a capitalist global political economy. I do not want to leave an impression that other factors are unimportant. This should be apparent from the section on alternative explanations, which considers the roles of size, rule of law, and property rights. These are important and necessary conditions but not sufficient conditions for a political economy to develop the ability to exercise liberal hegemonic leadership. In addition, one could easily isolate other contributors to a political economy's position in the global hierarchy and the capacity to exercise leadership. One could point to the importance of entrepreneurial spirit in unleashing creative processes and elevating a political economy in the hierarchy; the quality of educational infrastructure, which transforms human capital; the role of openness to immigration in infusing a political economy's labor pool with new and hungry members; or the ease of starting a new business. These all influence outcomes in a political economy and its trajectory in the global hierarchy. But in the end, these work only if national security sectors, entrepreneurs, immigrants, and start-ups can find access to capital efficiently and reliably. Everything takes us back to the centrality of financial mechanisms to modern political economies and to the global economy.

KEY CONCEPTS

capital markets (p. 238)	hegemony (p. 223)	price stability (p. 236)
hegemonic stability theory (HST) (p. 223)	lender of last resort (p. 235)	public debt (p. 235)
	liberal hegemon (p. 223)	

EXERCISES

1. What are the collective goods that a liberal hegemonic state provides?

2. What is at the essence of such collective goods?

3. How does a hegemonic leader overcome the collective action problem discussed in chapter 5?

4. What states have provided hegemonic leadership during the era of the modern Westphalian state system?

5. Why is liberal hegemonic leadership important for globalization and international cooperation?

6. Absent liberal hegemonic leadership, why might cooperation break down in the international system and damage globalization?

7. What does a lender of last resort do?

8. What is the tension between growth and stability that lenders of last resort often encounter in their policy deliberations?

9. How do the networks develop by which public and private policy makers in a liberal hegemonic state exercise their influence globally?

10. In recent times, critics have questioned the size of many governments' public debt obligations. Despite the question of size, why are public debt markets important in terms of social welfare?

11. Political scientists tend to focus on public governance, but the private sphere is also a critical component of hegemonic capacity. Explain.

FURTHER READING

Cox, Robert W. 1987. *Production, Power, and World Order: Social Forces in the Making of History.* New York: Columbia University Press.

Gilpin, Robert. 1981. *War and Change in World Politics.* Cambridge: Cambridge University Press.

Hamilton, Alexander. 1790. *Report on Public Credit.* Washington, DC: U.S. Treasury.

Kennedy, Paul. 1987. *The Rise and Fall of the Great Powers: Economic Change and Military Conflict from 1500 to 2000.* New York: Random House.

Keohane, Robert O. 1984. *After Hegemony: Cooperation and Discord in the World Political Economy.* Princeton, NJ: Princeton University Press.

Kindleberger, Charles P. 1986. *The World in Depression, 1929–1939.* Rev. ed. Berkeley: University of California Press.

Mearsheimer, John J. 2001. *The Tragedy of Great Power Politics.* New York: W. W. Norton.

Nye, Joseph S., Jr. 1990. *Bound to Lead: The Changing Nature of American Power.* New York: Basic Books.

Ruggie, John Gerard. 1982. "International Regimes, Transactions, and Change: Embedded Liberalism in the Postwar Economic Order." *International Organization* 36, no. 2: 379–415.

Sobel, Andrew C. 2012. *Birth of Hegemony: Crisis, Financial Revolution, and Emerging Global Networks.* Chicago: University of Chicago Press.

Strange, Susan. 1987. "The Persistent Myth of Lost Hegemony." *International Organization* 41, no. 4: 551–607.

7

Interest Groups and International Economic Foundations of Political Cleavage

The great task in the study of any form of social life is the analysis of [these] groups.... When the groups are adequately stated, everything is stated. When I say everything, I mean everything.

—*Arthur F. Bentley, The Process of Government, 1949*

Starting with the assumption that political and economic markets fail, this chapter combines models of international economic exchange with frameworks from micro political economy to construct a systematic framework for understanding the sources of political cleavage and coalition in societies. This chapter uses the concept of factors of production from international trade theory to identify systematically potential winners and losers in national economies resulting from the processes of globalization. Identifying such winners and losers can help us recognize the possibility for durable divisions—cleavages—in societies and the potential for political coalitions forming along such cleavage lines. These divisions are likely to recur and color the nature of policy debates in political economies across a wide range of issues, not simply those explicitly related to globalization. The ability to identify these divisions can be a useful tool for systematically anticipating policy variations within and across national political economies.

A PUZZLE: HOW TO ANTICIPATE POSSIBLE CLEAVAGES AND COALITIONS IN POLITICAL ECONOMIES[1]

Liberalism, a macro approach to international political economy, offers limited leverage for understanding variations in national policies toward international cooperation, trade, capital openness, and globalization. Why does a state lower trade barriers to some goods but raise barriers for other goods? Why does a state liberalize barriers to trade but maintain barriers to capital or human mobility? Why does a government discriminate against some goods from another state but not others? Why does a government cooperate with other governments on one occasion but not another? For governments that profess to adhere to the liberal economic tenets of the so-called Washington Consensus, any barrier to international exchange poses explanatory dilemmas. At the macro level of liberalism, unilateral free trade is unambiguously good for a nation's collective welfare, regardless of its trading partners' policies. The same case can be made for the exchange of capital, human mobility, and the exchange of ideas. Yet the empirical world persistently contradicts the macro theoretical world of liberalism, sometimes only marginally but at other times violently. As a macro theory, liberalism fails to provide a theoretical mechanism within its own boundaries to account for such variations and seemingly nonrational behavior. After all, from this macro perspective, governments that impose barriers to entry are reducing the collective welfare and wealth of society. Such governments appear be nonrational. But we started with the assumption of rationality. Is this a poor assumption, or can we find a rational explanation for such seemingly nonrational behavior?

How do investigators examine such variations in the policies adopted by governments and societies and interpret them as rational strategies within the boundaries of a macro liberal economic explanation? Often, they create atheoretical stories to account for why particular commodities encounter higher barriers to entry than some other commodities, why some capital finds more limited mobility than other capital, and why seemingly nonrational variations exist across products, capital, and states. These stories are attempts to preserve the liberal economic explanation, but at the macro level such accounts amount to ad hoc constructions on the part of investigators—they are not grounded in the theoretical framework of liberalism, but are appended to a liberal explanation. No mechanisms within the macro liberal economic framework seemingly offer a means for systematically understanding the deviations from liberal economic relations. This means that, *ex ante* (before the act), we could not use a macro liberal account to anticipate variations in national openness to global transactions or variations in willingness to embrace the processes of globalization.

Hegemonic stability theory performs a little better in anticipating and accounting for these variations, since it expects a hegemonic state to provide market access as a countercyclical

---

[1]This chapter draws heavily on the pathbreaking work of Ronald Rogowski in *Commerce and Coalitions: How Trade Affects Domestic Political Alignments* (Princeton, NJ: Princeton University Press, 1989).

good for the international system and recognizes that nonhegemonic governments will sometimes choose to free ride on the hegemonic power. The expectation of free riding means that those governments can, will, and probably should adopt at times nonliberal policies as rational policy choices, especially during times of economic duress. Yet HST also falters as an explanatory tool, as it cannot explain variations in the policies of the hegemonic state or in the policies of those states that choose not to free ride, even though free riding appears to be a rational policy.

HST expects that the United States, as a hegemonic power at the heart of a liberal global economy, will provide a handful of specific collective goods to the international system, and that these goods will reduce uncertainty and promote liberal economic exchange. But how, then, does HST account for enduring U.S. agricultural subsidies or other U.S. barriers to entry that disadvantage foreign agricultural producers, the imposition of steel tariffs during a time of global economic slowdown, or countless other examples that run counter to hegemonic stability expectations? Moreover, HST anticipates that nonhegemonic powers will free ride and defect from liberal exchange arrangements by erecting barriers to trade and attempting to intervene through nonmarket mechanisms in the flow of capital. Sometimes they do so, but often they do not, and—more problematically—the variations cannot be explained systematically within the logical framework of HST except by ad hoc accounts.

Of course, the social world is complex, and so we should not expect our theories to work perfectly and account for every variation, but we can search for theories and approaches that may perform better. Liberalism and HST implicitly assume monolithic nation-states wherein only collective interest and welfare exist. This assumption implies that individuals in societies share a similar preference ordering and make decisions based on a collective rationality—they evaluate outcomes only on how they affect the collective interest. But this schema neglects methodological individualism, an important focus of this book as explored in chapter 1, and the prospect for divergent individual preferences in society.

Explanations that account for deviations from the macro approaches often appeal to subnational-level devices such as organized special interests, but within the boundaries of macro theories, these explanations are ad hoc: they lack a theoretical mechanism that offers systematic tools for understanding why and when such variations occur. Yes, latent and active groups exist in societies, as demonstrated in chapter 5, but so far we have no systematic and theoretical means of anticipating those groups, their identities, and their motivations. Even if such ad hoc accounts appear to be correct on a case-by-case basis, they are nontheoretical constructions that fail to provide systematic mechanisms for anticipating and understanding future deviations. Successfully explaining deviations in theory means that they are not deviations but variations that may be accounted for systematically by mechanisms that are explicitly part of that theory. If a theory is robust, it ties these seeming deviations into an account that operates systematically and consistently across cases and contributes to the construction of a social science explanation that is cumulative, works in many settings, and is not unique to a particular setting. The likelihood of some political and economic market failure within states provides an opportunity to reconcile governments' profession of liberal economic beliefs with their adoption of protectionist measures, erection of barriers to entry, and intervention in the functioning of market mechanisms. Hopefully, we can create theoretical connections between the processes of globalization and the political bargaining within national political arenas that produces policies.

EXPLANATIONS GROUNDED IN MICRO POLITICAL ECONOMY

Looking inside states and building explanations based on methodological individualism explicitly recognizes the potential for diversity of interests, preferences, strategies, and capabilities at the subnational level. Earlier chapters examined the potential for failure in the social aggregation mechanisms of markets and politics, failures to accurately and efficiently compile and reflect the individual preferences of society's members to produce social outcomes. This helps to account for the breakdown in liberal and HST explanations. Our recognition of such failures in the mechanisms of social aggregation anticipates divisions in society that can strategically compete to manipulate outcomes for individual or narrowly defined group objectives regardless of a larger collective good. Many latent divisions exist within societies that can affect policy makers' choices, and these divisions may account for the variations that are unexplained by the mechanisms of the macro approaches. Unfortunately, this recognition of diversity does not simplify the problem of understanding behavior. There are a variety of means of constructing divisions in society.

Let's begin by shifting the focus of analysis to the level of individuals, businesses, and groups. Repeated interventions by governments to protect agricultural sectors or specific manufacturing producers and their labor—and to discriminate against foreign producers and labor—do not appear rational under a liberal economic framework. These actions hinder the functioning of market exchange and constrain the expansion of their societies' consumption possibilities and collective welfare. Yet we have assumed that policy makers are rational, which leads to the recognition of potential weaknesses in the macro explanations. If we shift our focus away from societal and state levels of analysis to the individual decision maker, we may find that what appears to be nonrational in the context of a macro-level explanation can be seen as rational within a micro political economic explanation.

Political and economic market failure are problematic for the collective welfare of society, serving as a potential boon to groups and individuals that can manage the failures to their advantage and a cost to those that fail to manipulate the failures to their advantage. Perversely, this phenomenon is also a boon for political scientists, for, without political and economic market failures, political scientists would have little to study, explain, or teach. Using micro political economic tools, which recognize that strategic action by individuals and groups can manipulate political and economic market outcomes to redistribute the gains and costs of exchange, we can demonstrate that such suboptimal collective outcomes occur as consequences of individual rational actions. Actions that seem nonsensical at the macro level make sense at the micro level of strategic behavior. The manipulation of government and market mechanisms for individual gain can be rational, regardless of the consequences for social welfare.

INTEREST GROUPS: FRAGMENTING MONOLITHIC PERCEPTIONS OF SOCIETY

Opening up the box of the nation-state, we shift our attention to civil society. This perspective will help us to recognize that divergent opinions on and preferences concerning policy exist within a society, and in the abilities of a society's members to make demands on government. Here we consider the ability of individuals with similar preferences to overcome barriers to collective action and act as concentrated and organized groups. These aggregations of individual preference into concentrated and organized coalitions are called **interest groups.** Overcoming barriers to group action and forming an interest group is a key step in communicating preferences to public policy makers and influencing their choices. This process involves transforming a latent, unorganized group of individuals into an organized, efficacious group that can represent the collective preferences of the group's members and try to exert influence over public policy choices. Such organization transforms the potential of diffuse and disconnected individuals into a group that has much greater capabilities in the political arena than do its members as individuals.

> **Interest groups** are voluntary associations of persons who share opinions on and endeavor to promote particular causes. The members of such groups have found ways to overcome the barriers to collective action discussed in chapter 5.

Latent interests that overcome barriers to collective action to form active and successful interest groups have some general similarities. First, enough individuals in a society must share some characteristic or common interest in obtaining a specific collective benefit, but shared interest is not sufficient. Even if enough individuals in a society are interested in a specific objective, an interest group may not form. As discussed in chapter 5, the barriers to collective action can be difficult to surmount, which accounts for the fact that many potential groups remain latent. Latent groups must exist as foundations for active and effective interest groups, but many fail to overcome the barriers to group action and remain latent.

Second, interest groups are often built around relatively narrow definitions of particular issues. Their issue domains can expand over time as they take advantage of their established organizational structure to piggyback new issues onto old, but interest groups generally begin with a relatively narrow focus, which helps them to overcome barriers to collective action and limits the identity problems (heterogeneity) that can hamper the effectiveness of groups with broadly defined interests.

Third, the success of an interest group is partly explained by its ability to gain access to relevant policy makers. What channels of access exist for any particular interest group? Are

On November 1, 2011, thousands of demonstrators took part in a protest march in Nice, France, against the Group of 20 summit in the nearby city of Cannes. Protest organizers successfully overcame barriers to collective action to mobilize thousands of antiglobalization protesters who demanded that the leaders of the world's leading industrialized and emerging economies "put people first, not finance."

those channels of access appropriate to furthering the agenda of the interest group? For example, the American Banking Association (ABA) will be far more successful at representing the interests of bankers if its channels of access include policy makers at the Federal Reserve and the Securities and Exchange Commission, the comptroller of the currency, members and staff of the House and Senate Banking Committees, and other relevant regulators. The ABA will be less successful if it cannot access those regulators and instead develops access to the Environmental Protection Agency or the Department of Transportation. In developing channels of access, interest groups make strategic choices regarding which government actors to cultivate, but their ability to develop such channels is also a function of the organizational structure of government and statutory restrictions. In considering the demands of civil society on government, we want to examine what groups organize, how their efforts are concentrated, and whether they have pathways that allow them to communicate their preferences to relevant policy makers.

Fourth, successful interest groups often form coalitions with other interest groups. How and why does this happen? Any particular interest group may be too narrow in its focus to mobilize sufficient public pressure to attract the attention of policy makers. Forming coalitions across interest groups may help overcome this problem by linking the interests and resources of multiple groups. By providing one another with support, interest groups that join together can place greater pressure on policy makers, as such alliances take advantage of specialization and the gains from trade in political markets.

BIOLOGICAL AND SOCIAL FOUNDATIONS OF CLEAVAGE

The framework of market failure explicitly recognizes the likelihood that differing beliefs and preferences exist in society, forming a basis for societal divisions. It begins with an assumption of competing interests, offers a lever to demonstrate weaknesses in the macro explanations, and challenges us to look beyond those explanations for more satisfying and useful theoretical frameworks. But it does not provide tools for anticipating the lines along which a society may divide. This is problematic if the boundaries and divisions in domestic society can affect preferences, strategies, capabilities, policy choices, and outcomes in the global political economy. Are such cleavages ad hoc, or is it possible to establish a systematic basis for anticipating cleavages in domestic society and their public policy interests? The previous discussion of interest groups does not offer any systematic leverage for understanding what cleavages and interest groups will appear in society. Why some divisions and not others? To move past ad hoc accounts and create a useful framework for explanation, description, and prediction, we will need tools that help us to recognize the sources of potential divisions in society.

Many sources of potential divisions exist, and investigators in comparative and American politics spend a great deal of time analyzing such divisions. As cleavages separate one group from another, they divide the large national community depicted in the macro explanation into smaller subcommunities. The very notion of community is one of erecting boundaries that separate one group of individuals from another, but often these boundaries are not cleanly drawn or mutually exclusive, as individuals can belong to a variety of communities. For example, an individual may identify herself as an American but also as a woman, an adherent of a particular religion, a member of a minority group, and an inhabitant of a geographic region smaller than the nation, as well as a member of a professional trade association, of multiple social organizations, and of a political party. Such subcommunities are part of the social fabric of civil society, often generating social capital that facilitates cooperation, but other times producing tensions that tear at that fabric. These subcommunities can overlap, but not completely. Some such cleavages in society get mobilized for political and social activities, while other divisions remain latent, never organizing or acting strategically as groups toward specific goals.

Cleavages can occur along lines generated by biological and social characteristics of individuals in society. Regardless of our normative preferences to the contrary, individuals often create groups and boundaries based on biological and social characteristics such as gender, race, ethnicity, and religion. Many biological and social characteristics are easily identifiable, which may contribute to their usefulness in creating a them/us mentality and erecting the boundaries necessary for group identity—even if key distinguishing characteristics are superfluous or unrelated to real differences in preferences and objectives. Unfortunately, history demonstrates that many cleavages and conflicts within societies occur along lines of race, religion, ethnicity, and gender.

Another characteristic that has been observed to create a basis for social cleavage is national heritage, despite the current citizenship of the people involved. The mass migrations of the 1800s, which were stimulated by globalization, provide a strong example of this characteristic at work, for those who migrated to the United States and became Americans also retained identities linked to their places of origin. Describing the U.S. population as a mix of Irish Americans, German Americans, Chinese Americans, Polish Americans,

Norwegian Americans, Jewish Americans, African Americans, and so on recognizes that current identities can be tempered by heritage. These identities grounded in heritage can be mobilized for political purposes that reflect different preferences and interests even though all are part of a larger community called Americans. The same holds true for other societies, as every nation has been socially constructed through the amalgamation of groups of differing identities.

Such social differences sometimes, but not always, provide a foundation for political cleavage. For example, the bloody and brutal hostilities in Kosovo during the 1990s are often portrayed as a conflict between Christian Serbs and Muslim Serbs that harks back to a battle that took place in the region in 1389. In that major battle, Christian Serbs fought and lost to the Ottoman Turks, but the defeat became celebrated in Serbian folklore and is often used to remind Christian Serbs of their separate identity. Yet for years, even centuries, Christian Serbs and Muslim Serbs lived side by side in communities, intermarrying, trading, socializing, and celebrating together. If heritage is so powerful in constructing group identity and producing societal cleavage, how could the members of these two ethnic communities get together for so many years, and why did social relations deteriorate along this particular characteristic of identity in the mid-1990s but not in the 1970s?

The variations observable in the historical experience in Kosovo suggest that there is something more at work in generating political cleavage than simply religious identity. Despite recent violence, the apparent absence of cleavage and conflict for many years could mean that religious identity alone was not a necessary or sufficient condition for political cleavage in Serbia—that some other division is masked by the appeal to religion. Biological and social differences are not necessarily divisive on their own; they need to be mobilized to create divisions in a society. For such social and biological characteristics to become sources of political cleavage, people must use them to construct distinct identities with wants and preferences that can be juxtaposed against those lacking the same characteristics.

INTERNATIONAL ECONOMIC SOURCES OF CLEAVAGE

Chapter 3 introduced a mechanism grounded in international exchange that provides a starting point on which to build a systematic foundation for understanding the international economic underpinnings of divisions in national political economies. The **Heckscher-Ohlin** framework of trade is built on the notion that economies differ in the distribution of factors of production—their factor endowments. This insight offers a strategy that allows us to begin connecting economic activity with political activity. Every nation has a particular distribution of land, labor, and capital. Variations in these distributions across states produce comparative advantages and disadvantages. The integration of national markets into a larger global market rewards some producers and laborers but penalizes others. The dynamics of economic exchange between states creates potential for differing interests and cleavages and provides some leverage for understanding political action within and across societies.

Building on the **Heckscher-Ohlin model,** we can focus on **factor endowments** to understand the resulting distribution of advantages and disadvantages and, consequently, to anticipate and explain systematically the potential political cleavages and coalitions in societies.

After building a framework for political competition and cooperation based on Heckscher-Ohlin and factors of production, we will consider its weaknesses. Then we will briefly explore two alternative approaches for examining the economic sources of cleavage and coalition in the international arena: economic sector and asset mobility. The first approach suggests that economies are divided into industrial sectors that may be more important sources of cleavage and coalition than are factors of production. The second focuses on the particular nature of economic assets and their mobility, asking whether a particular production asset (people, resources, or capital) can be easily reapplied to some other form of production or is relatively immobile and confined to a limited range of applications in producing commodities and services.

> The **Heckscher-Ohlin model** is an economic framework that states that differences in factor endowments across nations produce comparative advantages. A **factor endowment** is the distribution of factors of production (land, labor, and capital) in a specific economy; each economy has a different factor endowment based on the relative abundance and scarcity of its factors.

Factor Endowment: A Source of Preferences, Cleavage, and Coalition

The Heckscher-Ohlin model of trade asserts that with freer trade a nation will export commodities that are produced by relatively abundant factors of production in society and will import commodities that are produced by relatively scarce factors of production in that society. This is a function of the lower cost of factors in relatively high supply and the higher cost of factors in relatively tight supply as inputs to production. The Stolper-Samuelson theorem extends Heckscher-Ohlin to demonstrate that increased trade rewards abundant factors of production in a society and penalizes a nation's scarcer factors of production. Drawing on the logic of Heckscher-Ohlin and Stolper-Samuelson, we can anticipate that abundant factors of production should be more open to the processes of globalization generally and specifically should prefer more open trading arrangements than scarce factors of production. Holders of such factors of production are those most likely to benefit from greater exposure to the global economic geography of liberalism. Less abundant factors of production are likely to be more suspicious of the processes of globalization, perhaps even favoring more protectionist strategies that insulate their domestic political economies from the global economic geography of liberalism.

More open or more closed trading relations will affect the resources channeled to the different factors of production that may be applied to economic production or other activities, such as leisure, or to political action, such as lobbying, campaigning for elections, and public education. They may or may not choose to use such resources for political action, but the latent lines of division are established by the economic structure of the economy as revealed by exposure to the processes of globalization. As abundant factors of production gain under open trading relations, they will discover that as trade expands they enjoy an increase in the capabilities they may apply to political action. In this situation, scarce factors of production will face a decline in the resources that they can apply to political activities. Turning this logic around, slowdowns and interventions in globalization and trade will enrich scarce factors of production. If we assume that the willingness to engage in political action is equal across winners and losers from trade, we can predict that winners from changes in trade, either expansionary or contractionary, will gain political leverage. This assumption will be fragile if either the winners or the losers are more willing to devote disproportionate resources to political activities. Recognizing the fragility of the assumption of equal willingness, however, we can still observe that greater openness to globalization and trade economically enriches abundant factors of production but penalizes scarce factors of production, while less open trade economically enriches scarce factors of production but penalizes abundant factors of production. We assume that economic conditions affect policy preferences and beliefs, whether or not individuals act on those preferences and beliefs.

Now we have a plausible model that systematically links economic activity to political divisions and debates within national political arenas. This factor endowment framework defines the most basic cleavage lines in society, potential coalition partners, the nature of political conflict, and the likely winners of such conflict, if we assume that the change in political capabilities involves a simple extrapolation from changing exposure to trade. We can thus use the expansion or contraction of trade as a key independent variable for understanding shifts in capabilities, divisions, and coalitions in domestic political economies. This highly stylized framework—the argument reduced to its basic components—enables the construction of expectations about politics within states from knowledge only about factor endowments and whether trade is expanding or contracting. This can be a very powerful and elegant framework, if it works.

Some Stylized Examples

Capital is a factor of production that people construct, invent, or accumulate and then use to transform the other factors of production—land and labor—to make them more productive. Labor is the effort that men and women put into producing a commodity.

Imagine a state in a world of expanding trade. This state—let's call it State A—enjoys an abundance of capital and labor but suffers from a shortage of land, or resources. Capital and labor will benefit, facing fewer dislocations and growing richer and having more disposable resources to apply to more economic production or other activities such as leisure or politics. In this society, capital attains a higher return and more productive investment by transforming labor, the other abundant factor of production. State A's land resources, in contrast, will find themselves at a comparative disadvantage in a world of expanding globalization where they are exposed to competitors from land-abundant states, where land is a relatively less expensive input to production because of its supply. Given the factor endowments ascribed to this hypothetical state, we can predict the dominant form of production in this state and where such production would be located geographically. Because of its abundance of capital and labor, we can deduce that State *A*'s economy would specialize in the manufacture of goods and services rather than in agricultural or resource production, which would require an abundance of the land resource that is lacking here. With expanding trade, this economy would be conditioned by the global market to shift production toward commodities that are labor- and capital-intensive—the manufacture of goods and services. Such economic activity generally migrates to urban centers.

In State *A*, if labor and capital can translate their economic gains into political action, they may gain leverage in the political arena—not simply on trade-related issues, but on any issue. Holders of land, meanwhile, can use their diminishing economic gains to resist such changes. In this state, labor and capital have overlapping interests in promoting economic openness and are likely to discover that they have overlapping interests on other issues, such as social and educational policies, because of the connections of their economic interests. This overlap creates a potential for a political coalition between holders of labor and holders of capital against the interests of land. If these holders of abundant resources are able to form a political coalition and trade continues to expand, their coalition should gain even more capabilities and influence over time. At the same time, holders of land resources are likely to have different preferences than labor and capital, given their economic position and where gains and losses fall from expanding globalization. If this political cleavage emerges (labor and capital on one side, land on the other), it will translate into a geographic cleavage between urban and rural areas. As long as trade continues to expand, the urban areas in State *A* should continue to gain disposable resources that can be used to exert political influence. This does not mean they will use those resources for political purposes, just that they have more resources that can be applied to politics if they so desire.

Now, consider a second state, State *B*, with a different factor endowment, but still in a world of expanding international exchange. In this example, the country enjoys abundant capital and land but scarce labor. Again, because of the abundance of capital, this will be a relatively advanced economy. Unlike the previous example, however, State *B*'s particular set of factor endowments makes it internationally more competitive and productive in capital- and land-intensive commodities. The global market will reward activities involving capital applied to production and transformation and land-intensive activities such as mining, agriculture, and the production and refinement of metals or petroleum products. If trade continues to expand, capital and land will benefit and gain more disposable resources, resources that they can potentially employ for political activities. In this state, land and capital have overlapping interests in promoting economic openness and are likely to have overlapping interests on other issues, such as social and educational policies, given the connections of their economic interests.

This factor endowment divide creates a potential for a political coalition between holders of land and capital against the interests of labor. If the abundant factors of production in State *B* are able to form a political coalition and trade continues to expand, this coalition has the potential to gain political capabilities over time. Labor can use its diminishing economic gains to resist the policy changes preferred by the potential coalition partners of land and capital. This particular divide does not translate into the urban-rural geographic cleavage of the previous case but into a cleavage based on wealth and land versus labor—a class cleavage. Political debate and competition should fall along class lines.

In an environment of expanding international exchange, what does the factor endowment framework suggest for politics in capital-poor societies—societies that are less economically advanced than those considered in the above cases? Their lack of capital means that their land and labor resources remain relatively untransformed in comparison to those of their counterparts in capital-rich societies. Consider a state, State *C*, that is abundant in labor but scarce in capital and land. Since increasing trade rewards labor-intensive forms of production, land and capital will discover that they face a comparative disadvantage in the global economy.

At first glance, the dynamics here appear similar to those in State *B*: society faces a potential divide between a coalition of capital and land on one side and labor on the other. Again, this cleavage anticipates class conflict. Despite similar cleavages, however, who gains and who wins in State *C* under expanding trade differs from the example of State *B*, and this difference should eventually produce different political outcomes, even though the cleavage lines are identical. In State *B*, capital and land gain from expanding trade, but in State *C* labor gains from the expansion of trade. Labor will be gaining relatively more disposable resources that may be applied to political activity in this case, not diminishing resources as before. In State *C*, labor will become a more powerful political force as trade continues to expand, if gains and losses from trade and globalization translate directly into gains or losses in political capacity. If this capital-poor society accumulates capital with trade and the resulting economic expansion (which increases savings and investment), it eventually will transform to become a capital-abundant state. This is a goal of development. If this happens, we would anticipate a shift in coalition partners and a change in the political cleavages and coalitions of society.

Now, let's examine a capital-poor state, State *D*, that enjoys a relative abundance of land and relatively scarce labor. Trade is still expanding. At first glance, using the factor endowment framework, we anticipate the same divisions—the same lines of political cleavage and likely coalition partners—as in State *A*. We expect labor and capital, as relatively scarce factors, to be potential coalition partners, with the interests of land falling on the other side of the potential divide in society. This division predicts an urban-rural cleavage. Yet State *D*'s prospects differ from State *A*'s situation of urban-rural conflict. In State *A*, the urban coalition gained and the rural area lost capabilities as trade expanded. In State *D*, however, the rural area expands and the urban area loses capabilities as trade increases. With continued expansion of trade—and everything else remaining equal—we can extrapolate growth in the relative capabilities and disposable resources of land over those of the labor-capital coalition in State *D* and forecast that, over time, land will become increasingly successful in the political arena in obtaining its policy preferences, if it can translate those gains into political action. The divisions in society here mirror those in State *A,* but the political outcomes are likely to differ along with the differences in who wins and who loses in the arena of international exchange, if economic gains and losses translate directly into gains and losses in willingness and capacity to influence public policy. Again, if this capital-poor society accumulates capital with trade and the resulting economic expansion, it eventually will transform to become a capital-abundant state. If this happens, we would anticipate a shift in coalition partners and a change in the political cleavages and coalitions of society.

The expansion of trade is not inevitable. International trade and globalization of economic relations can shrink as a consequence of economic crisis, war, natural disasters, or the erection of political barriers to cross-border exchange. This will become apparent when we consider the beginning of the nineteenth century in Europe and the period between World War I and World War II in chapters 9 and 10, respectively. With trade contraction, political competition should fall along the same divisions as depicted in our stylized examples, as those states' factor endowments remain the same. But who gains and who loses economic resources as a result of the shrinkage will differ, as contractions in international exchange will reward scarce factors of production and penalize abundant factors of production. Changing a nation's relationship to the international arena from one of expanding trade to one of contracting trade reverses who gains and who loses economically in our examples, and consequently who gains and who loses resources that may be applied to political activities. Again, assuming that these gains and losses in capabilities translate into potential gains and losses in political influence, a situation of contracting trade anticipates very different political outcomes from an environment of expanding trade, even though political cleavages can remain the same.

The capabilities that factors of production can potentially expend in the political arena will change with the expansion or contraction of trade. What policies emerge from the divisions in society that are anticipated by the factor endowment framework will also depend on the ability of likely coalition partners to form coalitions and their willingness to expend their resources on political activities. The structure of international exchange reveals potential divisions in a society stemming from how that political economy's underlying structure meshes with the global economy, but such divisions are not limited to policy areas specific to globalization—trade, migration, or capital mobility. Such divisions reflect the basic structure of an economy, and consequently such fault lines might be mobilized for a broader range of issues than globalization—education, safety net provision, national security, monetary policy, and other fiscal policies.

An Empirical Example

The factor endowment framework offers an elegant theoretical specification about plausible connections between international economic relations and political activity in domestic political economies. The model may be elegant and internally consistent, but it remains a hypothetical story about the causal connections of one set of activities to another set of activities. Empirical testing is needed to evaluate its merit as a useful depiction of behavior. Happily, as the stylized examples above demonstrate, the model allows systematic derivation of testable proposals about political behavior—specifically, about winners and losers, cleavages and coalitions in national political economies. These testable proposals anticipate the nature and content of policy conflict in political economies, given knowledge of two key variables: a state's factor endowment and comparative advantage, and whether trade is expanding or contracting. Our initial assumption of rationality expects that players in the political arena can rank their preferences, evaluate strategies and their relative costs, and form coalitions with those that have compatible interests against those with less similar interests as a strategy to obtain their best outcome. History provides ample opportunities to test this elegant theoretical framework against the empirical world.

Let's use U.S. history to evaluate the factor endowment framework in action. The transformation of the U.S. economy over the past two hundred years allows us to consider different factor endowments at different times, all within a single national context. If the factor endowment framework is analytically useful, changes in factor endowment that occur as a consequence of economic growth and the interaction of the U.S. economy with the global economy should lead to predictable changes in domestic political cleavages, coalitions, and policy competition.

At birth and for almost a century thereafter, the United States was land rich but capital and labor poor. How do we know it was capital and labor poor during this period? The expansion of U.S. economic enterprises and infrastructure, such as railroads, relied heavily on financing from London's capital markets. New York's youthful capital markets provided some financing, but they could not meet the needs of the developing economy because there was insufficient capital accumulation in the United States. The U.S. banking house of Morgan established itself by selling bonds and engaging in dealings in London's financial markets for the promotion of U.S. enterprise. This tells us that even with a sophisticated financial organization such as Morgan, the New York markets were too small and undercapitalized for a rapidly expanding economy. Meanwhile, the movements of people from the Old World to Australia, Canada, the United States, and other regions of the New World speak to the labor scarcity in those areas.

By the late 1800s and early 1900s, the United States had transformed itself into an economy that enjoyed abundance in land and capital but still sustained a relative scarcity in labor. New York had become a major financial market, rivaling London in terms of capitalization and resources. This transformation in capital accumulation appears in a significant increase in per capita levels of industrial production from 1800 to 1913 (see chapter 9, table 9.4), which indicates a greater role for capital in the production of goods and services. Such a change can occur only with increasing access to affordable capital. So we can conclude that the accumulation and supply of domestic capital in the United States increased over the course of the century, and with this change, the U.S. economy went from being economically backward to being economically advanced. Labor remained relatively scarce, but immigration continued at a high rate. People tend to move to places where they find economic opportunity; the U.S. economy needed workers and paid relatively high wages, given the shortage of labor.

What does the factor endowment framework predict for U.S. economic activity, political division and coalition, and public policy competition during these different periods? During the earlier period, it expects that abundant land interests would gain economically with expanded trade, but scarce capital and labor would lose economically as they encountered competition from more competitive labor and capital in nations where those factors were abundant. During this period, the United Kingdom, one of the major trading partners of the United States, enjoyed a relative abundance of labor and capital but a shortage of land. For the first part of the nineteenth century, the United Kingdom protected its agricultural producers with the Corn Laws, which affected the prices and quantities of grains entering the English markets from abroad. This advantaged what would have been less competitive British producers who would have faced dislocations if trade were more open. With the repeal of British protections exacted by the Corn Laws and increasing British openness to trade, U.S. and other New World agricultural producers competed successfully in British markets because of their comparative advantage of abundant land, which enabled them to undercut their British competitors. In this case, expansion of trade led to a dramatic decline in British agriculture. But during this period, British capital- and labor-intensive commodities enjoyed a comparative advantage over similar U.S. products, as British manufacturers led the way during the Industrial Revolution. Only with government-erected barriers to entry— protectionism—could U.S. manufacturers compete against British manufacturers in U.S. markets during this period.

Conversely, with contractions in trade during this period, U.S. land resources should have suffered economic penalties, while the relatively scarce factors of labor and capital should have reaped economic gains. A variety of circumstances, including war, natural disasters, and economic distress, may prompt a contraction in trade, and the United States faced two such shocks during the nineteenth century: the Civil War and the depression of the later 1800s. But trade contraction can also be imposed by public policy interventions in the form of protectionist measures such as tariffs, quotas, and other barriers to entry, which can shelter all or part of an economy from the competitive forces of a larger global marketplace by ensuring domestic producers favored access to domestic markets.

The U.S. case initially anticipates an urban-rural cleavage. U.S. farmers should pursue freer trade, because their products are competitive in global markets. As the abundant factor of production in the U.S. economy, they should resist government obstructions to international exchange, for greater economic globalization rewards their efforts. In contrast, the urban coalition of capital and labor, the relatively scarce factors of production, should favor protectionism. With protections, U.S. farmers and consumers would pay more for labor- and capital-intensive commodities than they would without protections to bring the world market price for these commodities up to, or above, the price for similarly produced U.S. commodities. Moreover, in a protectionist environment that sheltered American labor and capital, American agriculture could face retaliatory measures by other governments, which could damage their comparative advantage.

Import substitution is a development strategy that advocates protecting the domestic market for domestic manufacturers in order to enable nascent domestic industries to emerge, gain strength, and eventually become competitive in the global economy.

"You ought to be ashamed of yourself!"

The 1896 U.S. presidential election provided the context for journalist L. Frank Baum's *The Wonderful Wizard of Oz,* which is a social and political commentary on the contemporary divisions in U.S. society and politics disguised as a children's story. Baum's story captures the tensions between eastern banking and industrial interests, the Wicked Witches of the East and West, and agrarian-labor interests, the Good Witches of the North and South.

The factor endowment story fits early American history quite well. Alexander Hamilton argued in a famous report to Congress that insulating U.S. manufacturing from the pressure of foreign competition by protecting the domestic market for U.S. manufacturers was essential to enable nascent U.S. industries to emerge and survive. This strategy, known as **import substitution,** was used intensively as a development strategy by Latin American governments during the twentieth century, but with notably less success than enjoyed by the United States in the 1800s. Open competition in manufacturing would have revealed the lack of U.S. comparative advantage in capital- and labor-intensive forms of economic activity versus producers of such commodities from the Old World. The growth of U.S. manufacturing would have been constrained without protectionism, and Thomas Jefferson's vision of an agricultural United States dominated by a rural elite might have survived and prospered. Slavery might have prospered and been extended to all the new territories, and the Civil War might not have come to pass.

Hamilton recognized the dilemma that free trade posed for U.S. capital and labor interests. Why did he favor protection of labor and capital instead of the interests of land (agriculture)? He may have had a grand vision of the United States as a manufacturing power, but it is also likely that his preferences were shaped by his regional attachment and professional expertise. His state of residence was New York, and his expertise was in finance. Farming was more difficult in the Northeast than in the South and the emerging West; fieldstone fences all over New England and New York testify to the difficulty of plowing the soil and managing crops in that region. The Northeast was emerging, instead, as a center of industry and the banking center of the young United States, but it faced more competitive finance and manufacturing from the United Kingdom and the Old World. Hamilton's vision of the United States differed from Jefferson's because Hamilton's regional concerns were bound up in the interests of labor and capital—even though these factors were lacking in comparative advantage—and not in those of land. This regional bias put him at odds with the farm states of the South and, if he had lived long enough, with the new territories of the West.

The urban-rural division that was based on economic interests expanded beyond the issue of trade. Rural interests, which resented capital's potential influence, formed farmers' cooperatives and alliances that became part of the foundation of populist and progressive movements in the United States. A deep and recurring theme in American history—the division between Main Street and Wall Street, including widespread distrust of New York bankers and financiers—reflects this cleavage. Andrew Jackson's election and the success of the early Democratic Party mobilized forces along this division, and by the mid-1800s the cleavage along production factor lines was captured in the division between the emerging Republican Party and the established Democratic Party. At this time, the workers and industrialists of the Northeast, representing the production factors of labor and capital, combined with the more capital-intensive interests of the upper Midwest to elect Abraham Lincoln over the objections of the Democratic Party, which enjoyed electoral success mostly in the Far West and the South. As we will see in chapter 9, this cleavage recurred in debates over issues such as the gold standard, price deflation, the formation of a national bank, farm indebtedness, and ownership and regulation of transport facilities—all issues that spilled over into the international arena.

But economies are dynamic. They change, often dramatically, as a result of capital accumulation and investment. The United States was an economically backward, capital-scarce nation during its early years, but with economic growth it accumulated more and more capital through earnings and savings that could be applied to investment in activities to transform and increase the productivity of land and labor. By the beginning of the twentieth century, the United States had shifted from a capital-scarce to a capital-abundant state. It was still labor poor, as evidenced by the great waves of immigration that continued through the gates of Ellis Island and other immigration centers, bringing Germans, Irish, Italians, European Jews, Norwegians, and others seeking economic opportunity and political refuge. These immigrants filled New York tenements and found employment, albeit often poorly paid and in dreadful working conditions, that greatly exceeded the dismal prospects they had left behind in the Old World.

Such a shift in the relative abundance of capital should lead to changes in the preferences of capital regarding trade restrictions and in coalition politics. The factor endowment framework predicts that the cleavage should shift to land and capital against labor, and that it should create tensions between more capital-intensive labor and less capital-intensive labor. The shift in the abundance of capital should have generated pressures for change in the Republican Party's policy preferences for tariffs and other barriers to entry while increasing conflict between the old coalition partners of labor and capital. Over time, we should anticipate a shift in the lines of political battle from the urban-rural cleavage of land against labor and capital to a cleavage reflecting class conflict, with land and capital allied against labor, and capital-intensive labor against capital-scarce labor.

Historically, the cost of capital declined with its transformation into a relatively abundant factor. Trade was expanding, which increased the gains to abundant factors. Consequently, U.S.-produced capital-intensive commodities became more competitive in global markets. As Democrats, who represented the interests of the abundant land factor, continued to press for reduction of trade barriers, the rewards to capital from expanded trade put pressure on the capital-labor coalition and placed the Republican Party in the difficult position of trying to manage a conflict between its two core constituencies. In effect, Republican politicians had to choose between policies that favored one coalition partner over another, and their choices could vary by political economic geography, depending on which coalition partner dominated in specific electoral districts. But over time, even though labor continued to find its greatest access to representation through Republican Party channels for many years, that party's support for labor preferences was becoming weaker compared with its positions on issues relevant to capital.

Republican politicians, who had long represented a capital-labor coalition that was urban and protectionist, began moderating their position on tariffs, moving away from the protectionist preferences of less capital-intensive labor. When President Theodore Roosevelt, a Republican, advocated tariff reform and increased exposure to the competitive pressures of the larger global market, his actions fed a growing rift in the Republican Party. This divide left labor, as the scarce factor of production, which had been allied with the Republicans since Lincoln, in an increasingly exposed position politically. As the gains from trade translated into political influence, expanding trade meant that capital was gaining strength while labor was weakening. Farsighted Republican politicians could envision the growing strength of capital if this trend were to continue, and they feared that if they ignored the trend, holders of capital would begin to defect from the Republican Party, taking with them their growing pool of politically influential resources.

Some of those engaged in capital-intensive industries and farms in the Midwest and East did indeed defect from the Republican Party and gradually shifted to the Democratic Party—the more free trade party. The election of 1912 reflects this trend and illustrates the Republican coalition split. In that year, President William Howard Taft, a Republican, ran as the incumbent. However, Theodore Roosevelt, a Republican who had served two terms as president and had stepped down in 1908 to support Taft, his handpicked successor, had since become dissatisfied with Taft and now challenged him for the Republican nomination. When Taft prevailed in this intraparty contest, Roosevelt decided to run as the candidate of a third party, the Bull Moose Party—and he took the progressive/populist wing of the Republican Party with him. With the Republican Party split, Woodrow Wilson and the more progressive/populist Democrats won the White House.

As a first cut, the factor endowment framework does fairly well in providing a connection between international economic activity and U.S. domestic political alignments and policies.

But the transformation in American economics and politics raises some additional dilemmas for which the factor endowment framework does not provide a ready explanation, such as the division of a specific factor of production into opposing interests. As some capital began to favor more open trading relations, some holders of capital resisted this change. Moreover, labor began to split, with some factions favoring more open trading relations and others favoring more restrictive trade arrangements. One plausible explanation for the divisions within capital is that the late 1800s was a transitional period; it took time for the holders of capital to recognize their new situation and to realign politically. Perhaps so, but how do we account for the divisions in labor? In terms of the factor endowment framework, there was no change in the scarcity of labor—labor was not going through a transition from being a scarce to an abundant factor of production.

We can adapt the factor endowment framework to address this problem and answer how a specific factor might divide into opposing interests, but this adaptation will also open the door to several alternative explanations. Remember, labor and land are naturally occurring assets, but capital is a human construction. Capital transforms other factors of production through investment, as we see in the application of capital to education, development of skills, shifts in social organization, improvements in plant and tools, and advances in technology and industrial organization. Capital invested in agriculture science makes land more productive than in its native state, and capital invested in labor makes labor more productive than in its native state. This transformative potential suggests that considering all land as alike or all labor as alike is problematic, and, indeed, we do observe differences in the capital intensity of some labor versus other labor forms of production, and in the capital intensity of some types of land-based production versus others. Perhaps in the U.S. example from the later 1800s onward, capital-intensive labor—the combination of a scarce and an abundant factor of production in an economic activity—would prefer policies different from those favored by less capital-intensive forms of labor.

If so, treating land, labor, and capital as monolithic factors of endowment can mislead us in our efforts to connect international economic activities with domestic political strategies. The factor endowment approach may be useful—as the analysis of the 1800s in the United States demonstrates—but it also has weaknesses. It initially fails to explain why labor in highly productive and capital-intensive industries (such as the manufacture of electrical equipment, cars, and communication technologies) began to advocate reduction in trade barriers while labor in less capital-intensive businesses resisted such change. We can adapt the framework to account for the transformation of a scarce factor of production by abundant capital, but other explanations may also offer analytical leverage here.

A Critique of the Factor Endowment Framework

As noted earlier, the factor endowment framework does fairly well as a first cut to connect international economic activity with political activity within nations and between nations.

But several significant problems can handicap the factor endowment framework and prompt us to pursue other explanatory tools. Let's consider three specific categories of problems:

1. The assumption that gains and losses from trade translate directly and proportionately into gains and losses in political influence

2. The failure to consider the possible impacts of different governmental organizational arrangements on the exertion of influence by societal factors such as land, labor, and capital

3. The determination of whether factors of production form the appropriate level of interest aggregation for analysis

The foundations of the first two problems are explored extensively in the discussion of interest groups earlier in this chapter, in the chapter 5 discussion of collective action, and in the chapter 8 discussion of institutions. Here we will focus primarily on the third category, offering in the remainder of the chapter two refinements that shift the focus from factors of production to other categories of interest aggregation.

Briefly, the first category of problems suggests that the factor endowment framework neglects the barriers, incentives, and disincentives to organizing for political action. The framework, as presented in this chapter, simply assumes that gains and losses will translate directly and proportionately into changes in political influence. But what if people elect not to use their gains for political activities? Political activity is a possible consumption choice, but those gaining additional disposable resources from the expansion of trade may decide instead to spend their gains on new cars, hot tubs, cases of wine, houses, their children's education, health care, or new clothes rather than on political influence. In other words, life is filled with complex choices that may limit ability and will to participate in political life. Gains from trade expansion do not necessarily translate dollar for dollar into expanded political influence. Those gaining from trade must make a conscious choice to spend such gains on political activity. Additionally, those losing from changes in trade exposure may decide to expend a disproportionate amount of their resources to protect the old status quo, wherein they profited. This unpredictability of consumption choices suggests that a dollar gained is not necessarily equivalent to a dollar lost in terms of the motivational effect of changing trade patterns on political activity. We cannot straightforwardly assume that the gains from trade will be directed toward political activity to protect globalization and international exchange. If we could, then we should expect a monolithic trend toward greater openness once abundant factors began to benefit and scarce factors lost from increased international exchange, but history is full of examples that demonstrate this does not always hold.

Even if those losing or gaining from trade decide to contribute their resources to political activities, substantial barriers to successful political organization remain. In politics, there is strength in numbers and in resources that can be brought to bear on a policy problem. This potential strength requires the coordination of numerous individuals, often unknown to each other, in a collective activity. Even assuming that factors of production are the appropriate level of aggregation, problems still hinder labor, capital, and land in functioning as blocs in the political arena. Deciding on appropriate policies in response to exposure to trade, communicating responsibilities and activities, sharing costs, and forming coalitions demand a tremendous amount of collective action among dispersed individuals. And, as was thoroughly explored in chapter 5, there are problematic barriers to such collective action.

The second category of problems, the failure to consider the influence of different governmental organizational arrangements on the exertion of influence by societal factors, reveals another potential weakness in the factor endowment framework as presented in this chapter. Since it essentially treats all governmental arrangements alike by neglecting the causal effect of different governmental forms—that is, governmental arrangements as an independent variable—the factor endowment framework is implicitly assumed to work identically in authoritarian states and democratic states, the same in winner-take-all electoral systems as in proportional electoral systems, the same in decentralized federal systems as in more centralized systems, and the same in a system with many checks and balances as in a system with few checks and balances.

If we simply assume that government style, structure, and operation make no difference in outcomes, we are implying that all governments are essentially alike and unimportant for understanding why some societal interests obtain better representation than others. For a political scientist, this proposition would be equivalent to saying that government has no independent causal influence on the observed outcome, nor does it interact at all with the hypothesized dominant mechanism, which here is factor endowment plus changing exposure to trade. Yet political science generates a tremendous amount of research investigating and demonstrating the independent influence of governmental structure and operation on outcome. So, although this problem is not fatal to the factor endowment framework, it does mean that the factor endowment framework—or any other framework for understanding political behavior and outcomes—should be considered within the context of different governmental arrangements. We consider these "institutional arrangements" and their differing effects more extensively in chapter 8.

The third category of problems concerns the determination of what level of interest aggregation awards the greatest and most efficient leverage for investigating the causal connections between changing exposure to international exchange and political competition within nations. At the end of the preceding section, we raised the prospect that another level of interest aggregation might prove more useful, as empirical dilemmas arise from the treatment of factors of production as monolithic. At that point, we circumvented this problem by suggesting that a monolithic factor of production such as land or labor might be divided into subcategories by level of capital intensity. But a variety of other alternatives—different types of aggregation devices—are available to connect expansion and contraction of international economic activity systematically with domestic political cleavages, coalitions, and policy competition. Here we briefly consider two promising but different refinements on the factor endowment framework. These alternative interest aggregation devices bypass factors of production and instead divide economies by focusing on two different aspects: industrial sector and mobility of the productive asset. The causal chain and logic remain similar to those of the factor endowment framework, but we substitute industrial sector for factors in one refinement and the mobility of the production asset for factors in the other refinement.

Industrial Sector as an Alternative Means of Interest Aggregation

Recognizing that factors of production are not monolithic is the same as asserting that some labor may have preferences that differ from those of other labor in society, that some capital may have preferences that differ from those of other capital in society, and that not all land resources in a society view the world through the same lens. Labor may disagree with labor over policy, land may disagree with land, and capital may disagree with capital. Identifying likely cleavages within a factor of production is thus problematic for a framework based on divisions between factors of production. We have suggested that we can circumvent this problem by determining whether a monolithic factor is fragmented by differences in the application of capital and then distinguishing between the preferences of more and less capital-intensive land, and more and less capital-intensive labor.

Alternatively, fragmenting an economy into some divisions other than factors of production makes sense if, with expanding or contracting trade, some labor gains and some labor loses, some land gains and some land loses, and some capital gains and some capital loses. The basic structure and causal mechanism of the factor endowment framework works remarkably well. Perhaps we can improve upon this framework, however, with modifications that shift the level of aggregation of the affected domestic groups. One alternative unit of aggregation is industrial sector. Replacing factors of production with industries as the unit of analysis recognizes that two different factors of production engaged in the same industry may share more common interests than a single factor of production that is spread across a wide variety of economic endeavors. This modification hypothesizes that labor and capital in a specific industry share more common interests than the labor in that sector shares with labor in other industrial sectors. For example, capital and labor in the U.S. automotive industry have more in common than does labor across the automotive and semiconductor industries. This hypothesis builds on a simple recognition that people within an industry share a common interest in their industry's future success, as their livelihoods stem from the same industry.

The basic argument from the factor endowment framework remains the same despite the substitution of industrial sector. Expansion of trade benefits those in industrial sectors that enjoy comparative advantage in relation to their global competitors, and it damages industrial sectors that are relatively less competitive in the larger global market. The reverse pattern holds true for the contraction of trade. But changing the focus of analysis to industrial sector makes it more difficult to describe policy conflict in a state as class or urban-rural cleavages. The foundations of political coalitions will originate instead across industrial sectors, which is a more decentralized basis for political division and coalition than factor of production for two reasons: (1) there are more industrial sectors than factors, and (2) factors span an entire economy, but any industrial sector is usually a compartment of an economy.

Switching from factor of production to industrial sector as the basic unit of aggregation places greater informational demands on investigators, but it may provide significantly more analytical leverage than the more elegant factor endowment framework. This trade-off between elegance and complexity is worthwhile if we gain important explanatory power over what appears to be incongruent behavior within the factor endowment or modified factor endowment framework. Making this switch does not mean that we should discard the factor endowment framework, but that we should work to recognize and define its limitations—under what conditions it will prove useful and under what circumstances problematic. By better specifying the conditions that are conducive or problematic to the factor endowment framework, we have gained at least one alternative in the industrial sector refinement. We can identify more than one refinement if we recognize the level of aggregation as a variable that we can manipulate and then feel free to choose another unit of analysis—plausibly spanning the range from factor to the individual—when appropriate. Let's move on to consider one other such unit of analysis, the individual as an asset of production.

Asset Characteristics as an Alternative Means of Interest Aggregation

It comes as no surprise that individuals participate in politics. So perhaps we should consider individual characteristics as a means for understanding political cleavage in society. The previous sections have clumped individuals into groups—as members of a factor of production or an industrial sector. The factor endowment framework divided individuals into three categories based on their common characteristic as a production factor, and then used this characteristic to anticipate their political activities. The industrial sector refinement clumped individuals into a particular industrial sector, hypothesizing that all individuals within that sector share a common motivating interest, and then used this characteristic to anticipate their political activities.

Individuals remain individuals, however, despite their group affiliations. Individuals within a particular grouping, be it a production factor or industrial sector, may behave differently in politics than do other individuals of that same grouping. Within a given factor, some individuals may be less motivated than others to act in their factor's interests. Within an industrial sector, some individuals may be less motivated than others to act in that sector's interests. Other individuals may act as if their interests are more tightly bound, more congruent, with their sector's or factor's interests.

Yet other individual-level characteristics may motivate people to resist or promote trade openness, or to behave differently in politics than do other members of their group as defined in the previous two models. What other individual characteristics might help to account for this variation? Do individuals vary in some key manner that motivates them to engage more or less in political activity, or makes them more or less likely to form coalitions with other people in similar circumstances?

Let's start by considering individuals and their capabilities as assets of production. Some individuals bring labor to their productive activities, others bring capital, and others supply land resources. This division fits with the factor endowment framework, but in the critique of that framework we recognized the potential for these assets to differ from individual to individual even if they are members of the same factor. Moreover, an individual may actually be a product of the interaction of several factors, especially in more economically advanced societies, where capital has interacted with other factors of production and transformed those factors. Training and education turn labor into a capital-intensive labor. The application of technology such as chemical fertilizers and biotechnology turns previously uncompetitive land into a fertile agricultural asset that can now compete well in the global marketplace. If individuals are actually an amalgam of factors of production, can a particular characteristic be identified that cuts across such interactions to provide insight into the question of who will be motivated to expend resources on political action?

Mobility of the asset of production is one such characteristic. *Mobility* means that the individual has the capacity to stop what she is doing and start doing something else in terms of economic production. Some labor is more mobile than other labor, can more easily switch jobs or careers than other labor. Some capital is more mobile than other capital; this quality is described as *liquidity*. For example, capital assets such as a house or a factory are more difficult to sell for reinvestment in other activities than is a portfolio of stocks on the New York Stock Exchange. Some land resources are more mobile than other land resources: a farmer may be able to change crops and use her land to produce another agricultural commodity, but a coal miner may not be able to find another use for her coal mine.

All transitions involve some dislocations to the individual. An economic shock such as changing exposure to international trade that forces an individual to seek other employment and opportunities clearly creates dislocation. But some individuals may be better prepared than others to manage that shock—their skills may make them more capable of finding other jobs. These people, who are more mobile because of their training and skill sets, will be less concerned about the shock than are individuals who are less mobile, and consequently more mobile individuals are less committed to resisting the changes that cause dislocation. This logic anticipates that those individuals with the greatest mobility are more likely to move on and participate in an alternative economic activity and less likely to engage in collaborative political activities to defend the status quo. They are less likely to define political cleavages or build political coalitions.

Here, asset mobility becomes an important independent variable as we try to understand the international contribution to national political cleavage, coalition, and competition. An asset's mobility or lack of mobility—the ability to exit and find other opportunities—intermediates the causal relationship between shifts in international economic activity and political outcomes. In this framework, the more restrictive the alternatives become for an asset, the less mobile the asset and the greater the incentives for that asset to work to protect its current economic activity. Consequently, this perception anticipates that less mobile assets are generally more motivated to engage in political action than are more mobile assets.

CONCLUSION

This chapter provides us with a framework, and several alternative approaches consistent with the basic logic of that framework, for anticipating where the lines of political cleavage and competition will be drawn in a society, and for understanding that some coalitions are more likely than others. As noted earlier, several problems burden the factor endowment framework, but the refinements developed here face similar handicaps. Most important, none of these frameworks provides a mechanism for overcoming the barriers to collective action. All these frameworks implicitly assume that if a factor, industrial sector, or asset has disposable resources, it will engage in political activity. But the empirical world is rife with examples of interests not coalescing into coalitions for political activity.

These frameworks are elegant and powerful, but their predictive utility is only part of the puzzle. The cleavage lines and likely coalitions identified by these frameworks are latent cleavages and coalitions, which need to organize and overcome barriers to collective action in order to exercise political influence. In chapter 5, we dealt explicitly with this problem of collective action. Now, by combining the lessons from that chapter with the frameworks concerning political cleavage that we have described in this chapter, we can develop a substantial understanding of political competition in national arenas over international and domestic policy issues. In chapter 8, we will add to our understanding of how domestic political arenas can influence political competition and outcomes by examining how different political institutional arrangements can affect the ability of interests to form coalitions and exercise their political voice.

KEY CONCEPTS

capital (p. 260)	Heckscher-Ohlin model (p. 259)	interest groups (p. 255)
factor endowment (p. 259)	import substitution (p. 266)	labor (p. 260)

EXERCISES

1. Consider India today. If you are not familiar with its resources, do a little research to determine its factor endowment. What factors of production are abundant in India, and which are scarce? What are the political coalitions that the factor endowment predicts? What is the nature of political conflict and competition anticipated by this framework?

2. China is undergoing rapid economic change. Twenty years ago it was clearly a developing political economy, today its economy is in transition, and twenty years from now it may well be a developed political economy. What was China's factor endowment twenty years ago? Today? If China succeeds in becoming a developed political economy in the next twenty

years, what will its factor endowment likely be then? What might such changes mean for political coalitions and the nature of political conflict in China over this span? Use this framework to hypothesize about the nature of Chinese trade policy in twenty years and the nature of Chinese educational policy.

3. Discuss briefly the problems with the factor endowment framework. Do these problems mean we should discount the whole framework?

4. Explain why we might prefer to use the automotive industry rather than factors of production as a level of aggregation to study political divisions and competition.

5. An alternative to focusing on factors of production to understand political competition in domestic political arenas is to consider the mobility of the asset of production. Explain asset mobility in the context of individuals. Hypothesize how asset mobility affects an individual's motivation to engage in political action.

6. Different factor endowments across nations can condition economic activity, affect level and type of economic development, and systematically shape political debate and conflict over public policies. If a nation is abundant in land and capital but scarce in labor, what type of economy does the nation have and what is likely to be the nature of political conflict and cleavage in that society? What type of trade policy should each factor of production in this economy prefer? In this scenario and with expanding trade, what factors gain and what factors lose in relative capabilities?

7. If a nation is abundant in land but scarce in labor and capital, what type of economy does the nation have and what is likely to be the nature of political conflict and cleavage in that society? What type of trade policy should each factor of production in this economy prefer? In this scenario and with contracting trade, what factors gain and what factors lose in terms of relative capabilities?

FURTHER READING

Frieden, Jeffrey A. 1991. "Invested Interests: The Politics of National Economic Policies in a World of Global Finance." *International Organization* 45, no. 4: 425–451.

Gourevitch, Peter. 1986. *Politics in Hard Times: Comparative Responses to International Economic Crises.* Ithaca, NY: Cornell University Press.

Hiscox, Michael. 2002. *International Trade and Political Conflict: Commerce, Coalitions, and Mobility.* Princeton, NJ: Princeton University Press.

Milner, Helen. 1988. *Resisting Protectionism: Global Industries and the Politics of International Trade.* Princeton, NJ: Princeton University Press.

Rogowski, Ronald. 1989. *Commerce and Coalition: How Trade Affects Domestic Political Alignments.* Princeton, NJ: Princeton University Press.

The Role of Institutions in Political and Economic Market Failure

What is the market? It is the law of the jungle, the law of nature. And what is civilization? It is the struggle against nature.

—*Edouard Balladur, Financial Times, December 31, 1993*

In this chapter we consider how institutions, what a Nobel Prize–winning economist defined as the rules of the game, can either help constrain or exacerbate political and economic market failures. Institutions structure the behavior of individuals in a community. They do so by shaping incentives, encouraging individuals to select some actions and not others. They essentially affect individual cost-benefit calculations across different courses of action. When successful, such rules of the game alter the structure of social interactions and consequently affect the costs and benefits of different choices to promote cooperative and productive social outcomes.

CONSTRAINING SOCIAL TRAPS AND MARKET FAILURE

In theory, Adam Smith's invisible hand in decentralized market exchange produces a nice social outcome wherein self-interested, rational, individual choices aggregate to produce an optimal social result in terms of the efficient use of resources. In this ideal world, we ask individuals to act only in their self-interest to produce a constructive social outcome. We also apply similar logic to individual choices in political environments such as democracies, anticipating good policy outcomes that efficiently and accurately reflect the aggregated

> An **institution** is any mechanism that guides the behavior of individuals within a given community. Institutions can be customs, norms, established patterns of behavior, and informal or formal rules. They are the rules of the game that structure our choices and actions.

preferences of members of society. But the bulk of this book demonstrates that, time and again, our real world falls far short of such an ideal—the invisible hand mechanism fails, democratic institutions falter, and we do not reach Eden. All too frequently, the rational actions of individuals aggregate to produce suboptimal social outcomes instead. Sometimes these outcomes represent only inefficient use of societal resources without serious social trauma, but at other times they generate tremendous social, economic, and political disruption. Left unrestrained or unguided, individual choices are far more problematic than classical economic theory or democratic theory describes. **Institutions** offer mechanisms to constrain individual behavior that could lead to socially unproductive outcomes, to create a scaffolding by which individuals can be encouraged to make choices that map onto better social outcomes and social orders.

The dilemma lies not in our assumption of human rationality but in the context of human interaction, which plays a major role in aggregating individual rational choices. Sometimes the aggregation process produces good and relatively efficient collective outcomes, as in the case of Adam Smith's theoretical invisible hand, but at other times the structure of human interactions and the mechanism that aggregates human choices lead to suboptimal collective outcomes. Worse, those outcomes often constitute strong and stable equilibrium. They are no fluke, but are slated to recur again and again. Rational individuals seem trapped by the structure of a situation that leads them to make choices that appear to be individually rational but result in perverse social consequences. Worse yet, in many of these situations an individual cannot unilaterally improve her situation independent of others' choices, even if she recognizes the problem. Obtaining a better individual and collective outcome requires coordination and cooperation by many decision makers, and often the situation works against such cooperation.

A variety of factors contribute to these situations, which we called social traps or market failures earlier in this book. The structure of human interaction may contribute to a social trap or market failure even if all those involved completely understand others' beliefs and preferences, their assessments of utility, and the structure of choice and interaction. Ironically, because of the strategic interaction of choices, in many of these cases individuals and policy makers can do better for themselves and their societies by opting for what appear to be suboptimal individual choices. In these situations, individuals often make choices that they know will lead to suboptimal outcomes because they are unable to secure a binding agreement among all the concerned parties to cooperate in order to obtain a better outcome. Each individual's fear that another may defect from such an agreement to cooperate leads her to defect. This is the starkest and most disturbing case of a social trap or failure in the social aggregation mechanism, as all participants are fully informed and aware of how to obtain a better outcome, yet they fail because the necessary cooperation and coordination are missing, as are the means to promote such cooperation and coordination. The suboptimal outcome then becomes a stable equilibrium, as confirmed expectations about the behavior of others lead to the same choices again and again. Good institutions can intervene in this process and constrain the structure of choice to enable individuals to cooperate, enter into agreements that are unlikely to be broken, and produce better social and individual outcomes.

More often, other factors intervene to create a social trap or market failure. Incomplete and asymmetric information about the structure of a social situation and about the processes by which choices aggregate, misperception of others' beliefs and preferences, and uncertainty over utility can confound rational choice. Here, expectations about the likely choices of others are unstable—we are unsure what to think, or we have a false consciousness about what to think, which leads to potentially poor decisions even though the process is systematic and rational. The very presence of incomplete and asymmetric information opens the door to the possibility of an individual strategically manipulating the information environment to influence others' choices in an attempt to advance her own interests at the expense of others' and of society as a whole. We cannot ask rational individuals to refrain from attempting such manipulation if they believe that others will not be so constrained.

Differences in capabilities and in the willingness to use those capabilities can transform a decentralized process into a hierarchical process in which those at the top of the hierarchy benefit at the expense of the larger society and of those beneath them in the hierarchy. If individuals attain disproportionate access to resources and capabilities that allow them to manipulate the distribution of goods in society, should we expect them to act in the best interests of society if it means that they will receive less? In the case of politicians and policy makers, should we expect them to act in the best long-term interests of society if doing so increases the prospects of their political demise? Ideally, we would want our leaders to select policies that are productive for society, but realistically, given our assumption of political survival, they will often make choices that improve their odds for political survival even if those choices are damaging to the broader social welfare. Differences in capabilities, in power, if unrestrained by law or some other institutional arrangements, can be a recipe for suboptimal social outcomes.

Societies face a number of dilemmas: how to constrain uncertainty and promote productive stable expectations versus destructive stable expectations; how to limit the manipulation of information for individual gain at the expense of others and of the broader society; how to constrain individual temptations to defect from cooperative contractual obligations; and how to transform the context of human interaction and the mechanisms that aggregate individual choices in order to produce good versus bad social and individual outcomes. Resolving such dilemmas is not easy; if it were, we would see a world full of economically productive and politically healthy states. Yet these dilemmas are also not insurmountable, as we have numerous examples of well-functioning societies in which year after year individuals find ways to cooperate and advance societal welfare. In the past several chapters, we have looked at a variety of mechanisms that can exacerbate or constrain social traps and market failures. In this chapter, we focus on the role of institutions and how they affect individual choices within social contexts—choices that aggregate to produce social outcomes. We will examine how various institutions can help to constrain economic and political market failures and social traps by limiting uncertainty and instability, promoting stable expectations, structuring the incentives of individual decision makers, overcoming barriers to cooperation and coordination, and containing the time-inconsistency problem, which ideally produces more socially efficient equilibrium. In an arena absent a formal rule of law and central adjudication and enforcement mechanisms (e.g., the international political economy), institutions that amount to informal rules of the game, customs, and practices can help overcome the traps that lead to dysfunctional outcomes.

INSTITUTIONS AS RULES OF THE GAME: INFLUENCING ACTIONS AND OUTCOMES

First, what are institutions, and what do they do? Douglass North, winner of the Nobel Prize in Economics for his work on institutions and institutional change, defines institutions as "the rules of the game in society, or more formally, the humanly devised constraints that shape human interaction." By this definition, institutions are not organizations; rather, they are rules, laws, customs, common practices, norms, and conventions. Often we resort to factors such as greed, nature, self-preservation, genetic fitness and fecundity, compassion, and the quest for power to explain human behavior. These are motivational primitives. In a state of nature, without any rules of interaction save survival of the fittest, such primitives are given primacy in explaining behavior. But institutions stand distinct from such factors as we try to account for why people do what they do, helping to distance our actions and choices from the primal state of nature. Socially constructed institutions attempt to intermediate between such primitive motivations and human actions.

If effective, institutions transform human activity and lead toward social outcomes different from those we would anticipate if only the laws of the jungle or nature applied. They do so by influencing the choices that individuals make in social settings and how those choices aggregate to produce social outcomes. Socially effective institutions transform a decision maker's information environment, reduce uncertainty in that environment, create stable expectations, extend time horizons, and, consequently, structure incentives for the decision maker to make collectively productive choices rather than others. Yet not all institutions are inherently good in how they affect human choices and social outcomes. Ineffective or socially dysfunctional institutions can feed uncertainty, contribute to unstable expectations, decrease the shadow of the future, and motivate individuals to engage in socially destructive activity.

As such, institutions impose important independent causal influence on social interaction. We can insert them as independent, or explanatory, variables in our models of human behavior. Variations in institutional frameworks, differences in rules of the game from one society to another, can help us to understand and anticipate differences in human activity from one social setting to another. Why do some societies experience economic growth and improvements in social welfare, while other societies prove dysfunctional, as their members repeatedly cheat, steal, and kill? Why can some nations engage in peaceful democratic transitions from one government to another, whereas others fall into the trap of coups, civil wars, and rebellions?

In chapters 1 and 4, we used several different games to demonstrate that there is no reason to believe that human physiology, psychology, or biology explains the differences between successful and failed states, productive and dysfunctional economies, or healthy and diseased societies. An educated individual (well trained, thoughtful, and analytical) may cooperate with others and act productively in one society, but if we place her in another society, she may lie, cheat, steal, or worse—the same individual, but different institutional settings and rules of the game. This means that any attempt to explain social activity with reference only to characteristics of the individual will fall short. Individual characteristics may be important and necessary to any account of social activity, but they are not sufficient once we move beyond the raw state of nature. Institutional settings become important variables as we try to fathom, anticipate, and change social activity. For example, a monetary policy maker in a broad-based democratic political economy faces a different constituency and set of pressures from those faced by a monetary policy maker in a right-of-center authoritarian state whose constituency is a much narrower slice of society. The different institutional settings of broad democratic representation versus narrow special interest may help explain why the more democratic state's monetary policy makers are concerned more with growth than with price stability, and why monetary policy makers in the less representative right-of-center state favor price stability ahead of growth. Such differences can also account for difficulties in obtaining cooperation across the monetary authorities of those states.

Difference between Formal and Informal Institutions

Consonant with his idea that institutions are the rules of the game, Douglass North notes that "political rules broadly define the hierarchical structure of the polity, its basic decision structure, and the explicit characteristics of agenda control. Economic rules define property rights, that is, the bundle of rights over the use and the income to be derived from property and the ability to alienate an asset or a resource. Contracts contain the provisions specific to a particular agreement in exchange."[1] But must institutions be codified in formal legal systems, as bodies of law and jurisprudence? Can institutions exist outside formal laws and

---

[1]Douglass C. North, *Institutions, Institutional Change, and Economic Performance* (Cambridge: Cambridge University Press, 1990), 47.

regulations? If so, how do such institutions differ from those we find embodied in formal legal statutes? For our field of study this is a particularly relevant question given the structure of international affairs and its absence of a central overarching authority. We can distinguish between formal and informal institutions. More than formal codification of the rules of the game, a presence of a third-party adjudication and enforcement mechanism separates formal from informal institutional arrangements.

Formal institutional arrangements involve third-party enforcement mechanisms with the authority and power to adjudicate disputes. Parties to an exchange or human interaction can appeal to this third party to referee, adjudicate, and enforce a resolution to a dispute. Moreover, individuals, whether they win or lose in the adjudication process, recognize the authority of the third party to intervene and mediate disputes. Such mediation is not random; it is guided by bodies of rules that get established and codified over time—a legal system. Such legal systems and rules guide expectations about the likely resolution of disputes and, consequently, can help preempt and deter disagreements or activity contrary to the rules of the game.

Constitutions, statutes, regulations, common laws, bylaws, contracts, and other rules and agreements create a hierarchy of formal rules of the game to guide political, economic, and social activity. Constitutions and laws amount to contracts between government and the governed. The government is also the third-party enforcement mechanism. Idealistically, we like to think that a good government stands outside disputes, does not have a stake in the resolution of a dispute one way or another but only in its resolution, and can fairly adjudicate disputes as an independent dispassionate party. This is the image represented by depictions of Lady Justice, holding the balance scales and blindfolded so as not to be swayed unfairly. But no government is independent of its society. Dispute resolution creates winners and losers and affects distributional outcomes in society. As a consequence, the design and construction of formal institutions and laws are targets of organized interests, who may use their capabilities to attempt to embed their preferences in the design of institutions and laws.

Informal institutions complement formal institutions, but, unlike formal institutions, they lack a third-party enforcement mechanism; they are self-enforcing. Parties to an economic, political, or social interaction adhere to the informal rules of the game because they want to play by such rules or because they fear that other parties to the interaction may impose sanctions or penalties if they do not follow the rules, but not because there is a threat of a centralized enforcer such as a government. Given our anarchical and self-help depiction of the modern nation-state system, the celebration of the concept of sovereignty, most institutions relevant to international political economy are by definition informal institutions. This is true regardless of whether they are enshrined as rules of the game within an international governmental organization such as the World Bank, the World Trade Organization, or the International Monetary Fund, or whether they are informal practices, customs, or norms that guide behavior across national boundaries. Similar to the realists' depiction of the nation-state system (discussed in chapter 2), informal institutions rely on self-help and on the parties to the exchange using their capabilities to enforce the rules and impose costs on those who renege on their obligations under the rules. Parties engaged in social interaction must resort to their own devices to ensure that others cooperate, follow the rules, and meet their obligations. Moreover, if informal institutions are to have traction and causal influence, they must be more than simply differences in capabilities or power. If we can explain why parties adhere to the informal rules of the game solely by focusing on differences in power, we do not need institutions to explain social outcomes, only assessments of power.

Norms, customs, conventions, common practices, and rules of the road communicate information and develop expectations about what is acceptable or anticipated behavior. Recognizing such patterns can reduce the costs of some choices and increase the costs of others. This set of informal rules affects the incentives and calculations of rational decision makers independent of differences in capabilities. For example, policy makers of relatively powerful governments often refrain from the sheer exercise of power over other governments to get their way in world affairs. These policy makers may have the capacity to force their will on others, but they do not do so because such intimidation would be outside the informal rules of the game, beyond the lines of acceptable behavior or convention in world affairs. They may resort to other tools of statecraft, even if it means they will be less successful, because an excessive use of power would be viewed as an inappropriate violation of acceptable practices and would induce significant costs. Certainly, U.S. policy makers had the capability to prevail during the Vietnam War if they had exerted the full military capacity of the United States to destroy the country. But such an exercise of power would have been disproportionate given the threat, and consequently it would have violated international norms of acceptable behavior in warfare, which potentially would have put U.S. decision makers at risk as possible war criminals in the court of global public opinion and imposed significant future costs on the United States. Remember our discussion in chapter 2 about matching the strategy of statecraft to the need in terms of costs and benefits. Informal conventions in the global arena work against such an excessive use of force by a superpower against a far weaker nation. In other words, winning is everything if we consider only power capabilities, but winning is not everything if informal institutions impose standards that are independent of power. Then, how one wins, loses, or socially interacts may well matter as much as, if not more than, simply prevailing in a contest of power.

Institutions as Social Bargains and *Ex Ante* Agreements

Institutions constitute *ex ante* agreements, which are contracts about current and future cooperation and interaction. Imagine a world full of social traps and strategic actors, but without institutions. Each day, decision makers would have to delve for information to reduce uncertainty, try to understand the preferences and capabilities of others, analyze different scenarios (potentially an unlimited number of scenarios), and then try to make a rational choice for every single decision they confront. Without some shortcuts or devices to organize the mass of information and reduce uncertainty, many—if not most—individuals

A street vendor markets pirated DVDs. Stores such as this one in Shanghai that sell pirated, black-market goods are common worldwide. They evade the constraints of formal property rights institutions and rely on informal practices and institutions to remain open in a society.

would be paralyzed. Absent a clear dominant strategy, the simplest choices would exhaust our resources.

Ever since early humans crossed paths with one another in the grasslands during their wanderings, migratory travels, and hunting and gathering, we have created devices to simplify our decision processes and save our energies for the more complicated and difficult choices. Without such tools, we would spend too much time on each individual choice and might never get to the important choices associated with complex situations. Moreover, without means for resolving the cooperation and coordination difficulties that occur frequently in social interactions, we would be more likely to select poor strategies and produce outcomes that were desired by none of the parties engaged in the interactions.

Therefore, sometimes intentionally and sometimes unintentionally, we have developed rules of the road, not only for the management of current problems but also to contain similar problems in the future. We develop such rules, or institutions, to help in constraining social traps and problems that we are likely to encounter again. The very existence of cooperation to manage one social trap can help to build foundations for cooperation to manage other social traps, as people develop familiarity, trust, and expectations about those with whom they interact frequently. Before the problematic situation recurs, an informal, perhaps implicit, social bargain emerges among the parties to a prospective social interaction about how to handle such situations. This advance bargain is an *ex ante* contract or agreement, which serves to reduce uncertainty, limit the need for information gathering and evaluation, and make the decision process far more manageable.

Formal institutions embed *ex ante* agreements in legal systems, whereby the parties to a social interaction understand the expected course of action and, if one party should wander off the expected path, know how to appeal and adjudicate the outcome. Aside from the added layer of third-party adjudication and enforcement mechanisms, a formal institution thus has the same *ex ante* implication as an informal institution. Given the anarchical nature of the modern Westphalian nation-state system, the absence of formal institutions in the international arena may differentiate social, political, and economic interactions within states from such interactions across state boundaries. If so, our focus on institutions in international affairs should be on how formal and informal institutions in the domestic arena constrain and motivate activity across borders and how informal institutions in the international arena influence that activity.

Institutions as Equilibria

Thinking about institutions as the structuring of incentives and *ex ante* agreements reduces uncertainty, but only if those involved in a problematic social exchange recognize the problem and the relevant institution for dealing with it. Rather than wondering about an extensive range of alternatives and analyzing different possible outcomes and their likelihood, individuals can converge on an *ex ante* agreement—if an appropriate one exists—to manage a particular type of situation. This predetermined set of expectations makes the decision process more efficient, as decision makers rely on choices that were structured in the past and embedded in an agreement, formal or informal. Instead of searching among a wide range of choices, individuals converge on a particular choice or limited set of choices. The institution structures and limits the set of potential choices. For example, over time since World War II the international trading regime, a set of informal institutions embedded in the WTO, has favored greater trade liberalization over less. Consequently, when governments enter into negotiations over market access, policy makers implicitly understand that their options are either to lower barriers to entry or to remain at the status quo; raising barriers to exchange is not an accepted option. The rules of the game that constrain international negotiations implicitly favor more over less access.

This mechanism can limit problems of multiple or suboptimal equilibria, and so contribute to cooperation and coordination. We have seen that in many social interactions multiple equilibria exist, and some produce social traps. Some of these equilibria are better than others, but all are stable. In other social traps, a single equilibrium exists, but it is a suboptimal stable equilibrium that is produced by a dominant strategy. In the former situation, institutions can alter the incentives and push individuals to select strategies that lead to a particular equilibrium and not others. In the latter situation, institutions can structure incentives and costs to help decision makers avoid the stable but suboptimal equilibrium by cooperating to produce better collective and individual outcomes that are stable, even if they do not constitute a stable equilibrium by definition. If such institutionally assisted outcomes are stable, we can

> A **structurally induced equilibrium** is a stable situation in which institutions have intervened to alter incentives and push individuals to select strategies that lead to a particular outcome among the range of possible outcomes.

consider them jointly as equilibrium because we do not anticipate movement away from the collective outcome. This situation is called a **structurally induced equilibrium.** Absent the institutional structures, individuals would make different choices, which would lead to different individual and collective outcomes, but the institutional arrangement has intervened to push human activity toward a particular outcome among the range of possible outcomes.

Institutions as Incentives and Path Dependence

Institutions can alter the costs of decisions and the costs of the process of decision making. If they reduce uncertainty in a decision-making environment by limiting the range of possible choices, they lower the costs incurred by decision makers in selecting one of those strategies versus expending resources to evaluate more uncertain alternatives. We say that institutions lower the transaction costs of an exchange, or the cost of transacting the interaction. Since we assume that decision makers are rational and are trying to balance costs and benefits, lowering decision-making costs should create incentives for decision makers to select among the range of alternatives structured by the institutional environment.

> **Path dependence**, or **path contingency**, is a characteristic of decision making in which past choices shape the direction of change and condition future choices.

If institutions influence expected costs and benefits among a range of possible choices, they are creating incentives for decision makers to make one choice over another. By doing so, they shape the direction of change and condition future choices, making those future choices somewhat dependent on previous choices. We call this phenomenon **path dependence** or **path contingency.** It simply means that knowing what people did in the past to address coordination and cooperation traps gives us a pretty good idea about what they will do in the future when they encounter similar situations—their choices of future actions are constrained by past actions. Consequently, limiting uncertainty by changing incentives and prompting one choice over another in a current interaction becomes embedded in institutional frameworks, which then make future choices contingent on past experience and choice.

For example, the GATT framework used rounds of negotiations to lower barriers to trade and expand liberal exchange. Each round incrementally extended and expanded upon agreements and practices constructed in previous rounds. Negotiators did not toss out the old framework and begin anew—instead, they kept what had worked in previous rounds of negotiations, tinkered with what had failed, and attempted to expand the trade agenda into new areas. The agenda for each new round of negotiation thus arose from the previous round. Even the extension of negotiations to new areas built on past lessons and practices institutionalized in the process of negotiation. The precedents and institutional advances of previous rounds of trade negotiations have heavily influenced the path for the current Doha Round of WTO negotiations. If we look closely, we can find commonalities that tie the negotiations of the first GATT agreement to those of the present day.

A Normative Caveat: Are Institutions Inherently Good?

We often think that institutions are normatively good human constructions that lead to better social outcomes. This is often the case, but not always. Institutions reduce uncertainty and make the decision process more efficient for individuals, but that does not necessarily mean that they produce good social outcomes. As they shape expected costs and benefits, institutions can just as easily create incentives to engage in activities that damage society.

For example, an authoritarian regime may construct an institutional framework that creates incentives for people to spy on their neighbors and report what they learn to the authorities. This practice can lead to tremendous distrust among neighbors, an unwillingness to share information for fear that it might be misused, and a breakdown in social goodwill and social capital—all conditions that promote contentious and socially damaging activity rather than cooperation that could advance overall social welfare. Why would a government construct such institutions and create such incentives? Perhaps the members of the governing elite benefit from a divisive society. Seeking to extract wealth and resources from their compatriots for private gain, such a governing elite may support institutions that weaken potential social opposition.

In another example, institutions that assist members of one particular group in overcoming barriers to collective action can lead to a better social outcome if the interests of the group that coalesces in this way overlap with the interests of the broader society. But groups such as cartels and criminal gangs also seek to overcome barriers to collective action, often to further their group and individual interests at the expense of the broader social welfare. A cartel may want to manipulate the price of a commodity, or a criminal gang may want to ensure that its members refrain from divulging information to the authorities in the face of prosecution. Yet, absent some device to promote cooperation, the individual incentives of the cartel members are to defect from the group objective and so reap extra rewards, and the incentive for the criminal is to squeal on her fellow gang members in order to receive a lesser prison sentence. In the case of successful cartels and gangs, the group develops institutions that promote cooperation and limit defection for individual gains. For example, if you cheat on the cartel, the other members will ostracize you; if you testify against the gang, your family will be killed. Such outcomes may be good for the cartel or the gang, but they are poor and destructive outcomes for society.

Institutional Effectiveness and Durability: Lasting Consequences

If an institution is to be effective in reducing uncertainty, stabilizing expectations, and creating individual incentives for preferred choices, it must have the ability to influence behavior and it must be durable. *Durability* refers to the persistence of an institution and its effects over time and over multiple social interactions. A durable institution sticks; it influences behavior again and again. Absent stickiness and persistence, a cooperative effort to overcome a social trap may be little more than an isolated incident and momentary success—not an institution. Such success may say little about expectations of future interactions. So what makes an institution durable? Why should one not simply renege on the rules of the game that constrain a social trap if doing so will promote one's individual well-being and benefit at the expense of others? Many times people do so—this demonstrates the absence or ineffectiveness of institutional arrangements to overcome social traps. But we also observe many examples of people and their governments cooperating, playing by the rules of the game, and limiting the pitfalls of social traps. A variety of pressures promote such institutional effectiveness and durability. Below, we focus on five general types of pressures: cost efficiency, third-party enforcement, reputation, status quo, and the shadow of the future. These types are not independent; rather, they overlap to create mutually reinforcing pressures.

Cost Efficiency

As an *ex ante* agreement about interactions, an institution can produce cost efficiencies for decision makers. In a social interaction, an institution can reduce the time and resources the parties spend on overcoming asymmetric information dilemmas, evaluating alternatives, monitoring the activities of others, and policing contracts. These effects limit the costs of interaction and constrain uncertainty over the appropriate course of action if all the parties in the interaction know and understand the rules of the game; the institution generates efficiencies in the process of the interaction—in the costs of doing business—regardless of whether it produces an optimal social outcome. For example, international investment can be hindered by information asymmetries across national borders. Investors may encounter uncertainty and questions about the investment environment and a host country's willingness to respect the integrity of an investment. Such uncertainty can be difficult and expensive to overcome, but several institutional mechanisms can help assuage the concerns of investors. First, once they become members of international organizations such as the World Bank or IMF, governments routinely supply these organizations with macroeconomic reports about their economies. Moreover, these organizations monitor and assess national economies and their problems and issue reports that provide additional data. These reports aid in transparency and lower the costs to private investors who are trying to learn about an investment environment and the risks they might encounter. Another institution is the provision of investment insurance, whether by the home government of the investor or by the Multilateral Investment Guarantee Agency (MIGA), a World Bank program. MIGA promotes foreign direct investment by providing risk insurance to investors and lenders against losses caused by noncommercial risks. Essentially, such insurance protects against information asymmetries and lowers the barriers to investment—reducing the time and resources investors must spend on overcoming asymmetric information dilemmas and monitoring the activities of others.

Institutions that create such efficiencies can be appealing in a world of uncertainty and limited resources, for they allow decision makers to conserve their time and resources for spending elsewhere. Routines, customs, and patterns of behavior enable people to interact in specific circumstances without expending too much energy evaluating and strategizing. As suggested, this mechanism may not produce optimal social outcomes, but it can lead to results that are good enough that people choose to adhere to the institutions in order to save

their scarce resources for more difficult or important interactions. This process of finding an outcome above a set threshold to be acceptable is called
satisficing (the term *satisfice* comes from the blend-
ing of the words *satisfy* and *suffice*).

> The process of **satisficing** is one in which,
> rather than seeking an optimal outcome, indi-
> viduals find any outcome above a set threshold
> to be acceptable. This practice can create an
> efficiency in the use of resources involved in a
> decision process.

Third-Party Enforcement

Formal institutions—those with third-party enforcement mechanisms—are the easiest
institutions to observe in society. Public and private governments act as third-party enforcement mechanisms for established rules that are intended to govern the relationships of
members of their groups. A fraternity's bylaws assign to the fraternity's governing body
responsibility for adjudicating categories of disputes between fraternity members. By their
rules, formation, and organization, the governing authorities of churches, synagogues,
mosques, and other religion-based groups act as third parties to mediate disputes among
their members. Public governments (states) are buttressed by extensive bodies of law that
confer on those in official positions the responsibility for mediating conflicts between the
state and its members, as well as between members of the state.

The authority of such governing bodies comes from a variety of possible sources, and
these sources influence the effectiveness of the formal institutions they are supposed to support. The capabilities and the willingness of the third party to use those capabilities can
determine the efficacy of a formal institution by influencing the costs of noncompliance.
Third parties often enjoy disproportionate capabilities on one or more dimensions. They
may be able to exercise coercion, which allows them to physically threaten, sanction, or compel compliance from those who renege on the formal institution. They may engender
respect, or even reverence, which endows their decisions with influence. They may control
levers of information dissemination, which enables them to advertise or disclose details
about members of the group who defect from the formal institutions and about those who
respect the institutions. This informational capability can generate reputations and reduce
uncertainty about members of a group, which can affect future interactions by creating long-
term costs or benefits for actions taken in the present.

The third party plays an important and effective role if its actions focus attention on those
who violate the formal institutions and produce pressures for compliance. Not all formal
institutions succeed in influencing behavior. Many fail to create incentives, constrain behavior,
or motivate compliance because the third party lacks either the authority or the willingness
to adjudicate violations and disputes, or has no ability to enforce its decisions even when it
does attempt to adjudicate disputes. Many governments adopt constitutions and bodies of law
that include provisions to protect the rights of their citizens or fairly adjudicate economic
disputes, but then they routinely ignore these bodies of law, enforce them only when doing so
meets government policy makers' needs, or enforce them in a seemingly arbitrary manner. We
like to think that such transgressions occur predominantly in developing or authoritarian

states, but we can also find examples of such problems in the more advanced industrialized democracies. For example, shortly after the end of the Civil War, passage of the Fourteenth Amendment to the U.S. Constitution guaranteed equal protection to U.S. citizens regardless of race. Despite this formal rule of law mandating equal protection, U.S. courts and authorities then stood by for almost one hundred years as many states and municipal courts systematically denied African Americans the rights and protections that were available to other citizens. In another set of examples, many developing democracies claim an institutional rule of law embedded in formal statute, yet policy makers in those states may ignore such institutions and award government contracts based on patronage, cronyism, and corruption.

Reputation

Reputation is a mechanism distinct from third-party enforcement of a formal institution. Obviously, a third-party enforcement device—such as labeling some party as reliable or as a scofflaw—can focus attention and generate costs and benefits in terms of reputation. Yet reputations that can affect the likelihood and form of social interactions may also emerge in the absence of a third party, as in decentralized relationships, where parties to a social, political, or economic interaction violate or adhere to the informal rules of a contract or game. If such compliance or violation is observable and broadcast to other members of society, then a reputation may develop that aids cooperative interactions or acts as a barrier to interaction.

For example, Hasidic Jews dominate the wholesale diamond trade in New York City. Their informal rules ask each trader to be fair and honest and to respect agreements that are consummated by verbal agreement, by a handshake, or by some other symbolic gesture that would be considered weak evidence, at best, in a court of law. Within this community, very little cheating occurs. Few disputes occur or require resolution despite the temptation inherent in handling millions and millions of dollars' worth of diamonds. What keeps individuals in this community from cheating and destroying such a system, especially since the state's courts would face difficulty resolving any disputes, given the nature of the contracting mechanism? A diamond trader's ability to function and thrive depends on his reputation. If one trader were to cheat another, the cheated trader would quickly inform other traders about the offense. The cheater's reputation would be damaged, and, depending on the severity of the offense, he could be penalized, ostracized, and perhaps forced to leave the diamond trade altogether. This kind of communal discipline occurs through self-enforcement, without resort to a third-party adjudicator and enforcer.

Fear of negative reputation costs can be self-enforcing, can limit cheating, and can protect an informal institution that serves to overcome barriers to cooperation and coordination. Conversely, a good reputation can produce rewards and increasing returns. Developing a reputation for adhering to the rules of the game, even if they are informal rules, helps to lower uncertainty about a party's honesty, reduces transaction costs, and builds trust that can lead to more beneficial interactions. Developing a reputation for fairness and evenhandedness, or for being a willing self-enforcer, offers reassurance to other parties in a social interaction that can affect their cost-benefit calculations and condition their choices. This status-enhancing effect holds for both informal and formal institutions. Research in the physical sciences and the social sciences demonstrates that long-term cooperation, as if guided by formal or informal institutions, can be a better strategy for individuals than maximizing choices that benefit themselves in the short term but create social traps and social aggregation failures in the long term.

Status Quo and Embedded Interests

Preferences for the status quo and embedded interests both operate to promote institutional stickiness. In a world of uncertainty, people often "prefer the devil they know to the devil they don't know," which simply means that the opportunity to alter or reject a current institution balances the consequences of the current institutional arrangement against the potential implications of a new institutional arrangement or the absence of an institutional arrangement. Given that we live in a world of uncertainty, we cannot completely anticipate the consequences of new institutional arrangements or a situation without an institutional constraint once the status quo institution has been damaged or dismantled. Some unknowns remain.

If we are somewhat dissatisfied with current institutional arrangements but also very unsure about the outcome of new ones, we may defend the current arrangements in order to manage our apprehensions of the unknown. In such cases, our willingness to defend the status quo depends on the extent of our dissatisfaction with the current rules, our estimation of potential benefits from changing the rules of the game, and our uncertainty about attaining the anticipated outcome. The prospect for institutional change increases along with our dissatisfaction with current arrangements, everything else being held constant. The greater the expected gains from institutional change, all else being held constant, the greater the likelihood of such change. But the greater the uncertainty or the lower the expected gains from change in the institutional context, the greater the likelihood of our maintaining the status quo, even if we are relatively dissatisfied with it.

Let's quickly consider how embedded interests work to maintain the status quo and to promote institutional durability independent of uncertainty. Most institutions that resolve difficult cooperation problems are not neutral in terms of the distribution of their effects—they create relative winners and losers in societies. As such, the design of institutions can become the target of political competition. From this perspective, formal or informal institutions are social constructs that reflect preferences about institutional design based on the different capabilities of societal actors and their ability and willingness to exert influence, and these different capabilities can affect the long-term efficacy of an institution. Those who profit from a particular institution can use their resources to promote the viability of that institution and to resist institutional change. The strength of their resistance to institutional change may depend on the size of the gains the status quo arrangement produces for those winners and the expected distributional consequences of institutional change. For example, warlords in the Sudan—those with disproportionate power in their society—have maintained social practices and political institutional arrangements that promote civil conflict, ethnic violence, famine, and starvation, and so damage the collective welfare of their society. It is hard to believe that local political leaders would resist institutional change amid such human tragedy, yet the warlords have adhered stubbornly to status quo arrangements as they seek to maintain their position of influence and continue to reward particular interests at the expense of the larger society.

The willingness of embedded interests to resist institutional change does not preclude such change, for those damaged by the status quo may willingly expend resources to promote change. This opposition of interests may lead to conflict and competition over institutional design. However, those benefiting from current arrangements may use the status quo to expand their capabilities, whereas the relative losers may suffer losses in capabilities—which suggests that, over time, the embedded interests (the winners) are likely to gain in ability to defend the status quo. All else being equal, this likelihood contributes to institutional durability.

The Shadow of the Future

All of the previously mentioned mechanisms that can contribute to institutional durability implicitly assume that people care about the future. Many human interactions take place between individuals, groups, and states that are likely to interact again and again. How people value such future interactions can affect how they behave in their current dealings. Those who live expressly for today—carpe diem!—and care little about tomorrow are essentially playing a one-shot game, in which they likely will seek to obtain their best possible outcome even if it damages social welfare, hurts their reputation, and risks ostracism from similar interactions in the future. After all, these people put little value or weight on the future, on the long-term consequences of their choices, or on the importance of cooperation in the future. Their actions may seem excessively self-centered and egomaniacal, yet the conditions of society can create incentives for such behavior. If a society is a violent and chaotic place, where people cheat, steal, or even kill without regard for the broader community and its long-term interests, it makes sense for individuals in that society to shorten their time horizons and take aggressive actions. In such situations, many people will act to ensure the short-term survival and well-being of their family and friends, even if their actions damage society further. In failing states, this logic creates a downward and vicious spiral of degenerating social, economic, and political conditions.

However, if people in a society find a means to extend their time horizons, boosting their interest in the future and their valuation of that future, the possibility of constructing bargains and institutions that guide current social interactions in order to protect future interactions increases. The greater the likelihood of repeated interactions in the future, the greater the incentives and prospects for constructing and maintaining institutions for overcoming barriers to cooperation, reducing transaction costs, and making social relations more stable and predictable. This dynamic is more than simply an economic calculation about future gains, for repeated interaction contributes to familiarity, which aids understanding and reduces uncertainty—good or bad—about the parties involved in the relationship. With greater familiarity, parties involved in social interactions can design institutions and contracts that take advantage of their different strengths and manage their weaknesses that can damage cooperation. The knowledge that comes from repeated interactions can lead to the development of institutions and rules that are robust in the face of pressures to defect.

Familiarity can also activate informal social pressures and build social networks that generate incentives to play by the rules. If productive, more frequent interactions build social momentum and trust that can produce slack, or flexibility, in social relations—a willingness to forgive or overlook some behavior that seems outside the rules of the game. Rather than allowing a single transgression to destroy the institution or relationship, other parties may give the transgressor a second chance, or even more. With repeated interactions, people develop expectations about the other parties. Behavior that deviates from such expectations may be unacceptable, but if it is unusual, familiarity may help to identify it as an aberration, and the other parties may then be willing to wait and see if it is repeated. Absent familiarity, such behavior might immediately undermine the social interaction and damage the institution built to promote that interaction.

Of course, successful institutions are *endogenous*—are themselves causal—to increasing the "shadow of the future." Causality runs both ways and is mutually reinforcing. An increasing shadow of the future improves the likelihood of institutional success, and institutional success increases the shadow of the future. Absent such an awareness of and concern for the future, even the most coercive enforcement mechanisms cannot prevent institutional failure and societal dysfunction. If people do not or cannot extend their time horizons, their incentives are often to opt for behavior that is damaging to themselves and to their societies—a social trap that creates a vicious cycle. For example, since World War II the General Agreement on Tariffs and Trade and its successor the WTO have promoted more liberal trade relations and lower barriers to trade. Governments appoint delegations of experts to such organizations. Over time, the trade experts from different states develop relationships and familiarity with one another. These relationships tend to aid understanding and cooperation, creating pressures for compromise and accommodation among the delegations regardless of politics at home. They expand the shadow of the future.

Distributional Implications of Institutions

Institutions affect distributional outcomes in society. They produce relative winners and losers, which creates the potential for boundaries within society and the formation of interests along such boundaries. For example, tax rules and regulations are part of the institutional makeup of any political economy. Some tax systems are more progressive than others; some are more regressive. A government's choosing a capital gains tax rate of 15 percent instead of 30 percent enables those who have surplus to invest, the wealthy, to retain more of their wealth. This reduces the progressivity of the tax system and places a greater burden on others in society to ante up to fund the government. Consequently, institutions and institutional design become targets of political competition. Power asymmetries influence, perhaps dictate, institutional design so as to advance particular distributional outcomes that favor some interests over others. Many institutional economists argue that because institutions reduce transaction costs and the uncertainties involved in exchange relations, they emerge in order to enhance efficiency. This is a functional argument—an explanation for a phenomenon based on its consequences. But enhanced efficiency may simply be a secondary or unintended result of institutional design that is intended to produce distributional advantage for some groups versus others.

In a social trap with great uncertainty, many different institutions can structure incentives, promote a better equilibrium, and improve efficiency and social outcomes. In such situations, a variety of institutional arrangements may lower transaction costs and improve social efficiency. But who benefits most, who benefits least, and who loses can shift across the variations in institutional arrangements. This is the multiple-equilibrium situation with distributional consequences discussed in chapter 1. Individuals and groups may disagree over variations in institutional arrangements even if every variation improves social outcomes, as the variations produce different gains and losses at the individual level. The creation of an institution can itself be a social trap.

Hence, institutions are not politically or normatively neutral—not even institutions that improve social outcomes. The rules of electoral systems, regulatory arrangements, administrative law, and judicial rights become targets of political competition as they affect who wins or loses and who may have greater or lesser influence over future policy discussions and institutional design. In political competition, winning at time t is often endogenous to winning at times $t1$, $t2$, and so on, as winning often helps to build capabilities and resources that will prove useful in future political and policy struggles.

Some political scientists use this view of institutional design and creation as a reason to downplay the importance of institutions for understanding social activity. They argue that if a society's institutions merely reflect the distribution of power in the society, we need only examine that power distribution in order to understand social outcomes—that is, institutions are unnecessary or secondary independent variables. Perhaps, but if institutions merely reflect the distribution of capabilities and influence in society, we would expect institutional change to correspond closely to societal shifts in power. The fact that societies are dynamic provides leverage for examining the relationship between power and institutional makeup. Societal distributions of wealth, resources, and power change, but institutional change lags behind. This disconnect between the distribution of influence in society and institutional change argues against looking only at the distribution of power. Institutions are sticky. Effective ones span changes in the distribution of influence and provide some durable structure to expectations.

Moreover, an institution can take on a life of its own, beyond what its designers envisioned, and create unanticipated by-products. Policy environments are uncertain. Policy makers may be motivated to resolve or manage a dilemma, but because of uncertainty they cannot anticipate all contingencies—especially given that many of those contingencies will appear only in the future and in the context of future change. If policy makers could anticipate all future possibilities, there would be no uncertainty to influence decisions.

For example, the policy makers who created the European Court of Justice never envisioned the extent to which the court would intervene in national polities to establish new rights and expectations across the European Union. Yet through their rulings, the justices of the ECJ have extended its mandate and reach beyond the boundaries anticipated by the court's creators. Individual member states of the EU have at one time or another become disgruntled by ECJ rulings that interfere in their domestic arenas and force governments to shift state-society bargains. Today, significantly reining in the institutional reach of the ECJ and returning to the intentions of its designers would require members of the EU to risk destroying the ECJ and endangering the cooperation that underpins the EU. An unwillingness to take such risks provides some insulation for the ECJ to continue to expand its mandate.

THE SOCIAL ORIGINS OF INSTITUTIONS: INTENTIONAL AND UNINTENTIONAL DESIGN

Institutions may be consciously designed and created with third-party oversight, as in the case of formal institutions, but they may also emerge without conscious design as a consequence of human activity that becomes regularized, generating expectations that influence future activity, as in the case of many informal institutions that are self-enforcing. Encountering uncertainty and risk, policy makers attempt to design institutions rationally to constrain some human behavior and create incentives for other human activity. Policy makers embark on the writing of constitutions, bodies of law and statutes, and regulations and administrative guidelines with conscious intent to steer, motivate, and engineer human activity, but conflicts in the processes of writing such rules may cloud their rational intentions. Difficult cooperation problems rarely engender universal agreement over institutional solutions, especially given the likely prospects of distributional consequences of different rules, and so institutional design often incorporates compromise that muddies intentions and distorts intended incentives. Nevertheless, these rules are *ex ante* attempts at rational institutional design with an objective of conditioning human activity. Of course, the success of institutions is more than simply a matter of their construction; success is also reliant on their subsequent acceptance, interpretation, and enforcement by society.

To have any chance at rationally designing a successful institution, one must have a keen understanding of the society, the preferences and capabilities of different groups and individuals in the society, the legacy of past institutional arrangements, the potential for the institution's interaction with other formal and informal institutions, and an ability to anticipate the consequences of a variety of hypothetical institutional arrangements. This is a formidable list of requirements, but policy makers who attempt to design institutions without such understanding are generally likely to fail, often quashing expectations and undermining confidence in the governments that have adopted the institutions. The world is littered with examples of failures of institutional design, despite good intentions. Policy makers at international development organizations as well as private consultants have counseled governments of developing and transitional states in the design of institutions that are intended to advance the transition toward more effective political economies. Often, they have simply transplanted institutions that worked in some of the advanced industrialized states to new arenas. More often than not, these institutions fail in their new environments or require substantial alteration before they can produce significant benefits.

Even with clear knowledge of a society—the different interests in the society and their preferences, and the path contingency of previous institutional arrangements—policy makers need substantial luck to design an institution that works as anticipated. As thorough and diligent as a group of intelligent policy makers may be, they cannot anticipate all contingencies. An institution that appears well designed beforehand can lead to unintended consequences that may undermine the institution or transform it to another purpose. Successful institutional design requires some luck and some art to accompany good social science engineering if the institution is to create incentives that actually lead to the intended outcome.

Many institutions and institutional changes, particularly informal ones, emerge from a far less deliberate process. As people interact, patterns may emerge that affect expectations about their future activity. These patterns often emerge incrementally, as small changes and frequent interactions add up over time to create a significant transformation in human activity. These patterns can reduce uncertainty, stabilize expectations, and create incentives to make some choices versus others. If so, they have intermediated the calculus of decision makers and imposed an independent effect on those calculations. If such patterns and expectations become firmer and more extensive in their reach across larger portions of society, they begin to have the effect of becoming rules of the game. Sometimes policy makers build formal institutions on the foundations of such informal institutions and established patterns of activity, and this correspondence between formal and informal practices often produces the most effective and durable formal institutions. For example, according to Nicholas Katzenbach, the U.S. attorney general in the Johnson administration, successful international law consists of the codification of existing practices. After World War II, the Allies tried German and Japanese officials as war criminals who had committed crimes against humanity. There was no formal basis in international law for such charges at the time, but the international tribunals established a precedent against such horrific actions that was later embedded in international treaties. Even so, not all nations were willing to sign such treaties. The United States signed the Genocide Convention adopted by the United Nations in 1948, but the U.S. Senate refused to ratify the treaty until 1988. Yet the United States still highlighted crimes against humanity during the period before ratification.

Institutions as Devices to Overcome the Time-Inconsistency Dilemma

As an *ex ante* agreement or bargain about future cooperation and interactions, an institution can help to overcome the time-inconsistency dilemma that hampers policy makers. This problem is the temptation that policy makers face to defect on long-term commitments to policies that benefit society in an effort to realize short-term political gains. Such defection could damage or undermine long-term societal gains for short-term and fleeting advantage.

A successful institution creates expectations about behavior that can limit this latitude and tie the hands of policy makers by increasing the costs of reneging on the agreement. Defecting from an institution that has gained traction and durability and has succeeded in establishing expectations and conditioning behavior is generally far more costly than changing policy or reneging in a social exchange that does not have institutional underpinnings. The development of reputation and value in the institution creates an investment in maintaining the rules of the game, which increases the cost of reneging on the institution. Violating the institution is thus more than a one-shot expense, for it damages the investment that went into building the institution.

Policy makers, faced with the temptation to defect on an agreement in order to obtain some short-term gain such as political survival, can design institutions intentionally to increase the costs of defection from long-term social bargains. Effectively, they use institutional design to attempt to tie their own hands so they will not succumb to short-term pressures to violate these long-term commitments. For example, policy makers face continual pressures to manage the economy—to promote growth or encourage price stability. Workers often want an expanding economy and job creation, while holders of capital worry about inflationary expansion that could eat away at the value of their assets. Such pressures become especially acute at election time or during crises of political survival, and politicians are then sorely tempted to use monetary policy to appeal to these interests even if they are likely to produce policy that undermines expectations and creates risks that may damage economic activity in the long term.

Ideally, societies would be happy with monetary policy that limits economic volatility, avoiding swings between too much inflation and too little economic stimulus. Such economic engineering is extremely difficult, as economies are complex and their causal mechanisms remain somewhat mysterious. But the difficulties of such engineering are compounded when politicians seek to manage monetary policy for short-term gains. We can look around the world and find political economies suffering under excessive inflation, languishing with low, even negative, real growth as they bounce from one extreme to another. Economic actors find such environments discouraging because they cannot estimate their risks or calculate an expected rate of return. If they have alternatives, they will avoid such environments. Perversely, policy makers' efforts to ensure their political survival by responding to constituent pressures can be the very source of this instability and volatility. Responsiveness to such pressures can do severe damage to a political economy's long-term prospects—another social trap.

Many states have enacted laws that, if enforced, create relatively independent central banks to manage monetary policy. These are government organizations, but their enabling legislation seeks to provide central bankers with some insulation from political pressures. To be successful at creating and maintaining a relatively autonomous central bank, policy makers must develop institutions and strategies that limit their ability to manipulate monetary policy for short-term political gain and allow the central bankers to manage monetary policy with a long-term view as to what is best for society. Effectively, politicians must tie their hands and transfer responsibility for monetary policy to more insulated policy makers. A host of strategies can help to limit the ability of politicians to renege on their commitments to an autonomous central bank and relatively apolitical monetary policy. Elected officials may appoint professional bankers and economists with specialized skills and knowledge that provide them with some insulation from political pressure. Central bankers may serve terms of longer duration than those of elected officials, or their terms in office may be staggered to avoid overlap with elections and political terms. Statutory requirements might demand that the governing board of a central bank be composed of politically diverse individuals. Board members may be protected from being fired by politicians or insulated from the budgetary mechanisms of the government, which would prevent other policy makers from pressuring the central bank through manipulation of the budget or threats of dismissal.

These strategies to limit the ability of politicians to interfere with the activities of central bankers are examples of institutional design that is intended to make a unit of government less responsive to political pressures—to protect a policy arena from democratic influence. Ironically, an independent central bank to manage monetary policy may seem philosophically inconsistent within democratic frameworks that encourage representation and responsiveness. The desire to construct institutions that encourage democratic responsiveness and, at the same time, insulate politicians from democratic but socially perverse short-term pressures poses interesting tensions and challenges for policy makers. We can find examples of similar institutions—such as the construction of an independent judiciary with lifetime tenure in order to insulate the law from short-term temptations for politicians to interfere in court proceedings. Many quasi-independent regulatory agencies in various countries are also constructed with an objective of overcoming the time-inconsistency problem. If such institutional devices succeed, they make short-term actions harmonious or consistent with long-term objectives. They increase the shadow of the future by tying present choices to goals that are more distant in the future.

IMPORTANT INSTITUTIONAL CONSIDERATIONS IN DOMESTIC AND GLOBAL AFFAIRS

Examples of institutions dot the landscape of domestic and global affairs. Institutions, rules of the game, play significant roles in our political and economic lives and history. The informal law of the market, when unimpeded, forces individuals to respond to the pressures of comparative advantage (another institution) as it creates incentives to either continue or change their productive activities. The Corn Laws, rules that intervened in market exchange and protected British agricultural producers from more efficient foreign competitors at the beginning of the nineteenth century, created incentives that allowed British farmers to continue engaging in inefficient agricultural production instead of finding more economically and socially productive outlets. The institution of most-favored-nation status (MFN) promoted the expansion of trade during the 1800s and again in the post–World War II era. The breakdown in domestic and global economic activity during the period between World War I and World War II was advanced by the adoption of informal and formal beggar-thy-neighbor rules. A cooperative set of rules and interactions broke down as the emergence of an "anything goes" rule created incentives for policy makers to raise trade barriers and engage in competitive currency devaluations. (See chapter 10.)

Negotiators at Bretton Woods in the mid-1940s designed a monetary system around a set of institutions that defined a currency's value in terms of other currencies, determined when a currency was incorrectly valued, and decided how a government could adjust its exchange rate. The Smithsonian Agreement in 1971 shifted those rules, but only marginally. Perhaps as influential as the institutions of the Bretton Woods and Smithsonian monetary system were for the post–World War II global economy, the adherence of governments to informal practices of restraint contributed to the success of postwar monetary arrangements. An institutional change, the Second Amendment to the IMF Articles of Agreement, eliminated the role of gold as a reserve asset, legalized floating exchange rates, and encouraged a stable system of exchange rates to replace the Bretton Woods system of stable exchange rates. (See chapters 11 and 12.)

Containment during the Cold War depended on formal and informal rules between the Western democracies about what should and should not be exported to the Eastern bloc political economies. Since World War II, the system of global capitalism has been extended by the adoption and creation of new institutions built on previous institutions. (See chapters 11–14.) Much institutional development is path contingent, but much uncertainty also remains. The incentives for public and private policy makers are not always consistent with global capitalism, and governments and firms often implement policies that produce barriers to cooperation and create risk for market exchange. Path contingency is not inevitable, as inconsistencies in policy making occur frequently. We place much of the blame for such outcomes on the problems of political and economic market failure and social traps.

We can look at institutional arrangements within and across states in order to discover how they affect policy outcomes, create or mitigate social traps, and influence the nature of politics and the resolution of cooperation and coordination problems. As a beginning, we can construct a broad framework of institutional considerations to assist us in examining human activity and recognizing why policy outcomes can differ from one national arena to another. We will quickly consider institutional variations in regime type, electoral systems, structure of government and relationships between components of governments, and social institutions. With respect to our interest in global affairs, such institutional considerations are important for distinguishing different national approaches to the processes of globalization, but they also help us to understand differences in domestic politics.

Regime Type: Democratic and Authoritarian Regimes and the Rules of the Game

At the most basic level, we classify regimes as either authoritarian or democratic. The rules of the game in democratic regimes accept, even encourage, involvement by a broader range of society in the affairs of governance than do the rules in authoritarian regimes. Usually, this democratic inclusiveness creates more varied demands on policy makers than are likely to be made in authoritarian regimes, and it can complicate the lives and decision processes of policy makers—more constituents to please to ensure political survival, and more who can be angered. This broader base also creates the possibility for countervailing interests to emerge and advance their cases in policy debates. Countervailing pressures work against each other, potentially constraining policy makers from moving too far in one direction or another. As a consequence of needing to appeal to constituents for reelection, democratic leaders must be more conscious of the implications of their policy choices for a broader range of society. Independent of other institutional considerations, simply having a broader swath of diverse and mobilized interests involved in policy debates can limit policy mobility and arbitrariness and promote compromise. Policy makers are likely to discover that their options are more limited when they are faced with a wider range of constituencies. Trying to please more people and constituencies, they limit their actions and often produce compromises that sit between the preferences of different groups—essentially splitting the difference.

Authoritarian leaders, while still facing constraints, rely on much narrower constituencies for their political survival, and there are fewer societal checks and balances to limit their policy flexibility. In successful democratic regimes, the rules of the game are embedded in bodies of formal law and informal practice, and changing those rules usually involves following established procedures that increase transparency and accountability to society. Authoritarian leaders, however, often enjoy greater unilateral influence over the rules of the game and can change those rules with less recourse to established practices and procedures. These leaders are usually more able than leaders of democratic regimes to replace members of their governments arbitrarily or to redesign their governments.

Democracies usually enjoy more established and transparent rules of transition or regime change. In successful democracies, elections occur at predictable intervals, and the shifting of the reins of power is accomplished with regularity and through established procedures. This regularity contributes to greater stability of expectations as one regime hands over governing power and responsibilities to another. Economic and social actors generally prefer such stability to wider variations that can constrain planning far into the future. Even less successful democracies tend to limit such variations, as they attempt to hold elections at predictable intervals using established procedures. Such electoral processes may be corrupted, but they are still more transparent and predictable than regime change in authoritarian states.

The rules of transition and regime change in authoritarian governments are far less transparent and predictable. The lines of succession are often ad hoc, which creates uncertainty as leaders become vulnerable owing to processes such as aging, increasing societal rejection, or elite disenchantment. Sometimes an authoritarian leader succeeds at stepping down and transferring power to a family member or other handpicked successor, but often regime change in authoritarian states takes place as a consequence of a coup or an episode of social disruption, sometimes violent. With the exception of monarchical succession, neither process is embedded in established procedures or rules that domestic and foreign observers can understand and anticipate. Lacking transparency and predictability, regime change in authoritarian states generates greater uncertainty and risk to economic and social actors than does regime change in democratic states. Even if some authoritarian rulers wield their power wisely and productively for their societies, there is no guarantee that their successors will be as wise and productive. This lack of certainty is also true in democratic regimes, but the ability of constituents to reject politicians at the polls and gain greater access to policy makers works to constrain policy makers, good or bad. Deficient policy makers in democratic societies burden their societies less than do similarly deficient leaders in authoritarian regimes.

In democracies, such constraints on dramatic and arbitrary policy shifts at the whim of a select few policy makers and segments of society can also act as a credible commitment mechanism, signaling commitment to a particular policy course. Given the potentially greater stickiness of policy in democratic regimes because of their lack of arbitrariness relative to authoritarian regimes, and the difficulty of enacting dramatic policy shifts with a broadly representative electorate that contains countervailing and politically costly pressures, democratic regimes have a simpler task of signaling a commitment to a policy once adopted. Policy making is costly, and arbitrariness is particularly costly to politicians in democratic arenas.

Electoral Systems: Influencing the Nature of Politics and Policies

Electoral rules and systems vary from one democracy to another, as do the pathways of ascension to office in authoritarian regimes. Such variations in rules and processes can influence the nature of politics and policies within states and, consequently, between states in the global arena. Let's focus on the electoral rules of democratic regimes, because they tend to be more transparent and durable than the means of ascension and succession in authoritarian states. They are more likely to constitute institutional arrangements than are the ad hoc transfers of power that often characterize authoritarian states. Some democratic polities elect their governments by a plurality rule, while many others use some form of a proportional electoral rule.

Only the leading vote getter is elected to office under a plurality or winner-take-all rule. Some plurality rules require that the winner receive a majority and not simply a plurality of the votes cast. Iran has such a rule for election of its president, and Louisiana uses such a rule for its statewide elected offices. In elections contested by more than two candidates, such majority rules sometimes lead to a run-off election between the top two vote getters when none of the candidates receives a majority of the votes cast in the first round. But most plurality electoral systems—most notably that of the United States—elect the candidate who simply receives the most votes. In such systems, a candidate may receive 49.9 percent of the vote yet fail to gain office. The term *winner-take-all* is apropos, as such systems potentially ignore the interests of those citizens who voted for the losing candidate even if they make up a significant portion of the electorate—the electoral process ensures that the winning candidate must pay attention to the voters who elected her and can choose to ignore the concerns of those whose candidate lost. These electoral losers must worry about minority rights even if they make up almost 50 percent of the electorate. For example, in a political economy like the United States with a winner-take-all rule, even though a significant number of Americans worry about climate change and carbon emissions, they are unable to convince the majority of Americans who worry more about employment during the economic slowdown following 2007–2008 to address the issue of climate change. This winner-take-all dynamic blocks U.S. policy makers from fully cooperating in international summits meant to address climate change, and consequently, because of the size of the United States, undermines significant global cooperation on efforts to address climate change, aside from nice public statements.

Parties in polities with proportional electoral rules (including most Western European democracies) gain office if they surpass an established threshold or proportion of the total vote—for example, a 10 percent threshold. This means that particular parts of an electorate or special interests can obtain representation in the legislature even if their proportion of the vote is relatively small. Minority candidates can target a specific issue or portion of the political spectrum and still gain office even while ignoring the preferences of the majority. This type of electoral system offers a greater likelihood that minority interests will be represented through the electoral process than does a plurality system. Proportional election rules can enable minority interests to advance their agendas, trade votes, wheel and deal, and participate in governing coalitions, whereas in a winner-take-all system, they would be left on the sidelines. In a highly fragmented proportional government, a small minority party can wield unusual influence and extract substantial concessions from far larger parties by providing the necessary votes to ensure a governing coalition. In proportional systems, larger parties may face substantial risk if they ignore the smaller groups that are often ignored in winner-take-all systems.

In proportional systems, voters often select their candidates from a party list—they are essentially voting for the party attached to the candidate's name. This process reinforces party unity and ideological attachment to a party, which helps to limit the "cult of personality" or candidate-centered campaigns that can dominate in winner-take-all systems such as the United States. Recognizing that voters are supporting a party more than a specific candidate, some proportional systems allow the transfer of votes to other candidates on the party list if one or more candidates exceed the threshold necessary for election. This device, known as a single-vote, transferable system, also helps to strengthen party cohesion, as the success of candidates depends on the success of their parties. Other proportional systems are single-vote, nontransferable. A variety of other plausible proportional systems reflect the efforts of policy makers to structure electoral systems to engineer particular types of outcomes and to overcome barriers to such outcomes. As such, electoral rules, like other institutions, are targets of political competition.

Differences in electoral institutions, from plurality to proportional systems, can affect party cohesion, determining whether politics and parties will converge on centrist policies and the median voter, or whether parties and politicians can be successful away from the center and the median voter. Differences in electoral rules influence whether a political arena can support three or more stable political parties or will inevitably converge on a two-party system. Consequently, electoral rules prescribe the nature of political competition in a society, as well as the manner in which interests will organize and the type of coalition building we should expect in legislatures and among interest groups.

For example, a winner-take-all electoral rule pushes political campaigns, political advertising and rhetoric, and electoral competition toward the political center as defined by the median voter in an election. This pressure works against the success of relatively extremist candidates and parties and rewards those who can move to the center. Of course, we are still assuming that politicians want to win and then to remain in office. Voters will vote for the party or candidate closest to their preferences, yet, even in a population with strong disagreements and a distribution of voters away from the middle, the median voter will dictate the long-term outcomes of an electoral process under a plurality rule, for politicians and parties must appeal to this voter in order to win. Their poor prospects for electoral reward force extremist elements to choose between supporting more centrist candidates or assisting the victory of a candidate who is even more distant on the political spectrum. Parties and candidates will converge, thus removing extremist debates and issues from the electoral agenda and possibly constraining the winner of an election from pushing such policies once elected if she worries about her electoral future. This centripetal effect makes it difficult, if not impossible, for a third party to emerge and remain politically viable over an extended period except as a spoiler to those whose interests are more similar than different.

Proportional electoral institutions enable a wider range of interests to gain political power and representation. Allowing access to electoral office based on a prescribed proportion of the vote, even if not a plurality, allows more specialized interests to hold to their policy positions, not moving to the center, and yet remain viable in the electoral arena. A more diverse range of societal interests can populate a legislature, influence a legislative calendar and agenda, and produce unpredictable coalitions as interests trade their votes to advance their particularistic objectives. Because electoral rules are likely to affect the organization of a legislature and government, producing differences in political agendas and coalition politics from one political arena to another, this institutional design has implications for the nature of political discourse and interest group activity in the broader society. In global affairs, such variations in electoral rules can contribute to state-by-state differences in policy debates over trade, immigration, national security, capital mobility, and economic policy, as well as willingness to cooperate and coordinate in the global arena.

Structure of Government: Domestic and Global Implications

Relationships between components of governments are strongly structured by institutions. In most states, constitutions provide the working plans for the structure of government.

A constitution, as an institution, influences the organization of authority in a state, assigns responsibilities, helps to define how the game of politics will be played between government authorities, and consequently serves to structure political activity throughout society. A government's form affects how it and its society functions and thus how its citizens and economy interact with those from other states. For example, a government may have a distinct national bias in its legal system, favoring the rights of nationals over those of foreigners. If so, this affects the willingness of foreigners to invest in that political economy and how they invest if they do. Foreign investors might be unwilling to expose their capital and property to possible expropriation through the legal system as a result of this bias, or they may enter into joint ventures with nationals from the country as a cloak of protection. Such institutions affect the willingness of foreigners to invest, which in turn affects investment and economic opportunities in the potential host country. Is the legislative arm separate from the executive arm of government? Is the judiciary independent, or are judges responsive to societal pressures or influence from other parts of government? Does the government have a federal or nonfederal structure—what are the lines of authority and the division of policy responsibilities between national and local governments? Are regulatory agencies exposed to political pressures, or are they relatively autonomous? Is the civil service based on meritocracy and professionalism or on patronage? How responsive must the country's bureaucracies be to their political masters?

Executive-Legislative Relationships

Relationships between executive and legislative functions fall into two broad categories in democratic systems: presidential and parliamentary. In presidential systems, the executive functions of government are separated by design from the legislative functions. The executive and members of the legislature seek election independent of each other. Their electoral hopes are clearly linked by issues, but voters have the opportunity to vote for members of one party to hold legislative office and for another party to hold executive office. This separation of electoral fortunes creates an opportunity for divided government, wherein different parties hold the reins of power in the legislature and the executive.

Even without divided government, the need to seek election independent of the other branch of government creates a potential wedge between the legislative and executive functions of government. Separating legislative and executive electoral outcomes introduces differing incentives that may not overlap between the executive and legislature, even among members of the same party. The executive or members of the legislature may find it useful to disagree or attack each other, even if within the same party. Legislators can undermine the policies of an executive from their party and damage her reelection chances without necessarily hurting their own political survival. In fact, showing a streak of independence from an executive within their own party can sometimes be a good electoral strategy for legislators in a presidential system, but hardly ever in a parliamentary system. The electoral separation of the executive and legislature in a presidential system can thus undercut party cohesion and allow external forces such as political and economic geography, regionalism, and other sectoral interests to garner influence through the legislature, even if the executive has a broader national objective. Conversely, an executive who is elected separately from the legislature may be able to resist pressures on some of her party's legislators that are tied to geographic or economic sectoral interests.

In parliamentary systems, the executive and legislative functions—and, hence, their fortunes—are tightly linked. The executive is elected as a member of the legislature and usually leads the party that controls the most seats in the legislature (although with coalition governments in a proportional system it is conceivable, if less likely, that a member of another party in the governing coalition could serve as the chief executive). Following an election, the head of state offers the leader of the party that has won substantial control of the seats in the legislature an opportunity to form a government. In most parliamentary systems, the head of state and the head of government are separate roles held by different individuals, whereas in presidential systems these roles are usually combined. In a parliamentary system, the head of government and the leader of the dominant party in the legislature are generally the same person.

Moreover, as head of the dominant party in the legislature, the executive appoints legislative members from her party, or from parties that make up a coalition government, to serve as ministers of the different executive bureaucracies (such as ministries of finance or treasury, defense, trade or commerce, foreign affairs, and interior). These ministers make up the executive's cabinet. Again, a minister is an elected member of the legislature who has been asked to run a department in the executive branch. This arrangement gives an elected legislative official, one who is responsive to an electoral base, control over a pool or portfolio of resources to allocate. Ministers can use this pool of resources to feather their electoral nests. In presidential systems, cabinet members are separate from the legislature; they are appointed, not elected, officials. Each cabinet member does control a pool or portfolio of resources, but a larger divide separates these appointed officials from the electoral base. Their political survival depends more on the executive and her reelection than on the legislature and its reelection. This dependence can influence their responsiveness to the electorate, to the executive, and to the legislature.

Because the executive is the head of the dominant party in the legislature in parliamentary systems, her electoral fortunes are tightly linked to those of the other members of the legislature from her party, as well as to those of members from the parties of the governing coalition. When the legislature overrides the preferences of the executive—signifying that enough members of the governing coalition have disagreed with the executive to reject her leadership—this action is called a "vote of no confidence," and it usually leads to the fall of the government in a parliamentary system. In presidential systems, legislatures can, and often do, vote against the expressed wishes of the executive without bringing down their governments. In a parliamentary system, a vote of no confidence can lead to a new election, but a new government can also be formed without an election. The dominant party may elect a new party leader, who then forms a new government, or, after an exercise of party discipline, party members may reaffirm their support for the present leader, who then gets to form a government anew. The parliamentary form of government gives the executive far more influence over the legislative agenda and legislative machinations than is exercised by the executive in a presidential system, but it also makes the executive more sensitive to her party's interests and acutely concerned about disagreements among members of her party in the legislature. It increases the importance of party cohesion.

For example, in the United States—a presidential system where the electoral fortunes of the executive are separate from those of the president's party in the legislature—legislative members of the president's party often break ranks with the president on trade issues such as agricultural subsidies. U.S. presidents are generally protective of free trade and resistant to policies that could damage trade, yet Congress has successfully supported agricultural subsidies that damage farmers in other economies who would be competitive with U.S. agricultural producers absent the subsidies. Members of the president's party can break ranks with the president to protect their electoral fortunes in their districts and not lead to a downfall of the government. The president and the legislature do not have to be in accord. In countries with parliamentary systems—where the electoral fortunes of the executive and her party's legislators are linked—the executive is likely to support the policies the legislators favor and vice versa. So in Europe, many executives and their legislators both favor agricultural subsidies in order to enhance their political survival and avoid a downfall of the government. This situation has led to agricultural policies among the advanced industrialized political economies that are frustrating to policy makers in developing nations and that have become a source of contention during the Doha Round of WTO trade negotiations.

Lines of Authority

The structures of political systems can also differ in the degree of centralization of authority. Federal systems divide responsibilities and authority between national and regional (state and local) governments. With federalism, regional governments enjoy significant autonomy and powers separate from those of the national government. The national government always holds the primary responsibility for national security, but the allocation of other responsibilities, such as education, economic management, fiscal policy, local policing, and adjudication, can vary from one federal system to another and, over time, within the same system. Such decentralization of responsibilities and authority creates a patchwork of rules and discontinuities both among subnational governments in federal systems and between the subnational governments and the national government. In the context of globalization, such decentralization of authority can mean that one regional government of a state responds differently to the processes of globalization than another regional government of that same state. Examples of this phenomenon include initiatives regarding illegal immigration passed by U.S. states in 2010 and 2011. From the outside, this patchwork can look schizophrenic.

Federal structures are sometimes considered inefficient in terms of governance because the rules of the game can shift from one subnational authority to the next, from one locality to another. Gray areas and ambiguity inevitably appear. Problems may arise between national and subnational governments over which level of government can exercise authority in particular policy areas and over where policy responsibilities—and blame for policy failures—should fall. Also, private actors can exploit such governmental fragmentation. Economic enterprises considering relocation routinely play one subnational government against another in federal systems, using competition among these regional governments as a bargaining strategy to extract concessions such as tax abatements or breaks, school improvements, infrastructure investments, and labor concessions. In federal systems, regional governments thus compete for investment, resources, people, and programs. In the best cases, this intergovernmental competition can feed policy innovation and creative destruction in the public sector. In the worst cases, it can increase disparities across regions or promote a race to the bottom, in which the governments lose revenue and sacrifice their ability to manage their local economies and cushion against volatile downturns, such as those produced by rapid economic change, sometimes a consequence of globalization.

On May 1, 2010, protesters gather outside the Arizona capitol in Phoenix to protest the state's controversial new immigration bill and argue that it conflicts with U.S. law. Activists outraged over Arizona's controversial immigration law demanded federal immigration reform.

In federal systems, the decentralization of authority provides a check on the exercise of authority. Disagreements between levels of government and across subnational governments can limit policy volatility and mobility, which helps to stabilize expectations. But such disagreements and discontinuities can also produce uncertainty and potential crisis if they create significant intergovernmental conflict. Often, such disputes involve constitutional issues that must be adjudicated by the courts responsible for constitutional questions. At other times, legislative action by the central government helps to manage such disputes by clarifying responsibilities and authority. Occasionally, however, such disputes turn into full-fledged constitutional crises, which can explode and threaten the legitimacy of the mechanisms of government, or even precipitate civil conflict.

Lines of authority are much clearer in nonfederal systems. Authority is more centralized, and subnational governments enjoy far less autonomy from the national government than in federal systems. Regional governments are extensions, or subunits, of the national government. What autonomy they do exercise is more a function of the authority expressly granted to them by the central government, or an unintentional side effect of their being out of sight and out of mind. In such systems, private citizens cannot easily shop around for government concessions, playing one government off against another, for the central government limits and directs such competition.

Institutional Independence and Professionalism

Let's quickly turn to one other set of considerations related to the institutional structure of government: the degree of independence and professionalism of the judiciary, regulatory agencies, and bureaucracies. The institutional designs of governments can vary in terms of whether members of the judiciary are insulated and relatively independent from societal and political pressures as they adjudicate cases or relatively exposed to societal pressures or influence from other parts of government. All judges are part of their societies, and they often recognize the political and societal limitations on their judicial discretion. Judges generally resolve disputes by seeking solutions that a majority of members of society will find tolerable, but judges who are relatively well shielded by institutional design from political and societal pressures are generally more able to rule consistently—and, ideally, fairly—than are judges who are less insulated by institutional design. A less insulated judiciary may shift rulings as the political winds change, or as different groups become mobilized. Institutional features such as lifetime tenure, required professional training and experience in the law, and nonpartisan election can help to shelter judges from the time-inconsistency dilemma that politicians often face.

The same institutional considerations of independence and professionalism apply to regulatory agencies and government bureaucracies. These institutional considerations are important variables to consider as we try to understand why governments do what they do in the global arena. How exposed are the employees of government agencies to political pressures? Do the rules of the game produce a civil service based on meritocracy and professionalism or one that is grounded in patronage and corruption? Does the institutional setup of government create incentives for bureaucracies to be responsive to their political masters, or are the incentives of bureaucrats structured to encourage them to do their jobs as professionals even if political winds blow in another direction? Earlier, we examined such considerations in the context of central banks, but the same questions apply across government agencies.

Social Institutions: Influencing Uncertainty and Risk through Social Bargains

Most of this chapter has focused on formal and informal political institutions. We would be negligent, however, if we failed to discuss the importance of social institutions, because they also help to make up the political arena, affect uncertainty and risk in society, and sometimes spill over to influence global affairs. For example, social institutions and practices such as labor-management agreements over work rules and wages shape the rules of the game in workplaces over extended periods. These practices can reduce uncertainty in labor-management relations, constrain dysfunctional conflicts between labor and management, limit such disagreements to proscribed periods and condition the form of conflict, allow economic enterprises to price their labor costs for a specified period, and overcome potential time-inconsistency problems and social traps that tempt both labor and management.

Following World War II, some societies produced a social bargain, a set of social institutions, known as *corporatism*. In corporatist social democracies such as Scandinavian states, labor, capital, and the government arrived at an informal agreement concerning the boundaries and nature of labor-capital conflict. Capital and labor agreed to bargain in good faith, with the goals of increasing wages and full employment in exchange for less disruption in the workplace. Governments acted as an insurance mechanism to the social institutional bargain with the provision of social welfare goods by the state to cushion workers during dislocations and the state's commitment to ensure a stable macroeconomic arena to protect the assets of capital. The parties involved in the creation of the informal bargains and institutions of corporatism hoped that by establishing such rules of the game they could avoid the disruptions, political extremism, and violent cleavages that had appeared during the interwar years.

Social institutions, like political institutions, may prove dysfunctional. Many of the labor institutions and social bargains that proved so effective and productive in European states in the postwar period now produce unintended and costly consequences. Today, labor institutions in much of the EU create disproportionately high labor costs for economic enterprise and produce incentives for companies to avoid adding new full-time employees. Many of the labor institutions require a transfer of resources to the state to subsidize social insurance programs for society. Because these costs are generally assessed for each full-time employee, many firms prefer to hire multiple part-time workers rather than individual full-time workers to fill positions. This preference has led to structural stickiness in European labor markets, relatively high unemployment, and a quandary for unions, management, and governments. Globalization through the mobility of capital and jobs has created pressures on such social institutions and on governments' abilities to finance the insurance mechanisms.

Labor bargains in the United States once promoted stability in labor relations and the development of a reliable workforce in many unionized industries, such as automobile and steel manufacturing. But today the durability of such bargains generates significant legacy costs for many of these industries. Many U.S. manufacturers owe significant pension and health care obligations to their retired, or soon-to-be-retired, workers as a consequence of past labor agreements. In the past, agreements to provide such benefits reduced labor strife, reduced uncertainty in labor-management relations, and contributed to the competitiveness of those companies, but in today's business environment, with its aging population, such obligations may affect competitiveness, as more and more of companies' revenues are committed to paying such legacy costs. These costs may reduce the amount of resources available for research and development, physical capital improvements, and worker training.

Social institutions can affect the nature and violence of societal divisions and disagreements. No society is homogeneous; group identities and interests fragment all societies—some more virulently than others. In some societies, social institutions have been created or have evolved to mitigate and manage potentially disruptive disagreements across group boundaries. In other states, the absence of social institutions to bridge groups and societal cleavages can reinforce incentives for groups to resort to discriminatory tactics, and even violence.

In the aftermath of the disintegration of the Eastern bloc and the Soviet Union, nongovernmental and governmental organizations have sponsored projects targeting the construction of civil society in transitional political economies. Such projects seek to advance the building of strong civil societies, which are characterized by an increasing density of social institutions that promote tolerance and bridge societal divisions. These initiatives are designed to promote stability and reduce uncertainty and risk in social relations, which can spill over to political and economic affairs—domestically and internationally.

VETO POINTS: INSTITUTIONAL CHECKS AND BALANCES IN A POLITICAL ECONOMY

Ideally, as social scientists interested in the influence of institutions on global affairs, we want to examine how institutional differences from one political arena to another may contribute to variations in social outcomes and policies. Do variations in the institutional makeup of political economies provide us with analytic insight for understanding differences in trade policies, monetary policies, policies regarding the external value of currencies, ability to attract foreign and domestic investment, incentives for economic enterprises to take risks on the future and expand their activities or to engage in corrupt practices and extract extralegal rents from economic actors, capacity of legal arenas to adjudicate disagreements fairly, or a society's proclivity for engaging in extralegal means of government replacement? Or does focusing on too many institutional variations from one society to the next serve to overwhelm the systematic analysis that can lead to useful, generalizable statements about the influence of institutions on social activity? Does describing too many differences from case to case simply undermine the search for commonality and generalizability by making each case appear to be unique? At some level, each case is unique, but we may find that by focusing on critical relationships in society we can make statements that often carry across societies—a difference that separates the social sciences from the humanities.

So, when we examine institutions, what are we trying to learn? Simply, we want to understand how the rules of the game constrain, motivate, or condition individual choices and social outcomes. How do institutions affect the incentives of individuals and policy makers to engage in political action, to overcome barriers to provision of collective goods, to form coalitions, and to act cooperatively or not? From this perspective, we would like to discover and report whether an institutional environment permits an individual to act without restraint or whether it limits her actions, penalizes her behavior, or counterbalances her individual actions. In effect, we seek to understand the checks and balances in institutional settings. This focus allows us to simplify the description of institutional settings and more easily compare one institutional setting to another. Instead of exploring the variety and nuances of institutional arrangements, we ask whether an institutional environment imposes more or less discipline in the form of checks and balances on policy makers—and how much more or less. Differences in electoral systems, structures of government, and regime types can be viewed as describing the constraints on policy makers.

> **Veto points** are constraints, checks, or countervailing pressures that affect policy makers' ability to select a course of action unilaterally.

We call such institutionally created checks and balances **veto points** in a political economy. Veto points are instances in which a policy maker faces constraints, checks, or countervailing pressures that limit her ability to select a course of action unilaterally. The fewer the veto points in a political economy, the greater the ability of a policy maker to decide policy unilaterally. Where there are more veto points, a policy maker must build support for policies among a wider range of constituencies. For example, in an authoritarian regime, a policy maker encounters far fewer institutional veto points than does a policy maker in a democratic regime with a federal structure and separation between the executive and the legislature. In democratic regimes the ultimate veto point is the will of a broad-based electorate. In an authoritarian regime the ultimate veto point is usually the will of a far smaller selectorate to which the ruler owes her power. A system with fewer veto points is conducive to a policy maker's unilaterally and arbitrarily shifting course if she so desires, which can feed policy volatility and uncertainty in political economies. Conversely, a policy maker facing multiple veto points or players generally has far less policy flexibility— which limits policy volatility and can reduce uncertainty.

We lose the nuance of institutional differences in such generalized characterizations of political economies, but we capture important comparable factors that help to explain variations in political behavior. There are limitations to such a summary approach to institutional settings. By definition, institutions are supposedly durable, which means that institutional settings are sticky and do not change quickly overtime. But policies can change, and if policies shift while the institutional setting as characterized by veto points remains the same, we may encounter a problem of assigning causal responsibility to the institutional setting. We can overcome this dilemma by disaggregating the veto points and examining specific institutions to discover whether institutional arrangements are or are not influential, but this disaggregation limits comparability and generalizability. The strength of the summary approach comes in comparisons across cases. Here, even though the summarization of the institutional setting and institutional checks and balances should vary little within each case, variations across cases can provide leverage that allows us to understand and anticipate the nature of political conflict or cooperation from society to society, the nature of policy volatility from state to state, and the different abilities of societies to overcome social traps and create productive social environments. This comparative process can lead to a fuller understanding of social behavior and provide insights that may help policy makers to design institutional settings that can improve the lot of their societies.

CONCLUSION

Institutions can reduce uncertainty, produce incentives, constrain options, induce equilibrium, influence the shadow of the future, create *ex ante* bargains over future actions, and affect the time-inconsistency problem. Normatively good institutions limit destructive individual actions, extend the shadow of the future, overcome the time-inconsistency problem, lead to better equilibria, and help societies to overcome barriers to cooperation and social traps. But dysfunctional institutions can generate perverse incentives that encourage individuals to engage in actions that damage social welfare, lead to poor equilibria, exacerbate the time-inconsistency problem, and perpetuate social traps. We have noted that many institutional alternatives exist across political economies. Differences in regime types, electoral systems, structures of government, social bargains and arrangements, and other institutional arrangements create tremendous variations in the nature of institutions and their potential effects across political arenas. Understanding the rules of the game that such institutional arrangements create can reduce uncertainty in social interactions, stabilize expectations, and guide individuals as they make choices about their activities within and across national boundaries.

KEY CONCEPTS

institution (p. 278)

path dependence (p. 286)

path contingency (p. 286)

satisficing (p. 289)

structurally induced
equilibrium (p. 285)

veto points (p. 311)

EXERCISES

1. Using the definition of an institution in this chapter, is the WTO an institution? Why or why not?

2. What is the difference between a formal and an informal institution? Give examples of each type, and explain why each fits its respective category.

3. Do formal institutions exist in international affairs, given the definition of a formal institution? Explain.

4. How can an institution be an equilibrium?

5. Give an example of an institution that affects global affairs and helps to overcome the time-inconsistency problem. Explain how it promotes time-consistent behavior.

6. Give an example of an institution that shortens the shadow of the future and encourages individuals to act against the well-being of their society. Why does it do this?

7. Give an example of an institution that extends the shadow of the future and encourages individuals to make choices that improve long-term social welfare. Why does it do this?

8. Provide an example of an institution that affects global affairs, and discuss the distributional implications of that institution. Who wins and who loses?

9. Explain why institutions may be sticky and durable. Why are many institutions slow to change?

10. Give an example of an informal institution in world affairs and explain why it is an institution.

11. Hypothesize how differences between a winner-take-all electoral system and a proportional electoral system might affect international trade policy. Explain your reasoning.

12. Central bank independence has become a popular institutional topic, explanatory mechanism, and variable in international and comparative political economy. How does central bank independence act as an institution?

FURTHER READING

Axelrod, Robert. 1984. *The Evolution of Cooperation*. New York: Basic Books.

Axelrod, Robert, and Robert O. Keohane. 1986. "Achieving Cooperation under Anarchy: Strategies and Institutions." In *Cooperation under Anarchy,* edited by Kenneth A. Oye. Princeton, NJ: Princeton University Press.

Calvert, Randall. 1995. "The Rational Choice Theory of Social Institutions: Cooperation, Coordination, and Communication." In *Modern Political Economy: Old Topics, New Directions,* edited by Jeffrey S. Banks and Eric A. Hanushek. New York: Cambridge University Press.

Clague, Christopher, Philip Keefer, Stephen Knack, and Mancur Olson. 1996. "Property and Contract Rights under Democracy and Dictatorship." *Journal of Economic Growth* 1, no. 2 (June): 243–276.

Cukierman, Alex, Steven Webb, and Bilin Neyapti. 1992. "Measuring the Independence of Central Banks and Its Effect on Policy Outcomes." *World Bank Economic Review* 6, no. 1: 353–398.

Filippov, Mikhail, Peter C. Ordeshook, and Olga Shvetsova. 2004. *Designing Federalism: A Theory of Self-Sustainable Federal Institutions*. Cambridge: Cambridge University Press.

Garrett, Geoffrey, and Peter Lange. 1995. "Internationalization, Institutions, and Political Change." *International Organization* 49, no. 4: 627–655.

Keohane, Robert O. 1984. *After Hegemony: Cooperation and Discord in the World Political Economy*. Princeton, NJ: Princeton University Press.

Knight, Jack. 1992. *Institutions and Social Conflict*. Cambridge: Cambridge University Press.

Krasner, Stephen, ed. 1983. *International Regimes*. Ithaca, NY: Cornell University Press.

Maxfield, Sylvia. 1997. *Gatekeepers of Growth*. Princeton, NJ: Princeton University Press.

McGillivray, Fiona. 2004. *Privileging Industry: The Comparative Politics of Trade and Industrial Policy*. Princeton, NJ: Princeton University Press.

North, Douglass C. 1990. *Institutions, Institutional Change, and Economic Performance*. Cambridge: Cambridge University Press.

North, Douglass C., and Barry R. Weingast. 1989. "Constitutions and Commitment: Evolution of Institutions Governing Public Choice in 17th Century England." *Journal of Economic History* 49: 803–832.

Olson, Mancur. 1993. "Dictatorship, Democracy and Development." *American Political Science Review* 87, no. 3: 567–576.

Schotter, Andrew. 1981. *The Economic Theory of Social Institutions*. Cambridge: Cambridge University Press.

Shepsle, Kenneth A. 1986. "Institutional Equilibrium and Equilibrium Institutions." In *Political Science: The Science of Politics*, edited by Herbert Weisberg. New York: Agathon Press.

Tsebelis, George. 2002. *Veto Players: How Political Institutions Work*. New York: Russell Sage Foundation and Princeton University Press.

Part III
Context

Around the World in Eighty Days: A Stage of Modern Globalization

Under a system of perfectly free commerce, each country naturally devotes its capital and labour to such employments as are most beneficial to each. This pursuit of individual advantage is admirably connected with the universal good of the whole. By stimulating industry, by rewarding ingenuity, and by using most efficaciously the peculiar powers bestowed by nature, it distributes labour most effectively and most economically: while by increasing the general mass of productions, it diffuses general benefit, and binds together by one common tie of interest and intercourse the universal society of nations throughout the civilized world.

—*David Ricardo, The Principles of Political Economy and Taxation, 1817*

The 1800s were dramatic in terms of changes in globalization and the economic geography of international exchange and finance. British hegemonic leadership provided the collective goods discussed in chapter 6, which helped overcome the risk and uncertainty that hampered international trade. With this scaffolding, the market exchange described in chapters 3 and 4 flourished and expanded across borders. Concurrently, national political arenas underwent transformations as suffrage expanded and individual choices exercised through elections and other representative mechanisms, as described in chapter 4, became more and more common. British public and private financial capabilities promoted global economic expansion and state development, and stabilized the global economy at times of stress. Mass migrations transformed the political economies of the New World and the Old World, particularly those countries that have come to be categorized as the *Atlantic economy.* These political economies seemed to be embarking on a golden era of liberal market exchange and democratization.

GLOBALIZATION IS NOTHING NEW

Globalization became a popular topic toward the end of the twentieth century. At that time, much of the commentary approached globalization as a fascinating new phenomenon that would radically transform relations within and between states. This perspective, which still dominates in the early twenty-first century, is naive because it neglects the historical record. In fact, the globalization of market relations and the accompanying transformation in political and social relations was under way well before the latter half of the twentieth century. Modern globalization began more than a century earlier, linking the political economies that made up the Atlantic economy and helping to fuel their economic and political transformations. Its roots date even earlier if one includes the activities of the Dutch from the 1600s. Economists, philosophers, and policy makers of the eighteenth and nineteenth centuries devised the theoretical underpinnings of today's economic globalization and pushed for the policy reforms that started us down the road of increasing interdependence and global capitalism. The changes they unleashed helped to reshape the global hierarchy as well as the social and political contracts within states. The forces of economic transformation and globalization also pressed for increased political rights and democratization of political spheres. Those states that partook of globalization—the movement of goods, capital, services, information, and people across national boundaries—experienced tremendous surges in economic welfare and in the advance of political rights and liberties.

The United Kingdom played the central role in the evolution, invention, and implementation of ideas, policies, and technologies that provided the scaffolding for the political and economic changes of globalization and democratization in the 1800s. As the dominant political economy of the nineteenth century, it embarked on what came to be known as the Industrial Revolution before other political economies did so. British scientists, industrialists, and markets invented and funded technologies that brought distant societies closer together, lowered the costs of transport, and reduced the time lapse of distant communication. British economists and philosophers created ideas that set an intellectual agenda for capitalism and market exchange within and across state boundaries. British politicians and policy makers adopted those ideas and turned them into commercial, monetary, and military policies that lowered barriers to international exchange. British financiers developed instruments and strategies that helped finance technological and scientific advances that lowered barriers to international exchange and helped manage the risks that had hindered such exchange. London succeeded Amsterdam as the center of global finance. The significant size of London's capital markets and the effectiveness of those markets established the British as the bankers to the expansion of global capitalism.

Intentionally or not, British policy makers and private financiers provided a handful of the important collective goods discussed extensively in chapter 6: supporting a relatively open market for distress goods, providing countercyclical and stable long-term lending, supporting a stable system of exchange rates, promoting the coordination of macroeconomic policies across states, and acting as a lender of last resort to the international system among others. Remember the discussion of collective goods in chapter 5. Sometimes called a *public good* or a *common good*, in its simplest form a collective good is a commodity

> The **principle of nonexclusion** holds that if any member of a group can consume a good, then any other member of that group must also be able to consume that good.

that, if consumed by one member of a group, cannot be withheld from others in the group. Any such commodity that is available to one member of a group must be available to all members of that group—this is the **principle of nonexclusion.** There are other characteristics of a collective good, but let's focus on the impossibility of excluding members of a group from consuming the commodity in question. In the case of nineteenth-century Great Britain, the collective was defined much more broadly, to include those engaged in the global economy.

These collective goods provided mechanisms that increased liquidity, capital, in the international economy during good times and bad. Capital as a primary input to production is critical to productive economic activity, which helps limit economic tensions and conflict between states. Such liquidity underpinned economic expansion, international exchange, and the interstate cooperation necessary to productive globalization. The collective goods provided by British markets and government actions increased the gains from cooperation around liberal market exchange across borders, raised the costs of defection from such policies, reduced temptations for national policy makers to adopt policies that would shift costs of adjustment to economic dislocations abroad, and helped manage crises that could threaten stability and growth in the global economy. These collective goods provided scaffolding that helped lubricate and sustain international cooperation and socially productive economic interactions during good times and assisted in managing and limiting dislocations during bad times. Their availability furnished resources and markets that encouraged growth, stabilized expectations of economic actors, helped reduce volatility and crises in the global arena, and allowed those actors to overcome their fears about the risk of investment and exchange across state boundaries. Other states also took advantage of such goods, to help manage the risks involved in globalization and lower the potential costs of exchange. Other nations contributed to the first big wave of modern globalization, but the United Kingdom took the lead and set the pace.

The bout of globalization that began around the beginning of the nineteenth century was rooted in an evolution of intellectual thought, public policy change, technological shifts, and the activities of private economic actors in markets for goods and capital. Changes in these arenas led to lower national barriers to international exchange, increasingly integrated commodity markets, convergence in prices across many economies, development of a global capital market based in London, and mass migrations from one state to another. Such changes linked national economies and created winners among those who profited from the tremendous expansion of trade in goods, services, and capital. But those changes also created losers in societies. Those who were losing from the changes wrought by economic modernization and globalization were confronted by a choice between making costly adjustments to the changing state of affairs and using the political arena to resist such changes and defend the old status quo. This chapter considers the activities and changes that fueled globalization in this early period.

INTELLECTUAL CHANGE: COMPARATIVE ADVANTAGE AND EFFICIENCY IMPROVE SOCIAL WELFARE

Despite the tendency of pundits, policy makers, businessmen, and others to downplay the contributions of academics and their ideas in comparison to the activities of those in business and government, academics have played an important role in the progress of civilization. The economist John Maynard Keynes, who developed ideas that helped to transform political economy in the twentieth century, put it elegantly:

> The ideas of economists and political philosophers, both when they are right and when they are wrong, are more powerful than is commonly understood. Indeed the world is ruled by little else. Practical men, who believe themselves to be quite exempt from any intellectual influences, are usually the slaves of some defunct economist.[1]

Indeed, the advance of globalization and global capitalism owes a great debt to intellectuals such as David Hume, Adam Smith, and David Ricardo. In 1817 Ricardo published a series of essays titled *On the Principles of Political Economy and Taxation*. In one of those essays, Ricardo, an intellectual, economist, stockbroker, and member of the British House of Commons, created one of the most elegant and influential ideas in economics. "The Political Economy of International Trade" would prove revolutionary because it introduced the idea of *comparative advantage*. With this essay, Ricardo supplied the intellectual underpinnings for trade among nations regardless of their productive capabilities and advantages.

We discussed the economics of comparative advantage extensively in chapter 3, but we should recognize the historical significance of Ricardo's discovery as well. Paul Samuelson, one of the most influential economists of the twentieth century, called comparative advantage perhaps the only truly important discovery in economics. The principle of comparative advantage represented a revolution in economic thought that challenged and soon replaced absolute advantage as the accepted trade theory of the time. Extending intranational market exchange to the international arena required overcoming intellectual, political, and physical barriers to cross-border exchange that were entrenched in the public policies of the early 1800s. Economists had made arguments for free trade between states before Ricardo's essay, but they had justified it only under conditions of absolute advantage. Ricardo's innovation was in showing that international trade could be advantageous even for a state that enjoyed absolute advantage in every form of production. Comparative advantage demonstrated that

---

[1]John Maynard Keynes, *The General Theory of Employment, Interest and Money* (1936; repr., New York: Classic Books, 2009), 328.

gains from trade depend not on absolute efficiencies and advantage in producing commodities but on differences in relative efficiencies and advantage within and across states. Ricardo's insight meant that differences in labor productivity—and, in later versions such as the Heckscher-Ohlin model, diversity in the distribution of factors of production across nations—created the potential for welfare gains from specialization in production and broader exchange. The combination of specialization and exchange leads to increased benefits, increased welfare, and expanded consumption possibilities for a society—even if it enjoys absolute advantage in the production of every commodity.

Ricardo's arguments about comparative advantage became the center of trade policy debates during the first half of the 1800s, providing powerful leverage for those favoring the expansion of international exchange to use against those opposing the lowering of obstacles to trade. Later, his innovation would become accepted wisdom among economists and policy makers—even when it was ignored. Ricardo's pivotal recognition of the political economy of trade was echoed by John Stuart Mill, who wrote that the "benefit of international trade is a more efficient employment of the productive forces of the world."

SHIFTS IN PUBLIC POLICY AFFECT INTERNATIONAL EXCHANGE

Physical barriers such as mountains and oceans can impose obstacles to the expansion of cross-border exchange. More important than such physical barriers, however, are the human obstructions that such exchange can face, in the form of policies that include tariffs, immigration laws, subsidies, taxes, sanctions, differences in standards such as the gauge of railroad tracks or the type of electrical current, blockades, wars, food and health regulations, currency restrictions, boycotts, export restraints, and other human-made devices that can hinder the flow of commodities, capital, information, and people across state boundaries. Sometimes these policies intervene unintentionally in international exchange, but more often they are created intentionally by governments that shape public policy in response to some preferences in their domestic societies or in exchange for the support of some domestic constituency.

> **Mercantilism** is a system of political economy that dominated Europe after the decline of feudalism. It assumed that government control of foreign trade was important to increase the sovereign's, or government's, access to capital resources that could be used to ensure the prosperity and military security of the state. **Protectionism** is the use of government policies and tools (such as tariffs, quotas, subsidies, restrictive regulations, and tax policy) to restrict trade, usually with an intention of advantaging a political economy's domestic producers and labor at the expense of foreign producers and labor.

Mercantilism and Protectionism as the Legacy of War

The 1800s began with a human-made legacy of **protectionism** and **mercantilism.** From a mercantilist perspective, trade and the international flow of capital were good if they disproportionately fed the coffers of the state's sovereign versus those of foreign sovereigns, and consequently contributed to the political-military might and position of the state. Exchange across borders was viewed as a zero-sum interaction, whereby gains for one side in political-military influence were presumed to be balanced by comparable losses on the other side. This presumption made all parties suspicious of exchange, as they often could not be sure whether they were gaining or losing in this framework.

The mercantilist legacy was a function of interstate conflict. During the seventeenth, eighteenth, and early nineteenth centuries, costly conflicts that originated in Europe colored exchange across boundaries in Europe and between Europe and the New World. These conflicts were trade distorting, which means that trading relations would have looked very different absent those conflicts. By definition, any shift in what states would import or export as a result of conflict, especially prolonged conflict, would also influence production structures in political economies because producers, labor, and consumers would alter their behaviors in response to changes in the price of commodities caused by the intervention of trade-distorting conflict. By 1815—the year of Napoleon's defeat at Waterloo by troops under the command of the Duke of Wellington—the flow of goods, capital, technology, and people had been heavily influenced by military events.

This legacy proved durable, carrying over into the peace that followed the years of intermittent conflict. By then, the production structures of the European economies had adapted to limited trade and the conflict-generated distortions in trading patterns, from which many economic interests had profited. British beer production and consumption had expanded as war interrupted French wine imports. The cross-Channel hostilities reduced food imports from the Continent. British rural and agricultural interests profited from the barriers to exchange, as their crops replaced imports even though continental producers were generally more efficient in the production of many agricultural commodities.

The wars' end raised fears of declining competitiveness for such producers, and not only in Great Britain. Absent the threat of blocked sea-lanes and trading channels, agricultural producers in other European states began to fear the productive capabilities of the New World and of nations on the European periphery, such as Spain and Portugal. In England, members of Parliament from the ruling Tory party reacted by passing legislation to protect British agricultural interests from their new exposure to more efficient foreign producers. The British Corn Law of 1815 limited the sale of imported grain when the price of domestically produced grain fell below a specified level. This law had the effect of sometimes closing British markets to foreign grain and thus inflating the price of domestic grain by limiting market supply. It allowed inefficient British producers to avoid searching for more efficient production strategies or, worse, to change enterprises entirely.

As predicted by the Heckscher-Ohlin model of trade, these protections sheltered and rewarded the less abundant factors of production—in the British case, the rural land interests—while the relatively more abundant factors of production, capital and labor, which were located in the cities, lost out as the costs of food increased. By now the United Kingdom had embarked on the Industrial Revolution, the first political economy to do so. This revolution in economic production radically transformed the use of capital and other factors of production to increase output dramatically, which led to an increase in wealth, economic opportunity, consumption possibilities, and collective welfare. British capital-intensive labor and land production produced the highest-paid workers in the world as their efforts were rewarded by the Industrial Revolution and expanding globalization. The Corn Law protections worked against the interests of those benefiting from the Industrial Revolution and expanding trade. This pattern of protection for less abundant factors of production was repeated across Europe. Some nations protected agriculture, while others, such as Sweden, Russia, and France, limited the importation of manufactured products in order to shield less competitive domestic producers. In a sense, these protections were an attempt to maintain the status quo by locking in the gains created by the French-British wars' massive intervention in trading patterns. Governments enacting such protections sought to resist the dynamic forces that would be unleashed on production structures by more liberal trading relations.

The Rise of British Protrade Political and Policy Pressures

The British Parliament revised the Corn Law in 1828, replacing the prohibitions against grain imports tied to domestic prices with tariffs that varied inversely with the price of grain in the domestic market—higher grain prices in the domestic market meant lower tariffs, while lower prices brought higher tariffs. However, the protections of both the original and revised versions would soon come under attack and be whittled away as a policy competition developed between opposing interests in British society. Rural agricultural interests favored the Corn Law protections because they maintained relatively high prices for agricultural commodities and kept their products competitive against those of foreign producers. But these artificially high agricultural prices penalized labor and capital, which made up the manufacturing sector, thus feeding a growing rural-urban divide in British politics. Rural interests dominated the Tory party, while the urban interests sought representation through the Whig party. Under the leadership of Richard Cobden, opponents to the Corn Law formed the Anti–Corn Law League, which drew its strength from the manufacturing centers of Manchester and other cities.

Political Reform and Expansion of Suffrage Affect Market Exchange

Pressures for political institutional reforms, which would change the nature of representation and elections in the United Kingdom, coincided with the growing divide over trade and boosted the momentum for a shift to more liberal trade policies. Demographic changes had led to a growing disconnect between British society and the House of Commons, supposedly the representative institution in the British political system. Never very representative of the broader British society, the House of Commons had become even less representative as the weight of the English population shifted northward and into the industrial urban centers.

Because the voting franchise was extremely limited—the right to vote restricted predominantly to major landowners—a small number of men, many who were members of the House of Lords, elected most of the House of Commons. A significant portion of these powerful lords reflected the interests of the southern and rural regions even as the United Kingdom was becoming more urban.

As revolutionary disturbances on the Continent echoed across the English Channel, reformers sought to transform the electoral rules for selecting members of the House of Commons to make that body more representative of British society. A Whig electoral reform proposal was rejected in 1830 by the Tory government, led by the Duke of Wellington (of Waterloo fame), who served as prime minister. His unwillingness to compromise led to a loss of confidence in the Tory government, however, and the Whigs took over control of the government. After several failed attempts, the Whigs succeeded in passing an electoral reform bill in the House of Commons. It passed the Tory-dominated House of Lords and became law in 1832, but only after rioting threatened the foundations of British government.

The Reform Bill of 1832 expanded suffrage—increased the size of the electorate. The changes in electoral law began to redistribute electoral power by class and geography and injected increasingly active two-party competition into British politics. The size of the electorate grew by more than 50 percent, although still only about one-eighth of the total British adult male population had the right to vote after this reform. This political institutional shift increased the representation of those in British society who benefited from expanded international exchange. Labor and the middle classes gained political power, particularly in the industrial towns and among the business interests. Ironically, after the changes wrought by the Reform Bill, the conservative Tories became the advocates for industrialized labor, promoting restrictions on child

PAPA COBDEN TAKING MASTER ROBERT A FREE TRADE WALK.

Papa Cobden.—"Come along, Master Robert, do step out."
Master Robert.—"That's all very well, but you know I cannot go so fast as you do."

In an 1845 political cartoon published in the magazine *Punch,* Richard Cobden, founder of the Anti–Corn Law League, leads British prime minister Robert Peel to free trade. To rally opposition to the protectionist Corn Law, Cobden and other free trade advocates appealed to the preference of consumer, urban, and industry interests for low-priced imported corn and other grains. Peel rejected the protectionist interests of his Conservative Party and embraced the concept of free trade. The adoption of free trade as a policy principle helped the United Kingdom expand its trading empire, position itself at the heart of the emerging liberal global economy, and build its hegemonic leadership.

labor and a ten-hour workday. Despite these reforms and the political advances of the industrialized middle classes, labor still suffered, and its continued disproportionate exclusion from elections and government fed a rising interest in socialism and Chartism, both anticapitalist movements that advocated the formation of labor unions and working-class representation in elections.

Repeal of the Corn Laws

By the mid-1830s, British prime minister Robert Peel, a Tory and son of a cotton manufacturer, began to reverse course on the Corn Law protections and to decry the government barriers to trade. In opposition to the majority of their party, Prime Minister Peel and the Duke of Wellington joined forces with Cobden and his Anti–Corn Law League to seek the repeal of the Corn Laws. Peel was reacting to a changing political and economic landscape. Shifts in English economic activity because of the accelerating Industrial Revolution transferred economic importance away from rural agricultural landlords and toward the capital and labor of manufacturing and industrial production located heavily in urban areas. A growing intellectual awareness—owing to the work of Ricardo and other economists—of the gains from trade was also contributing to changes in political discourse. Finally, Peel realized that the increased prices for food caused by the Corn Laws damaged the living standards of middle- and working-class people, who were gathering economic power and political influence. His recognition of these circumstances helped to transform Peel from a protectionist to a free trader; in 1846 the Corn Laws were repealed, largely as a result of his efforts.

Peel's conversion to **free trade** took considerable political courage, even with the shifting political economic landscape, because it conflicted with the immediate interests of his political party and its most influential constituents. The strife his actions created within the ranks of the Tory party effectively destroyed his political career. Perhaps the repeal was inevitable, given the growing importance of British manufacturing and the Industrial Revolution, but Peel's courageous stand was a key element in the liberalization of trade barriers and helped to unleash a new chapter in world history.

> **Free trade** is international trade that is free of government intervention such as tariffs, quotas, subsidies, restrictive regulations, tax policy, and other instruments used to shield domestic producers from foreign competition.

Further Expansion of Suffrage in Britain and the Continent Heightens Domestic Pressures on International Exchange

Most of the British male population still lacked the right to vote, despite the significant advance in political liberties brought by the Reform Bill of 1832. However, the forces of economic change, increased labor movement activity, and the promotion of socialism and Chartism fueled demands for greater enfranchisement. In 1867 a Conservative government passed the Second Reform Bill, which extended suffrage to more than one-third of the adult male population. Enlarging the electoral base expanded the range of interests to which elected officials must appeal and thus transformed representation. Protrade interests in society gained more and more electoral clout, reducing the influence of the more protectionist agricultural and rural sectors of society. Hoping to avoid revolution and rebellion, other European nations began to follow the British lead in peaceful transition to wider enfranchisement. Democratic initiatives of differing degrees arose across the Atlantic economy, from the adoption of constitutional monarchies to broad expansions of suffrage, altering the political landscapes and reshaping policy makers' attitudes toward protection and trade.

Initially, the expansion of suffrage tended to empower politically those who gained from international exchange, especially given the United Kingdom's central role in the liberalization of trade policy. But expansion of suffrage is a double-edged sword: those who were disadvantaged by trade—the holders of scarce factors of production—could also be empowered through the pathways of representation and a more accessible political arena. Wider enfranchisement initially supported greater liberalization, but extended suffrage does not inevitably equate to the promotion of protrade policies. With the expansion of representation, all policies became more vulnerable to mass pressures, as politicians recognized that they must appeal to a broader constituency to survive. Because all power is relative, the expansion of political suffrage meant that the middle and working classes inevitably gained political influence and the landed elites lost influence. With greater mass participation, those who successfully organize for political action to advance their preferences can increasingly influence the outcomes of policy debates over the openness of an economy.

Bilateral Trade Treaties and Most-Favored-Nation Status

With the British move to embrace more open trading relations, freer trade was aided by **bilateral trade negotiations**—that is, negotiations between nations. Perhaps even more influential than the repeal of the Corn Laws, the Cobden-Chevalier Treaty of 1860 removed or reduced many of the trade barriers between the United Kingdom and France—the two largest European economies at the time. A host of trade agreements followed Cobden-Chevalier, as Prussia, Belgium, Spain, and other nations signed treaties reducing barriers to international exchange.

Bilateral trade negotiations occur when two nations engage in negotiations with the intent of constructing a reciprocal trade agreement that is undertaken by the two sides and is binding on both parties. **Most-favored-nation status (MFN)** is an international trade mechanism that automatically extends to nations that have such status any trade concessions, such as a lower tariff barrier, that one nation might grant to another.

Cobden-Chevalier introduced a novel and productive mechanism called **most-favored-nation status (MFN)** to international trade agreements. MFN automatically extended any trade concession, such as a lower tariff barrier, to the British or French that either might grant to a third nation. This reciprocal arrangement helped in principle to create a foundation of nondiscrimination, limiting governments' abilities to use trade policy to extend privilege to one country but not to others. Many of

TABLE 9.1	Average Tariff Rates on Manufactured Products, 1820–1913 (in Percentages)		
	1820	*1875*	*1913*
United Kingdom	45–50	0	0
France	*	12–15	20
Germany	8–12	4–6	13
United States	35–45	40–50	44
Italy	*	8–10	18
Russia	*	15–20	84
Japan	*	5	30

Source: Data extracted from Paul Bairoch, *Economics and World History* (Chicago: University of Chicago Press, 1993).

Note: Asterisks indicate that restrictions in importation of manufactured products make calculations of tariff rates insignificant.

the bilateral trade agreements that followed Cobden-Chevalier included MFN clauses, creating a network of bilateral agreements in which a concession to one trading partner would cascade to other trading partners. This automatic extension of market concessions created a potential for more and more liberal trade arrangements systemwide, even though negotiations took place nation by nation through bilateral trade agreements. Little steps could produce large changes. Table 9.1 displays tariff levels for some key states in the global economy. In general, there was a decline in tariff levels during the mid-1800s, which reflected a greater openness to trade.

Other Liberalizing Policy Shifts and a Caveat

Other British policy shifts around this same time helped promote globalization. Loosening of the Navigation Acts, which for years had limited British colonies to trade only with the mother country, and only on British ships, allowed those colonies to begin trading with other nations. A Tory government also lowered emigration barriers that had hindered the emigration of skilled British workers. Both reforms enhanced the international mobility of important economic assets.

Such policy reforms certainly contributed to increased globalization. However, we should keep this history—the repeal of the Corn Laws, the advent of liberalizing bilateral trade agreements, and other policy reforms—in perspective. They may have been *necessary conditions*, but they were not *sufficient conditions* to account for the expansion of global exchange. Even after the lowering of formal barriers to international exchange, those willing to engage in the processes of globalization still faced significant obstacles. Risk, uncertainty, physical difficulties, and other barriers still created impediments to the cross-border mobility of goods, services, people, and information. Let's now consider these other obstacles that needed to be overcome.

THE INFLUENCES OF RISK AND UNCERTAINTY ON INTERNATIONAL TRADE

Those engaged in trade face uncertainties that may affect their willingness to engage in international exchange. They worry about risk arising from contractual commitments across national boundaries and legal jurisdictions. Is a contract in one state considered binding by another government? What are the prospects for one party or another to default on cross-border contractual obligations? Parties to exchange have to assess the stability of exchange rates between different national currencies, as trade across borders involves contracts in a variety of currencies. Will an exchange made today be worth the same tomorrow, next week, or in a month? And the parties have to worry about trade financing and liquidity in the international arena. Will there be sufficient resources available to ensure continued economic expansion and access to capital so that parties to trade can pay their bills?

With the lowering of trade barriers, private economic actors must be willing to take advantage of the new, more open environment if exchange across borders is to succeed and contribute to the expansion of economic welfare. But other factors may affect their willingness to play in the international arena if those factors generate risk or uncertainty that threatens to outweigh the returns on their activities. If risk, or perceived risk, becomes too large, economic actors may decide to refrain from engaging in cross-border economic activity altogether, or demand higher compensation for such activities in order to offset the additional risk. Either way, the elements of risk and uncertainty can limit global exchange even if formal barriers such as tariffs are lowered.

At the heart of these issues of risk and uncertainty are key differences between international exchange and exchange within domestic arenas. Unlike trade conducted within a domestic context, international exchange takes place across multiple legal jurisdictions and legal frameworks, as well as across multiple currency areas. The sheer multiplicity of these structural conditions creates some degree of uncertainty for those engaged in international exchange. If the associated risk factor becomes sufficiently daunting, the prospects for international exchange can break down or be damaged.

Managing Risk and Uncertainty: Incomplete Contracting, Default Risk, and Banker's Acceptances

Participating in international trade requires entering into contractual relationships across borders. An exporter or producer in one nation contracts with an importer in another nation to deliver a particular commodity. Large-scale and efficient exchange rarely involves "cash on the barrelhead." Instead, such exchange almost always uses some form of *credit*— one of the more significant economic inventions in history. Credit is a commitment to pay for today's exchange at some future time, which means that an importer can obtain commodities from an exporter with a promise to pay for those goods by a set time in the future. This arrangement gives the importer time to sell her goods and so obtain the capital necessary for payment. It also allows her to import more goods than she would be able to afford if constrained by her cash on hand. Her inventory can therefore be larger and more diverse, providing her customers a greater range of choice. The terms and value of such exchange are specified in a contract. Often the terms are formally spelled out in legal documents, but sometimes contracts are less formal, as in the diamond trade, where trading frequently takes place over a handshake. Occasionally an importer obtains credit from an exporter, but more typically some third party such as a bank or other financial institution extends credit to the importer. In such situations the exporter is paid promptly and the importer owes money to the banker at some time in the future.

What if one party attempts to change the terms of a contract by delivering something or some amount other than what is expected, or an importer delays or reneges on payment? A buyer or borrower reneging on payment, partially or wholly, consti-

> **Default risk** is the threat that a borrower or a buyer may renege on payment, either partially or wholly.

tutes a **default risk** to the seller. Who adjudicates such a dispute? If the exchange takes place within one legal jurisdiction, this problem is fairly straightforward, although it can still prove problematic. German law governs exchange that takes place between contracting parties within German borders, and German courts adjudicate in the case of disputes between such parties; likewise, U.S. law governs exchange within U.S. borders, and U.S. courts adjudicate disputes. But what about an exchange between a German party and an American party that takes place across national boundaries? Who adjudicates a dispute in such a case, when there is no overarching international authority, international court, or international trade police to assert and enforce a binding resolution?

Short-term incentives almost always exist for one party to renege on an agreement—this is why contracts exist. If there were no incentive for attempting to change the terms of a deal unilaterally, there would be no need for contracts, lawyers, and judges to adjudicate disputes, for disputes would be nonexistent. Consequently, those who specialize in writing contracts (generally members of the legal profession) try to specify the terms and obligations of a deal so as to limit the possibility of one party or another unilaterally changing the terms. Unfortunately, all contracts are incomplete, since even the specialists cannot foresee all the contingencies that may threaten a deal. Moreover, a good contract alone may not be sufficient if one party can later simply state, "I lied," without fear of significant penalty. International trade raises concerns about the likelihood of fair adjudication and enforcement of the terms of a contract across borders. If one party to an exchange is uncertain about the other party's commitment to abide by the contractual terms of the deal, and the mechanisms of adjudication and enforcement are ambiguous because multiple national jurisdictions are involved, beneficial trade may simply not occur.

Fortunately for international exchange, shrewd bankers, first in Amsterdam in the 1600s and then in London in the 1700s and 1800s, solved part of this problem of uncertainty in international trade contracts by expanding and extending ingenious financial instruments called **banker's acceptances** and **letters of credit** to those engaged in such trade. These devices are financial guarantees that a party to an exchange can obtain from her bank to lower the risk and uncertainty of nonpayment of a contractual obligation across national boundaries. How? They replace the individual importer's commitment to pay for an international transaction with the commitment of her bank to pay for that transaction. A trader purchases this service from her bank, which guarantees payment to the other party's bank. A banker's acceptance or letter of credit replaces individual credit with institutional credit (the credit of the bank), thus substituting a bank's reputation for an individual's reputation as a guarantee of payment.

> **Banker's acceptances** are financial instruments that a party to an exchange can obtain from a bank to lower the risk of nonpayment of an obligation across national boundaries. They are promises of future payment drawn on deposits at a bank and guaranteed to be paid by that bank. **Letters of credit** are financial instruments that, similar to banker's acceptances, lower the risk and uncertainty of nonpayment of an obligation across national boundaries. They are issued by financial institutions and are generally irrevocable.

Banks do business with other banks frequently and repeatedly, within and across borders, which means that the costs to a bank for reneging on a contract are high—a bank would not want to develop a reputation for unreliability among other banks, as it would then encounter increasing difficulty in conducting business. Meanwhile, the importer must agree to pay her bank for the banker's acceptance or letter of credit, thus incurring a legal obligation to the bank. Because this credit contract usually takes place within one nation's boundaries, any contractual dispute that occurs between the importer and her bank gets adjudicated within the importer's national courts. This poses a more credible and binding threat of adjudication and enforcement on the importer than would be the case if the dispute were to involve some form of cross-border adjudication. Banker's acceptances and letters of credit thus serve to limit uncertainty and risk about payment obligations across national boundaries.

Managing the Problems of Currency Risk: Monetary Regimes

Multiple currencies also create risk and uncertainty for those engaged in international exchange. Unlike trade between Connecticut and New Hampshire, in which the inhabitants of both states use the dollar, trade between the United States and Germany involves two different currencies, the dollar and the euro. These currencies fluctuate in relation to each other, and, at any given time, one may be more stable or valued as money (a tool of exchange, a storehouse of value, and a unit of accounting, as defined in chapter 3). This situation of flux is called a foreign exchange or **currency risk.** If, in a trade contract, the importer or the importer's bank promises to pay a specified amount in a particular currency at some point in the future, any relative decline in the value of that currency before that time means that the exporter or the exporter's bank receives less than anticipated for the exchange. Over the course of the contract period, the exchange has declined in value for the exporter and increased in value for the importer. Conversely, if the currency in which the trade is denominated appreciates in value, the reverse hap-

> **Currency risk** is uncertainty about exchange rates owing to the fluctuations of currencies vis-à-vis each other. An **international monetary regime** is a set of formal and informal rules, conventions, and norms that govern international financial transactions—the monetary and financial relations between states. It specifies what policy instruments governments may use, what those instruments can legitimately target as policy, and when they can be used.

pens. Some currency fluctuation is a risk that is accepted as part of the cost of doing business, especially if the movements in currency values are relatively predictable. Indeed, large markets in currency futures have emerged since the mid-1970s to help manage such risks by allowing those engaged in international exchange to "lock in" a future price for a currency. But what if great uncertainty exists over the valuation of national currencies? Then traders who cannot comfortably anticipate the future value of their exchanges may become reluctant to engage in exchange priced in those currencies, or they may simply demand immediate payment, which also reduces trade.

The problem of pricing one currency vis-à-vis another is a function of what we call an **international monetary regime** or system. Such a regime is a set of formal and informal rules, conventions, and norms that govern international financial transactions—the monetary and financial relations between states. A monetary regime specifies what policy instruments governments may use, what those instruments can legitimately target as policy, and when they can be used. In the early 1800s, a variety of monetary systems existed across national economies. Some countries used gold as the standard of value for their currency, others used gold and silver (called *bimetallism*), and a few found other standards. These differences in state preferences and choices spilled across borders to create uncertainties in the valuation of currencies internationally and so posed obstacles to international exchange. In *Globalizing Capital: A History of the International Monetary System* (1996), economic historian Barry Eichengreen notes:

> The international monetary system is the glue that binds national economies together. Its role is to lend order and stability to foreign exchange markets. . . . Nations find it difficult to efficiently exploit the gains from trade and foreign lending in the absence of an adequately functioning international monetary mechanism.

Beliefs about currency risk can either undermine or facilitate trade. Too much risk and uncertainty about a currency or currencies can drive exchange away from those currencies by triggering **Gresham's law,** which states that bad money drives out good

> **Gresham's law** is an economic principle that states that bad money drives out good money, but it generalizes to any market or exchange wherein people encounter difficulties distinguishing between good and bad versions of a commodity.

money. Centuries ago, a coin's value was determined by its precise weight—the amount of gold or silver it contained. Some people would shave the edges off their coins, harvesting small amounts of gold or silver each time; when they had enough metal, they would mint a new coin. But this process left the shaved coins no longer worth their specified value. If enough uncertainty existed over whether coins were shaved or not, merchants might decide not to accept any of the coins in question, whether good or bad. Hence, bad money (the shaved coins) would drive out, or devalue, good money (the unshaved coins). Many coins today have ridges on their edges to discourage shaving, or at least to allow the parties to an exchange to recognize that a coin has been shaved. Gresham's law is specifically about commodities that serve the function of money, but its logic generalizes to any market or exchange where people encounter difficulties distinguishing between good and bad versions of a commodity. Overcoming currency risk and uncertainty requires convincing parties to international exchange either that fluctuations in a currency's value are unlikely to occur or that they are predictable and manageable. Parties to an exchange must be reasonably confident that the exchange will not lose its expected value because of currency risk. The potential unpredictability of the relative prices of currencies has led traders to prefer denominating their trade contracts in currencies that have track records and reputations for relative reliability and stability—a statement not just about the particular currency but also about the government that issued that currency.

THE GOLD STANDARD AND STABLE EXCHANGE RATES

In the mid- to late 1800s, currency risk and uncertainty were reduced, and stability of expectations enhanced, by convergence on a particular international monetary regime and exchange-rate system called the **gold standard.** The governments of the Atlantic economy enhanced beliefs in the stability and value of their currencies by making commitments to maintain the value of their currencies vis-à-vis gold. British finance, both public and private, underpinned the success of this exchange-rate system.

The **gold standard** is a monetary regime in which governments set their currency values relative to gold.

By setting their currencies to gold, governments established the exchange rates of their currencies in relation to other currencies that also were fixed to gold. Gold became the mediation mechanism, stabilizing the number of French francs that an economic actor would exchange for a British pound, the number of American dollars for a British pound or a German mark, and so on. Table 9.2 displays the values of national currencies in gold—their exchange rates—during the gold standard era of the latter 1800s.

At the beginning of the nineteenth century, prior to the convergence on the gold standard, a mix of different national monetary arrangements coexisted. Great Britain was on a de facto gold standard, while the Scandinavian states, Russia, the German states, and others used a silver standard for their currency and international payments. France, the United

TABLE 9.2	**Currency Values in Terms of Gold during the Late 1800s**		
Country	Currency	Value of 1 unit of national currency in U.S. dollars ($)	Value of 1 ounce of gold in national currency
Australia	Pound	4.86	4.2
Austria-Hungary	Corona	.202	102.32
Belgium	Franc	.193	107.09
Denmark	Krone	.268	77.13
Finland	Markka	.193	107.09
France	Franc	.193	107.09
Germany	Mark	.238	86.85
Great Britain	Pound	4.86	4.25
Greece	Drachma	.193	107.09
India (British)	Rupee	.444	46.55
Italy	Lira	.193	107.09
Romania	Leu	.193	107.09
Russia	Ruble	.514	40.21
Spain	Peseta	.193	107.09
Sweden	Krona	.268	77.13
United States	Dollar	1	20.67

Source: Adapted from Hugo S. Cunningham, *Gold and Silver Standards* (1999); http://www.cyberussr.com/hcunn/gold-std.html.

States, and most others employed a bimetallic standard based on gold and silver. A range of systems based on different mixtures of gold, silver, and copper served as the basis for settling international obligations—the deficits and surpluses in the balance of payments.

The convergence toward gold as the official reserve asset began by accident in the eighteenth century when the British mint, the maker of coin, set too low a price for silver. Speculators then exchanged other assets for British silver and moved their silver holdings abroad to where they would be worth more, thus draining silver from circulation in the United Kingdom. Absent the availability of silver coin in the United Kingdom, gold coin became the British standard. As the result of a poor pricing decision by the British mint, which created arbitrage opportunities for investors, and without any official declaration, the United Kingdom thus informally adopted a gold standard.

Portugal, which enjoyed significant trade with the United Kingdom partly as a result of the British-French wars of the latter 1700s, shifted solely to gold in 1854. This reduced currency uncertainty for the Portuguese with importers in their principal market abroad. France and other European states moved away from bimetallism to gold in the 1870s. Germany's adoption of the mark in 1871, based on gold, moved another large political economy into the gold column and added momentum to the convergence on gold. By 1879, the United States also was on the gold standard for all intents and purposes, albeit unofficially. By the end of the century, most European nations had switched to gold, either de jure or de facto.

Debates over Alternatives to the Gold Standard

Although some believe that the gold standard is unique in reducing risk and uncertainty, other international monetary arrangements can provide stability and limit currency risk just as well. Governments could have supported some standard other than gold. Why not converge on some other standard, as long as it meets the three functional conditions of money—tool of exchange, unit of accounting, and storehouse of value? Any commodity or item that meets these conditions and is accepted by enough parties could serve as the core of an international monetary regime. In fact, gold had some troubling shortcomings that would eventually threaten its role as the monetary standard.

For many, a monetary system based on something other than gold was preferable. In the early 1800s, prospects existed for other monetary systems, such as a silver standard or a bimetallic standard based on gold and silver. At midcentury, gold was in much more limited supply than silver. An influx of gold from discoveries in California and Australia temporarily improved the balance between gold and silver, which led to a decline in the price of gold in relation to silver. In 1859, however, large silver discoveries in Nevada reversed that trend and brought a flood of silver into the international markets. Maintaining a bimetallic standard became more difficult for governments. Large swings in the quantity and value of gold against silver played havoc with nations on a bimetallic standard, alternately causing large gold inflows and large silver outflows, followed by large gold outflows and large silver inflows. This threatened the stability of exchange rates. In particular, France and the United States found the resulting swings in exchange rates troubling. The intense variability in capital flows placed pressures on national mints and treasuries, and on prices in international exchange. Those on silver or bimetallic standards faced threats of **inflation** as the abundance of silver worked to drive up prices in those economies—remember Hume's arguments about the positive relationship between the size of the money supply and prices, discussed in chapter 3. Despite the resulting variability in prices, the threat of inflation from the growing supply of silver, and the apparent stabilizing benefits of a shift to an international gold standard, some governments on bimetallic or silver standards resisted converting to a more stable gold standard. Why?

Political dissension and policy debates over bimetallism versus gold affected many national political arenas. Silver-mining interests and agricultural interests resisted convergence on a gold standard. Demand by government mints for silver as part of bimetallic regimes propped up the price of silver. Silver-mining interests—those who owned or worked in silver mines—benefited from the demand for silver, which would shrink if it ceased to be a key component of national monetary regimes. Agricultural producers preferred silver for another reason: its abundance relative to gold could promote increases in agricultural and other commodity prices, while a standard based on a scarcer resource such as gold threatened to cause a decline in the price of those commodities, a phenomenon known as commodity price deflation.

> **Inflation** is a persistent increase in money supply that leads to a rise in the level of consumer prices for commodities and services and a decline in the purchasing power of money. It is caused by an increase in available currency and credit beyond the proportion of available goods and services. **Deflation** is a persistent decrease in the level of consumer prices for commodities and services, or a persistent increase in the purchasing power of money because of a reduction in available currency and credit relative to the supply of commodities and services.

Debates over gold versus silver were compounded by the advance of the Industrial Revolution, which increased the production of goods available for consumption and generated more downward pressure on the prices of commodities and services—remember Hume's arguments about the relationship between the size of the money supply and prices. This effect, price **deflation**, hit the agricultural sector particularly hard. Prices fell dramatically in the late 1800s (see table 9.3), causing severe recessions and hardships among agricultural producers. Wheat prices, for example, fell by more than 69 percent from 1867 to 1900. Workers and producers in sectors that were particularly hard-hit by deflation preferred a currency regime based on a commodity or metal in greater supply, such as silver.

The unofficial move by the United States to the gold standard in 1879 failed to end the virulent debate among policy makers and others in American society. The policy competition persisted, finally culminating in 1896 with the presidential election between William Jennings Bryan and William McKinley—an election that demarcated a major turning point in the U.S. outlook on world affairs. Bryan, a Democratic Populist, attracted strong support among agricultural and mining interests located in the South, the Midwest, and parts of the West. He campaigned for bimetallism and warned that the gold standard would crucify American farmers "on a cross of gold." McKinley, a Republican, drew strong support from the banking and manufacturing sectors, which preferred the price stability of the gold standard. McKinley's victory in this pivotal election confirmed the U.S. commitment to the gold standard. It also represented a victory for those anticipating a growing U.S. role and responsibility in the global arena over those favoring more insular and inward-looking policies.

The 1896 election provided the context for journalist L. Frank Baum's *The Wonderful Wizard of Oz,* a biting social and political commentary on the contemporary divisions in U.S. society and politics disguised as a children's story. Baum's story captures the tension between

TABLE 9.3   Price Deflation of Agricultural Commodities, 1867–1900

Commodity	1867	1870	1873	1876	1879	1882	1885	1888	1891	1894	1897	1900	Decrease over this period (%)
					Prices								
Barley	1.22	0.853	0.963	0.685	0.599	0.631	0.557	0.591	0.522	0.437	0.343	0.407	66.6
Corn	0.781	0.521	0.483	0.361	0.364	0.481	0.322	0.331	0.398	0.451	0.26	0.35	55.2
Cotton				9.71	10.28	9.12	8.39	8.5	7.24	4.59	6.68	9.2	5.3
Hay	14.3	14.45	14.4	9.8	9.63	9.99	10.07	9.24	8.65	8.98	7.21	9.78	31.6
Oats	0.587	0.426	0.374	0.349	0.326	0.371	0.279	0.27	0.306	0.32	0.21	0.253	56.9
Wheat	2.01	1.04	1.17	1.04	1.11	0.888	0.772	0.927	0.831	0.489	0.809	0.621	69.1
Potatoes	1.51	1.18	1.16	1.1	0.72	0.91	0.73	0.65	0.6	0.89	0.92	0.72	52.3
Sweet potatoes	1.93	1.61	1.42	1	1.02	0.93	0.86	0.9	0.88	0.92	52.3		

Source: U.S. Department of Agriculture, National Agricultural Statistics Service.

eastern banking and industrial interests, the Wicked Witches of the East and West, and agrarian-labor interests, the Good Witches of the North and South. The Wizard is President McKinley, Oz is the abbreviation for *ounce* (the common measure of gold's weight), Emerald City represents Washington, D.C., and Dorothy and her admirable companions on the Yellow Brick Road are those opposed to the "cross of gold" policies that favored banking and industrial interests. Dorothy's silver slippers click on the yellow bricks, thus suggesting the bimetal mix of gold and silver. The Cowardly Lion symbolizes William Jennings Bryan, the witless Scarecrow represents farmers, and the rusty Tin Man typifies industrial workers. The American spirit is celebrated in their bravery, their wisdom, and their heart, and by Dorothy's wholesome goodness. You'll never see Judy Garland's character in the same light again!

Why Converge on a Gold Standard?

Why did gold prevail as the standard, rather than bimetallism or some other reserve asset? Why did enough governments converge on gold to make it the heart of an international monetary system? Once again, Great Britain played a pivotal role, as British trade and monetary policies generated pressures on others to converge on the gold standard. British economic capabilities, especially in public and private finance, placed the United Kingdom at the center of the global economy and gave it the

THE SACRILEGIOUS CANDIDATE.

While advocating populist causes and during a run for the presidency in 1896, William Jennings Bryan warned against crucifying U.S. agricultural producers on "a cross of gold." The adoption of a gold standard ensured price stability. However, the government's inability to increase money supply during a period of great increases in productivity and rapid economic expansion contributed to severe price deflation in primary products, resulting in a recession in the agricultural sector that devastated its producers. Appealing to banking and industrial interests, William McKinley prevailed in the election, and the United States continued to adhere to the gold standard.

capacity to act as the hegemonic stabilizer (as described in chapter 6) and influence the choices of other states over exchange-rate and trade policies. With a rapidly expanding economy resulting from the Industrial Revolution and the accompanying rise in household incomes, British consumers had more disposable income to lavish on commodities than did consumers in other countries. As lower barriers to trade made it possible for them to decide to spend part of this new prosperity on foreign goods, British markets became increasingly attractive outlets for foreign producers and soon emerged as the center of the globalizing economy. The attractiveness of selling goods to the British markets gave the British political economy disproportionate influence over the choices of others in the global arena. This included British preferences over trade, monetary, and exchange-rate policies.

The United Kingdom led the drift toward a gold standard with its early and de facto, albeit accidental, adoption of the standard in the eighteenth century. The rise of British prowess in international finance and trade gave British preferences disproportionate weight over international monetary policies. The British choice of a gold standard influenced foreign parties that sought to borrow money in London's capital markets or to trade with British merchants. As the international financial center and a source of capital for economic expansion and nation building, London drew borrowers and savers from other nations, who accessed capital and invested in capital markets that were located in a nation adhering to a gold standard. On the trade side, because British markets were the dominant international outlet for foreign producers, the concerns of British importers over exchange-rate risk influenced policy debates in other political economies that wanted to export to British markets—good business requires that producers address their best customers' needs. The attractiveness of Britain's markets, its market power, effectively endowed the British with influence over international monetary and trade matters, whether intentionally manipulated by British policy makers or not. A similar pattern is repeated today in the global economy, as many governments adjust their exchange-rate policies to match those of their dominant trading partners, with the intention of stabilizing currency risk in their most important international economic relationships.

By the early 1870s, the incentives to reduce currency risk in major trading relationships accelerated the convergence on a gold standard. When France and Germany joined the United Kingdom on a gold standard, pressures increased on other nations to demonetize silver—to move away from silver and bimetallism. The expansion of trade made it increasingly difficult for nations to resist the impetus to converge on a gold standard. The pressure increased further with the de facto move to gold by the United States, which was rapidly expanding and moving toward becoming the largest economy in the world. By the late 1800s, with the four largest commercial and trading nations (the United Kingdom, United States, Germany, and France) on the gold standard, most other nations adopted gold as well.

Even with the problems presented by price deflation and the political resistance to gold in some nations, it was extremely difficult and costly for any single nation to maintain a bimetallic standard. A nation's unilateral rejection of the gold standard while others switched to gold would result in the draining of that nation's gold reserves. Speculators would have economic incentives to purchase that nation's gold with silver and then move it abroad. The resistant nation would be left holding only silver reserves, but then would need gold to settle its international payments; this outcome would only make trade more expensive. Once the major nations and markets moved to gold, it became costly for other nations to resist the gold standard without incurring economic costs to their national economies even if specific sectors might benefit from such resistance. This effect has been called a **network externality,** wherein the globalization of trade and finances created

> A **network externality** is a dynamic whereby previous choices made by policy makers in the system spill over to push convergence of future choices on the original choices. It is an artifact of and a contributor to increasing interdependence.

benefits for switching to gold and costs for retaining silver or bimetallism. Silver did not disappear as money, but it no longer served as a major reserve asset. Many nations continued to employ silver coin as well as gold, and many supplemented their gold reserves with reserves of foreign currencies.

The gold standard of the late 1800s and early 1900s enjoyed some notable success in stabilizing the expectations of those engaged in international economic activities and reducing the currency risk that hampered international trade and lending. To the extent that it worked, it succeeded for several key reasons. First, governments converged on a common standard and cooperated to support that standard. Second, governments committed to **convertibility** of their currencies on demand, each agreeing to exchange its currency for gold or for another currency at the established rate of exchange upon request. Committing to convertibility and living up to that commitment, especially when challenged, helped to build governments' reputations and contributed to the stability of the gold standard.

> **Convertibility** is a government's practice of exchanging its currency for another currency or reserve asset at the established rate of exchange upon request.

At the heart of this system sat the British and their commitment to the stability of the exchange-rate mechanism of the gold standard and to convertibility regardless of the choices of other governments in the international arena. Early on, the British government committed to exchanging gold for British pounds sterling upon demand. Its position as the center of global finance and the largest economy helped to make this commitment to convertibility credible—if any government and economy could maintain that commitment, it was that of the United Kingdom. Over time, the British guarantee of convertibility gained increasing credibility as the British Treasury continued to live up to its commitment. Because the United Kingdom was the largest, most influential economy and global capital market, a credible British commitment to convertibility provided the global economy with an important collective good.

Convertibility as a Collective Good

The United Kingdom's credible commitment to convertibility reduced the risks of holding the British pound sterling, which therefore became "as good as gold." People and governments grew more willing to hold the pound sterling for long periods of time and to use it as the currency of choice to settle transactions. Other governments and economic actors increasingly held British pounds as a reserve currency in addition to gold, while more and more contracts and payments in international exchange took place in pounds. Both of these practices lowered currency risk, reduced transaction costs associated with the exchange of gold as part of the international payment process, and further elevated the importance of British capital markets and policy preferences over the rules of the global game. The rise of the pound sterling as an international, extraterritorial money gave the British a tool of substantial influence in world affairs, as the pound's reach extended well beyond the borders of the United Kingdom and the British Empire. As a consequence, the British gained even more influence over the rules and direction of the global economy.

Why Would a Government Renege on a Commitment to Its Currency Price?

Commitment to convertibility and maintenance of a stable exchange rate seem like worthwhile, even obvious, goals for governments. Yet they are not simple tasks for national policy makers as they try to juggle diverse demands from their constituencies. If an exchange-rate system is to stabilize currency prices and reduce the currency risks in international exchange, however, governments' commitments to the prices of their currency and to the rules of the monetary system must be credible, especially for a state whose currency is used heavily in international exchange. In the case of the gold standard, this meant that a government's commitment to the price of its currency in gold, as well as its commitment to convertibility, must prove convincing. If a government could renege on such commitments by simply stating that it had lied about the value of its currency or its willingness to convert its currency on demand, or if private traders believed that such a scenario were probable, then any claims about commitment to such a standard would be viewed as insincere, cheap talk. Why would a government renege on a commitment to its currency price?

Let's think about why a government would lie, mislead, or change its policy toward the commitment to a specific price for its currency or its willingness to convert that currency to some other asset. What might induce a government to undermine its own credibility in this way? Political economy provides some insights. Consider two dynamics that might pressure a government to defect from its commitments: the effect of the exchange-rate mechanism on the competitive stature of the state's economy or sectors in that economy, and the potential for draining the state's monetary reserves.

The **tradable sector** is that portion of an economy where domestic producers of goods and services compete with overseas producers, whether in overseas markets or at home.

First, as we discussed in chapter 3, the exchange-rate mechanism influences pricing in international markets and plays a central role in the adjustment of the balance of payments. A nation's exchange rate affects the prices and competitiveness of its commodities and services both in international markets and in the tradable sector more generally. The **tradable sector** is that arena where domestic producers of goods and services compete with overseas producers, whether in overseas markets or at home. Since the value of a nation's currency affects the competitiveness of the nation's commodities and services, a government may encounter difficulties in committing credibly to a standard whereby its currency is overvalued vis-à-vis other currencies. Moreover, since economies are dynamic and change over time in their productivity and advantages, an exchange rate that is good at one time may become problematic at a later time. Domestic producers and labor in the tradable sector, recognizing the ability of the exchange rate to influence the global competitiveness of their industries, may pressure their government to manipulate the price of its currency against others in the global trading arena. The more such pressures threaten politicians' ability to persevere in office, the more they are likely to respond with policies that are designed to enhance the competitive stature of their domestic producers. Policy makers can address these pressures by adopting trade policies such as tariffs, subsidies, or quotas, or they can use monetary policies that manipulate their currency's value.

A less expensive or undervalued currency will make a nation's commodities and services less expensive in comparison to other nations' commodities and services in overseas markets, while making overseas commodities and services more expensive in its domestic markets. Conversely, a more expensive or overvalued currency will make a nation's commodities and services more expensive in overseas markets in relation to other nations' products and services, and overseas goods and services less expensive in its domestic markets. Such relative differences in prices can affect consumption decisions by individuals and businesses both in the domestic economy and abroad. A less expensive currency will help to swing the current account of the balance of payments toward a surplus, and a more expensive currency will push the current account toward a deficit. Consequently, a state's tradable sector can be made more competitive through the manipulation of a single policy instrument. A government facing a persistent balance-of-payments deficit as well as pressures from domestic producers might be tempted to address both situations by manipulating the value of its currency. A unilateral shift in the exchange rate by a nation affects the prices of all its goods and services in the tradable sector, including the price of labor, or wages.

Under the second dynamic that might lead a government to renege on its commitments, the issue of convertibility can pose another dilemma. The convertibility commitment exposes a nation's monetary reserves (gold, foreign currencies, or some other reserve asset, depending on the international monetary system) to potential depletion if some individual,

company, or government perceives an opportunity to convert that nation's currency into a reserve asset and then move it overseas in order to purchase another currency or commodity that is relatively undervalued (that is, yielding more for the money). This dynamic can lead to a draining of the target nation's monetary reserves. The conditions for such speculative activities—which are known as **arbitrage opportunities**—exist when people believe that a currency is systematically overvalued or undervalued, or when they believe that a government may not be committed to defending its currency at the stated price. A government can act to defend its currency in such situations, but if enough distrust undermines the valuation of its currency, the pressures of convertibility may lead to the draining of the nation's reserve assets and force the government to revalue its currency.

> **Arbitrage opportunities** are situations in which an individual can purchase in one market an asset that she believes is systematically undervalued and then move it to another market to sell it for a gain, or use it to purchase another asset.

BRITISH CONTRIBUTIONS TO OTHER COLLECTIVE GOODS

Other factors contributed to the central role of the United Kingdom in promoting globalization in the late nineteenth and early twentieth centuries. In addition to their commitment to freer trade, gold, and convertibility, the British provided other collective goods to the global arena that helped to reduce risk significantly and advance globalization and economic expansion. In particular, they offered the international arena liquidity, a systemic lender of last resort, and market access under duress. These were all means of pumping capital into the international arena during both good and bad economic times, capital that was necessary to promote continued economic expansion during good times and to stimulate growth at times of economic dislocation that threatened cooperation and globalization. British private and public finance were both critical. Private British capital markets provided the liquidity, or supply of capital, that fostered economic expansion and political development. The Bank of England and H.M. Treasury acted as the lender of last resort, or central bank, for the system in managing financial crises and economic downturns in the international arena. And even during periods of economic stagnation or decline, the British retained their commitment to free trade and kept the entry barriers to their markets low, thus maintaining market access under duress. All these activities, which acted as key financing mechanisms for globalization, were underpinned by British public and private finance sitting at the hub of a network of relationships, a financial network that spanned national borders and acted as the global nervous system or thermostat managing activity.

Liquidity: Fuel for a Global Economy

National unification, governance, and economic development required capital to finance armies, ports, railroads, roads, communication infrastructure, and economic enterprise. Some of this capital was raised locally, within the states where the capital was to be applied to projects. But British financiers had created highly efficient capital markets that attracted capital looking for investment opportunities, as well as opportunities looking for capital. London's capital markets provided much of the liquidity—a statement about how much capital is available, how mobile a capital asset is, and how easily capital assets can be bought and sold—that helped to fund state formation and economic development across Europe, the Americas, Australia, and other nations. British willingness to pump the pound sterling into the global economy turned that currency into a reserve asset that was used to settle accounts between states and private economic actors across boundaries. It also served to expand the supply of good money in the global economy, which fueled investment in economic enterprise, helped to maintain or increase prices (the opposite of price deflation), and contributed to improvements in social welfare.

London's capital markets helped to finance unification of the disparate German and Italian regional states into single nation-states. Latin American governments borrowed in London to finance a variety of public infrastructure projects. U.S. railroad developers sought and obtained financing in London for systemic improvements that would link regions, advance westward expansion, create more efficient internal trade, and spur the economic development that was rapidly transforming the United States from a developing economy into the world's largest and most advanced economy (see table 9.4). Table 9.5 gives some indication of the changes and magnitude of global borrowing in London's markets.

The importance of London's capital markets for growth, development, and state building gave British policy makers, public and private, valuable leverage over the choices and actions of others wanting capital for economic and government enterprise. Using the emerging global financial network and the ability to obtain financial assistance or impose financial

TABLE 9.4	Index of per Capita Levels of Industrialization, 1750–1900					
	1750	*1800*	*1830*	*1860*	*1880*	*1900*
United Kingdom	10	16	25	64	87	100
Belgium	9	10	14	28	43	56
United States	4	9	14	21	38	69
France	9	9	12	20	28	39
Germany	8	8	9	15	25	52
Austria	7	7	8	11	15	23
Italy	8	8	8	10	12	17
Russia	6	6	7	8	10	15
China	8	6	6	4	4	3
India	7	6	6	3	2	1

Source: Paul Bairoch, "International Industrialization Levels from 1750–1890," *Journal of European Economic History* 11 (Fall 1982): 294.

Note: The index is scaled to the United Kingdom; 1900 = 100.

TABLE 9.5	The Shift in British Capital Markets toward Increased Overseas Lending, 1850–1913

Foreign investment as percentage of domestic savings (at current prices)

1850–1854	12.3*	1885–1889	46.5
1855–1859	30.2*	1890–1894	35.3
1860–1864	21.5*	1895–1899	20.7
1865–1869	32.2*	1900–1904	11.2
1870–1874	38.0	1905–1909	42.7
1875–1879	16.2	1910–1913	53.3
1880–1884	33.2		

Source: Kevin H. O'Rourke and Jeffrey G. Williamson, *Globalization and History* (Cambridge: MIT Press, 1999), 209.

Note: Asterisks indicate numbers that are calculated from original current-account data, rather than gold-adjusted data.

sanctions, British policy makers extended their sphere of influence and leveraged policies in support of an increasingly global economy.

Globalization's costs as well as its benefits soon became apparent. The exposure of London's markets to overseas economic activities brought rewards but also carried new risks. The prospect of lucrative returns on investments in the New World attracted financial speculation. Some investments and speculation paid off handsomely, but other ventures collapsed and left creditors exposed when some borrowers failed to meet their debt obligations. In some of these latter cases, the markets were roiled by financial crisis, which exposed major British and European financial institutions to extreme risks and threatened the global economy. Argentina, the fifth-largest economy in the world by the end of the 1800s, borrowed so much capital that its economic crises threatened to unhinge the European financial system and collapse British capital markets. Earlier in the century several defaults by developing American states threatened the stability of the European banking system. Speculative financing of American railroads would also disrupt British capital markets during the century.

The global financial crises that occurred in the late twentieth and early twenty-first centuries had antecedents in the crises of the mid- to late 1800s. The financial crises created by defaults of U.S. borrowers in the mid-1800s and by Argentine borrowers later in the century are comparable to such recent events as the Third World Debt Crisis of the 1980s, the peso crisis of 1994, the Asian financial crisis of 1997, the Russian ruble crisis of 1997, the Internet bubble that burst in 1999, the global credit crisis that emerged in 2007–2008, and the recent sovereign debt crisis in Europe spurred by problems in Greece and other weaker economies in the EU. When London's investors were outraged and severely damaged by the U.S. defaults in the 1800s, the preeminent European banker of his time, Baron Rothschild, emphatically asserted that U.S. borrowers would find no access to new loans and that the "United States could not borrow a dollar, not a dollar." Sydney Smith, a clergyman, wrote:

> There really should be lunatic asylums for nations as well as individuals. . . . America is a nation with whom no contract can be made, because none will be kept; unstable in the very foundations of social life, deficient in the elements of good faith, men who prefer any load of infamy, however great, to any pressure of taxation however light.[2]

Lender of Last Resort: Managing Economic Crises

The emerging network of global finance—the central nervous system of the global economy—provided Great Britain with disproportionate influence over the direction of the global economy, but it also exposed Britain and the global economy to new risks and challenges. British capital markets provided the capital liquidity that helped generate economic

---

[2]Sydney Smith, *The Works of the Rev. Sydney Smith*, vol. 2 (1859).

expansion during good economic times, but bad economic times or financial crises threatened the provision of capital as private lenders and investors became risk averse. The British government, led by the Bank of England and the British Treasury, helped to coordinate the activities of private European financial institutions

> A **lender of last resort** is a nation or bank that acts countercyclically to ensure an adequate supply of capital during economic crisis, providing a collective good.

and multiple governments to ensure an adequate supply of capital during such crises. The British thus took on the function of systemic **lender of last resort,** another collective good, as described in chapter 6.

A lender of last resort acts to ensure the supply of capital to a financial system at a time when other financial institutions face a liquidity shortage that can threaten the solvency of those institutions or when they are risk averse and reluctant to pump capital into the system. Such liquidity shortages may occur as a consequence of excessive demands during an economic cycle or as a result of a crisis that unnerves the holders of capital. At some points during economic cycles, private banks and financial institutions may find themselves either lacking the capital to meet the demands of their depositors and clients or unwilling to lend the capital they have to borrowers and economic enterprises—a liquidity shortage that can constrain economic activity.

For example, planting seasons create economic cycles in agricultural areas, producing large fluctuations in demand on bank resources. At the beginning of planting season, farmers need capital to purchase seeds, to pay labor, and to buy or fix equipment. But they cannot bring their crops to market for months, so they must either draw upon their savings or borrow from their banks. This need generates a major seasonal demand on their banks' resources—usually far more than the banks have on hand. At the other end of the farming cycle, farmers sell their crops and then either deposit their earnings in the banks or pay down their loans. The banks are now faced with too many deposits on hand. As they have to pay interest on those deposits, they must use them to earn money, so the banks lend some of those deposits to borrowers. These loans, in turn, limit the banks' resources on hand when the farming cycle begins anew. When banks in agricultural areas face such a liquidity shortage because of seasonal demand, they may reach up the banking food chain to borrow funds from banks in urban areas, which are subject to a different economic cycle and so are not facing the same liquidity problem. The demand for capital to meet the seasonal needs of the agricultural cycle can thus cascade up the banking chain. Ideally, this upward reach will address the liquidity problem of the rural banks; if it does not, they—and perhaps other banks as well—may face a solvency dilemma that can turn into a larger economic crisis. Alternatively, banks in such situations may access funds from a national central bank devised intentionally to address such liquidity dilemmas—a national lender of last resort.

Similar liquidity problems can occur as a consequence of unexpected crises. Whatever the cause, the problem remains a shortage of capital that threatens the ability and willingness of financial institutions to lend capital to economic endeavors. Capital supply can shrink dramatically during an economic crisis, as holders of capital become risk averse and reluctant to invest in economic activities, preferring to sit on their surplus capital in order to protect it—figuratively or literally hiding money in mattresses or coffee cans. A decline in the supply of capital as the result of the reluctance of investors to lend their surplus increases capital costs for borrowers, who must then pay more to comfort the fears of investors and entice them to lend. Because capital is an important factor of production, such changes in its price and supply affect the costs of economic enterprises as well as the range of enterprises that can obtain capital. This effect influences the prices of commodities produced by those enterprises, as well as consumption choices and choices about economic activities. Shrinkage in capital supply following a downturn can lead to further decline in economic activity and turn a temporary crisis into a more serious, long-term problem—a vicious cycle.

A **countercyclical policy** is a policy that works to oppose and counteract the current trend. Examples are public policies that provide liquidity when private liquidity becomes scarce and low levels of tariffs when others are raising tariffs. A **procyclical policy** is a policy intended to support and promote the current economic trend.

A lender of last resort is the final safeguard against a liquidity crisis. The party that fulfills this function seeks to keep banks and financial institutions operating productively, providing liquidity, by ensuring the availability of sufficient capital to prevent a crisis. A lender of last resort enacts **countercyclical policies,** or policies against the trend. (Going along with a trend is **procyclical policy** behavior.) Pursuing a countercyclical policy strategy, a lender of last resort attempts to interrupt the trend of a downward cycle by injecting capital into a system at the very time that capital is being drained from the system as others become risk averse and withhold their capital. This strategy is an attempt to mitigate recessionary downturns, to make them shorter and less painful, by providing capital to promote the economic activity necessary to grow out of a downturn. A lender of last resort can use the same countercyclical approach to constrain a too-rapid economic expansion that creates inflationary pressures, by withdrawing money from the system. By raising interest rates or using other policy instruments to reduce the supply of money and increase its costs, the lender can slow an expansionary trend in an economy.

We can easily understand why a lender of last resort would act countercyclically to promote growth at times of economic contraction, but why would it work countercyclically to slow an expansionary economy? After all, growth is good! It generates jobs, income, and consumption, and it improves welfare. When a lender of last resort acts to shrink the money supply, the expressed objective is usually to constrain economic expansion that threatens to bring on inflation, which undermines the value of money and thus can be dysfunctional for an economy. If the money supply grows too fast, that money loses value and purchases less and less. As people lose confidence in the value of that money, they are less willing to hold it over extended periods. Long-term investments decline in value, and this decline generates incentives for individuals and firms to consume for today rather than invest for the future.

Most often, governments have performed the lender-of-last-resort function for their domestic economies, although there have been instances of private entities undertaking this function. For example, the large money-center banks in New York cobbled together an arrangement to perform such a function for the United States during the period from 1837 to 1913, when the United States lacked a public central bank. But such examples are far less frequent than governments' attempts to act as lenders of last resort for their economies. Private providers have also had a more problematic history in providing this service, as their natural incentives are to become risk averse and protect their enterprises at the very time that the lender-of-last-resort function is most needed by a political economy.

Governments, their central banks, and their treasuries can attempt to act as lenders of last resort for their domestic economies, but only a very wealthy economy, or handful of economies, with significant financial reserves, can perform this function in the larger global arena. Whether or not it was the original intention of the British Treasury and Bank of England, the prominence of London's capital markets, banks, and financiers meant that, for the 1800s, only the United Kingdom enjoyed such capabilities and position in the global arena. If other states attempted to act as lender of last resort for the system at large but without British participation, those governments would discover that their capabilities were insufficient to stem a global liquidity crisis. Their gold and currency reserves would be drained and the international predicament would remain unresolved. Even France, a far larger political economy demographically and geographically than the United Kingdom, did not have the capacity to act as systemic lender of last resort.

Market Access under Duress

The British commitment to freer trade, regardless of the actions of other nations and in the face of domestic protectionist pressures, constituted another collective good during the late 1800s. Economic recessions and dislocations during this period increased domestic pressures for protectionism against imports and prompted some states to temper and even reverse their movement toward freer trade (see table 9.1). These pressures were strongest in agricultural sectors, which were experiencing severe price deflation related to the gold standard and to surplus production. If the United Kingdom, the largest consumer economy and the hub of the global trading system, had raised barriers along with these other nations during a time of global economic slowdown and duress, the growth of trade would have been further curtailed. Economic activity would have faced more severe challenges, and recessionary trends would have been amplified.

Instead, the United Kingdom's resolve to maintain relatively open markets for international goods at this time of economic duress, even as other governments moved to restrict access to their domestic markets, provided an outlet for foreign economic enterprises to sell their products in the British market and an opportunity to temper and counter the recessionary trend in other economies. This collective good of maintaining a market for distress

Market access under duress is a countercyclical policy of maintaining relatively open markets for international goods at a time of economic crisis and providing an outlet for foreign economic enterprises to sell their goods in order to counter recessionary trends.

goods has become known as **market access under duress.** This collective good (which is discussed in depth in chapter 6) is also a financing mechanism to provide liquidity to the global economy, especially at times of economic weakness. Revenues from selling goods into the British markets could help finance economic activities that would stimulate economies. British policy makers, by maintaining relatively open access to their markets, kept a pathway open for capital to flow to slowing economies, which could lead to economic expansion. Although it was a countercyclical policy, this action was not selfless or altruistic. As the largest trading country, the United Kingdom stood to gain if other economies grew and their consumers increased their consumption, some of which would inevitably involve increased purchases of British goods. But this strategy required a long-term perspective on the part of British policy makers and an ability to resist short-term demands from domestic interests as British producers and labor were being damaged in the short run by economic downturns and increasing barriers to entry in some foreign markets.

Again, only a wealthy and dominant (or near-dominant) nation can provide this collective good to the global system and have the desired countercyclical effect. A small political economy, even if it kept its barriers to trade low, could not possibly consume enough goods to turn around the global economy.

TECHNOLOGY'S ROLE IN THE GROWTH OF GLOBALIZATION

Any accounting of nineteenth-century political economy that neglects technology ignores some pivotal changes that empowered globalization and transformed social relations. Certainly, new economic ideas, political reforms, the absence of international conflict, and the stable monetary regime anchored by the United Kingdom fueled the growth of a global economy in the 1800s. These conditions may have been necessary to account for the extent and depth of globalization, but they were not sufficient.

Barriers such as great distance, seemingly impassable deserts or mountain ranges, vast oceans, pandemic disease, and other forces of nature can obstruct and hinder international exchange even when political economies are open to such exchange. Such obstacles make transit difficult perhaps, but they are not insurmountable, as demonstrated by the will and creativity displayed by such determined human adventurers as Hannibal, who crossed the Alps to invade Rome in 218 B.C.E.; the Portuguese mariner Vasco da Gama, who navigated the Horn of Africa in 1498, searching for rewards from exploration and trade in Eastern goods; and Christopher Columbus, who crossed the Atlantic in 1492 in search of an easier and faster route to the lucrative spice trade of the Orient, only to discover the New World. These conquerors and explorers benefited from technological change and discovery.

Hannibal harnessed the technology of animal husbandry, as his armies employed war elephants to battle the Romans. Breakthroughs in navigational technology empowered the efforts of Columbus, da Gama, and other explorers.

Technological and industrial revolutions transformed production in the states of the Atlantic economy. These revolutions generated economic pressures that pushed people to move from rural to urban areas, dramatically increased wealth while decreasing the number of people subsisting on day-to-day earnings, lowered the cost of transport, reduced the time of communication across great distances from days and weeks to near-real-time messaging, and inspired a search for raw materials to feed industrial engines. The Industrial Revolution diffused wealth across more and more of the population, creating middle and working classes with disposable income and growing consumption appetites, which in turn fed the demand for more goods and services. Technological inventions and innovations in transport—railroads, steam engines, screw propellers, and steel hulls—introduced greater efficiencies that allowed larger quantities to be transported and at far smaller cost. The advent of refrigeration meant that perishable goods could be shipped over great distances and time to arrive in faraway markets as fresh as many local goods.

Transportation Leads to Greater Efficiency and Market Integration

Technological advances in transport revolutionized the movement of goods and people, lowered costs, rapidly increased shipping capacity, and reduced the time of getting goods from producers to consumers in distant markets. Such improvements in transportation capabilities contributed as much as any other factor to the integration of markets and national political economies. These changes also empowered the specialization and comparative advantages produced by differences in national factor endowments; production structures shifted as global market exchange rewarded some producers and penalized others.

Construction of canals, harbors, and navigable inner waterways produced the first breakthroughs in transport. Water transport was dramatically more efficient and cheaper than shipping by road—especially the dirt roads that dominated the internal transportation networks of states. The states of the Atlantic economy invested heavily in canal construction and the installation of locks on existing waterways to create and expand transport capabilities. British investments produced a huge increase in navigable waterways in the United Kingdom: shipping costs on such waterways undercut those on roads by 50 percent or more in the early 1800s. In the United States, the Erie Canal, constructed between 1817 and 1825, decreased shipping time between Buffalo and New York City by almost two-thirds and reduced shipping costs by more than 80 percent. Other canals and waterways, such as the Baltimore and Ohio Canal, created comparable productivity gains. Europeans garnered similar gains as international cooperation harnessed the Rhine River system. The opening of the Suez Canal in 1869, in tandem with the steamship (needed because the still air of the Suez was not friendly to sailing ships), generated similar cost and time improvements for trade between the Far East and Europe, and restored the Near East to a position in world trade that it had not enjoyed for centuries.

The railroad, another major innovation in transport, also brought markets together. At an 1869 ceremony in Utah, dignitaries gathered to drive the last spike that completed the first transcontinental railroad in the Americas. Motivated partly by the desire of the U.S. government to link the East and West for national security reasons during the Civil War, this development in transportation foreshadowed the emergence of a national market in the United States, in which prices in Los Angeles converged with prices in Chicago, St. Louis, New York, and Boston. A rapid expansion of rail lines across the Atlantic economies (as shown in table 9.6) linked distant markets and led to an increase in the frequency and density of economic interactions within and across national borders. Commodity prices converged in markets linked by rail and water networks.

Railways, canals, and the improvement of national navigable waterways led to large productivity gains as domestic shipping costs fell and more and more tonnage could be shipped efficiently. Goods produced at a distance became increasingly competitive with goods produced nearby. The benefits of railways and newly navigable freshwater passages reached across national boundaries when nations were contiguous, but the economic gains and pressures for market integration they produced could not be extended to those separated by seas without technological gains in ocean transport. It was fortunate, therefore, that underpinning the railroad revolution was the development of the steam engine, which also found its way into the design of merchant shipping.

TABLE 9.6	The Expansion of Railway Mileage, 1850–1910			
	1850	1870	1890	1910
Argentina	—	637	5,434	17,381
Australia	—	953	9,524	17,429
Austria-Hungary	954	5,949	16,489	26,834
Canada	66	2,617	13,368	26,462
China	—	—	80	5,092
France	1,714	11,142	22,911	30,643
Germany	3,637	11,729	25,411	36,152
India	—	4,771	16,411	32,099
Italy	265	3,825	8,163	10,573
Japan	—	—	1,139	5,130
Mexico	—	215	6,037	15,350
Russia (in Europe)	310	7,098	18,059	34,990
United Kingdom	6,621	15,537	20,073	23,387
United States	9,021	52,922	116,703	249,902

Source: John Hurd, "Railways and the Expansion of Markets in India, 1861–1921," *Explorations in Economic History* 12 (1975).

Steam engines and other technological inventions such as the screw propeller, steel hulls, and subsequent advances in engine design led to rapid increases in the size of oceangoing ships, the weight they could transport, their speed, and the reliability of shipping schedules no longer at the mercy of wind and weather. British steamships began to traverse the English Channel regularly by the second decade of the 1800s, and transatlantic steamer service began in 1838. By 1870, the tonnage of ships powered by mechanical engines exceeded the tonnage of shipping powered by wind and sail.

Larger, faster, and more predictable ocean shipping reduced delivery times and lowered the costs of transport. Domestic producers now faced price competition from abroad: consumers in Liverpool could choose between British domestic grain and lower-cost grain from the United States, Argentina, or Canada. Ironically, Indians found that cotton shirts made in the United Kingdom were cheaper than shirts made in Bombay, even though the raw cotton often had come from India. Consumers enjoyed expanded consumption possibilities—a greater range of choice and value—as the transport revolution reduced costs, increased productivity, linked markets, and expanded opportunities for efficient producers.

By the mid-1800s, journeys that decades earlier had taken weeks and months took far less time. New Orleans and New York were highly separated markets in 1800, but by 1850 they had become highly integrated, as, increasingly, were London and New York, Paris and London, and Rotterdam and Boston. Differences in commodity prices declined with the advances in navigation; technological change interacted with political change, and world trade expanded rapidly—as can be seen in figure 9.1 and table 9.7. Improvements in overall social welfare corresponded to increases in international exchange and the resulting specialization of national production structures.

Still, not everyone benefited from these changes. Inefficient producers and labor, once protected by great distance and expensive shipping, now faced competition from more distant and efficient producers and labor. Grain and other agricultural exports from the New World challenged agricultural producers in Europe. At first, only agricultural goods that did not easily spoil made the long journey. New World producers of such commodities quickly demonstrated their competitive advantage over European producers. Farmers in Europe responded to this initial loss of competitive advantage by shifting production away from grain and toward animal husbandry, supplying perishable goods such as fresh beef and dairy products. Even with the advances in transportation technology that reduced shipping times and lowered shipping costs, these goods still faced the prospect of spoilage during transit.

The advantage and security of animal husbandry were short-lived, however, as the development of refrigeration technology in midcentury soon overcame the problem of spoilage. By the 1870s and 1880s, agricultural producers in the United States, Argentina, Canada, Australia, New Zealand, and other New World economies were shipping meats, butter, and other perishables under refrigeration to European markets. Soon the European agricultural producers, hurt by these innovations in transport, responded to their loss of comparative advantage by pressuring their governments to raise tariffs and other protections. Inefficient

FIGURE 9.1	Change in the Tradable Sector, 1800–1910: The Expansion in Trade, as an Aggregate of Imports and Exports, for Each State

9.1a Fast and Significant Change

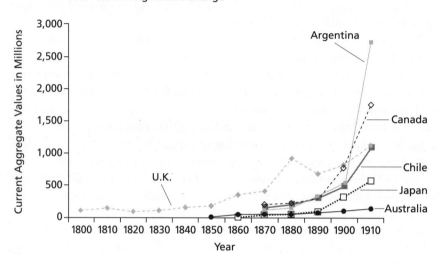

9.1b Extraordinary Change

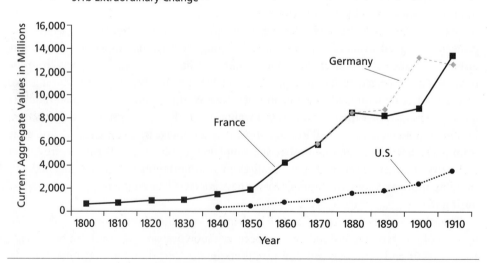

Source: Data from B. R. Mitchell, *International Historical Statistics* (New York: Palgrave Macmillan, 2003).

producers thus sought government intervention to delay or avoid their costs of adjusting to the new global economy and to force the costs of adjusting onto others. Despite the midcentury trend toward lower and lower barriers to entry, tariff rates ceased their decline after 1870. Consumers and foreign producers were penalized by the increases in tariffs, which meant they paid higher prices and sold fewer goods.

The Industrial Revolution and Migration Transform Political Economies

Technological invention and innovation transformed far more than transport. The Industrial Revolution involved the application of new ideas and technology to economic processes and organization, which led to a shift from agrarian to industrial production. The resulting transformation in economic and industrial activity is illustrated above in table 9.4. Such economic transformations created a need for workers in the emerging industrial centers. As industrial production tended to concentrate in urban areas near transportation arteries, people moved from the rural areas to urban centers to find employment. The states of the Atlantic economy in particular experienced rapid shifts in their rural-urban population distribution, which tore at the social and familial networks based in agricultural communities and resulted in populations that were more mobile and amenable to relocation. The safety nets of rural life provided less support for those who moved to the urban centers.

The industrialization of economic activity also changed the relationship between workers and their economic activities. Prior to the Industrial Revolution, both agricultural and nonagricultural production tended to involve workers who owned their means of production. Working as craftsmen and apprentices, they owned their own labor and sold the fruits of their labor. With industrialization, however, workers increasingly worked for wages—becoming commodities

TABLE 9.7	World Trade, 1720–1913	
	Volume index	Annual growth (%)
1720	1.13	
1750	1.9	1.75
1780	2.18	0.46
1800	2.3	0.27
1820	3.1	1.5
1830	4.3	3.33
1840	5.4	2.3
1850	10.1	6.46
1860	13.9	3.25
1870	23.8	5.53
1880	30	2.94
1890	44	2.97
1900	57	3.5
1910	81	3.87
1913	96	4.34

Source: Data from W. W. Rostow, *The World Economy: History and Prospect* (Austin: University of Texas Press, 1978).

themselves as they sold their labor to the owners of the factories—and they no longer owned what they produced. This economic revolution transformed the workers' relationships to what they produced and to the emerging power of capital, which in turn led to a shift in their political outlook. Labor, Chartist, and socialist movements arose to voice their demands within political economies, and by midcentury such movements were threatening the foundations of monarchist political authority in Europe. These pressures culminated in 1848 with short-lived revolutions and governments' swinging to the left, only to give way to a quick retrenchment as conservative, but increasingly democratic, governments reasserted dominance.

The economic draw of urban areas, the weakening of the rural social fabric by the movement to the cities, and agricultural distress at midcentury weakened the incentives of individuals to remain in rural regions. These factors, combined with increases in disposable income and the declining costs of transit, encouraged migration. Individuals who had previously been constrained by social ties and limited finances discovered that they had sufficient resources and incentives to purchase passage. Migration increased dramatically by the mid-1800s. Some left their homes to seek dreams and opportunity, many fled economic hardships such as the Irish famine, and others migrated to escape political and religious persecution. At first, much of this movement was from rural to urban areas within nations, and then from one European nation to another, but soon the leading destinations were in the New World of the Americas and Australia. Political economies in the New World suffered from a shortage of labor, whereas the states of the Old World generally enjoyed a surplus of workers. Such differences in the supply of labor produced a higher wage level in the New World compared with the Old World, which, on top of the availability of employment opportunities, acted as a draw for migration. More than sixty million individuals migrated across national boundaries during the 1800s, headed predominantly for economic opportunities in the New World. They were heavily male, young, and low skilled. Table 9.8 shows the growth and magnitude of international emigration by origin. The British Isles, for example, lost approximately fifty to sixty people per thousand of its population through emigration for almost every decade of the mid- to late 1800s. Political, economic, and religious opportunities existed abroad long before the great migratory movements of the nineteenth century, but people did not emigrate much in those earlier times. The economic and technological transformations of the 1800s are pivotal to accounting for why major migrations occurred in the latter half of that century and not earlier.

Technological Advances in Communication Promote Globalization

Trade, migration, and the flow of capital linked societies as part of the process of globalization, but the communication of ideas and the development of more and more sophisticated communication networks also connected societies, economies, and

TABLE 9.8	Emigration Rates by Decade, 1851–1910 (per 1,000 Mean Population)					
Country	1851–1860	1861–1870	1871–1880	1881–1890	1891–1900	1901–1910
Austria-Hungary			2.9	10.6	16.1	47.6
Belgium				8.6	3.5	6.1
Denmark			20.6	39.4	22.3	28.2
Finland				13.2	23.2	54.5
France	1.1	1.2	1.5	3.1	1.3	1.4
Germany			14.7	28.7	10.1	4.5
Ireland			66.1	141.7	88.5	69.8
Italy			10.5	33.6	50.2	107.7
Netherlands	5.0	5.9	4.6	12.3	5.0	5.1
Norway	24.2	57.6	47.3	95.2	44.9	83.3
Portugal		19.0	28.9	38.0	50.8	56.9
Spain				36.2	43.8	56.6
Sweden	4.6	30.5	23.5	70.1	41.2	42.0
Switzerland			13.0	32.0	14.1	13.9
United Kingdom	58.0	51.8	50.4	70.2	43.8	65.3

Source: Data from Kevin H. O'Rourke and Jeffrey G. Williamson, *Globalization and History: The Evolution of a Nineteenth-Century Atlantic Economy* (Cambridge: MIT Press, 1999), 122.

financial markets. The invention of the telegraph, for instance, increased the availability of timely information that might affect economic choices in such markets and sped capital market integration domestically and internationally. Time and information are key factors in the calculus of investment. Delay in the transmission of information relevant to economic activity or in the ability to purchase or sell a financial investment increases risk, which can affect investors' willingness to invest or lend capital and the costs they charge for that capital. Any such increase in risk can constrain economic activity and reduce investment.

Prior to the invention and widespread application of the telegraph, investors located far from their investments faced long delays in their access to price information and other data that might be relevant to their investments. During the Napoleonic Wars, some financiers used carrier pigeons to obtain the latest news from the battlefield so they could base their financial decisions on the most current information—giving them an information advantage over investors who waited for news carried by horseback. Even more time challenged were investors in New York or Boston, who had to anticipate the price of a financial instrument in the London markets weeks into the future. Two weeks was the average time required for a transatlantic voyage, and, since each transaction required one transit to bring the news from London and another to deliver the investor's instructions back to an agent there, these Americans were making their investment decisions in the only global capital market, London, on the basis of a minimum four-week lag in information at the time of the actual trade.

The time delay was longer for investors in Australia, and shorter for investors on the European continent. Regardless, foreign investors were basing their financial activities on old information, and even those investors situated in London were trading on old information if the loans and investments they were funding were located overseas. Imagine that you were a British investor with a financial stake in an American economic enterprise at midcentury, and you were at least two weeks behind in information as you contemplated increasing or decreasing your investment. What would happen if during that time the Southern states seceded from the United States, or the battles of Bull Run, Antietam, or Gettysburg took place? Any such event could influence the expected value of your investment, but as an investor in London you would be acting with no knowledge of it.

The introduction of the telegraph meant that investors were suddenly able to trade with at most a day's delay in current information about the price of an investment and other news that could affect its prospects. The United Kingdom and continental Europe were linked by telegraph in 1851, with the laying of an underwater cable from Dover to Calais. In the United States, the major centers of New York, Philadelphia, Boston, Washington, D.C., Hartford, and Baltimore were quickly connected by telegraph, and a transcontinental connection linking the East and West coasts opened in 1861. A transatlantic cable was first put into operation in that same year, but more permanent service lagged until the laying of sturdier cables in 1865 and 1866.

The telegraph radically transformed the transmission of information, making people in one part of the world aware of activities in other parts of the global arena with increasing speed (as shown in table 9.9) and at rapidly increasing levels of traffic (as shown in table 9.10). The telegraph helped to integrate financial relations and activities across national boundaries, advancing London's position as the center of global finance. It encouraged more investment and created more opportunities for investors and borrowers alike. It also increased the transmission of financial shocks, as well as benefits, from one market to another. In terms of intrastate dynamics, this technological change made the greatest difference in countries with

TABLE 9.9 The Speed of Travel of Information to London, 1798–1914

Event	Date	Place	First Times of London report	Miles per hour
Battle of the Nile	8/1/1798	Egypt	10/2/1798	1.4
Battle of Trafalgar	10/21/1805	Portugal	11/7/1805	2.7
Earthquake, Kutch, India	6/16/1819	India	11/16/1819	1.1
Treaty of Nanking	8/29/1842	China	11/21/1842	2.8
Charge of the Light Brigade	10/25/1854	Crimea	11/11/1854	4.0
Indian Mutiny, Delhi Massacre	5/12/1857	India	6/27/1857	3.8
Treaty of Tien-Sin	6/26/1858	Tianjin, China	9/16/1858	2.6
Assassination of President Abraham Lincoln	4/14/1865	DC, USA	4/27/1865	11.7
Assassination of Archduke Maximilian	6/19/1867	Mexico	7/1/1867	19.2
Assassination of Czar Alexander II	3/13/1881	Russia	3/14/1881	118.7
Nobi earthquake	10/28/1891	Nobi, Japan	10/29/1891	245.8
Messina Strait earthquake	12/28/1908	Italy	12/29/1908	398.0
Assassination of Franz Ferdinand	6/28/1914	Sarajevo	6/28/1914	118.6

Source: Adapted from Gregory Clark, *The Conquest of Nature: A Brief Economic History of the World, 10,000 BC–2000 AD,* chap. 12, "The Great Divergence: World Economic Growth since 1800," 20; http://www.econ.ucdavis.edu/faculty/gclark/globalhistory/conquesthome.html.

TABLE 9.10	Telegraph Traffic, 1850–1920 (in Millions of Telegraphs)							
	1850	*1860*	*1870*	*1880*	*1890*	*1900*	*1910*	*1920*
United Kingdom			8.60	29.90	66.50	89.60	86.70	88.00
France		0.70	5.70	17.00	27.00	40.00	50.00	51.00
Germany	0.04	0.73	8.66	13.50	22.20	39.70	48.20	79.60
Italy		0.10	2.00	5.90	8.30	9.40	15.20	20.70
United States			9.20	29.00	56.00	63.00	75.00	156.00
Canada							10.00	17.00
India			0.58	1.66	3.41	6.50	13.09	19.05
Japan			0.01	2.03	4.21	16.23	28.64	70.93
Argentina						3.90	8.80	10.00
Australia			0.86	3.68	9.25	8.38	12.49	18.41
New Zealand			0.24	1.31	1.96	3.90	8.36	14.00

Source: Data from B. R. Mitchell, *International Historical Statistics* (New York: Palgrave Macmillan, 2003).

large territories, such as the United States, as the telegraph shrank those distances to no more than a day in terms of trading time and information lag.

THE DARK SIDE OF GLOBALIZATION IN THE 1800S

So far, our discussion may have suggested that the process of globalization in the nineteenth century produced a win-win situation for all those involved—as if economic growth, political liberalization, and improved social welfare accrued to all those who participated in globalization. This would be a mistaken conclusion, however, as might be seen in the case of those European agricultural producers faced with competition from more efficient New World producers of the same goods. Nineteenth-century globalization generated substantial improvements in the lives of many, but it also produced dislocation, discomfort, trauma, and outright disaster for some of those touched by the phenomenon. Inevitably, market exchange leads to some temporary dislocations as a result of economic change and transformation, but many of these effects should fade as people adjust to the discipline of the market mechanism. But in the nineteenth century, the processes accompanying globalization also created a more enduring and troubling legacy in the form of colonialism.

Creative Destruction and Dislocation

With expansion of market exchange and the integration of national markets into a larger global market, producers and labor were exposed to the forces of comparative advantage and market discipline across national boundaries. Some discovered that they were less competitive than producers and labor located in other political economies. Competitive markets push producers and workers to adjust in order to regain their competitiveness. This could involve learning new skills, discovering another form of production in which they enjoy a comparative advantage, or relocation. A competitive market forces such transformation on producers and labor, generates waves of structural change, and creates economic advance in society.

> **Creative destruction** is the disciplinary mechanism of competitive markets that forces transformation on uncompetitive producers, generates waves of structural change, and creates economic advance in society.

In 1942 Joseph Schumpeter, an economist at Harvard College, used the term **creative destruction** for this process. Theoretically and in the long run, if markets work as anticipated, creative destruction produces more socially efficient outcomes and increases collective welfare.

Unfortunately, this transition can be painful in the real world. The adjustments brought on by creative destruction include transaction costs that are absent from the world of neoclassical economic theory—the costs of finding a new job, learning new skills, and adapting to a more competitive environment can range from negligible to overwhelming. Such costs can be quite high in the short term for many and in the long term for some, particularly for older people or those with dependents. It is not easy to shift to a new type of employment, which may require different skills or even relocation to a new setting. Being compelled to change practices, seek new jobs, learn new skills, and adapt to a newly competitive environment can be a harsh experience for individuals, for their families, and for their communities. Many benefit from such creative destruction and discover they are better off after the transition, but some fall behind and discover they are now working at lower-skilled jobs and at lower compensation. Some industries simply disappear in the face of competition from abroad.

The rapid pace of globalization in the nineteenth century left some individuals, families, and communities damaged even as their larger societies benefited. Poorhouses, charities, community organizations, and nascent governmental social welfare programs provided threadbare safety nets that provided only subsistence-level support and most certainly afforded no dignity. Charles Dickens exposed the cruelty of this state of affairs in *A Christmas Carol*, when the character Scrooge replies to a request for a charitable donation for the indigent by asking indignantly, "Are there no workhouses, are there no poorhouses?" It is not a random coincidence that we observe the beginnings of the modern social welfare state during this era. The increasing exposure of workers and producers to the risks arising from the market discipline of capitalism, from the rapid economic transformation of communities associated with the Industrial Revolution, and from globalization increased the potential for social, political, and economic instability. The shift of populations to urban areas made such dislocations and risks to individuals more visible than in earlier times, when the poor in rural areas could still farm their fields and raise animals for sustenance. With democratization, policy makers encountered greater demands to manage such risks. The modern social welfare state emerged and coevolved with the processes underpinning the Industrial Revolution, modern capitalism, and globalization.

In focusing on the improvement in *overall* social welfare and efficiency, we risk overlooking the costs that befall *individuals* and their immediate communities. Such localized and individual costs are inevitable products of a globalization process based on competitive market exchange—a part of the process of creative destruction. These costs persist in twenty-first-century globalization as well, but the manifestations of such dislocation are often masked by the modern social welfare state, which affords a better safety net. The expansion of market exchange and global capitalism presents societies and governments with the policy dilemma of capturing the collective gains of globalization while managing the individual costs. This tension plagues all political economies as they become more integrated into a global economy. Failure to manage the individual costs humanely can lead to political and social instability and attacks on the process of market exchange itself, which may damage collective outcomes.

The Dominance of Colonialism and Imperialism

A far more disquieting phenomenon further tainted nineteenth-century globalization. Colonialism, the expansion of imperial control, appeared as one of the more unfortunate outgrowths of globalization. Centuries earlier, European traders and explorers had connected societies that were highly differentiated by religious and social practices. Their travels and activities foreshadowed the development not only of modern trade relations but also of European colonial empires. Early in this period of expanding trade and economic exchange, the tentacles of European territorial ambition were limited to protecting the market centers and fueling stations that were critical to the flow of commodities across great distances. With the stark exception of the struggle for conquest of the Americas, early European commercial exploits built on trade with indigenous populations. As the European merchants traded for local goods, they generally avoided explicit or heavy-handed interference in local forms of production and social organization. They generally recognized local governance structures, worked with those structures, and did not try to impose their own governing institutions. Only occasionally were troops or naval vessels dispatched to resolve disputes between the European traders and local elites. These ventures were basically trading regimes rather than political-military empires.

Napoleon's defeat in 1815 left the British as the only significant colonial empire for almost sixty years. By 1870, however, the colonial ambitions of many powerful political economies—at first the French, Spanish, Dutch, and Germans, who were later joined by the Americans and Japanese—had emerged as a significant aspect of international political and economic affairs. In the rush to build their colonial empires, these emerging world powers partitioned much of the earth, dramatically altering the geopolitical face of the globe. Maps 9.1a and 9.1b show the expansion and consolidation of this new and different form of colonial empire.

The new colonialism, **imperialism,** involved far more intrusive political and economic domination. Market forces no longer tempered the activities of producers and labor in the colonies. Under imperialism, the disciplining mechanism that altered production structures had little to do with global forces of supply and demand, which would reveal weak-

> **Imperialism** is the intrusive political and economic domination of overseas colonial possessions. Imperial powers employ the political-military tools of hierarchy, not markets, to manage their colonial possessions and change production structures in their colonies.

nesses and reward strengths based on comparative advantage and specialization. Instead, heavy-handed political dictates by an invasive colonial administration determined production strategies and the goods produced. Imperial powers employed the tools of hierarchy, not markets, to manage and change the production structures of the colonized, and they developed large bureaucracies devoted to managing their colonial possessions. Moreover, those production structures did not face the direct discipline of the global marketplace. The economic geography of production in the colonies was not the decentralized geography of global capitalism; rather, it conformed more to the political geography of the nation-state system. And, thanks to the Industrial Revolution, the military capabilities of the colonial powers now dwarfed any local resistance by those being colonized. For the colonial powers, the military resources needed to maintain control were actually relatively small.

Native industries languished as colonial powers invested only in the production of commodities for export and in the infrastructure to assist those exports. Production shifted to extractive industries and cash crops such as rubber, cotton, jute, gold, diamonds, tin, cocoa, and coffee. Investments in roads, railways, ports, plantations, factories, and other infrastructure were designed to address the needs of the colonial power, not those of the colonized. The shift in production structures toward cash crops reduced economic diversity, which left the colonies increasingly exposed to perverse shifts in the global economy. By the beginning of the twentieth century, societies that had once been capable of feeding themselves were debilitated, at the mercy of the global economy and their colonial masters. Declines in prices elsewhere decreased the gains from trade in the colonies and reduced the purchasing power of the indigenous populations.

The rationales offered for colonial expansion were many. One was the search for raw materials and inexpensive inputs to sustain the colonial powers' industries and standard of living. Another rationale advanced the need to invest surplus capital abroad in order to limit

Map 9.1a	U.S., British, and Japanese Colonialism, c. 1900

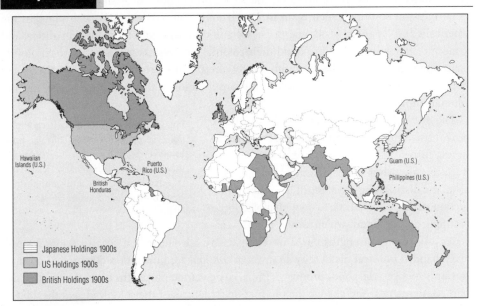

Map 9.1b	European Imperialism in Africa, c. 1914

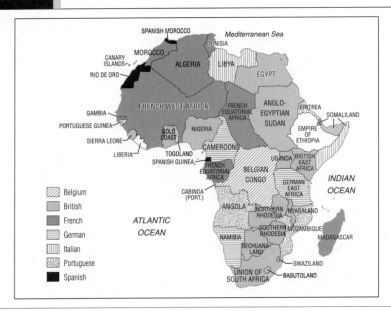

Sources: Map 9.1a, Bruce Buena de Mesquita, *Principles of International Politics* (Washington, DC: CQ Press, 2003). Used by permission. Map 9.1b, from http://exploringafrica.matrix.msu.edu and information supplied by the author.

inflationary increases at home. Another argued the advantages of captive markets and self-contained trading empires, where the colonial powers' commodities could escape the competitive pressures of an open global economy. Ironically, under these rationales, Great Britain, the home to modern liberal economic thought, celebrating the efficient collective outcome produced by market exchange, was using its colonies to shelter itself from market forces. Yet another argument for colonialism was expressed by Rudyard Kipling in his poem "The White Man's Burden" (1899):

> Take up the White Man's burden—
> Send forth the best ye breed—
> Go bind your sons to exile
> To serve your captives' need;
> To wait in heavy harness,
> On fluttered folk and wild—
> Your new-caught, sullen peoples,
> Half-devil and half-child.

Kipling thus romanticized the white man's burden as a crusade to bring modern civilization, European rationality, to those of non-European origin.

Whatever the rationale, the reality was that of political, military, and economic domination. Although the European and American governments advanced notions of political liberty and rational constitutionalism—and were themselves experiencing a golden era of political and economic enlightenment—those same nations denied those very concepts to the peoples they colonized. In the Spanish-American War of 1898, U.S. troops marched off purportedly to liberate Cuba and the Philippines from Spanish colonial domination, only to replace Spanish colonial domination with U.S. colonial administration. The imperialism and colonialism that emerged in the latter 1800s besmirched both rational constitutional governance and the reputations of the European powers, Japan, and the United States. Extending their political and economic spheres by military means and imposing governance structures on indigenous populations, these colonial imperialists sullied the record of nineteenth-century globalization, contravened the market forces propelling that globalization, and tainted the international relations of the twentieth century.

CONCLUSION

A combination of public and private inventions and policy shifts promoted the processes of globalization during the nineteenth century. The principle of comparative advantage, policy shifts that lowered human-made barriers to trade, the invention of MFN in bilateral trade treaties, and transportation revolutions promoted the expansion of cross-border exchange. Public and private innovations helped to manage the currency and default risks of international exchange. Banks intermediated cross-border default risk through the issuance of financial instruments, while governments stabilized expectations about currency values and exchange-rate risk through convergence on the gold standard and the commitment to convertibility. These measures promoted international trade by making the risks more predictable and acceptable to the individuals and firms engaged in such trade. The primacy of London's capital markets—dominated by those holding firmly to liberal economic beliefs—and the nurturing role of such British governmental institutions as H.M. Treasury and the Bank of England helped to reduce procyclical pressures during economic downturns by supplying capital liquidity that could stimulate economic investment and activity. These mechanisms worked well enough that British financiers and public officials found themselves at the core of the expanding global economy. Some observers attribute the long peace of the nineteenth century—the relative absence of international conflict that colored the 1700s and 1900s—to the influence of British finance.

KEY CONCEPTS

arbitrage opportunities (p. 341)

banker's acceptances (p. 330)

bilateral trade negotiations (p. 326)

convertibility (p. 339)

countercyclical policy (p. 346)

creative destruction (p. 359)

currency risk (p. 331)

default risk (p. 329)

deflation (p. 335)

free trade (p. 325)

gold standard (p. 332)

Gresham's law (p. 331)

imperialism (p. 361)

inflation (p. 335)

international monetary regime (p. 331)

lender of last resort (p. 345)

letters of credit (p. 330)

market access under duress (p. 348)

mercantilism (p. 321)

most-favored-nation status (MFN) (p. 326)

network externality (p. 338)

principle of nonexclusion (p. 319)

procyclical policy (p. 346)

protectionism (p. 321)

tradable sector (p. 340)

EXERCISES

1. What were the purposes of the Corn Laws and the Navigation Acts? Who benefited and who lost?

2. What makes a good a collective good?

3. What collective goods did the United Kingdom provide in the late 1800s, and how did they affect globalization?

4. The collective goods that Britain provided in the late 1800s seem intricately connected to the maintenance of a cooperative environment conducive to the international exchange of goods, services, and capital. Are these factors independent or dependent variables in relation to globalization? Explain.

5. Explain why the United Kingdom was able to provide such collective goods but other governments could not, even if they so desired.

6. Name a collective good other than those already mentioned and explain why is it a collective good.

7. Explain MFN and its significance to international affairs.

8. In the late 1800s, the United Kingdom and the United States adhered to the gold standard. If a creditor in Great Britain loaned money to someone in the United States, and then the United States were to switch to a bimetallic standard, what implications would this have for the British creditor?

9. Explain creative destruction and how it serves to increase the collective welfare of society.

10. Explain the difference between absolute advantage and comparative advantage as they relate to the agricultural producers of the late 1800s who were affected by advancing transportation technology.

11. Technological change played a key role in the globalization of the 1800s. Provide several examples of technological change that helped to increase economic exchange across borders during this period and explain how they worked to promote globalization.

12. Some of the collective goods provided by the United Kingdom during the 1800s were countercyclical public policies. What is a countercyclical policy and why is it important?

13. The expansion of suffrage in the late 1800s is said to have been a two-edged sword in respect to free trade. Explain.

14. What made governments' commitments to the gold standard credible, rather than cheap talk?

FURTHER READING

Cohen, Benjamin J. 1998. *The Geography of Money*. Ithaca, NY: Cornell University Press.

Eichengreen, Barry. 1996. *Globalizing Capital: A History of the International Monetary System*. Princeton, NJ: Princeton University Press.

Findlay, Ronald, and Kevin H. O'Rourke. 2007. *Power and Plenty: Trade, War, and the World Economy in the Second Millennium*. Princeton, NJ: Princeton University Press.

Hobsbawm, Eric. 1989. *The Age of Empire: 1875–1914*. New York: Vintage Books.

———. 1996. *The Age of Capital: 1848–1875*. New York: Vintage Books.

Hume, David. (1741) 1987. "Of the Balance of Trade." In *Essays, Moral, Political, and Literary*. Reprint, Indianapolis: Liberty Fund.

Irwin, Douglas A. 1996. *Against the Tide: An Intellectual History of Free Trade*. Princeton, NJ: Princeton University Press.

Kennedy, Paul. 1989. *The Rise and Fall of Great Powers*. New York: Vintage Books.

O'Rourke, Kevin H., and Jeffrey G. Williamson. 1999. *Globalization and History: The Evolution of a Nineteenth-Century Atlantic Economy*. Cambridge: MIT Press.

Pahre, Robert. 2007. *Politics and Trade Cooperation in the Nineteenth Century: The "Agreeable Customs" of 1815–1914*. New York: Cambridge University Press.

Ricardo, David. (1817) 1996. *The Principles of Political Economy and Taxation*. Reprint, Amherst, NY: Prometheus Books.

The World between the Wars: A Breakdown in Globalization

By 1914, there was hardly a village or town anywhere on the globe whose prices were not influenced by distant foreign markets, whose infrastructure was not financed by foreign capital, whose engineering, manufacturing, and even business skills were not influenced by the absence of those who had emigrated or by the presence of strangers who had immigrated. . . . Not everyone was happy with the new global economy. . . . Rich landowners demanded protection from cheap farm products. Workers pointed to unfair competition from imports made with cheap foreign labor and claimed their jobs were being robbed by immigrants. Capitalists in declining import-competing industries argued that it was only fair that they get compensation for the losses they suffered on sunk investments. And domestic policymakers began to feel they were losing their ability to manage prices, interest rates, and markets; they felt increasingly vulnerable to financial panic, industrial crisis, and unfavorable price shocks generated in distant corners of the globe.

—Kevin O'Rourke and Jeffrey G. Williamson, Globalization and History, 1999

This chapter examines the period between the two world wars of the twentieth century. Why did rational policy makers adopt policies that unraveled the cooperation and globalization that had been so beneficial to their societies during the 1800s? We consider how the social context of those choices, the interdependence of those choices, and the absence of a hegemonic leader created a social trap for national policy makers and their societies, a trap that led them to choose policies that fed a vicious cycle and undermined the global economy.

WHY THE REVERSAL IN GLOBALIZATION AND ECONOMIC ADVANCE?

The long peace, stability, and growing prosperity of the 1800s proved too good to last. Industrialization, globalization, market exchange, and the growth of rational governance had all contributed to economic and political transformation, especially in the Atlantic economy. Despite the unqualified improvement in the human condition in the major economies of the Atlantic economy, the conditions that spawned such development were fragile. The seeds of breakdown were sown in the successes of globalization. Increasing trade and the Industrial Revolution produced significant gains in wealth, which funded the expansion of the state into new areas of social welfare, but these factors also underwrote an enlargement of states' military capabilities. Public education advanced the development of national identity through the teaching of citizenship and improved the quality of the labor available for economic activities, but it also increased the pool of stakeholders willing to sacrifice for the state in case of military conflict. Improvements in government bureaucracies and the increased use of the census led to better accounting of populations, which improved the ability of the state to conscript soldiers and also enhanced its ability to extract taxes to pay for the training and materials for a military. The same transformations that fed economic and political development also increased the potential for violence in interstate conflict if it were to occur.

World War I, the Great Depression, and World War II interrupted and reversed the trend toward globalization. The Depression, which began in 1929 and lasted until the beginning of World War II, imposed great hardships on the peoples of the world. The gains of the 1800s made a U-turn during this period. Economies that had been growing by leaps and bounds slowed to a halt and then shrank. Statistics can describe the declines in gross domestic product and international trade, as well as the increases in unemployment and food lines, but they cannot convey the full harshness of the suffering, the loss of dignity and the cost in lives and communities that overwhelmed the populations of many states. Traditional family structures broke down as parents found themselves unable to feed their children. Fathers deserted their families in humiliation and embarrassment. Mothers were known to boil shoelaces to add some nutrition and flavor to the water that served as a meal. Indeed, the effects of the Depression proved as violent an assault on people and communities as the world wars that were its bookends. The worldwide suffering served as a breeding ground not only for noble attempts at political reform and experimentation but also for extremist politics, as societies and communities sought solutions to the burdens of their people.

What precipitated the Great Depression? Why did the market system falter and fail so dramatically instead of redressing its inefficiencies through market corrections? Why did the mechanisms of supply and demand fail to regulate the system and restore equilibrium? Why did monetary and fiscal policies fail to halt the downward spiral of economic activity? Why did these shocks spill across national borders to create an international economic crisis of stunning magnitude and pain, producing violent political dislocations? Various explanations have been offered to account for the breakdown in globalization that coincided with the two major world wars and the Great Depression. Some focus on the years between the wars, highlighting the collapse of national economies and the failure of governments to manage divisive forces in their political economies. Others emphasize the role of the 1929 market crash, or the failure of U.S. monetary policies to address the building crisis, or shifts in trade policies and rising protectionism. This chapter focuses on several major factors that contributed to the breakdown of the global and national economies during the interwar years.

First, the legacy of the 1800s began to pose difficult decisions for policy makers, as they sought to limit, manage, and allocate the adverse effects of globalization that were threatening some of their constituents. Second, World War I devastated national political economies, presenting them and the global economy with severe challenges. These included catastrophic losses in labor, instability and pressures in the exchange-rate mechanism, debt and reparation demands, shortages of liquidity and vulnerability of credit mechanisms, growing obstructions to international trade, increasing willingness of governments to intervene in their economies to shift the costs of globalization abroad and so damage their neighbors, and an absence of international leadership. As polities faced increased economic hardship, national policy makers faced difficult questions about who would carry the burden of adjusting to economic dislocations at the same time that their resources and capacity for action were sorely diminished by the ravages of war. These problems led to a breakdown in the provision of key collective goods that helped to promote globalization in the 1800s; conditions conducive to the rise of political extremism became more common.

ALLOCATING COSTS OF ADJUSTMENT

This book began with several core assumptions. One was that policy makers act as if they are rational. So we must try to understand the twentieth-century reassertion of government obstructions to international trade and labor mobility and other policy choices as rational, goal-oriented choices regardless of their outcomes. Another assumption was that politicians want to survive, which involves being responsive to those they represent, whether that constituency entails a broad swath of society, as in democracies, or a smaller segment of society, as in less democratic regimes. Varying degrees of constituent satisfaction or dissatisfaction with politicians are registered in elections, coups, assassinations, and other forms of regime change or regime validation.

With the expansion of suffrage and democratic governance in the 1800s, politicians in the states of the Atlantic economy faced increasingly difficult tests of survival in elections. Wider enfranchisement broadened the diversity of interests demanding representation from these democratically elected officials. Increased representation provided pathways for those damaged by economic change to lobby their elected officials for barriers to globalization, if they could organize successfully for political action. Growing political participation increased the prospect of policy makers encountering a **time-inconsistency problem,** in which constituent groups' short-term goals were at odds with the long-term welfare of society, which could affect politicians' political survival. Many of these short-term pressures demanded redistribution of the costs and

> A **time-inconsistency problem** is a policy dilemma in which the short-term demands on policy makers are at odds with the long-term welfare of society.

> The **costs of adjustment** are the challenges and dislocations that people and societies confront as they adapt to economic and social change.

benefits of economic progress through the policy and regulatory mechanisms of the state.

Societies and governments decide how to allocate the **costs of adjustment** that inevitably accompany the creative destruction caused by competitive markets or the turmoil produced by any other significant process of change. Costs of adjustment are the challenges and dislocations that people and societies confront as they adapt to economic and social change. Such costs are unavoidable in dynamic economies. Unwillingness to accept them represents a resistance to change and an unwillingness to take a chance to obtain new gains. Costs of adjustment may include the costs of unemployment, lost income, and the dilemma of making ends meet; the costs of searching for new employment and, possibly, relocating to find new opportunities; the costs of retraining and education; the costs of lost opportunities in the future; and social costs such as divorce, alcoholism, family violence, and breakdown in community.

Governments and societies have three choices in the face of these costs of adjustment: (1) to let those personally experiencing the negative effects of economic change bear the full costs of adjustment; (2) to redistribute the costs more broadly to the domestic society at large through the safety net mechanisms of the social welfare state; or (3) to export the costs abroad through the linkages of globalization, placing them on other nations' workers, producers, and voters. If those experiencing a dislocation are successful at organizing for political action and placing their concerns on the political agenda, they may succeed in avoiding the full costs of adjustment and shifting some of those costs to others in their society, abroad, or both. Despite the rapid advance of globalization during the late nineteenth century—and the many gains that accrued to societies from exchange of goods, services, capital, people, and information across national boundaries—groups and segments of society that were being affected negatively by global pressures began to criticize the processes of globalization and to pressure their governments to redistribute the costs of adjustment. Politicians, worried about their chances of political survival, could not afford to ignore these societal pressures if they were well organized and politically influential.

THE LEGACY OF RAPID CHANGE IN THE 1800S

By the late 1800s, trouble was brewing in national economies that could spill over into international affairs. Price deflation in key economic sectors created dislocations in national economies that led to pressures on politicians to resist further trade liberalization and, in some cases, to reverse the trend toward lower tariffs and greater openness. Policy makers in several nations began to restrict immigration, which was one of the central processes driving globalization and factor price convergence across national political economies. New World economies such as the United States, Canada, Australia, and some Latin American states—where labor was a relatively scarce factor of production—had fueled their economic expansions with the labor of Irish, Italian, German, Norwegian, and Russian immigrants, along with immigrants of other nationalities. Despite a need for more labor, however, California passed a series of initiatives in the 1880s designed to limit the immigration of Asians, and other governments also began to impose more restrictive barriers to entry for immigrants.

Governments were proactive in the mid-1800s in creating conditions favorable to globalization and economic progress, but by the late 1800s they increasingly implemented restrictive trade and immigration policies that threatened to interrupt the gains from globalization and undermine their societies' welfare. These policy changes limited potential gains from specialization of production and mobile labor markets. Policy interventions to slow and restrict globalization constrained the consumption possibilities for societies overall, but they improved the lot of a few at the expense of many. Why would politicians adopt policies that interrupted processes so beneficial to their societies?

Agriculture and Costs of Adjustment

The recessions of the late 1800s affected every economic sector, but especially agriculture and the producers and labor in the primary product sector, which included agriculture, minerals, metals, and other primary commodities. Producers and labor in these sectors were hard-hit by price deflation, which led to declines in incomes. (In chapter 9, table 9.3 shows the deflation in prices of agricultural commodities.) At the crux of their dilemma was too much production, not enough consumption, and the tight money supply policies associated with the gold standard. With the Industrial Revolution, more and more commodities were being produced, but with disproportionately smaller increases in the labor force as the result of natural processes (births and increased longevity) and more limited expansion of the money supply because of its ties to gold. The limit on money supply interacted with the increase in supply of goods and services to generate downward pressures on prices. This linkage returns us to Hume's recognition of the relationship between the size of money supply and prices—if downward pressures are severe enough, price deflation results.

Farm income could increase if the supply of agricultural commodities were to decline. In a **laissez-faire** global political economy, this contingency would require that farmers limit their production, either voluntarily or through some form of coordination, or that a sufficient number of agricultural producers go out of business as a part of the process of creative destruction. But voluntary constraints on production require an amazing amount of coordination across vast geographic space and, given the global nature of agricultural markets, across national boundaries. Such coordination is unlikely without some coercive mechanism, because individual farmers would have incentives to defect on such voluntary constraints, particularly if other farmers did limit their production. By defecting they would increase their incomes at the expense of others—in other words, they would be free riders.

> A **laissez-faire economy** is one in which private transactions are relatively free from state intervention in the form of regulation, taxes, or rule of law.

Consequently, if a farmer believed that other farmers were going to defect—free ride—by overproducing, she would be foolish not to overproduce as well. Even though such actions would contribute to an oversupply of farm commodities and aggravate price deflation, why should she let other farmers reap all the incremental gains of overproducing? This situation offers another example of a social trap in which individual rationality undermines collective welfare. The individual incentives in this dynamic led to more and more overproduction as each farmer planted more cropland in an attempt to make ends meet, but this individual rationale just added fuel to the problem of price deflation and oversupply in agriculture. Moreover, the process of creative destruction—the weeding out of inefficient farm producers through business failures—proved uncertain, for farmers could live off the land even as their economic enterprises faltered. Farmers were resistant to weeding out! This peculiarity made agricultural producers slower than other producers to adapt to the discipline of global capitalism—a legacy that persists today.

Agricultural producers were threatened with bearing the full costs of adjustment to price deflation, which could lead to a drastic increase in farm failures and bankruptcies. Unable to resolve their problems through concerted, voluntary coordination of production targets, producers and laborers in agriculture and other sectors turned to government to redistribute their costs of adjustment. Farmers were particularly well placed to appeal to government for policies to address their dilemma because in many societies they had substantial ties to political representatives because of history and geography. Historically, landowning was a prerequisite of political enfranchisement, so rural areas and farmers had been overrepresented in legislatures before the expansion of suffrage, and this legacy persisted. Geographically, farmers were distributed across broad areas and, consequently, could often appeal to large numbers of elected representatives.

Two alternative mechanisms were available to address this problem of dwindling farm income: (1) increasing the money supply, which could reverse price deflation; and (2) limiting the supply of a commodity and increasing its price through some government intervention. Global convergence on the gold standard and the slow growth in gold resources limited the possibilities of dramatically increasing the money supply. Even if an alternative to the gold standard were adopted at a national level, the ability of capital to migrate would undermine this alternative unless the alternative standard were to be adopted across many political economies. Unilateral adoption of an alternative monetary system by a state would lead to a drain of that state's national gold reserves, as people would convert their currency holdings to gold. Because increasing the money supply would undermine the exchange-rate system and generate uncertainty and instability, it was not a viable option; the only strategy available to agricultural producers was to limit supply, but the difficulties of exercising voluntary constraints across the entire community remained formidable.

Retrenchment of Trade Barriers

Unable to coordinate an effort of self-restraint, agricultural and other commodity producers sought to limit the supply of commodities from abroad. These communities succeeded in overcoming the barriers to political action by mobilizing to exercise their political voice in favor of shifting the costs of adjustment to others. They lobbied government to halt the decline of trade barriers, and in many states they succeeded in halting the decline and even restored higher barriers to entry. As table 9.1 in the preceding chapter shows, tariff rates initially declined in the mid-1800s, but they started to climb again in many nations by the late 1800s. The United Kingdom maintained its open-border policy and continued to provide the collective good of market access under duress, but other major economies and markets raised tariffs and other barriers to entry.

While not affecting supply, a tariff or import tax on a foreign product artificially increases the price for that good. A tariff on foreign commodities would increase the prices of those commodities relative to their domestic counterparts, and domestic producers hoped that consumers faced with such a change in the prices of foreign commodities would alter their consumption choices, given their **budgetary constraints.** When

> **Budgetary constraints** are limits on the amount of money or resources that one can spend, which thus affect consumption choices.

such barriers did change domestic consumption decisions by shifting consumption from foreign-produced products to domestic-produced products, the tariffs forced the costs of adjustment onto the backs of foreign producers and labor, whose products lost market share, and onto the broader domestic society, where prices for those commodities (domestic and foreign) increased.

This process of retrenchment did not necessarily mean an absolute rejection of globalization, but it did moderate the processes and mechanisms promoting globalization. Such actions were harbingers of the embedded tensions between the economic geography of globalization and the political geography of the state system. The processes of globalization operated within a social context of separate nation-states, where global economic processes interacted with national political and social processes. Those disadvantaged by global processes could appeal to national mechanisms for redress. These tensions contributed to the dilemmas facing governments during the years leading up to World War I.

THE UNSETTLING LEGACY OF WORLD WAR I IN THE INTERWAR YEARS

Political scientists and historians continue to debate the reasons World War I occurred. Some base their explanations on the technological imperatives of particular military force structures and the dynamics of military mobilizations. Others suggest that the cognitive frameworks of the different national leaders contributed to misperception, miscommunication, and missed opportunities for peaceful settlement and diffusion of the looming military crisis in 1914. Others argue that the dynamics of domestic political economies contributed to the onset of the conflict. Some claim that the development of national identity and expansion of the notion of citizenship enhanced the likelihood of conflict by promoting jingoism, which only ensured a greater level of violence than in previous wars. Others point to the structure of balance-of-power politics and the inflexibility of alliance structures in dealing with power shifts in international relations. Still others highlight the importance of critical events such as the assassination of Archduke Franz Ferdinand of Austria and his wife in Sarajevo in June 1914.

Regardless of its definitive cause or causes, many agree that World War I was a war few really wanted. Sadly, the world stumbled into a conflict of tragic proportions. Here, however, we are less interested in the war's causes than in its consequences for the global political economy. Called "the war to end all wars," World War I produced a ghastly amount of death and destruction in a four-year period. It also left a troubling legacy of great dislocation and uncertainty in the global political economy—traumas that inhibited postwar recovery, unsettled the global political economy, contributed to the slide into the Great Depression, fanned the fires of political extremism, and fueled animosities leading to the eventual resumption of global hostilities in World War II. Indeed, the two world wars were less separate conflicts than a single war with an intermission.

World War I interrupted globalization, and after it ended, the nations of the Atlantic economy sought to rebuild their political economies. The aftermath of any war challenges policy makers as they try to regain the economic and political stability that is critical to advancing prosperity and welfare during peacetime. After this war, they faced particularly difficult obstacles as they sought to recapture the economic and political hopes of the late 1800s, for the legacies of the war hindered economic recovery and left a residue of political animosity within and between nations. In this environment, a combination of poor policy choices by some leaders and the sheer inability of some nations' policy makers to implement good policies even when they tried handicapped the rebuilding of national political economies. Let's consider several important legacies of World War I that presented major obstacles to the restoration of stable political economic life.

Post–World War I Population Loss as a Barrier to Economic Activity

The war to end all wars revolutionized the technology of warfare and produced a quantum leap in the violence of war. World War I debilitated the material, human, and social resources of the European combatants, leaving only the United States relatively unscathed, largely because of its late entry into the war and its geographic separation from the main fields of battle. As the major combatants turned away from war and took up the task of peacetime rebuilding, they encountered sluggish economies and barriers to reconstruction. Economies that had been supplying the materials of war now had to be retooled to produce goods for private and peacetime consumption. Such retooling required the key inputs of labor and capital for economic activity, but both of these factors were lacking in postwar Europe as a result of the high material and human costs of the conflict.

Growing economies need labor to work the factories, harvest crops, teach in schools, and provide productive energy and creativity, and the war's toll of death and disability severely constrained the supply of labor. Approximately 10 percent of the population of the European combatant states (twenty million men) joined the fight in the first months of the conflict; far more soon followed as grist for their nations' war machines. The proud soldiers who marched off to war in 1914 bore little resemblance to the armies at the turn of the previous century. These modern warriors had been strengthened by significant gains in economic welfare, improvements in health care and diet, and the expansion of education. These men, their fathers, and their grandfathers provided the labor, energy, and creativity that transformed the economies of Europe in the mid- to late 1800s. This cream of European progress, however, was soon devastated by four years of brutal trench warfare. Graveyards along the western front, "cities of the dead," serve as grim reminders of the horrors of World War I, in which entire generations were killed, crippled, or traumatized. Table 10.1 details the

TABLE 10.1	**World War I Mobilization and Casualty Rates**			
Country	Mobilized	Killed	Wounded	Missing/POW	Casualties (as % of mobilized)
Germany	11,000,000	1,773,700	4,216,058	1,152,800	65
Russia	12,000,000	1,700,000	4,950,000	2,500,000	76
France	8,410,000	1,375,800	4,266,000	537,000	73
Austria-Hungary	7,800,000	1,200,000	3,620,000	2,200,000	90
United Kingdom	8,904,467	908,371	2,090,012	191,652	36
Italy	5,615,000	650,000	947,000	600,000	39
Romania	750,000	335,706	120,000	80,000	71
Turkey	2,850,000	325,000	400,000	250,000	34
United States	4,355,000	126,000	234,300	4,526	8
Bulgaria	1,200,000	87,500	152,390	27,029	22
Serbia	707,343	45,000	133,148	152,958	47
Belgium	267,000	13,716	44,686	34,659	35
Portugal	100,000	7,222	13,751	12,318	33
Greece	230,000	5,000	21,000	1,000	12
Montenegro	50,000	3,000	10,000	7,000	40
Japan	800,000	300	907	3	0.1
Totals	65,038,810	8,556,315	21,219,252	7,750,945	58

Source: Data from Susan Everett, *The Two World Wars,* vol. 1, *World War I* (Lincoln, NE: Bison Books, 1980).

numbers of men who went to war, the numbers killed or wounded, and the proportion of their national militaries that were casualties. Even those who stayed home did not escape the suffering. Spouses, parents, and siblings were victims of the war as well as they awaited word of their loved ones. Such waiting imposes mental and physical trauma that wears on the human spirit and diminishes the ability of individuals to contribute productively to societal outcomes. Table 10.1 does not reflect the lingering damage to the psyches and capabilities of those who survived the war.

Clearly the breadth and depth of the losses incurred in World War I denied the major combatant nations the fruits of the labor of their most economically valuable citizenry. Several generations of men who were in their prime years of productivity and creativity were snuffed out in the trenches of Europe. Evaluating the human costs of war goes far beyond considering the numbers of those killed and wounded, for costs are, by definition, the paths not taken when a course of action is chosen. The costs of World War I were what Europe might have become politically, economically, and socially had the war not occurred. Of course, this counterfactual is impossible to assess accurately. We can only speculate, but we do know that ideas and creativity died with those victims of the conflict. Who can say what processes and inventions were not created, what talents were not brought to bear on public and private dilemmas, what leaders never entered politics or industry, or what students never went to universities to become teachers and investigators? We cannot predict what those people would have created or contributed, but we can be fairly sure that their contributions would have made for a different world.

THE EXCHANGE-RATE MECHANISM: CURRENCY INSTABILITY AND CONVERTIBILITY

Chapters 6 and 9 discussed the importance of both an effective exchange-rate mechanism and a currency that is trusted to settle international accounts as collective goods critical for overcoming obstacles to international exchange. Instabilities in exchange rates create currency risk and uncertainty, which affects the expected value of exchange. In the prewar years, a fixed-exchange-rate system that was based on gold produced stability, which limited the currency risk that could hinder international exchange. The Bank of England and London's private capital markets helped to manage the system and maintain stability in the price of currencies, and this stability was abetted by the British commitment to convertibility. World War I, however, introduced several major problems for stability in the exchange-rate mechanism.

The financial demands of war led governments to disassociate their currency values from the prewar gold standard and created imbalances in the value of currencies in relation to each other. Gold provided the discipline to constrain inflation, but this discipline disappeared with the fiscal demands of World War I. Governments cannot tax enough to employ a pay-as-you-go system during a major international conflict. They must find means in addition to tax revenues to finance costly war expenditures. Governments have a variety of ways of financing such an extensive international conflict. They tax, borrow against the future through sovereign debt instruments, and, inevitably, if the conflict is costly enough, resort to printing money. All governments inflated their currencies as a means of financing their efforts in World War I, some more than others. Money supply in the United States increased by about 250 percent during the war; prices about doubled, but U.S. gold reserves also doubled, which supported the expanded money supply. Germany's currency base expanded by 400 percent during the war, and prices increased tenfold. France expanded its money supply by 350 percent, and prices increased by more than threefold. In Great Britain the money supply more than doubled, going from about five billion to twelve billion dollars, with a 250 percent increase in prices.

In response to the pressing financial demands of a major war, governments suspended both convertibility and their commitment to maintain the prewar par value of their currencies vis-à-vis gold. Currencies were allowed to float, which meant that market forces determined their prices. Imbalances in this floating-currency mechanism could hurt those in the tradable sector in one country and help those in the tradable sector in another country if one state's currency became overvalued relative to the other's. Imbalances in exchange rates threatened to hinder the rebuilding of trade relations, as governments faced pressure from their domestic constituencies to address the imbalances—to manipulate the value of a state's currency to the advantage of its domestic producers. In this environment, policy makers sought to restabilize currency values. Many, the British in particular, argued for a return to the par value of currencies that had existed before the war. As nations tried to return to the gold standard by the mid-1920s, the continuing problem of imbalances in exchange rates was compounded by price deflation in commodity sectors and the difficulty of promoting economic expansion in the context of a scarce money supply.

Remember that prices in a fixed-exchange-rate system should eventually adjust through changes in the money supply, which result from capital flows to pay for trade. But a rigid system with fundamental imbalances in exchange rates puts pressure on governments to deal more rapidly with such problems by changing the value of the currency or resorting to other policies that can affect trade. If governments respond to such pressures by devaluing their currencies in order to make their goods more competitive in the global arena, they can threaten the stability of currency prices, as well as the stability of the exchange-rate mechanism itself.

British commitments to rebuilding an exchange-rate system based on the gold standard and the collective good of convertibility, which had helped to generate confidence in the prewar gold standard, were also in question. A credible commitment to the gold standard and convertibility requires that a government maintain sufficient gold reserves to exchange for its currency on demand. If other governments and people believe that a commitment to convertibility is credible—that a government does have sufficient reserves to meet demands to convert and will meet those demands—then demands to convert should be manageable and not threatening to monetary and macroeconomic stability. But several factors challenged the relationship between gold reserves and currencies in the postwar period and threatened the credibility of any commitment to convertibility and the exchange-rate mechanism.

Even before the war, the costs of mining and the limited discovery of new gold veins had constrained growth in gold reserves. This slow growth limited expansion of the money supply even as production of many commodities increased. This led to deflationary pressures on commodities, particularly agricultural products. Economic sectors that were feeling the strains of deflation pressured their governments to increase the money supply to inflate prices—even if this increase would lead to a shift in the ratio of gold reserves to currency. All governments engaged in World War I had done this to varying degrees to help finance their efforts in the conflict. After the war, governments continued to face pressures within their polities to increase money supply to aid in reconstruction, even if such actions might produce inflation. As some governments acquiesced, the amount of currency in circulation grew faster than the world's supply of gold. The resulting discontinuity between additions to official gold reserves and growth in the money supply threatened the credibility of a commitment to convertibility, as paper currency far exceeded official gold reserves.

Regardless of the limitations of world gold production, World War I placed such demands on governments that convertibility would have been very difficult to maintain as official policy. The need to finance the war, which represented a huge leap in the size and degree of conflict and hence in its costs, taxed the capital resources of the European combatants. The war effort demanded a tremendous amount of very expensive materials, for which the United Kingdom and its allies turned to the United States. Initially, as they paid for such materials with their gold reserves, these governments limited convertibility and imposed controls on gold exports so that they could afford to pay for the war materials. In times of such dire need, governments were no longer willing to exchange their gold forcurrency.

Even with such drastic changes in policy, the Allied governments quickly spent their reserves paying for war materials. And although they taxed their publics heavily to raise funds to pay these expenses, increasing tax revenues could not make up the budget shortfalls. As they had during past wars, the governments had to borrow to pay for their continued war efforts. The United States extended credit in the form of loans that conferred obligations to tax the supply of capital that would be available in the future. By the end of the conflict, the United Kingdom, France, and other war-torn economies faced massive debts (see table 10.2).

Governments were able to incur debt to pay for their purchases of war materials abroad, but they still needed to find a means to meet their domestic economic obligations. They began to issue money that was not backed by gold, further divorcing money supply from gold reserves. This money was called **fiat money** or **fiat currency.** The creation of fiat money created inflationary pressures. Differences in the rate of fiat money creation across countries led to differences in their inflation rates. Because these differences affected domestic prices, they prompted significant variations in exchange rates. Inflation and exchange-rate instabilities persisted in the aftermath of the war. In this context, changes in the supply of currency, fiat money, and limited gold reserves created uncertainties over the price of currencies.

> **Fiat money** or currency is any money that is defined by a government as legal tender, which means it is acceptable to that government for payment of taxes and settlement of obligations. A **fiat currency** obtains its value through government regulation and decree.

> **Weak-currency countries** are those with state economies in which there are relatively large discrepancies between money supplies and reserve assets. **Strong-currency countries** are those with state economies in which there are relatively small discrepancies between money supplies and reserve assets.

With the end of the war, why did governments not return immediately to the stability of the pre-war gold standard and convertibility? Because they were already facing serious gold reserve shortages, an immediate return to the gold standard would have led to a further gold exodus from **weak-currency countries**—those states with the greatest differences between their gold reserves and their expanded supplies of currency. Despite their prewar reputations for financial responsibility and diligence, Germany and the United Kingdom had become weak-currency states. Much smaller discrepancies existed between money supply and gold reserves in **strong-currency countries.** A return to convertibility would have prompted an exchange of weak currencies for gold or for strong currencies as people worried about the prospects of such currencies holding their value or declining in value through further inflation. People would have sought to purchase a strong currency that was more likely to maintain its value or to hold their assets in gold. Such exchange would have led to an exodus of gold from weak-currency states to strong-currency states, exacerbating the economic problems of those states most damaged by the war. Only the United States, a strong-currency country, maintained the convertibility of its currency in this environment. Given the vast amount of U.S. gold reserves and the strength of the U.S. currency, there was little likelihood of a gold exodus from the United States.

Despite the barriers to returning to the gold standard and convertibility immediately following the war, many policy makers hoped to do so sometime in the future. They looked back at the economic expansion of the 1800s, the growth of trade, and the stability of the gold standard with fondness. By the mid-1920s, government attempts at stabilization and return to the gold standard appeared near success. Many governments began to restore stability to their exchange rates by constraining inflation. But this effort involved limiting the money supply, which ran the risk of reviving deflationary pressures in national economies, so most governments sought to stabilize and fix their exchange rates at current levels rather than at prewar levels.

TABLE 10.2	War Debts of Major World War I Combatants

Country	Debt total (in $ millions)
United Kingdom	4,277
France	3,405
Italy	1,648
Belgium	379
Russia	192
Poland	159
Czechoslovakia	92
Yugoslavia	52
Romania	38
Greece	27
Austria	24
Estonia	14
Armenia	12
Finland	8
Latvia	5

Source: Data from Thomas A. Bailey, *A Diplomatic History of the American People,* 10th ed. (Englewood Cliffs, NJ: Prentice Hall, 1980).

The United Kingdom, in its quest to support stability in the exchange-rate system and to recover its prestige and central role in managing the global economy, sought to return to the prewar gold standard and the prewar value of the pound (its par value). Restoring the pound to its prewar par value meant that the British needed to increase the pound's value in relation to other currencies, such as the French franc, even though it was already overvalued. By the mid-1920s, the United Kingdom had returned to the prewar par value of its currency, but this exchange-rate imbalance proved perverse for British producers and labor. British commodities that already were relatively expensive in global markets became more so, and the British balance of trade suffered in relation to nations with relatively undervalued currencies. This situation led to capital outflows from the United Kingdom and other countries with fixed, overvalued currencies.

The war and war debts severely wounded the United Kingdom's ability to continue playing the dominant role it had played in the promotion of globalization before World War I. It could no longer credibly support convertibility or manage problems in the exchange-rate system. The credibility of any nation to perform such functions relies on the nation's having access to sufficient financial resources, or at least the belief by others in the system that it has sufficient financial resources. Such belief can be enough to prevent a rush to convert currencies into gold and thus to motivate private economic activity and investment. Unfortunately for the British, the financial resources that had been so integral to their success in promoting the expansion of the global economy in the late 1800s were now in New York. The United Kingdom's gold reserves had declined tremendously. If people now believed that the British Treasury and the Bank of England could not access sufficient gold reserves to be able to exchange currencies for gold on demand, adherence to the prewar gold standard and the policy of convertibility would run the risk of increasing the incentives for others to exchange their currencies for British gold before there was no gold left in the British Treasury. No one wanted to be at the end of the line if the British ran out of gold, so the individual incentives of firms and governments to get there before no gold was left could produce a run on the British Treasury. Without sufficient official gold reserves, the pound was no longer perceived as "good as gold." The British were caught in a dilemma.

Even if the British government could marshal enough official gold reserves and capital resources at home through London's financial markets, trying to support the prewar price of the pound in gold imposed large costs on the British people in terms of unemployment, tighter money at home, and slower domestic recovery. Maintaining the prewar value of the pound in gold would damage British producers and workers if the value of other currencies declined in relation to gold or the pound. Wartime inflation had led to changes in the relative prices of national currencies. They almost all fell in value relative to gold, but some became undervalued and others were overvalued in relation to each other. The prices of commodities from nations with overvalued currencies became less competitive, while the prices of commodities from nations with undervalued currencies became more competitive.

The return to the gold standard and convertibility in the mid-1920s, even at markedly devalued exchange rates for many states, failed to restore the stability and prosperity of the prewar years in the global political economy. Severe constraints on money supplies resulted from limited gold supplies in weak-currency states, increasing balance-of-payment deficits in such states as a consequence of gold outflows caused by the return to convertibility and worsening imbalances in trade. Currency crises related to gold and capital outflows from the weak-currency states occurred with greater and greater frequency.

Many central banks raised interest rates to counteract gold and capital flight, attract capital inflows, and maintain confidence in their currencies. Here the United States differed. Benjamin Strong, the president of the Federal Reserve Bank of New York, intentionally held U.S. interest rates down to discourage capital outflows from Europe to the United States. By keeping U.S. interest rates low, Strong was trying to help the Europeans rebuild their capital structures and their economies, and support their efforts to restore the gold standard. But the pressure of gold outflows on money supply and higher interest rates—even though designed to work at counterpurposes—fed deflationary pressures on prices. There was less money chasing the same amount of commodities and services. Higher interest rates failed to restore confidence, strengthen currencies, and attract sufficient capital inflows to counteract capital flight. Meanwhile, the higher interest rates imposed by a state's central bank worked to slow domestic economic activity and increase unemployment. These results led to greater pressures for currency devaluation. Policy makers were caught in a horrible bind, in which strategies to fix one problem exacerbated another problem, and all the problems were serious.

To counteract deflationary pressures arising from the linkage between gold reserves and money supply, many governments again began to limit convertibility to prevent further decline in their gold reserves. Many also adopted currency-exchange controls to try to maintain and increase domestic money supply and protect against deflationary pressures. When these policies failed, many states moved to sever the connections between gold and currency

A **floating exchange rate** is an exchange-rate mechanism in which a currency's value is determined by market forces rather than fixed by a government.

values further by letting their currencies float. By the 1930s, many nations had formally moved away from the gold standard to a **floating exchange rate.** The return to the Holy Grail of the gold standard had lasted only about five years, 1926–1931.

Beggar-Thy-Neighbor Policies and Currency Devaluation

Economic distress, price deflation, and imbalances in the exchange-rate mechanism led to increased pressure on national policy makers to devalue their currencies strategically in order to assist their domestic producers and labor. Currency devaluation might address a dislocation within a national political economy, but a policy of currency devaluation shifts the costs of the economic dislocation overseas and imposes economic burdens on other nations' producers and labor. Policies that shift the costs of adjustment from one political economy to another are called **beggar-thy-neighbor policies.** These efforts are designed to promote the welfare of one nation's producers and labor at the expense and relative impoverishment of other nations' producers and labor.

Beggar-thy-neighbor policies use fiscal, trade, or monetary policies, such as regulations, tariff systems, or the exchange-rate system, to promote the welfare of one nation's producers and labor at the expense, and relative impoverishment, of other nations' producers and labor. **Tit-for-tat policy reactions** are retaliations in kind against burdens imposed by unilateral changes in another nation's policies.

Absent international cooperation and agreement on exchange-rate adjustment, such unilateral currency devaluations can lead to a round of retaliatory and potentially destabilizing competitive devaluations. Why should any nation's producers and labor willingly and quietly accept burdens imposed by unilateral changes in another nation's policies? Why should British producers and workers, for example, be expected to accept a greater likelihood of unemployment and family economic hardship so that U.S. producers and workers can benefit? Unilateral changes in policies that impose burdens abroad run the risk of encouraging **tit-for-tat policy reactions,** or retaliation in kind.

Imbalances in the exchange-rate mechanism and unilateral attempts to manipulate exchange rates in the post–World War I era generated a recipe for severely stressing the global political economy. An absence of sufficient multilateral cooperation to coordinate national policies, the United Kingdom's inability to manage pressures on the exchange-rate mechanism as it had done before the war, and the inexperience and inability of the United States to play a constructive leadership role posed serious obstacles to globalization and economic recovery. Beggar-thy-neighbor policy pressures spilled over into other policy arenas, particularly trade policy and other monetary policies. Governments confronted by growing distress in their national political economies increasingly turned to macroeconomic and trade policies that shifted costs of adjustment abroad and invited retaliation. The problems in the exchange-rate mechanism would convince later policy makers that monetary disorder, currency devaluations, and floating exchange rates contributed to the economic disaster of the

Great Depression and the political-military catastrophe of World War II. Right or wrong, these lessons would color the design of the post–World War II system.

Breakdown in Liquidity and Lender-of-Last-Resort Collective Goods

The shortage of capital resources in London created another significant barrier to economic revitalization during the interwar years. Modern economies need mobile capital—liquidity—for growth. A shortage of labor or relatively expensive labor can be overcome through the adoption of capital-intensive strategies such as substituting capital for labor and increasing the productivity of relatively scarce labor. In fact, increasing productivity through the use of technology and the application of capital has been the primary reason for the development of modern economies. In the late 1700s, English labor was considerably more expensive than labor in almost all other states—the exceptions being the Netherlands and the American colonies. The English responded by substituting capital for labor, which helps explain why the Industrial Revolution initially took place in England. With the devastation imposed on Europe's human resources by the war, the need for capital became even more important for reconstruction. Capital was necessary to invest in labor, to rebuild and retool industrial plants, to educate, and to enable consumers to spend. Without sufficient capital, businesses and individuals quickly confronted limitations on their abilities to rebuild and to take chances on the future.

Prior to the war, London's financial markets sat at the heart of a rapidly expanding global economy, providing liquidity for public and private enterprise, domestically and internationally. These markets became amazingly efficient at transferring capital from savers to borrowers. Investors found that they could move in and out of investment positions more quickly in British markets than in other financial markets, thus limiting their risk exposure. This discovery created an increasing return dynamic. More and more borrowers sought out British merchant banks to help raise funds for their endeavors as the size, depth, and liquidity of these markets increased. The position of London's capital markets and the connections between British financiers and the Bank of England placed the British at the center of the global economy and endowed them with capabilities for crisis management during economic downturns. Their capital resources were critical not only for providing procyclical stimulus but also for injecting countercyclical stimulus during periods of distress. The former was important to continuing a cycle of economic expansion, while the latter helped to constrain economic downturns that might otherwise provoke politicians to respond to short-term domestic political pressures with policies that could be counterproductive for the global economy.

Unfortunately, the war diminished the capital resources available in London and other European capital markets. Some investors in Europe still enjoyed a capital surplus despite the flows of capital to the United States, but those investors faced uncertain macroeconomic conditions in Europe, such as the postwar inflation in Germany, deflation in other economies, and instabilities in the exchange-rate mechanism. These conditions tended to make investors risk averse with their capital and restricted their investments in European reconstruction. Today, with modern monetary policy instruments, governments would provide more economic stimulus by increasing the money supply, lowering central bank interest rates, or purchasing government securities. But modern monetary policy had yet to be created. Money supply during the prewar period was a direct function of gold reserves. There was little room for improvisation. Confronted by the dilemmas of the postwar period, governments had no intellectual foundations or established policy experience to guide their use of monetary policies. Benjamin Strong had engaged in some ad hoc monetary experiments in New York, but it was John Maynard Keynes in the mid-1920s who began to develop the foundations of modern macroeconomic monetary policy. In addition, in the immediate postwar period many governments were also trying to contain inflation and restore stability to the price of their currencies; increasing the money supply would have counteracted these efforts. The reduction in capital caused by the war and the need to fight inflation and restore stability thus limited the availability of capital resources passing through the London markets. In the early 1920s, New York's capital markets faced no such constraints on capital availability, but New York financiers were relative newcomers to the world of global finance. Their inexperience limited their ability to recognize and play the role British financiers and markets had played during the expansion of economic globalization in the later 1800s. Moreover, the financial crises of the late 1920s and early 1930s were to place severe constraints on liquidity in U.S. capital markets and banks.

The Effects of War Debts and Reparations on Liquidity

The Treaty of Versailles in 1919 formally ended World War I. The European allies of the United States emerged victorious but also suffused with great hostility toward the losers and burdened with staggering debt obligations to the United States. Their animosity and frustration were reflected in the terms of the treaty, which imposed stringent conditions on Germany. These included limitations on German military forces and demands for vast reparations to be paid by Germany. Reparations—payments by the losers to cover the winners' costs from a conflict—were not new in the history of warfare. The United Kingdom had exacted payments from France following the defeat of Napoleon. France had paid reparations to Bismarck's Germany following the Franco-Prussian War of 1871. Northern carpetbaggers extracted resources from the South during the Reconstruction period following the U.S. Civil War. But World War I far outstripped previous conflicts in size and costs, and the pressures of war debt facing the European allies, their need for capital to rebuild, and lingering bitterness over the conflict materialized in unusually severe reparation expectations. The French, whose territory was left scarred by trench warfare, were particularly resolute in their demands for reparation. Both the Allies' debt to the United States and Germany's reparations debt to the Allies added significantly to the liquidity dilemma in world markets.

Officially, the Treaty of Versailles established a principle of reparation, which led to the formation of a commission that was to determine amounts. In the spring of 1921, the commission determined that Germany owed 132 billion gold marks, or $33 billion, in reparations to the Allies. Germany faced approximately fifty years of reparations payments, during which time a significant portion of any gains from German economic activity would go to the French and British instead of being channeled into improvements in the German standard of living or per capita income. The reparations demanded were well beyond the ability of even an economically healthy Germany—and postwar Germany was far from economically healthy. Perhaps the French and British could have been more magnanimous, but the governments in Paris and London each also owed billions of dollars to Washington, and the United States expected repayment. Germany immediately encountered difficulties in making reparations payments. Unlike France, German territory was unscathed by the horrors of trench warfare, but the German population and economy were as devastated as those of the Allies by the years of conflict. The excessive demands for reparations created hostility within the German population, a feeling that political extremists would later exploit to mobilize German public sentiment against domestic groups such as the Jews, opposition parties, and the Allied combatants from World War I.

In his treatise *The Economic Consequences of the Peace*, John Maynard Keynes warned that the terms of the peace were dangerous for Europe and for the global economy. An economist and consultant to the British and German governments, Keynes argued for suspension of the reparations and forgiveness of the Allies' war debts, which, he worried, would constrain liquidity and create formidable obstacles to global growth and recovery. Fearing that the treaty undermined German economic prospects and insulted German national pride, Keynes anticipated that Germans would turn increasingly bitter toward the imposed reparations and that this bitterness would lead to a renewal of German nationalism based on feelings of persecution and unfairness. Such resentments, he warned, could eventually lead to a resumption of hostilities.

Keynes's entreaties fell on deaf ears. The victors, owing huge war debts to the United States and facing a liquidity crunch, put tremendous pressure on Germany to keep up with its reparations payments. When the Germans threatened to default on the reparations, the British were willing to revise the payment schedule—even to forgo reparations—but they tied their position to the war debts they owed to the United States. If the United States were to forgive the Allied nations' war debts, the British would be willing to forgo reparations. Such an accommodation might have provided breathing room to reduce tensions between the former combatants, liquidity to prime the growth pump in Europe, and room for more moderate political forces to prevail over extreme nationalist parties. Unfortunately, U.S. policy makers rejected the Allies' appeal to rescind their war debts. President Coolidge responded at different times, "They hired the money, didn't they?" and "They borrowed the money, yes or no?"

Even if the United States had agreed to forgive the Allies' war debts, the French might have refused to reconsider reparations, which they considered their due. As the Germans fell behind in their payments, in 1923 French troops occupied the Ruhr region of Germany, a coal- and steel-producing area that was key to German economic recovery. Seizure of the region exacerbated Germany's difficulties in rebuilding, injected greater stress and rancor into Franco-German relations, and further scarred the German national psyche. German workers in the Ruhr factories and mines responded to the French occupation with passive resistance, sabotage, and even violence. Adolf Hitler used the occupation to mobilize support for his emerging National Socialist (Nazi) movement. Hitler's movement played on national pride, incorrectly asserting that Germany had been defeated in World War I by forces within Germany and not by the military strength of its adversaries. The German government's acquiescence to the French occupation therefore provided fodder for those who rationalized Germany's defeat in the war by blaming domestic factors.

U.S. loans to Germany might have relieved some of the pressures of German reparations payments, but U.S. policy makers and financiers were reluctant to lend funds without revision of the reparations schedule, and the Allies were unwilling to alter their reparations expectations without war debt forgiveness. These competing pressures constructed a vicious social trap, with the United States as the key obstruction to escape from the trap. Reparations and war debts affected both the prospect of obtaining commercial loans for economic expansion and the costs of such loans. Lenders in capital markets considered the risk of default in their calculations about whether or not to make loans, and at what price—deriving information about the risks to their capital from delays in making payments or threatened defaults. Governments that delayed or reneged on their payments could thus affect the ability of enterprises in their societies to obtain commercial loans. Policy preferences and the linkages among war debts, reparations, and new loans left little room for constructive compromise. Table 10.3 summarizes the four major nations' policy preferences on the issues of debt and reparations. The international economic obligations between nations as a consequence of war debts, reparations, and foreign borrowing spilled over to distort domestic political debates and economic activities.

The United States was the potential linchpin of any positive resolution of the liquidity dilemma produced by the countervailing obligations of war debts and reparations. The debts owed to the United States provided U.S. policy makers with a tool they might have used to break the stalemate if they were willing to forgive the Allies' war debts as a lever to pressure the British and French to forgo German reparations. The British were already willing to accept such a compromise, although lasting French bitterness toward Germany and the prospect that capital inflows from reparations might exceed outflows for payment of war debts made the French more reluctant to forgive reparations. Unfortunately, American policy makers chose not to exercise their leverage.

The issues of war debt and reparations dominated much of the international agenda of the early 1920s, feeding the liquidity problems that confronted political economies seeking to rebuild and expand. The Bank of International Settlements (BIS) was created during this period to address reparation issues. Disagreements over these intersecting issues created tensions that spilled over into other international discussions and created barriers to the kinds

TABLE 10.3	**Policy Preferences on War Debt, Commercial Debt, and Reparations**
Country	*Preferences*
United Kingdom	Is willing to cancel German reparations, but only if its war debts are forgiven
France	Refuses to forgive German reparations, but wants its war debts forgiven
Germany	Wants reparations canceled, but wants to meet commercial debt obligations to maintain creditworthiness
United States	Refuses to connect war debts to reparations; will not forgive war debts, but will accept a moratorium on both

of cooperation that would have been useful in managing the economic crises that would erupt in the late 1920s and 1930s. Some international attempts were made to address the problems caused by reparations, war debts, and currency instability. Most notable among these efforts were the Dawes Commission in 1923 and the Young Commission in 1928. The Dawes Commission (chaired by Charles Dawes, a U.S. banker) sought to stabilize the German budget and currency by rescheduling reparations payments and arranging for substantial loans from the United States to Germany. The Young Commission (chaired by Charles Young, the chairman of General Electric) led to another rescheduling of German reparations in 1929. Both commissions' attempts produced false hopes.

German Hyperinflation Threatens Monetary and Political Stability

In the period preceding the Dawes Commission's proposal of its solution, known as the Dawes Plan, the German government and central bank, fearing the political consequences of reparation demands, increasing unemployment, and poor domestic economic conditions, started to increase Germany's money supply, with the short-term goal of meeting payrolls and constraining unemployment. Unfortunately, absent real economic growth such policies can prove inflationary to prices. Recall that price inflation occurs when the money supply increases at a faster pace than the supply of goods and services—more and more money chases a relatively stable supply of goods and service. This process can lead to a rapid increase in the nominal prices of goods and services and a decline in the purchasing power of a currency. German government policies aimed at maintaining payrolls and limiting unemployment thus turned perverse and unleashed strong inflationary pressures on the German economy. The monetary stimulus quickly got out of hand, generating extraordinary **hyperinflation,** which destroyed the value and purchasing power of the German reichsmark.

Hyperinflation is extremely rapid inflation that leaves a country's currency virtually worthless.

From May 1921 to July 1922, nominal prices in Germany increased by more than 600 percent. Prices jumped another 18,000 percent from July 1922 to June 1923, and then registered a whopping 850 billion percent increase from July 1923 to November 1923. To place this situation in comparative perspective, before World War I the German mark, the French franc, and the Italian lira all had about equal value, and all exchanged at the rate of four or five to the dollar. By the end of November 1923, the exchange rate between the dollar and the mark was 4.2 trillion marks to one dollar (see table 10.4). The printing presses at the Reichsbank ran twenty-four hours a day to try to keep up with this hyperinflation of prices, only adding to the crisis.

What did this mean for Germans?

> A student at Freiburg University ordered a cup of coffee at a cafe. The price on the menu was 5,000 Marks. He had two cups. When the bill came, it was for 14,000 Marks. "If you want to save money," he was told, "and you want two cups of coffee, you should order them both at the same time."[1]

On a trip through Germany during the hyperinflation period, novelist Pearl S. Buck described the situation as follows:

> The cities were still there, the houses not yet bombed and in ruins, but the victims were millions of people. They had lost their fortunes, their savings; they were dazed and inflation-shocked and did not understand how it had happened to them and who the foe was who had defeated them. Yet they had lost their self-assurance, their feeling that they themselves could be the masters of their own lives if only they worked hard enough; and lost, too, were the old values of morals, of ethics, of decency.[2]

Shoppers showed up at bakeries, butcher shops, and grocery stores using wheelbarrows to carry the necessary quantities of marks to purchase foodstuffs. Notes of 20 million marks attained common usage within a very short period of time. This period of hyperinflation, with its crushing impact on German welfare and its pernicious effect on German politics, left a strong memory. In the years since, that memory has played a significant role in the monetary politics of Germany and what is now the European Union. Excessively fearful of inflation, the Bundesbank and now the European Central Bank of the EU have been dominated by a focus on monetary stability at the expense of promoting growth. This has hindered both institutions from being effective lenders of last resort during economic downturns or crises.

---

[1]Adam Smith (George J. W. Goodman), *Paper Money* (New York: Summit Books, 1981), 59.

[2]Quoted in Smith, *Paper Money*, 62.

The Rise of Political Extremism in Germany

Many investigators blame hyperinflation for the rise of political extremism in Germany, the success of the German National Socialist Party (the Nazi Party), and the ascension of Adolf Hitler to power. Certainly the pressures of hyperinflation did damage confidence in the nascent democratic government and helped to fuel the rise of extreme political movements in postwar Germany. Household purchasing power drastically eroded on a daily, hourly, and minute-by-minute basis. Saving was pointless. The effects were particularly pernicious for lower-income, working-class households. The Nazi and the Communist movements, at opposite ends of the political spectrum, both grew rapidly in this environment. Hitler garnered confidence as his Nazi Party won thirty-two seats in the first postwar election. Yet the hyperinflation of prices provided only one motivation for the drift toward political extremism in Germany and other European states. For Hitler and the Nazi Party, rancor over the government's management of the domestic economy added fuel to an already burning fire of political unrest. Political dissent was rooted in a broader national dissatisfaction with the way the war had ended. Many Germans shared widespread beliefs that the Treaty of Versailles was too harsh and inequitable, that it produced economic ills, and that the German military had been abandoned on the field of battle by politicians and undermined by enemies within the German state.

Strategically, Hitler paired the economic dislocations arising from hyperinflation with the disagreements over the harsh peace treaty to boost his political movement from

TABLE 10.4	The Exchange Rate of the Dollar to the Mark, 1914–1923
Period	*Rate*
Prior to 1914	US$1 = 4.20 Mk
End of 1914	4.60
1915	5.00
1916	5.50
1917	6.40
1918	7.00
1919	42
1920	70
1921	185
1922	7,350
January 1923	4,000
February 1923	27,300
March 1923	20,975
April 1923	29,800
May 1923	69,500
June 1923	154,500
July 1923	1,000,000
August 1923	10,000,000
September 1923	160,000,000
1 October 1923	242,000,000
10 October 1923	3,000,000,000
20 October 1923	12,000,000,000
31 October 1923	73,000,000,000
1 November 1923	130,000,000,000
10 November 1923	630,000,000,000
15 November 1923	2,000,000,000,000
End of November 1923	4,200,000,000,000

Source: Data extracted from Baltimore Philatelic Society, http://www.balpex.org/philatelist.html.

a small band of disaffected military veterans into a significant political party. The Nazi Party grew rapidly in this environment, but it remained a minority party even with the economic distress of the people. In the midst of the hyperinflation crisis, Hitler overestimated both the extent of public animosity toward the democratic government, the Weimar Republic, and the degree of support for his movement within the military. In November 1923 he gambled that a coup he attempted in Munich—the so-called Beer Hall Putsch—would mobilize public dissatisfaction over hyperinflation and the military's discontent over its emasculation as a result of the Treaty of Versailles, leading to the overthrow of the current regime and the establishment of a new regime under Hitler's control. But he miscalculated. The coup failed, as the military remained neutral and the police quelled his attempt. Imprisoned for nine months, Hitler redirected his efforts to gain control of the government by focusing on a constitutional ascension to power through the ballot box.

The economic crisis eased, the German economy recovered, and political extremism faltered in the mid-1920s. Supported by the assistance provided under the Dawes Plan, the German government implemented stringent measures that conquered hyperinflation, stabilized the value of the currency, and restored the credit mechanisms necessary for economic growth. German industry revived, and unemployment fell. By itself, the hyperinflation in the German economy of the early 1920s was not sufficient to account for Hitler's rise to power. The difficult period of hyperinflation provided Hitler the opportunity to expand the foundation of the Nazi Party early in the decade, but support for the party stagnated with economic recovery.

The world economy soon encountered another economic crisis, however. The onset of the Great Depression following the collapse of capital markets beginning in 1929 undermined the provision of liquidity that was so critical to the continued expansion of the German economy and other economies recovering

After World War I, excessive monetary stimulus in Germany led to hyperinflation that quickly eroded the value of the German reichsmark. German economic activity declined as the reichsmark dramatically lost purchasing power. With hyperinflation, Germans soon needed laundry baskets of currency to collect pay packets or make daily purchases. In this environment, Hitler and other political extremists sought to build a political base.

from World War I. Like other economies, starved of the fuel of capital, the German economy staggered, slumped, and then retreated. In September 1929, a month before the New York stock market crash, German unemployment stood at 1.32 million people in a nation of approximately 60 million. As the new economic crisis took hold, that number grew to approximately 3 million by September 1930, around 4.5 million by September 1931, and more than 6 million by early 1932.

In this stressful economic environment, dissatisfaction with the government grew. Political movements of the far right (the Nazis) and left (the Communists) found greater traction. Hitler exploited the tremendous economic distress and dislocation that arose in Germany after 1929 to expand the base that he had built earlier. This enabled his rise to power through the ballot box and legitimate constitutional means. Hitler's party won a plurality of legislative seats in the 1932 election. Following some political machinations, he was asked to form a coalition government by the head of state, Paul von Hindenburg. After gaining access to the levers of power through a series of democratic elections and government formation, however, Hitler turned sharply authoritarian, suspending parliamentary powers. With Hindenburg's death in 1934, Hitler consolidated his authority as both the head of state (president) and the head of government (chancellor) into a single position (führer), thus destroying the democratic Weimar Republic.

U.S. Financial Market Speculation and the Crash

The liquidity crunch that hampered postwar economic recovery and expansion improved significantly in the mid-1920s. In the early and mid-1920s, Benjamin Strong, in his role as president of the Federal Reserve Bank of New York, intentionally kept U.S. interest rates low to discourage capital flight from Europe to the United States. U.S. banks and investors responded by shifting their balance sheets and capital structures away from U.S. government bonds and toward foreign sovereign debt, corporate securities, and real estate. Ironically, even though this helped the liquidity crunch in Europe during the mid-1920s, it also changed the risk exposure and capital adequacy of U.S. banks, a problem that would surface and prove devastating with the 1929 stock market crash. By the end of the decade a new liquidity shortage, grounded in the exposure of the U.S. banking system to higher-risk investment strategies, would hit the global economy and undo these hard-won economic gains. Let's look at this new crisis, which undermined the economic recovery and led the world into depression.

Many popular accounts single out the October 1929 New York Stock Exchange (NYSE) crash as the primary cause of the liquidity crunch that contributed to the Great Depression. Clearly, the market crash was a significant factor. Before World War I, the United Kingdom provided liquidity to the international system, acted as lender of last resort, and supported a stable international monetary system, but the war drained the nation's capital reserves and undermined its ability to continue credibly playing such a role. Postwar attempts by British policy makers and financiers to provide these collective goods imposed unsustainable costs on British workers and producers—unemployment, lack of investment capital at home, and threats to the competitiveness of British products in global markets—which led the policy makers to suspend such efforts.

The United States, and New York City specifically, replaced London as the center of capital and global financial holdings. The purchase of war materials during World War I, the resulting war debts, and reparations payments generated massive capital flows into the New York markets, fueling growth in stock prices and trading, and further enhancing the attractiveness of these markets to holders of capital in the United States and abroad. As noted, Benjamin Strong used the price of interest rates on U.S. government securities to alter the incentives of holders of capital in order to stem capital inflows to the United States and support European reconstruction and efforts to return to the gold standard. This worked only to a limited extent. Capital did shift away from U.S. Treasury securities, with their low rates of return, and it sought out investments with higher rates of return, such as foreign sovereign debt and corporate securities both abroad and at home. These were investments with higher rates of return but higher risks, which would prove problematic later in the decade as banks shifted their balance sheets and capital structures to capture higher rates of return.

This change in incentives caused by differences in rates of return contributed to a surge of capital into U.S. corporate securities in the New York markets. Prior to the 1920s, the Dow Jones Industrial Average (DJIA), a financial index based on core industrial companies' performance, had bounced around within a trading range for most of the century without breaking out to the upside or the downside. At the beginning of the 1920s the DJIA bottomed out at 67 but then climbed to more than 150 by 1925 and continued to boom until the 1929 crash. From the beginning of 1928 to just before the crash, the DJIA grew twofold, as did the number of market transactions. With increases in market valuations, an increasing return dynamic took hold as New York markets acted as a magnet for surplus capital from around the world. This made these markets key to international capital liquidity. However, financial panic set in on Black Thursday, October 24, 1929, and a still bigger shock hit on Black Tuesday, October 29, when 16.4 million shares were traded—a record trading volume that stood for almost the next half century. The October 1929 collapse in New York followed significant declines in markets elsewhere. The German markets encountered rough sailing by early 1928, London markets fell in mid-1928, and Paris dropped in February 1929. Confidence in financial market mechanisms was already being tested before October 1929.

The 1929 market crash was important, but it was not sufficient by itself to precipitate a decade-long global depression. The stock market expansion of the 1920s was not disconnected from changes in the underlying economy. Despite rapid price and market expansion, stock prices were not terribly out of line with earnings for firms listed on the NYSE. The U.S. industrial base emerged healthy from the war, and it expanded significantly in the years preceding the crash. For example, the increase in U.S. automobile ownership generated growth in a core industrial sector that spilled over to those industries that supplied automakers. Steel and oil producers, upholsterers, electronics manufacturers, and builders of the expanding network of roads and infrastructure related to modern transport all gained from the expansion of automotive production. Jobs were created as cars were built and bought and roads constructed. Modern transport also improved agriculture and shipping.

Moreover, comparable stock market crashes have occurred that did not lead to depressions or even significant recessions. Not all market crashes precipitate liquidity shortages. No other significant market crash during the twentieth century or in more recent times was accompanied by a liquidity crisis comparable to that leading to the Great Depression until the credit crisis of 2007–2008. Nevertheless, the 1929 stock market crash, the resulting decrease in wealth, and a decline in confidence in modern capital markets were all connected to a crisis in capital liquidity that undermined economic activity.

Crisis in the Credit Mechanism

A greater dilemma than the actual 1929 crash lay in the mechanisms that provided credit in the United States and the fact that those mechanisms were increasingly intertwined with the stock market. People, firms, and governments borrow capital through credit mechanisms to finance a host of activities—home mortgages, plant expansion, school construction, and other projects. In the 1920s, banks, as credit institutions, obtained much of the capital they loaned from the deposits of their account holders and the earnings on those funds. Individuals and businesses deposit money in banks, and banks pay their depositors interest on that money. Deposits are essentially loans by those with surplus capital to banking institutions. The interest that banks pay to their depositors is the cost of capital to the banks. Banks must find a way to make those deposited assets earn money, so that they can pay interest to the depositors, make enough money to pay for their own operation, and have some left over as profit. Banks thus take those deposits and lend them to individuals and enterprises experiencing shortages of capital; they invest the capital seeking a good rate of return. The actions of the New York Federal Reserve Bank regarding U.S. interest rates had already shifted the preferences of U.S. bankers regarding where to lend their capital. U.S. Treasury securities provided too low a rate of return. Real estate, corporate securities, and foreign sovereign securities offered far more lucrative returns, but with the higher returns came added risk in bank capital structures.

Add to this the rapid stock market expansion of the 1920s. Then greed overtook reason and common sense. Speculators began to borrow, and borrow heavily, to purchase equities in the stock market. People did not want to miss the opportunity to garner wealth. Stockbrokers borrowed funds from domestic and foreign credit institutions (banks) and then loaned those funds to their clients to purchase stocks. An investor could thus purchase a large position in stocks with only a small amount of her own money up front. Credit from her broker financed the rest of her purchase, which she anticipated paying off with the gains made from the sale of her stock. More and more stock positions were supported with borrowed capital. This trend was sustainable as long as stock prices were stable or continued to rise, people were willing to purchase stocks at such price levels, and credit institutions could continue to provide additional credit at attractive prices. Under such conditions, those who borrowed to purchase their stocks could sell some stocks to pay off their loan obligations, and the credit institutions could then afford to make new loans. At the very least, a borrower could turn over the asset, the stock, to the credit institution that loaned the capital used in the stock purchase. The merry-go-round would keep spinning.

So far so good, but what if a stock's value were to fall substantially below the value of the loan obligation? What if a lot of stocks should fall substantially below the value of the loan obligations—so that the loans became significantly more expensive than the stock asset? In fact, this was the situation that confronted investors, speculators, brokers, credit institutions, and central bankers during and after the 1929 market crash. As the value of their loans now exceeded the value of the underlying asset, the bankers began to worry about their ability to recover their funds and about the viability of the brokers to whom they had loaned capital. Moreover, with brokers owing funds to multiple banks, each banker feared being last in line to demand payment of such loan obligations. This fear generated a first-come, first-served pressure on banks to beat the others to the punch. Foreign and domestic credit institutions, worried about their exposure, began calling in their loans to brokers.

Brokers, confronted with demands by credit institutions to repay their loans, called in the loans that they had extended to investors to finance their stock purchases. Investors then rushed to liquidate their stock positions in hopes of meeting their loan obligations and limiting their losses. This frenzied liquidation was like throwing gasoline on a fire—it increased the supply of stock for sale, which produced even greater downward pressure on stock prices.

The social dynamic, the interaction of individual choices, thus exacerbated a downturn and turned a market correction into a market collapse. Individuals made rational and prudent decisions, but those decisions aggregated to create a destructive social trap—a **fallacy of composition.**

A **fallacy of composition** is a strategic situation in which the outcome is different from simply the sum of the parts, either greater or less.

The rush by credit institutions to recall their loans threatened to reduce capital liquidity in the market—to shrink the amount of money available. This effect, in turn, could lead to further collapse in stock prices, as there would be less money chasing the same amount of stock, and, potentially, to a full-scale reduction in capital liquidity that would extend beyond the immediate setting of stock prices. Recognizing this potential, New York banks and the Federal Reserve attempted to check the panic and restore stability by taking over loans from outside credit institutions and injecting their own capital to shore up the faltering market. The Federal Reserve attempted to maintain the money supply through manipulation of the discount rate (the rate at which it lends capital to banks) and through its open-market operations (by which the Fed can inject money into the economy by purchasing government securities). Milton Friedman and his coauthors Rose Friedman and Anna Schwartz assert that the efforts by the Federal Reserve were too conservative to address the scope of the crisis. They argue that more liberal monetary expansion would have contained the crisis and prevented the Great Depression. Perhaps, but the Federal Reserve of then is not the Federal Reserve of today. The Federal Reserve was still relatively new and had never faced a crisis of such magnitude. The charters of the Federal Reserve banks were also temporary charters and due to expire in 1934. The powers of the Federal Reserve were far more limited than they later became, and policy makers' comprehension of the use of monetary policy for macroeconomic management was just beginning to evolve beyond that of linking money supply to gold reserves.

In addition, changes in the capital structures of most U.S. private financial institutions had created massive risk exposure. Many such institutions were merely illiquid, but many were insolvent, and simply expanding money supply might not have prevented the banking crisis to come. Banks can face an illiquidity problem when they encounter an imbalance between short-term demands by depositors and borrowers and long-term less liquid assets. They have the assets to meet short-term demands, but those assets are locked up in longer-term assets that are hard to liquidate quickly. Many banks during this era faced an ongoing problem of liquidity due to agricultural and other economic cycles. The Federal Reserve was created to help manage this dilemma—particularly liquidity constraints related to seasonal fluctuations in demand for credit in agriculture—by providing a short-term lending facility. Insolvent banks are those that are undercapitalized given their risk exposure or because they made poor investment choices with depositors' assets. Even if they could liquidate their investments, insolvent banks would not have enough capital to meet the demands of depositors and creditors.

Central banks did attempt to use their policy instruments as lenders of last resort to quell the emerging liquidity crisis. They lowered their discount rates and increased money supply. Many actually succeeded in increasing money supply over the next year, but economic expectations are heavily influenced by psychology and perceptions, particularly in the short term. Central banking policies can succeed only if they convince private holders of capital to act consistently with those policies. These actions by the central banks proved insufficient to stem the fears of private credit institutions or those providing capital to those institutions. Perhaps the central banks could have averted the crisis by adding more to the money supply, but, by 1930, the reluctance of private actors to expand credit began to shrink the money supply in spite of central banks' efforts to the contrary.

When the stock market collapsed, the large amount of market speculation funded by credit spilled over to threaten the viability of the credit institutions themselves. Banks depend on revenues from their loan portfolios to pay off their depositors and fund new loans. Providing credit in the form of new loans is critical to ensuring liquidity for economic expansion and activity. But if enough outstanding loans cease to provide the necessary revenues, the banks can neither pay their depositors nor extend new loans. If depositors cannot withdraw their capital from the bank, they will stop depositing funds there, or perhaps even panic, as many depositors need those funds to pay bills and purchase necessities. The credit institution itself may fail, and certainly the amount of capital in the system will decline.

For example, imagine you have $5,000 and you borrow $95,000 to purchase an asset, a house, for $100,000. Then the real estate market in your community collapses and your house declines in value to $60,000. You have been making your monthly mortgage payments, but you still owe $90,000. Are you going to continue meeting your loan obligation and so pay the credit institution $30,000 more than your property is worth? Rationally, you may decide instead to default on your loan. The bank will likely foreclose and own your house. It will then turn around and sell the house, but for only $60,000, which is its new market value. The bank has lost $30,000 on this set of transactions—not a good business deal, for it now has $30,000 less to fund new loans and meet depositor demands.

> A **structural condition** is an event or something in the social environment that affects everyone in the community. It is not a function of an individual's activities independent of those contextual or structural conditions.

Now remember, the real estate market in your community has collapsed, which means that you are not the only home owner in this position. The collapse in real estate prices is a **structural condition**—it affects everyone in the entire community. All credit institutions anticipate some defaults as a course of normal business, because people occasionally mismanage their affairs, miscalculate, or encounter unanticipated shifts in their economic conditions. But a structural downturn generates conditions under which many borrowers default on their loan obligations, even if they have managed their affairs wisely. The cumulative amount of defaults may begin to exceed the expectations of the lenders and their capacity to manage their losses. The banks are destabilized, becoming unviable—unable to extend new loans or to make good on obligations to their depositors—as their balance sheets run damaging deficits. Such insolvency is more likely to occur if the downturn is structural.

Essentially, this was the problem facing credit institutions and societies after the 1929 stock market crash. In the aftermath of the crash, many banks were excessively exposed as a consequence of the speculative use of credit in the stock market. Many found themselves illiquid, but significant numbers were either fully or nearly insolvent. Both conditions meant that in the short term banks lacked the funds to extend new credit or to meet their depositors' requests for withdrawals. With time, banks can sometimes weather such problems by attracting new deposits, selling assets, and increasing their earnings. But in the aftermath of the crash, depositors began to fret over the security of their deposits in banks that were beginning to look vulnerable, while those with a capital surplus became increasingly reluctant to deposit their capital in banks. Worried depositors began to withdraw their funds in anticipation that the banks might not have sufficient funds to meet all depositor demands—another instance of the "first come, first served" pressures of a social trap. Many banks actually did not have sufficient funds to meet depositor demands and suspended operations (see table 10.5), which only confirmed public fears and so escalated the credit crisis. The public lost confidence in the intermediary mechanisms—the banks and credit markets—that sat between those with a surplus of capital and those needing capital for their economic endeavors.

TABLE 10.5	**Numbers of U.S. Banks and Bank Suspensions, 1929–1934**	

	Number as of December 31	
Year	Total banks	Banks with suspended operations
1929	24,633	659
1930	22,773	1,350
1931	19,970	2,293
1932	18,397	1,453
1933	15,015	4,000
1934	16,096	57

Source: U.S. Census Bureau, *Historical Statistics of the United States: Colonial Times to 1970,* vol. 20–30 (Washington, DC: Government Printing Office, 1975), 912; http://www.census.gov/prod/www/abs/statab.html.

With retrospective vision, clues of such weaknesses in the U.S. financial system had been evident for some time. The agricultural downturn of the 1920s revealed the fragility of the U.S. system. More than five thousand banks failed between 1921 and 1929, well before the onset of the Great Depression, or roughly 10 percent of the institutions active in the money markets. The problems of liquidity were significant, but the failures mostly involved insolvent banks that were undercapitalized given their risk exposure or that had made poor investment choices with depositors' assets—often speculating in hot real estate, corporate and foreign bond, or equity markets. The brewing crisis in the money markets was to worsen. As noted earlier, during the 1920s the balance sheets of U.S. financial institutions such as commercial banks, savings and loan associations, credit unions, and insurance companies shifted dramatically from conventional loans and U.S. government obligations to foreign and corporate bonds, real estate, and equity markets. Some of this shift in bank balance sheets was directly a result of banks building larger positions in these asset categories, but there was also an indirect shift occurring in the risk exposure of banks' capital structures because of the nature of their loans. Stockbrokers and investors borrowed heavily from the banks to finance purchases in more risky markets, particularly margin purchases. This change in the capital structure and balance sheets of financial institutions was fine as long as prices continued to rise or remained relatively level, but it created a potential for disaster in the money markets if prices started to collapse in real estate, foreign or corporate bonds, or equities.

The market crash of October 1929 revealed this problem when the rapid decline in stock prices led to margin calls, a significant number of which could not be met. This led to liquidation of stock positions and further downward pressures on stock prices. The sizable unfilled margin calls acted as a contagion and spread distress to the banks. Many banks found their reserves drained by speculative investments and margin calls. This crisis in the credit markets, the banking system, was to drag on and worsen. The transition to Franklin D. Roosevelt's presidential administration revealed the extent of the banking crisis. Bank failures soared, peaking in 1933 with more than four thousand bank suspensions. Immediately after Roosevelt's inauguration in March 1933, the new president's first major action was to declare a bank holiday and place the weight of the federal government behind stabilizing the banking system and restoring confidence. By the end of the extended bank holiday, a four-day closure, the new government had dramatically restructured the U.S. banking industry. Government auditors closed many insolvent banks, consolidated others, and acted to ensure the solvency of the banking system and address a crisis of confidence as well as liquidity. Bank failures declined dramatically after the government intervention and were not an issue for years to come.

Restoring confidence once so shaken proves a sticky problem, however. Beaten and bruised by the market crash and the banking failures, in many cases life investments and savings destroyed, investors refused to return to the securities markets. Trading volume on the New York Stock Exchange took until the mid-1950s to return to precrash levels. Depositors, even though badly traumatized, did respond positively to dramatic government actions meant to build confidence in the safety and stability of the money markets. Following the national bank holiday, depositors quickly regained confidence in the banks as safe havens for their savings. By the end of 1934 the banking system was on sound footing. Actions by the new administration, the Federal Reserve, the Reconstruction Finance Corporation, and other federal initiatives transformed a teetering system with thousands of insolvent banks, and even more illiquid banks, into a fully solvent system with rebuilt capital structures and federal insurance.

Following the bank holiday, the difficult problem to overcome in the money markets proved to be not the fears of depositors but the willingness of banks to make loans or of prospective borrowers to borrow capital. Commercial loans continued to decline. The liquidity crunch became a liquidity trap as borrowers and lenders alike became risk averse. The mechanisms to preclude such destruction of confidence or to manage such a crisis in confidence were not in place until after the 1933 reforms introduced by the Roosevelt administration, but by then it was too late to prevent a crisis of confidence. Simply providing more liquidity through Federal Reserve actions may not have been sufficient to unclog the system given the evidence of completely rebuilt bank capital structures but declining loan portfolios.

To make matters worse, the credit that speculators borrowed to invest in the stock market came from a much broader range of institutions than U.S. commercial banks located in New York City. If only New York commercial banks had faced the threat of numerous defaults from such speculation, the crisis might have been contained by their coordination with the

U.S. Federal Reserve Bank. But stockbrokers borrowed capital to lend to speculators not only from banks in New York City but also from banks located elsewhere in the United States, from nonfinancial U.S. firms, from foreign credit institutions and firms, and from other sources. This extensive borrowing created a broader network, a global financial web, along which the credit crisis spread. The stock market crash of 1929 migrated to become a full-blown crisis for all credit market mechanisms. Financial institution after financial institution faced liquidity and insolvency issues after 1929 that only got worse until 1933. The market crash had long-term negative effects because of the widespread breakdown in the credit mechanisms, which created the most severe wave of liquidity problems to befall nations during the interwar years and paved the way for a decade of economic misery and political extremism.

The Breakdown in Trade Erodes the Benefits of Global Exchange

The market crash, the liquidity trap, and the insolvency crisis in banking and credit institutions led to reduced consumption and placed pressures on production structures in national economies. With less money and less access to credit, and fearing worse things to come, people reduced their consumption of domestic- and foreign-produced commodities. Prices declined as less money and credit chased the same amount of commodities (remember Hume). Producers faced increasing difficulty in meeting their obligations and in employing workers. Unemployment jumped as conditions worsened.

Scared and angry, producers and workers pressured their governments for relief. Policy makers, fearing a threat to their political survival, responded with policies that sought to protect domestic markets for domestically produced goods. Hoping to redistribute the costs of the economic downturn away from their workers and producers and onto the backs of workers and producers abroad, governments intervened in international trade by increasing tariffs and other barriers to trade. Such beggar-thy-neighbor policies rejected the gains from comparative advantage, specialization, globalization, and the discipline of exchange in a larger market. They also imposed costs on nontradable sectors of political economies and consumers because they influenced the prices of the goods and services consumed. Seeking to protect specific segments of a political economy, these policies damaged the broader political economy at home and abroad.

Trade slowed and then began to decline. In the first four years of the Great Depression, international exchange fell by 60 percent, as shown in figure 10.1. Sometimes such protective policies work as intended to redistribute costs abroad and shelter specific segments of national political economies, but even when successful, they impose costs on the broader economic welfare. A protected sector benefits at the expense of the broader national society and to the detriment of economic welfare in other national political economies. In this case, the initial imposition of higher trade barriers turned into a sustained policy of economic warfare. Governments retaliated and resorted to more and more strategies to protect their domestic markets and advantage their domestic producers in international exchange. Rather than

| FIGURE 10.1 | The Decline in World Trade, 1929–1933 |

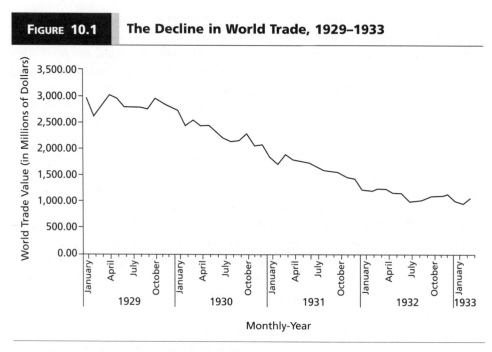

Source: Charles P. Kindleberger, *The World in Depression, 1929–1939,* rev. ed. (Berkeley: University of California Press, 1986), 170.

bringing the anticipated relief, this economic warfare by means of beggar-thy-neighbor policies damaged the very sectors those policies were designed to protect. The breakdown in trade imposed large costs on the tradable sectors of economies. The trends toward lower revenues, lower wages, and increased unemployment accelerated. These costs then spilled over into other parts of national economies, as the breakdown in trade eroded consumption choices and gains from specialization. Trade could have been a pathway to the expansion of economic activity and welfare, a means to grow out of the economic downturn, but government policies in response to constituent pressures closed this route. This breakdown in international exchange contributed significantly to the severity and duration of the Great Depression.

Let's take a closer look at this breakdown in trade, the lessons of which remain critical today, as public debates over trade and outsourcing raise many of the same issues and appeal to the same fears. Threats to international trade began to emerge before World War I. After lowering tariffs and negotiating bilateral trade agreements that contributed to the expansion of trade in the mid- to late 1800s, many governments found themselves facing pressures in their political economies to slow or reverse the trends toward trade liberalization. Expanding democratization in the 1800s pulled more and more of the national populations into the electorate, thus changing the representative demands on politicians. The increasing connections between political elites and the masses translated into new temptations on the part of politicians to manipulate trade policy to shift costs away from their own vocal and politically mobilized constituents and onto other governments' constituents and those less politically mobilized in the domestic arena. This response can be an appealing electoral strategy, even if overall society would benefit more from free trade—it all depends on who votes and why.

In this environment, many governments started to increase tariffs and to adopt other protectionist measures for specific economic sectors, particularly agriculture. Through such policies, governments sought to protect against price deflation and maintain aggregate demand for the output of their domestic businesses and labor—to protect jobs and revenues. Government interventions in trade attempted to redistribute the costs of adjustment and to shelter those parts of the economy threatened by the dynamics of comparative advantage, specialization of production, and creative destruction. Protections for a specific sector's goods imposed higher costs for those goods on a broader domestic base, affecting their consumption choices and economic welfare, although consumers often did not notice, or did not mind, the impact of a nickel here and a dime there on their personal budgets. The willingness of the broader society to bear such costs in order to protect the economic activities of a narrow segment of the society might seem noble, but the protections also imposed costs on other nations' labor, producers, and societies. The protections beggared (impoverished) neighbors who had no representation in the nation raising barriers to trade.

The prewar pressures for trade protections continued to grow in the years following the war. As currency instability, slow economic recovery and growth, and other economic stresses posed threats to workers and enterprises in the tradable sector, policy makers tried a variety of strategies and policy tools to manage these pressures on their domestic producers. Production subsidies, tariffs, price controls, international attempts to arrive at production targets to control supply, **imperial preferences** (whereby a colonial power and its colonies enjoy privileged

> **Imperial preferences** are a set of economic arrangements whereby a colonial power and its colonies, or former colonies, enjoy privileged access to each other's markets.

access to each other's markets), and government purchase and storage of surplus production in order to reduce supply in the marketplace were some of the tools employed in attempts to manage the political and economic difficulties in tradable sectors.

National policy makers were surely aware of the threat posed by protectionism. The economic profession accepted as gospel Ricardo's theory about the benefits of trade and comparative advantage from a century earlier. During the 1920s, several international conferences—some held under the auspices of the League of Nations—attempted to address these trade issues and to constrain the inclination of government officials to protect their domestic sectors from the price pressures of the global market. These efforts failed to stem the increasing protectionist pressures, however, and national policy makers continued to enact intrusive tariff legislation that nibbled away at trade openness. The British adopted the Safeguarding of Industries Act of 1921. The U.S. Congress passed the Fordney-McCumber Tariff Act of 1922, which raised tariffs on a range of imports in the United States and allowed the president to raise or lower tariffs on any product by up to 50 percent after advisement by the U.S. Tariff Commission. Other countries followed suit. In 1925, France and Italy increased duties on cars, India on piece goods, and Australia on a variety of commodities. Italy raised duties on wheat in 1925, which led to an escalation of protections on this commodity as other nations reciprocated with similar protections. Germany returned to tariffs on wheat after 1926.

Despite such protections, trade expanded during the 1920s. This upsurge should not be too surprising, given the drastic break imposed on international trade by the hostilities of World War I. War is not good for trade, and world war is especially harmful. So the end of hostilities offered an artificially low baseline for international trade, setting the stage for an increase despite the adoption of trade protections by many governments. By the end of the 1920s, however, the growing liquidity crunch, ensuing price deflation, and economic fears threatened more and more producers and labor. As tradable sectors faced increasing hardships, politicians faced increasing pressures from their constituents to adopt protectionist strategies.

In 1930, the largest and most significant political economy, the United States, enacted the Smoot-Hawley Act, one of the worst pieces of legislation ever crafted by Congress (recall the discussion of Smoot-Hawley at the beginning of chapter 1). In spite of its noxious potential, the act passed overwhelmingly. More than one thousand economists signed a letter to President Hoover decrying the irresponsibility of the legislation and beseeching him to veto the bill. Many other governments also warned U.S. policy makers about the damage that Smoot-Hawley would do to international trade. Nevertheless, Hoover signed the bill into law. Even with its history as a protectionist political economy, the United States previously had not attempted any measure comparable in size and range to Smoot-Hawley. The act imposed the largest tariff increases ever across twenty thousand commodities. Its provisions raised tariffs above the already high rates established under Fordney-McCumber eight years earlier. Not content to sit by and let their citizens be beggared by U.S. policy, other governments, predictably, responded by raising their tariffs. Smoot-Hawley thus unleashed tit-for-tat retaliation by Switzerland, Canada, Italy, Spain, France, Cuba, New Zealand, Australia, and many others states.

Tit-for-Tat Retaliation Beggars International Trading Partners and Hinders Recovery

This retaliation, while rational and understandable from a politician's perspective, only made matters worse. Although many governments engaged in beggar-thy-neighbor policies, Smoot-Hawley was perhaps the most damaging given the size of the U.S. economy and market, and its potential for stimulating a countercyclical market for distress goods. As the largest economy by far, the United States possessed policy capabilities that were critical to interrupting the downward economic trend, if possible. If its policy makers had adopted a countercyclical strategy of maintaining market access under duress and promoting exchange, the Great Depression might well have been shortened or contained. But U.S. policy was, instead, procyclical. It added fuel to the forces threatening globalization and peace in the global political economy. It made little economic sense for policy makers in other states to persevere with countercyclical, protrade policies when the largest market had adopted procyclical, antitrade policies. The U.S. policy simply precipitated a stampede to the fire exits.

Governments started with tit-for-tat increases in trade protections. When those tools failed to improve the conditions of producers and labor in the tradable sector, policy makers shifted to other beggar-thy-neighbor policy instruments to promote domestic interests at the expense of foreign interests. Next, policy makers resorted to currency devaluation as a means to affect their producers' prices in domestic and overseas markets. Devaluation is a centralized, broad-range strategy that affects the prices of *all* goods produced in a nation vis-à-vis other nations' commodities. But, like the tit-for-tat retaliation in tariffs, devaluation engendered tit-for-tat devaluations that undermined currency stability and created further barriers to international exchange. The devaluations sabotaged any efforts to maintain the reconstructed gold standard; figure 10.2 shows the dramatic decline in the percentage of the world's nations adhering to the gold standard during the 1930s as a result of pressures to devalue. The exchange-rate policy arena became a free-for-all.

It is unlikely that Congressman Willis Hawley, R-Oregon, and Senator Reed Smoot, R-Utah, are congratulating each other on severely damaging the global economy and driving the world into a severe depression—which is what they helped do in 1930 with the passage of the Smoot-Hawley Act on tariffs. The act led to a dramatic increase in U.S. tariffs at a time when the United States was running a balance-of-payments surplus and had emerged as a creditor nation. Because of the economic strength of the United States and the difficulties facing other nations, the attempt to divert U.S. demand away from foreign goods added to a growing crisis in the global economy and invited other governments to retaliate.

The rapid tit-for-tat rise in trade barriers in 1929–1930 and the ensuing tit-for-tat currency devaluations led to dramatic declines in exports. As mentioned earlier, the value of world trade fell precipitously after 1929, contracting by more than 60 percent between 1929 and 1933 (see figure 10.1). The decline in trade exacerbated economic contraction, increased liquidity shortages, limited efficiencies from specialization, decreased consumption

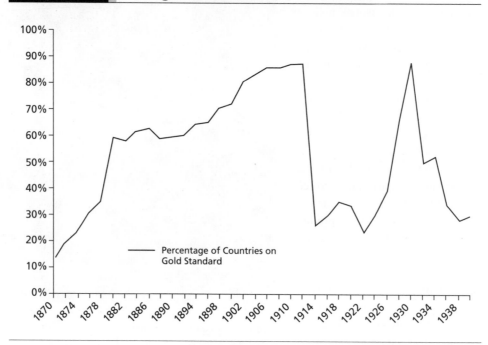

Source: Antoni Estevadeordal, Brian Frant, and Alan M. Taylor, "The Rise and Fall of World Trade, 1870–1939," National Bureau of Economic Research, Working Paper 9318, November 2002.

possibilities, increased unemployment, and fed the growing depression. A decline in social welfare was the perverse consequence of behavior intended to protect domestic economies. Instead of protecting domestic industry and labor, tit-for-tat responses to beggar-thy-neighbor policies wreaked even more damage. This paradoxical outcome demonstrates, again, the fallacy of composition dilemma raised earlier in the discussion of the growing liquidity crunch, whereby individually rational actions interact to damage individual interests and the larger political economy.

THE ABSENCE OF HEGEMONIC LEADERSHIP IN THE INTERNATIONAL SYSTEM

Chapter 6 explores the importance of liberal hegemonic leadership to overcome barriers to mutually beneficial international cooperation and to promote market-based economic exchange in the global economy. Such leadership, or **hegemony,** helps manage the social trap created by the political geography of the state system. It does so by providing incentive-compatible collective goods that alter the cost-benefit calculations of policy makers in major countries' governments, inducing them to select mutually productive—versus destructive—policies. During the 1800s, the British provided such leadership and collective goods to overcome barriers to cooperation in the global arena and promote the expansion of a liberal global economy. They acted as the hegemonic leader described in chapter 6. This leader helped to manage and overcome seemingly incompatible policy preferences across governments, established the rules of the game, and assumed a disproportionate share of the costs of maintaining those rules. Foremost among those collective goods was the liquidity essential to economic expansion. Growth that creates jobs and opportunities can hide a lot of social ills and insulate policy makers from perverse pressures.

> **Hegemony** is the predominance of one state over other states and the rules of the game in the system. A **liberal hegemon** is that state with the capacity to unilaterally promote, manage, and stabilize a system conducive to liberal economic relations.

As discussed above, in the immediate aftermath of World War I the reviving global economy faced some significant challenges. Perhaps the most critical of these challenges was the absence of a system leader in the postwar period—a leader capable of resolving the dilemmas produced by incompatible policy preferences or able to assume the costs of leadership and provision of the collective goods needed to promote liberal exchange and economic expansion. Even if they had the will, the British no longer enjoyed the capacity to provide the collective goods that greased the wheels of the global economy in the mid- to late 1800s. Other major combatants were similarly strained, except for one. The United States emerged from the war with the world's largest and healthiest economy. Indeed, the United States actually profited from the war. Expansion of the U.S. military, in anticipation of the conflict, meant that more troops needed to be clothed, fed, quartered, and armed, and so the military mobilization helped to expand the U.S. industrial base. Training also proved a boon to the education and health care of poorer U.S. citizens, improving their future capabilities as labor, should they survive the conflict.

As a late entrant to the war, the United States avoided the horrible devastation of its draft-age population that other countries suffered. The economic gains from the mobilization of its population and industrial base were not lost to death and injury on the battlefield. As U.S. industry sold war materials to the combatants, European capital reserves flowed to the United States to pay for those materials. Later, when those reserves were exhausted, the extension of credit to Allied governments to fund more purchases produced war debts that were really obligations of future transfers of liquidity from Europe to the United States. Such transfers would help fund U.S. economic expansion, but they would hinder European recovery following the war. Effectively, the war and its financial consequences moved the United States to the center of the network of global finance. Many European policy makers, such as the chancellor of the Bank of England, Montagu Norman, wanted U.S. engagement in Europe and worried about the prospects of a U.S. retreat to isolationism.

In the aftermath of the conflict, did the United States have the capacity to take up the role that the British had played in the expansion of globalization in the nineteenth century? Charles Kindleberger, an economic historian, argues that the United States had the capacity but not the will to act as the hegemonic leader, the stabilizer in the system. The U.S. economy harbored tremendous wealth relative to others. A huge percentage of the world's gold reserves had become U.S. assets (see table 10.6). As the largest and healthiest economy in the world, perhaps the United States had sufficient economic resources to provide the collective goods of liquidity and convertibility that had been a cornerstone of the prewar monetary system. Perhaps the United States also had the capacity, if its policy makers desired, to provide countercyclical lending and market access during times of economic downturn. But U.S. policy makers failed to take up the mantle of responsibility from the British. If the United States did have the capacity to act as the stabilizer and provide the collective goods that underpinned international cooperation and productive economic expansion and international engagement, then its failure to do so places significant responsibility for the Great Depression, the resulting international uncertainty and decline, and the rise of extremist political regimes in Europe at the doorstep of U.S. policy makers.

Perhaps the United States had more will than Kindleberger claims, but less capacity for leadership. Let's examine this puzzle more carefully within the context of the discussion in chapter 6 about the foundations of liberal hegemonic leadership. Certainly U.S. policy makers' prewar beliefs and practices heavily influenced their postwar thinking about the global arena—we are all influenced by our past experiences and beliefs. Many resisted shifting from the traditional U.S. isolationist, reactive stance to a more proactive and liberal engagement with the world. Early in its history, the United States adopted protectionist trade policies to promote the growth of its nascent industries. Generations of American policy makers heeded Washington's and Jefferson's admonitions against binding political engagement with Europe. After World War I, many U.S. policy makers wanted to return to their prewar policy positions of opposing more open trade or more proactive internationalist policies, but not all.

A virulent debate within the U.S. policy community over U.S. engagement with the world and its responsibilities as a leader in the global community began years before World War I. The empirical evidence about will and capacity is more complicated than Kindleberger suggests. The United States exhibited what might be labeled schizophrenia in terms of will. Policy makers were tugged between past policies of protectionism and isolation and the desire and potential to become more engaged in global affairs. The 1896 and 1900 presidential elections reflected this schizophrenia. The Republicans under McKinley advocated high tariffs but also the gold standard as a responsible form of engagement in the global economy. McKinley pushed global affairs to center stage by advocating the annexation of Hawaii, opposing Spanish atrocities in Cuba, and eventually launching the Spanish-American War.

TABLE 10.6   Gold Reserves of Central Banks and Governments, 1913–1935 (as Percentage of Total Reserves)

Country	1913	1918	1923	1924	1925	1926	1927	1928	1929	1930	1931	1932	1933	1934	1935
United States	26.6	39.0	44.4	45.7	44.4	44.3	41.6	37.4	37.8	38.7	35.9	34.0	33.6	37.8	45.1
Russia/USSR	16.2	—	0.5	0.8	1.0	0.9	1.0	0.9	1.4	2.3	2.9	3.1	3.5	3.4	3.7
France	14.0	9.8	8.2	7.9	7.9	7.7	10.0	12.5	15.8	19.2	23.9	27.3	25.3	25.0	19.6
Germany	5.7	7.9	1.3	2.0	3.2	4.7	4.7	6.5	5.3	4.8	2.1	1.6	0.8	0.1	0.1
Italy	5.5	3.0	2.5	2.5	2.5	2.4	2.5	2.7	2.7	2.6	2.6	2.6	3.1	2.4	1.6
Argentina	5.3	4.5	5.4	4.9	5.0	4.9	5.5	6.0	4.2	3.8	2.2	2.1	2.0	1.9	2.0
United Kingdom	3.4	7.7	8.6	8.3	7.8	7.9	7.7	7.5	6.9	6.6	5.2	4.9	7.8	7.3	7.3
India	2.5	0.9	1.3	1.2	1.2	1.2	1.2	1.2	1.2	1.2	1.4	1.4	1.4	1.3	1.2
Canada	2.4	1.9	1.5	1.7	1.7	1.6	1.1	0.8	1.0	0.7	0.7	0.7	0.6	0.6	0.8
Brazil	1.9	0.4	0.6	0.6	0.6	0.6	1.1	1.5	1.5	0.1	—	—	0.1	0.1	0.1
Spain	1.9	6.3	5.6	5.5	5.5	5.4	5.2	4.9	4.8	4.3	3.8	3.6	3.6	3.4	3.3
Japan	1.3	3.3	7.0	6.5	6.4	6.1	5.7	5.4	5.3	3.8	2.1	1.8	1.8	1.8	1.9
Netherlands	1.2	4.2	2.7	2.3	2.0	1.8	1.7	1.7	1.7	1.6	3.2	3.5	3.1	2.6	2.0
Belgium	1.0	0.7	0.6	0.6	0.6	0.9	1.0	1.3	1.6	1.7	3.1	3.0	3.2	2.7	2.7
Switzerland	0.7	1.2	1.2	1.1	1.0	1.0	1.0	1.0	1.1	1.3	4.0	4.0	3.2	2.9	2.0
Australia	0.5	1.5	1.5	1.5	1.8	1.2	1.1	1.1	0.9	0.7	0.5	0.4	—	—	—
All other	9.9	7.8	7.1	6.9	7.4	7.3	7.4	7.3	7.0	6.3	6.4	6.0	6.9	6.7	6.6

Source: Data from Barry Eichengreen, *Globalizing Capital: A History of the International Monetary System* (Princeton, NJ: Princeton University Press, 1996).

Bryan and the Democrats argued for bimetallism and against imperialism and opposed the annexation of the Philippines. The debates were about the role of the United States in world affairs, but neither side recommended abdication of that role; rather, the two sides disagreed about its manifestation. U.S. policy makers were battling over how the United States could be a great power, torn between the past and debates about the future. With the end of World War I, Wilson's strong defense of democracy and support of international institutional initiatives placed the United States at the center of global politics, even though the United States did not join the League of Nations.

As previously noted, Benjamin Strong, president of the New York Federal Reserve Bank, intentionally kept U.S. interest rates low to stem the outflow of capital from Europe and encourage foreign access to U.S. capital. Keynes, in *A Tract on Monetary Reform,* explicitly recognized the efforts of U.S. policy makers to move the United States to center stage when he wrote about the implicit emergence of a dollar standard instead of a return to the prewar gold standard: "A dollar standard was set up on the pedestal of the Golden Calf. For the past two years the U.S. has *pretended* to maintain a gold standard. *In fact* it has established a dollar standard."[3] Other events and actions suggest the movement of the United States to the center of global finance and a will, if not the capacity, to exercise leadership. The Dawes and Young Plans to address the reparations crisis demonstrated a willingness by the United States to lead at a time of economic crisis, even though both plans would fail. U.S. policy makers remained central to major international negotiations and agreements, such as the arms control Kellogg-Briand Pact and other multilateral treaties, which were precursors to the United Nations Charter. The historical record on international negotiations in both economic and security arenas does not find U.S. participation missing but integral and often leading. One can debate the merits of the policies and agreements that came from such forums, or the capacity to follow through on policies, but U.S. will was not the problem.

The question of capacity is also not straightforward. The United States became the world's largest economy by the turn of the century. It had yet to achieve the United Kingdom's per capita level of industrialization at the dawn of the 1900s, but it was closing in quickly and in absolute terms had by far the largest industrialized sector. By the end of World War I the United States led the world in per capita level of industrialization. As table 10.6 shows, the United States enjoyed an abundance of gold reserves. So Kindleberger's assertion has support in terms of absolute size, but chapter 6 demonstrates that although economic size may be a necessary condition, it is not sufficient for hegemonic leadership. Neither the Dutch Netherlands nor the United Kingdom was the largest political economy when it emerged as a commercial and financial hegemon. Consistent with Kindleberger's assessment of U.S. capacity was the trail of borrowers from around the world showing up in U.S. capital markets.

---

[3] John Maynard Keynes, *A Tract on Monetary Reform* (London: Macmillan, 1924), 198.

Foreign enterprises and governments found U.S. financial markets and banks more attractive after World War I. The war produced an outflow of capital and official reserves from Europe to pay for war material. This outflow continued as a consequence of the cascade of war reparations and debts that funneled capital to the United States. This excess of capital and actions by the Federal Reserve to keep interest rates low to support a return to the gold standard kept capital costs relatively low vis-à-vis the British and other European financial markets. This began to place U.S. financial markets and institutions nearer the hub of global finance.

Even with the world's largest economy and greatest capital reserves, the United States probably did not have in place the institutional mechanisms it needed to provide the collective goods necessary to promote stable and productive international economic relations. The U.S. financial system was not as solid in its institutional makeup as the British system of the 1800s. Despite the deep pool of global capital accumulating in the United States, questions about the reliability of U.S. markets and the dollar as a reserve currency persisted. The New York Stock Exchange had been a haven for market manipulators and speculators for much of its history. U.S. financial problems revealed with the NYSE crash had deep roots in U.S. history. A series of troubling financial crises, each more damaging than the previous, had hit the U.S. economy with some regularity since the 1870s. These crises threatened the U.S. financial system and also the willingness of others to use the dollar as an international reserve asset to settle accounts in international trade or as a storehouse of value. Such crises eventually led to investigations and debate that culminated in the creation of the Federal Reserve and adoption of other reforms.

Significant as the early reforms were, they were insufficient to preclude the financial problems that appeared in the 1920s and the early 1930s. The 1920s revealed massive problems of crony capitalism, insider trading, fiduciary irresponsibility, conflicts of interest, excessive speculation, transparency, and, by definition, insufficient regulation. With the financial crisis, the organizations central to U.S. financial markets, the banks and stock exchanges, lost credibility at home and abroad. Yet the evidence suggests that U.S. policy makers went to extraordinary lengths to address problems of insolvency, illiquidity, and confidence. Despite ideological reluctance, the Hoover administration, and then a more aggressive and activist Roosevelt administration, created agencies and enacted programs that amounted to a revolution in state-market relations with the objectives of shoring up and unlocking money and capital markets, saving households, preventing agricultural collapse, and restoring growth in the United States. Roosevelt, the Federal Reserve and the Reconstruction Finance Corporation, new federal banking and securities regulators, and the advent of depositors' insurance stemmed the rash of bank failures and improprieties on Wall Street that had produced a global liquidity crisis. Illiquid U.S. banks that Roosevelt closed with a national bank holiday in March 1933 were reopened and recapitalized with far healthier and more robust balance sheets. Yet, even with the restructuring of bank balance sheets and the recapitalization of the banking system, a lack of confidence led to either an unwillingness of banks to supply capital for investment or a lack of demand for that capital.

Under such conditions, the ability of U.S. capital markets to provide liquidity to the global arena and of the United States to be the global lender of last resort is questionable.

The economic downturn challenged the capacity of the United States to act as a liberal hegemon, but not because of size. Main Street's distrust of banks and of Wall Street had produced a financial system that created obstacles to the sound financial management and coordination necessary for the United States to act as the world's financial center and lender of last resort. Whereas the British Treasury, the Bank of England, and private financiers in London cooperated to manage and contain many global financial and economic crises during the 1800s, the U.S. system did not yet have the organizational capacity to replace the British. In the 1920s, the United States did not have the regulatory institutions or financial arrangements to absorb the severe shocks of the 1929 market crash and the banking crisis and still be able to sit at the heart of a network of relations that would have enabled it to act as the stabilizer in the system. Fear, distrust, and a desire to avoid repeating mistakes disrupted the network of global financial relations that might have enabled policy makers to manage the crisis. The financial crises of the interwar years were widespread, not confined to a specific sector of the economy, and threatened every household and community. They severely damaged confidence in capitalism. Households and businesses, their confidence in the system shaken, were slow to overcome the fear created by the breakdown in the financial system. Firms were reluctant to borrow and invest in job creation, households were scared to borrow, recapitalized banks raised their lending standards and appeared hesitant to lend, and investors avoided returning to the bond and equity markets. The liquidity crunch of the early 1930s turned into a liquidity trap.

U.S. policy makers demonstrated their will as they leapt into the world of policy unknowns and made valiant efforts to manage insolvency, create liquidity, and restore confidence. The United States experienced a revolution in governance, a massive shift in state-market relations that would transform U.S. finance. Those transformations took time to gain credibility and confidence. The foundations being built by government regulatory reforms in response to the financial crises of the 1920s and 1930s were to be central to a scaffolding for U.S. leadership following World War II, but they were new, untested, and without the credibility to overcome the fears of those hurt by the crisis. It took years of extraordinary measures and effort to restore confidence and overcome the fear that paralyzed investors, savers, borrowers, households, and firms. Without those actors actively engaged in the financial arena, the United States did not have the financial capacity to underpin the provision of those key collective goods necessary to act as the stabilizer in the system. Until U.S. households and U.S. and foreign firms returned to the money and capital markets through saving, investing, and borrowing to support consumption, job creation, and production, the private component of U.S. hegemonic capacity could not contribute to U.S. leadership, despite the will and capacity of public officials. The United States would have found it extremely difficult, if not impossible, at that time to provide financial collective goods to the global political economy.

CONCLUSION

The troubles and travails of the interwar years contributed to the breakdown in the global political economy and, eventually, to World War II. The inability of U.S. policy makers to assume hegemonic leadership and provide the collective goods that would promote liberal economic activity and expansion, the United Kingdom's inability to provide liquidity and act as lender of last resort, instability in the exchange-rate mechanism, German reparations and Allied war debts, the stock market crash, and the undermining of credit institutions severely damaged growth prospects in the global arena. Perhaps if the victors of World War I had been more generous to the vanquished at Versailles, if credit mechanisms had been better regulated to prevent excessive speculation and the risk of insolvency, or if central banks had created more liquidity by lowering their interest rates and pumping capital into the system, the Great Depression and the rise of tyrannical political leaders could have been avoided. But this is pure speculation.

Policy makers learned some critical lessons from their mistakes in the interwar period; in their deliberations over the design of the post–World War II global political economy, they would seek to avoid committing the same mistakes. In that later case, deliberations over the makeup of the postwar global political economy—over the rules of the game—began well before the fighting ended. Allied policy makers began their discussions at summits and conferences during the war. Chapter 11 considers these important lessons, examining their effects on the design of postwar international economic organizations, the rules of the game for the global economy, domestic safety nets, state and society bargains, and the global order. In particular, the negotiations that would help structure the post–World War II global political economy would center on the United States as a hegemonic leader willing and able to provide key collective goods to the system that promoted mutually beneficial cooperation and globalization, a critical absence during the interwar years.

KEY CONCEPTS

beggar-thy-neighbor policies (p. 382)

budgetary constraints (p. 373)

costs of adjustment (p. 370)

fallacy of composition (p. 394)

fiat currency (p. 379)

fiat money (p. 379)

floating exchange rate (p. 382)

hegemony (p. 405)

hyperinflation (p. 388)

imperial preferences (p. 401)

laissez-faire economy (p. 371)

liberal hegemon (p. 405)

strong-currency countries (p. 379)

structural condition (p. 396)

time-inconsistency problem (p. 369)

tit-for-tat policy reactions (p. 382)

weak-currency countries (p. 379)

EXERCISES

1. World War I demanded a tremendous amount of resources from the nations involved. The United States provided loans to help its allies pay for their war efforts. What implications did these loans have for the future of the debt-ridden Allies? How did the loans contribute to the Great Depression?

2. Describe a political method a government might use to allocate unemployment costs caused by competitive foreign market prices, and give an example. Who bears the costs of adjustment? How?

3. The United Kingdom was at the center of the first modern international financial system. How did World War I affect its performance in this capacity?

4. What negative effects did increased tariffs and immigration restrictions have on globalization? Why would nations adopt policies that might undermine their societies' welfare?

5. What key shift occurred in the relationship between individuals and their governments in the late 1800s that put pressure on governments and politicians to reconcile increasing international trade with domestic welfare concerns? Explain.

6. In the late 1800s and early 1900s, more and more commodities were being produced with only marginal increases in the labor force and only marginal increases in the money supply because of its ties to gold. What was the result of this trend?

7. Societies and their governments have choices about how to allocate the costs of adjustment that inevitably accompany economic transformation. Name and explain one of these possible choices.

8. We normatively view expanded suffrage, which endows greater political and civil rights on a wider population, as a positive development. But such changes may have made World War I more violent and deadly. How?

9. An absence of liquidity caused by war reparations and debts, instability in international monetary affairs, and the loss of a productive generation fed domestic distress and created problems for governments and their economies. Break down this statement and identify the independent and dependent variables.

10. Identify each of the following and explain its significance to the study of world politics:

    Time-inconsistency problem

    Smoot-Hawley Act

    Beggar-thy-neighbor policies

Hyperinflation

Structural condition

11. Debilitated by World War I, the European nations struggled to rebuild their economies. What factor deprived Germany of the capital it sorely needed to stimulate its economy and to fund rebuilding?

12. In the late 1800s, the United Kingdom had a smaller population and fewer natural resources than such other major European powers as France, Germany, and Russia. Yet it assumed a hegemonic role in that period. What does it mean to be the hegemon in a liberal global political economy? What does a hegemon do to provide stability in this situation?

13. What is the difference between a fixed-exchange-rate mechanism and a floating-exchange-rate mechanism?

14. How did the absence of a hegemonic leader during the interwar years affect the global economy and international cooperation? Why?

FURTHER READING

Ahamed, Liaquat. 2009. *Lords of Finance: The Bankers Who Broke the World*. New York: Penguin Press.

Bernanke, Ben S. 1983. "Non-monetary Effects of the Financial Crisis in the Propagation of the Great Depression." *American Economic Review* 73: 257–276.

Carr, E. H. 1946. *The Twenty Years' Crisis, 1919–1939*. 2nd ed. London: Macmillan.

Eichengreen, Barry. 1992. *Golden Fetters: The Gold Standard and the Great Depression, 1919–1939*. New York: Oxford University Press.

———. 1996. *Globalizing Capital: A History of the International Monetary System*. Princeton, NJ: Princeton University Press.

Friedman, Milton, and Rose D. Friedman. 1979. "The Anatomy of Crisis . . . and the Failure of Policy." *Journal of Portfolio Management* 6, no. 1: 15–21.

Friedman, Milton, and Anna Jacobson Schwartz. 1963. *A Monetary History of the United States, 1867–1960*. Princeton, NJ: Princeton University Press.

Keegan, John. 1989. *The Second World War*. New York: Penguin Books.

Kennedy, David M. 1999. *Freedom from Fear: The American People in Depression and War, 1929–1945*. New York: Oxford University Press.

Keynes, John Maynard. 1924. *A Tract on Monetary Reform.* London: Macmillan.

Kindleberger, Charles P. 1978. *Manias, Panics, and Crashes: A History of Financial Crises.* New York: Basic Books.

———. 1986. *The World in Depression, 1929–1939.* Rev. ed. Berkeley: University of California Press.

Polyani, Karl. 1944. *The Great Transformation.* New York: Rinehart.

Sobel, Andrew C. 2012. *Birth of Hegemony: Crisis, Financial Revolution, and Emerging Global Networks.* Chicago: University of Chicago Press.

Temin, Peter. 1989. *Lessons from the Great Depression.* Cambridge: MIT Press.

11

The Bretton Woods System: The Rebuilding of Globalization

In the long sweep of time, America's half-century-long ideological, political, and military face-off with the Soviet Union may appear far less consequential than America's leadership in inaugurating an era of global economic interdependence. . . . Who could have foretold that the nation that had flintily refused to cancel the Europeans' war debts in the 1920s would establish the World Bank in 1945 . . . ? That the country that had embraced the Fordney-McCumber and Smoot-Hawley tariffs would take the lead in establishing the General Agreement on Tariffs and Trade, and . . . would create the International Monetary Fund in 1944? . . . And who could deny that globalization—the explosion in world trade, investment, and cultural mingling—was the signature and lasting international achievement of the postwar era, one likely to overshadow the Cold War in its long-term historical consequences?

—*David M. Kennedy, Freedom from Fear, 1999*

Toward the end of World War II, Allied policy makers, led by the Americans and British, began to consider how to avoid the mistakes of the interwar years that undermined mutually beneficial cooperation and globalization, and eventually led to economic and then military warfare between states. The United States as the most influential and important political economy exercised dominant influence over the construction of new rules of the game for the postwar global economy. The United States assumed the mantle of the system's liberal hegemonic leader. U.S. public and private policy makers, particularly in the arena of finance, devised policies, organizations, and mechanisms that provided key collective goods and would serve as scaffolding for the expansion of interstate cooperation, global capitalism, and globalization. The Soviet Union would create a competing sphere of influence with dramatically different approaches to the aggregation and allocation of resources, capital, goods, and labor.

PAST MISTAKES AND A NEW FRAMEWORK FOR INTERNATIONAL COOPERATION

World War II grew out of an acrimonious and unworkable peace, a deep and widespread depression in the global economy, a failure by states to overcome barriers to international cooperation and economic exchange, an inability of politicians to resist pressures from their domestic political economies to shift costs of adjustment overseas and across borders, and a lack of mechanisms and strategies within states to insulate their politicians from such pressures. This chain of policy choices and defaults produced social and political conflicts within and between states that aided the rise of extremist politics and authoritarianism and eventually led to the most horrific war in human history. The supposedly civilized states of the industrialized world outdid the violence of any past human conflict. The American Civil War heralded the application of modern technologies of destruction to the battlefield, but its costs in human casualties, though excessive for the time, were constrained by its nature as a civil conflict. World War I and World War II demonstrated the brutality of modern technological warfare on a global scale. As described in chapter 10, the number of human casualties of World War I was breathtaking given previous international conflicts, but World War II was even more mind-numbing, as reflected in one military historian's catalog of the breadth of the tragedy:

> Some 50 million people are estimated to have died as a result of the Second World War. . . . By far the most grievous suffering among the combatant states was borne by the Soviet Union, which lost as least 7 million men in battle and a further 7 million citizens; most of the latter, Ukrainians and White Russians in the majority, died as a result of deprivation, reprisal and forced labour. In relative terms, Poland suffered the worst among the combatant countries; about 20 per cent of her pre-war population, some 6 million, did not survive. About half of the war's Polish victims were Jewish, and Jews also figured large in the death tolls of other eastern European countries, including the Baltic states, Hungary and Romania. Civil and guerrilla war accounted for the deaths of a quarter of a million Greeks and a million Yugoslavs. The number of casualties, military and civilian, were far higher in eastern than in western Europe. . . . In three European countries, however, France, Italy and the Netherlands, casualties were heavy. Before June 1940 and after November 1942 the French army lost 200,000 dead; 400,000 civilians were killed in air raids or concentration camps. Italy lost over 330,000 of whom half were civilians, and 200,000 Dutch citizens, all but 10,000 of them civilians, died as a result of bombing or deportation.
>
> The Western victors suffered proportionately and absolutely much less than any of the major allies. The British armed forces lost 244,000 men. Their Commonwealth and imperial comrades-in-arms suffered another 100,000 fatal casualties (Australia 23,000, Canada 37,000, India 24,000, New Zealand 10,000, South Africa 6000). About 60,000 British civilians were killed by bombing. . . . The Americans suffered no direct civilian casualties; their military casualties, which contrast with 1.2 million Japanese battle deaths, were 292,000. . . .

> Germany, which had begun the war and fought it almost to Hitler's "five minutes past midnight," paid a terrible price for war guilt. . . .
>
> . . . Over 4 million German servicemen died at the hands of the enemy, and 593,000 civilians under air attack. . . .
>
> It seems possible that a million Germans died in the flight from the east [to escape the advancing Soviet forces] in the early months of 1945. . . . In the winter of 1945 most of the remaining Germans of eastern Europe . . . were systematically collected and transported westward. . . . [I]t is calculated that 250,000 died in the course of the expulsion from Czechoslovakia, 1.25 million from Poland and 600,000 from elsewhere in eastern Europe.[1]

Even before the war ended, Allied policy makers began to discuss how to construct a new peace and the postwar system. They sought to avoid missteps of the past and build foundations for a healthy global political economy that would constrain the anarchy of the global arena and the temptations to resort to political, economic, and military violence. Both the distribution of power and a basic conflict of ideologies presented challenges. World War II left two states with disproportionate influence at the top of the power hierarchy in the international system: the United States and the Soviet Union. These states had competing views about the organization of economic and political life, but Operation Barbarossa, the German attack on the Soviet Union in 1941, had made strategic allies out of these ideological enemies.

The industrial machinery of the United States, still stagnating from the Great Depression, shifted into high gear for the production of war materials and served as a bulwark against fascism. Sheltered by oceans from the ravages of war, the renewed industrial capabilities of the United States provided material assistance to the British and Soviets as they manned the front lines against the German aggressors. American trucks, tanks, aircraft, food, and other materials flowed into the United Kingdom and the Soviet Union to help stem and then reverse the German onslaught. American trucks provided Soviet forces with greater mobility and transport capacity than their foes could match, while felt boots made in America protected Soviet soldiers' feet against the brutally cold Soviet winters.

Unlikely partners, Joseph Stalin, Winston Churchill, and Franklin Roosevelt (and later Harry Truman) met at conferences in Tehran and Potsdam to discuss the conduct of the war and to initiate postwar planning. The end of the war brought high hopes for peace and prosperity, but history, suspicion, competition, and ideological differences between the communist Soviet regime and the democratic capitalist systems of the United States and the United Kingdom made the wartime alliance a fragile structure, one that would unravel quickly with the end of military conflict. Almost immediately after the war, tensions arose over Allied responsibilities in an occupied Germany and the rules of the postwar global political

---

[1]John Keegan, *The Second World War* (New York: Penguin Books, 1989), 590–593. Published by *Hutchison.* Reprinted by permission of The Random House Group Limited. Copyright © John Keegan; Copyright © J.R. Fowles Ltd.

economy. The United States and Britain favored a system of decentralized market exchange with limited state intervention in the economy, while the Soviets preferred a system with intensive state intervention in the economy and state-directed allocation. These incompatible preferences would divide the global political economy into two hostile spheres of influence, lead to a cold war, and color international affairs for most of the next fifty years.

In this environment, U.S. and British policy makers began to design a framework that would avoid past mistakes, promote international economic cooperation, resolve disputes, and embed liberal economic relations in a nation-state system. Recognizing that laissez-faire market exchange in a nation-state system had contributed to the downward spiral of the global economy, they faced the dilemma of how to embed liberal economic relations in a self-help nation-state system. Their answers involved the construction of cooperative international arrangements that would restrict beggar-thy-neighbor inclinations, rebuild trade, and create an international monetary order based on a system of stable exchange rates. U.S. military and economic capabilities would be crucial to establishing a politically and militarily secure arena conducive to trade, obtaining cooperation from partners who might disagree on specifics, financing the provision of important collective goods, and supporting institutional arrangements to restrict damaging choices by governments that could unravel economic exchange and cooperation. The United States assumed hegemonic responsibility for providing key collective goods that were essential to obtaining the cooperation necessary for a productive capitalist global economy. The United States had both the capacity and the will to act as the global stabilizer and leader, as described in chapter 6.

Policy Making and Time Inconsistency: Lessons from the Interwar Years and the Postwar Dilemma

Numerous mistakes of the interwar years had damaged the global economy and led to the renewal of tensions and then war. To avoid making the same mistakes in the future, policy makers after the war needed to come to terms with the pathologies of the interwar years that had undermined rational constitutional governance, fed the rise of political extremism, promoted unbridled economic nationalism, led to the unraveling of the global economy, and ultimately brought on the most devastating conflict in human history. We will focus here on a handful of critical lessons that policy makers took from the experiences of the interwar years.

Conducting their historical autopsy, policy makers learned several vital lessons from the descent into global chaos. First, *market exchange is not necessarily self-correcting and self-sustaining.* Laissez-faire economics taught that markets were, indeed, self-correcting and self-sustaining, and this approach seemed to do pretty well for much of the nineteenth century and the beginning of the twentieth century. Market economies experienced sustained growth as exchange within and across borders expanded. This early success, however, generated false confidence in the ability of markets to discipline unproductive behavior, reward productive activities, and produce inexorable economic growth. Governments in market economies grew hesitant to intervene to regulate economic activity. Yet evidence already existed in the 1800s of potential dysfunction in market exchange. A series of troubling financial crises, each more damaging than the previous, had hit the U.S. economy with some regularity beginning in the 1870s and had led to discussions of reform and regulation. The 1907 financial crisis pushed the debate about reforms over the threshold. The crisis led to congressional hearings that revealed a concentration of economic power and vulnerabilities in the U.S. financial system. The creation of a national central bank with the passage of the Federal Reserve Act in 1913 was an explicit reaction to problems revealed by the 1907 crisis and earlier crises. Agricultural depressions during the latter 1800s and problems of commodity price deflation sent similar signals about the potential limitations of markets' ability to self-correct. Finally, the experiences of the 1920s and 1930s starkly demonstrated that markets could become dysfunctional and extraordinarily problematic for social and political stability.

Policy makers in the wake of World War II embraced the idea that market exchange requires government support to ensure that societies can reap the welfare gains from functioning markets. Governments must provide the domestic and international scaffolding that protects efficient market exchange and limits market failure. Domestically, this need suggested a greater role for government regulation of market exchange to constrain economic actors when their choices could seriously damage confidence in markets. Internationally, protecting market exchange would require developing mechanisms for promoting cooperation between governments in order to overcome potential barriers to exchange across borders and to ensure the provision of the collective goods that reduce obstructions to international exchange. As we have seen, the British provided many of these collective goods during the 1800s and early 1900s.

This necessity led postwar policy makers to the second major lesson: *economic nationalism and international economic instability can be devastating if carried to extremes.* During the economic hard times preceding World War II, governments had resorted to beggar-thy-neighbor policies to shift the costs of economic adjustment overseas and across borders. Policy makers had used protectionist policies and currency devaluations to protect their domestic producers and labor at the expense of those in other states. They used the tools of the state to transfer economic dislocations from their constituents to citizens of other states. These policies of economic nationalism explicitly sought to advance the interests of one state's constituents over those of other states, the health of one state over the health of others. The history of trade protection shows that governments sometimes get away with such beggar-thy-neighbor intervention in market exchange, but the experience of the interwar years demonstrated that this strategy can be dangerous if it invites retaliation that substantially obstructs cross-border exchange. The beggar-thy-neighbor policies of the interwar years provoked tit-for-tat retaliation and construction of formidable barriers to international exchange. These factors undermined the exchange necessary to promote growth, which contributed to worsening international economic instability.

This lesson highlights the tension between sovereignty and interdependence, between political and economic geographies. Domestically, policy makers react to constituent pressures, but with growing interdependence they must become more cognizant of the cross-border influences and consequences of their policy choices. Movement from relatively closed to more open economies means that policy makers cannot select policies in a vacuum. But a puzzle remains: Why would tension exist between sovereignty and interdependence if international exchange improves the economic welfare of society? Why would governments adopt policies that are adverse to the welfare of their societies?

At the core of this puzzle is the time-inconsistency dilemma discussed in chapters 8 and 10. Ideally, we want our policy makers to develop policies that are time consistent—good today and good tomorrow—so that they will not face pressures to change these policies from period to period. But creating time-consistent policies can prove difficult, given that politicians want to remain in office—a difficulty that is particularly acute in democratic societies, where elections pose regular threats to political survival. Politicians worried about short-term political survival in more representative environments may have to respond to the demands of organized groups by creating policies that can damage the long-term welfare of the larger community. Narrow special interests in societies may find easier paths to overcoming the problems of collective action described in chapter 5 than may more diffuse and latent interests, and consequently they may be able to advance policies that are good for a specific slice of society even if damaging to the greater social welfare. Policy makers anxious to please such organized interests, and less concerned about latent unorganized interests, face significant temptations to succumb to the whims of those who are organized and vocal, even if the policies are societally damaging in the long term. Failure to pass such penny-wise, pound-foolish policies can be political suicide for politicians in these political economies. Ironically, expanded suffrage and interdependence, both considered normatively good objectives, can interact to increase the time-inconsistency problem and the provision of policies that damage social welfare. This perverse situation cropped up across the Atlantic economy in the interwar years, creating a democratic trap for policy makers who might have hoped instead to encourage international cooperation and exchange.

This perception of political vulnerability led the postwar policy analysts to a third critical lesson: *the interaction of rational choices by policy makers in a self-help system can produce unexpected and destructive outcomes.* If only one government in the Atlantic economy had faced a time-inconsistency problem, perhaps only that society's long-term social welfare would have been damaged, as other governments could select policies that promoted long-term gains. But, in fact, many governments faced such short-term pressures, and so the desire of politicians to remain in office across many states led to the implementation of tit-for-tat, beggar-thy-neighbor policies that severely damaged the global economy. The interaction of rational choices by policy makers of many states in a self-help system produced the interwar crisis.

Addressing these harsh lessons from the interwar years posed daunting challenges for the statesmen who met to design a system that would promote growth and exchange in a self-help nation-state system. In order to avoid the traps that had mired their counterparts during the interwar years—and still lurked in the background of any such system—the makers of policy sought to construct arrangements and institutions that would do all of the following:

- Constrain economic nationalism
- Embed liberal economic interactions into the system
- Insulate politicians from pressures for short-term electoral gain that could damage trade and undermine long-term gains
- Ensure the provision of key collective goods and limited social traps

The challenge confronting policy makers was to construct domestic and international mechanisms that could manage the time-inconsistency problem, restrain governments from adopting policies that could undermine a liberal economic system, and promote cooperation between governments so market exchange could function. They needed to create both intra-governmental mechanisms to lessen the pressures on democratic governments to respond to constituent pressures and intergovernmental scaffolding to reduce international obstructions to market exchange. Because international trade was not only an important engine of growth but also a means to translate dislocations across borders, it was essential that they design mechanisms that would protect politicians from the temptation to manipulate trade and exchange-rate policies for short-term gains, and, ideally, would enable them to risk promoting policies that would invest in the future even if other polices were more popular in the near term.

The leadership of the United States was essential to any set of arrangements and institutions that would reflect these lessons and avoid falling into past traps. The inability of the United Kingdom and the United States to provide key collective goods during the interwar years contributed to the beggar-thy-neighbor momentum, but the United States was now far more capable than it had been after World War I. Because the U.S. economy dwarfed all others in the aftermath of World War II, attempts by other nation-states to address the lessons of the interwar years would be meaningless and futile if the United States did not play the central role of underwriting collective goods and promoting cooperation.

Using Monetary and Fiscal Policies to Manage Economies: Postwar Domestic Strategy and Mechanism Design

John Maynard Keynes and Franklin Roosevelt were major figures in redesigning the relationship between governments and the economy, between states and markets. Upon taking office in 1933, President Roosevelt tried one policy experiment after another in a determined effort to restart economic growth in the United States and battle the dislocations of the Great Depression. The U.S. economy grew at faster rates from 1934 through 1937 than at any other time during the twentieth century with the exception of World War II. Roosevelt's experiments helped redefine state-society relations and the role of government in the economy in democratic advanced industrialized states. His experiments were controversial, provoking debate and some virulent opposition, but voters rewarded Roosevelt by reelecting him again and again.

Roosevelt improvised and moved from one policy experiment to another, searching for strategies that would reduce economic hardship and improve the economy. Meanwhile, Keynes, a British economist, advanced a comprehensive framework that challenged prewar economic thinking. The ideas presented in his seminal works, *A Tract on Monetary Reform* and then *The General Theory of Employment, Interest and Money,* made Keynes perhaps the most influential economist of the twentieth century. The prescriptions of Keynesian economics dominated the postwar design of capitalist political economies and postwar government economic policy until the 1980s, when they were challenged by the ideas of other economists, most notably Milton Friedman and Friedrich Hayek. Before the Great Depression, economic policy in the democratic capitalist economies was dominated by a strict monetarist approach based on the classic gold standard. Under the classic gold standard, money supply was a function of official gold reserves, which left little leeway to use **monetary policy** to manipulate the supply of money. Modern monetary policy and its intellectual foundations did not yet exist. In *A Tract on Monetary Reform,* Keynes began to provide the foundations for modern monetary policy. He advocated a looser connection between money supply and official gold reserves and a more activist use of monetary policy to manage macroeconomic conditions—expanding money supply to promote growth during an economic downturn or contracting it to restrain inflation during rapid economic expansion. Benjamin Strong, president of the Federal Reserve Bank of New York during much of the 1920s, had been experimenting with such policies, but he was basically innovating on the fly. In his later work, *The General Theory of Employment, Interest and Money,* Keynes argued that such use of monetary policy was good for the long-term management of macroeconomic conditions in an economy, but the consequences of monetary manipulation would kick in too slowly during harsh times. Significant segments of an economy could be exposed to continued severe dislocations while waiting for the alteration in money supply to work its way through an economy. Keynes worried that these lags exposed politicians to societal demands for redress, which could lead to economic nationalism, other detrimental policies over time, and damaging social and political instability. The history of the interwar years backed his assertions.

> **Monetary policy** is a government strategy to manage economic activity in a society by manipulating the supply of money, either expanding it to promote growth during an economic downturn or contracting it to restrain inflation during rapid economic expansion.

Keynes believed that the design of government institutions and policies could counteract such pressures, protect society from the extremes of such downturns, and insulate politicians from demands that would prove perverse in the long term. This approach would involve a restructuring of state-society bargains (the social contract) as it transformed the role and responsibilities of the state versus those of society. Keynes proposed that governments aggressively employ other policy tools in their arsenals to complement monetary policy. During particularly difficult times of economic downturn, governments should be more proactive in stimulating economic activity and cushioning those who fell on hard times. Keynes suggested that a countercyclical use of **fiscal policy** (tax and expenditure measures) would kick in faster and supplement

> **Fiscal policy** is a government tax and expenditure strategy designed to influence investment and economic activity. **Countercyclical fiscal policy** involves expanding government expenditures and/or reducing taxes during a downturn and reducing government expenditures and/or increasing taxes during an expansion.

monetary policy by priming the economic pump of a stagnating economy or slowing activity in an inflationary economy. **Countercyclical fiscal policy** involves expanding government expenditures and/or reducing taxes during economic downturns and doing the opposite during periods of too-rapid growth. Keynes also thought that governments should be willing to engage in deficit spending to stimulate their economies during periods of decline. Careful use of fiscal and monetary policy would allow governments to manage their economies more successfully and would act as a safety valve by moderating economic downturns or constraining inflationary growth and preventing them from running their course.

Keynes also advocated the creation of government programs to provide temporary relief for those suffering dislocations, whose plight otherwise could feed discontent and produce demands for detrimental economic nationalist policies. Keynesian fiscal and monetary policies sought full employment, but recognizing the impossibility of attaining such a goal and the need for some mobility in labor markets, Keynes advocated safety nets to cushion workers from the costs of adjustment caused by economic change, whether from globalization or some other transformation in productive relations. This approach led to the rise of unemployment assistance and social insurance programs to protect workers and their families from economic changes beyond their control. These programs shifted some of the costs of adjustment resulting from economic change from individuals to the broader society. Instead of leaving individuals to bear the full brunt of economic dislocation, governments could redistribute part of the burden by taxing their societies to provide some form of temporary social insurance. In their programs of experimentation, Roosevelt and leaders of other governments had already adopted some social insurance policies, but Keynes provided a systematic argument that linked monetary, fiscal, and social welfare policies.

The transformation of government's role in the economy from simply managing money supply based on gold reserves to the far more activist and interventionist use of monetary, fiscal, and social welfare policies to manage the economy and individual risk represented a tremendous shift in governance and state-society relations. The social contract was redefined. Both governments' obligations to their citizens and the citizens' expectations of their governments were being radically reshaped. The warfare state was transforming into the welfare state. This redefinition of state-society relations, development of more interventionist policy tools to manage national economies, and expansion of social safety nets were important to the expansion of market exchange across borders and globalization. Without such innovations in their policy toolbox, national policy makers could face irresistible pressures to limit the processes of globalization, even if such processes brought greater gains than losses in social welfare.

SUPPORTING HEGEMONIC LEADERSHIP WITH IGOS: POSTWAR INTERNATIONAL STRATEGY AND MECHANISM DESIGN

Policy makers recognized a need for international governmental organizations to buttress U.S. hegemonic efforts in providing collective goods beneficial to growth and international exchange, promoting international macroeconomic stability, assisting stable monetary relations, limiting the social traps of the self-help nation-state system, and embedding liberalism within this system. These IGOs would supplement the international activities of U.S. hegemonic leadership. They would also complement the domestic strategies of Keynesian economic management and social safety nets, working as safeguards in case domestic strategies to protect liberal economic relations failed to insulate politicians from pressures to adopt beggar-thy-neighbor policies. By building IGOs to promote cooperation, policy makers sought to avert these dangerous choices by governments. But would sovereign governments delegate enough of their authority to make such international organizations useful? Constructing IGOs could help by creating specialized networks of communication between governments, promoting greater familiarity between policy makers of different states, offering formal complaint and adjudication mechanisms, and developing professional bureaucracies within governments that had a stake in the objectives of the international organization.

Again, leadership by the United States was critical to the construction of postwar IGOs. While the rest of world emerged from World War II physically and economically devastated, the United States left the battlefield with incomparable military, technological, and economic superiority. In 1945 the United States produced 40 percent of the world's total output of goods and services, and it held 574 million out of the total 965 million ounces of gold in all nations' official reserves. This huge gap in capabilities and the need of many nations for U.S. economic and security assistance endowed the United States with unparalleled and disproportionate influence in the global arena.

The period after World War I had demonstrated what could happen absent a hegemonic state with the capabilities and will to act as the stabilizer in the system by providing key collective goods to promote productive international cooperation, exchange, and growth. U.S. policy makers now embraced the challenge of designing a framework for the global political economy. Their willingness to exercise leadership was not based on altruistic good nature, but on a self-interested desire to promote a system of global capitalism and liberal economic relations that would best mesh with U.S. domestic economic activity and U.S. security interests. The experiences of the interwar years had educated U.S. policy makers about the need for such leadership to protect liberal economic exchange, so they threw their resources aggressively into the construction of a postwar system that would avoid the mishaps that had followed World War I. Moreover, U.S. and British policy makers recognized the military prowess of the Soviet Union, and they wanted to design postwar global economic arrangements to counter the growing communist threat on the horizon. They sought to promote global economic arrangements that were conducive to democratic capitalist political economic systems.

The United States emerged from World War II as a major creditor nation, just as it had done in the aftermath of World War I. Because the wealth and productive capabilities of the United States had bankrolled the fight against the Axis powers, the Allied nations once again owed substantial war debts to the United States. But U.S. policy makers had learned an important lesson from the interwar years about the need for liquidity to rebuild economies and the negative consequences of excessive debt and reparations for reconstruction and economic activity. President Truman moved quickly to forgive the war debts and reject reparations, but he would go further: he would soon support massive capital lending and rebuilding grants to many war-torn nations.

Displaying leadership early on, the United States hosted international negotiations in the midst of World War II to discuss the design of the postwar global economic system. Bretton Woods, New Hampshire, played host to some of these meetings, where negotiations and agreements led to the framework for what became known as the Bretton Woods system. The United States and the United Kingdom dominated the negotiations. Policy makers discussed how to construct a market-oriented, nondiscriminatory trading system that would reduce barriers to trade and restrain governments from resorting to protectionist tactics; how to build a monetary system that would manage pressures on trading mechanisms and balance of payments; and how to promote reconstruction and development.

Active leadership and commitment of resources by the United States was essential to any agreement that hoped to survive the stresses of a self-help nation-state system and the pressures that could arise within domestic political economies. The design of the postwar system, begun at Bretton Woods, is best reflected in the three IGOs that became the foundation of the postwar global political economy. The General Agreement on Tariffs and Trade, the International Monetary Fund, and the World Bank constituted the three organizational and institutional cornerstones that would embed liberalism in a global political economy made up of nation-states.

Promoting Freer Trade: The GATT

Discussions at Bretton Woods recognized the importance of trade for economic expansion and a healthy postwar system that could avoid the pitfalls of the interwar years. Policy makers understood that state intervention to protect domestic markets for domestic producers and labor had been a major part of the beggar-thy-neighbor policies that fueled the economic and political calamity of the interwar years. Negotiations focused on reducing barriers to trade and promoting its expansion. After many disagreements and debates, negotiators compromised and built a rule-driven system that promoted nondiscriminatory trading arrangements and initially emphasized the reduction of tariffs. Because it is more robust in the face of changes, a system based on rules that guide government policy making differs from a system that targets quantities in trading relations.

Tariffs affect the prices of imported goods by adding taxes on top of the prices. If tariffs on imported goods become sufficiently large, they can influence consumer choices in favor of domestic goods. Tariffs were an important part of economic development strategies in the 1800s and had provided a significant share of government revenues. Yet, if pushed too far or too high, tariffs can become counterproductive. Ironically, economic theory suggests that the focus on tariff reduction and the neglect of other obstructions to trade—such as quotas, subsidies, and discriminatory trade blocs—target the least offensive government intervention and leave other, more troublesome, interventions alone. Tariffs give domestic producers an advantage in the domestic market, but those producers do not usually retain the proceeds of the tariffs. Tariffs are taxes that governments collect and usually redistribute in the form of government programs; at least part of the penalty that domestic consumers pay as a tariff is returned to the broader society. Other trade interventions, such as quotas, allow domestic producers to keep the consumers' cost of the trade intervention; economists call such interventions a complete **dead-weight loss** to the economy.

> A **tariff** is a government tax on imports or exports, increasing the price of those goods. A **dead-weight loss** is a pure social inefficiency even though some individuals may benefit, as in a government intervention, such as a quota, that allows domestic producers to keep the consumers' cost from the obstruction of trade. **Nondiscriminatory trading arrangements and institutions** can be used as a strategy that seeks to inhibit governments from using trade policy to extend privilege to one country but not to others and to prevent political manipulations that could translate into structural inefficiencies that detract from the economic gains from trade.

Trade policy is a domestic policy tool that can be used to foster development of nascent industries in the face of more competitive foreign producers, but it can also be a foreign policy tool used to strengthen alliances and extend special privileges. Before World War II, governments employed trade policy to discriminate among potential trading partners—to exclude some and include others. Used this way, it created distortions that limited the gains from trade and the growth of interdependence. **Nondiscriminatory trading arrangements and institutions,** in contrast, seek to inhibit governments from using trade as a policy instrument to extend a privilege selectively to one country but not to others. They seek to protect the tools of trade policy from political manipulation, which can create economic distortions in international exchange that can translate into structural inefficiencies in productive endeavors and detract from the economic gains from trade.

The willingness of U.S. policy makers to promote freer trade represented a significant shift from the past, in which U.S. trade policy had built on a history of protectionism to shelter U.S. markets and promote the growth of U.S. manufactures. By 1900, the United

States had become an economy with significant concentrations in manufacturing and service, which looked to export markets, yet policy change lagged behind. Only after the onset of the Great Depression did U.S. policy makers recognize the pitfalls of this beggar-thy-neighbor protectionism and the importance of more open trade for domestic economic welfare. Still, protectionist forces remained strong in the United States and hampered the ability of Congress to reduce tariffs. In 1934, as a roundabout strategy, Congress passed the Reciprocal Trade Agreements Act (RTAA), which delegated to the executive branch authority to reduce tariffs by up to 50 percent through bilateral negotiations that extracted similar concessions from other states. Since this authority did not require the president to submit a bilateral agreement to Congress for approval, the delegation of authority provided congressional members with some insulation from protectionist pressures.

Negotiations begun at Bretton Woods produced an agreement to form the International Trade Organization (ITO), but the ITO proved unacceptable to Congress because it reached far beyond the narrow bounds of trade policy to include mandates for full employment and economic development. A temporary agreement in 1947 produced a substitute for the ITO: the General Agreement on Tariffs and Trade. Twenty-three states initially signed the GATT, which provided a multilateral framework of rules to promote the nondiscriminatory expansion of trade and to govern what governments could do to affect trade.

Lower tariffs on manufactured goods dominated GATT negotiations from the beginning. This priority reflected the economic and political strengths of the early GATT signatories, the industrialized states, which enjoyed advantages in the production and export of manufactured goods but were less competitive in the production and export of agricultural goods. However, since farmers in many industrialized nations enjoyed significant political power, negotiators were persuaded to develop a system that lowered barriers to manufactured goods while allowing protectionist assistance such as commodity price supports and subsidies to remain for agricultural sectors. The Common Agricultural Policy (CAP) of what is today the European Union is a prime example of such a policy. CAP is a legacy of the political power of farmers in European states. With CAP, a significant portion of EU resources subsidizes inefficient European agricultural production. Other industrialized nations, including the United States, also subsidize agricultural production, albeit to a lesser degree. The exclusion of agriculture in the GATT's early years thus discriminated against farmers in developing states. This bias continues today. Ironically, Mexican farmers, the ancestors of the prehistoric people who domesticated maize, find it difficult if not impossible to compete with corn producers in the United States. This cannot be a result of differential costs of labor.

The GATT was built around three core strategies: the use of multilateralism and most-favored-nation status to reduce tariffs, recurring rounds of negotiations to address barriers to trade, and dispute resolution. These strategies seem to have paid off. Tariff levels fell dramatically, trade expanded, and governments brought their disputes to the adjudication processes of the international organization rather than resorting to unilateral response. In 1995 the GATT was replaced by the World Trade Organization, which had 153 members as of July 2008. Today, the WTO and the world trading system continue to face challenges because the political geography of the Westphalian state system ensures that states retain their sovereign ability to act unilaterally and could at any time choose to defect from the principles established under the GATT.

Multilateralism and MFN

The adoption of multilateralism was a significant departure from the bilateralism that had dominated trade policy in the 1800s and early 1900s. Bilateral trade agreements (those between two nations) tend to decrease the transparency of negotiations and to increase the opportunity to use trade policy as a discriminatory tool of foreign and industrial policy. The ability to use bilateral trade policy to discriminate across states—to include some and exclude others—encouraged the use of trade as a tool of alliance. We saw in chapter 10 that bilateral trade negotiations that incorporated MFN clauses did produce an expansion of trade in the 1800s, but bilateralism was a relatively inefficient strategy for expanding trade even when used in a nondiscriminatory manner. If the objective was to expand trade by extending identical privileges to many nations, a multilateral agreement could accomplish more than many bilateral agreements linked by sequential bargaining, one bilateral negotiation after another. With many parties participating, a multilateral negotiation offered greater transparency, less vulnerability to secretive manipulations, and lower likelihood of special targeted provisions that could discriminate among states.

The mechanism of MFN, discussed in chapter 9, sat at the heart of the multilateral GATT. Very simply, a trade concession to one signatory of the GATT became a trade concession to all the signatories who enjoyed MFN status. MFN transformed bilateral agreements between GATT members into multilateral concessions that diffused across all GATT signatories with MFN status. For example, the United States and the United Kingdom were signatories of the GATT. If, in a bilateral negotiation, the United States reduced tariffs on British steel in exchange for a British tariff reduction on U.S. autos, the United States then had to apply that tariff rate to the steel of all other members of the GATT that enjoyed MFN status, and the United Kingdom was obliged to apply the same tariff rate to autos from other GATT signatories with MFN status. Multilateralism and MFN limited the use of trade concessions as discriminatory tools of foreign and industrial policy, and constrained the prospects for reemergence of the discriminatory trade blocs that had damaged trade during the interwar years.

Recurring Rounds of Negotiations

Policy makers hoped that multiple rounds of trade negotiations would create an inertia that would build on and reinforce the success of the original GATT. Some label this the "bicycle approach"—if you stop pedaling, you fall off, but if you continue to pedal, you continue to make progress. Multiple rounds of negotiations target a series of gradual changes instead of a single large shift. Creating a coalition among a large number of negotiating parties to support a single dramatic shift generally proves more difficult—perhaps impossible—than obtaining agreement for smaller incremental shifts. Over time, however, a series of incremental changes can produce dramatic shifts. Frequent rounds of negotiations can also improve relations across borders by building reputation, trust, and familiarity. The GATT and its demands for frequent negotiations led to the development of professional domestic and international bureaucracies with personal and professional commitments to the GATT's mission and success. Policy makers from different states could use their personal and professional ties to help sidetrack protectionist pressures by promoting discussions and compromise at times when protectionist pressures arose.

Multiple rounds of negotiations produced significant tariff reductions. Eight rounds of negotiations occurred under the GATT, beginning with the Geneva Round in 1947 and ending with the Uruguay Round, which concluded in 1994 (see table 11.1). Since 2001, the WTO, the successor to the GATT, has been engaged in a new round of negotiations called the Doha Round. The first five rounds of GATT negotiations were restricted to reducing tariffs, while other barriers to trade remained untouched. The average tariff at the end of the Uruguay Round stood at 4 percent, which represents a huge decline in tariff barriers since the beginning of the GATT. Meanwhile, the scope of negotiations has expanded to include nontariff barriers (NTBs) as well.

TABLE 11.1   GATT and WTO Rounds of Negotiations

Year	Round	Subjects covered
1947	Geneva	Tariffs
1949	Annecy	Tariffs
1951	Torquay	Tariffs
1956	Geneva	Tariffs
1960–1961	Dillon	Tariffs
1964–1967	Kennedy	Tariffs, antidumping measures, development
1973–1979	Tokyo	Tariffs, nontariff barriers
1986–1994	Uruguay	Tariffs, nontariff measures, rules, services, intellectual property, agriculture, textiles, dispute settlement, WTO creation
2001	Doha (WTO)	Agriculture, services, intellectual property, nontariff barriers, investment, technology transfer, regional trade agreements, transparency

Dispute Resolution

The GATT and WTO established mechanisms to manage disagreements and adjudicate disputes among members. These are public processes created by international agreement. Formal dispute mechanisms shine the light of day on disagreements. If a government concludes that its producers are being slighted, having a dispute process in place provides an alternative to resorting immediately to unilateral punitive policies that could prompt retaliation and further damage trade. The GATT/WTO adjudication process may find no damage or inappropriate activity, but if the process discovers a violation of the GATT/WTO agreements, it can authorize remedies such as punitive tariffs. Participation in the dispute process endows such penalties with legitimacy and inhibits the offending party from then engaging in tit-for-tat retaliation. More often than not, states found by the dispute process to be in violation of the GATT/WTO rules remove the offending policies before penalties are imposed. This is not always the case, however; sometimes governments are willing to incur the penalties to protect segments of their societies.

Dispute adjudication mechanisms can help to establish reputation in the international community. If a formal adjudication process finds a state in violation of the GATT/WTO trading regimes, this finding generates reputation costs. Governments generally resist being defined as pariah states, or scofflaws, in an adjudication process they have supported by signing an international agreement. Finally, a formal dispute resolution process allows time for disagreements to cool and be negotiated rather than escalating to beggar-thy-neighbor policy contests in the heat of anger.

NTBs, Escape Clauses, and Regional Trade Agreements

Despite the GATT's focus on tariffs, many NTBs such as quotas, voluntary export restraints (VERs), and structural impediments present more significant and difficult obstacles to trade. A quota caps the amount of a particular commodity that can be imported. VERs are bilateral agreements wherein one state and its producers voluntarily promise to limit exports to another state. Of course, the term *voluntary* is open to interpretation. When the Japanese government and its automobile manufacturers first agreed to limit their exports to the United States at the urging of the Reagan administration, the implicit understanding was that if the Japanese refused, the U.S. Congress was likely to impose far harsher, nonvoluntary restrictions. Assuming there is consumer demand, artificially limiting the supply of a commodity increases its price. Domestic producers benefit from such limits on foreign imports, as unmet consumer demand will turn to domestic products even if consumers prefer the foreign product. Both domestic and foreign producers may even be able to increase their prices as the result of the supply effects of a quota. Structural impediments are aspects of an economy that may limit the supply of goods available to consumers. Distribution networks, cultural practices, warehouse availability, exclusive contracting arrangements, and special financing arrangements that favor domestic producers over foreign producers can all influence the supply of foreign goods.

In a shift to broaden the GATT's reach, the last three rounds of GATT negotiations included discussions about NTBs. The Tokyo Round created rules to guide governments' use of tools such as countervailing duties and antidumping restrictions. The last GATT round of negotiations, the Uruguay Round, took more than seven years and broached issues of intellectual property, trade in services, financial liberalization, structural impediments to trade, telecommunications, and pharmaceuticals such as AIDS treatments among others. The Doha Round of the WTO continues this trend and at the behest of developing states has expanded the boundaries of negotiations to include agricultural subsidies. This reflects the awareness that significant barriers to trade persist and recognizes the changing role of developing countries in the negotiations.

Governments use other tools to intervene in trade, sometimes aiding politically influential economic sectors by means of **subsidies,** which are government financial assistance to producers. In many cases, absent such subsidies, producers would be forced to sell their products at above-market prices in order to earn a profit; but then consumers would not purchase those products, and the producers would lose, or perhaps go out of business. Alternatively, these producers could sell their products at market prices, but if their costs of production exceeded the market prices, again they would lose. Subsidies allow such producers to remain in production. In other cases, competitive industries may receive subsidies simply because they are politically effective. In both situations, taxpayers foot the bill—the many subsidize a few.

> **Subsidies** are government financial assistance to economic sectors or industries, many of which are uncompetitive without subsidies. **Dumping** occurs when a foreign producer sells its products below their production costs; this predatory behavior is designed to drive competitors out of business and grab market share.

Policy makers also resort to the threat of antidumping investigations to discriminate against foreign producers. **Dumping,** which occurs when a producer sells its products below its production costs, is predatory behavior designed to drive competitors out of business and grab market share. After dumping damages or eliminates the competition, the dumping producer raises its prices. Dumping is defined under GATT and WTO rules as an unfair trade practice that governments can penalize. A government must first begin an antidumping investigation to determine whether dumping occurred. This process involves determining what the real costs of production are for the foreign producer and what constitutes fair value. Determining fair value is not straightforward because labor costs, production techniques, and other inputs to production vary significantly from one state to another. Since the process involves such ambiguities, however, policy makers can manipulate antidumping investigations to favor domestic producers regardless of whether or not dumping actually occurred. Domestic producers who recognize this systematic bias increasingly use the threat of antidumping investigations to deter foreign competitors or to force them to raise their prices. If a foreign producer receives notification of an antidumping investigation and realizes that it is likely to lose in the dispute after paying significant legal costs, it may simply withdraw from the market or change its pricing structure to avoid the process.

Quotas, subsidies, and other NTBs can provoke retaliation by governments in the form of **countervailing duties (CVDs),** which, under GATT and WTO rules and authorization, impose legitimate tariffs to penalize foreign producers who have received unfair government assistance and, as a consequence, are damaging domestic producers who otherwise would be legitimately competitive. Because they assess punitive damages and are authorized by the adjudication process of the IGO, CVDs are a legitimate response to protect domestic industries from such damaging foreign intervention. But, like any policy tool, they also can be used strategically to create barriers to trade. Policy makers sometimes find that applying a loose definition of a subsidy allows them to claim the existence of a subsidy where one may not actually exist, and then to apply a CVD to protect their own producers.

> **Countervailing duties (CVDs)** are legitimate tariffs, sanctioned by WTO rules, that are imposed to penalize foreign producers who have received unfair government subsidies and as a consequence are damaging domestic producers who would otherwise be legitimately competitive. **Escape clauses** are special provisions included in the GATT (and now the WTO) organizing treaties that allow governments to protect their domestic industries temporarily—allowing them to escape from the discipline of the market—under special circumstances in order to provide time for adjustment and to ease dislocations.

The GATT (and now the WTO) have allowed governments to protect their domestic industries under special circumstances by means of **escape clauses** that permit temporary protection of an industry to provide time for adjustment and to ease dislocations. The need for inclusion of an escape clause demonstrates again the tension between interdependence and sovereignty. Without such loopholes, would states want to risk becoming parties to agreements such as the GATT? Unfortunately, however, governments sometimes abuse these escape-clause mechanisms to circumvent the spirit of more open trade.

In recent years, **regional trading agreements** and **free trade areas** have affected trade by creating blocs of states that agree to lower or eliminate barriers to trade between members. Such agreements combine multiple smaller markets into larger unified markets. Although this practice discriminates between members of these agreements and nonmembers, which is seemingly antithetical to the MFN principle, GATT and WTO rules provide exclusions for such agreements if they conform to certain requirements—for example, no increase in the tariffs imposed against nonmembers. The GATT's sanction of what appears to be discrimination in these cases reflects some legitimate confusion about what free trade areas and regional trading agreements are likely to produce in the long term. They may expand aggregate world trade as trade increases between members of the agreements. If they create significant new trade between members while only

> **Regional trading agreements** occur when blocs of states agree to lower or eliminate barriers to trade between members; such agreements combine multiple smaller markets into larger unified markets. **Free trade areas** are created when blocs of states agree to eliminate tariffs or barriers to trade between member states; the GATT (and now the WTO) provide exceptions for such exclusionary principles if they conform to certain requirements, such as not raising tariffs for nonmembers.

marginally diverting trade between members and nonmembers, they may increase consumption possibilities for consumers without seriously damaging specialization of production and social efficiency. But they could be damaging to long-term social welfare if they significantly divert trade between members and nonmembers, distort production structures, and embed structural inefficiencies in the system. These potential dangers lie at the heart of controversies over such agreements.

The European Union is the largest example of a regional trading agreement, with twenty-five member states. The North American Free Trade Agreement among Canada, Mexico, and the United States is another example of a free trade area. In 2005 the Central American Free Trade Agreement, or CAFTA, expanded free trade arrangements in Latin America, and ongoing discussions hold the promise of enlarging NAFTA by bringing in new members from Latin America. The United States also partners with Israel in a free trade agreement. The Andean Pact is a regional trading agreement between Colombia and Venezuela. Mercosur eliminated barriers among Argentina, Brazil, Paraguay, and Uruguay. The U.S. Congress passed three new trade pacts with Colombia, Panama, and South Korea in 2011. Agreements between states to create regional markets are appearing in Asia and Africa as well. This ongoing expansion of regional trade agreements magnifies the importance of determining whether such agreements are trade creating and liberalizing or trade diverting and protectionist.

Monetary Arrangements and the International Monetary Fund

At Bretton Woods, Harry Dexter White led the U.S. mission and John Maynard Keynes headed the British mission. White and Keynes sought to balance their respective states' priorities in constructing a system of stable monetary relations, which they viewed as an essential handmaiden to trade and economic expansion. Such a system needed to manage balance-of-payments problems, insulate the exchange-rate mechanism from short-term political manipulations, provide an orderly means to adjust exchange rates when currencies were fundamentally over- or undervalued, limit currency risk, and constrain the international transmission of financial shocks.

Many systems were plausible, but White and Keynes faced the task of producing an agreement that balanced a set of objectives that were not fully compatible. Keynes and the British sought, first and foremost, a system that would promote full employment. The British worried that unemployment could become the adjustment mechanism for balance-of-payments problems. They feared that idle workers were a source of political instability. Keynes argued for a system that would allow governments the latitude to restrict capital mobility, erect trade restrictions, and change their exchange rates if necessary to promote full employment.

U.S. negotiators sought instead to promote capital mobility, limit the ability of states to shift their exchange rates, create an international oversight mechanism to oversee changes in exchange rates, and link the construction of an international monetary system to the principle of nondiscrimination in trade. The last of these objectives was a direct blow to the

British imperial preference system, which provided Commonwealth states and colonies preferred access to each other's markets—a discriminatory trade restriction that, from the U.S. perspective, disadvantaged U.S. producers and labor.

Demands on Monetary System Design: Exchange Rates, Balance of Payments, Reserve Assets, and Capital Mobility

Let's stop and ask, What is a monetary system? It is a set of arrangements, rules, and conventions that govern monetary and financial relations between states. It specifies what policy instruments governments may use, what those instruments can target, and when they can be used to influence the exchange-rate mechanism. Exchange rates, the price of countries' currencies, affect international trade, competitiveness, and the means of adjustment to economic dislocations. Policy makers generally prefer a monetary regime with rules and conventions to chaos, but, as the interwar years demonstrated, policy makers can rationally choose polices that result in chaos by using exchange rates to shift the effects of economic dislocations abroad. The breakdown in monetary relations during the interwar years produced a system with only one rule: governments can use any instrument or policy to intervene in monetary relations, and at any time. This was the worst form of monetary system, a free-for-all, and one that designers of the new system sought to avoid.

The U.S. and British negotiators at Bretton Woods considered three key questions in the design of a monetary regime: (1) What role would exchange rates play in the balance-of-payments adjustment process? (2) What would be the reserve asset? and (3) How much capital mobility should be allowed or encouraged? Let's first consider the role of exchange rates in the balance-of-payments adjustment process. Recall from chapter 3 that the balance of payments reflects a state's economic interactions with other states. It is an accounting of all the goods, services, and capital exported and imported across national borders. At any moment, a state's balance of payments is going to be in surplus or in deficit, but a balance-of-payments position cannot be permanently in surplus or in deficit. It adjusts over time, tending toward a long-run equilibrium as the current and capital accounts balance each other. Often, such adjustments are gradual and relatively seamless, but occasionally a persistent balance-of-trade deficit or surplus signals a fundamental imbalance in an economy and demands more drastic adjustment, manipulation, and intervention to restore balance.

A variety of mechanisms can produce an adjustment in the balance of trade and balance of payments. These include changes in domestic prices, in employment, or in exchange rates. In an adjustable-exchange-rate system, movements in the exchange rate alter relative prices in the system, which changes the prices of one state's goods and services vis-à-vis those of other states, thus influencing consumption choices and moving the balance of trade toward equilibrium. A fixed-exchange-rate system forecloses this adjustment mechanism, forcing the balance-of-trade adjustment on either domestic prices or employment.

For example, a persistent balance-of-trade deficit signals a relatively expensive currency in a fixed-exchange-rate system such as the classic gold standard, but the price of the currency cannot shift to affect the balance-of-trade adjustment. This situation puts downward pressures on domestic prices in the economy with the relatively expensive currency, what Hume recognized as reduced money supply chasing the same quantity of domestic goods in his specie flow model. If prices on domestically produced goods and services in that economy quickly adjust downward, then domestic price deflation generates the balance-of-trade adjustment as the cost of domestically produced goods and services becomes relatively cheaper in the economy's domestic and global markets. This prompts a shift in consumption and helps to adjust the balance of trade. If domestic prices adjust downward too slowly, however, the price of domestic commodities remains relatively expensive compared with foreign commodities. Sales of domestic commodities suffer, and domestic producers must lay off employees or reduce wages. Either of these actions reduces consumption and leads to the balance-of-trade adjustment.

The second question for design of a monetary regime asked what the reserve asset in the system would be. Obviously, gold was the reserve asset under the gold standard of the latter 1800s and early 1900s, but it was not the only plausible system. In the early to mid-1800s, some governments had opted for bimetallism, wherein gold and silver served as reserve assets. Postwar policy makers were wary of a return to the pre–World War I gold standard, because economic expansion had outpaced the growth in the supply of gold in the late 1800s and led to price deflation, which produced excessive hardship in economic sectors such as agricultural commodities.

Third, how much capital mobility should be allowed? Should capital flow freely across borders, or should states erect barriers to capital mobility using policy tools such as capital controls, exchange restrictions, export and import licensing, or other regulatory restrictions? What should be the connection between national financial markets? Few state barriers to capital mobility had existed during the globalization of the late 1800s, when global capital sought out investment opportunities across borders, financed development in emerging states such as the United States and Argentina, enabled investors to diversify their portfolios, and imposed penalties on states and their economic enterprises that disappointed global capital. This flow of global capital promoted rapid economic change and development. But the interwar years also demonstrated a downside to high capital mobility and dense connectivity of national capital markets. The New York markets attracted capital from around the world that could have rebuilt economies after World War I, but, instead, this flow of capital fed a financial bubble that eventually burst and shocked capital markets worldwide.

As Keynes, White, and their delegations met, they recognized that a robust exchange-rate system needs the following qualities: (1) an accepted and legitimate process to effect relative price adjustments to address fundamental disturbances without promoting retaliation, (2) compatibility with the pursuit of robust monetary policies, and (3) the capacity to contain market pressures. Inevitably, a state will suffer economic disturbances, many of which can adversely affect its balance-of-trade position. The most troubling of such disturbances is

Fundamental disequilibrium is a situation in which a nation's balance-of-payments mechanism fails to adjust in response to economic disturbances—such as inflation, chronic unemployment, and stagnation—that can adversely affect the nation's balance-of-payments position and persist over time; for some reason, the prices of a large number of domestically produced goods and services in the state's tradable sector are overvalued, so that changes in a large number of domestic prices will be required to address the underlying problem.

one that persists over time, a **fundamental disequilibrium**, in which the balance-of-trade mechanism fails to adjust. A fundamental disequilibrium signals that for some reason the prices of a large number of domestically produced goods and services in a state's tradable sector are under- or overvalued, which means that changes in a large number of domestic prices will be required to address the underlying problem. Most governments rarely worry about a fundamental disequilibrium where a large number of domestically produced goods and services are underpriced. This usually results in persistent balance-of-trade surpluses, which domestic producers and labor generally enjoy even if the situation contributes to dislocations in other states. Policy makers in a state running a persistent balance-of-trade surplus owing to a fundamental disequilibrium may come to worry about this condition if it becomes a matter of international tension. But a fundamental disequilibrium where a large number of domestically produced goods and services are overpriced because of the exchange rate is another matter. Here domestic producers and labor face stiff headwinds in global markets, which can lead to political pressures on national policy makers for redress.

A state or society facing the problem of a persistently overvalued currency can effect such relative price adjustments with a variety of instruments. It can erect protectionist barriers to increase the relative costs of foreign commodities. It can reduce wages or lay off workers, which changes consumption. It can increase efficiency and productivity, producing more for the same labor and effectively cutting prices on those goods. Or it can adjust its currency's exchange rate and devalue, which effects a relative price adjustment across all prices. But the negotiators at Bretton Woods realized that pushing governments toward trade protections to address fundamental disturbances would be dysfunctional if trade was to sit at the heart of the postwar global economy. The British commitment to full employment limited the use of labor markets to address fundamental disturbances, which left exchange-rate adjustment as the policy instrument of choice to address a fundamental disequilibrium. But how much change should be anticipated, when, and how often? Too-frequent changes can create currency risk and threaten expectations in trade. Legitimating exchange-rate manipulation to address a fundamental imbalance also creates greater opportunities for policy makers to use the exchange rate as a beggar-thy-neighbor policy tool. So the negotiators sought an adjustment mechanism that could address a legitimate fundamental disequilibrium, but one that policy makers would be reluctant to employ.

Creating a robust adjustable-exchange-rate mechanism means balancing the tension between the gains from stability and the gains from flexibility. How do policy makers commit to monetary policies and restrain the temptation to realign their exchange rates to address problems other than fundamental imbalances? If a state's policy makers can too easily realign the value of the state's currency, they may be tempted to force adjustment costs overseas through the exchange-rate mechanism, whether the underlying problems are fundamental or temporary. Robust monetary policies are those that withstand such pressures and commit to effecting shifts in relative prices through the exchange-rate mechanism only under severe dislocations. This commitment requires developing an ability to resist pressures to manipulate the exchange rate. Because resisting those pressures can disappoint constituents and threaten political survival—a time-consistency problem—policy makers have resorted to a variety of strategies to tie their hands and signal commitment to robust monetary policy, including central bank independence, currency control boards, development of a reputation for changing rates only when faced with a fundamental disequilibrium, and transparency.

Financial markets and societal pressures eventually challenge even the most seemingly robust monetary and exchange-rate policies. It is then that we can discover how robust a government's commitment is to those policies and whether it can resist or contain the market and societal pressures that challenge its monetary and exchange-rate policies. Today, policy makers hope that traders in currency markets will remain indifferent to the value of their currencies. If currency traders think that a fundamental imbalance may exist in a given nation—signaled by persistent balance-of-trade problems, high unemployment, inflation, or some other macroeconomic indicator—they may shed their indifference and bet against the government's commitment to the price of its currency. With such challenges, traders are betting that the currency is over- or undervalued. They sell a currency if they believe it is overvalued (called shorting the currency), going to depreciate and lose value; they buy a currency (called going long in the currency) if they think it is undervalued, going to appreciate and gain value. If traders sell or buy enough of a currency, they can change the supply of that currency in currency markets and effect a real change in its price. Then the question becomes whether the government will attempt to defend the value of its currency, and whether it has the capacity to do so.

The Bretton Woods Monetary System Establishes the International Monetary Fund and a Framework for International Cooperation

The Keynes and White missions wanted to limit the incentives and abilities of governments to export negative domestic economic conditions to other states through monetary instruments. They produced two plans for postwar monetary arrangements—a British plan and a U.S. plan—both of which sought to use institutional design to insulate monetary relations from domestic political pressures. The plans overlapped, but they also differed significantly. The eventual reconciliation of the differences across the Keynes and White plans laid the foundation for the Articles of Agreement of the International Monetary Fund and the postwar system. The U.S.-British compromise produced a system that differed from the gold standard in three critical characteristics: (1) a central coordinating organization, the IMF, with the ability to extend credit to finance balance-of-trade shortfalls and a charge to exercise oversight of national economies; (2) an adjustable-pegged exchange rate; and (3) accepted limitations on capital mobility.

First, the gold standard had been constructed from the bottom up. States opted into the gold standard through decentralized policy choices, government by government, and not as a result of a compromise formulated by negotiators at an international conference and coordinated by an international organization. No international organization oversaw the gold standard to smooth out differences between states. No international organization existed for use by policy makers to try to prevent anarchy in monetary relations. Policy makers met instead at ad hoc international conferences or in the back rooms of the Bank of England when crises loomed, but there was no established organizational framework or expertise to help governments avoid such crises or provide crisis management. The IMF was created to avert some of the problems of too much decentralization, to provide an established framework and staff to supply national policy makers with expertise and knowledge, to offer a forum with rules and procedures that could help member states discuss threats and coordinate their actions, and to try to limit the economic nationalist proclivities of policy makers in an anarchical nation-state system.

The IMF's Articles of Agreement directed the organization to reduce monetary obstacles to trade, exercise surveillance over member states' economic policies, and extend financing to cover temporary balance-of-trade shortfalls. Providing a mechanism to finance temporary balance-of-trade deficits helped to insulate governments from pressures to manipulate currency values and domestic economic policies. Temporary shortfalls were assumed to be self-correcting, but it was recognized that some time might be required for the pendulum to swing back and restore balance. The short-term financing facility sought to offer governments some breathing space and so constrain them from resorting to actions such as tariffs, impediments to trade, and predatory devaluation to redress their balance-of-trade deficits.

Temporary financing would be extended to a state based on a formula tied to its state quota, which was determined by economic size. States faced limits on their ability to draw on their IMF quotas. Access to the IMF financing facility became progressively more difficult as account deficits grew larger. This limiting factor gave the IMF a lever to discipline states with persistent balance-of-trade deficits. If a state's balance-of-trade deficit persisted, as a condition to that state's accessing financing the IMF could ask the state to address specific national economic problems that IMF experts had determined to be contributing to the problem. This ability to impose conditions on the extension of further credit is called **conditionality.** Imposing the right conditions would require the IMF to have sufficient expertise and information about the member economies and their economic policies, which meant that the IMF needed to exercise surveillance over its members.

> **Conditionality** is the imposition of restrictions on the extension of financing pending some change, as when the IMF asks a government to address specific national economic problems that IMF experts have determined are contributing to the state's persistent balance-of-payments problems.

The second difference from the gold standard's fixed exchange rate was the adjustable-pegged exchange rate established by the IMF's Articles of Agreement. Many adjustable-rate systems are possible, from freely floating rates to more rigid adjustable pegs. Seeking to limit instability, the IMF's Articles of Agreement created an adjustable peg, which allowed adjustments in a currency's exchange rate, but only under unusual circumstances. The Bretton Woods system permitted exchange-rate adjustment when a state faced a fundamental disequilibrium in its economy and balance of payments, but only after the state had notified the IMF for changes up to 10 percent devaluation. Larger changes required IMF approval. Providing an orderly and legitimate process through which a government encountering a fundamental disequilibrium could adjust exchange rates recognized that governments need to sustain growth and promote employment. Devaluation was preferable to chronic unemployment or economic ills that could prompt unilateral beggar-thy-neighbor policies. Orderly devaluation with international oversight was an escape mechanism for governments that also restrained the tendency of national policy makers to view monetary and exchange-rate shifts as an easy way out of domestic economic ills. The requirement to notify the IMF prior to devaluation created costs for governments and encouraged states to resort to devaluation only after they had tried other policies. For the most part, this strategy seemed to work, because states hesitated to devalue under the Bretton Woods arrangements.

The IMF's Articles of Agreement provided for an adjustable peg but also sought to limit exchange-rate volatility and keep currencies within a narrow trading range. The Articles of Agreement directed the United States to declare a **par value** of the dollar. This fixed the dollar's value to gold (one ounce gold = $35). Other countries then declared their currencies' par values in terms of gold or in a currency convertible to gold, such as the dollar. The Articles of Agreement required governments to maintain their exchange rates within 1 percent of their par values. The United States committed to supplying the collective good of convertibility, convincing others to hold dollars willingly as a reserve asset as long as they believed in the U.S. commitment to convertibility. This arrangement, and the commitment by the United States to convert dollars into gold on demand, made the dollar the leading currency and reserve asset in the system. More than sixty years later, the dollar is still used for pricing and settling the majority of international transactions and accounts for more than 60 percent of hard currency reserves in national treasuries.

> **Par value** is the stated value of a currency, usually in relation to a reserve asset or currency.

The dollar's prominent role gave the United States advantages in the postwar system, but it also constrained U.S. policy makers. The United States could run balance-of-payments deficits as long as others were willing to hold dollars in place of gold. Other governments and the IMF ignored U.S. balance-of-payments deficits because dollars flowing from the United States created reserves and liquidity abroad. The system depended on dollars for liquidity. The desire of others to build dollar reserves allowed U.S. policy makers to escape the discipline of the balance-of-payments mechanism and enabled the United States to finance its deficits at relatively low interest rates and without much exchange-rate risk. It also gave the United States disproportionate influence over the policy choices of other governments. President Charles de Gaulle of France would come to criticize this exorbitant privilege, but it persisted. On the downside, the latitude of U.S. policy makers to change their currency's par value was far more limited than that of policy makers in other states. All other states set their currencies' par values in dollars, so any change in the dollar's price would change prices throughout the system and potentially create price instability internationally, which could threaten economic activity. With the dollar as the leading reserve currency, the United States could turn to the exchange-rate mechanism only as a last resort to address domestic economic dislocation. Power and privilege have their rewards, but also their price.

The third difference from the gold standard was the new monetary system's willingness to limit capital mobility. White favored full capital mobility, but Keynes argued for the ability of governments to restrict capital flows that could create destabilizing volatility and threaten balance-of-payments positions and full employment. The preferences of the British prevailed. They pointed to the 1929 New York financial shocks, which had quickly spread across the globe, to emphasize the destabilizing potential of volatile capital flows. They also worried that capital outflows in the aftermath of the war could drain an economy of the liquidity necessary to rebuild and generate employment. To promote reconstruction, governments were likely to adopt inflationary policies that could provoke capital outflows if holders of capital lost confidence in a currency's value. But governments that needed to stimulate growth and promote employment had little choice, because opting for more fiscally conservative policies would risk deflation, stagnation, and increased unemployment. With governments unwilling to constrain government expenditures and with barriers to changing exchange rates, unrestrained capital flows would operate as the adjustment mechanism in the balance of payments. This situation could threaten employment. The Bretton Woods agreement therefore accepted, even encouraged, constraints on capital mobility to avoid losses in the capital account, regulate the unsettling downside of financial markets, encourage growth, and promote the full-employment goal of the postwar social contract in many nations. After the experience of the interwar years, with competitive devaluations, extreme currency risk and uncertainty, and beggar-thy-neighbor free-for-all exchange-rate relations, the Bretton Woods monetary system contained threats of currency risk, encouraged interstate cooperative monetary relations, and provided a stable international monetary system that was conducive to the expansion of international trade. The Bretton Woods system was at the heart of postwar international cooperation and the expansion of globalization, which fueled growth, created jobs, and improved social welfare.

Development and the World Bank: Encouraging Economic Expansion

The World Bank supplied the third pillar of intergovernmental cooperation in the postwar global economy. The World Bank is an intergovernmental financial organization like the IMF, but with a different role in the postwar system. The IMF was created to manage international monetary arrangements and promote stability in the exchange-rate mechanism. The World Bank was created to provide economic aid and technical expertise in rebuilding war-damaged economies and promoting the development and expansion of economic infrastructure in developing economies. Reconstruction and development were viewed as critical to insulating policy makers from pressures to adopt beggar-thy-neighbor policies. Economic expansion, by offering individuals the prospect of being better able to work and support their families over time, hides a lot of ills that can push politicians to adopt policies that safeguard their short-term political survival but damage society in the long run.

Initially, the World Bank focused primarily on the reconstruction of the European and Japanese economies damaged by war, and only secondarily on promoting economic growth in the developing nations. This priority was set partly because of the geopolitical importance of the European and Japanese political economies in the emerging tensions between the U.S. and Soviet spheres of influence and partly because of the relative absence of developing nations on the scene owing to the persistence of colonial empires after the war. Despite having fought a war to make the world safe for democracy, U.S. policy makers looked the other way as the European powers reasserted their prewar colonial claims and authority.

The World Bank was built around three financing facilities, or windows, each designed to extend loans to promote development. The main lending window is the International Bank for Reconstruction and Development (IBRD), which targets middle-income economies. Initially the IBRD was designed primarily to aid in postwar reconstruction by supplying assistance to stimulate economic development. Today, it borrows in capital markets and lends capital to developing states at a small markup that is needed to help cover the World Bank's operating expenses. Because investors view the World Bank as an excellent risk, the IBRD can borrow at the best rates and then make loans to developing nations at rates far below what they could expect if borrowing on their own. A second and smaller window, the International Finance Corporation (IFC), also borrows in markets and then makes loans to emerging economies. A third window, the International Development Association (IDA), extends loans or grants to states facing the most difficult barriers to growth. Today, approximately 70 percent of IDA funds are awarded as grants.

The multilateral resources of the World Bank proved too limited to meet the pressing reconstruction needs of the European and Japanese political economies, given the immediate problems of countering economic dissension in their polities and the prospects of domestic communist parties succeeding at the ballot box. Under President Truman, the United States therefore bypassed the multilateral mechanism of the World Bank and filled the gap in these regions with a tremendous infusion of bilateral economic and technical assistance called the **Marshall Plan.** The Marshall Plan budgeted $16.5 billion for the

> The **Marshall Plan**, an economic policy initiative of the Truman administration, was designed to promote post–World War II reconstruction and to provide a bulwark against the rise of domestic communist movements in the Western European states.

A Maasai man and his cattle gather at a pond that was built with financial help from the World Bank in Kajiado, Kenya. Programs like the one that created the pond, funded by the World Bank and similar institutions, provide economic assistance to governments and encourage the growth of national and regional stability, as well as greater economic prosperity.

program, which was on top of the $6 billion already extended in postwar assistance by the United States. It was an extraordinary amount of assistance at the time—not much less than current U.S. foreign assistance in nominal dollars. This targeted U.S. effort left the multilateral World Bank to shift its emphasis from reconstruction to development.

With the explosion of independence movements, the dismantling of colonial empires, and the emergence of newly sovereign states in the developing regions of the world, the challenges facing the World Bank multiplied. For approximately sixty years, the World Bank has been the key institution funneling financial assistance and expertise to developing nations from developed political economies. World Bank programs bring capital, technical expertise, and research to developing societies in attempts to improve the lots of the people living there. To date, such programs have helped governments and societies lift billions of people out of extreme poverty and other conditions that can feed national and regional instability. But even as the relative number of people living in extreme poverty as a proportion of the global population has declined, the absolute number of people living in such conditions has increased with global population growth. Are we making progress or falling further behind?

Challenges of Development Prompt Policy Experimentation

The World Bank faces the most daunting task of all the postwar liberal economic IGOs. Unlike the GATT and IMF, which manage economic tensions and relations between states, the World Bank targets the microfoundations of economic activity within states. It seeks to transform those foundations into healthy, developed economies so that their societies prosper and their governments can more easily cooperate to create harmonious relations across states. One of the assumptions implicit in the World Bank's undertaking this task is that greater disparities across states place greater strains and demands on cooperation. Promoting growth is intended to reduce such disparities and improve the conditions for cooperation.

Unfortunately, the problems addressed by the GATT and the IMF look like child's play in comparison with the problems of development that the World Bank faces. Economists and policy makers have long recognized that development is one of the stickiest and most impenetrable of the world's policy problems. Despite the efforts of generations of smart economists and the lessons learned about economic activity in relatively developed economies, the lack of success in developing economies signals the paucity of knowledge about transforming developing economies into developed economies, the substantial obstacles that need to be overcome, and the difficulty in simply applying lessons from one context to another—one size does not fit all.

To date, economists have proved better at understanding established economic behavior than at analyzing dynamic transformations. Economic historians describe such transformations, but the causal explanations that inform good policy prescriptions fall short or do not travel well to other contexts. Theories have led to policy experimentation, but the evidence suggests that those theories remain incomplete and insufficient to the task of generating growth and transforming economies. In retrospect, this is not surprising. The industrialized states of Europe, North America, and northeastern Asia did not emerge fully developed, nor did they follow the same development paths, nor were their paths linear and continuous. The economic histories of developed nations are full of meandering experimentation and failure—one step forward, two steps back, and then two steps forward, one step back. Some call economics the "dismal science," not because of poor science and lack of effort, but because of the difficulty and complexity of identifying causal economic mechanisms.

Despite the earnest efforts of organizations such as the World Bank, the problems of poverty, nutritional deficiency, illiteracy, gender discrimination, ethnic and racial violence, disease, and idleness abound. The percentage of the earth's population living in extreme poverty has declined even as the absolute number of people living under such conditions has grown. Is this improvement or failure? In some developing states, the daily wage remains below one dollar. The infant mortality rate in the richest quintile of states is four deaths per thousand, but in the poorest quintile, it is two hundred deaths per thousand. In developing states, millions of children die annually from dehydration, and millions more from pneumonia, tetanus, polio, measles, and other diseases that can be treated easily and cheaply with vaccines and antibiotics. Deficient diets lead to caloric, vitamin, and nutritional shortfalls that cause blindness, thyroid problems, anemia, mental impairment, and death. The desperation that grows from such suffering drains societies by taxing the resources of caregivers, diverting labor that could be used for more economically productive activities, and promoting slavery and debt bondage. Children in desperate societies turn to prostitution or war, unenviable professions for adults but even more obscene and immoral for children. Gender inequality and discrimination are greatest in poor societies, where spousal abuse of women is often simply a matter of happenstance and expectation. Money may not buy happiness, but people living in poor and desperate societies routinely have terrible things happen to them. This affects individuals' views of the future and their willingness to take risks and invest in the future versus just living day to day.

Dozens of slave children, held in a police vehicle, receive bagged water after they were apprehended en route to the Republic of Benin. Child trafficking in Nigeria provides cheap labor to the economy. Human trafficking has become so lucrative in parts of the developing world that it has become a significant source of crime and regional instability. There are now reports of maternity clinics raising babies specifically for sale into this market. Human trafficking, just like drugs and arms dealing, spans national borders.

Yet literacy, economic welfare, and gender equality have been improving decade by decade in many regions, albeit not nearly fast or far enough. Latin American states have made some progress since World War II, while Japan, South Korea, Taiwan, and Singapore have achieved stunning successes, becoming the poster children for development. The rapid expansion of the Chinese economy since the thawing of China's political economic relations with the West and the adoption of economic reforms at home continues apace. But many African states although doing better recently fell behind where they were a decade ago, two decades ago, or three decades ago. Even where conditions have improved, significant problems remain and the potential for backsliding is very real. Lagging development is more than a burden for the people living in poverty in those nations, for its related problems can spill across borders to damage international security and economic affairs. Failed economies are failed polities that nurture the seeds of violence, discrimination, human and drug trafficking, and international terrorism. The track record of the World Bank and other development organizations in addressing the root causes that fuel such problems is unsatisfying, but not for a lack of trying. Frustration with the relative lack of success so far may tempt some to turn a blind eye to development problems, but ignoring them will only risk greater dislocations and violence.

Strategies to Promote Development

The World Bank has tried a variety of strategies to overcome barriers to growth. Abstractly, economic theory posits that change in growth is a function of changes in three factors: *capital, labor,* and *technology or knowledge.* Increases or improvements in the supply of labor, increases or improvements in physical and human capital, and, most important, technological and informational changes that transform the inputs of land, resources, and capital should affect economic activity, increase output per capita, and improve economic welfare. The economic history of the West supports this elegant framework and informs the World Bank's development activities. World Bank programs attempt to improve a state's labor pool, increase its human and physical capital investment, and provide technology and knowledge to improve the productivity of its labor, resources, and capital.

Initially, World Bank programs targeted a perceived **financing gap** in developing states—the difference between the level of domestic investment considered necessary to promote economic growth and the level of domestic savings. Believing that an inadequate level of capital was hindering the economic activity that could transform developing states into developed states, policy makers at the World Bank and other development organizations started programs to close this financing gap by extending financial assistance to developing states. This was much of the World Bank's focus during the 1950s and early 1960s. When this assistance failed to spark development, however, the World Bank directed its strategies toward improving the quality and supply of physical capital. While continuing to provide funds to address a perceived financing gap, World Bank programs shifted to helping fund the physical infrastructure of development. Programs provided industrial and agricultural machinery and assistance in the development of infrastructure such as roads, buildings, and communication networks. Unfortunately, poverty proved remarkably resistant. In many countries, such efforts even seemed to lead to less economic activity, more income inequality, more poverty, and more violence, as this well-intentioned international assistance was captured by small segments of society who used it to advance their narrow interests at the expense of their larger societies.

> A **financing gap** is the difference between the level of domestic investment considered necessary to promote economic growth and the level of domestic savings.

Discovering that the manipulation of financial and physical capital was insufficient to stimulate growth, the World Bank turned to strategies to influence the quality and supply of labor. It funded efforts to increase literacy and improve the skills of workers—a capital improvement in the quality of labor. Today, many developing states have basic literacy rates that are comparable to those of the developed states, but they still have not achieved stable growth. Contrary to expectations, there appeared to be little correlation between education and growth in many developing states. Conjecturing that perhaps quantity, not quality, of people was the problem, the World Bank and other development organizations next turned to population planning. These programs assumed that high birthrates act as a brake on growth. But, like previous strategies, this tactic failed to overcome the barriers to growth. In retrospect, the evidence suggests that wealth does lead to lower birthrates, but little evidence supports the contrary proposition that lower birthrates lead to development. In the developed states, birthrates declined after growth took hold, not before. It turns out that children provide insurance against violence, predation, economic instability, neglect in old age, and highly uncertain future opportunities. Once societies achieve stable economic growth, security, and more predictable shadows of the future, parents decide to have fewer children and spend more of their surplus income on other commodities.

The **Washington Consensus** is a policy agenda that places emphasis on the corrective pressures of market discipline and seeks to reduce government regulation and intervention in the economy by promoting economic openness in trade and capital movements, liberalization of financial markets, fiscal policies that lead to balanced budgets, anti-inflationary monetary policies, stability in exchange-rate relations, expansion of private enterprise, and reduction in state-owned enterprises. The name of this system reflects the prominence of Washington, D.C., and the organizations located there, in international economic affairs.

Beginning in the 1980s, the World Bank and other development organizations started to tie developmental assistance to regulatory reforms in states' political economies. This strategy, part of the **Washington Consensus,** recognized that governments could help or hurt economic activity, and so it pushed for reforms of government policies and institutions that conceivably were handicapping market exchange. The Washington Consensus promoted stable and clear property rights, a rule of law with transparent adjudication and enforcement mechanisms, independent central banks, reduction of corruption and cronyism, and responsible macroeconomic policies. This approach emphasized the role of governments in creating a context conducive to growth so that investments in labor, capital, and technology might work as expected. Unfortunately, this strategy also appears to have fallen short.

Many celebrities—including film and television actors and pop musicians—have been drawn to the problems of the human condition and have tried to use their stature and influence to mobilize development initiatives. Bono, of the music group U2, has used his public notoriety to garner attention for **debt forgiveness** as a development strategy. Proponents of this strategy argue that the debt burden of developing states acts as a ball and chain, slowing or retarding these states' investment in economic activity because they must send their capital abroad to pay off loans instead of investing in their domestic economies. This reasoning returns to the logic of the financing gap, and, as with strategies based on that logic, debt forgiveness has been tried in the past as a means of addressing this problem, with little success. Worse, much of the evidence shows that debt forgiveness has led states with newly clean slates to run up new debt burdens without stimulating economic development, thus further damaging their credit reputations. Perhaps a problem here is that the debts of the wrong states have been forgiven. In the past, the states with the worst records have enjoyed the greatest amount of debt forgiveness.

Debt forgiveness is a development strategy involving cancellation of the debt burden of developing states in order to relieve them of the need to send capital abroad to pay off their loans instead of investing in domestic economic activity.

Despite the commitment of substantial financial, human, and physical capital and emotional resources, no panacea or silver bullet has yet been uncovered that provides a clear means for overcoming the obstacles to development. The problems associated with economic stagnation, the handful of unambiguous successes in Asia, and some partial successes in other parts of the world motivate continued efforts to discover and unleash the mechanisms of growth, but the history of development efforts and the stubbornness of poverty should make us wary of quick fixes and overblown claims about building healthy political economies, especially in places such as Afghanistan and Iraq, which are doubly burdened with political conflict. We have had almost no success in transforming under-developed, dysfunctional authoritarian political economies into modern democratic political economies. South Korea is one of the few and most notable success stories of the post–World War II period. Economic history strongly suggests that we do not yet know how to unlock the economic growth model so that changes in capital, labor, and technology will produce the expected growth. Otherwise, we would have a world filled with modern, developed political economies.

ACTIVE ENGAGEMENT AND THE TRUMAN DOCTRINE

The reconstruction of the European political economies proceeded slowly after World War II despite U.S. willingness to forgive war debts, the Bretton Woods arrangements to promote trade and stability in the exchange-rate mechanism, and assistance from the World Bank. The citizens of these damaged states suffered through several harsh winters, drought and agricultural failures, recession and high unemployment, and hunger. With the Eastern European political economies already under Soviet influence, President Truman became increasingly concerned that the inability of the Western European political economies to rebuild after the war promoted internal dissension and threatened to bring national communist parties to power by the electoral process in Greece, Turkey, Italy, and other places. If national communist parties succeeded at the ballot box, Truman feared, the Soviets could extend their sphere of influence over Western Europe through legitimate electoral means. The major European allies of the United States, the United Kingdom and France, were hardly better-off economically than the states where national communist parties were knocking on the electoral door, so they were incapable of extending economic assistance to the others.

Truman faced a difficult task in convincing Americans of the emerging communist threat in Europe. After the war, many Americans turned their focus inward and adopted an increasingly isolationist posture. In particular, the Republican members of Congress from the Midwest and West opposed foreign engagement and lengthy overseas commitments. However, several factors worked to counter the isolationist forces. George Kennan, a U.S. diplomat based in the Moscow embassy, sent the policy memorandum that has become known as the Long Telegram to his superiors at the State Department. Kennan's Long Telegram detailed the incompatibilities between the Soviet and U.S. systems, the upcoming Soviet challenge to the West, and strategies for responding to the threat. The memorandum became renowned and highly influential in U.S. policy circles. A version of Kennan's analysis appeared in the influential periodical *Foreign Affairs* in 1947 under the pseudonym Mr. X. Next, a U.S.-Soviet confrontation over Berlin in 1948–1949 and the Soviet detonation of an atomic bomb in August 1949 helped Truman and his secretary of state, General George

Marshall, convince Americans and their congressional representatives to abandon their isolationism and confront the communist threat, including the growing electoral prospects of domestic communist political parties in Western Europe.

President Truman's restatement of U.S. foreign policy strategy, the **Truman Doctrine,** was perhaps the most important shift in U.S. foreign policy since the American Revolution. Unveiling this new policy in a speech to Congress in 1947, Truman asserted, "I believe that it must be the policy of the U.S. to support free peoples who are resisting subjugation by armed minorities or by outside pressures." The Truman Doctrine thereby inserted U.S. policy makers proactively into world affairs to support states oriented toward democratic governance mechanisms and market-based economic mechanisms. Truman claimed the authority to challenge nondemocratic, nonmarket political economies that threatened the political economic order he believed was most conducive to U.S. well-being. Rather than the passive and reactive stance maintained by previous generations, the Truman Doctrine advanced a strategy of active engagement, using the tools of power to challenge communist influence and expansion and to mold world affairs. The two pillars on which the Truman Doctrine was built were containment and the Marshall Plan.

> The **Truman Doctrine** was a foreign policy enunciated by President Truman that committed the United States to a strategy of active engagement, "to support free peoples who are resisting subjugation by armed minorities or by outside pressures."

Economic and Military Containment

Containment involved the use of military and economic capabilities to encircle and challenge the Soviet Union and its sphere of influence. Kennan first used the term in his Long Telegram. In practice, this strategy involved constructing collective security pacts among states. In Europe, it became the motivation for the formation of the North Atlantic Treaty Organization. Since the European allies of the United States lacked the capabilities to contain the Soviets militarily should they move west, Truman recognized that credible military containment required the redeployment of U.S. troops and support capabilities to Europe. This military presence was intended to signal to the Soviets the U.S. commitment to the defense of the Western European democracies. Several hundred thousand U.S. troops could not stop an invasion of Soviet forces by conventional means, but their physical presence committed U.S. nuclear weapons to the defense and safety of Western Europe. Successive U.S. presidents extended this policy of containment by deploying U.S. military and covert capabilities to challenge threats, real or not, of communist expansion in Asia, Latin America, and Africa.

Containment also involved policies that were designed to constrain Soviet economic progress, create economic dislocations within the Eastern bloc economies, and promote economic activity within the Western alliance and friendly nonaligned nations. By means of systematic economic sanctions, containment sought to deny to the Eastern bloc nations gains from trade and exchange with the larger global economy. The long-term objectives of economic containment were to undermine Soviet capabilities in the competition between communism and capitalism, to create economic hardships within the Eastern bloc political economies, and to breed dissatisfaction among the publics of the Eastern bloc nations. This strategy is based on the logic underpinning the use of any form of economic sanctions.

How did economic containment work? First, Western governments limited Eastern bloc access to Western markets, goods, capital, technology, and ideas that could contribute to post-war rebuilding, construction of healthy competitive economies, or the development of military technologies. Limiting such exchange denied the gains from specialization associated with trade, investment, and transfer of technology and production strategies. This constraint imposed inefficiencies on the production structures of the Eastern bloc states and detracted from their economic capacities. The important counterfactual question is this: What would the Eastern bloc economies have looked like without containment? Viewing military and economic containment as security threats from the West, the Eastern bloc governments exacerbated the inefficiencies and distortions in their own production structures by shifting assets toward production of national security goods and away from consumables. The designers of containment hoped that this excessive allocation of Eastern bloc productive capabilities to national security needs would strain the Soviet bloc in terms of unmet consumer demand and breed consumer dissatisfaction, which could grow into political discontent and pressures for reform of communist governments—maybe even a rollback of communism.

The policies of constraint, denial, and sanction extended to the IGOs created at Bretton Woods. These organizations were dominated by the United States and United Kingdom, which exercised their disproportionate voting power to ensure that these organizations would refuse to extend assistance to political economies in the Soviet sphere. Many of the restrictions were relaxed during the period of East-West détente that began in the late 1960s, but many—such as technological export restrictions—remained active until after the breakup of the Eastern bloc and demise of the Soviet Union in 1991.

Excluding the Eastern bloc from the larger global economic exchange also denied the Western nations gains from trade with the Eastern bloc. Western policy makers, however, calculated that the costs to the West would be far smaller than the costs to the East from this loss of trade. Larger arenas of economic exchange, such as that of the Western bloc, tend to produce greater gains from exchange than do smaller arenas, like that of the Eastern bloc; consequently, the denial of gains from trade between the East and West would be proportionally more damaging to the Eastern bloc economies. So even if the economic sanctions imposed under the policy of containment were damaging to Western economic interests, the potential long-term political strategic gains were considered worth the cost.

The Marshall Plan's Strategy to Promote Economic Growth

For Truman, "support[ing] free peoples who are resisting subjugation by armed minorities or by outside pressures" involved not only constraining the threats to free peoples but also promoting their economic, political, and military well-being. Truman therefore asserted that the United States must help to strengthen the political, social, and economic arenas in friendly states that appeared vulnerable to Soviet pressure or to domestic communist movements. If successful, the strategy of promoting growth in political economies tied to the Western markets while limiting economic gains in the Eastern bloc economies would expand the relative disparities between the Western and Eastern blocs and highlight the superiorities of democracy and market exchange. The Soviet threat thus provided the United States with additional leverage to exert leadership over the postwar political economy. U.S. policy makers used U.S. aid to push for more liberal trade within Western Europe, while granting Western European producers greater access to U.S. markets than U.S. producers found in Europe. They hoped that this encouragement would help to strengthen the Western European states, produce a healthy economic bloc, and create a bulwark against Soviet influence. This U.S. policy served as a step toward formation of the European Economic Community.

At the Harvard College commencement ceremony in 1947, General George C. Marshall, Truman's secretary of state, announced the policy initiative known as the Marshall Plan. It was designed to promote postwar reconstruction and to provide a bulwark against the rise of domestic communist movements in the Western European states. The Marshall Plan asked Congress to support a massive infusion of U.S. aid to states trying to rebuild their war-torn economies. Seeking to avoid a liquidity crunch like the one that hindered rebuilding after World War I, Truman sought to use the wealth of the United States to ensure a sufficient supply of capital for rebuilding. The Truman administration argued that such a program would promote U.S. economic health by creating economies that would purchase U.S. goods but would also advance U.S. security interests by creating healthy economies tied to the U.S. economy and undermining the success of communist parties. U.S. policy makers hoped to form a strategic bond of economic cooperation between the United States and recipient nations.

Truman invited governments to submit plans for their economic recovery. The Soviets and states within their sphere of influence were invited to participate, but this gesture was a mere public relations ploy, because these states could not accede to the conditions attached to the promised assistance. Moreover, the Soviet leadership would not permit states in their sphere of influence to participate. The Marshall Plan proved extremely successful, as massive amounts of U.S. aid flowed abroad, creating liquidity for growth and providing materials for revamping production. U.S. manufacturers benefited, as this financial largesse was cycled back to the United States to purchase industrial machinery, farm equipment, and other inputs to economic activity. The Marshall Plan budgeted $16.5 billion for the program, but it cost only about $12.7 billion over a three-year period. From 1947 to 1952, U.S. financial assistance, including Marshall Plan grants and private loans, rose at times to nearly 2 percent of U.S. GNP—an astounding commitment of resources in comparison to the diminutive size of Western foreign aid budgets today.

The Marshall Plan worked as a catalyst for economic recovery. By 1952, Western Europe was surpassing prewar industrial and agricultural production levels, and the benefits of this phenomenal economic revival extended beyond Western Europe. More than two-thirds of European imports during this period came from the United States, which created opportunities for U.S. workers and producers. As U.S. manufacturers and labor profited from the renewed economic vitality in Europe through trade, their support for expanded international trade and greater integration into the global economy increased. This was not a trivial matter, considering U.S. preferences for protectionist policies during the interwar years and the damage done by such policies.

The Marshall Plan complemented military containment by creating healthy and connected market-oriented economies. The greater economic integration wrought by the extension of assistance and the growth of trade provided an economic bulwark against communist expansion, which helped to improve political-military relations and solidify opposition to the Soviet Union. The initial fear of significant electoral success by indigenous communist parties disappeared with the revival of domestic economies in Western European states.

The Truman Doctrine was an important volley in the conflict between competing ideological views and blocs in the global power hierarchy. With both sides seeking to avoid a catastrophic military confrontation, the conflict between the Soviet Union and the United States morphed into a cold war in which one side confronted the clients of the other but the two sides never confronted each other directly. This cold war occasionally threatened to turn hot with potential confrontations in Europe, Korea, Cuba, Vietnam, and the Middle East, but U.S. and Soviet leaders averted any direct shooting confrontations between their own forces. So an uneasy peace continued into the 1960s and 1970s, when tensions thawed and the doors opened to détente and more constructive East-West engagement.

BREAKDOWN IN THE BRETTON WOODS MONETARY ARRANGEMENTS

Policy makers designed the Bretton Woods monetary system as a handmaiden to the expansion of trade and interdependence of markets for goods and services. But this system of monetary arrangements carried the seeds of its own destruction. Problems began almost as soon as the ink had dried on the Articles of Agreement that created the International Monetary Fund and the Bretton Woods monetary system. Many of these problems were manageable in the short run, but eventually cracks appeared in the system that would undermine the foundations of the adjustable-peg arrangement. The Bretton Woods monetary system lasted until August 15, 1971, when President Richard Nixon unilaterally suspended convertibility of the dollar and demanded renegotiation of the dollar's value. During the twenty-five years of the Bretton Woods era, economic trade and growth expanded at a fairly remarkable rate. U.S. growth averaged about 3 percent, the Western Europeans experienced even stronger growth as they recovered from the devastation of war, and Japan rebuilt and became a major industrial power with a compounded growth rate of approximately 12 percent during the 1950s. Most industrialized nations experienced good price performance with low inflation.

Suspension of Convertibility and Imposition of Capital Controls

> **Capital mobility** is the ease or difficulty of moving capital across national borders or of transforming one financial asset into another.

Initially, the Bretton Woods signatories committed to openness to capital flows and convertibility of their currencies into gold or another currency, but these promises fell by the wayside immediately as most governments created barriers to **capital mobility** and suspended convertibility. Policy makers worried that balance-of-payments positions, convertibility, and capital flight could prevent access to the capital needed to stimulate domestic economic activity. They feared that capital mobility could also be destabilizing and limit policy makers' ability to regulate financial markets. Policy makers in war-torn economies faced persistent balance-of-payments deficits, as their enterprises and governments borrowed capital abroad and imported goods and services to rebuild their industrial and agricultural enterprises. Under the gold standard system, deflation and David Hume's specie flow would address this balance-of-payments adjustment problem, but the need to restore employment levels made deflationary policies politically unacceptable. Technically, a change in the adjustable peg would provide an adjustment mechanism, but it would also signal a fundamental disequilibrium or crisis in an economy. Policy makers refrained from taking this course because signaling an economic crisis would likely cause more problems for capital flows than an adjustment in exchange rates could fix.

Indeed, governments suspended convertibility and imposed capital controls (restrictions on who could acquire foreign currencies and when) in order to manage the balance-of-payments problem and limit the outflow of capital. Suspending convertibility protected hard currency reserves and gold reserves in a state's treasury. Capital controls to restrict the outflow, and sometimes the inflow, of capital were permitted under the Bretton Woods arrangements, although the long-term goal was capital mobility. Governments used import licenses and exchange restrictions to help limit capital outflows. These measures helped governments to manage their balance-of-payments positions by limiting the demand for imports and constraining potentially destabilizing currency flows. In 1959, many governments restored current-account convertibility. As conditions improved, some governments relaxed their capital controls and allowed importers to acquire foreign currencies to buy goods abroad without special licenses. As the return to convertibility placed greater strain on the adjustable peg, many policy makers confronted increasing pressures to adjust their states' currencies' pegs. The use of capital controls and limits on convertibility helped governments manage their societies' exposures to the global economy and to manage the tensions between growing interdependence and the national policy autonomy that policy makers needed to address problems and tensions within their selectorates.

The Leading Currency Problem and the Triffin Dilemma

A greater threat appeared at the end of the 1950s and beginning of the 1960s, when currency and gold traders began to question the connection between the dollar and gold.

The dollar acted as the reserve currency for the system, a substitute for gold. Governments and other investors were willing to hold dollars as a reserve asset as long as the dollar was perceived as being as good as gold. The U.S. commitment to convertibility, to exchange dollars for gold or some other currency on demand, underpinned the willingness of others to hold dollars as a reserve asset, but it also exposed the system to two fundamental and eventually unsurpassable challenges to the Bretton Woods system: the leading currency problem and the Triffin dilemma. First, to avoid chronic price instability in the Bretton Woods system, at least one currency had to restrain itself from exchange-rate changes vis-à-vis other currencies. This guardian of stability was the dollar. The United States declared a par value of the dollar—fixed its value in relation to gold. Other countries then declared the par values of their currencies in terms of dollars. As the dollar's role as the leading currency and reserve asset increased under the Bretton Woods system, the system depended more and more on the success of the United States in maintaining the dollar's par value. If any other state declared a fundamental disequilibrium and adjusted its exchange rate, all the prices in that state's tradable sector would be affected, but if the leading currency country were to announce a fundamental disequilibrium and adjust its exchange rate, then prices throughout the entire system would be affected. This situation is known as a **leading currency problem.** Every other economy's preference for a stable and passive leading currency limited the ability and willingness of U.S. policy makers to change the dollar's par value, but it also gave them enormous leverage to escape the constraints faced by policy makers in other governments. Other states had to give the United States latitude in its balance-of-payments and macroeconomic management as they sought to avoid price instability. President Charles de Gaulle of France, however, believed that this situation allowed U.S. policy makers to pursue irresponsible economic policies and shift some of the costs of those polices abroad.

A **leading currency problem** is a dilemma created when the leading currency country, the dominant reserve currency state, encounters a fundamental disequilibrium and contemplates adjusting its exchange rate, which would thereby affect prices throughout the system and potentially unsettle international economic transactions. The **Triffin dilemma**, first articulated by Yale economist Robert Triffin, is a long-term inconsistency between persistent U.S. balance-of-payment deficits in the Bretton Woods system, which created liquidity for the system and led to a growing number of dollars being held outside the United States, and the size of U.S. gold reserves, convertibility, and the value of the dollar.

Second, Robert Triffin, a Yale economist, noted a logical inconsistency in the Bretton Woods dependence on the dollar as the reserve currency. This inconsistency became known as the **Triffin dilemma.** As trade and economic activity expanded, a fixed-rate system would require an increase in usable reserves—an increase in the supply of acceptable money to finance trade and investment. As a reserve asset, however, gold was a very limited quantity, and new supplies were increasing very slowly. At its established price and supply, gold would be insufficient to meet the liquidity needs of the system. This was the same problem that had burdened the gold standard of the pre–World War I era. The Bretton Woods arrangements addressed the shortcoming of gold as a reserve asset by encouraging the use of the dollar as a reserve asset. But this use meant that the only mechanism to pump liquidity into the system—to expand the number of dollars in the system—was that of U.S. balance-of-payments deficits. Initially, these deficits resulted from an imbalance between the capital and current accounts: the United States enjoyed a substantial surplus in its current account but a significant deficit in its capital account. More dollars flowed in than out to pay for goods and services, but even more flowed out than in as investments and loans. Triffin saw a long-term inconsistency between persistent U.S. balance-of-payments deficits, which created liquidity for the system and led to a growing number of dollars being held outside the United States, and the size of U.S. gold reserves that backed convertibility and the value of the dollar.

With the notable exception of Charles de Gaulle, most non-U.S. policy makers ignored the persistent balance-of-payments deficit of the leading currency country. As the banker to the system, lender of last resort, and provider of collective goods, the United States provided an outward flow of dollars that stimulated the economic activity essential to postwar reconstruction and the building of a liberal global political economy. Expanding political economies needed the liquidity provided by U.S. balance-of-payments deficits. Foreign governments and banks rebuilt their economic foundations with dollars. By adding dollars to their reserves, other states were able to restore convertibility by the late 1950s. The vitality of the U.S. economy masked the threat posed by the Triffin dilemma for many years. As long as they perceived the U.S. economy as fundamentally healthy and dominant, and the dollar therefore as good as gold, other governments could ignore the deficits. This perception underpinned the willingness to hold dollars as a reserve asset rather than convert them into gold. But if the number of dollars held abroad continued to increase, the total would eventually exceed the U.S. official gold reserves. Such a situation could provoke questions about whether the dollar was, in fact, as good as gold, and could threaten confidence in convertibility.

By 1960, the amount of dollars held overseas did exceed U.S. official gold reserves. This dollar overhang (dollar holdings outside the United States) began to raise questions about whether the dollar was as good as gold. The growing imbalance between U.S. gold reserves and dollars held abroad placed increasing pressure on the decision to convert dollars to gold at the U.S. Gold Window (a metaphor for the exchange process at the U.S. Treasury). No one wanted to undermine confidence in the dollar, but neither did anyone want to show up at the U.S. Gold Window with dollars after U.S. gold reserves had been exhausted. This dynamic created the potential for a rush to exchange dollars for gold—an unsustainable dilemma that injected new risk into the system. If governments were to start exchanging dollars for gold, the United States would have to either suspend convertibility or change the par value of the dollar. This destabilizing outcome was the ultimate threat posed by the Triffin dilemma.

Growing Pressures on the Dollar-Gold Relationship Threaten the Bretton Woods Monetary System

Other changes at the end of the 1950s and during the 1960s eroded confidence in the health of the U.S. economy, raised questions about the relationship of the dollar to gold, and threatened the Bretton Woods monetary system. In the late 1950s, the U.S. economy went through a temporary but sharp recession. The Federal Reserve lowered U.S. interest rates to promote growth, but this reduced the incentives to hold dollars or dollar-denominated financial instruments and increased the incentives to convert dollars into gold or other currencies in order to pursue higher rates of return. As a consequence, the United States lost about 10 percent of its official gold reserves in 1958. Then, as the recession eased, interest rates rose and the incentives to exchange dollars for gold or other currencies diminished, but the loss of gold reserves and the run on the dollar had impressed traders in financial markets. They began to worry about the connection between dollars and gold. Was the dollar as good as gold? Could the United States sustain its commitment to convertibility and maintain the dollar's par value despite the increasing imbalance between official gold reserves and dollars in the system?

The United States continued to lose gold reserves over the next several years, but at a slower rate than in 1958. However, in October 1960, just before the tightly contested presidential election between Kennedy and Nixon, a shock hit the gold markets. The price of gold in private markets shot up to $40/ounce, although its official par value remained at $35/ounce. Such a disparity between the public and private values of gold had never happened before under the Bretton Woods system. It reflected growing uncertainty over the relationship between the dollar and gold, and uncertainty about the policies a Democratic president might adopt in regard to the exchange rate and convertibility. Perhaps the dollar was overvalued at $35/ounce of gold. Was there a fundamental disequilibrium? If so, an overvalued dollar made U.S. commodities in the tradable sector relatively expensive vis-à-vis foreign commodities and acted as a drag on U.S. growth. A Democratic president would be more likely to represent economic interests that favored growth over price stability (e.g., labor), whereas a Republican president would be more likely to represent economic interests that favored price stability over growth (e.g., bankers and owners of financial assets). In his campaign, in fact, Kennedy had advocated more aggressive growth policies.

If this disparity were to persist, it could lead to a run on official reserves, for it constituted an arbitrage opportunity with an extremely attractive rate of return if financial traders could buy gold for $35/ounce from governments committed to convertibility and then sell it for $40/ounce in the private markets. Realizing that concerns about the relationship between the dollar and gold could affect his electoral prospects, Kennedy reacted immediately, stating his unwavering support for the current par value of the dollar. Gold returned to $35/ounce in private markets and the market perturbation ended, but the seeds of doubt sown in 1958 had been reinforced. Financial traders began looking more closely at the U.S. economy for signs of vulnerability that could foreshadow a looming crisis of the Triffin dilemma. They did not have to look for long.

U.S. Financial Constraints and International Reactions Challenge U.S. Leadership

For the first time since World War II, the United States began to experience the external financial constraints that other nations had faced all along. President Kennedy entered office promising to end a recession and expand the economy. His administration had a variety of monetary and fiscal tools available to stimulate the economy, but the exchange-rate problem constrained his choices. Governments use monetary policies to affect the supply and cost of capital as they attempt to prod or restrain their economies. Kennedy's government could increase money supply or lower interest rates to stimulate investment and economic activity, but the Federal Reserve had already eased interest rates at the end the Eisenhower presidency. Lowering the rates further or increasing the supply of dollars could raise questions about U.S. commitment to the dollar's value and produce destabilizing speculative market pressures on the dollar. Alternatively, the Kennedy administration could reinforce the U.S. commitment to the dollar's value by pushing more restrictive monetary policies, but this would risk another recession, violate the president's campaign promises to expand the economy, and threaten his reelection prospects. Kennedy turned to fiscal policy. He reduced taxes in an effort to stimulate investment and also increased government expenditures for defense and domestic programs. Tax cuts plus rising expenditures ran the risk of enlarging public deficits and debt if the economy did not grow fast enough to offset the change in tax rates. Kennedy might have avoided this gamble by using monetary policy to stimulate the economy, if not for the constraint of the exchange-rate mechanism.

Perversely, the success of U.S. postwar efforts also raised questions about U.S. policies and leadership. U.S. postwar leadership had proven remarkably successful in rebuilding a liberal global economy. The revitalization of Japanese and European political economies was a good outcome, but the growing economic strength of these trading partners made them more assertive in international economic discussions. Some observers pointed to the growing assertiveness of others in international forums as evidence of U.S. hegemonic decline, which could undermine the willingness and ability of the United States to provide collective goods to maintain the postwar arrangements. In the early 1960s, new international cooperation and institution building indicated potential instability in the Bretton Woods system.

In 1962, ten states (Belgium, Canada, France, Germany, Italy, Japan, the Netherlands, Sweden, the United Kingdom, and the United States) agreed to provide additional credit lines to the IMF in case its resources were insufficient to support one of the system's key currencies. This arrangement, the General Agreements to Borrow, meant that substantial funds ($6 billion) would be made available to defend against speculative attacks on key currencies. Although small for an emergency bailout or backstop fund by today's standards, it was a significant line of credit given financial crises to that date in the postwar system. Hidden between the lines, the arrangement's veiled intent was to ensure that the IMF and the United States had the resources to defend the dollar without forcing U.S. policy makers to sell U.S. gold reserves. Because a loss of U.S. gold reserves might signal weakness to markets, which could encourage speculation and undermine confidence in the dollar, the signatories agreed to intervene in gold markets to ensure stability in the monetary system by maintaining gold's price at close to $35/ounce. These ten states became known as the Group of 10 (G-10). Switzerland later became a member of this elite club, which would meet regularly to coordinate actions in defense of stable international monetary and financial relations. The formation of the G-10 led to the creation of other intergovernmental groups (G-7, G-5, and so on) to promote cooperation and manage threats to global economic relations. But the advent of all these new groups raised a question: If the Bretton Woods system was not at risk, why construct new international scaffolding to defend it?

Despite the willingness of other governments to engage in such concerted market interventions to protect the dollar's value, growing capital-account deficits continued to worry U.S. officials. The growth of multinational corporations (MNCs), predominantly based in the United States, was increasing the dollar overhang outside the United States, as U.S. MNCs borrowed in U.S. capital markets to fund their overseas activities. Hoping to escape the Triffin dilemma and threats to dollar convertibility, the Kennedy and Johnson administrations searched for strategies to restrict dollar outflows. They could have used monetary policies to raise the rate of return on dollar-denominated financial instruments in hopes of attracting foreign capital to the United States and reducing, or maybe even reversing, the net outflow of dollars, but such policies would, at the same time, increase the costs of borrowing in U.S. capital markets. This effect could have decreased the outflow of dollars if borrowers moved to overseas markets to borrow capital, but use of these policies was politically difficult because they would increase the costs of capital for all borrowers, whether for domestic or overseas use, and likely damage an economy that was recovering from a recession. Pushing for monetary policies that slowed U.S. economic activity would also have violated Kennedy's campaign promise to revitalize the economy—potential political suicide.

Policy makers in the Kennedy and Johnson administrations looked elsewhere to slow the outflow of dollars. They recognized that the relative efficiency of U.S. capital markets, which were far more flexible and attractive than overseas markets, contributed to dollar outflows. Because of the efficiency and flexibility of U.S. capital markets, U.S. MNCs and other states' firms and governments preferred to finance their non-U.S. operations by borrowing in the New York capital markets. Capital was more available and cheaper in New York than in overseas markets, all else being equal. Policy makers therefore pondered how to reduce the attractiveness of U.S. capital markets, making them more costly and less efficient sources of capital for overseas activities without raising interest rates, which could slow the U.S. economy. They could enact capital controls, but this would signal a sharp philosophical break with postwar U.S. preferences for liberal trade and capital movement. It would amount to a fundamental change in the rules of the game by the system leader. Such a dramatic reversal of course by the system leader would likely create more, rather than less, of a crisis. A less disruptive alternative would be to tax capital borrowed for overseas use, which U.S. Treasury experts thought might produce the same effects on capital outflows as capital controls or higher interest rates, but without the unsettling stigma of capital controls or the risk of slowing economic activity within the United States. Such a tax would be a policy substitute for a capital control.

In this vein, the Kennedy administration adopted the Interest Equalization Tax (IET) of 1963, which was expanded two years later. The IET lasted until 1974, when it was repealed by the Nixon administration. The IET placed a tax on capital borrowed in U.S. bond markets that was to be used abroad. It was intended to push borrowers away from U.S. markets by artificially raising the cost of capital and constraining the efficiency of U.S. markets—to make borrowers indifferent between borrowing their capital in the United States or abroad. When the IET failed to stem dollar outflows, in 1965 the Johnson administration adopted the Voluntary Foreign Credit Restraint Act (VFCR) in another attempt to limit outflows. The VFCR established voluntary quotas on U.S. bank lending to U.S. MNCs for their foreign direct investments. The quotas became mandatory in 1968.

The **euro markets** are markets trading financial instruments that are denominated in a nation's currency outside the boundaries of that nation.

In response to the IET and the VFCR, U.S. MNCs and others did shift some borrowing overseas. This shift encouraged the development of markets in dollar deposits and dollar securities abroad. This was a significant development in the global financial infrastructure. Despite the fact that they are not specific to Europe or the euro currency, these new venues are called **euro markets.** Euro markets trade financial instruments denominated in currencies beyond the national boundaries of those currencies. Nevertheless, the IET and the VFCR failed to reduce dollar outflows enough to reverse the brewing threat to the Bretton Woods arrangements.

About the same time as the United States adopted the IET and the VFCR, French president Charles de Gaulle recognized the vulnerable linkage between the dollar and gold and began a campaign to unsettle the dollar's role as the dominant reserve asset in the system. De Gaulle believed that the dollar's position in the system afforded the United States enormous privilege in global affairs; allowed U.S. policy makers to escape the discipline faced by other states, as the liquidity needs of the system benefited from persistent U.S. balance-of-payments deficits; and permitted U.S. policy makers to export the effects of their policies rather than implementing politically difficult policy changes at home. His position had merit, but his solution was problematic. He called for a return to the gold standard, which would create a slew of other problems. De Gaulle's call for return to the gold standard likely was not sincere; rather, it was probably a strategic ploy to call attention to the increasingly vulnerable link between the dollar and gold. The French pressured U.S. policy makers by slowly exchanging dollars for gold, which drew attention to the imbalance between dollars in the system and U.S. official gold reserves.

Pressures on the dollar-gold relationship grew. In 1968, the G-10 nations decided to stop transferring public gold into the private gold market—refusing to sell official gold reserves to private citizens. This decision removed the possibility for arbitrage and amounted to a confession by governments that they could no longer be confident of maintaining a market price of $35/ounce. It essentially shifted the terms of convertibility. The rate for official exchanges between nations remained $35/ounce, but the value of gold in private markets was now divorced from its public price. Going forward, two different prices for gold—a private price and a public price—became the norm. Discrepancies between public and private prices suggested what traders in private gold markets believed was the real value of the dollar. They signaled that they believed the dollar was significantly overvalued.

Meanwhile, the Vietnam War had become a political, military, and economic quagmire for U.S. policy makers. Aside from the tensions that the war imposed on U.S. political relationships with allies who disagreed with U.S. involvement in Vietnam, many governments believed that U.S. economic policies related to the war were exporting inflation into the global system. U.S. defense expenditures exploded during the Vietnam War, but U.S. policy makers, worried about public dissent, refrained from raising taxes to pay for them. Instead, they financed the war through public borrowing and increases in the money supply. During the same period, the Federal Reserve resisted raising interest rates. Together, these U.S. policies led to inflationary growth, and, because the United States was the largest and most influential member in an increasingly global political economy, its economic policies spilled over into other economies. Other nations' policy makers, thinking that the United States was exporting its inflation through the outflow of dollars and unsettling price stability in other nations, expressed increased interest in system reform.

Suspension of Dollar-Gold Convertibility

In the late 1960s, with confidence waning in the dollar-gold relationship, doubts growing about the ability of the United States to maintain convertibility at $35/ounce, and questions being raised regarding the soundness of the U.S. economy, the United States reported its first balance-of-trade deficit since World War II. U.S. balance-of-payments deficits since the war had been related to the capital account, not the current account, for the United States had enjoyed a trade surplus over that same time. With the United States running both a capital-account deficit and a current-account deficit, confidence in the U.S. economy was threatened, as was the belief that the dollar was as good as gold. Countries cannot run balance-of-payments deficits without the pendulum swinging back toward surpluses, except in cases of a fundamental disequilibrium that signals structural problems in an economy. The United States had run such deficits for most of the time since World War II in spite of the logic of the economic mechanism. This was because of its special position as the leading currency country, the dollar's role as the primary reserve asset, and the need for dollars to provide liquidity to fund reconstruction and postwar expansion. As provider of system liquidity and lender of last resort, the United States was encouraged to increase its money supply and run balance-of-payments deficits. U.S. policy makers thus could adopt policies that in other states would signal poor economic management and a fundamental disequilibrium.

Other states' policy makers and the IMF willingly looked the other way because the system needed dollar outflows and they believed in the fundamental health of the U.S. economy. Dollar outflows had provided the liquidity necessary to support growth. Policy makers took the continued success of U.S. producers in the global economy, the U.S. balance-of-trade surplus, as a signal of U.S. economic vibrancy and health. Even though the current and capital accounts did not balance, they both pointed in the right direction to undercut fears about balance-of-payments adjustment pressures on the United States. But beginning in the late 1960s, the U.S. current-account deficit raised fears about pressures on U.S. leaders to address a fundamental disequilibrium, either by affecting the dollar exchange rate or adopting some other policies such as protectionism. This possibility threatened to throw the system into disarray and increased the pressures to convert dollars into gold before U.S. policy makers changed the rules. Like a snowball rolling down a hill, the system was building momentum for change.

The balance-of-trade deficit signaled a brewing domestic dilemma for U.S. policy makers. Current-account deficits suggested that a fundamental imbalance in the dollar's value was penalizing U.S. producers and labor in the tradable sector. With postwar rebuilding and economic expansion, foreign producers had grown increasingly competitive vis-à-vis U.S. producers. Their gains were assisted by an overvalued dollar. This situation was less problematic when the U.S. producers dominated trade by wide margins, since a buffer existed to cushion the blows of creative destruction. But the trade deficit signaled the end of this buffer and rising problems for U.S. politicians as the effects of the overvalued dollar were felt in U.S. labor markets.

As the leading currency country, the United States wanted to avoid changing the value of the dollar in order to preserve price stability in the system. Devaluation would generate a large shock that could undermine confidence in the dollar and in U.S. leadership. U.S. politicians faced quite a dilemma. They could maintain the dollar's value and face discontent among U.S. labor and producers that could lead to protectionist pressures and electoral losses, or they could devalue the dollar to redress a fundamental disequilibrium and assist the competitiveness of U.S. producers and labor. The latter would improve their electoral chances at home, but potentially create a systemic economic crisis.

The trap was inescapable. By 1971, U.S. policy makers could no longer resist the dynamics and continue to defend the Bretton Woods monetary system. The dollar was fundamentally overvalued by at least 10 percent. Worried that Congress might adopt trade policies that would undermine the embedded liberalism of the global political economy, President Nixon unilaterally changed the system on August 15, 1971. He suspended convertibility and demanded renegotiation of the value of the dollar. Convertibility would be restored only under a reformed monetary system and a realignment of exchange rates that would address the fundamental disequilibrium and make U.S. companies more competitive. Rather than devalue the dollar, Nixon sought to have the major trading partners of the United States revalue their currencies. The economic effects of such a move would be similar for the United States, but the political consequences would differ because the responsibility for the system dysfunction would fall more heavily on others. Obviously, policy makers in other states preferred devaluation of the dollar to revaluation of their currencies. The negotiations were extremely contentious and threatened to disrupt international cooperation, but thirty years of postwar cooperation had built a robust foundation. The discussions culminated in the Smithsonian Agreement in December 1971. This agreement retained the adjustable-peg system, but with several key changes. The dollar was devalued, and bands of the peg were expanded to 2.25 percent from par value. When he signed the new agreement, an exuberant President Nixon declared the Smithsonian Agreement the greatest monetary agreement of all time. Yet it would last less than two years! Many pundits and analysts interpreted the demise of the Bretton Woods monetary system, and its successor the Smithsonian Agreement, as an indication of U.S. hegemonic decline, but the United States unilaterally changed some of the most important rules of the game that guided postwar expansion of liberal market exchange across borders and globalization. Moreover, U.S. policy makers were pivotal to guiding the construction of new rules of the game in the exchange-rate system and the evolution of the IMF.

CONCLUSION

The planners at Bretton Woods laid the foundation for a liberal global political economy. Having learned from the missteps of the interwar years, they constructed a framework of national agreements, domestic governance mechanisms and safety nets, and international governmental organizations that sheltered politicians from domestic political pressures to shift the costs of economic dislocations abroad. They had learned a great deal about how to use fiscal and monetary policies to promote stable growth and avoid destabilizing swings in their economies. Not trusting the ability of policy makers to resist unilaterally the beggar-thy-neighbor pressures from their domestic constituencies, the Bretton Woods designers also devised IGOs in the form of the World Bank, the GATT, and the IMF to limit the policy mobility of national policy makers and to provide resources and pathways for safeguarding and reinforcing liberal economic exchange in a self-help nation-state system. The United States acted as the hegemonic leader, the system stabilizer, by providing key collective goods and bankrolling the system at a time when other governments found themselves devastated and impoverished by war. These all helped to build a liberal global political economy, which strengthened in the years following the war. This growing economy combined with political-military policies to form a bulwark against the communist political economies of the Soviet sphere. Despite the eventual, and inevitable, breakdown in the Bretton Woods monetary system, the efforts of the planners succeeded well beyond anything they could have imagined when they first met in the mountains of New Hampshire.

KEY CONCEPTS

capital mobility (p. 452)

conditionality (p. 438)

countercyclical fiscal policy (p. 423)

countervailing duties (CVDs) (p. 432)

dead-weight loss (p. 426)

debt forgiveness (p. 446)

dumping (p. 431)

escape clause (p. 432)

euro markets (p. 458)

financing gap (p. 445)

fiscal policy (p. 423)

free trade areas (p. 432)

fundamental disequilibrium (p. 436)

leading currency problem (p. 453)

Marshall Plan (p. 441)

monetary policy (p. 422)

nondiscriminatory trading arrangements and institutions (p. 426)

par value (p. 439)

regional trading agreements (p. 432)

subsidies (p. 431)

tariffs (p. 426)

Triffin dilemma (p. 453)

Truman Doctrine (p. 448)

Washington Consensus (p. 446)

EXERCISES

1. What critical lessons did policy makers learn from the interwar years that they needed to confront as they discussed arrangements for the post–World War II global political economy?

2. Why did the failures of the interwar years require both domestic and international policy reforms?

3. How did delegating some authority to the executive branch in the Reciprocal Trade Agreements Act (1934) affect U.S. trade policy and why?

4. Name three nontariff barriers. How do they work to influence the pattern of trade?

5. How does Keynesian economic policy differ from monetarism?

6. What is a fundamental disequilibrium? What does it signal?

7. How did the dollar's role as leading currency and reserve asset hinder/help the United States?

8. Explain the logic behind the policy of economic and military containment. How did the Marshall Plan contribute to containment? What did U.S. policy makers hope to accomplish with containment and the Marshall Plan?

9. Explain the dynamic underpinning the Triffin dilemma.

10. Explain why President Nixon suspended convertibility in 1971.

FURTHER READING

Bates, Robert H. 2008. *When Things Fell Apart: State Failure in Late-Century Africa.* Cambridge: Cambridge University Press.

———. 2009. *Prosperity and Violence: The Political Economy of Development.* 2nd ed. New York: W. W. Norton.

Bhagwati, Jagdish. 1988. *Protectionism.* Cambridge: MIT Press.

Collier, Paul. 2007. *The Bottom Billion: Why the Poorest Countries Are Failing and What Can Be Done about It.* New York: Oxford University Press.

Easterly, William. 2002. *The Elusive Quest for Growth: Economists' Adventures and Misadventures in the Tropics.* Cambridge: MIT Press.

Eichengreen, Barry. 1996. *Globalizing Capital: A History of the International Monetary System.* Princeton, NJ: Princeton University Press.

———. 2011. *Exorbitant Privilege: The Rise and Fall of the Dollar and the Future of the International Monetary System.* New York: Oxford University Press.

Gardner, Richard N. 1980. *Sterling-Dollar Diplomacy in Current Perspective: The Origins and Prospects of Our International Economic Order.* New York: Columbia University Press.

Kennan, George F. 1985. *American Diplomacy.* Chicago: University of Chicago Press.

Keylor, William R. 2006. *The Twentieth-Century World and Beyond: An International History since 1900.* 5th ed. New York: Oxford University Press.

Keynes, John Maynard. 1924. *A Tract on Monetary Reform.* London: Macmillan.

Ruggie, John Gerard. 1982. "International Regimes, Transactions, and Change: Embedded Liberalism in the Postwar Economic Order." *International Organization* 36, no. 2: 379–415.

Triffin, Robert. 1960. *Gold and the Dollar Crisis: The Future of Convertibility.* New Haven, CT: Yale University Press.

The World Post–Bretton Woods: Globalization Advances

Of all the changes of the world economy of recent decades, few have been nearly so dramatic as the resurrection of global finance. A half century ago, after the ravages of the Great Depression and World War II, financial markets everywhere—with the notable exception of the United States—were generally weak, insular, and strictly controlled, reduced from their previously central role in international economic relations to offer little more than a negligible amount of trade financing. Starting in the late 1950s, however, private lending and investment once again began to gather momentum, generating a phenomenal growth of cross-border capital flows and an increasingly close integration of domestic financial markets.

—*Benjamin J. Cohen, The Geography of Money, 1998*

The end of the Bretton Woods system and its successor, the Smithsonian Agreement, marked a fundamental shift in global political economic relations, especially in global financial relations. The Bretton Woods and Smithsonian international monetary systems had been built around a narrow-peg exchange-rate mechanism with the objectives of limiting exchange-rate risk that could damage international trade and constraining competitive manipulations of currency rates that could damage international cooperation and globalization. The end of these systems generated apprehension as policy makers remembered the exchange-rate free-for-all of the interwar years that proved so destructive to international cooperation, globalization, and social welfare. The presence of U.S. hegemonic leadership and the international and domestic scaffolding (see chapter 11) constructed to support and encourage mutually beneficial liberal exchange and cooperation proved up to the task of managing the new and uncertain environment. Embedded liberalism worked, and as the new arrangements took hold, globalization advanced with the dramatic restructuring and liberalization of national exchange mechanisms and financial arenas. The linkages across national political economies became denser, more frequent, and more complex. The years following 1973 brought increasing rejection of narrow-peg exchange-rate mechanisms, the adoption of floating-rate mechanisms with potential for much greater exchange-rate volatility, attempts at resurrecting collective-currency pegs through cooperative action such as the European Monetary System and the European Monetary Union, a shift in the role of monetary policy in national arenas, a rebalancing of the role of state and market mechanisms, increasing global capital mobility, and greater financial liberalization. Altogether, these shifts marked a distinctive transformation in global financial relations—a reawakening of financial globalization that would lead to greater integration of national political economies into a larger global political economy, thereby challenging the policy autonomy of governments.

FUNDAMENTAL SHIFTS IN GLOBAL FINANCE

Under Bretton Woods and the Smithsonian Agreement, policy makers used monetary policy—the manipulation of money supply—extensively to maintain the stability of a currency's value as well as to manage growth and inflation. With the end of the Smithsonian, the adoption of floating exchange rates by many states represented a dramatic shift in international monetary arrangements and in the use of monetary policy. Monetary policy became liberated from the stability of the exchange rate and freer to address domestic economic pressures.

Keynesian beliefs had colored postwar planning at Bretton Woods, rebalancing the role of markets and governments in managing international economic relations. The demise of Bretton Woods brought a shift away from Keynesian strategies, which included heavy reliance on fiscal and monetary policies, domestic social protections, controls on capital movements, and collective international management. Instead policy makers placed greater emphasis on the role of markets in rewarding or penalizing economic activity. This shift toward market forces and away from state allocation mechanisms, which is known as **neoliberalism,** led to greater capital mobility across borders, increased the global integration of national economies, and constituted a potential sea change in state-society relations.

> **Neoliberalism** is a shift away from Keynesian strategies such as fiscal policies, domestic social protections, controls on capital movements, and collective international management and toward greater emphasis on the role of markets in conditioning, rewarding, or penalizing economic activity.

Changes in the activities of the International Monetary Fund and other IGOs and governmental bodies would reinforce this neoliberal shift. The IMF had managed the Bretton Woods monetary system, coordinated defense of its narrow-peg system, alleviated short-term balance-of-payments pressures, and provided a systematic procedure for addressing fundamental balance-of-payments disequilibrium related to the exchange-rate mechanism. After losing its raison d'être with the demise of the Bretton Woods system, the organization re-created itself by building on the skills of its staff economists to become a source of expertise for managing national economies. IMF prescriptions and assistance increasingly constrained government intervention in national economies, promoted market reforms, and advocated market discipline to temper economic forces. The IMF inserted

The **Washington Consensus** is a policy agenda that places emphasis on the corrective pressures of market discipline and seeks to reduce government regulation and intervention in the economy by promoting economic openness in trade and capital movements, liberalization of financial markets, fiscal policies that lead to balanced budgets, anti-inflationary monetary policies, stability in exchange-rate relations, expansion of private enterprise, and reduction in state-owned enterprises; the name of this system reflects the prominence of Washington, D.C., and the organizations located there, in international economic affairs.

itself into state policy arenas by attaching policy prescriptions and conditions to its financial assistance, most often at times of economic crisis, when governments had little ability to refuse its assistance and directives. This shift reached beyond the IMF to involve the participation of other important organizations, such as the World Bank and departments of the U.S. government. Together, they formulated what has become known as the **Washington Consensus,** a policy framework that relies on the notion of self-correcting markets to discipline governments and economic enterprises. We return to the Washington Consensus later in this chapter.

POST–BRETTON WOODS MONETARY ARRANGEMENTS

Even though the Bretton Woods system ended in 1971, its basic framework persisted through the Smithsonian Agreement until its failure in February 1973. The two pacts' influence continued to linger in global monetary affairs until 1978, when the Second Amendment to the IMF Articles of Agreement (the IMF's charter) eliminated the role of gold as a reserve asset and legitimated the floating-exchange-rate mechanisms that some states had adopted. A patchwork of monetary arrangements emerged post–Bretton Woods and Smithsonian that included the following features:

- Floating rates
- Collective-currency pegs, such as the European Monetary System
- Monetary unions, such as the European Monetary Union
- Loose, adjustable pegs of a state's currency to the currency of its major trading partner
- Currency control boards that tightly pegged a state's currency to the currency of its major trading partner

These arrangements run the gamut from a float, whereby supply and demand in currency markets determine a currency's value, to a tight peg, whereby a government commits to its currency's value and defends that value through intervention in currency markets, managing its money supply, international cooperation, and the use of other policy instruments.

Both Bretton Woods and the Smithsonian pegged exchange rates either to gold or to another reserve asset, such as the dollar. Both systems aimed to constrain changes in the prices of currencies tightly in order to limit uncertainty and instability in the exchange-rate mechanism, which could hinder international exchange. The designers of these systems hoped to protect politicians from constituent demands for beggar-thy-neighbor policies such as using their exchange rates to force the costs of adjustment to trade and growth abroad, onto other nations' producers and labor.

Unlike the inflexibility of the gold standard, the Bretton Woods and Smithsonian arrangements offered a means by which state policy makers could adjust their exchange rates. Policy makers could ask the IMF to adjust the par value of their currency if their state faced persistent trade deficits that constituted a fundamental balance-of-payments disequilibrium, reflecting structural problems in the nation's economy or a seriously misaligned exchange rate. Such adjustments could be politically expensive, for they required a state's politicians to notify or appeal to the IMF for approval. This action suggested a surrender of sovereignty and potentially involved admitting partial mismanagement of their domestic economy. Such adjustments in the par value of a currency did occur during the postwar period, but they were relatively limited given the potential appeal for politicians to manipulate a nation's exchange rate to improve the nation's competitiveness in the tradable sector of the economy.

The imposition of capital controls by many governments at the beginning of the Bretton Woods system provided their policy makers with leeway in responding to serious balance-of-payments pressures that signaled fundamental misalignment of their currencies. The perception that a currency was seriously misaligned (overvalued or undervalued)—and therefore likely to prompt the sponsoring government to seek an adjustment in its par value—could lead to massive outflows or inflows of capital, absent capital controls. Such capital flows could force rapid and destabilizing shifts in the value of a currency. Limits on the ability of capital to exit allowed policy makers to resist adjusting their currency's par value and consequently supported the narrow-peg system. Even if they proved unsuccessful at addressing the balance-of-payments pressures and maintaining a currency's par value, capital controls afforded policy makers the opportunity to seek a stable adjustment in the currency's par value. In practice, governments sought readjustment only when their currencies were overvalued and damaging to workers and producers in their states' tradable sectors.

The gradual liberalization of capital controls and the reawakening of global financial markets beginning in the 1960s led to increases in international capital mobility. And with greater capital mobility, many policy makers found themselves under greater and greater pressure to adjust their currencies because of changes in their balance-of-payments positions. It became increasingly difficult for them to maintain their commitment to the narrow pegs of the Bretton Woods and Smithsonian monetary systems. They defended parity within the bands of the system, but this arrangement did not remove balance-of-payments pressures that signaled a fundamental misalignment in the currency. Such pressures continued to build.

As capital controls were relaxed, policy makers realized that the mere suggestion that a state was going to adjust its currency's par value could lead to outflows of capital and potential crisis. The situation was increasingly troubling for policy makers across many states, and by 1973 the system was in crisis. President Nixon's "greatest monetary agreement of all time" tottered and began to collapse. As some currencies moved beyond the 2.25 percent bands established by the Smithsonian system, that system became too costly, economically and politically, for the United States. An overvalued dollar helped European and Japanese exporters, as their nations ran surpluses in their trade accounts with the United States, but American producers and labor in the tradable sector suffered. The United States experienced persistent balance-of-payments pressures and repeated attacks on the dollar. These attacks required U.S. and other states' monetary authorities to intervene to support the dollar's par value actively.

Seeking a Stable System of Exchange Rates amid a Variety of Exchange-Rate Mechanisms

U.S. policy makers were inclined to let the dollar float. As the dominant currency in international transactions, a floating dollar would put tremendous corrective pressures on the currencies of states running surpluses. Because they benefited from the dollar's plight, and the stability and certainty of a narrow-peg system, the Europeans and Japanese preferred a system of adjustable-peg rates, intended to maintain the par values of an adjustable peg. This arrangement would place the burden on the United States to adjust. Negotiations intended to address the frailties of the system attempted to save the adjustable peg, but they failed to produce a resolution. Finally, finance ministers from the United States, the United Kingdom, France, Germany, and Japan—known as the Group of 5 (G-5) and also as the Interim Committee—became the locus of negotiations.

In the G-5 deliberations, the Europeans and Japanese continued to push for an adjustable peg, but U.S. policy makers resisted. As holder of the key reserve currency, the United States held the position central to the final outcome. Instead of adopting a system of pegged but adjustable rates, as preferred by the Europeans and the Japanese, the G-5 advocated a stable system of exchange rates. Let's consider the difference: instead of stable rates (pegged rates), the G-5 proposed a stable system based on expectations that members would support stable exchange-rate policies by implementing sound macroeconomic and monetary policies. It did not advocate a specific exchange rate for each currency, but a stable system of exchange rates. Conceivably, a variety of different exchange-rate mechanisms could coexist, as long as governments worked to maintain a relatively stable relationship among those different mechanisms and to limit shocks that could transmit instability across the system.

The G-5 proposal led to the Second Amendment to the IMF Articles of Agreement in 1978, which formally legalized floating exchange rates and eliminated the role of gold as a reserve asset. Under the new system, governments were responsible for managing their domestic economies so as to reduce economic and exchange-rate instability. The IMF thus gained a responsibility to oversee economic activities by its members that could affect the stability of the exchange-rate system.

The new system brought a variety of exchange-rate arrangements. The United States and some other states moved to a float, whereby currency prices were determined primarily by supply and demand in currency markets, with relatively limited intervention by the currency's home government's monetary authorities to manipulate currency values explicitly. Instead, monetary policy authorities focused primarily on growth and inflation, which would nevertheless affect currency values. Those governments were more flexible, more willing to allow market forces to determine the values of their currencies, and less willing to intervene in currency markets. Both the persistent U.S. current-account deficit, which had provided the liquidity essential to rebuilding and economic expansion since World War II, and the inflationary policies adopted by the United States during the Vietnam conflict created a vast supply of dollars in the international system and downward pressures on the dollar's value. After the adoption of a float, the dollar depreciated dramatically against many currencies, while the deutschmark, the yen, and the pound sterling appreciated quickly. Many feared that a floating-rate system would generate wild and recurring swings in the value of currencies, which would create currency risk damaging to international exchange. Others predicted that market forces would quickly push rates to their equilibrium levels, with little volatility after the initial change in values. Neither prediction was accurate. Floating exchange rates proved more volatile than the pegged systems, but usually the volatility did not approach the instability feared by supporters of an adjustable peg, although occasional crises were to occur. After the initial exchange-rate perturbations, any further extreme shifts in currency values tended to reflect the effect of currency markets disciplining governments for mismanagement of their economies.

Floating exchange rates did not mean that all governments refrained from intervening to manage the price of their currencies. Many actively intervened in currency markets to adjust the supply of their currencies. They used monetary and fiscal policies to affect a currency's price. They became buyers and sellers of currencies, affecting price through supply and demand. Some used capital controls to limit capital inflows or outflows, changed reserve and deposit requirements for foreigners in their banking systems, placed limitations on foreign purchases of domestic securities, and engaged in international cooperation to influence currency prices.

The decline in the value of the dollar reversed by the late 1970s, as U.S. monetary policies and inflows of foreign capital to the United States strengthened the dollar and increased demand for dollar-denominated financial instruments. In 1979, Paul Volcker, newly appointed as chairman of the Federal Reserve Board by President Carter, moved to throttle the inflation in the United States that was feeding stagnation in the global economy. He used Federal Reserve policies to raise interest rates and increased reserve requirements for banks. These policies reduced money supply, which pushed up the value of the dollar. As gaps between foreign and U.S. interest rates grew, foreign capital discovered that U.S. interest rates provided a greater rate of return on their financial investments. Demand for dollar-denominated assets increased, the demand for dollars increased, and the value of the dollar appreciated.

President Reagan's policies during the 1980s reinforced the inflow of foreign capital into the United States and the appreciation of the dollar. When the Reagan administration cut taxes even as it was undertaking a dramatic expansion in national security outlays, government revenues fell further behind government outlays. To pay for this expanding public deficit, the U.S. government sold government bonds—debt obligations. As its deficit increased, the government had to sell more and more bonds and offer more and more attractive rates of return to draw in investors. This policy pushed interest rates (the rate of return) on U.S. government bonds up, which made U.S. government debt even more attractive to investors. U.S. government debt was regarded as relatively risk-free, and it offered rates of return better than many investment opportunities in the global market that carried substantially greater risk. As these financial instruments were denominated in dollars, investors needed dollars to buy them, so the demand for dollars increased and the value of the dollar appreciated further. Adding even more fuel to the upward pressures on the value of the dollar was the fact that private industries had to increase the rates of return on their debt offerings in the United States in order to compete with the U.S. government for capital. Interest rates rose in both U.S. public and private debt markets.

The dollar's rise continued until 1985, as the Reagan administration refrained from manipulating the exchange rate. The Europeans and Japanese were slow to push the United States to manage the dollar's value because their tradable sectors benefited from the dollar's appreciation. But by the mid-1980s, U.S. producers and labor were pressuring Congress for relief, demanding the adoption of protectionist trade measures. The rise of these protectionist pressures worried the Europeans and the Japanese—who feared that erection of U.S. trade barriers would limit their ability to sell in U.S. markets and damage their producers and labor. The Reagan administration also grew concerned that such protectionist pressures could undermine its neoliberal agenda of promoting market forces over government management of economic affairs.

Faced with a choice between more active management of the exchange rate or protectionism, policy makers in the Reagan administration decided to promote a stable and orderly depreciation in the value of the dollar vis-à-vis other currencies. This gradual adjustment process required substantial cooperation among the monetary authorities of the major states. By now, the size of currency markets precluded unilateral intervention by a state's monetary authorities to shift a currency's value significantly. Producing an orderly shift in a currency's value required a sustained commitment of resources, and even then currency traders might not have confidence in a state's willingness or ability to pay such costs. If currency traders were not *indifferent* to a state's commitment, they might bet against the government's position in the currency markets. Only a joint commitment by the monetary authorities of the major nations to a currency's value could convince traders to be indifferent to that value. Such commitment was essential to an orderly realignment of a currency such as the dollar. In 1985, the G-5 met at the Plaza Hotel in New York and adopted a joint policy to reverse the appreciation of the dollar. The value of the dollar fell after the Plaza Accord and the sustained intervention it brought about. Within a year it had declined between 30 percent and 40 percent against its major trading partners.

This substantial depreciation in the dollar affected the competitiveness of non-U.S. producers in the tradable sector and led to pressures on other governments to stem the appreciation in their currencies. In 1987 the G-5 met at the Louvre in Paris to discuss whether to stabilize the dollar's value or to continue letting it depreciate, and, if they were to agree on stabilization, what policies should be adopted in support of stabilization. The ministers agreed to stop the dollar's decline, stabilizing it at current levels. Central banks, acting together, then intervened in currency markets to prop up the dollar. The joint efforts that led to the dollar's depreciation and stabilization demonstrated the capacity for cooperation across the major governments to protect the global economy. U.S. policy makers sat at the center of this cooperation and coordination, again demonstrating the importance of hegemonic leadership to manage potential traps that could undermine the interstate cooperation essential for sustained globalization.

After the Louvre Agreement halted its decline, the dollar rose in value for the next several years. But by 1989, it began to decline again, benefiting U.S. producers and labor and the competitiveness of their products in the tradable sector. Within a few years, the fall in the value of the dollar was again creating problems for non-U.S. producers and labor abroad. Japanese producers and labor faced the most serious problems. In the early 1990s a real estate bubble burst in Japan, threatening the stability of financial credit institutions, slowing domestic consumption and investment, and leading to stagnation in the Japanese economy. A declining dollar added to Japanese economic woes, and it also hindered economic expansion in the European economies.

Despite these foreign concerns, Presidents George H. W. Bush and Bill Clinton allowed the dollar to continue to decline through benign neglect. No strong interests in U.S. society argued for strengthening the dollar, as compared with the mid-1980s, when U.S. producers and labor had pushed for the dollar's depreciation. Why was domestic pressure forthcoming in one instance and not the other? Overvalued currencies create significant problems for their nations' producers in the tradable sector, as the prices of their goods increase relative to those of other nations' producers; undervalued currencies have the opposite effect, lowering the prices of their producers' goods in the tradable sector. In nations with undervalued currencies, consumers may be hurt, as they encounter higher-priced imports and an increased likelihood of inflation. But, compared with producers, consumers are a diffuse and unorganized interest. They encounter difficulties in presenting a united front, agreeing on common objectives, voicing those objectives, and acting in a concerted manner to demand government policy change. Producers in the tradable sector are a more concentrated interest, and, as a consequence, they are more likely to overcome barriers to collective action and appeal to governments for redress.

Strategies to Limit Exchange-Rate Volatility: Currency Pegs, Currency Control Boards, and Limited Monetary Policy Flexibility

Many governments feared the potential volatility of a floating exchange rate. Many policy makers remembered the last systematic experience with floating exchange rates during the interwar years, which did not inspire confidence. Policy makers in small, developing political economies were particularly fearful of exchange-rate instability, because exports often constituted a relatively large portion of their overall economies. Moreover, they looked to foreign assistance and investment inflows to promote economic expansion, and they worried that excessive exchange-rate volatility could create currency risk, damage their domestic producers in the tradable sector, deter foreign investment, and promote capital flight. Hoping to reassure foreign investors and create stable expectations, therefore, many of these states pegged their currencies to the currencies of their major trading partners. Many of the Latin American states pegged their currencies to the dollar, many former British colonies pegged their currencies to the pound, and many former French colonies pegged their currencies to the franc.

A **currency control board** tightens the trading band of a currency and limits a government's latitude for responding to political pressures to manipulate money supply and the exchange rate. **Hard currency** is any monetary unit that can readily be used and accepted in international transactions; such currencies are desirable because they are considered likely to hold their value over time and so present relatively little currency risk to the parties involved in an international transaction.

Most governments that took this step chose to adopt a peg with some flexibility in its band, which meant that their currencies could trade within a reasonable range of the dominant currencies to which they were pegged and still remain within the peg. But some states adopted either an extremely narrow version of a peg or a **currency control board,** both of which are designed to tighten the trading band of a currency. The statutory provisions that created a currency control board generally dictated the ability of the government to affect money supply. These provisions tied government monetary policies to **hard currency** reserves in the national treasury—those currencies that can readily be used and accepted in international transactions because they will hold their value over time and present relatively little currency risk to the parties in a transaction. Today, most international transactions are conducted in the hard currencies of the dollar, the pound, the euro, the yen, and a few others. As hard currency reserves increased, the government increased money supply, and as reserves decreased, it was mandated to decrease money supply. Generally, the connection between hard currency reserves and money supply was transparent and tied to a specific formula, which limited the ability of policy makers to change money supply independent of the changes in hard currency reserves. Effectively, a government tied control of its currency and money supply to its success in trade and the monetary policies of its major trading partner. Adoption of a currency control board was an extreme policy with the aim of constraining national policy makers, limiting inflation, and importing the stability and discipline of a major currency.

Governments often maintained capital controls to support their pegs. They hoped that controls could limit the outflow of capital during speculative attacks on their currencies, provide them with added resources to combat such attacks, and consequently limit attacks that could damage their economies and place the governments at risk from their societies. But with growing financial globalization (the increasing openness and integration of national financial markets), governments found it more difficult to maintain capital controls and currency pegs. Governments needed to intervene in currency markets to maintain their currencies' value within a prescribed trading range, but the amount of hard currency reserves necessary for such active intervention steadily increased given the growth in the size of currency markets. By pegging the value of its currency to the currency of its major trading partner, a small state exposed itself to the demands of the macroeconomic and monetary policies of its larger trading partner.

For example, monetary policy choices by the Federal Reserve or U.S. budgetary choices that affected the value of the dollar would require governments and central banks in states pegged to the dollar to adjust their policies. This meant that small governments with very limited resources would be exposed to policy choices by big governments with vastly greater resources. To compound this problem, the governments of the larger states usually make their policy decisions based on the anticipated consequences of those choices for their domestic political economies, with little or no concern regarding the outcomes of their choices for their smaller trading partners.

Well-intentioned policies to limit exchange-rate volatility, such as capital controls or a narrow peg, often backfire. They create opportunities for currency traders to bet against a government, which could raise barriers to investment. If enough traders in currency markets believe that a government's currency is fundamentally misaligned and doubt its ability to maintain its pegs and capital controls, this belief increases the likelihood of a speculative attack. Moreover, the ability to get in and out of an investment—mobility—is a means to limit risk. Controls limiting the mobility of capital could stymie investment if investors prefer arenas that allow easier entrance and exit. Many of the financial crises of the 1990s, including the Mexican peso crisis, the Russian ruble crisis, the Asian financial crisis, and the Argentine crisis, resulted from pegs that came under attack in currency markets by traders who viewed those pegs as fundamentally misaligned. Attacking the governments' commitments to maintain their pegs, the currency traders overwhelmed the ability of these governments to defend their currencies. These attacks led to significant profits for those who succeeded in overwhelming government defenses of their currencies and resulted in massive devaluations, in some cases almost 30 percent, in the prices of their currencies. Those devaluations degraded the purchasing power of people in those countries and imposed significant economic hardships, particularly on lower-income groups.

A Collective-Currency Peg to Limit Exchange-Rate Volatility: The European Snake

Like the policy makers in developing states who worried about trade and investments in their economies, policy makers in some of the advanced industrialized nations were concerned about the potential volatility of a floating-rate system. The tradable sectors in many Western European states constituted larger portions of their economies than was the case in the United States and Japan. By design, the Western European economies had grown increasingly connected by trade. The European Coal and Steel Community (ECSC) and its successor, the European Economic Community (EEC), were created to increase European economic interdependence. The objective of greater interdependence was to control German aggressiveness by integrating Germany's economic fortunes with those of its neighbors and to limit beggar-thy-neighbor policies by creating a network of cooperative agreements. As a result, European interstate trade and the exposure of European national economies to the global arena increased, which meant that these economies were more sensitive to shifts in exchange rates. With the demise of the Bretton Woods and Smithsonian frameworks, European policy makers seeking to protect and promote this greater interdependence were confronted by uncomfortable memories of the exchange-rate instability of the interwar years.

> The **European Snake** was a collective-currency peg that constrained the trading range of European currencies; it was created in response to fears about post–Bretton Woods floatation and designed to limit exchange-rate volatility.

Seeking to constrain exchange-rate instability, many European states cooperated to create a collective-currency peg that came to be called the **European Snake.** The parties to the Snake specified a fluctuation band that would limit the trading range of their currencies vis-à-vis each other, defined the responsibilities of the members to intervene and support their currencies and those of other members, and created financing facilities to help states with weak currencies remain within the trading band. The parties to the Snake agreed to retain the 2.25 percent bands of the Smithsonian Agreement.

The Snake quickly came under pressure as the global economy was hit by oil shocks in the 1970s. Energy costs reduced the competitiveness of the European economies at the same time the dollar began to depreciate. This combined effect put divergent pressures on the Snake, as some currencies grew weaker and others remained relatively strong. Weak-currency countries pushed the bottom boundary of the Snake, while strong-currency countries pushed at its upper boundary. Differences in domestic monetary and fiscal policies added to the pressures, as currencies threatened to move outside the band of the Snake. Facing economic slowdown and increased unemployment, the French enacted expansionary policies to promote growth, but these actions weakened its currency. The German central bank, the Bundesbank, fearing inflation more than slow growth, reacted against the inflationary pressures of increasing oil prices, thus limiting the adoption of expansionary policies in Germany and keeping the German currency strong. Such differences in macroeconomic policies sent mixed messages to traders in the currency markets, which increased the potential for speculative attacks.

The Snake was being pulled in different directions by its two major currencies. Each government wanted the other to intervene and realign its currency, but neither wanted to realign its own currency. Other members faced the same tension, and the debate focused on whether the weak or strong currencies should be the currencies to realign. The size of the German economy and the strength of its currency had made the deutsche mark the core currency of the Snake, but the weaker-currency countries had no means to affect the policies of the Bundesbank. Unable to influence German monetary policy or to coordinate the policies of member states, weak-currency states faced the choice of surrendering control over their monetary policies (adopting Germany's anti-inflationary price stability stance) or withdrawing from the European Snake when they could no longer defend their currencies. Arguments continued throughout the 1970s, and, after numerous attempts at realignment, France, the United Kingdom, Italy, Denmark, Sweden, and Norway were forced to withdraw from the Snake at one time or another.

Balancing Strong- and Weak-Currency States: The European Monetary System

By the late 1970s, the inability of many states to stay within the 4.5 percent band of the European Snake led to discussions, particularly between the Germans and French, over the formation of the **European Monetary System (EMS).** At the heart of the negotiations was a tension between strong-currency states and weak-currency states over who

> The **European Monetary System (EMS)** is a collective-peg monetary arrangement formed in 1979 that targeted ±2.25 percent bands for members of the peg, but allowed some weaker-currency states (such as Italy) a wider, transitional band of 6 percent.

would adjust to protect the collective-currency peg if national currencies threatened to move beyond the boundaries of the peg. Commitments by the German Bundesbank and other states' central banks to price and currency stability helped make their currencies strong. But in other states, such as France, policy makers faced electoral pressures, constituent demands, labor unrest, and other societal pressures that prompted progrowth policies even at the risk of inflation. Elevating growth over price stability as a policy objective led to increases in money supply that could depreciate the value of a currency. States implementing such policies drifted toward the bottom of the band of the currency peg. The Snake had no agreement over who was to adjust if some currencies became too weak relative to the strong currencies, or if some currencies became too strong relative to the weak currencies.

Bilateral discussions between France and Germany paved the path to the EMS. French-German agreement was critical. The French wanted strong-currency states to adopt expansionary policies and weak-currency states to implement contractionary policies in defense of the peg. They also sought to have strong-currency states intervene in currency markets in defense of the collective peg to strengthen weak currencies by using the strong currency to buy the weak currency. German policy makers also recognized the need to intervene to help weak-currency nations, but they feared that a commitment to intervene and purchase weak currencies could create moral hazard problems for policy makers in those weak-currency states and could flood the currency markets with too much of the strong currency. This could undermine the strength of a strong currency and damage the anti-inflationary commitment to price stability in the strong-currency nation. And it could enable policy makers in the weak-currency states to avoid making politically costly but presumably economically sound choices in the management of their domestic economies.

The French-German negotiations finessed this divide by linking Bundesbank intervention to the ability of weak-currency states to reestablish their rates within the peg or to their willingness to realign (devalue) their currencies. If a weak-currency state could not adjust its policies to remain within the peg even with the intervention of strong-currency countries, or if a weak-currency state was unwilling to devalue, the Bundesbank could decide not to intervene in support of a weak currency. Intervention by Germany or other strong-currency states thus depended on the willingness of weak-currency states to either adjust their policies or devalue. Each side had an out, but both made the necessary gestures to promote cooperation and obtain international agreement.

The **exchange-rate mechanism (ERM)** is a mechanism that determines the value of one currency versus another and provides a means of adjustment in the balance-of-payments mechanism.

The French-German agreement provided a basis for the European Community member states to form the EMS in 1979. The EMS targeted a collective peg with 2.25 percent bands, but allowed some weaker-currency states (such as Italy) a wider, transitional band of 6 percent. Governments could implement capital controls in defense of their currencies to provide some policy autonomy. All but one EC nation, the United Kingdom, joined this **exchange-rate mechanism (ERM)** at the start. This collective peg worked remarkably well during the 1980s, as none of the original parties to the ERM moved beyond the band. Pressures did arise that threatened the system, but orderly devaluations of weak currencies helped to manage the stresses. By the early 1990s, the EC had expanded, and almost all its members were operating within the ERM. Stability in the EMS encouraged European leaders to broach greater European integration. Encouraged by success in the exchange-rate regime, policy makers thought greater integration was possible and predicted that it would help European economic producers compete more successfully with U.S. and Japanese economic enterprise.

In the early 1990s, a global economic slowdown, declining European competitiveness, increasing European unemployment, and a desire to assist Eastern European political economies after the breakdown of communist rule in 1989 increased pressures on the EMS, which limited the ability of the EMS states to manage tensions within the ERM. As the strong-currency anchor of the ERM, Germany faced a special problem. West Germany's financing of the political and economic unification of the two Germanys transformed Germany from one of the largest creditor states into one of the largest debtor states overnight. Germany borrowed heavily to finance unification, which led to increases in European interest rates because of Germany's dominant position in Europe. The EMS was being taxed by global events.

By the last quarter of 1992, the EMS came under attack as currency traders began to speculate regarding the future of European monetary cooperation. Currency traders bet against the willingness and ability of EMS governments to defend currencies that contributed to European unemployment and economic stagnation. Weak currencies fell to the lower boundary of the band, and then below the band. The British pound, Italian lira, Portuguese escudo, Spanish peseta, Swedish krona, Irish punt, Danish krone, and French franc faced increasing pressures as currency traders challenged governments to keep their currencies within the bands of the EMS. Governments defended these currencies with a mixture of tools, including raising interest rates, intervening in currency markets through their central banks and finance ministries, tightening capital controls, and increasing reserve requirements based on bank assets and liabilities. All were strategies intended to stabilize currency prices and convince currency traders it would be costly to bet against governments—to convince them to be indifferent. Governments of rich, powerful states and currency traders were engaged in a strategic game that reflected a shifting balance between Keynesianism and the neoliberal approach of the Washington Consensus, with its greater reliance on market discipline. Both strong- and weak-currency governments dipped deeply into their hard currency reserves to defend the EMS. Currency traders remained skeptical about the will and capacity of these governments to sustain a defense of their currencies—about the will and capacity of strong-currency countries to risk inflation and the will and capacity of weak-currency governments to risk unemployment. Both could threaten political survival in democratic states.

By mid-September 1992, the United Kingdom and Italy had withdrawn from the ERM and allowed their currencies to float. But the crisis did not subside, as currency traders kept the pressure on other weak EMS currencies. More devaluations followed. By the end of July 1993, the EMS appeared ready to collapse completely—the financial reserves of a group of advanced industrialized governments could no longer withstand the currency market pressures. The EMS governments capitulated by expanding the ERM bands to 15 percent—not quite a float, but still quite a large change in the band. Moreover, currency traders learned that it was incredibly lucrative to challenge government policy commitments with the discipline of the market if the traders could prevail, marking a new chapter in the tension and conflict between state and market forces.

The European Monetary Union: Balancing Greater Monetary Integration with Fiscal Autonomy

The European Coal and Steel Community, the predecessor of the EEC, had hoped to reduce the prospect of European conflict by linking German and French economic fortunes. The EEC built on this foundation with cooperative agreements that aimed to increase European economic interdependence. The level and robustness of monetary cooperation in the EMS, even if only partly successful, was quite remarkable, given the willingness of the United States and Japan to let their currencies float and the declining competitiveness of European economic enterprises vis-à-vis U.S. and Japanese industries. The prospect of defecting from the collective-peg system offered the temptation of a more competitive exchange rate, but the relationships created by a framework of cooperative agreements during the postwar years withstood the temptation to defect. Members withdrew from the ERM only after a period of concerted and severe crisis in 1992.

During the mid-1980s, discussions advanced over greater monetary integration in Europe. Such unification had been envisioned as early as the late 1960s, but governments had been unwilling to surrender monetary sovereignty and accept the elimination of national monies. On the trade front, meanwhile, declining competitiveness and increasing unemployment pushed the agenda of integration and monetary union. In 1986 the Single European Act targeted the creation of a unified European market in order to take advantage of economies of scale and scope, to increase the competitiveness of European producers, and to reduce unemployment. As this goal would require removing obstructions to exchange within the EC, the Single European Act promoted the harmonization of regulatory arrangements across the EC states and the dismantling of other barriers to the flow of goods, services, and inputs to production within the EC.

Nonetheless, national monies were viewed as obstacles to greater integration. They gave governments tools to escape the costs of adjustment from greater market integration, or to shift those costs onto EC neighbors. EC members could still be pressured by protectionist constituents to use monetary policies, the exchange rate, capital controls, and other policy tools that would hinder trade and limit long-term gains from economies of scale and scope. This persistent vulnerability to protectionist pressures placed monetary unification at the center of discussions about greater integration.

In 1988–1989, the Delors Commission (named for Jacques Delors, then president of the European Commission) advocated monetary union and the adoption of a common currency, the removal of capital controls, and the elimination of autonomous national monetary authorities. Those authorities were to be replaced by the creation of the European Central Bank (ECB), which would centralize monetary authority. National central banks would become agents of the ECB. Some hoped for greater political unification, but the Delors Commission resisted explicit recommendations to promote political unification and avoided centralization of fiscal policies, protecting national policy autonomy in this area. This would create an odd mix of centralized monetary authority located in the ECB and decentralized fiscal authority remaining in the hands of national governments. This structure came under serious criticism, yet the EU moved forward. Recognizing the inherent tension in this structure, which many critics considered a serious if not fatal design flaw, the commission did advocate constraints on deficits, a government debt ceiling, and other macroeconomic targets that could limit some fiscal policy autonomy. It envisioned that monetary union would be easier to attain if member economies were more alike than different—that greater macroeconomic alignment across members was necessary to reduce the stress on monetary union. The criticisms of this odd institutional and seemingly incoherent mix of centralized monetary policy in the hands of the ECB and decentralized fiscal authority under the control of national policy makers located in different national capitals would prove prescient with the onset of the European sovereign debt crisis that began to develop in 2010.

The Delors Commission's report led to formal intergovernmental negotiations that in 1992 produced the Maastricht Treaty, which created a three-stage timetable for monetary unification (see table 12.1). Stage I, which began in 1990, sought the end of capital controls, which would remove barriers to the formation of a unified financial market. Borrowers from across the EU, public and private, would compete in a unified market that would discipline governments and industries seeking to borrow capital if they implemented policies that investors considered uncompetitive. Investors could essentially reward good performance with lower capital costs (interest rates) and penalize what they perceived as poor activity with higher capital costs. The end of capital controls, which had provided some insulation from such pressures, reduced the ability of governments to adopt macroeconomic policies that were inconsistent with the policies of other member states.

| **TABLE 12.1** | **The Maastricht Treaty** |

Stage	Components
I	An end to capital controls
	• Removed barriers to forming a unified financial market
	• Reduced governments' ability to adopt macroeconomic policies inconsistent with those of other member states
II	Harmonization of macroeconomic policies through convergence goals
	• Established the Maastricht criteria
	• Established the European Monetary Institute to help coordinate policies
	• Reduced divergent pressures that could threaten monetary union
III	Monetary union
	• Retained distinct national currencies at first, with fixed exchange rates
	• Phased in the euro to replace national currencies
	• National central banks ceded authority to manipulate monetary policy (money supply and interest rates)

The **Maastricht criteria** are a set of macro-economic convergence goals, established by the Maastricht Treaty (1992), that European governments had to meet by 1997 if they were to move to Stage III of the European Monetary Union.

Stage II targeted the harmonization of macro-economic policies by establishing convergence goals, the **Maastricht criteria**, that governments had to meet by 1997 as they moved to Stage III. As part of Stage II, Maastricht created the European Monetary Institute (EMI) to aid EC members in coordinating their policies as they worked to meet the convergence criteria. EU policy makers believed that these convergence goals were central to reducing divergent pressures that could threaten the success of monetary union. The underlying assumption was that if political economies were more alike than different in their policy beliefs, expectations, and practices, they would respond similarly to stress. This was critical if monetary authority was to be centralized but fiscal authority was to remain decentralized. EU governments were expected to achieve certain targets by 1997 if they wanted to qualify for the European Monetary Union (EMU) and a common currency. If states met the following criteria, it was believed that they shared similar approaches to long-term government borrowing, deficits, inflation, and exchange-rate stability:

- Government deficits below 3 percent of GDP
- Government debt below 60 percent of GDP
- Inflation rate not to exceed by more than 1.5 percent the average of the three best-performing members of the EU
- Long-term government bond yields (interest rates) not to exceed by more than 2 percent the average of the three best-performing members of the EU
- Maintenance of currency within the ERM bands for two years

Stage III, monetary union, was set to begin on January 1, 1999, even if only a minority of the EU members met the convergence criteria. Initially those states qualifying for the EMU would retain their national currencies, but these currencies would fix exchange rates vis-à-vis each other. Functionally, fixing exchange rates creates a single currency with conversion rates between different denominations of cash, much like the relationships among pennies, nickels, dimes, quarters, and dollars. A new currency, the *euro*, would be phased in over a multiple-year period and eventually replace national currencies. In Stage III, national central banks would cede their ability to manipulate monetary policy to the ECB. They would no longer control money supply or interest rates. EU members remaining outside the EMU could join an ERM anchored by the euro and with bands up to 15 percent.

In late 1991, the EU appeared fully committed to implementing the three stages, but economic conditions and a crisis in the ERM in 1992 began to hollow out support for monetary union. A growing proportion of the publics in member states began to question the wisdom of surrendering monetary policy to the EU. Monetary unification was easier to promote during the good economic times of the late 1980s. It became much more difficult as member economies stagnated in the early 1990s. Public opinion polls in the EU revealed a growing indifference toward, and even dislike for, the EU agenda. By June 1992, a Eurobarometer poll showed support for the single-market program at 44 percent—a decline of 13 percent from its highest level of public support in 1987. Enthusiasm for the EU fell least in less economically advanced states such as Greece, Portugal, Spain, and Ireland, and most in the original EEC member states of Luxembourg, Belgium, France, and Germany.

The Danish referendum to ratify the Maastricht Treaty in June 1992 reflected the growing shift in public sentiment. After the Danes voted against ratification, suddenly the Maastricht Treaty, monetary union, and the EU were seen to be in danger. Currency traders viewed the Danish referendum and growing public resistance to the Maastricht Treaty as a lack of credible commitment by EU members. Traders began to challenge the ERM in currency markets, thus contributing to the 1992 ERM crisis. The crisis was eventually resolved in the second half of 1993 and the bands of the ERM expanded to 15 percent. A French referendum on Maastricht passed in September by a narrow margin as the pro–monetary union forces prevailed.

Despite threats, the EMU stayed on schedule. Stage III went into effect in January 1999. Eleven EU members initially joined the EMU, placed their monetary policies under the ECB, and, for all intents and purposes, adopted a single currency. The central banks of Austria, Belgium, Finland, France, Germany, Ireland, Italy, Luxembourg, the Netherlands, Portugal, and Spain thus transferred their ability to manipulate monetary and exchange-rate policies to the ECB. Financial institutions, financial markets, and governments immediately began using the euro as a unit of account and settlement. Although it would be three years before people on the street started using euro notes and coins, conversion rates between EMU members' currencies became fixed, essentially creating a single currency. Greece met the convergence criteria and joined the EMU in January 2000. Then, on January 1, 2002, euro notes and coins entered everyday circulation, and by the end of February 2002, the Austrian schilling, Belgian franc, Dutch guilder, Finnish markka, French franc, German mark, Greek drachma, Irish punt, Italian lira, Luxembourgian franc, Portuguese escudo, and Spanish peseta were all removed from circulation. As of 2012, seventeen states had adopted the euro as their currency.

To the degree that the EMU lowered real and cognitive barriers to cross-border exchange and capital mobility within the EMU area, it increased competitive pressures on producers, fueled greater integration of the single market in goods and services, and bolstered connections across financial markets and instruments. The real size of these effects in the tradable sector remains a matter of empirical debate. The EMU also promoted the integration of fragmented financial markets into larger and deeper markets with greater liquidity. Governments and industries would compete for capital in increasingly unified financial markets, which would help investors and borrowers by creating more opportunities to lend and borrow capital, to manage risk through portfolio diversification, and to obtain more efficient pricing of capital. Moreover, the run-up to Stage III led to greater policy discipline, increased EU cooperation, and coordination of national macroeconomic policies, including fiscal and labor market policies as well as monetary policies. Even EU members that did not join the EMU used the Maastricht criteria to limit government intervention that supported uncompetitive practices. With greater financial market integration, such markets could penalize those that adopted policies contrary to EMU guidelines, thus placing anti-inflationary and price stability pressures on all EU members. As time would tell, the discipline that states adhered to on their way to joining the euro zone proved fragile in the face of domestic constituent pressures.

Monetary union helped to reassert Europe's influence in the global political economy, many times for the better but sometimes perversely as the events beginning in 2010 revealed. The economic, demographic, and physical size of the EMU, the growing international use of the euro, and the increasing size of integrated European financial markets reinforced the role of Europe in international affairs. A large, integrated market with a single currency tends to be more influential than many smaller markets with many currencies. The use of the euro as a reserve currency and means of denominating international trade expanded—the euro is a tool of exchange, a unit of account, and a storehouse of value. Monetary union can add fuel to the pressures for political unification if greater alignment of economic interests helps to create shared values and identities that lead to greater convergence on domestic and foreign policies. But such union can also prove dangerous if governments fail to meet their commitments; these failures are sometimes costly and can threaten political survival.

The EMU is an extraordinary and remarkable experiment in governance. Monetary union transferred governance of an important policy tool of sovereign governments—monetary policy—from national central banks to a supranational institution, the ECB, by means of an international treaty among sovereign states. Nevertheless, EU members have maintained their identities as distinct states in the international system, indicating that theirs is a hybrid experiment that muddies the very basis of the Westphalian state system. For the first time since the establishment of the modern nation-state system following the Treaty of Westphalia, a potential alternative means of organizing political space emerged, and it came into being trying to reduce the inconsistencies between the organization of political and economic geographies that had characterized the Westphalian system. The size of the EU already surpasses the size of the U.S. economy. Monetary union, if successful, holds the prospect of leading to closer and closer coordination of member states' policies, and across a wider range of issues then monetary policy. It could prove to be the foundation for coordinating fiscal policies, foreign policies, and national security policies. Only time will tell. But the closer cooperation and coordination involved in monetary union elevated the EU on the world stage and led to speculation about closer coordination, and even similar unions, in other parts of the global arena, such as an expansion of NAFTA beyond trade and its current partners as a Western Hemisphere response to the EU and EMU, or a union of Asian powers across similar policy areas. Again, only time will tell, but it is a very intriguing shift in the nation-state system.

FINANCIAL GLOBALIZATION AND LIBERALIZATION: UNLEASHING NATIONAL FINANCIAL MARKETS AND REVIVING GLOBAL FINANCE

The post–Bretton Woods period witnessed three distinct trends that transformed global finance and altered state-market relationships: (1) a reawakening of *financial globalization,* whereby national financial systems became increasingly connected to one another; (2) *financial liberalization and innovation,* as the market forces of supply, demand, price competition, and creativity were unleashed in financial markets; and (3) dramatic changes in *international capital mobility,* defined by the ease or difficulty of moving capital across borders or transforming one financial asset into another. Changes in financial globalization, financial liberalization and innovation, and international capital mobility are some of the most significant changes observed in social relations during the latter part of the twentieth century—affecting how governments and industries borrow, their costs of capital, public and corporate governance, the connections across political economies, and the influence of financial markets on global economic relations.

Financial globalization involves the lowering of barriers to cross-border capital flows. This practice leads to an expansion in **global capital,** or capital that can move from one nation to another. Financial globalization includes **foreign direct investment (FDI)**—cross-border capital flows that result in significant ownership and management control of overseas economic enterprises, as well as all cross-border portfolio financial transactions such as lending and borrowing, trading in currencies or some other form of financial instrument (bonds, equities, or some financial derivative), or the provision of any financial service. These cross-border flows fall into two categories: money market flows and capital market flows. **Money markets** involve the trading of financial instruments that have a maturity of less than one year; **capital markets** issue and trade financial obligations with maturities longer than a year. Traders in money markets exchange currencies, currency futures and options, and other short-term obligations. Capital markets involve the exchange of capital for longer-term economic activities such as investment in plant and people. On average, money market flows are more volatile and liquid. This mobility across state boundaries affords holders of capital an ability to reward or penalize economic and governmental activity—to impose discipline.

> **Global capital** is capital that can move from one nation to another. **Foreign direct investment (FDI)** is investment in control of productive facilities overseas—usually defined by an investment that amounts to control of 10 percent or more of a company's equity. **Money markets** are markets that involve the trading of financial instruments that have a maturity of less than one year; these short-term obligations include trading in currencies, currency futures, and options. **Capital markets** are financial markets where enterprises and governments issue and trade financial obligations with maturities longer than a year.

The late 1800s saw the mechanisms of capital accumulation and allocation reach across national boundaries to connect lenders and borrowers of diverse nationalities. Active global capital markets based primarily in London played a major role in the economic development of the states of the Atlantic economy before the stock market crash of 1929 and the Great Depression, but the breakdown in financial globalization in the early twentieth century and the postwar design to limit financial globalization meant that the mechanisms of capital accumulation and allocation were predominantly national for much of the twentieth century.

Financial globalization reemerged after decades of stagnation. International borrowing accelerated in the 1960s. A trickle of cross-border interactions turned into a deluge as global capital flows expanded to levels unseen since before the Depression (see figure 12.1). Global capital markets now play essential roles in influencing economic activity within and across states. They influence who can get capital and at what price. They affect prospects for economic advancement and improvements in social welfare, create networks of interdependence that link societies across national boundaries, obstruct regulatory oversight and control, and produce pathways for transmission of economic improvements as well as dislocating shocks from one nation to another. Financial globalization feeds

| FIGURE 12.1 | **International Borrowing, 1960–1993: Mid- and Long-Term International and Foreign Bond and Loan Instruments** |

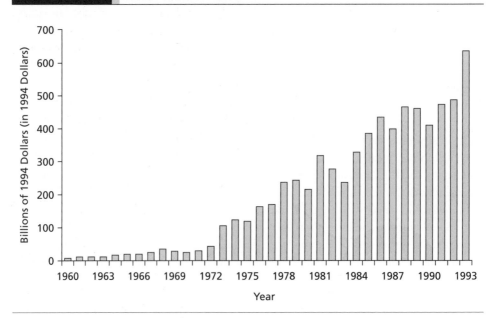

Source: Data from *OECD Financial Statistics Monthly.*

interdependence and alters conceptions of owner-ship, risk, investment, geography, and the state.

Financial globalization constitutes only one component of this late-century shift in capital rela-tions. Financial liberalization and innovation con-stitute another component: market liberalization in the financial sector, or the unleashing of market forces of supply, demand, price competition for capital, and creativity. Financial liberalization and deregulation prompted innovation in financial instruments, services, and strategies, as well as cre-ative destruction in the financial arena. Regulatory liberalization in the major markets encouraged

> **Disintermediation** is a process in which eco-nomic enterprises shift their borrowing away from commercial banks, which guarantee spe-cific rates of return to savers and intermediate their risks, and toward securitized financial instruments such as bonds and equities, in which the investor accepts the full risk of the loan to a borrower but also can reap a greater reward. **Securitization** is the transformation and packaging of financial liabilities into financial instruments, such as bonds and stocks, that can be sold in financial markets.

competitive pricing of capital and greater disintermediation and securitization of borrow-ing. **Disintermediation** involved shifting large-scale borrowing by economic enterprises away from commercial banks, where the banking institutions guaranteed specific rates of return to savers and intermediated their risks, and toward securitized financial instruments such as bonds and equities. **Securitization** took financial liabilities and transformed or packaged them into financial instruments, such as bonds and stocks, that could be sold in financial markets. Together, disintermediation and securitization meant that the saver (investor) accepted the full risk of the loan to a borrower but also reaped the full reward. With liberalization, those seeking to borrow capital increasingly preferred issuing securi-tized financial instruments (bonds and equities) in disintermediated markets over using commercial loans in intermediated markets.

Figure 12.2 displays the activities of borrowers in OECD states (the advanced industrial-ized political economies), developing states, and the Eastern European states of the former Soviet sphere of influence in intermediated and disintermediated global financial markets. Borrowers in the advanced industrialized economies accessed these markets far more heav-ily than did borrowers from other political economies, enjoyed a disproportionate rate of increased access, and increasingly favored disintermediated instruments. Borrowers from non-OECD political economies found potentially greater access to global financial resources than they had in the past, but more often they were limited to less flexible and more costly intermediated financial instruments. The processes of liberalization and inno-vation generated increasing complexity and linkages within and across markets. Financial infrastructures within nations deepened, even as financial interactions between nations expanded.

Financial globalization and liberalization afford tremendous opportunities and corre-sponding challenges for public and private policy makers, offering new opportunities and strategies for individuals, firms, and governments to acquire capital, lower capital costs, and

FIGURE **12.2**

Intermediated and Disintermediated Borrowing by Borrower, 1973–1993: Mid- and Long-Term International and Foreign Instruments

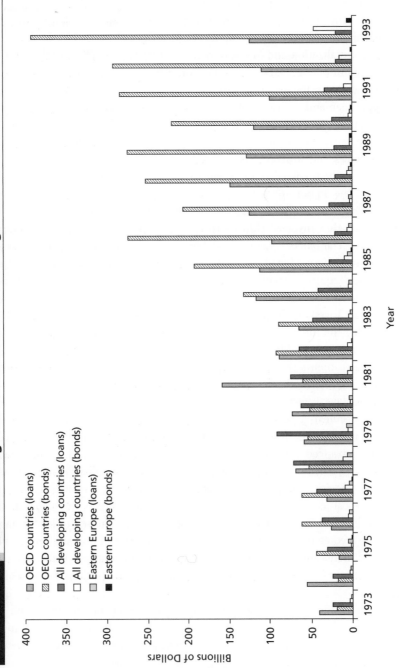

■ OECD countries (loans)
▨ OECD countries (bonds)
■ All developing countries (loans)
□ All developing countries (bonds)
■ Eastern Europe (loans)
■ Eastern Europe (bonds)

Source: Data from OECD Financial Statistics Monthly.

manage risk. Borrowers can increasingly access capital at home and abroad, seeking lower-cost capital in more efficient and liquid markets. But these trends can also strain national political economies, pose dilemmas for policy makers, and constrain national policy autonomy. Even though globalization and liberalization generally help many borrowers in terms of improved access and lower capital costs, the transformation in global financial relations systematically helps some more than others. Financial globalization divides those who can borrow in global capital markets from those who cannot (see figures 12.2 and 12.3). This effect raises tremendous normative implications for the distribution of wealth, opportunities, and influence in the global political economy. Systematic variations in access to capital separate the haves from the have-nots, creating or exacerbating tensions and divisions in and across societies. Nations with poor economic growth and low levels of opportunity are economic disasters for their populations, but they also can spawn political discontent and serve as breeding grounds for political violence and terror, which can damage national polities and spill across national boundaries.

The relative paucity of access to global capital markets for borrowers from developing nations does not mean that such disparities in capital flows exist across all forms of investment capital. One area of investment capital in which borrowers from developing nations have gained some footing is foreign direct investment, cross-border capital flows that result in significant ownership and management control of overseas economic enterprises. In developing nations, FDI has grown at a much faster rate than the ability to borrow in global capital markets (see table 12.2). Of course, this form of international capital mobility, which produces foreign ownership of economic activity in domestic spheres, raises questions of domestic control and management of the economy, and it sometimes sparks nationalist discontent and protectionist policies even as it creates economic opportunity.

Decision makers must now consider the reaction of global capital to their decisions. Some believe that financial globalization and liberalization provide public and private policy makers with new resources, but many fear that this increased cross-border capital mobility may diminish the autonomy and capabilities of national policy makers, constraining their abilities to enact policies that redistribute resources from holders of capital to the social safety nets that many societies have constructed. Regardless, the role of financial globalization and liberalization is an increasingly important consideration in international affairs. Policy makers are growing more attentive to movements in financial markets and cross-border mobility of capital. James Carville, President Bill Clinton's 1992 campaign manager, noted the growing influence: "I used to think that if there was reincarnation, I wanted to come back as the president or the pope. But now I want to be the bond market: you can intimidate everybody."[1]

---

[1]Quoted in *The Economist,* October 7, 1995, 3.

International Borrowing by Category of Borrower, 1960–1993: Mid- and Long-Term International and Foreign Bonds and Loans

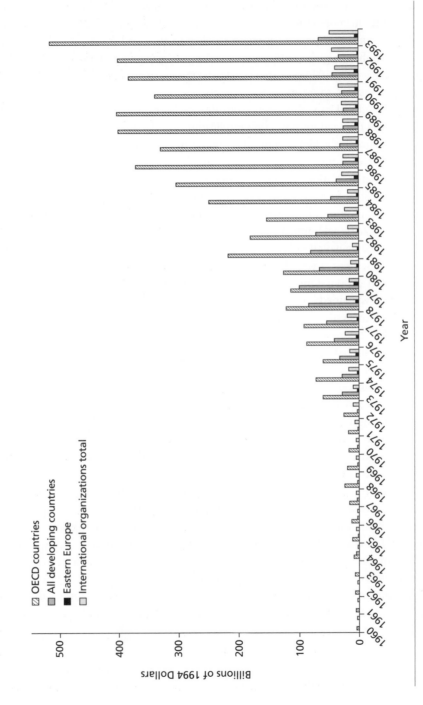

Source: Data from *OECD Financial Statistics Monthly.*

Explanations for Globalization: Technology, Competition, Politics, and Policy

Recall the discussion in chapter 1 about looking for causality in global affairs. In our systematic investigation of the phenomenon of globalization, we should be able to identify how independent variables may cause the dependent variables. Could such factors as technology and competition or changes in politics and policy cause financial globalization and liberalization? We have already considered these different forms of explanation in examining the expansion of globalization in the 1800s (in chapter 9) and the contraction in globalization during the period between World War I and World War II (in chapter 10).

TABLE 12.2	**Foreign Direct Investment in Developing Nations, 1982–1991 (Annual Averages)**

Period	Investment
1982–1986	$19 billion
1983–1988	$19 billion
1987–1991	$31 billion

Source: Data from United Nations Conference on Trade and Development, *1995 World Investment Report: Transnational Corporations and Competitiveness,* Annex table 1, 391–396.

Technology and Competition

Many accounts of the transformation in global financial markets highlight either the importance of technological changes in communication and financial instruments or the pressures of international competition, emphasizing **systemic factors** that work across borders. Rightly or wrongly, technological change and competitiveness receive both the blame and the accolades for much of financial globalization. These accounts offer systemic perspectives, as the forces driving change reside outside the domain of any specific national arena and operate across all national arenas. Competitiveness and technological change are the independent variables in this framework, and financial globalization and liberalization are the dependent variables. Clearly, such factors are important components of any explanation of financial globalization and liberalization, but are they sufficient?

> **Systemic factors** are forces that reside outside the domain of any specific national arena and operate across all national arenas.

History poses tough analytical problems for such explanations, which may prove to identify necessary conditions but not sufficient conditions. First, what startling changes occurred in technology or international competition during the 1960s and 1970s that correspond to the equally dramatic takeoff in financial globalization and liberalization? Does examination of that period reveal breakthroughs in communications and information technologies that sweep across nations as a systemic shift? Can we observe a dramatic shift in competition across nations and markets? Changes in satellite communications and computer processing and the invention of new financial instruments did occur during this period, but did these developments fuel revolutionary advances in terms of their influence on economic interactions? An increasing density of economic interactions across borders did feed cross-national competitive pressures, but these changes had been taking place since World War II.

Second, financial globalization and liberalization were well under way in the late 1800s and early 1900s, when London was a sophisticated financial center that supplied capital for economic activities and nation building around the world. But financial globalization and liberalization slowed in the early 1900s and then actually regressed with the Great Depression, after which global capital markets disappeared as major factors in the global political economy for almost forty years. Assuming the causality of technological change or competitiveness, backward induction would lead us to conclude either that technological change had reversed itself or that the pressures of competitiveness had declined from World War I to the 1960s.

Yet history shows that technology did not reverse direction in 1929 and again in the 1960s. Transformations in communications, advances in information processing, and financial developments within national markets provide abundant evidence of ongoing technological development throughout the twentieth century, even as global capital markets stagnated. Nor did participants in the global economy lose their competitive zeal in the 1920s, only to regain their competitive instincts in the 1960s. Technological change and competitiveness may be necessary conditions, but given the movements of our independent and dependent variables, they cannot be sufficient conditions.

Politics and Policy

Giving primacy to government choices, and domestic policy competition over those choices, offers another causal path to understanding globalization, liberalization, and changes in world affairs. In this category of explanations, decisions by key governments in response to domestic pressures to lower their barriers to capital mobility, alter their exchange-rate mechanisms, and enact financial regulatory reforms within their domestic financial markets spilled across national borders. Here, government policy change is a critical independent variable for understanding financial globalization and liberalization. Unlike technology or competitiveness, governments can reverse policy course.

In the 1920s and 1930s, government actions reversed the movement toward financial globalization. Instability in their exchange-rate mechanisms, strategic manipulation of exchange rates to transfer costs of adjustment abroad, and policies that detracted from liquidity in the system added to economic instability and created barriers to recovery after World War I. After World War II, as policy makers sought to avoid the same mistakes, many governments adopted capital controls to limit capital outflows. They were concerned that unrestrained capital mobility might encourage capital flight and create liquidity problems in rebuilding economies, expose political economies to destabilizing movements, and limit governments' ability to regulate financial markets. Meanwhile, some states, worried about destabilizing short-term capital inflows, imposed controls to limit such inflows. Policies such as foreign exchange restrictions, licensing special agents to engage in foreign exchange markets, limits on amounts of money that travelers could take in and out of a country, and regulation of institutional transactions across national borders were obstacles to global capital mobility. For years, such limits on capital mobility inhibited the expansion of global finance, except in the United States.

Post–World War II, the United States was noteworthy for its lack of capital controls. Along with the availability of capital, this feature placed U.S. capital markets at the center of the global economy. A persistent U.S. capital-account deficit provided liquidity and helped to fund the rebuilding of national and global economies, but the expanding size of this deficit began to concern U.S. policy makers. Over the course of twenty years, a massive dollar overhang emerged (the Triffin dilemma), whereby overseas dollar holdings exceeded U.S. official gold reserves. This disparity threatened convertibility and confidence in the dollar. But the growing pool of overseas dollars also created prospects for a significant capital market in dollar-denominated assets outside of the United States. This emerging offshore (outside the United States) market in dollar-denominated assets was underdeveloped and relatively inefficient compared with markets in the United States.

The Kennedy and Johnson administrations' efforts to limit the dollar outflow and reduce the threat to Bretton Woods—the Interest Equalization Tax of 1963 and the Voluntary Foreign Credit Restraint Act of 1965—created incentives for borrowers to access the overseas pool of dollars despite its inefficiencies. The IET and VFCR failed to protect the dollar and Bretton Woods monetary arrangements, but they did spur the development of the euro markets. U.S. private financial institutions exported their better skills and technologies to the euro markets. Recall from chapter 11 that euro markets trade financial instruments that are denominated in a nation's currency outside the boundaries of that nation. So *dollar*-denominated instruments that trade in Europe or Japan are euro markets, *yen*-denominated instruments that trade in the United States are euro markets, and *euro*-denominated instruments that trade in Tokyo are euro markets. By the time President Nixon suspended dollar convertibility in 1971, the euro markets had expanded dramatically and had become far more efficient.

The expansion of the euro markets was an important step toward financial globalization. Suspension of convertibility and the U.S. movement to a floating exchange rate after the demise of Bretton Woods and the Smithsonian Agreement removed the rationale for the IET and VFCR. They were repealed in 1973 and 1974, lowering barriers to U.S. capital markets. Moreover, many other advanced industrialized economies began to drop their capital controls in the 1970s, as the success of postwar reconstruction eliminated the rationale for them. The end of such controls in the advanced industrialized nations dismantled barriers to global capital mobility. The removal of controls in the United Kingdom and Japan in 1979 and 1980, respectively, proved especially significant, as these states were the two most sophisticated financial centers outside New York. International borrowing and capital flows expanded dramatically in the wake of such policy shifts.

Seignorage is an intentional overexpansion of money supply so that a government can extract an inflation tax to pay its bills and finance its programs without a more explicit use of fiscal tax policy.

Several other important governmental actions contributed to globalization and liberalization of finance from the late 1960s onward. First, government expenditures in the industrialized nations expanded during this period. When faced with financing dilemmas, governments avoided politically unpopular avenues such as limiting programs, increasing taxes, or resorting to **seignorage.** (Seignorage is a source of revenue for governments that uses inflation. By expanding money supply—issuing more currency—a government can redistribute resources to the issuer of the currency, the government, and away from those who hold and use the currency. It amounts to an inflation tax that a government uses to pay its bills and finance its programs.) Instead, government borrowing in disintermediated markets increased. Such borrowing helped to increase the size of these markets. In many cases, the borrowing reached far beyond domestic capital markets, as governments of successful economies, or governments of economies that looked like they were going to overcome barriers to growth and development, were able to access capital in global markets. Since the 1980s, as much as a third of U.S. government and private debt has been financed by overseas capital.

Second, many governments privatized much of their public sectors. That is, many governments that owned railroads, airlines, banks, telecommunications enterprises, defense firms, and other companies transferred ownership of these state-owned enterprises (SOEs) to private shareholders by selling off assets in private financial markets. In Europe, these issues led to large increases in financial market capitalization, liquidity, and efficiency.

Third, after the collapse of the Bretton Woods and Smithsonian monetary arrangements, the dollar, the yen, and some other currencies began to float. Floating exchange rates can add currency risk to trade and affect people's willingness to engage in international exchange.

Financial futures markets are markets in which traders purchase financial instruments in particular currencies and lock in the prices of those instruments at some future date; such betting on the future value of currencies allows hedging against exchange-rate risk and supplies insurance mechanisms to manage currency risk.

With greater variability in exchange rates, currency markets (short-term money markets) and financial futures markets became extremely important for managing such risk. In particular, **financial futures markets** in currencies—betting on the future value of currencies—allow hedging against exchange-rate risk and supply insurance mechanisms to manage currency risk. In such markets, traders purchase a currency future and lock in the price of that currency at some future date. Commodities markets already traded futures in tangible goods such as pork bellies, rice, grains, cattle, oil, corn, and coffee, but intangibles such as financial instruments were not traded as commodities in any substantial way before the 1970s.

Financial instruments began trading as commodities in futures markets in the early 1970s, after legislation in the U.S. Congress redefined what constitutes a commodity.

Defining intangibles as commodities allowed the construction of financial futures and derivatives and meshed with the need to manage currency risk in a floating-exchange-rate system. Trading in currencies and currency futures exploded. Growth in this type of trading increased international mobility in short-term money markets, enhanced the prospects for short-term financial movements in the international system, and led to a more tightly interconnected financial infrastructure across markets. Futures trading in other financial commodities and derivatives also expanded.

Markets in financial futures can lower currency risk, but they also connect financial markets, enable currency traders to speculate against a government's commitment to its macroeconomic policies and exchange rate, and may transmit shocks during a crisis. Currency traders can reward governments for adopting and maintaining policies they perceive as good and sustainable, or they can pressure governments and destabilize a currency, and maybe even an economy, if they believe that a government cannot sustain its commitment to the price of its currency or its commitment to macroeconomic policies. As noted earlier, traders challenging governments in currency markets set off crises involving the European Monetary System, the Mexican peso, the Russian ruble, and a handful of Asian currencies during the 1990s.

Beginning in the 1960s, regulatory changes, the demise of capital controls in the industrialized nations, and other public policy shifts helped to liberalize financial markets and opened international avenues for those with surpluses of capital to trade with those needing capital. In this changing regulatory environment, bankers, institutional investors, financiers, and market entrepreneurs harnessed technologies to unleash financial innovation and competitive market pressures. These opened national doorways to capital flows and awakened global financial markets. Financial globalization and liberalization offered a more efficient allocation of capital as they expanded the capital pool that borrowers could access. Changes in technology and competitive pressures acted as intermediate factors, but they were insufficient by themselves to account for the shifts in financial globalization and liberalization.

The increasing density and volume of global financial relations and their ability to link national political economies can produce tremendous economic opportunities and gains. Despite their promise, these connections across financial markets and national borders are not well understood, however, because of their growing complexity. The consequences of reforms can be difficult to comprehend fully. As sophisticated as the practitioners of global finance appear to be,

> A **contagion network** is a web of transactions and connections that transmits opportunities, dislocations, and risks across societies.

they are continually learning about the linkages across boundaries and financial markets. Often these discoveries arise out of crises that damage societies and people. The increasingly complex web of global finance can transmit opportunities, but it can also serve as a **contagion network** that communicates dislocations and risks across societies.

Challenging the Emerging Global Financial Infrastructure: Petrodollars and a Debt Crisis

No sooner had the Smithsonian Agreement failed and the world embarked on a new system of global financial relations than a series of events and processes began that would challenge the stability of this newly emerging infrastructure and reveal some of its potential pitfalls. By 1973, the Organization of Petroleum Exporting Countries had already begun pushing for increases in the price of oil. For years, Western oil companies had controlled the production of oil in the Middle East—they paid a price to local governments for each barrel produced within their boundaries, but the companies owned the drilling rigs and the oil extracted. Now, however, the OPEC states sought to increase their share of oil revenues. Libya, a key member of OPEC, had garnered limited success in raising the price of oil when Muammar el-Qaddafi seized power in that nation and demanded a price increase. For leverage, Qaddafi threatened to nationalize oil production—to seize ownership of Western-owned production facilities and transform them into an SOE. In 1970 the Western oil companies agreed to Qaddafi's demands. The other OPEC states took note: the Libyan initiative had succeeded without provoking intervention or retaliation by Western governments.

Over the next several years, OPEC pushed for more price increases. In 1971, OPEC and the oil-production companies agreed to a five-year pact that increased oil's price from $1.80 to $2.29 per barrel over the period. An agreement in 1972 among several of the Arab OPEC members and the oil companies provided for gradual transfer of control over production to the governments in those states. Learning to flex its muscles, OPEC had obtained increases in price and a gradual nationalization of production. In this context, OPEC is an excellent example of the successful collusion and collective action discussed in chapter 5 that can lead to oligopolistic price setting and market failure (chapter 4). Given the nature of the commodity, the sensitivity and dependence of the world on that commodity, and the inelasticity of demand for that commodity regardless of price, successful OPEC collusion was a significant change in the rules of the game in the global political economy. Oil was becoming a tool of international political as well as economic influence. The locus of global influence in the oil sector was shifting from the big oil companies of the Western industrialized states to the governments and SOEs of the oil-producing countries.

Then, in October 1973, the outbreak of a new Arab-Israeli war galvanized the Arab OPEC membership. Overcoming barriers to collective action in response to the military situation, the Arab members of OPEC colluded in an attempt to use oil as a political economic tool for applying pressure on other governments to withdraw their support for Israel and change the global geopolitical landscape. By mid-October of that year, the Arab oil-producing states unilaterally raised the price of their oil to $5.12/barrel. By the year's end, the price sat at $11.65, and OPEC, not the Western oil companies, now controlled the price of oil. Taking advantage of this opportunity, the OPEC states pressured the oil companies to transfer either majority or total ownership of their facilities to the governments of the states in which they were located—a revolutionary change in the ownership and production of oil. The large

Arab oil-producing states—Saudi Arabia, Iran, and Kuwait—could use their significant production capacity to manage the global oil supply system. This situation provided the OPEC states with tremendous political economic leverage, which they began to exercise on the world stage.

The Arab OPEC states partly succeeded in their agenda of isolating Israel. Many governments shifted their policies toward Israel, and some states, particularly developing political economies, severed diplomatic relations with the country. Israeli aid and agricultural development teams were sent home from states where they had been providing expert assistance. Post-1973, Israel found itself increasingly isolated in the United Nations, relying more and more on the willingness of the United States to use its veto power in the U.N. Security Council to protect Israeli interests.

By 1974–1975, the price of crude oil floated around $30/barrel. It peaked near $50/barrel during the Iranian Revolution in 1978, when Iranian oil exports ceased. Iran had contributed between 15 and 20 percent of OPEC's total oil exports. At this point, the rising price of oil only marginally affected the demand, for consumers still needed oil to heat their houses and to power their cars, and industries still needed energy to operate their plants. The price increases thus translated into tremendous oil revenues for the OPEC states. Decisions by the national governments of Arab and Persian oil-producing states, and later events in the Iranian domestic arena, spilled over to the international political economy and created oil shocks, price shocks, and economic disruptions. The oil shocks were transmitted as a contagion, demonstrating the interdependence of national political economies.

> **Petrodollars** are the revenues that accrue to oil-producing states from the sale of oil; much of this revenue is recycled into the global economy either through increased consumption or through bank deposits in Western banks located in the large financial centers, which then lend those petrodollars to borrowers.

The OPEC states recycled these revenues, known as **petrodollars,** into the global economy by two paths: increased consumption and bank deposits. The increase in oil revenues was so dramatic that no conceivable level of consumption could recycle all the petrodollars. OPEC governments deposited vast sums into private banks. The bulk of such deposits went to Western banks located in the large international financial centers. The banks owed interest on these deposits, and, consequently, they faced the task of making these deposits perform by lending them to borrowers and charging those borrowers interest on the loans.

The banks found that potential borrowers in oil-consuming countries—particularly developing states—faced with significantly larger energy bills because of the increase in oil prices, were happy to borrow petrodollars to pay for their current-account deficits. This created a cycle. Oil-producing states raised oil prices and earned large revenues, which they deposited in banks. Unable to reduce oil consumption significantly, oil-consuming states ran large deficits and borrowed the deposited petrodollars to finance their deficits. They owed the bank interest on these loans. Unfortunately, the increased costs of oil crowded out other consumption and slowed economic activity. Exports of nonoil commodities then slowed, limiting earnings of the hard currency reserves necessary to pay loan obligations. This looming shortfall of hard currency reserves in developing nations should have signaled the need for caution, but the banks had so many petrodollars to recycle that they just floated more and more loans, thereby connecting the well-being of financial institutions in the large Western money centers (New York, London, Paris, Tokyo) to the economic well-being of developing countries. The stability of the entire banking system was increasingly connected to the cycling of petrodollars.

Many of the loans made to borrowers in developing countries were adjustable-rate loans, which meant that the cost of capital (the interest rate on the loan) was tied to some interest rate such as the U.S. federal funds rate or a U.S. Treasury bill rate. If those rates decreased or increased, the interest rate on the loan would decrease or increase in response. During the mid-1970s, these rates were relatively low, so even though developing countries were borrowing heavily to finance economic development and to shore up their current-account deficits because of higher energy costs, while their hard currency earnings were declining because of the crowding out of nonoil commodity consumption, the relatively low interest rates enabled them to still meet their loan obligations.

In 1979, however, the cost of capital began to rise, and quickly. The U.S. economy had been burdened by inflation and stagnation since the end of the Vietnam War. This was partly a consequence of choices by U.S. policy makers to hide the real costs of the war by inflating money supply rather than raising taxes or increasing borrowing. As noted earlier, President Jimmy Carter appointed Paul Volcker as chairman of the U.S. Federal Reserve in 1979. Volcker, who was known as an inflation hawk, set out immediately to reduce inflation by rapidly increasing the cost of capital in the United States. He used the tools of the Federal Reserve to raise interest rates and increase reserve requirements. These reduced the supply of dollars in circulation and increased their cost, which slowed the global economy because the dollar was the dominant hard currency used for international exchange and maintaining hard currency reserves by other states' central banks. Production and consumption slowed in the global economy. For the developing political economies, this proved disastrous. Already faced with trade deficits because of higher energy prices, which limited their hard currency earnings and forced them to borrow to finance their deficits, they now confronted an even greater shortfall in export earnings as consumption in the Western economies declined with the rise in interest rates, decreased money supply, and the resulting economic slowdown.

Moreover, the cost of the capital borrowed by the developing political economies was rising quickly. Much of the capital had been borrowed under adjustable-rate agreements, and those rates were now climbing fast as international interest rates soared. Under Volcker, the U.S. prime rate—the interest rate available to the lowest-risk borrowers—climbed from around 7 percent to more than 20 percent in one year. The interest rates on mortgages, car loans, business loans, and other loans doubled and tripled in many cases. Borrowers in developing countries were in a quandary. They owed money from borrowing to finance their trade deficits, but now those loans were dramatically more expensive. At the same time, their revenues from exports were falling quickly. Under other circumstances, their political economies could work harder to pay the interest on their loans, but with the decline in consumption in the advanced industrialized states, this option was not viable. Faced with economic dislocations at home that could destabilize their polities, many political leaders in developing nations increased government expenditures to promote growth and provide some safety net. But these desperate measures only exacerbated the fiscal problems and deficits of these states.

Developing countries were caught in a debt trap, and, by connection, so were the banks that had recycled the petrodollars in loans to these countries. By 1982, the debt exposure of the most indebted countries had increased by more than 300 percent over their levels of indebtedness in the mid-1970s. Argentina was the first to be overwhelmed—it suspended payments on $37 billion in debt obligations following the Falklands War in 1982. Other countries faced similar, if not worse, problems. In August 1982, the Mexican government announced that it could not meet its payments on obligations of $85 billion. By December, Brazil, with $91 billion in loan obligations, followed the lead of Argentina and Mexico. By the end of 1983, almost all Latin American and many African states were in trouble and had threatened to suspend the servicing of their debts. This debt trap has been labeled the Third World Debt Crisis.

There is an old adage: if you owe the bank a hundred dollars, it's your problem, but if you owe the bank a billion dollars, it's the bank's problem. As the connections across markets and across state boundaries tied together the fortunes of developing political economies and the Western banking infrastructure, the major banks of the world faced a potential default of more than $200 billion in obligations. The IMF, the U.S. government, other Western governments, and the Bank for International Settlements (an international organization based in Switzerland that oversees accounting and settlements of international transactions) moved to stem the crisis. They provided short-term credit and bridging loans to help the governments of developing states meet their short-term obligations. They cajoled the creditor banks to delay the collection of debt-servicing fees for several months. Finally, they arranged debt rescheduling in exchange for austerity programs on the part of developing states and additional financing from the creditor banks. The United States and its policy makers, acting as the system stabilizer and lender of last resort (as discussed in chapter 6), were central to reaching a productive outcome and resolving the Third World Debt Crisis, but many governments of the developing world paid a heavy political and economic price during the process.

IMPLICATIONS OF FINANCIAL GLOBALIZATION: DOES MOBILE CAPITAL GAIN DISPROPORTIONATE ADVANTAGE AND ERODE NATIONAL POLICY AUTONOMY?

Increasing interdependence has prompted debates between advocates and critics of globalization. Some praise globalization for its potential to enhance social welfare, promote

Ministers of the Organization of Petroleum Exporting Countries discuss production targets, pricing policy, and the use of oil as an instrument of political leverage at a December 1973 meeting in Kuwait. The outbreak of the October Arab-Israeli war and failed negotiations with oil companies to revise prices led OPEC, dominated by Arab states, to overcome barriers to collective action. Members raised prices and cut production, and most joined in limiting oil shipments to Western industrialized supporters of Israel. The quadrupling of oil prices sparked a worldwide recession in 1974–1975.

universal harmony and common interests, and constrain governments from adopting policies damaging to their publics. Others warn that globalization undermines sovereignty and state autonomy, erodes the ability of governments to provide social welfare goods, promotes the growth of inequity and injustice, and dismantles distinct cultural identities. Globalization generates substantial social welfare gains through specialization and comparative advantage, but not without posing significant costs and risks to individuals and groups that find themselves less competitive in the face of global market forces. Post–World War II planners feared that if such risks were not contained, they could turn into demands on politicians to interfere in liberal economic exchange. The postwar social welfare state helped to manage such risks by redistributing costs away from those dislocated by change to the broader society.

Today, both critics and supporters of globalization worry that the winners from globalization will use their resources to influence public policy, escape tax burdens, and limit the redistribution that underpins the social welfare state. They worry that these advantages might exacerbate disparities, mobilize disaffected groups, and produce backlashes that could ultimately damage both globalization and social welfare. In particular, the increasing mobility of capital has become a lightning rod in these debates. What are the implications of increasingly mobile capital for state-society bargains and for the ability of governments to adopt and implement policies? Could financial globalization affect the ability of governments to produce public policies, enact and implement economic regulation, and generate social welfare goods that manage the risks to individuals, groups, and communities? In order to address these concerns, we need to examine two frameworks: the capital mobility hypothesis, which applies to all societal and governmental bargains involving mobile capital, and the "unholy trinity," a more specific framework that explores the relationships among exchange-rate policy, monetary policy, and capital mobility. In chapter 14 we will consider some of the substantive consequences of global financial integration, but here we focus on two theoretical frameworks that suggest linkages between financial globalization and the abilities of policy makers to enact the domestic policies of their choosing.

The Capital Mobility Hypothesis: The Use or Fear of Bargaining Leverage

The **capital mobility hypothesis** posits an inverse relationship between the mobility of capital and the policy autonomy of government or less mobile assets of production. This hypothesis speculates that more mobile economic actors gain disproportionate bargaining power in political and societal arenas, as increased openness enables

> The **capital mobility hypothesis** is a conjecture that posits an inverse relationship between the mobility of capital and the policy autonomy of government or less mobile assets of production.

those with mobility to exit or threaten to exit. This threat of exit empowers highly mobile economic enterprises with bargaining leverage to constrain government policies, avoid taxation, limit regulation, or reduce the redistributive demands of the social welfare state. This situation could expose less mobile assets of production to added risk, shift the burdens to fund state programs to those actors, or alter the balance in negotiations between management of more mobile industries and their labor. Whether the hypothesis is well-founded or not, increasingly the *fear* of capital mobility is used strategically as a lever to extract concessions in labor negotiations and discussions with policy makers. The dynamic of the capital mobility hypothesis underpins debates over the outsourcing of jobs, the relocation of industry, and the offering of tax abatements and incentives to attract and retain industry.

Using the logic of the capital mobility hypothesis, we can produce testable expectations about a rollback in state autonomy, a tit-for-tat race to the bottom of minimal provision of government services and regulation, and an increasing shift of globalization's costs of adjustment to those put at risk by openness. For example, if capital gains bargaining leverage with greater openness, the following effects may be expected:

- Capital should be able to find greater escape from redistributive tax burdens in more open societies than in less open societies.
- Capital should be able to create larger barriers to redistribution and social welfare programs in more open societies than in less open societies.
- The growth of state sectors should be smaller in more open societies than in less open societies.
- Tax burdens should increasingly fall on less mobile factors.

The effects of capital mobility on state autonomy, on state-society bargains, and on the distribution of the costs of adjustment remain ambiguous despite attempts by holders of capital to threaten exit. The empirical world offers conflicting evidence. Contrary to the expectations of the capital mobility hypothesis, state sectors have grown with globalization. More open economies generally have bigger governments than do less open economies. The advanced industrialized nations with the larger tradable (that is, more open) sectors maintain larger social welfare states, impose more regulatory demands on business, and operate with more rigid labor market agreements. Today, as throughout the post–World War II period, most cross-border flows of capital go from one advanced social welfare state to another, from one regulated economic arena to another, from one political economy with a relatively large state sector to another, and not to smaller social welfare states, relatively unregulated economic arenas, or political economies with relatively small state sectors. This is consistent with the evidence from earlier periods. In the 1800s, the growth of economic and financial globalization coincided with the origins of the modern social welfare state. As governments added social welfare functions to their national security functions, it was states with greater openness and mobility that led this shift in state responsibilities.

This ambiguity suggests that perhaps we need to examine the capital mobility hypothesis more closely. Exit, outsourcing, and relocation of production facilities constitute one set of strategies for maintaining and improving competitiveness. Improving productivity through human and physical capital investment, innovation and invention, and restructuring of industrial organization are other strategies that can help companies maintain their competitiveness and undercut a need to relocate to other settings. Industries may dislike some regulatory and statutory policies of governments but appreciate those same governments' abilities to deliver stable and enforceable property rights, good contracting mechanisms, consistent and transparent rule of law, good infrastructure, and well-educated workers. Governments still fund social welfare goods, but in many cases they have shifted away from demand-side social welfare goods, such as unemployment insurance and other safety net policies, and toward provision of supply-side goods, such as education, prenatal care, family leave policies, health care, and infrastructure, which can improve the efficiency of productive factors. The relationship between capital's choices to relocate and government policies is much more complicated than a single policy.

The capital mobility hypothesis also assumes that policy makers will respond to the demands of mobile capital because they fear the effects of its departure on social welfare, as well as its threat to their political survival. If, as we assumed at the beginning of this book, policy makers value political survival, they will formulate their policies in response to the preferences of those who can credibly commit to participating in the domestic political arena. Therefore, the ability to exit easily may actually undermine the impact of mobile capital's demands, since politicians may also be concerned about less mobile assets that have no alternative but to remain in their communities and participate in political life.

The Unholy Trinity: Three Policy Tools and an Inherent Tension

The **unholy trinity,** a framework based on a model developed by economists J. Marcus Fleming and Robert Mundell, examines the relationships among exchange-rate policy, monetary policy, and capital mobility. The **Fleming-Mundell model** predicts an inherent tension among the three elements of currency stability (which derives from a condition of relatively fixed exchange rates, whether the narrow peg of the Bretton Woods system or a broader but stable peg), capital mobility, and monetary policy autonomy. Governments can intentionally obtain two of the three components of the trinity, but not all three at the same time, unless by fluke. Policy makers may want to control all three tools, but they cannot. Indeed, the tension among the components of the unholy trinity was at the root of the major currency crises of the 1990s, as governments sought to have all three. During these crises, traders in currency markets saw what they considered to be an incompatibility between a state's stated exchange rate and its government's monetary policy.

> The **unholy trinity** is a framework that describes the relationships among exchange-rate policy, monetary policy, and capital mobility; governments can obtain two of the three components of the trinity, but not all three at the same time. The **Fleming-Mundell model** is a theory that predicts an inherent tension among currency stability, capital mobility, and monetary policy autonomy.

The absence of capital controls, a relatively new phenomenon in many states and an increasingly common characteristic of post–Bretton Woods national monetary arrangements, is key to the unholy trinity. Capital openness allows traders to use the mobility of capital to challenge government policies, to exit or vote with their feet. Capital controls limit the mobility of capital across state boundaries, as well as the ability of currency traders to attack a government's management of its monetary policies or a pegged exchange rate. With capital controls the state retains greater control over the amount of its currency in circulation outside the state and, consequently, limits the ability of others to challenge the value of its currency. Without capital controls, currency markets can more easily challenge a state's monetary and pegged-exchange-rate policies that appear inconsistent.

Let's list the different permutations of the unholy trinity (see figure 12.4). First, a government can preserve exchange-rate stability and monetary policy autonomy by limiting capital mobility. Second, a government can maintain exchange-rate stability and openness to capital flows, if it surrenders monetary policy autonomy to markets. Third, if a government wants to preserve openness to capital flows and the possibility of enacting monetary policy, it can escape exchange-rate pressures by forgoing a peg and letting its currency float. When a government floats its currency, it is no longer imperative for the government to defend the value of that currency if it comes under attack. Rather than fending off a speculative attack, a float allows market pressures to determine a currency's value.

How do such challenges occur? If a government with a pegged currency adopts monetary policies that are inconsistent with its balance-of-payments position, it creates a significant balance-of-payments disequilibrium. Such disequilibrium, produced by the tension between a government's stated value for its money and its attempt to influence the amount of money in circulation, prompts currency traders to question the government's commitment to its

FIGURE 12.4	The Unholy Trinity: Exchange-Rate Policy, Monetary Policy, and Capital Mobility
If governments . . .	*they can preserve . . .*
Limit capital mobility	Exchange-rate stability + monetary policy autonomy
Surrender monetary policy autonomy to markets	Exchange-rate stability + openness to capital flows
Allow currency to float (escaping exchange-rate pressures)	Openness to capital flows + monetary policy autonomy

monetary policies or to its pegged exchange rate. Since they do not believe the nation's currency will hold its value, traders will reduce their holdings of that currency by using it to purchase more stable currencies. This process can lead to capital flight from the offending state, an increased supply of its currency in currency markets, and downward pressure on the price of the currency. In defense of their currency, a central bank and finance ministry must then use their hard currency reserves to purchase their currency in order to reduce its supply in currency markets. A reduction in their hard currency reserves, however, will exacerbate the balance-of-payments problem, as the hard currency reserves necessary for paying off their international obligations have disappeared.

If the government persists in trying to maintain a stable peg and implement an independent monetary policy in the face of such pressures caused by the mobility of capital, a currency crisis is likely. Confronted by such pressures and constraints, a government has three alternatives: to accept market discipline and forgo independent monetary policies, to obstruct capital movements by imposing some form of capital controls, or to surrender its defense of the pegged rate. Increased capital mobility and the resulting integration of financial markets has unleashed the force of speculative capital, which can punish inconsistencies in government macroeconomic policies with destabilizing flows of speculative capital. Not even the strongest central banks can unilaterally withstand such pressure if it becomes intense enough.

GOING FORWARD: THE IMF AND THE WASHINGTON CONSENSUS

Under Bretton Woods, the IMF focused on maintaining stable pegged rates, addressing balance-of-payments pressures that threatened the peg, and, if necessary, overseeing an orderly process of adjustment in currencies from one par value to another. The end of the peg, along with growth in global capital markets and capital mobility, posed dilemmas for the IMF. The Bretton Woods arrangements had legitimated an intergovernmental structure that monitored, coordinated, and supported a system of stable exchange rates. The breakdown in that system left governments without an intergovernmental agreement about what constituted legitimate exchange-rate policies. This lack of coordination increased the risk that governments might manipulate their exchange rates to gain competitive advantage. Recalling the disaster of unilateral, beggar-thy-neighbor monetary affairs that took place during the 1920s and 1930s, policy makers feared that such actions could produce monetary disorder, thereby threatening trade, investment, and interdependence.

The growth of global financial markets and capital mobility could discipline a government that was strategically manipulating its currency to affect its balance of payments or competitiveness, but what if many governments went down this path? Would it lead to a social trap? In the absence of a legitimate intergovernmental authority to coordinate, monitor, and negotiate differences in monetary arrangements, policy makers feared that market discipline would prove insufficient to contain monetary disorder. They recognized the need to build a new framework for international monetary arrangements that would act as a rule of law, accommodate new exchange-rate strategies ranging from floating to pegged, complement the discipline of international financial markets, and contain the prospects of monetary anarchy. Such concerns led to negotiations that transformed the IMF's responsibilities and expanded its reach beyond managing monetary arrangements to advising governments on their macroeconomic policies.

Earlier we discussed the disagreements between U.S. and French policy makers over monetary relations after Bretton Woods and the Smithsonian. The French sought to retain pegged rates and the use of capital controls, and they wanted to constrain the role of the dollar as the central currency in the international system. They believed that it gave U.S. policy makers disproportionate political and economic influence in the global arena as well as the ability to export their economic ills, what has been called *exorbitant privilege*. In contrast, U.S. policy makers favored the free mobility of capital, as well as the ability of governments to let their currencies float. The resolution of this French-U.S. disagreement sits at the heart of the Second Amendment to the IMF's Articles of Agreement, adopted in 1978. The Second Amendment eliminated the role of gold as a reserve asset and legitimated floating exchange rates. It assigned to the IMF the responsibility for overseeing an effective international monetary system and, most important, restored a legal basis for the management of international monetary arrangements that would help to guide IMF activities and government policies, thereby restraining monetary anarchy. Instead of a system designed to promote stable par values, the revision of the Articles of Agreement directed the IMF to promote a stable system of exchange rates by reducing any undue volatility that could spread from one nation to another.

To help the IMF in carrying out this mission, the Second Amendment to the Articles of Agreement expanded the IMF's surveillance of its members' economic affairs. Member states were expected to provide the IMF with economic information and to consult with the IMF if requested. IMF data gathering and surveillance thus moved beyond monitoring exchange-rate policies and current-account balances to overseeing other aspects of economic activity that could affect exchange rates. The expansion of surveillance recognized that macroeconomic policies could have substantial influence on exchange rates. Labor markets, inflation, deficit spending and debt, tax policy, corruption, financial regulatory arrangements, trade policies, and other economic policy areas became legitimate targets of IMF interest in the pursuit of stability in the exchange-rate system.

As a function of their sovereignty, governments naturally resent outside interference in their domestic arenas. The revision to the Articles of Agreement addressed this potential threat to sovereignty by including a general proposition that required the IMF to respect members' domestic political and social policies. Still, its charge to exercise surveillance and to promote an effective monetary system allows the IMF to move beyond technical consultation—to use its financial reserves, and its ability to borrow more, as a carrot in exchange for commitments from governments to implement IMF-recommended policy reforms.

As of the beginning of the European sovereign debt crisis in 2010, no advanced industrialized state had accessed the IMF's financial reserves since the 1970s to address balance-of-payments problems, structural economic difficulties, or macroeconomic dilemmas that could threaten international monetary affairs and stability. Instead, these states had been able to access global financial markets, enabling them to avoid IMF intervention. The sovereign debt crisis that began in Greece and Ireland and spread throughout Europe has challenged the ability of these countries to use private finance instead of IMF resources to manage their problems, but developing and transitional political economies continue to rely heavily on IMF resources in times of crisis. Many have neither sufficient hard currency reserves nor the ability to borrow in global financial markets to defend their currencies or monetary policies against concerted attacks. In such difficult situations, they often turn to the IMF for financial assistance to stem the crises. Such crises provide the IMF with opportunities to use its capital reserves to leverage commitments from governments to reform their economic policies.

During its early years the IMF initially limited its assistance to addressing short-term liquidity problems that contributed to currency and economic instability. With its transformation post–Bretton Woods, the IMF expanded its assistance to include medium-term loans targeted at more stubborn structural problems. This change of focus recognized that short-term liquidity problems, which threaten a currency's stability, might be symptomatic of deeper structural problems. Providing short-term liquidity during a currency crisis may address a symptom and offer a government some respite, but such action is unlikely to repair the structural macroeconomic conditions that produced the crisis. Without addressing these deeper structural problems, governments face a likelihood of recurring short-term crises.

The IMF extends assistance, but usually only after a government signs a **letter of conditionality,** which includes a commitment to address problems that purportedly brought on the crisis in the state's currency and may require domestic reforms that the IMF believes address more fundamental problems in the nation's economy. In a letter of conditionality, the IMF trades financial assistance for policy reforms. The ability to offer financial assistance to governments needing such resources thus gives the IMF leverage over government economic policies, inserts the IMF into the management of domestic macroeconomic arenas, and makes it a central player in the management of crises that threaten international monetary stability.

> A **letter of conditionality** is a letter, signed by representatives of a government, that specifies the government's commitments to address systemic problems in its domestic economy in exchange for financial assistance from an international organization such as the IMF.

The IMF's increasing focus on the macroeconomic conditions of its members is part of a broader shift in the relationship between states and markets that is known as the Washington Consensus. The postwar Bretton Woods system was built on Keynesian foundations, which rejected the laissez-faire notion that markets are self-sustaining and self-correcting. Bretton Woods sought to ensure liberal economic exchange by encouraging governments to employ countercyclical fiscal and monetary policies to mitigate destabilizing economic swings. It recognized that social welfare policies were important tools to limit dislocations, which otherwise could lead to pressures on politicians to adopt policies that would damage market exchange. It created international cooperative mechanisms that could be used to constrain beggar-thy-neighbor policies at times of crisis. The Bretton Woods era saw a shift toward greater government regulation of the economy, with the objectives of limiting the harsher aspects of market discipline, constraining market failure, and protecting market exchange.

The Washington Consensus shifted course by placing greater emphasis on the corrective pressures of market discipline and sought to reduce government regulation and intervention in the economy. Thus, with the swing of intellectual and policy pendulums, the Washington Consensus, and what were labeled neoliberal policy prescriptions, began to supplant the Keynesian framework of the Bretton Woods era. The name of this new approach reflected the prominence of Washington, D.C., and the organizations located there, in international economic affairs. The Washington Consensus promotes economic openness in trade and capital movements, liberalization of financial markets that are open and transparent, fiscal policies that lead to balanced budgets, anti-inflationary monetary policies, stability in exchange-rate relations, expansion of private enterprise, and a reduction in state-owned enterprises. Financial openness, market liberalization, and transparency are its central values. Financial markets provide the discipline that rewards or penalizes political economies, but governments are critical to creating the macroeconomic conditions that these markets mediate—too much or too little intervention gets penalized, while the right amount attracts investment and exchange.

The need for economic assistance for development or for managing economic crises has empowered the Washington Consensus and prompted dramatic reforms in domestic political economies. IMF and U.S. Treasury assistance often comes with conditions attached that push the agenda of the Washington Consensus. In many states, this leverage has led to the privatization of SOEs, increased fiscal constraint by governments, restructuring of labor bargains and markets, financial liberalization, removal or reduction of capital controls, and increased trade openness. In some nations, the pressure to constrain the public sector and meet prescribed macroeconomic targets has produced constraints on the size of the public sector and on social welfare provisions, and has even led to recommendations to privatize aspects of national social welfare systems.

The emphasis on openness, capital mobility, and market pressures is increasing the density of linkages that connect national political economies and is expanding the sensitivity of workers, producers, companies, and markets in one country to those in others. Doubts about the Washington Consensus provoke vigorous debates about which framework is most likely to be conducive to stable monetary relations, to promote growth, to improve social welfare, and to manage volatility. The intellectual pendulum could swing back as economic crises and disparities generate complaints and challenges to the Washington Consensus. The conditionality imposed by the IMF and the Washington Consensus in response to financial crises has occasionally produced hardships in domestic political economies, failed to generate expected economic rewards, rattled politicians as they seek to survive in their political arenas, and created opportunities for speculation about alternatives.

For example, the Washington Consensus pushes fiscal restraint on developing nations at the very time that increasing globalization exposes their citizens to greater risk. By requiring constraints on government deficits and debt, conditionality limits the ability of developing states to fund safety nets when they are most needed to insulate politicians from constituent demands that could damage globalization. Without adequate safety nets, constituents may press for less globalization rather than more. In the wake of the 1997 Asian financial crisis, which led to significant devaluations in many states' currencies in that region, the IMF and other organizations making up the Washington Consensus offered financial assistance that was tied to stringent conditions. These conditions required adoption of neoliberal policies—fiscal and monetary constraint, greater trade openness, and no capital controls—whose underlying idea was that the discipline of the global market would correct the ills that were presumed to have created the financial crisis. Instead, these policies slowed economic activity, imposed hardships on low- and middle-income workers, and created domestic political unrest for governments. Rejecting such policy demands and assistance, the president of Malaysia instead instituted capital controls and reimposed state management of globalization. Ironically, the historical experiences of the developed nations are quite different from the path laid out by the policy prescriptions of the Washington Consensus. In the 1800s, the industrializing nations paced the globalization of that era, but they also led the way in the development of fiscal expenditures and social safety nets that cushioned their citizens from the increased risks that accompanied globalization.

The harsh aftermath of the Asian financial crisis of 1997 and other financial crises produced some soul-searching within many of the organizations that make up the Washington

Consensus. Whichever way the pendulum swings next—toward greater reliance on market discipline or toward increased government regulation—events on the world stage, economic crises, the temptations of beggar-thy-neighbor tactics, and a need to find the means to cooperate will continue to provoke debates, policy experimentation, and new insights and reforms.

CONCLUSION

The breakdown in the Bretton Woods and Smithsonian adjustable-peg monetary systems and the movement to a wide range of monetary arrangements worried many policy makers who remembered the floating-exchange-rate system of the interwar years, as well as the resulting monetary anarchy and breakdown in globalization. Instead of these results, however, the post–Bretton Woods era witnessed a tremendous explosion in global capital mobility, global lending, and financial innovation that challenged state boundaries and encouraged greater globalization, not less. Trade continued to expand as it had during the Bretton Woods era, but the developments in global finance helped to rearrange state-society relations and complemented a shift away from Keynesian economic management toward neoliberal policies.

In this brave new world of global finance, markets enjoy greater ability to reward or punish government policy choices. In this environment, the prospects for governments and societies that get policies right are favorable, but those governments and societies that manage their political economies poorly can face harsh discipline. The shifts in the international political economic system increase the likelihood of greater disparities between those who can play the game of global finance and those who cannot. These changes also add to the uncertainty about how national political economies are connected. The innovations of the post–Bretton Woods era increase the complexity and density of linkages across national political economies. Both good and bad effects can be conveyed across linkages that are not completely understood and are consequently difficult to manage and mitigate, in the case of bad effects.

In the language of causality introduced in chapter 1, the changes in global finance, by creating great complexity, have muddied our understanding of how the global economy operates and how events in one state influence activities in other states. Much of the time better outcomes result from these changes in globalization, but sometimes our ambiguous understanding of this new, more complex environment limits our ability to recognize and avoid potential crises. The challenge for policy makers, public and private, is to develop better understanding of a system of economic and political interactions that is undergoing tremendous change. Otherwise, they will be continually surprised by shocks that travel along this evolving and increasingly dense network of interdependence. Such shocks, if severe and frequent enough, could undermine support for continued globalization among members of polities and encourage governments responsive to such concerns to use their policy tools to constrain the processes of globalization broadly instead of addressing specific deficiencies in global financial networks.

KEY CONCEPTS

capital markets (p. 483)

capital mobility
  hypothesis (p. 499)

contagion network (p. 493)

currency control board
  (p. 472)

disintermediation (p. 485)

European Monetary System
  (EMS) (p. 475)

European Snake (p. 474)

exchange-rate mechanism
  (ERM) (p. 476)

financial futures
  markets (p. 492)

Fleming-Mundell model
  (p. 501)

foreign direct investment
  (FDI) (p. 483)

global capital (p. 483)

hard currency (p. 472)

letter of conditionality
  (p. 505)

Maastricht criteria
  (p. 480)

money markets (p. 483)

neoliberalism (p. 465)

petrodollars (p. 495)

securitization (p. 485)

seignorage (p. 492)

systemic factors
  (p. 489)

unholy trinity (p. 501)

Washington Consensus
  (p. 466)

EXERCISES

1. What is the EMS?

2. In the post–Bretton Woods era, international organizations such as the IMF shifted away from their emphasis on Keynesian policies in their recommendations to governments. What do we call the set of policy prescriptions that replaced those of the Bretton Woods era, and what principles does it emphasize?

3. What is the Washington Consensus? What types of public policies does it promote? Give two examples.

4. What are the three policy components of the "unholy trinity"? Explain the tensions among them.

5. Explain the difference between a system of stable exchange rates and a stable system of exchange rates.

6. You work in the finance ministry of a Latin American nation. For the past several years, your nation's currency has demonstrated unusually high levels of inflation and volatility. In addition to the price and welfare effects they create in your domestic markets, persistent inflation and volatility affect the willingness of international investors to invest in your nation. Your nation is also being pressured by the IMF to address these problems. One of your Latin American neighbor countries has adopted a currency control board to address such policy concerns.

What is a currency control board and what are its strengths and weaknesses? Should your nation also adopt a currency control board?

7. Technological change has helped to lower obstacles to the international flow of capital. Many attribute primary responsibility for financial globalization to such changes. Did technological innovation cause financial globalization? What other factors contribute to it? How?

8. How does financial globalization differ from financial liberalization?

9. Summarize the three stages created in the Maastricht Treaty. What are the convergence criteria of the Maastricht Treaty? What is the logic underpinning the need for the convergence criteria?

10. Generally, financial globalization improved access to capital resources for many, but some have gained disproportionately. Who has gained disproportionately and why? Who has suffered from the disparity?

11. According to the capital mobility hypothesis, what is the relation between capital and political bargaining power? How does this work?

FURTHER READING

Cohen, Benjamin J. 1998. *The Geography of Money*. Ithaca, NY: Cornell University Press.

Eichengreen, Barry. 1996. *Globalizing Capital: A History of the International Monetary System*. Princeton, NJ: Princeton University Press.

———. 2011. *Exorbitant Privilege: The Rise and Fall of the Dollar and the Future of the International Monetary System*. New York: Oxford University Press.

Garrett, Geoffrey. 1998. *Partisan Politics in a Global Economy*. New York: Cambridge University Press.

Goldstein, Morris. 1998. *The Asian Financial Crisis: Causes, Cures, and Systemic Implications*. Washington, DC: Institute for International Economics.

Helleiner, Eric. 1994. *States and the Reemergence of Global Finance: From Bretton Woods to the 1990s*. Ithaca, NY: Cornell University Press.

Keylor, William R. 2006. *The Twentieth-Century World and Beyond: An International History since 1900*. 5th ed. New York: Oxford University Press.

Maxfield, Sylvia. 1997. *Gatekeepers of Growth*. Princeton, NJ: Princeton University Press.

Mosely, Layna. 2003. *Global Capital and National Governments*. New York: Cambridge University Press.

Pauly, Louis W. 1997. *Who Elected the Bankers? Surveillance and Control in the World Economy.* Ithaca, NY: Cornell University Press.

Rodrik, Dani. 1997. *Has Globalization Gone Too Far?* Washington, DC: Institute for International Economics.

———. 1999. *The New Global Economy and Developing Countries.* Washington, DC: Overseas Development Council.

Ruda, Nita. 2008. *Globalization and the Race to the Bottom in Developing Countries: Who Really Gets Hurt?* New York: Cambridge University Press.

Sobel, Andrew C. 1994. *Domestic Choices, International Markets: Dismantling National Barriers and Liberalizing Securities Markets.* Ann Arbor: University of Michigan Press.

———. 1999. *State Institutions, Private Incentives, Global Capital.* Ann Arbor: University of Michigan Press.

13 Détente and the End of the Cold War: Globalization during Transition

There are many people in the world who really don't understand, or say they don't, what is the great issue between the free world and the Communist world. Let them come to Berlin. . . . All free men, wherever they may live, are citizens of Berlin, and, therefore, as a free man, I take pride in the words "Ich bin ein Berliner."

—*President John F. Kennedy, Berlin, June 26, 1963*

General Secretary Gorbachev, if you seek peace, if you seek prosperity for the Soviet Union and Eastern Europe, if you seek liberalization: Come here to this gate! Mr. Gorbachev, open this gate! Mr. Gorbachev, tear down this wall!

—*President Ronald Reagan, Berlin, June 12, 1987*

Any discussion of world affairs in the twentieth century must consider the superpower tensions between the United States and the Soviet Union, the Cold War between Eastern and Western blocs, the thawing and renewal of East-West economic relations that began with détente, and the dismantling and disintegration of communist regimes from 1989 to 1991. Following a long period of hostile, sometimes violent, confrontation between competing forms of political economic relations, tensions began to ease. Trade, migration, capital flows, and the exchange of information and culture improved across the East-West divide, creating connections that brought the communist Eastern bloc into active engagement with the larger global capitalist political economy.

COLD WAR TO POST–COLD WAR TRANSFORMATION

For twenty to thirty years following World War II, the United States and the Soviet Union, and their allies, were involved in a cold war. Following the Cuban Missile Crisis in 1962, both Soviet and American leaders began to seek out ways to ease tensions between the two blocs.

East-West economic linkages improved in fits and starts, and by the end of the century, the communist governments of the Eastern bloc nations had fallen and their successor regimes had started down a path of significant economic and democratic liberalization, albeit with different degrees of success. The Soviet Union and its domination of the Eastern bloc became an artifact of historical memory. Aside from a dramatic change in political-military relations, the end of the Soviet empire removed the twentieth century's most significant threat to a global political economy built on market transactions. With greater integration and the ongoing political economic transformation, these nations have become significant contributors to the global economy and important actors in global affairs. They have educated populations, some have potentially large domestic markets, and some are rich in raw materials.

THE COMMAND ECONOMIES GRADUALLY JOIN THE GLOBAL ECONOMY

The increasing integration of the Soviet, Eastern European, and Chinese economies into the global economy began in the 1960s, but the most dramatic changes took place in the post–Bretton Woods era, and they deserve special attention. When these states were under communist rule, from the end of World War II until the events of 1989–1991, we called them **command economies** because of the hierarchical organization of their economic activity. In a command economy, economic activity is centrally directed through the hierarchical mechanisms of the state, unlike the decentralized organization of economic activity in a market economy (recall the discussion in chapter 1 of centralized and decentralized economies). After 1989 and the breakdown in Communist Party control in these states, we began calling them **transitional political economies,** since they began to change the organization of their political, economic, and social relations to allow greater political competition and decentralized economic exchange—a shift from hierarchical communist political economies to more democratic, market-oriented political economies. Some of these transitional political economies—such as Poland, Slovenia, Hungary, the Baltic states, and the former East Germany—have made significant strides in their transitions, even qualifying for membership in the European Union, but others lag behind.

> **Command economies** are systems in which allocation mechanisms are centrally directed through the hierarchical mechanisms of the state, unlike the decentralized organization of economic activity in a market economy. **Transitional political economies** are states that are trying to change the organization of their political, economic, and social relations to allow greater political competition and decentralized economic exchange. **Containment** was the name given to the policy of using military and economic capabilities to encircle, restrict, and challenge the Soviet Union and its sphere of influence.

For years following World War II, the command economies of the Soviet Union and its Eastern bloc remained largely separate from the broader global economy. This isolation was partly a matter of policy choice by the Soviet leadership, which sought to consolidate its authority within its sphere of influence, and partly a function of the policy of **containment** adopted by the United States and the Western bloc in the late 1940s as the cornerstone of their Cold War strategy. Eastern bloc participation in market-oriented global finance and trade remained relatively limited for many years as domestic economic policy preferences and international tensions hampered East-West economic interactions. Eastern bloc nations traded heavily with each other, although Soviet bureaucrats and policy makers directed much of this trade from their positions in the power hierarchy. The bulk of economic activity in the Soviet Union and the Eastern bloc centered on a series of five-year plans that established production targets. Such economic activity and trade faced no market discipline; specialization occurred as a matter of bureaucratic fiat rather than market-driven creative destruction. Eastern bloc nations participated in an organization called the Council for Mutual Economic Assistance (Comecon), which was the economic equivalent of the Warsaw Pact (the Soviet-led political-military alliance).

A gradual thawing of East-West political economic relations from the mid-1960s onward led to an influx of ideas, advice, goods, technology, assistance, and investment from the Western bloc into the Eastern bloc economies. The pace of such inflows quickened following the dismantling of the Eastern bloc and the disintegration of the Soviet Union between 1989 and 1991. The expanding participation and increasing integration of the Eastern bloc nations into the global economy required significant changes in the foreign policies of East and West, as well as major shifts in the domestic political economic policies in the East. The changes advanced in two stages: first, a thawing of political-military relations in the late 1960s and early 1970s promoted the initial integration of these economies into the global political economy; and second, domestic economic and political liberalization in the late 1980s and early 1990s fueled further integration. Shifts in the domestic political economies of the Eastern bloc nations, changes in the perspectives of policy makers in the Western bloc, and events and lessons in global affairs combined to promote greater cooperation and integration, but the changes and lessons took time, and many were painful and costly, as has been shown in earlier examples of growing international exchange. The remainder of this chapter covers these two aspects of integration between East and West, between command economies and market economies.

DÉTENTE AND SHIFTS IN THE INTERNATIONAL POLITICAL-MILITARY CONTEXT LEAD TO IMPROVED ECONOMIC RELATIONS

The end of World War II left Europe divided into two camps—a Soviet-led Eastern bloc and a U.S.-led Western bloc—that were separated by distinct ideologies and approaches to the organization of political economic life that made them inherently hostile to each other. Although the Soviet Union and the United States had been allies during the war, relations between these two leading states soured quickly after the defeat and division of Germany. A series of confrontations over the status of Berlin, a nuclear weapons race, the Korean War, the construction of the Berlin Wall, and other crises punctuated the Cold War, in which U.S. and Soviet combat troops faced each other in central Europe and U.S. and Soviet military advisers aided opposing sides in many regional conflicts around the globe. But the super-powers themselves never engaged in direct physical combat with each other—at least not admittedly.

Détente is the reduction of political-military tensions and improvement of economic relations between the United States and the Soviet Union that began in the late 1960s.

The Cold War continued into the 1960s, but the East-West showdown peaked and then relaxed during that decade. This easing up led to **détente,** a reduction of political-military tensions and improved economic relations. Several political-military factors helped to promote more constructive engagement. First, the peaceful resolution of the Cuban Missile Crisis and the narrowing of the U.S.-Soviet strategic weapons gap led to greater East-West cooperation to reduce the possibility of catastrophic military conflict. Second, the ascension of Willy Brandt and his political agenda in West Germany promoted the resolution of issues that had persisted since the end of World War II and obstructed a political settlement in Europe. Third, the conclusion of the U.S. intervention in Vietnam removed important obstacles to more amicable relations between East and West. Fourth, discontent within the Communist bloc created opportunities for the West to seek rapprochement with both the Chinese and the Soviets.

The Cuban Crisis and a U.S.-Soviet Strategic Gap Lead to Greater Cooperation

In 1962 the Cuban Missile Crisis brought the world to the precipice of nuclear confrontation, terrifying policy makers and their publics. Premier Nikita Khrushchev's attempt to base Soviet intermediate-range missiles in Cuba revealed weaknesses in the Soviet Union's strategic weapons capabilities and proved its inability to challenge U.S. supremacy as a global power beyond the Eurasian land mass. The Soviet retreat in the face of U.S. ultimatums embarrassed Khrushchev and caused many in the Soviet leadership to lose confidence in him, which fueled his downfall and the ascendancy of Leonid Brezhnev to power. The Cuban face-off uncovered strategic shortcomings and diplomatic limitations that could generate miscommunication, foster misunderstanding, impose dangerous time pressures on decision makers, and introduce instabilities into the U.S.-Soviet bargaining relationship. These problems increased the likelihood of potential missteps, which could lead to dangerous policy choices, including an otherwise avoidable use of nuclear weapons.

The lessons of the Cuban crisis prompted changes in U.S. and Soviet diplomatic and military practices that would help improve East-West relations within a decade. Soviet policy makers shifted away from the confrontational approach that had led to the crises in Berlin and Cuba, and those on both sides sought to change the dynamics of the nuclear relationship in order to reduce the likelihood of unintended nuclear confrontation. Soviet and U.S. policy makers engaged in a series of arms control discussions to limit destabilizing weapons, reduce uncertainty, and promote dialogue in the superpowers' relationship. The Nuclear Test Ban Treaty, the Hot-Line Agreement, the Outer Space Treaty, the Nuclear Non-proliferation Treaty, the Strategic Arms Limitation Treaties (SALT I and SALT II), the Mutual and Balanced Force Reductions talks that led to the Conventional Armed Forces in Europe Treaty, and other agreements arose from this diplomatic engagement that started in the aftermath of the Cuban crisis. These negotiations restructured the international political-military landscape, eased East-West tensions, increased stability in interbloc political-military relations, and created precedents for interbloc cooperation.

Concurrent with these political initiatives to reduce potentially catastrophic mishaps in the nuclear relationship, the Soviets sought to achieve strategic parity with the United States. They increased the pace of their long-range weapons programs, built up their strategic intercontinental missile forces, improved their intermediate-range nuclear weapons for the European theater, enlarged their submarine-based nuclear missile capabilities, and created an oceangoing surface fleet capable of projecting Soviet power beyond the Eurasian land mass. The Soviets achieved the goal of nuclear parity with the United States by the time of the Nixon administration, ensuring that each side had the ability to inflict horrifying and unacceptable losses on the other side, even after suffering an initial attack by the other side. This situation of **mutually assured destruction (MAD)** became the status quo, increasing stability and decreasing the likelihood of the unthinkable.

> **Mutually assured destruction (MAD)** is the Cold War situation in which each side had the ability to inflict unacceptable losses on the other side, even after suffering an initial attack by the other side.

It may seem paradoxical that the improvements in Soviet strategic capabilities that led to nuclear parity actually contributed to improving interbloc relations and the integration of the Eastern bloc economies into the global economy, but in fact the shifts in Soviet military strategy and weapons development empowered Soviet policy makers to undertake a diplomatic shift toward more constructive engagement with the West. The emergence of strategic equivalence between the superpowers removed the possibility of one-sided nuclear intimidation and extortion, punctuated the threat of mutual destruction, illuminated the dysfunctional nature of an uncontrolled arms race, and created a foundation for negotiation between equals. Both sides became increasingly interested in limiting the expensive nuclear arms race and the destabilizing competition between them. The Cuban Missile Crisis revealed the dangers of previous policies and force structures. Recognizing the threat pushed the United States and the Soviet Union toward arms control negotiations, changes in force structures, more constructive engagement, and improvement in the channels of communication between them.

The Two Germanys and Political Settlement in Europe Transform the Global Context

Even with improvements in East-West diplomatic relations, unresolved issues regarding the status of East and West Germany hampered rapprochement between the two sides. The fate of the two German states and of Berlin, along with West German territorial disputes with Poland and Czechoslovakia over the redrawing of national boundaries in 1945, remained serious obstacles to normalization of relations (see map 13.1). Following the division of Germany into two states in 1949, West German chancellor Konrad Adenauer rejected East German sovereignty and announced the objective of a unified German state. The Hallstein Doctrine enshrined this position in 1955, claiming for the West German government the sole right to represent all Germans.

The Hallstein Doctrine denied the authority of the East German state and declared that the West German government would regard diplomatic recognition of East Germany as an unfriendly act. West Germany severed diplomatic relations with Eastern European governments that recognized East Germany, with the exception of the Soviet Union. Over the same period, the West German government refused to renounce its claims on territory awarded to Poland and Czechoslovakia following World War II. West Germany's hopes for unification and a redrawing of postwar boundaries, its refusal to accept the political and

| Map 13.1 | **Europe at the End of the Cold War** |

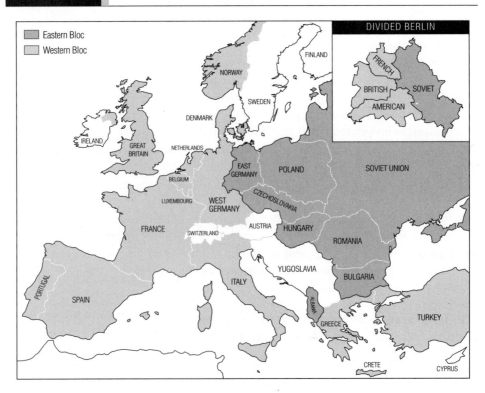

territorial status quo, kept alive Soviet and Eastern European fears of a resurgent Germany and restrained Soviet allies from seeking normalization of relations. This implicit threat posed a major obstacle to a thawing of the Cold War and a normalization of economic relations.

West German intransigence softened in 1966 with the election of a new governing coalition, which elevated Willy Brandt (a Social Democrat) to the position of foreign minister, where he signaled a significant shift in the West German position with his policy of **Ostpolitik**, or Eastern policy. *Ostpolitik* sought the normalization of relations between West Germany and Eastern European states, even if this meant forgoing both unification and claims on the territories ceded to

> *Ostpolitik* (Eastern policy) is the policy pursued by West Germany in the 1960s that sought the normalization of relations with Eastern European states.

Poland and Czechoslovakia at the end of World War II. Brandt did not reject unification as a goal, but *Ostpolitik* dropped it as a precondition for the normalization of relations. West Germany established formal diplomatic ties with Hungary in 1967 and continued working toward the normalization of political and economic relations with other Eastern European states. Prospects for the political settlement of German issues improved further with the West German elections in 1969, in which Brandt's Social Democrats dominated the coalition government that emerged and Brandt ascended to the chancellorship.

As chancellor, Brandt continued his efforts to normalize relations with Eastern Europe. He reduced Soviet fears of a reawakened, aggressive Germany by signing the Nuclear Non-proliferation Treaty and negotiating a nonaggression agreement with the Soviets that recognized the territorial status quo in Europe. Next, West Germany entered into a nonaggression treaty with Poland that accepted the German-Polish boundaries imposed at the end of World War II. In 1973, West Germany recognized the existing German and Czechoslovak borders and renounced the Munich Pact of 1938, abandoning any claims on the Sudetenland. The West German territorial claims that had posed obstructions to a political settlement in Europe no longer existed.

East German sovereignty and the question of Berlin were the major remaining barriers to improved European political relations. The resignation from office of the East German leader Walter Ulbricht in 1971 and the rise of Erich Honecker as his successor opened the door for the removal of these remaining stumbling blocks. The four occupying powers in Berlin (the United States, the United Kingdom, France, and the Soviet Union) formally recognized the "special relationship" between West Berlin and West Germany and rejected East Germany's demand that it control access to the entire city. In December 1972, the Soviets pressured East Germany to sign the Basic Treaty with West Germany, which called for greater commercial ties between the two Germanys and the exchange of diplomatic missions. In 1973, East and West Germany gained membership in the United Nations as individual sovereign states. The successful resolution of all these matters—German territorial demands, the Berlin dilemma, and sovereignty issues—underpinned the political settlement in Europe, transformed the global context, and substantially lowered barriers to improved East-West commercial relations.

The Vietnam War's Resolution Contributes to Improved East-West Relations

U.S. military involvement in Vietnam imposed another obstacle to improved East-West relations. The United States became engaged in Indochina in the 1950s, providing support for French colonial and neocolonial activities. The United States recognized the French puppet government of Emperor Bao Dai and subsidized a significant portion of French military costs during the French-Vietminh conflict. However, the Vietnamese nationalists under Ho Chi Minh persevered, clinching victory with a stunning defeat of the French forces at Dien Bien Phu. This was a defeat of a military of an advanced industrialized Western political economy by nationalist forces from a non-Western peasant economy—a harbinger of anti-colonial success and the power of nationalist sentiments in the face of modern, sophisticated military opposition. In 1954, after eight years of conflict, the French signed a peace treaty in Geneva and withdrew from Indochina, but the United States remained involved. The Geneva Agreement divided Vietnam temporarily, leaving Ho Chi Minh and the Vietminh as rulers north of the 17th Parallel, while Ngo Dinh Diem, an anti-Communist and U.S.-educated Catholic, led the government south of the line (see map 13.2).

The treaty called for a national plebiscite to be held within two years under United Nations auspices, in order to unify the country and determine its sole government. But U.S. president Dwight Eisenhower, anticipating that such an election would produce a united Vietnam governed by Ho Chi Minh and his supporters, blocked the national vote. Instead, in 1954 policy makers from the United States and other countries agreed to form a regional security pact called the South East Asia Treaty Organization (SEATO), which committed the member states to defend South Vietnam and other regional governments against Communist aggression. Under the guise of SEATO obligations, U.S. military and economic support flowed in to assist Diem and the South Vietnamese government. U.S. assistance expanded over time, as a guerrilla war broke out in the South following the cancellation of the plebiscite. Meanwhile, the Soviet Union and the People's Republic of China provided Ho Chi Minh's government with military and economic aid.

Diem's government proved incredibly corrupt and oppressive, stimulating non-Communist opposition, which formed a coalition with the Communist Viet Minh to oppose Diem. The number of U.S. military advisers to the South Vietnamese government continued to grow. Only about 300 U.S. military advisers had been assigned to the South Vietnamese government after the Geneva Agreement in 1954, but this number had more than doubled before the end of the decade. When President Kennedy took office in 1961, there were almost 900 U.S. advisers helping to train the South Vietnamese forces. This number then tripled before the end of the year, and it exceeded 16,000 by the time of Kennedy's assassination in 1963.

Map 13.2	**Divided Vietnam**

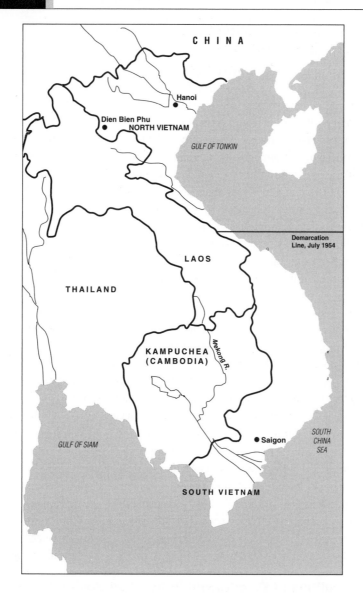

By 1965, the United States had moved beyond its advisory role to become an active combatant on the ground. At first, President Lyndon Johnson sent in two battalions of U.S. Marines, but the number quickly increased to more than 184,000 ground troops by year's end. The number of U.S. troops involved in military operations in Vietnam swelled to almost 550,000 at the height of U.S. engagement. The Soviets, Chinese, and other members of the Eastern bloc could go only so far down the road of normalization of relations with the West as long as U.S. troops were actively engaged in military conflict with a nation in the Communist sphere.

Resistance by North Vietnamese regular army troops and Vietcong guerrillas frustrated U.S. and South Vietnamese efforts. As casualties mounted and time wore on, domestic disagreements over U.S. involvement created significant cleavage and dissension within the U.S. polity, coloring American electoral politics. Under President Nixon and Secretary of State Henry Kissinger, the United States and North Vietnam finally negotiated a settlement that led to U.S. military withdrawal from Vietnam in 1973. Without U.S. military backing, it was only a matter of time before the government and military of South Vietnam faced defeat by the North. In 1975 North Vietnamese troops triumphed over the South Vietnamese, occupying Saigon and the South, and the two Vietnams became a single state.

Resolution of the conflict in Vietnam and the resulting decrease in U.S. adventurism created an opening for improved East-West political and economic relations. The U.S. experience in Vietnam revived the nation's isolationist leanings, increased American wariness of foreign entanglements, and made U.S. policy makers think twice before they engaged in military adventurism in distant parts of the world. Vietnam educated U.S. policy makers and their public about the limitations of U.S. power and about the need for domestic consensus in foreign policy, and it led to U.S. political-military retrenchment in the global arena. As U.S. policy makers became more cautious about U.S. military commitments overseas, questions arose in Europe about the commitment of the United States to its Western European partners. The European allies of the United States faced the possibility of a reduced U.S. military commitment to Europe, which could force politically unpopular increases in their own defense expenditures. Reduction of East-West political-military tensions in Europe offered a more appealing alternative to such defense expenditures.

As the American public grew disillusioned with the Cold War and U.S. foreign policy became more cautious, Western European governments, fearing a U.S. retrenchment in Europe, sought to improve relations with the Eastern bloc. In Europe, all the major parties recognized the advantages of normalizing East-West relations, pursuing détente, and stabilizing military relations. The Mutual and Balanced Force Reductions negotiations in Vienna and the European Security Conference in Helsinki in 1973 grew out of this recognition. American withdrawal from Vietnam also removed a major obstacle to Soviet-American and Sino-American rapprochement. With the U.S. withdrawal from Vietnam, the Soviets and Chinese lost an important motivation for a common front, and long-standing Sino-Soviet tensions reemerged.

Global Implications of Discord within the Sino-Soviet Alliance

From its onset, the Sino-Soviet alliance had proved to be an uneasy coalition. Prior to the victory of Mao Zedong's Communists over Chiang Kai-shek's Nationalists in 1949, the Soviets had recognized the Nationalists as the official government of China. Although some U.S. policy makers advocated exploiting the potential division in the Communist bloc by recognizing the triumphant Chinese Communist regime on the mainland, the Korean War destroyed any prospects for Sino-American rapprochement during the 1950s and pushed the Soviets and Chinese closer together. Despite earlier Soviet recognition of the Nationalist government, the Chinese Communists looked to the Soviets for assistance. Responding with military assistance during the Korean War and committing to long-term development loans, the Soviet Union became China's primary trading partner in the 1950s.

But Soviet assistance came at a price that was sometimes distressingly high for the Chinese. The Soviets required repayment for the military assistance extended during the Korean War. Moreover, the level of Soviet economic assistance proved disappointing. Economic development aid extended to India and other non-Communist states by the Soviets actually exceeded their aid to China. Much of the Soviet assistance to China came tied to Soviet access to Chinese resources. In 1957, the Soviets offered technical assistance to China's nascent nuclear program, but only if China agreed to Soviet control of Chinese nuclear weapons and greater coordination of the two nations' foreign policies. When the Chinese rejected this demand as an infringement on their sovereignty, the Soviets responded by withholding assistance to China's nuclear program.

Significant territorial disputes fueled Sino-Soviet tensions. Officially, the Soviet Union remained neutral during the 1959 Sino-Indian territorial dispute over Tibet and the Himalayan frontier, and also when bloody border clashes again broke out between China and India in 1962. But India, a non-Communist state, was receiving substantial economic and military assistance from the Soviet Union before, during, and after the Sino-Indian conflicts. The Soviets remained silent during the Quemoy and Matsu crisis between the mainland Chinese Communists and the Nationalists on Taiwan. Border disputes between China and the Soviet Union itself provided more dramatic and prophetic signs of tense Sino-Soviet relations. When the Chinese disputed Soviet claims to territory that Russia had obtained by treaties during the 1800s, the disagreement turned violent as Chinese and Soviet troops clashed along the border. As such military confrontations escalated, the Soviets redeployed troops, aircraft, and nuclear weapons from Eastern Europe to the Chinese frontier.

Sino-Soviet disagreements grew after the Soviet embarrassment in the Cuban Missile Crisis. The expanding Sino-Soviet rift spilled over to other nations in the Communist sphere. By the mid-1960s, the West sensed an opportunity to exploit the increasing divisions in the Communist bloc, but Vietnam continued to overshadow Sino-Soviet divisions. However, Vietnam began to fade as an obstruction by the end of the decade, as the Nixon administration took office in 1969 and pursued settlement with North Vietnam. Hoping to take advantage of Sino-Soviet tensions, the United States embarked on a diplomatic strategy to normalize relations with China and exploit the split in the Communist bloc.

U.S. policy makers began playing the so-called **China card**, embarking on policies such as relaxation of American trade and travel restrictions, ping-pong

> The **China card** describes a U.S. diplomatic strategy to normalize relations with China in order to exploit the growing split between China and the Soviet Union.

diplomacy, shuttle diplomacy by Secretary of State Henry Kissinger, support of Pakistan against China's enemy India, and significant changes in U.S. policy toward Taiwan. These measures paved the way for President Nixon's groundbreaking visit to the People's Republic of China in 1972. Sino-American rapprochement allowed China to balance the Soviet military buildup on its borders by redeploying troops to the northwestern Chinese frontier. Détente, the end of U.S. involvement in Vietnam, and the growing divisions in the Communist bloc thus transformed the international political-military context and created opportunities for improvements in East-West relations.

DOMESTIC SHIFTS IN THE EASTERN BLOC AND CHINA GENERATE GREATER INTERNATIONAL EXCHANGE

At the same time that the global political-military context was becoming more conducive to improved East-West relations, domestic conditions in the Eastern bloc were feeding growing interest among Eastern bloc policy makers in greater interaction with the global economy. Comecon's inability to keep pace with Western European economic growth, food riots in Poland in 1970, and increasing tensions over the Soviet Union's economic exploitation of its Eastern European allies roused significant concerns and dissatisfaction over Eastern bloc economic policies. Unmet domestic consumer demands led to increasing frustration among the Eastern bloc polities and produced domestic pressures for increased economic openings to the West. These pressures led Eastern bloc policy makers to seek greater exchange with the West to provide them with materials, capital, skills, and information that could promote faster economic expansion and address the unmet needs of Eastern bloc consumers. In the end, a series of policy changes led to economic and political liberalization that undermined Communist Party control in most Eastern bloc states.

President Richard Nixon and Chinese premier Zhou Enlai enjoy a stroll in Hangzhou, China, in February 1972 during a historic visit that resulted when Nixon took advantage of dissension in the Communist bloc to play the "China card." Secretary of State Henry Kissinger laid the groundwork for improved U.S.-Sino relations during secret trips to the People's Republic. Nixon's opening to China represented a dramatic move toward the normalization of U.S.-Sino relations and the integration of China into the global political economy.

Access to Western Markets, Technology, and Capital Encourages Development

In 1964, a faction led by Leonid Brezhnev and Alexei Kosygin pushed Nikita Khrushchev from power following the Cuban Missile Crisis. Brezhnev, who by 1969 had outmaneuvered Kosygin for the Soviet premiership, viewed improved economic and diplomatic ties with the West as a pathway to stimulating Soviet economic growth. The East-West arms race had led to swollen military budgets, tying up capital that could be invested in economic growth if it were not being spent on an arms race that no one could win. Greater economic integration with the Western bloc economies would promote economic specialization and improve access to materials, information, skills, and capital that could promote economic advancement. What a nation imports is more critical to the nation's development than what it exports. The Eastern bloc states turned to the West for capital, technology, and other assistance to develop their raw materials and modernize their industrial bases. In retrospect this was a clear indication that the long-term strategy of containment was working and the U.S.-led global political economy was prevailing in the Cold War.

Despite the trend toward improving relations, political and economic détente stalled in the late 1970s. The direction of trade quickly turned disturbingly one-sided, as Eastern bloc exports to the West slumped. Large increases in energy costs produced by the OPEC crises squeezed non–energy export markets and led to further reduction of Eastern exports to the West. This increasing gap between imports and exports hindered the Eastern bloc states' ability to finance development through hard currency earnings from exports, but it also signaled a potential balance-of-payments crisis if the shortfall in earnings should prevent them from meeting their international payment obligations. As noted in chapter 12, hard currencies are those that can readily be used and accepted in international transactions because they will hold their value over time and present relatively little currency risk to the parties of such transactions.

Eastern bloc policy makers could limit Western imports—goods, technology, and expertise—in order to reduce the balance-of-payments pressures, but doing so would delay the development of the East's resources, slow the construction and conversion of industrial plants, and add to the dissatisfaction among Eastern bloc consumers. Rather than thus limiting imports, delaying modernization, and risking more disaffection in their polities, Eastern bloc policy makers turned to the global capital markets as an alternative. Borrowing in global capital markets offered an avenue through which they could cover their chronic balance-of-payments deficits and finance continued economic expansion. Global borrowing by Comecon states more than doubled in 1974–1975, as these states accessed approximately $2.1 billion in commercial loans and $140 million in bond issues in the global capital markets. Western investors and bankers were happy to extend capital, assuming that centralized control of those economies and the economic strength of the resource-rich Soviet Union limited risk and secured such loans. Eastern bloc engagement with Western capital markets and consumption of Western goods, technology, and expertise increased the connections and interdependence across the blocs.

Seconds Thoughts, Overleveraged Political Economies, and International Lending

By the late 1970s, Western governments and financiers began to pull back from extending such liberal credit to the Eastern bloc states. Worries grew about the sizes of the trade deficits of most Comecon nations and their growing debt obligations in relation to hard currency earnings from exports. Questions arose about the ability of Eastern bloc borrowers to service their growing debt obligations, about the potential consequences for the stability of the global economy if they should fail to meet those obligations, about the risks to Western political economies from this threat, and about the wisdom of greater integration under these circumstances. Western public and private decision makers had assumed, mistakenly or not, that the centralized management of the Eastern bloc economies could protect against these economies' possible failure to service their external debt obligations and that the Soviet Union would stand behind the debt obligations of its allies. But the lack of information about their indebtedness, creditworthiness, and economic projects began to feed uncertainty and to affect the willingness of Western financial institutions to extend credit to Eastern bloc borrowers. Senator Henry Jackson expressed these worries openly before a congressional investigating committee in April 1977:

> By all accounts, Soviet and East European indebtedness to the West has reached major proportions. And yet, estimates of that debt vary widely—from about $27 billion to about $45 billion overall. By any measure, these sums are substantial—and they are growing. It is all the more disturbing that official and private estimates of that debt diverge so greatly. An apparent inability to gain consistent and reliable information about the extent of Soviet and East European borrowing is, itself, a significant part of the problem.
>
> Large-scale loans to the Soviet Union and the East European countries were once thought of as a way to gain "leverage" over these governments. What may be happening instead is that the debtors are on the verge of obtaining leverage over Western governments by the substantial interest in repayment that the Western banking system may be acquiring. . . .
>
> Are we on sound ground if we assume that the Soviet Union and the states of Eastern Europe will be able to earn enough hard currency to repay their mounting obligations?

Ironically, the activities undertaken to increase relations across blocs and to integrate the Eastern bloc into the Western-dominated global economy, which generated a rush by Western financiers to capitalize on new access, also created some financial risks and exposure for Western capital markets. The recognition of such risk would become more apparent with the Third World Debt Crisis in 1983, when many developing political economies found it impossible to service their debt obligations to Western financial institutions. At this point, Western bankers realized they had similar exposure and similar limited information about their loans to Eastern bloc political economies.

Renewal of Political-Military Tensions
Interrupts the Eastern Bloc's Global Economic Integration

On the political front, East-West rapprochement also stalled despite the achievement of the 1975 conference held in Helsinki, Finland, that marked the formal end of the Cold War in Europe. The Helsinki conference resolved territorial and sovereignty issues that had plagued East-West relations since World War II. Yet Cold War tensions and the nuclear arms race reemerged as U.S.-Soviet arms control negotiations stumbled over technological advances in Soviet weaponry. Theater nuclear weapons—those limited by range to a particular area of operations—in Europe became problematic as the Soviets replaced old intermediate-range missiles with more capable systems. Under pressure from European allies and seeking to reinforce the credibility of the U.S. deterrent umbrella over Western Europe, President Carter committed a new generation of intermediate-range nuclear weapons to deployment in Europe.

Then, in late 1979, Soviet troops entered Afghanistan to support the pro-Soviet government in Kabul against militant opposition. This action marked the first time since World War II that Soviet troops had formally intervened outside Eastern Europe. Earlier that year, the overthrow of the shah of Iran by Muslim fundamentalists had severely damaged U.S. strategic capabilities in the oil-rich region and produced a significant cutback in Iranian oil production, which caused long lines at gas pumps and contributed to a global economic slowdown. In the context of this shift in the regional geopolitical landscape, President Carter viewed Soviet military adventurism in Afghanistan as a threat to vital U.S. interests—specifically, access to oil resources, which is a recurring theme in U.S. foreign policy.

Carter announced that the United States would use all resources necessary to protect vital U.S. national interests in the region. This commitment became known as the Carter Doctrine. In response to Soviet intervention in Afghanistan, U.S. policy makers repaired damaged relations with the military regime in Pakistan, sought military facilities in the region to replace those lost in the downfall of the shah, provided assistance to the Afghan rebels fighting the Soviet-supported Kabul government, created a rapid deployment force for the Persian Gulf region, and increased U.S. military capabilities throughout the region. Ironically, the U.S. assistance to Afghan resistance forces included aid to a young Saudi named Osama bin Laden, thus helping his rise to influence.

The Reagan administration continued and accelerated these initiatives. At the beginning of his first term in office, President Reagan dramatically increased U.S. defense expenditures, thereby exploding government deficits and debt but reaffirming the military versions of the U.S. policy of containment that had been the cornerstone of U.S. foreign policy since the Truman administration. These additional U.S. defense expenditures raised the costs and stakes of the U.S.-Soviet arms race. The renewal of Cold War tensions, uncertainty about the ability of Eastern bloc nations to service their growing debt burdens, and the Third World Debt Crisis all coincided to slow or interrupt the integration of Eastern bloc states into the global economy. This interruption would prove temporary, and China offered a hint of the future.

China Takes Steps toward Liberalization

Under the leadership of Deng Xiaoping, China rejected lingering inclinations toward the self-reliant and centralized development strategies of Mao Zedong, moving instead to embrace export-oriented production, a limited free market, and an increasing amount of private ownership. The Chinese actively sought overseas development assistance and direct loans by requesting United Nations Development Program assistance in 1978; China soon became the largest recipient of UNDP funds.

China joined the World Bank, the IMF, and the Asian Development Bank, and in 1980 it began receiving IMF and World Bank assistance. By mid-decade, the country had obtained more than $5.5 billion in World Bank funds. Chinese policy makers moved cautiously, trying to constrain China's level of external indebtedness even as they sought overseas capital, but they abandoned their restraint by the mid-1980s. More than $7 billion of foreign direct investment flowed into China between 1979 and 1987. This flow of capital and investment to China reflected not only the appeal of China's potentially huge domestic market but also the success of Sino-American rapprochement and mutual apprehension over Soviet military adventurism in Afghanistan. The invasion of Cambodia by Vietnam, a Soviet client, reinforced Chinese and U.S. concerns. Political-military events that exacerbated Soviet-American tensions thus strengthened Sino-American relations. The most populous political economy in the world, and a major Pacific Rim nation, was moving from the shadows of the global capitalist political economy to becoming integral to that global arena. While not fully adopting the rules of the Washington Consensus, Chinese policy makers were at least engaged with the major institutions of the Washington Consensus. The continued transformation of the Chinese economy over the next twenty years would lift more that 400 million Chinese out of poverty, creating new consumers, producers, and markets in the global economy.

Arms Control, Perestroika, and Glasnost Change the Political Economic Landscape

During this period, the Soviet Union was burdened with unstable leadership, experiencing four changes in leaders in a little more than three years: Brezhnev died in 1982; his successor, Yuri Andropov, in early 1984; and Konstantin Chernenko, Andropov's successor, in 1985. When Mikhail Gorbachev ascended to the leadership of the Soviet Communist Party in 1985, he began moving to halt and reverse the deterioration of the Soviet economy, to limit the costly political-military competition with the United States that was diverting resources from the expansion of economic welfare at home, and to reduce U.S.-Soviet tensions. He also introduced important policy changes that ultimately led to the dismantling of the Eastern bloc and the breakup of the Soviet Union.

Internationally, Gorbachev sought to curtail the arms race with the United States that was sapping resources that could be directed to productive enterprises in the Soviet economy. After nearly a decade of stalled arms control negotiations, the United States and the Soviet Union reached several agreements. In 1987 the two parties signed the Intermediate-Range Nuclear

Forces Treaty (INF), which led to the removal of intermediate-range nuclear missiles from the European theater. The Conventional Armed Forces in Europe (CFE) talks in 1990 produced a treaty that provided for a balance of conventional forces in Europe, while the Strategic Arms Reduction Talks (START) in 1991 led to a treaty limiting the numbers of long-range missiles and nuclear warheads. Gorbachev's diplomacy and these successful arms control negotiations led to further improvements in East-West relations.

> **Perestroika** refers to the economic reforms introduced by Mikhail Gorbachev that ushered in market mechanisms and pressures to the economy of the Soviet Union in the 1980s. **Glasnost** refers to the political reforms initiated by Gorbachev that helped to unleash individual choice and provide for broader citizen participation in the political life of the Soviet Union in the 1980s.

Domestically, Gorbachev moved daringly to restructure the Soviet political economy. Economic reforms, known as **perestroika**, introduced limited market mechanisms that encouraged consumer demand, decentralized decision making and industrial management, and supported private economic initiatives. The political reforms of **glasnost** accompanied these economic reforms. Whereas perestroika encouraged consumer choice and individual initiative in the economic arena, glasnost promoted greater choice and participation in the political sphere.

Eastern European supporters of reform gained strength from the introduction of glasnost and perestroika in the Soviet Union, and they too pressed hard for changes in their domestic arenas. Eastern European governments came under even more severe pressures from their polities, however, as demands for reform outpaced those in the Soviet Union. In 1989 the populations in several Eastern European states rejected Communist Party rule, and the rest of Eastern Europe soon followed. Unlike they did in Hungary in 1956 or Czechoslovakia in 1968, this time the Soviets refrained from intervening to halt the sweeping changes unleashed in their satellite nations. By late 1990, the two Germanys had reunited, the Warsaw Pact had disappeared, and Comecon had disbanded. Popular pressures and uprisings led to the demise of Communist leadership throughout Eastern Europe and the transfer of political leadership into new hands.

The political transformations achieved within the Soviet satellites pale in comparison with changes in the Soviet Union itself. Glasnost and perestroika raised expectations, but economic conditions barely improved. For many Soviets, conditions even deteriorated, as agriculture and oil production declined and GNP fell. Economic stagnation and a shortage of basic goods plagued Soviet leadership and fed pressures for greater political decentralization. Nationalist and ethnic pressures grew in the Soviet republics. The Baltic republics pushed for autonomy and secession, and the legislatures in other Soviet republics voiced preferences for greater autonomy. Conflict between Christians and Muslims arose in the Caucasus. In the fall of 1991, the Soviet Union disintegrated as republic after republic announced its secession and independence. Privatization and democratization led to perhaps the most stunning transformation of the European political economic landscape in the twentieth century. No longer did the U.S.-dominated global political economy face a competing model of political economic relations. The Cold War politics and economics of the post–Word War II period had come to an end.

CONCLUSION

Global integration by the Eastern bloc economies increased following détente in the late 1960s and early 1970s, decelerated with the resumption of East-West tensions at the end of the Carter administration and during the early years of the Reagan administration, and then accelerated again with the increased Chinese integration into the global economy and a new easing of East-West tensions. Integration again slowed temporarily amid the revolutionary changes of the late 1980s. These trends can be seen in the data on international borrowing by these political economies reported in figure 13.1.

Examination of more data suggests significant differences in how the former Eastern bloc political economies and China have fared in terms of their transitions and integration into the larger global economy. Ironically, China, the state with the least amount of political liberalization, has emerged as the most integrated in terms of trade volume, becoming an attractive destination for development assistance and foreign direct investment. As a group, the former Eastern bloc political economies lag behind China, despite their greater movement on political liberalization and transition. Figure 13.2 displays changes in trade exposure for these political economies, figure 13.3 shows changes in official development assistance extended to these transitional economies, and figure 13.4 displays shifts in foreign direct investment.

| FIGURE 13.1 | Soviet/Russian and Eastern European Borrowing in Global Capital Markets, 1971–1993 |

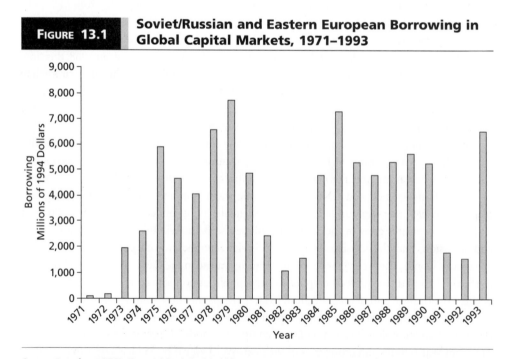

Source: Data from OECD Financial Statistics Monthly.

| FIGURE 13.2 | **Commodity Trade of the Transitional Political Economies, 1980–2004** |

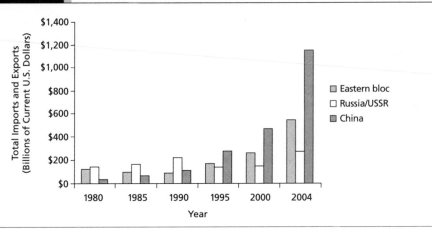

Source: Data from World Trade Organization Statistics Database, http://stat.wto.org.

Note: The Eastern bloc consists of Albania, Bulgaria, Czechoslovakia (the Czech Republic and the Slovak Republic), Hungary, Poland, and Romania.

| FIGURE 13.3 | **Official Development Assistance (ODA) and Official Aid to the Transitional Economies, 1985–2000** |

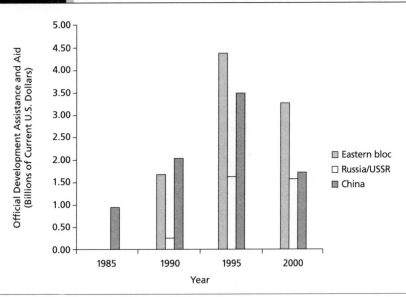

Source: Data from World Bank World Development Indicators, http://www.worldbank.org/data.

Note: The Eastern bloc consists of Albania, Bulgaria, Czechoslovakia (the Czech Republic and the Slovak Republic), Hungary, Poland, and Romania.

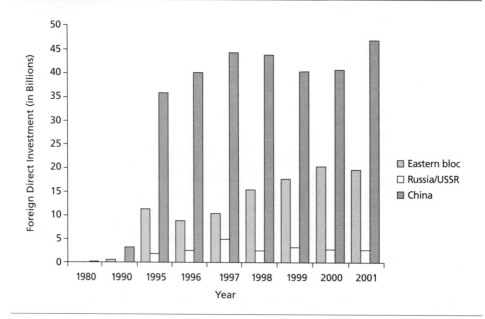

FIGURE 13.4 **Foreign Direct Investment (FDI) Inflows to the Transitional Economies, 1980–2001**

Source: United Nations Conference on Trade and Development, http://www.unctad.org.

Note: The Eastern bloc consists of Albania, Bulgaria, Czechoslovakia (the Czech Republic and the Slovak Republic), Hungary, Poland, and Romania.

All the transitional political economies of the Eastern bloc and China have enjoyed some success at becoming more involved in the global economy. Twenty years after the fall of the Berlin Wall, we find former Eastern bloc political economies as members of the European Union or seeking ascension to the EU. The Chinese embrace of market mechanisms and state capitalism has led to stunning growth rates in China, transforming a dysfunctional, lagging peasant economy into the second-largest economy in the global arena. China still has a long and uncertain journey to travel, however, before it qualifies as a modern advanced industrialized political economy, despite the rhetoric of some Western pundits and policy makers. Much of China's population remains relatively untouched by the transformation. Chinese per capita (nominal) income was $3,735 in 2010, a far cry from U.S. and EU per capita (nominal) incomes of $46,860 and $33,052, respectively, for that year. Significant challenges, including an aging population, growing income inequality, inflation and a potential property bubble, and potential political dissension in the one-party state, could interrupt or hinder the Chinese transition.

Many hurdles remain as these governments attempt to liberalize further in order to expand their economies and develop productive civil societies, undergoing difficult political reforms and transitions in the process. Some are farther along on the political spectrum, while others are advancing more rapidly on the economic dimension. These societies have undergone radical transformations in a relatively short period of time. There are no historical precedents, and reversals are possible.

KEY CONCEPTS

China card (p. 521)

command economies
  (p. 512)

containment (p. 512)

détente (p. 514)

glasnost (p. 527)

mutually assured
  destruction (MAD)
  (p. 515)

Ostpolitik (p. 517)

perestroika (p. 527)

transitional political
  economies (p. 512)

EXERCISES

1. What was the U.S. government's motivation for reestablishing diplomatic relations with China during the Nixon administration?

2. What was the Carter Doctrine, and what was its political context and motivation?

3. What are glasnost and perestroika? How did they change the political and economic arenas in the Soviet Union?

4. Explain the meaning and significance of détente to world affairs.

5. Explain the meaning and significance of *Ostpolitik*.

6. The Cuban Missile Crisis demonstrated the depth of distrust and hostility between the East and the West, but it also contributed to a thawing in East-West relations. Explain.

7. Construct a causal model/explanation with independent variables in which the dependent variable is the thawing in East-West relations. Justify your inclusion of each independent variable and explain how it is causally related to the dependent variable.

8. Assume that the year is 1949 and you are a top foreign policy and defense adviser in either the United States or the Soviet Union. Both nations have now exploded atomic bombs. You are being asked whether your nation should proceed with research and development for a bomb that is far more deadly than the atomic bomb—a superweapon called the hydrogen bomb. The preferences of the two sides are as follows: Each seeks security and survival, greater strength than the other, and the ability to set the rules of the game. Neither wants to be left behind or dominated. Each has two available strategies: to build or not to build the H-bomb. There are costs involved. If one side builds and the other does not, the side that does not will be left behind and will be exploited in global affairs. If both build, little if any geopolitical advantage accrues to one or the other. Arsenals cancel each other out, but at very substantial

costs—there will be fewer dollars and rubles for education, health care, economic investment, and so on. Moreover, any war waged with such weapons would lead to massive devastation (immense costs). We can put the choice of strategies and their outcomes into a game matrix as in chapters 1 and 4:

	USSR	
U.S.	Build	Don't build
Build	Arms race	U.S. dominance
Don't build	Soviet dominance	Arms limitations

Build a preference ordering for each player independent of the other. What outcome is the intersection of these two preference orderings likely to produce? Is this the best social outcome? Why or why not? If it is not the best collective outcome, what is? Is it a stable outcome? (The social trap depicted in this game is known as the *security dilemma*.)

FURTHER READING

Ambrose, Stephen E., and Douglas G. Brinkley. 2011. *Rise to Globalism: American Foreign Policy since 1938*. 9th rev. ed. New York: Penguin Books.

Bacevich, Andrew J. 2010. *Washington Rules: America's Path to Permanent War*. New York: Metropolitan Books.

FitzGerald, Frances. 2002. *Fire in the Lake: The Vietnamese and the Americans in Vietnam*. Boston: Back Bay Books.

Gaddis, John Lewis. 2006. *The Cold War: A New History*. New York: Penguin Books.

Kaplan, Fred. 1991. *The Wizards of Armageddon*. Stanford, CA: Stanford University Press.

Kennan, George F. 1985. *American Diplomacy*. Chicago: University of Chicago Press.

Keylor, William R. 2006. *The Twentieth-Century World and Beyond: An International History since 1900*. 5th ed. New York: Oxford University Press.

Lafeber, Walter. 2002. *America, Russia, and the Cold War, 1945–2002*. 9th ed. New York: McGraw-Hill.

Schelling, Thomas C. 2008. *Arms and Influence*. New Haven, CT: Yale University Press.

Sheehan, Neil, Fox Butterfield, Hedrick Smith, and E. W. Kenworthy. 1971. *The Pentagon Papers as Published by the New York Times: The Secret History of the Vietnam War*. New York: Times Books.

Into the Future: Political and Economic Market Failures and Threats to Globalization

The King is dead. Long live the King!

At the beginning of the twenty-first century, the Washington Consensus seemed firmly established as the dominant rules of the game in the global political economy. Built on strong domestic foundations of governance and public and private finance, the United States had acted as the system stabilizer during the post–World War II period. As the liberal hegemonic leader, the United States had promoted and maintained rules of the game conducive to the expansion of global capitalism and globalization. The mechanisms of U.S. public and private finance had provided key collective goods—described in chapter 6— that helped lubricate and sustain international cooperation and socially productive economic interactions during good times and managed and limited dislocations during bad times. The actions of U.S. policy makers and financial markets helped to ease the tensions between the increasingly global geography of economic exchange and the political geography of autonomous nation-states. With the disintegration of the Eastern bloc and the Soviet Union, as described in chapter 13, the United States was left as the sole superpower. Close observers, however, were aware that the system was already showing signs of problems that could threaten U.S. leadership and raise questions about the Washington Consensus.

In this chapter we consider threats to continued international cooperation and globalization in the twenty-first century from the transformation of global financial relations caused by financial and regulatory liberalization in domestic political arenas. We examine the role of U.S. hegemonic leadership in managing such threats. In so doing, we recognize the foundations of such leadership in the mechanisms of U.S. public and private finance and the global networks built around those mechanisms as described theoretically in chapter 6. We explore the prospects for U.S. decline and the capacities of other states to provide the collective goods described in chapter 6, which are essential to stabilizing the system and avoiding threats to continued cooperation and globalization if the United States falters.

REGIONAL AND FINANCIAL INSTABILITY GROW INTO A SYSTEMIC THREAT

Several important changes took place in the global political economy in the late twentieth and early twenty-first centuries. At the beginning of the twenty-first century, turmoil in the Middle East captured the attention of publics, policy makers, and the media. The terrorist attacks on the World Trade Center and the Pentagon of September 11, 2001, led the United States to engage in two wars in the Middle East, each lasting longer than any previous war in U.S. history. These conflicts were not universally welcomed by U.S. allies or their publics, who began to question U.S. leadership in the global arena. In 2011, events in Tunisia led to a popular uprising against an authoritarian regime and a relatively peaceful overthrow of that regime. Rapidly expanding global news networks and social networks enabled by the Internet transmitted images and information about the Tunisian "Arab Spring" across borders. These images and information acted as a contagion. Soon popular uprisings appeared in Egypt, Yemen, Bahrain, and then Syria. Some of these led to tense but relatively nonviolent regime change, but others were met by governments that responded with violence—in the case of Syria, extreme violence. Other Arab governments adopted political reforms, such as more representative elections and bigger social welfare transfers, to undercut political opposition to their regimes. At the time of this writing, tremendous uncertainty exists about the direction of the Arab Spring, the extent and stability of the changes that have occurred, their implications for regional affairs, and the consequences for the global political economy more broadly. Discussion of these events must wait for a later edition, when their importance to the global political economy and their implications are clearer and better understood.

The most significant changes in political economic relations across the advanced industrialized countries during the last quarter of the twentieth century and the beginning of the twenty-first century have been the liberalization and accelerating globalization of public and private finance. National financial arenas had been incredibly stable and the most tightly regulated sectors of the advanced industrialized states since the 1930s and the Great Depression. Beginning in the 1970s, this world began to change, slowly at first but then with increasing speed. We have been experiencing both the benefits and the costs of that transformation. This chapter focuses on the implications of those changes for U.S. hegemonic leadership, continued global cooperation, and the prospects for mutually beneficial outcomes as contrasted with socially destructive outcomes.

The financial liberalization and innovations described in chapter 12, which began in the mid-1970s in the United States and then spread to London's markets, then Tokyo's, and then to other markets, created a denser, more complicated network of financial relationships within states and across national boundaries. The 1990s saw strong economic growth globally, driven in part by historically disproportionate growth in the United States that produced low unemployment and higher-than-normal consumption. American consumers helped drive rapid economic expansion and transformation in China and other economies. By 2011, more than 400 million Chinese had been lifted out of poverty by the economic transformation taking place in China since the early 1980s—the most remarkable shift in human poverty in history. Globalization and international cooperation around the tenets of the **Washington Consensus** appeared to be the only game in town. Some academics and pundits spoke about the end of history, meaning that the rules of the game built on global capitalism, neoliberalism, and the Washington Consensus no longer faced competition from other alternatives. U.S. hegemonic leadership appeared more firmly ensconced than at any time since the immediate post–World War II period.

> The **Washington Consensus** is a policy agenda that places emphasis on the corrective pressures of market discipline and seeks to reduce government regulation and intervention in the economy by promoting economic openness in trade and capital movements, liberalization of financial markets, fiscal policies that lead to balanced budgets, anti-inflationary monetary policies, stability in exchange-rate relations, expansion of private enterprise, and reduction in state-owned enterprises; the name of this system reflects the prominence of Washington, D.C., and the organizations located there, in international economic affairs.

But events would soon generate questions and doubts about the uniform claims of the benefits of such financial liberalization and globalization, even stirring questions about the stability of U.S. hegemonic leadership and capacity. After decades of tight regulation of national financial sectors and a relative absence of major financial shocks and crises that could threaten global economic stability, financial crises began to appear beginning in 1980 in the wake of regulatory reforms that liberalized market access and practices. These appeared with increasing frequency and severity over time. At first they appeared at the local and regional levels, but they became larger and more systemic threats to the global economy and productive international cooperation. With the growing intensity of these shocks, policy makers began to ask questions about the financial reforms that had liberalized financial markets and encouraged innovation and invention, but had also created greater connections across markets and states. What might have been smaller local crises under previous regulatory arrangements now spilled across borders, transmitted economic hardships from one political economy to another, and challenged policy makers to address the economic ills or confront threats to their political survival. Dissension within and across governments about how to respond to such financial and economic shocks also spilled over to threaten cooperation on nonrelated issues such as global climate change.

By the second decade of the twenty-first century the landscape had shifted dramatically. A century that had begun with unrestrained optimism about the future now faced a far more daunting path to maintaining productive globalization and mutually beneficial cooperation across national boundaries. National policy makers, worried about their political survival, faced demands from their selectorates to address economic slowdowns, fiscal problems, persistent and high unemployment, and general crises in confidence. Governments faced barriers to finding the consensus and will to address many of the concerns threatening their political economies. Under such conditions, politicians might be tempted to shift the costs of adjustment abroad, which could threaten the international cooperation that underpins productive globalization and turn a virtuous cycle of cooperation into a vicious cycle of tit-for-tat defection. Earlier chapters in Part III demonstrated the importance of a hegemonic leader, a state that provides the key collective goods described in chapter 6, for stabilizing the system and encouraging others to follow the virtuous path. Let's consider the prospects for continued U.S. hegemonic leadership and provision of the collective goods central to productive economic globalization and crisis management, as well as the possibility that another state could provide such collective goods.

THE FUTURE OF U.S. LEADERSHIP IN THE TWENTY-FIRST CENTURY

Questions of hegemonic capacity and will have been important throughout the history of globalization and capitalist expansion. From a policy perspective, understanding such processes is never more important than when the global political economy slows and faces heightened uncertainty about future prospects for economic growth and vitality, when national policy makers entertain notions of transferring the costs of economic adjustment to other nations' populations, and when those at or near the top of the global hierarchy begin to wonder about hegemonic decline or replacement. The early twenty-first century just might be such a time, as a financial crisis rooted in the United States spread across national borders. We observe a growing global dissatisfaction with U.S. foreign policies related to the war on terror. Concerns are rising about the growing fiscal exposure of the United States because of expanding trade and budget deficits and a declining dollar. Moreover, the rapid economic expansion of China and India is prompting questions about possible hegemonic replacement.

In chapter 12 we examined some of the public and private actions and innovations that led to financial liberalization, a deepening and widening of global financial integration, and expanded economic opportunity. These accompanied U.S. influence in the international system. They also had the potential for being disruptive to the global economy. The increasing returns dynamic of global financial integration creates a potential for systemic risks if the tentacles of financial integration convey severe dislocations from society to society, just as the same network transmits opportunities for economic advancement. Denser linkages increase the likelihood of transferring good information and growth across national boundaries, but such connections can also spread misinformation and shocks as quickly. Transmission of shocks, poor information, and fear can undermine the intentions of national macroeconomic policy manipulations, raise concerns about foreign ownership of domestic economic enterprises, present monitoring and compliance dilemmas, and increase speculative pressures and volatility in the markets. International trade in financial services adds complexity to already sophisticated financial markets, increases the sensitivity and vulnerability of markets to each other, and highlights the tension between economic interdependence and sovereignty. This is the back of the hand of financial deregulation, liberalization, and globalization.

The financial liberalization that began in U.S. markets in the 1970s and then spread to London, Tokyo, and other markets amounted to a seismic change in global financial relations and a deepening of financial integration, a reawakening of global finance, which had lain dormant for much of the post–World War II period. This expanded the global capital pool and lowered capital costs, fueling a great deal of sound economic activity, but the added liquidity and looser regulation also created opportunities for financial crises and bubbles that, if severe enough, could raise questions about the rules of the game and U.S. leadership. Ironically, the same mechanisms that had endowed U.S. public and private actors with such global influence were putting that influence at risk.

The global economy avoided systemic financial crisis for much of the time since the Great Depression. Beginning in the 1980s, however, markets that previously were relatively stable and free from systemic shocks began to experience such shocks with increasing frequency. Financial institutions, enabled by deregulation and increased capital mobility, were at the center of these major financial crises. Threats to global economic stability from the Third World Debt Crisis in 1983, the October market crash in 1987, the savings and loan crisis at the end of the 1980s, the Russian ruble crisis, the peso crisis, the Asian financial crisis, the bursting of the technology bubble in 1999–2000, and the credit market freeze in 2008 were partly the unintended consequences of the liberalization that unleashed financial innovations and at the same time increased integration. U.S. policy makers, primarily at the Federal Reserve and the U.S. Treasury, were central to putting together coalitions to manage these shocks. Each successive shock raised more and more questions about the rules of the game that produced such shocks and about the wisdom of U.S. leadership even as U.S. policy makers were central to constructing the global cooperation necessary to manage those shocks.

This raises an interesting paradox and dilemma for policy makers. The reforms that promoted greater liberalization and global financial integration also created the opportunities for the increasing frequency of shocks and disruptions that could potentially threaten the foundations of economic globalization along with the gains in specialization and social welfare produced by such globalization. U.S. leadership, which supported the expansion of financial liberalization, globalization, and the extension of the network of U.S. influence, is put at risk by the unintended and negative consequences of that liberalization and globalization. Reforms and liberalization that can be credited with the production of wealth and economic opportunity have a dark side when crises diffuse across borders and produce pressures on policy makers to rein in globalization or to look elsewhere in the system for alternatives to U.S. leadership.

A Network of Financial Relations Creates Self-Sustaining, but Not Stable, Leadership

An exploration of the potential for such crises to damage globalization requires a thorough assessment of the prospects for continued U.S. leadership and the ability of the United States to provide key collective goods to the global arena. Chapter 6 provides a framework for understanding the role of hegemonic leadership in promoting globalization and engendering cooperation among policy makers across national borders. This conception of hegemonic leadership includes explicit and intentional hierarchical attempts to manipulate relations in the system, but only as a subset of a larger set of relations that incorporates both intentional and unintentional influences that arise from reforms in governance and in public and private finance. These reforms, if successful and embraced by others in the global arena, place a political economy at the hub of a network of global financial relations—a global nervous system. This network of financial relations is produced by the aggregation of small public and private decisions. It emerges over time and enables policy makers from the hegemonic political economy to promote cooperation and manage downturns that threaten globalization. This involves providing other decision makers in the system with a set of incentive-compatible collective goods that encourage the cooperation essential to globalization. This leaves a deeply embedded structural leadership, which is not imposed but built. Such leadership, once created, exhibits self-sustaining and self-reinforcing tendencies because of increasing returns, which enhance its stability. Yet those self-reinforcing increasing returns do not inevitably make such leadership forever more stable and uncontested. The current leadership can be challenged by crises and processes that undermine confidence in that leadership, leave an absence of leadership, or produce a shift in capabilities for leadership elsewhere in the system.

Chapters 9, 10, and 11 used the history of globalization during the 1800s, its breakdown in the years between World Wars I and II, and the post–World War II period to show the essential role of hegemonic leadership and its provision of a handful of important collective goods based in public and private finance for mutually beneficial cooperation and productive globalization. After World War II, the United States emerged as the system's **hegemon** and stabilizer. This leadership role for the United States was created through the interaction of choices by U.S.

A **hegemon** is a leader who helps to manage seemingly incompatible policy preferences across governments, establishes the rules of the game, and assumes a disproportionate share of the costs of maintaining those rules.

public and private policy makers in governance and financial arenas with choices of public and private decision makers elsewhere in the system.

The increasingly frequent crises since the early 1980s, which have disturbed systemic stability and some of which originated in the financial arena of the hegemonic state, are the types of shocks that could undermine confidence in the abilities and wisdom of the leader. Even as public and private actors in the hegemonic state are key to managing those crises, the very existence of the crises can raise questions about the financial mechanisms that produce such unexpected and devastating shocks. In 2008, after a year of building financial crisis, a meltdown in global credit markets began in the United States after the collapse of Lehman Brothers and the decision by U.S. policy makers to allow Lehman to fail. The crisis was built on a record of sustained questionable behavior in the credit markets, which was enabled by regulatory reforms and lack of oversight. Questions were raised about the U.S. financial arena as economic autopsies revealed markets where the rules of the game were corrupted by cronyism and a disturbing amount of shortsighted greed driven by perverse incentive structures, an absence of transparency in the clearinghouse and information mechanisms that disproportionately advantaged insiders, and poor internal risk controls at major private financial institutions. The average market participant was faced with the dilemma of no longer knowing what products were good or bad—a market failure dilemma. Seventy years after the Great Depression and the adoption of regulatory and market reforms to ensure confidence in the reliability, fairness, and transparency of U.S. financial markets, questions were again being raised about the quality of those markets.

The crisis was managed with aggressive action by the U.S. Treasury, which oversaw an emergency congressional financing package for troubled financial institutions, and by even more aggressive action by the Federal Reserve, which provided lines of credit and purchased trillions of dollars of financial assets from private financial institutions teetering on the brink of disaster. The Federal Reserve provided support to both U.S. and foreign financial institutions at the time. It was an extraordinary display of lender-of-last-resort capacity, but one brought on by the unintended consequences of thirty years of regulatory liberalization and laxity in the financial markets. Not since the banking crisis of the 1930s had the system come so close to complete collapse. Even with aggressive action by U.S. policy makers and public financial authorities abroad, the global economy fell into a severe recession with high levels of unemployment.

Public and Private Domestic Financial Practices Threaten U.S. Hegemony

The same liberalization and regulatory reforms that enhanced financial integration and brought huge benefits also limited the abilities of regulatory overseers to rein in excessive behavior and created incentives for individuals and firms to engage in activities that can fundamentally damage the system. Such problems might undermine the confidence and the network that endow the United States with hegemonic capacity. Activities in U.S. public and

Federal Reserve Board chairman Ben Bernanke, center, poses with board members at a two-day meeting of the Federal Open Market Committee, the Federal Reserve's interest rate–setting body, in Washington in March 2009. The Federal Reserve has been the U.S. lender of last resort since its origin in 1913, and effectively the global lender of last resort since the end of World War II. During the 2007–2008 global credit and liquidity crisis, which brought the global economy to the brink of another great depression, the Federal Reserve pumped trillions of dollars of liquidity into the global economy by expanding its balance sheet. These actions helped stabilize the global economy. After this meeting the Federal Reserve announced the purchase of longer-dated Treasury securities to help end a deepening U.S. recession.

private finance might be the biggest threat to continued U.S. leadership if they undermine confidence in the U.S. rules of the game because of the creation and transmission of socially destructive and economically destabilizing crises.

Along with the regulatory problems revealed in the U.S. financial architecture by the increasing frequency of crises leading up to the major systemic crisis of 2007–2008, growing public fiscal issues in the U.S. economy could damage confidence in U.S. public and private financial arrangements, potentially undermining the credibility of the U.S.-supported rules of the game and threatening the microfoundations of U.S. hegemonic capacity. These fiscal issues are partly an outgrowth of the regulatory dilemmas revealed by the 2007–2008 crisis. Before that financial crisis hit, the U.S. gross public debt–to–GDP ratio was approximately 55 percent in 2000, which means that U.S. gross public debt amounted to 55 percent of U.S. annual GDP. The proportion of debt to GDP grew during the Bush administration to almost 65 percent by 2006 because of outlays for overseas conflicts and tax cuts that reduced revenues. The United States was spending more on national security in the early twenty-first century than all the other states in the global arena combined. This ratio of gross public debt to GDP was affordable and not nearly as large as those of most other advanced industrialized economies, but the U.S. gross public debt–to–GDP ratio was to shift dramatically after the financial and economic crisis hit.

The financial crisis and ensuing recession led to significant decreases in tax revenues as unemployment rose to near 10 percent, consumption slowed, and corporate revenues declined. At the same time, unemployment and resulting economic hardship led to an expansion of entitlement and safety net expenditures such as unemployment insurance, Medicaid and Medicare, Aid for Dependent Children, and school lunch programs. An expanding differential between public revenues and expenditures is typical at times of economic distress in an advanced industrialized state with sophisticated social safety net programs. In such cases the U.S. government acts countercyclically to reduce hardship and provide benefits to cushion citizens against hardship, at the same time that tax revenues are constrained or decreasing. Added to this expanding gap between public revenues and expenditures was the Emergency Economic Stabilization Act of 2008, enacted at the end of the Bush administration, which produced the Troubled Asset Relief Program (TARP) to stabilize the banking sector, and the American Recovery and Reinvestment Act of 2009, which was the economic stimulus package passed at the beginning of the Obama administration.

In this June 2010 photo, a demonstrator holds a sign during a rally organized by the Philadelphia Unemployment Project. High unemployment and unsustainable levels of debt and budget deficits in Europe and the United States led to slow growth in the global economy.

By the the time of the presidential election in November 2008, the U.S. gross public debt–to–GDP ratio had grown to approximately 80 percent and was headed higher as the U.S. economy continued to experience weak growth. By 2010 the ratio had passed 90 percent and was forecast to level off around 105 percent by 2012. Two economists, Carmen Reinhart and Kenneth Rogoff, undertook a historical analysis of major financial crises and found that a 90 percent public debt–to–GDP ratio was a troubling threshold in terms of economic stagnation—not necessarily applicable to any specific crisis but on average a troubling threshold. Questions about the United States' leadership, its fiscal conditions, and its mechanisms of public and private finance are more than simply questions about the United States. Given its position in the global economy—the U.S. economy is about a quarter of nominal global GDP—U.S. domestic financial and fiscal crises quickly become systemic crises for the global political economy.

The U.S. public fiscal dilemma is not explicitly the size of the debt or its ratio to GDP; rather, the dilemma lies in the willingness and ability of U.S. policy makers to make the politically difficult choices to finance the debt by increasing revenues (raising taxes), by cutting popular programs that are backed by influential constituencies, or both. Despite American popular opinion, the United States has one of the lowest and least progressive tax structures among the world's advanced industrialized political economies. After major changes in the U.S. tax structure during the Roosevelt administration in the 1930s, which increased rates and the progressivity of those rates, the marginal tax rates remained remarkably stable until the mid-1960s. Since then, they have been steadily declining and becoming less progressive, with a few interruptions. This has been true for both individual and corporate marginal tax rates. Moreover, the United States is not nearly as burdened as most other advanced industrialized societies, or even developing political economies such as China, by a rapidly aging population that is shifting the ratio of workers to pensioners and placing greater strains on public fiscal practices. The United States is fortunate to enjoy relatively stable worker replacement because of comparatively high birthrates for an advanced industrial state and because of migration.

So the United States has the means to raise tax rates to increase revenues to address the expanding ratio of gross public debt to GDP or to constrain spending, but do U.S. policy makers have the political will? The question of will goes to the credibility of U.S. public financial mechanisms, which if damaged can spill over to affect confidence in U.S. private financial markets and arrangements—already potentially damaged by the regulatory shortcomings revealed by the 2007–2008 crisis. The lessons of British hegemonic leadership, the absence of such leadership during the interwar years, and the postwar period of U.S. hegemony are instructive about the connections between the fiscal arena and hegemonic capacity. During the construction of British and American hegemonic capabilities, those societies were among the highest per capita tax states and had relatively progressive tax structures. U.S. tax rates were significantly higher and much more progressive during the emergence of U.S. hegemonic capacity and for years following. Today, the U.S. tax structure is the lowest and least progressive it has been in decades. The United States has plenty of room to adjust taxes or spending to address the potential fiscal dilemma, but does it have the will? The answer to this question could be critical to continued U.S. hegemonic capacity.

Challenging the Health and Efficacy of U.S. Global Economic Leadership

Questions are beginning to arise about U.S. commitments to sound and credible policies in both regulatory and fiscal arenas. Such questions become more apparent, and more threatening, when conflicts arise in Congress concerning regulatory reforms in the financial sector of the economy, whether to raise the U.S. debt ceiling (the amount the United States can borrow to finance deficit spending), and the size and nature of public programs in light of revenues. This is not a crisis yet in terms of U.S. hegemonic capacity, as global capital still flows into dollar-denominated assets at times of potential systemic distress. Even when that distress originates in the United States, the dollar is still the preferred reserve asset, interest rates on U.S. public debt remain relatively low, and the U.S. Federal Reserve and the Treasury continue to sit at the apex of crisis management in the system by providing the lender-of-last-resort collective good. But, depending on policy responses to regulatory and fiscal issues, chinks may or may not appear in U.S. hegemonic capacity.

Questions about the health and efficacy of U.S. leadership are not new. Beginning in the late 1970s, concerns over *Pax Americana*'s decline began to appear, and with increasing frequency. Such arguments cited overstretched military commitments, the revival of Western European and Japanese economies, U.S. retreat from unilateral management of the international economic system, disagreements in international economic summitry, the end of the Bretton Woods system and fixed exchange rates, persistent U.S. budget and trade deficits, and a weakening dollar. Such concerns faded during the 1990s with the disintegration of the Soviet Union and the Eastern bloc, stagnation in the Japanese economy, and vibrant growth in the U.S. economy. Concerns over U.S. leadership resurfaced in the early twenty-first century as a financial crisis rooted in the United States spread across national borders, the war in Iraq led to widespread global dissatisfaction with U.S. foreign policies, some began to worry about the growing fiscal exposure of the United States resulting from expanding trade and budget deficits and a declining dollar, and the rapid economic expansion of China and India raised questions about the vitality of U.S. leadership in the global economy and the ability of the United States to provide important collective goods and responsible leadership.

Questions about the health of U.S. leadership, or the prospects for any potential hegemonic leader, are critical not simply for Americans but also for others around the globe, because such leadership is critical to the provision of key collective goods that help reduce uncertainties involved in cross-border exchange, manage the risks involved in such exchange, extend the time horizons of economic actors, encourage those actors to risk exchange and investment across time and geographic space, and support a network of relationships that can mobilize cooperation and manage countercyclical downturns or crises. The answers to these questions inform us about the prospects for severe economic disruptions, excessive and destructive economic nationalism, peaceful adjudication and resolution of international disagreements, conflict arising from competition, the maintenance and expansion of productive exchange across borders, the stimulation of growth and development, and the reduction of obstacles to cooperation and coordination in the global arena.

Concerns about U.S. leadership may or may not be warranted, but we can determine that only by examining the state of that leadership, the implications of U.S. decline, and whether another political economy could step into the position of leader and provide the collective goods described in chapter 6. Without better understanding, responding to such fears might easily prove to be an overreaction if policy makers miscalculate the prospects for U.S. decline and Chinese or Indian rise. Such an overreaction could damage continued cooperation, limit the capacity and willingness of governments to coordinate their policies to limit activities detrimental to productive economic activities, and even produce the very outcome policy makers sought to avoid with their policy choice—a self-fulfilling prophecy. Let's use the road map from chapter 6, which emphasizes the centrality of the mechanisms of governance and public and private finance to global leadership, to evaluate empirically the prospects for U.S. leadership surviving in the twenty-first century, as well as potential successors to U.S. leadership.

POTENTIAL HEGEMONIC SUCCESSORS TO STABILIZE THE SYSTEM AND PROMOTE COOPERATION

This is more than an empirical exercise to satisfy our curiosity. The absence of a liberal hegemonic state can be disastrous for the economic cooperation essential to promoting economic globalization and reaping the gains from such globalization. Without a hegemonic political economy to provide liquidity, act as lender of last resort, and induce the cooperation necessary to manage downturns in the wake of a crisis—to act as the stabilizer in the system—economic distress can lead to increasing pressures on policy makers to adopt policies that damage international exchange. As in the 1920s and 1930s, there would be no safety mechanisms to constrain self-interested behaviors that may make sense in the short run but have perverse long-term consequences. Perhaps the United States is in decline, perhaps not, or perhaps the crises of the past thirty years, culminating in the 2007 crisis, will serve as a wake-up call. U.S. policy makers were beginning to revisit the regulatory reforms of the past thirty years even before the 2007 crisis, in attempts to limit the negative unintended consequences of those reforms while preserving the gains. In some cases new regulatory demands were initiated, and the 2007 crisis led to even more significant financial regulation—regulation intended to create greater transparency, improve oversight, identify and limit the prospects for systemic risk, and ensure confidence. Such regulation might serve to buttress continued U.S. hegemonic leadership. Ironically, even with the crisis originating in the United States, the flight to quality brought even more capital to the United States. Even with a crisis that should have damaged confidence in U.S. markets and U.S. policy makers, holders of capital still preferred U.S. markets and assets to others.

If U.S. capacity for leadership is in danger of failing, does another political economy exist that could pick up the slack and provide those collective goods important to promoting continued international cooperation and globalization? Chinese, and to a lesser extent Indian, economic success has led to speculation about the possibility of another political economy replacing the United States as the global leader. In particular, pundits and others focus on China as it gains economic size—becoming the second-largest economy in the world—and becomes increasingly assertive in world affairs. By mid-2008 public opinion surveys in the United States showed that a majority of Americans believed, erroneously, that China had already surpassed the United States as the preeminent economy in the global system.

For some this is a question of global competition, a zero-sum game over which political economy is going to be king of the hill, where one society's gain is another's loss. By now, however, it should be clear that the relevance of liberal hegemonic leadership is not about global competition but about global cooperation, stabilizing the global arena during times of duress, and promoting the expansion of globalization and international exchange that enhances social welfare. There is no reason to anticipate that any political economy that might surpass the United States in capacity to act as a liberal hegemon would dramatically alter the rules of the game that enabled such economic success.

Let's consider potential successors to the United States as the hegemonic political economy—not from the viewpoint of competition, but as a matter of concern that without a political economy with the capacity to provide the collective goods that reduce transaction costs and barriers to exchange and globalization we might all be far worse-off. In addition to China and India, whose rapid growth suggests that these political economies are becoming powerhouses of sufficient size to pass the threshold for hegemonic leadership, let's also consider the European Union, which is comparable to the United States in demographic and economic size and wealth. We will not examine the prospects for Japan, even though it is a wealthy and large political economy. Japan was considered extensively as a hegemonic contender in the 1970s and 1980s, when persistent U.S. trade deficits and expanding public deficits, U.S. economic stagflation, weakness in the dollar, and the rise of Japanese economic prowess fueled a discussion over the prospects of U.S. decline and the ability of the United States to continue to act as the commercial and financial hegemon in the global arena. In retrospect, this was much ado about nothing, as the U.S. economy recovered and demonstrated its vitality and Japanese economic expansion faltered because of a bursting real estate bubble, a shift in demographic makeup, and economic stagnation that has persisted for at least two decades at the time of this writing. Given Japan's aging demographic profile and its continuing economic travails, there is little to suggest that Japan will regain its position as a potential contender.

Considering the Microfoundations of Hegemonic Capacity for China, India, and the European Union

Let's return to the first principles discussed in chapter 6 and used in Part III of this book to examine the historical incidence and role of hegemonic leadership. First, a political economy must be of sufficient size to generate and attract sources of domestic and foreign capital that can be redirected to promote globalization or manage threats to global economic stability. Second, good property rights are essential. Third, a handful of public and private arrangements in finance and governance underpin the provision of key collective goods that provide the scaffolding for globalization and cooperative global economic relations. These are all connected to providing liquidity and financing mechanisms for economic expansion, cross-border exchange, and globalization during good times. During bad times, they provide capital that encourages continued international cooperation, limits economic downturns, and prevents the chipping away at the processes of globalization. Five key aspects of public governance and public finance have been highlighted as underpinning the capacity for leadership: rule of law, taxation, public debt, ability to act as a lender of last resort, and the willingness to expose one's national currency to international use as a reserve currency and a means to settle international transactions. In the arena of private finance, chapter 6 emphasized the importance of capital market size, market diversification, market depth and liquidity, transparency and good clearinghouse mechanisms, and the relative absence of barriers to cross-border participation.

Table 14.1 compares these first principles, the microfoundations of hegemonic capacity, across the three cases of potential successors to U.S. leadership. Size and property rights are two characteristics that sit at the heart of other explanations of leadership. Clearly these aspects of a political economy are critical components of hegemonic capacity, but history demonstrates that a hegemon might not be the largest political economy in the system, nor

TABLE 14.1	**Domestic Microfoundations of Liberal Hegemonic Capacity**		
	China	*India*	*European Union*
Economic size GDP ppp*	$9.05 trillion	$3.862 trillion	$14.77 trillion
Nominal GDP	$4.98 trillion	$1.236 trillion	$16.41 trillion
Per capita GDP (nominal)	$3,735	$1,032	$33,052
Per capita GDP (ppp)	$6,778	$3,015	$29,729
Property rights**	–	–	+
Rule-of-law:** clarity, burden, stability, corruption	–	–	+
Taxation: fair/avoidance	–	–	+
Public debt market	+/–	+/–	+
Lender-of-last-resort role: growth and stability	+	+	–
International reserve currency	–	–	+
Capital market size	–	–	+
Depth and liquidity	–	–	+
Market diversification	–	–	+
Transparency and clearinghouse mechanisms	–	+/–	+
National bias	–	–	+

Source: Adapted from Andrew C. Sobel, *Birth of Hegemony: Crisis, Financial Revolution, and Emerging Global Networks* (Chicago: University of Chicago Press, 2012), Table 7.1.

*IMF data, 2009–2010. For comparison, U.S. gross domestic product purchasing power parity (GDP ppp) is $14.53 trillion, U.S. GDP nominal is $14.53 trillion, U.S. GDP per capita (ppp) is $46,860, and U.S. GDP per capita (nominal) is $46,860.

**Based on International Property Rights Index.

might it be the only political economy with sound and stable property rights or the best property rights. Size as a predictor and explanation would have been wrong in the majority of cases of hegemony since 1600. Size alone cannot account for Dutch commercial and financial hegemony in the 1600s and 1700s, British leadership in the 1700s and 1800s, or the absence of U.S. leadership during the interwar years. Property rights are a function of the rule of law, which will be addressed as a separate category. History also shows that good property rights are a necessary condition for commercial and financial leadership, but they are not a sufficient condition. The cases of Dutch, British, and American hegemony enjoyed relatively good property rights, but they were not alone in their eras. Many nations are sufficiently large but do not acquire the capacity for hegemony. Many nations develop sound property rights yet fail to lead and provide important goods to support international cooperation. Several nations are both large enough and possessed of sound property rights, yet fall short of being able to act as the liberal hegemon despite a desire to do so.

Gross Domestic Product

In terms of size, using 2009–2010 **gross domestic product purchasing power parity (GDP ppp)** data, China and the EU both appear to be above the size threshold. Using GDP ppp, China is the second-largest nation-state. The EU is larger still, but it is a federation of states. Both have demonstrated an ability to marshal surplus capital from their domestic economies and redirect that capital.

> **Gross domestic product purchasing power parity (GDP ppp)** is the total value of goods and services produced within a nation during any given year, but it is adjusted for relative costs of living and inflation across countries. **Nominal GDP** is the total value of goods and services produced within a nation during any given year. It is calculated using official government or market exchange rates. **Per capita income** is the average income within a political economy, calculated by taking an aggregated measure of all income in an economy—such as GDP—and then dividing that measure by the total population within the economy.

China has accumulated surplus capital as a function of its trade surplus and has administered much of that surplus centrally through the public mechanisms of the sovereign wealth funds, the Bank of China, and the Ministry of Finance. India is more problematic using GDP ppp. For comparative purposes, **nominal GDP** of the Chinese and Indian economies shrinks dramatically, but the EU actually grows.

The ability to provide the collective goods and liquidity that promote economic exchange, expansion, and globalization is a function not simply of aggregate economic size but also of per capita size. The requisite collective goods and liquidity involve a redistribution of capital from the hegemonic state to other states, especially at times of economic turmoil in the system. **Per capita income** provides some measure of a political economy's ability to generate surplus capital that is above and beyond the amount of capital an individual or family needs for essential goods. The larger the per capita income, the more individuals in society are living above the poverty line and the more surplus they have that can be used for consumption or can be saved, invested, or taxed. These are all means of injecting liquidity into the system and promoting economic activity. Political economies with lower per capita incomes have less domestic capital resources available for financing key collective goods for hegemonic leadership or injecting liquidity into the system during good or bad times.

The per capita numbers tell a story different from that of the aggregate GDP numbers. Per capita GDP (ppp) for the EU is quite large. It is not as large as the United States, but it is more than sufficient to support the capacity for hegemonic leadership in the modern arena. Individuals in the EU live far above the poverty threshold, and this indicates a significant surplus of capital that could be tapped to provide liquidity to the system and underwrite the provision of collective goods that promote globalization and international cooperation. GDP per capita (nominal) is even larger.

Per capita GDP numbers for China and India, both nominal and ppp, show that both states, even though they are large in the aggregate, are still developing political economies with a long way to go before they are solidly in the category of advanced industrialized economies. The per capita numbers show that individuals and families in China and India are living much closer to the poverty line than are those in the United States or the EU. Consequently, there is far less domestic surplus capital to be used through the processes of consumption, savings, investment, and taxation to support the capacity for hegemonic leadership. China circumvents this problem somewhat with the aggregation of surplus wealth from trade in sovereign wealth funds that the government centrally controls. Such central control could be a plus during economic crises—when private individuals and firms become risk averse—by placing more resources in centrally administered public hands that are more likely to act countercyclically. However, this limits the resources at the disposal of private individuals and firms in China, which might hinder the development of China as an economy at the hub of a network of economic relationships built on private consumption and investment choices. Private market activity was a key factor in the emergence of Dutch, British, and American influence.

Regardless of where the surplus capital is stored, there is far less surplus in China and India, and not nearly enough to underpin hegemonic capacity. These numbers are trending up, so it is entirely conceivable that sometime within the next century China and India may attain sufficient per capita economic size to be able to support the provision of key collective goods and liquidity for hegemonic capacity. Given the demographic trends of aging in China and the EU, however, it is likely that an increasing portion of their surplus will be directed toward the provision of safety net goods for domestic society.

Property Rights and Rule of Law

Given that governments generally exercise dominant control over the tools of coercion in a society, respect for property rights and rule of law reflects the willingness of a government to exercise self-constraint in its actions, refrain from arbitrary behavior, and adhere to a society's rules of the game. Good rule of law includes stable and predictable processes of regime change. Good rule of law underpins stable and productive property rights, which define the ownership properties of capital and other commodities and how those can be exchanged—key to productive economic activity. In the realm of finance, rule of law defines the responsibilities of government, market organizations, borrowers, and lenders. This helps address uncertainty and possible market failures that can affect incentives to accumulate, lend, and invest.

The EU does well on both property rights and rule of law. The EU member states, including the newcomers, enjoy a relatively stable and productive rule of law, which constrains the risks and uncertainties that can hinder economic activity. Comparatively, the EU looks very good in any assessment of property rights or corruption, such as the International Property Rights Index or the measure generated by Transparency International. The rules of regime change, economic exchange, property ownership, bureaucratic process, complaint and adjudication, and enforcement are clear, stable, and relatively unencumbered in the EU as compared with most political economies.

China and India are quite different stories. As in most developing political economies, in these two states many property rights remain ambiguous. This is evident in the amount of piracy of intellectual property—such as music, films, and software—seen in both countries. Weak property rights hinder exchange and limit the ability of individuals to use property as collateral to secure loans that could finance greater economic activity. Part of this problem for China and India may simply be that they are working through the processes of development as they develop better mechanisms of governance that will embed a rule of law clarifying property rights and the processes of exchange, complaint, adjudication, and enforcement. However, the development of sound property rights and productive rule of law can be difficult if historical or cultural legacies and inefficiencies exist that work against such development. The pressures of corruption and the willingness of governments to engage in arbitrary actions can lead policy makers to change the rules of the game when it is in their short-term interest, regardless of the long-term interests of society. Both China and India face obstacles to developing good property rights and stable rule of law that will increase clarity, reduce uncertainty, constrain the risks from corruption and arbitrariness, and promote stable expectations that encourage productive economic activity.

India may have some advantages over China in building a sound rule of law. India has enjoyed a stable process of regime change since independence despite the assassinations of leaders, ethnic unrest, and domestic turmoil. This means that Indian policy makers have abided by their constitutionally defined path of regime change even if it meant giving up the reins of power in society—a strong demonstration of self-constraint and commitment to an emerging rule of law. China has the added difficulty of not having a stable process of regime change or political competition. If anything, to date, Chinese policy makers have demonstrated a willingness to obscure or change the rules of the game when they believe threats exist to their political survival, engaging in arbitrary behavior that undermines stable expectations.

Taxation

Taxation is another important microfoundation to hegemonic capacity, affecting a society's ability to provide collective functions that contribute to economic success and ultimately underpin hegemony. Good tax systems are deep and broad, covering a wide swath of society.

These enable governments to develop reliable sources of capital; to draw on that supply at times of crisis; to reallocate surplus to address societal needs such as public safety, infrastructure, education, and public health; to anticipate reliable revenues from year to year; and to plan for the future. A good tax system is fair and encourages contribution rather than avoidance.

The member states of the EU have relatively progressive and productive tax systems. All tax systems have loopholes that are designed and exploited by those seeking to limit their tax contributions—often reflecting disparities in political and economic power. No one really likes to pay taxes, but the level of tax avoidance in the EU is relatively low compared with that of most states in the global arena. Moreover, the EU member states' tax systems do not contain extensive national bias—that is, they do not discriminate excessively between national and foreign individuals and firms. Such characteristics make for a broad and deep tax base from which governments can draw capital.

The Indian and Chinese tax systems are not nearly as broad and deep, contain far more loopholes, enable tax avoidance, and discriminate between foreign and domestic taxpayers. Despite the recent economic success and rapid growth of China and India, their tax systems do not compare well with those of the EU and the United States in terms of fairness, progressivity, or level of avoidance. Part of this is a dilemma of good information and accounting systems, but part of the deficiencies in Chinese and Indian taxation arise as a consequence of corrupt practices, political cronyism, and disparities in wealth and power.

Public Debt Markets

Effective taxation has impacts on other mechanisms of raising capital, affecting liquidity and the allocation of financial resources. Taxation contributes to a government's ability to borrow by providing resources to finance debt. Even successful governments face emergencies that defy foresight and overwhelm funds set aside for crises. Delaying responses until taxation produces sufficient capital can create social unrest and instability, and can even threaten political survival. An active public debt market provides prospective lenders with information about a government as a borrower—about the likelihood that the government will fulfill its financial obligations, renege by outright default, or engage in questionable practices such as renegotiating the terms of a loan or inflating a currency that erodes the value of an investment. Such information affects the risk and uncertainty that lenders consider when determining whether or not to lend to a government and at what price. A government's good reputation as a borrower will increase the likelihood that it will find financing and reduce its borrowing costs. A public debt market with low risk premiums reflects a political economy that has developed financial tools to handle emergencies and expenditures and has also overcome the short-term temptations of policy makers to renege on their obligations. An active public debt market also helps in the development of private markets.

Table 14.2 shows the sizes of the public debt markets and the costs of that debt in the United States, China, India, and the EU. The data reflect both the need to borrow to finance

TABLE 14.2	**Public Debt Size, Public Debt Costs, and Private Equity Market Capitalization***			
	United States	*China*	*India*	*European Union*
Public debt**	$9.33 trillion	$986 billion	$880 billion	$12.17 trillion‡
Debt costs (%)***				
1 year	0.0	2.58	6.82	‡‡
5 year	1.375	3.65	7.40	‡‡
10 year	2.65	4.02	8.21	‡‡
30 year	4.25			
Equity****	$12.83 trillion (NYSE)	$2.8 trillion (Shanghai)	$1.63 trillion (Mumbai)	$3.6 trillion (LSE)
	$3.65 trillion (NASDAQ)	$2.68 trillion (Hong Kong)	$1.59 trillion (NSE)	$2.99 trillion (Euronext)
				$1.39 trillion (German Bourse)

Source: Adapted from Andrew C. Sobel, *Birth of Hegemony: Crisis, Financial Revolution, and Emerging Global Networks* (Chicago: University of Chicago Press, 2012), Table 7.2.

*The data in this table do not include private debt markets, venture capital markets, derivative markets, commodity markets, money markets, OTC markets, or foreign exchange markets. The European NASDAQ OMX Group is not included.

**Public debt data are from The Economist Intelligence Unit. These data reflect just the debt of the central government held by the public as of fall 2010 and do not include municipals, intragovernmental holdings, and so on.

‡Data are from Eurostat. EU public debt is less straightforward to assess, given that the member states are the issuers of government debt, and consequently the figure shown is the cumulative outcome of all member states. As of late 2010 EU public debt was estimated at approximately 79 percent of EU GDP.

***Data are from Bloomberg and as of mid-December 2010.

‡‡EU rates depend on the borrowing country. The rates can vary quite dramatically, reflecting perceptions of differing risk. Yields for the best risks look similar to those for the United States, but those for more problematic political economies are significantly higher.

****Equity markets data are from the World Federation of Exchanges monthly statistics reports as of October 2010. The numbers are based on the value of listed stocks. Only the largest national markets are included. Regional exchanges are omitted.

public expenditures and the capacity to borrow. Many fear and bemoan a large public debt, but a large public debt market shows the willingness of those holding a surplus to lend it to the government. This, along with the costs of the debt, provides some useful information about the reputation of the government as a reliable borrower.

The United States has the largest public debt in absolute size, although U.S. public debt is smaller than the public debts of many other nations relative to GDP, including Japan and many of the EU member states. The reputation of the U.S. government as a borrower underpins a large and deep U.S. debt market that allows policy makers to borrow great sums and stretch the costs of public policies over time, even over generations. This enables U.S. policy makers to support policies and programs that their current tax base could not sustain, allowing the U.S. government and society to live beyond immediate government revenues obtained by taxation. It also enables the government to borrow during emergencies at a time when many less capable and less reputable governments encounter obstacles to borrowing and those in private capital markets become risk averse. This gives U.S. policy makers a cushion of financial resources to address situations that could create instability at home or abroad and to use to encourage cooperation across governments by providing liquidity.

Together, the EU states have a public debt that exceeds that of the United States both in absolute size and as a portion of the GDP. The absolute size of Chinese and Indian public debt is less than one-tenth that of the United States or the EU—even smaller as a percentage of national GDP. The size of Chinese and Indian public debt partly reflects the amount of time that those governments have been able to borrow and build debt and partly indicates the capacity of those governments to use surplus capital in a productive manner. For China, the size of the public debt market also reflects the ability of the central government to capture and reallocate substantial gains from international trade.

The size of the EU debt market suggests an ability by the EU and its member governments to respond to national crises, but the EU debt market also is burdened by national boundaries and lacks central coordination to address EU problems or emergencies beyond EU boundaries. These factors detract from the EU's potential capacity as a global lender of last resort. Such national barriers to EU cooperation and quick action were evident during the sovereign debt problems of some member states that began in mid-2010. The slow, and uncertain, response by the EU to the sovereign debt problems enabled the problems to fester, spill across borders, and slow economic recovery from the recession of 2007–2009. Those problems remain unresolved and threatening to the stability of the global economy at the time of this writing.

China and India do not face the hindrances that the EU's federal structure imposes on quick, decisive policy making that involves deficit financing, but the Chinese and Indians are limited by the size of their debt markets. Both are approximately the size of the U.S. stimulus legislation for 2009–2010, which was enabled by deficit financing and was just one of the U.S. government's responses to the economic crisis that attacked the U.S. and global economies. The ability of the United States to borrow huge sums quickly underpins the capacity of U.S.

policy makers to react to domestic and international crises promptly and, ideally, to constrain such crises. The Chinese and Indian debt markets are not yet of sufficient size to enable such a role in the global economy. One could view Chinese investments in U.S. public debt as implicit support of U.S. capacity to engage in global stabilizing activities.

The costs of public debt reveal important differences across states. Given the decentralization of the EU public debt markets, the costs of EU public debt vary by member state. Consequently, it is not easy to contrast the costs of EU public debt with the costs of U.S., Chinese, and Indian public debt. For example, the costs of German public debt are not much different from the costs of U.S. public debt, but the costs of public debt for Greece, Ireland, Spain, and Eastern European EU members are significantly higher.

Even though the absolute and relative size of Chinese and Indian public debt is far smaller than U.S. public debt, the United States pays significantly lower costs for its capital (see interest rates in table 14.2). With the effective cost of short-term public debt (loans of one year or less in duration) in the United States at 0 percent, the Chinese and Indians pay infinitely more for short-term capital than does the United States. Compared with the United States, the Chinese pay two to three times more to borrow for five years and almost twice as much for a ten-year note. Public borrowing is even more expensive in India.

Differences in costs across states reflect differences in the perceptions of lenders about the potential risks to their capital. Public debt markets with low risk premiums reflect political economies that have developed stable, reliable, and credible mechanisms of governance that constrain the short-term temptations of policy makers to renege on their obligations and have constructed the financial tools to handle emergencies and expenditures beyond the immediate capacity of the tax system. China and India have developed large and relatively affordable public debt markets for developing political economies, but their size and costs of capital are still far from that necessary to support the hegemonic capacity to create and infuse sufficient liquidity to stabilize the broader system during times of systemic crisis.

Lender of Last Resort

All modern political economies have some organization, or organizations, that act as **lender of last resort.** A hegemon's lender of last resort effectively plays that role for the hegemon's domestic economy and for the international system. A global lender of last resort must address the tasks of both price stability and growth. Many central banks have price stability as the principle objective of monetary policy, but a global lender of last resort must be willing to trade off between price stability and growth. This is a difficult task given the inherent tension between stability and growth. A global lender of last resort must be willing to promote growth and risk inflation by manipulating money supply to inject liquidity into

> A **lender of last resort** is a nation or bank that acts countercyclically to ensure an adequate supply of capital during economic crisis when no other institution or market will, providing a collective good.

the system to stimulate economic activity countercyclically, and to do so without hesitation at times of crises and during contractions.

The Chinese and Indian central banks and ministries of finance have demonstrated a willingness to try to balance the tasks of supporting price stability and growth in their domestic arenas. Central bankers in China and India have used the levers of monetary policy to try to slow growth that is considered inflationary, in order to enhance price stability, but also to stimulate growth during slowdowns. Moreover, China has demonstrated a willingness to engage in lender-of-last-resort activities regionally to address economic and financial crises. The Bank of China provided financial assistance to the Hong Kong Stock Exchange during the 1987 market crash, helped regional governments support their currencies during the 1997 Asian financial crisis, and engaged in massive infrastructure stimulus during the economic crisis that began in 2007. In late 2010 the Chinese indicated a willingness to provide financial backstopping to the EU during its emerging sovereign debt crunch. Yet China and India do not have the capacity to act as lender of last resort for the international system given the sizes of their capital markets, their access to capital, and the limited extent of the global network centered on the lender-of-last-resort institutions in China and India.

The EU is another matter in terms of access to capital and extent of global networking. The European Central Bank is well situated in terms of the global financial nervous system to operate as a potential global lender of last resort, but it faces two massive obstacles. First, the ECB's statutory commitment is to price stability above all else, with only a very limited statutory charge to promote growth. For the ECB there is no inherent tension between promoting price stability and promoting growth, as price stability reigns supreme as a policy objective regardless of economic circumstances. Second, the federal structure of the EU creates obstacles to quick policy response, as such response requires deliberation across national finance ministries. Unlike the U.S. federal structure, where the most significant tools of lender-of-last-resort action rest in the hands of the central policy makers in Washington, D.C., many of the major tools of EU economic policy, particularly fiscal policy, are distributed across the capitals of the member states. This may make for good and thoughtful deliberation, but not for quick policy making.

With constraints on the ECB's ability to inject massive amounts of liquidity quickly into the global arena at times of systemic economic distress, its capacity to act as global lender of last resort and to elicit cooperation across governments is fatally flawed, despite the ECB's favorable positioning in the global financial network and its access to capital. Given the statutory constraints, which are heavily influenced by Germany's historical experience and resulting chronic fear of inflation, there is little likelihood, absent a major crisis that challenges and upsets the status quo, that the ECB mission will change sufficiently to enable it to operate as the system's lender of last resort or stabilizer. The European sovereign debt crisis that began in 2010 and festered may provide such a crisis and opportunity. Time will tell.

International Reserve Currency

A potential hegemon must be willing to have its currency become a transactional currency with a geography that extends beyond its national borders, an **international reserve currency**, and a currency used to settle international accounts. This requires a commitment to open capital flows and an absence of capital controls. Exposing their state's currency to extensive international use can create complications for policy makers as well as provide some advantage—a tension between losing some control over money supply and being able to manipulate the rules and conditions of the global economy. Exposing one's currency internationally sits at the heart of the reach of a potential hegemon's monetary policies and its ability to influence liquidity in the global economy. The extensive international use of a potential hegemon's currency is key to the construction of a network to promote economic expansion and to manage systemic threats.

> An **international reserve currency** is a currency that is held by many governments and institutions as a significant part of their foreign exchange reserves. It is often used to price transactions that cross national borders.

Table 14.3 details the use of currencies as foreign reserve assets. The data reflect the willingness of governments to expose their currencies to international use and the willingness of others in the system to use those currencies as reserve assets and to settle international accounts. Foreign exchange reserves are those held as official reserves by government finance ministries and central banks. These are also called *hard currencies*. Outside their own currencies, governments are usually willing to hold substantial reserves of other states' currencies only if those currencies are willingly, perhaps exclusively, used by others in the system to settle cross-national accounts, are likely to hold their value over significant periods of time—especially during times of duress—and are useful to manage the foreign exchange value of the domestic currency. At times of crisis there is often a flight to such hard currencies to manage risk and uncertainty that could damage asset values.

Table 14.3 shows that the dollar continues to be the preferred foreign reserve currency by an overwhelming margin. This is partly the legacy of the international monetary arrangements created for the post–World War II era, but it also reflects the continued position of the United States as the largest, most dominant political economy with the most attractive consumer markets. Ironically, even a bit perversely, others rushed into dollar positions in the wake of the 2008 global financial crisis and liquidity crunch that began in U.S. markets.

What about other states that could potentially attain hegemonic capacity? The Chinese and Indian currencies are not yet considered hard currencies that are likely to be held as official foreign exchange reserves. First, Chinese policy makers have been unwilling to expose the yuan to use as an international reserve asset, keeping a tight rein on its dissemination outside China. This is partly a consequence of Chinese policy makers' desire to keep close control of the tools of monetary policy in order to address domestic stability during the

TABLE 14.3   **Currency Composition of Official Foreign Exchange Reserves (in Percentages)**

Currency	1995	2000	2001	2002	2003	2004	2005	2006	2007	2008	2009
						Year					
U.S. dollar	59.0	70.5	70.7	66.5	65.8	65.9	66.4	65.7	64.1	64.1	62.2
Swiss franc	0.3	0.3	0.3	0.4	0.2	0.2	0.1	0.2	0.2	0.1	0.1
Pound sterling	2.1	2.8	2.7	2.9	2.6	3.3	3.6	4.2	4.7	4.0	4.3
Yen	6.8	6.3	5.2	4.5	4.1	3.9	3.7	3.2	2.9	3.1	3.0
Deutsche mark	15.8										
French franc	2.4										
Euro		18.8	19.8	24.2	25.3	24.9	24.3	25.2	26.3	26.4	27.3

Source: Adapted from Andrew C. Sobel, *Birth of Hegemony: Crisis, Financial Revolution, and Emerging Global Networks* (Chicago: University of Chicago Press, 2012), Table 7.3.

Note: Data in this table are from IMF, *Currency Composition of Official Foreign Exchange Reserves;* and ECB, *The Accumulation of Foreign Reserves.*

remarkable growth of the Chinese economy. Yet Chinese policy makers are not enthralled by the preeminence of the dollar as the international reserve asset and as the preferred means to settle international transactions. They have suggested creation of an international currency that is a basket of currencies—similar to the IMF's special drawing rights—to serve as an international reserve and alternative to the dollar. Second, others in the system have not reflected much interest in holding yuan even if the capital control obstacles to its circulation did not exist. Questions about the yuan, how it would adjust, and a relative absence of deep and liquid markets in yuan futures act as barriers to its use as an international reserve asset or a currency to settle international transactions. The Chicago Mercantile Exchange just began trading in yuan futures in late 2011. These problems are compounded by the lack of a predictable rule of law in China that would act as a constraint on arbitrary behavior such as strategic manipulation of the currency.

Indian policy makers are less protective than Chinese policy makers of their currency's international use, but others in the system are not receptive to the rupee's international use, even regionally. This reflects the inherent uncertainty regarding the stability of a currency from a developing country where the economy is experiencing rapid change and has much more change to come if it is going to develop into a stable advanced industrialized political economy. Here, India has the advantage over China of a tested rule of law, but by itself this is not sufficient to make the rupee attractive as an international reserve asset.

Once adopted, the euro emerged as the second-largest preferred foreign exchange reserve asset, far outpacing the Japanese yen. The euro is viewed as relatively stable and likely to hold its value during times of stress. This is largely because of the ECB's commitment to price stability, which helps convince economic actors that the ECB will not play fast and loose with the value of the euro in the face of domestic political and economic pressures. Embedded in the ECB commitment to the euro's stability is the legacy of the deutsche mark and the Bundesbank. Yet the very constraints on the ECB's flexibility in monetary affairs that quickly convinced economic actors about the stability of the euro also serves as a limitation on the EU's ability to fill the role of a liberal hegemon and on the euro's capacity to become the dominant reserve asset. Even though the euro's stability is attractive, without the ability for the ECB to act countercyclically to inject substantial liquidity quickly during global economic threats, the euro will have a difficult time replacing the dollar as the prime reserve asset.

Capital Market Size

Private financial characteristics also contribute to the capacity of a political economy to exercise leadership, for they affect the capacity to provide **liquidity** to the system. Chapter 6 noted that capital market size, financial market diversification, the depth and liquidity of financial markets, transparency and clearinghouse mechanisms, and the relative absence of barriers to cross-border private capital flows and market participation

> **Liquidity** is a measure of how mobile an asset is or how easily it can be exchanged; for example, cash is more liquid than land.

are particularly important. The importance of capital market size should be evident given that a hegemon's capacity for leadership depends on an ability to supply liquidity cyclically and countercyclically—during good times to promote continued economic expansion and exchange across borders and during difficult times to stabilize the global economy, promote cooperation that limits damaging economic nationalism, and fuel recovery.

Private capital markets are among the primary mechanisms for injecting liquidity during good times, when investors and savers are more willing to accept risk and to put their capital to work. Table 14.2 displays information about the size of the major private equity markets in the United States, China, India, and the EU. The data do not include smaller equity markets, private debt markets such as bank loans or bond issuances, derivative markets, money markets, or venture capital markets—all of which are quite substantial in the United States and the EU, and some of which are significant in China and India.

Even omitting other forms of financial intermediation and disintermediation, which would increase the relative capitalization of U.S. private finance over the other political economies, the comparisons are informative and serve as good proxy indicators of the disparities in private finance from state to state. The major U.S. private equity markets far outpace those in other political economies. The cumulative capitalization of the major U.S. private exchanges is more than twice as large as that of the major exchanges in the EU, almost three times as great as that of the major Chinese exchanges, and more than five times larger than that of the major Indian exchanges.

Political economies can evolve along different paths to finance private economic activity. For example, German industrial financing depends heavily on debt through bank loans, whereas U.S. firms rely far more heavily on bond and equity issuances. Variations in tax structure, financial infrastructure, industry-banking relations, business culture, and path dependence contribute to such national differences in private finance. Yet, regardless of such variations in domestic financial infrastructure, the data in table 14.2 are a good approximation of U.S. financial capacity relative to the other political economies given the global trend toward greater disintermediation that began in the 1970s and 1980s. U.S. private capital formation capacity far outpaces that of other political economies, and, more important, much of this capital comes from and finds its way abroad.

Market Diversification

Capital markets in successful political economies take a variety of forms—banking, securitization of debt, equity markets, money markets, derivatives and futures, venture capital, and so on. Some political economies are more diverse than others in terms of their capital market structures. Any potential hegemon must have a diversified portfolio. London was more diversified than other major financial centers in the 1700s and 1800s. The two centers of U.S. private and public finance, New York and Washington, D.C., became more diversified than other major centers as the United States moved to center stage in the 1900s.

Market diversification encourages competition and financial innovation. Competition and innovation can produce a range of financial instruments and strategies that enable holders of capital to find different levels of risk and reward. At the same time, borrowers can find lower costs of capital and a wider range of strategies to tailor their borrowings. This results in improved efficiency and the increased attractiveness of markets, which can induce an increasing returns dynamic that helps attract more and more domestic and foreign capital. Such a dynamic contributes to the construction of a network of global financial relations and results in increased market depth and liquidity. Market diversification is key to creating a critical mass of capital and a network of relations that can be influenced by policy makers to create liquidity for the system cyclically and countercyclically.

China and India are just at the early stages of significant market diversification. As noted, although both have sizable public debt and equity markets and both have sizable banking sectors, neither approaches the capacity to create the liquidity for a political economy to act as the system stabilizer. Even if those markets were larger, the lack of greater market diversification would hamper China's or India's capacity to attract sufficient capital at home or abroad to create the critical mass necessary for leadership. Undeveloped or underdeveloped futures and derivatives markets, currency markets, commodity markets, and venture capital markets limit a state's ability to attract a wide range of global investors and borrowers seeking different levels of risk and reward. The limited market structure constrains the ability of investors and borrowers to hedge their risks. Consequently, Chinese and Indian policy makers are limited in their capacity to manage their private and public financial mechanisms to address international dilemmas that could threaten cooperation and globalization.

The EU does enjoy diverse and sophisticated financial markets, with the weak link perhaps being venture capital. The EU is home to robust currency markets, deep public and private bond markets, extensive banking systems, a global equities market, healthy money markets, and many of the major euro markets—markets in which a nation's currency and similarly denominated financial instruments are traded outside of that country. Again the drawbacks are the EU's lender-of-last-resort focus on price stability and lack of emphasis on growth, and the federal structure that hampers quick action. Despite the EU's having a strong private financial foundation that could have the capacity to exercise leadership, statutory constraints on the mission of the ECB and the awkward supranational structure that leaves critical powers in the hands of national governments means that EU policy makers would have difficulty in harnessing the capacity of those private markets to act as the system stabilizer.

Depth, Liquidity, Transparency, and Clearinghouse Mechanisms

A hegemon's capital markets are deep, liquid, and relatively transparent, and they have good clearinghouse mechanisms. All these characteristics help promote participant confidence and limit risks to investors. Deep and liquid markets are generally more orderly and less volatile. In deep and liquid markets investors can quickly get in and out of large positions without creating the price volatility that can upset stability. Deep and liquid markets are partly a result of good transparency, which ensures that market participants have the opportunity to be well-informed, and good clearinghouse mechanisms, which transfer property rights quickly and unambiguously. Clarity and efficient completion of exchange help to manage risks from asymmetric information, incomplete property rights, time, cronyism and corruption, and manipulation. All these qualities contribute to a capital market's appeal, potentially feeding a virtuous cycle that attracts more and more capital and produces deeper and more liquid markets.

Again, the EU does very well on the dimensions of market depth, liquidity, transparency, and clearinghouse mechanisms. The size of EU financial markets and their settlement mechanisms limit investors' risks from price volatility that results from thin markets and from the inability to get in or out of market positions quickly. Moreover, the rule of law in the EU and its accompanying regulatory oversight of financial dealing and disclosure requirements increase transparency, which limits market risks from asymmetric information, corruption, and unfair manipulation. These contribute to investor confidence, as do good clearinghouse mechanisms that ensure the quick transfer of property rights to settle transactions without ambiguity.

The Chinese and Indian markets, particularly their private financial markets, do not enjoy the same advantages as those of the United States or the EU in terms of depth, liquidity, relative transparency, and good clearinghouse mechanisms. Despite their overall size, in practice they are much thinner markets with far smaller trading volume, which is often concentrated in a handful of financial instruments. This creates the potential for large price swings and difficulties in moving quickly in and out of positions. This is especially true for foreign investors, who effectively work at much greater distance than do locals and have less familiarity with market practices. Moreover, the Chinese and Indian markets are far less transparent than those in the United States or the EU, and they do not enjoy as efficient and unambiguous settlement mechanisms. This limits the attractiveness of these markets for large foreign institutional investors and for foreign corporations interested in listing their stocks or bonds abroad.

Consequently, the Chinese and Indian private financial markets are overwhelmingly national markets for listing of domestic financial instruments. The rapid growth in the Chinese and Indian economies has increased the participation of foreign institutional investors, but such activity remains a relatively small portion of those markets. This limits the capacity of the markets to have any significant effect on global liquidity. The Chinese markets are particularly hampered by the absence of a clear rule of law that underpins disclosure requirements, market practices, and settlement procedures. The rules appear open to seemingly arbitrary change. The prospect for arbitrary changes in market practices is a fundamental threat to the transparency and the clear transfer of property rights that underpin stable expectations, which are necessary to attract the amount of capital essential for hegemonic capacity.

National Bias

To emerge at the hub of the network of global finance, a political economy must be relatively porous to capital flows. This requires a state's willingness to allow its currency to become an international transactional currency and to reject capital controls. Such choices are made in public arenas, but a mix of other public and private activities can also affect openness. Informal practices can discriminate against nonnational investors and borrowers. Strong national bias can create barriers to entry and obstacles to participation. Some national bias is inevitable, but a global market has a relative absence of such bias.

Chinese and Indian financial markets reflect an almost exclusive national bias despite their recent economic success, their increasing exposure to international trade, and the rapid growth in their private financial markets. This national bias is partly a consequence of statutory constraints and a legacy of regulatory limitations, but it is also an artifact of business practices and culture. Market access differs between domestic and foreign participants. The Shanghai Stock Exchange, unlike the Hong Kong Stock Exchange, is not completely open to foreigners. The market is divided into two classes of shares—A and B shares. Trading in A shares is restricted to domestic investors (with some qualified exceptions). Trades are priced in yuan in this class. Both domestic and foreign investors can trade in B shares, which are priced in U.S. dollars. Currently only Chinese firms can list securities on the Shanghai exchange. The Hong Kong exchange is a different story because it had exposure to foreign capital and participants before the British transferred rule of Hong Kong to China in 1997. More than one hundred foreign firms were listed on the Hong Kong exchange at the end of 2010—predominantly from Taiwan, with the remaining mostly from Australia, Indonesia, Japan, Malaysia, Singapore, the United Kingdom, and the United States. Even though such firms are listed, there is relatively little trading in foreign shares.

National bias is at least as strong in the Indian financial markets as in Shanghai. The same limitations that apply in Shanghai for listing of foreign firms are true for the two major Indian stock exchanges—one of which listed its first foreign company in June 2010 as a depository receipt. Differences in taxation and investment rules that discriminate against foreign capital have hindered foreign participation in the Mumbai markets in the past. Despite financial reforms and liberalization, particularly in the area of capital controls, lingering legacies from past regulatory and tax structures continue to create obstacles to equal treatment. Such national bias in China and India limits the flow of international capital into and from their national markets. Even though the Chinese and Indian economies are increasingly connected by trade to the global economy, a strong national bias constrains the integration of their financial markets into a global financial network that links economic activity, private and public actors, and regulators across borders. They still sit somewhat apart from the global financial nervous system.

The EU is quite a different story. Perhaps because of the legacy of London as the predominant global financial center at one time, perhaps because of the role of international trade in European economic success, or perhaps because of the evolution of financial regulation and liberalization, the EU has a long history of being open to international capital flows. Europe was completely open to the flow of capital across borders in the late 1800s during an earlier era of extensive globalization, and even back then there was a distinctive lack of national bias in London's markets. Statutory barriers to capital flows were erected following World War II to guard against the outflow of capital necessary to rebuild war-torn European economies. Such controls all but disappeared by the early 1980s. By 2010, the London Stock Exchange had even more foreign corporations listing their securities than did the NYSE, and foreign capital made up a sizable portion of daily trading in London's equity market, Frankfurt's bond market, and other European-based financial markets.

The EU's financial markets are well integrated into the global financial network. Again, it is not a problem of sufficient size, property rights, rule of law, taxation, capital market size, diversification, depth, transparency, clearinghouse mechanisms, or national bias that limits the capacity of the EU to act as the stabilizer and provide the leadership in the global economy that surmounts problems that could undermine cooperation and damage productive globalization. The EU does well on all microdimensions necessary for hegemonic capacity except for one: it falters on the lender-of-last-resort function with its overriding commitment to price stability and the barriers to quick action posed by its decentralized federal decision-making structure.

CONCLUSION

The United States emerged from World War II with overwhelming military, technological, and economic capacity. In response to the financial and economic crises that reversed globalization and created the massive economic hardship of the Great Depression, reforms in governance, regulation, and public and private finance during the 1930s put U.S. financial markets and mechanisms on firmer foundations with greater transparency, more oversight, better clearinghouse mechanisms, and improved assurances of fair and honest markets without corruption, cronyism, unfair manipulation, or insider dealing. World War II interrupted the opportunity for such changes to gain credibility. The end of the war saw confidence restored in U.S. financial markets, as they were now on a firmer regulatory foundation. The United States had become the preeminent political economy in terms of wealth, influence, and resources essential to rebuilding a stable, productive global economy based on market exchange.

The postwar period brought additional changes in public and private finance that helped cement U.S. financial capacity and leadership. The Marshall Plan advanced massive foreign assistance—most often in dollars—to help political economies facing domestic economic and political turmoil with their postwar rebuilding efforts. International governmental organizations were established to promote global exchange, reconstruction, and development, and to help manage international monetary relations. These organizations created scaffolding that buttressed U.S. hegemonic capacity and helped place the dollar at the center of a global network of financial relationships—public and private. The outflow of dollars from the United States because of postwar monetary relations helped further. The dollar became the reserve currency in the Bretton Woods monetary system, the dominant currency to settle international accounts, and the primary unit of accounting for international organizations. These circumstances gave U.S. leaders, public and private, disproportionate leverage to influence the well-being of the global economy—to promote continued expansion, exchange, and globalization, and to manage dislocations that threatened such expansion.

The Bretton Woods system and its successor came to an end in the early 1970s, creating some uncertainty over international monetary affairs and increasing the role of market mechanisms. More reforms and liberalization further increased the role of market mechanisms. The end of foreign exchange restrictions, the increased fungibility of currencies, the lowering of market barriers, and financial liberalization led to an increase in the density and pace of financial interactions domestically and internationally. These fueled an increasing return dynamic that actually boosted the ability of U.S. policy makers to sit at the center of the global financial nervous system and manage dislocations. In the 1970s, 1980s, and 1990s, reforms and financial liberalization reduced government oversight and unleashed new waves of financial innovation. Much of this innovation fueled new productive economic activity but also unintentionally created opportunities for injecting unanticipated risks into financial markets. This new, heavily deregulated global financial landscape would promote invention and innovation, new access to capital, and greater global integration of national economies—a denser global financial nervous system. Such integration also created channels for financial crises to spread across borders. These threaten to destabilize the processes that had produced the postwar economic expansion and globalization.

The threats to global economic stability of the successive and increasingly severe shocks of the Third World Debt Crisis in 1983, the October market crash in 1987, the savings and loan crisis at the end of the 1980s, the Russian ruble crisis, the peso crisis, the Asian financial crisis, the bursting of the technology bubble in 1999–2000, the credit market freeze in 2008, and the European sovereign debt crisis that began in 2011 were partly unintended consequences of the liberalization that unleashed financial innovations and at the same time increased integration. U.S. policy makers, primarily at the Federal Reserve and the U.S. Treasury, were central to advancing policies and putting together coalitions to manage these shocks. Each successive shock raised more and more questions about the rules of the game that produced such shocks and about the health and wisdom of U.S. leadership, even as U.S. policy makers were central to constructing the global cooperation necessary to manage those shocks. Other problems add to the questioning of U.S. capacity for leadership, such as the persistent U.S. trade imbalance, U.S. economic stagflation, weakness in the dollar, and increasing disagreements over U.S. unilateralism in political and military foreign policies.

More recently, the economic successes of other states, particularly China, have led to speculation about continued U.S. leadership in the system and the possibility of another political economy replacing the United States as the global leader. Questions about the health of U.S. leadership, or potential successors to that leadership, are critical if such leadership underpins the provision of key collective goods that ensure the liquidity that is essential to promoting economic growth, helping reduce uncertainties involved in cross-border exchange, managing the risks involved in such exchange, extending the time horizons of economic actors, encouraging those actors to risk exchange and investment across time and space, and supporting a network of relationships that can mobilize cooperation and manage countercyclical downturns.

For some this is a question of global competition, a zero-sum game over what political economy is going to be king of the hill, where one society's gain is another's loss. Yet it should be clear that the relevance of liberal hegemonic leadership is not about global competition but about the global leadership and cooperation necessary to stabilizing the global arena during times of duress and promoting the expansion of globalization and international exchange that enhances social welfare. If U.S. capacity for leadership is at risk, does another political economy exist that could pick up the slack, assume the role of a liberal hegemonic leader, and provide those collective goods important to promoting continued international cooperation and globalization?

The answer to this last question is an unambiguous no. Table 14.1 summarizes the key findings. The rapidly developing political economies of China and India are far from obtaining the capacity to provide the key financing mechanisms that underpin hegemonic capacity. The EU is actually quite close on many dimensions but falls short on one of the most important characteristics of hegemonic capacity: the ability to act as lender of last resort with the capability of emphasizing growth over price stability and acting quickly in response to a systemic crisis.

At the beginning of the twenty-first century, U.S. policy makers have demonstrated a remarkable resilience in their ability to respond to systemic crises, but such crises seem to be more frequent and more threatening since the financial liberalization and globalization that took place after the 1970s. The Emergency Economic Stabilization Act of 2008, which produced TARP, the American Recovery and Reinvestment Act of 2009, and revelations in late 2010 about the Federal Reserve's injection of massive liquidity into the global economy by purchasing trillions of dollars of domestic and foreign corporate obligations demonstrate the capacity of the United States to continue to act as the global fireman during systemic crises. Ironically, activities in U.S. public and private finance may be the biggest threats to continued U.S. leadership if they undermine confidence in the U.S. rules of the game because of the creation and transmission of socially destructive and economically destabilizing crises. Paradoxically for now, the United States is the only political economy with the capacity to address such systemic crises or to coordinate an international response, yet the United States might be the biggest threat to continued U.S. hegemony and leadership in the twenty-first century, and consequently to continued mutually beneficial cooperation and globalization.

KEY CONCEPTS

gross domestic product
purchasing power parity
(GDP ppp) (p. 547)

hegemon (p. 538)

international reserve
currency (p. 555)

lender of last resort (p. 553)

liquidity (p. 557)

nominal GDP (p. 547)

per capita income (p. 547)

Washington Consensus
(p. 535)

EXERCISES

1. Why is liberal hegemonic leadership important for globalization and international cooperation?

2. What does a lender of last resort do?

3. Why should we worry about the state of U.S. hegemonic leadership?

4. Is hegemony a zero-sum relationship in the global arena? If so, why? If not, why?

5. The EU could be a possible successor to the United States as system stabilizer. It is large and wealthy, has deep and liquid capital markets with good transparency and clearinghouse processes, has a strong rule of law, and good tax systems. Explain what dilemma the EU faces that might prevent it from acting as the system stabilizer.

6. Use the European sovereign debt crisis that began in 2011 to explore the EU's ability to act as a system stabilizer.

7. China has developed rapidly over the past thirty years. It is now the second-largest economy in the world. Analyze China's capacity to become a liberal hegemonic leader.

FURTHER READING

Cox, Robert W. 1987. *Production, Power, and World Order: Social Forces in the Making of History.* New York: Columbia University Press.

Henning, C. Randall. 1994. *Currencies and Politics in the United States, Germany, and Japan.* Washington, DC: Peterson Institute.

Johnson, Simon, and James Kwak. 2010. *13 Bankers: The Wall Street Takeover and the Next Financial Meltdown.* New York: Pantheon.

Kennedy, Paul. 1987. *The Rise and Fall of the Great Powers: Economic Change and Military Conflict from 1500 to 2000.* New York: Random House.

Keohane, Robert O. 1984. *After Hegemony: Cooperation and Discord in the World Political Economy.* Princeton, NJ: Princeton University Press.

Kindleberger, Charles P. 1986. *The World in Depression, 1929–1939.* Rev. ed. Berkeley: University of California Press.

Mearsheimer, John J. 2001. *The Tragedy of Great Power Politics.* New York: W. W. Norton.

Nye, Joseph S., Jr. 1990. *Bound to Lead: The Changing Nature of American Power.* New York: Basic Books.

Reinhart, Carmen M., and Kenneth S. Rogoff. 2009. *This Time Is Different: Eight Centuries of Financial Folly.* Princeton, NJ: Princeton University Press.

Ruggie, John Gerard. 1982. "International Regimes, Transactions, and Change: Embedded Liberalism in the Postwar Economic Order." *International Organization* 36, no. 2: 379–415.

Sobel, Andrew C. 1994. *Domestic Choices, International Markets: Dismantling National Barriers and Liberalizing Securities Markets.* Ann Arbor: University of Michigan Press.

———. 1999. *State Institutions, Private Incentives, Global Capital.* Ann Arbor: University of Michigan Press.

———. 2012. *Birth of Hegemony: Crisis, Financial Revolution, and Emerging Global Networks.* Chicago: University of Chicago Press.

Strange, Susan. 1987. "The Persistent Myth of Lost Hegemony." *International Organization* 41, no. 4: 551–607.

Index

Photo Credits

About the Author

Andrew C. Sobel specializes in the politics of global finance with a focus on domestic explanations of international behavior. He earned his Ph.D. in political science from the University of Michigan. He is on the faculty of International and Area Studies at Washington University in St. Louis, a member of the Academic Board of Directors of the Center for New Institutional Social Sciences, and on the Faculty Advisory Council to the Center for the Interdisciplinary Study of Work and Social Capital at Washington University. He has won numerous teaching awards. He has published many articles and is the author or editor of six books, including *Domestic Choices, International Markets* (1994); *State Institutions, Private Incentives, Global Capital* (1999, 2002); *Political Economy and Global Affairs* (2006); *The Challenges of Globalization* (2009); and *Birth of Hegemony: Crisis, Financial Revolution, and Emerging Global Networks* (2012).

⑤SAGE research**methods**

The essential online tool for researchers from the world's leading methods publisher

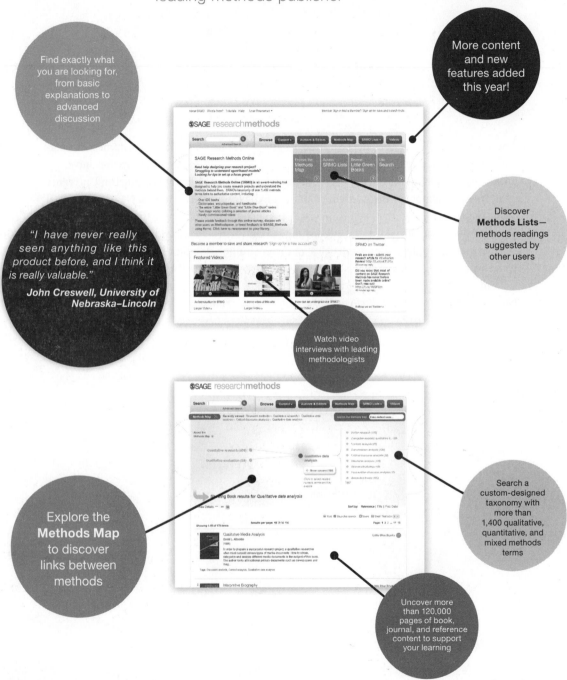

Find exactly what you are looking for, from basic explanations to advanced discussion

More content and new features added this year!

"*I have never really seen anything like this product before, and I think it is really valuable.*"
John Creswell, University of Nebraska–Lincoln

Discover **Methods Lists**— methods readings suggested by other users

Watch video interviews with leading methodologists

Explore the **Methods Map** to discover links between methods

Search a custom-designed taxonomy with more than 1,400 qualitative, quantitative, and mixed methods terms

Uncover more than 120,000 pages of book, journal, and reference content to support your learning

Find out more at
www.sageresearchmethods.com